CID Cisco® Internetwork Design

Thomas M. Thomas II

Doris E. Pavlichek

McGraw-Hill
New York Chicago San Francisco
Lisbon London Madrid Mexico City
Milan New Delhi San Juan
Seoul Singapore Sydney Toronto

Osborne/**McGraw-Hill**
2600 Tenth Street
Berkeley, California 94710
U.S.A.

To arrange bulk purchase discounts for sales promotions, premiums, or fund-raisers, please contact Osborne/**McGraw-Hill** at the above address. For information on translations or book distributors outside the U.S.A., please see the International Contact Information page immediately following the index of this book.

CID Cisco® Internetwork Design

1234567890 DOC DOC 01987654321

Book p/n 0-07-212651-5 and CD p/n 0-07-212652-3
parts of

ISBN 0-07-212653-1

Publisher
Brandon A. Nordin

Vice President & Associate Publisher
Scott Rogers

Acquisitions Editor
Francis Kelly

Project Editor
Mark Karmendy

Acquisitions Coordinator
Alex Corona

Technical Editor
Andrew G. Mason

Copy Editors
Claire Span
Barton Reed
Lisa Theobold

Compositor and Indexer
MacAllister Publishing Services, LLC

This book was composed with Quark XPress 3.32.

To my lovely and strong wife, without whom I would have a much harder life. Through her faith in the Lord and in me we have been able to work as a team and build a wonderful life together.

—Thomas M. Thomas II

This book is dedicated to my family, without whose support I would not have been able to write this book. Their patience, love, and encouragement during many long nights and weekends of work helped me to remain focused on the end goal. For their amazing generosity in allowing me to take on this project, I will be eternally grateful.

—Doris Pavlichek

ABOUT THE AUTHORS

Thomas M. Thomas II, CCSI™, CCNP™, CCDP™, CCDA™, CCNA™, is the founder of NetCerts.com (**www.netcerts.com**) and the Certified Professional Association Worldwide (**www.cpaw.org**). He was previously a Course Developer for Cisco Systems and a Group Leader of MCI's Managed Network Services Advanced Engineering Team. He is currently working as a Senior Consulting Engineer for Ericsson IP Infrastructure and as the Cisco Content Director of CCPrep.com.

Doris E. Pavlichek is a Product Marketing Manager for Ericsson IP Infrastructure in Rockville, MD, where she produces technical content for the marketing of Ericsson router products and works closely with product management. Formerly, she led the team of senior engineers performing Tier 3 support of Ericsson routers and switches. She has 15 years of networking experience including design, implementation, and advanced troubleshooting in both government and business environments. She has also spent time teaching, performing site surveys, and specializing in both network management and security. She currently holds a CCNA™ and CCDA™, is pursuing other Cisco certifications, and is working toward completion of her BSCS.

ABOUT THE TECHINICAL REVIEWER

Andrew G. Mason, CCIE™ #7144, CCDP™, CCNP™ Security, is the CEO of CCStudy.com limited (**http://www.ccstudy.com**), a UK-based Cisco Premier Partner specializing in Cisco consulting for numerous companies. Andrew has 10 years experience in the networking industry and is currently consulting for Energis, the largest ISP in the UK. He is involved daily in the design and implementation of complex secure hosted solutions utilizing products from the Cisco Secure product range. You can contact him at **andrew.mason@ccstudy.com**.

CONTENTS

ACKNOWLEDGMENTS

Doris has been a strong part of my life during the past year and she has been both a wonderful friend and respected co-worker. Francis Kelly has been an awesome professional throughout this process; if only all books could be accomplished so seamlessly. Of course, without Lou Rossi and Cary Riddock of CCPrep, the world would be far less interesting.

—Thomas M. Thomas II

Any project of this magnitude is a combined effort of many people, not just the authors. I would first like to thank Tom Thomas for granting me the enormous responsibility for this project and for his guidance throughout the entire process. To Paul Pavlichek, thanks for your significant contribution to the chapter on BGP and for your support. I would also like to thank the staff of Ericsson IP Infrastructure for being my sounding board, reality check, and cheerleading team. I would especially like to acknowledge the following people: Larry Dwyer, Ronan McLaughlin, Rajah Chowbay, and Ayman Nassar. These folks were instrumental in assisting me with questions, technical review, and other detailed information. Special thanks, also, to Andrew Mason for the valuable work on the technical reviews. The staff of Osborne/McGraw-Hill was fabulous throughout the entire project—especially Franny Kelly, Alex Corona, and Mark Karmendy, in whom I found a fellow movie buff. To my comrades in the world of network design—at Science Applications International Corporation and Network Solutions, especially—I would like to offer my gratitude. Without a place to grow my skills, I never would have gained the experience to pursue my certifications. Finally, in recognition of the man who allowed me to first get my foot in the door of the networking world, I would like to thank Thomas Demarest. Thanks for seeing my potential and letting me blossom.

—Doris Pavlichek

INTRODUCTION

When first presented with the proposed outline for this project, we found it to be more than a little daunting. After all, the scope of the Cisco Internetwork Design course, as presented by Cisco Systems training partners, is a five-day, intensive workshop designed to deluge the student with all sorts of network designs, architectures, and functions. It is not a configuration course, nor is it a troubleshooting course.

So, whereas you will find that this book describes problem areas and how to solve them, as well occasionally providing sample configurations or commands, the purpose of this book is not to teach you to configure Cisco routers. It is designed to do two things–give you the tools to pass the Cisco CID exam (part of the CCDP certification track) and to create scalable network designs throughout your career.

Designing networks that scale well is only a small part of what we hope you gain from reading this book, however. Hopefully you will find that you learn more about the inner workings of a desktop or "legacy" protocol than you knew before. Perhaps you will discover something new about a particular piece of Cisco equipment or a new way to use a piece of equipment with which you are already familiar.

Creating a design, presenting it, and seeing it through to reality is one of the most rewarding parts of a networking career. Reading this book and testing your retention of the material with the enclosed CD-ROM is only part of what will make you successful. The part that no one can write for you or script for you is the practical part of learning to design networks–actually putting it all together.

To those of us who have been in this field for many years, there is probably nothing more annoying than meeting a person who is certified on paper only. Fortunately, most Cisco exams are designed to weed out the candidates who have no practical experience with the equipment and the technology. So before you attempt the CID (or any other) Cisco exam, study the material presented in this book, create some network designs, and get yourself into a lab so that you can test your proposed designs.

The chapters in this book contain a lot of information that needs not be read in order, from start to finish. You can use this book as a study guide, a reference book, or truly as a start-to-finish read-through on network design. You will find that we have included study hints to help you organize the material you really need to know—hands-down—before taking the CID test. We have also included CCDP tips, which are essentially a summary of the chapter topics and notes, case studies, and frequently-asked questions, where appropriate.

Here is a quick overview of the material contained in each chapter in this book.

Overview of Chapters

The chapters in this book are arranged logically and in sync with the syllabus of the Cisco CID course itself. The first section introduces you to the Cisco design model, followed by an introduction to campus LAN design and technology. This is followed by two chapters on the most popular protocol in use today—TCP/IP. The next few chapters will take you through routing protocol design and desktop protocol design. Finally, we conclude with several chapters on WAN design and WAN protocols—including BGP.

Chapter 1—Introduction to Internetwork Design As we open our discovery of internetwork design, we offer this short chapter about the design goals and issues you may encounter. We will also discuss design methodology as it applies to the creation of Cisco design models.

Chapter 2—Hierarchical Design Model The basis for Cisco internetwork design is the hierarchical model—three-layered in form. In this chapter, we show you the important reasons for this model and how it will apply to all of the chapters that follow.

Chapter 3—Campus LAN Overview The purpose of this chapter is to introduce you to the elements and terminology used in the campus LAN environment. It will also point out several areas to consider as we move forward into the next chapters.

Chapter 4—Campus LAN Technology The meat of our discussion on campus LANs is covered in Chapter 4. Not only will we discuss the topologies from which you may select an appropriate choice for your design, but we will also explore connection methods, Virtual LANs (VLANs), and more about LAN Emulation (LANE).

Chapter 5—Campus LAN Design Models As a final note on campus LANs, this chapter gives examples of the different types of LAN design models. In addition to taking a look at the typical models, it will also introduce you to the usage of ATM in the LAN through (LANE).

Chapter 6—TCP/IP Design Overview One of the most important areas that you must understand when pursuing an internetworking career is how to design for a TCP/IP network. This chapter serves as an introduction and springboard to the chapter that follows. It will also explain some basic facts about TCP/IP networks, such as logical versus physical networks and how TCP/IP is structured.

Chapter 7—TCP/IP Addressing Design Building on Chapter 6, this chapter introduces the reader to the intricacies of creating the TCP/IP addresses for the design. This is a complex topic that we have presented in easy-to-understand sections on addressing (including VLSM), address management, multicast, and security. This is a chapter you will want to bookmark for future reference.

Chapter 8—Routing Protocol Design Chapter 8 will introduce you how routing works. It will also describe routing protocol design, giving you an overall understanding of how routing metrics work and how a routing protocol selects the best path to a destination. You will gain an understanding, too, of switching methods and of the difference between static and dynamic routing.

Chapter 9—OSPF Network Design OSPF is one of the most popular, yet complex, routing protocols available for interior gateway routing. It is the protocol that can give you the best scalability and convergence when used properly in internetwork designs. Unfortunately, it is also the most often misunderstood protocol. This chapter should give you a solid foundation in OSPF.

Chapter 10—IGRP-EIGRP Design Cisco's proprietary routing protocols are discussed in this chapter. You will learn the differences between IGRP and EIGRP, the functions of the timers and how to set each one, and how convergence works.

Chapter 11—Desktop Design Overview This rather brief chapter will introduce you to what is unique to designing for desktop protocols. It will also give you overviews of IPX, AppleTalk, and Windows networking.

Chapter 12—IPX Design IPX is the protocol used by Novell's networking software. While some people consider it to be a legacy protocol, it is still very much alive in some businesses and government facilities around the world. This chapter will give you an understanding of how IPX works, special considerations you should note when designing for this protocol, and how to use it within the context of routing protocols such as EIGRP.

Chapter 13—AppleTalk Design AppleTalk is used in many schools and facilities where graphics-heavy work or the simple elegance of the Mac OS is favored over more complex desktop protocols. This chapter will introduce you to the unique terminology related to AppleTalk and will show you how easy it is to design for it.

Chapter 14—Windows Networking Design The most commonly used desktop protocol is Windows networking software. Within this chapter, we cover domain structures, name resolution, common problems, and how to best design for this protocol.

Chapter 15—WAN Design Overview This brief chapter introduces you to the topics that will follow in the next few chapters. It will also describe how to optimize the WAN design for efficiency, performance, and availability.

Chapter 16—Dedicated Lines In the WAN it is quite common to use dedicated lines to connect point A to point B. In this chapter, we discuss not only the different speeds and types of lines, but also the architecture and encapsulation methods associated with these lines.

Chapter 17—Frame Relay Design Frame Relay remains one of the most popular WAN connectivity methods in use today. This chapter describes the terminology used in conjunction with Frame Relay as well as the resilient topologies and interface selections appropriate for this WAN technology.

Chapter 18—X.25 Design One of the most valuable chapters, you may find, is this chapter on X.25 design, because it is unlikely that you have had much contact with this protocol. Most of the networks still using X.25 are financial networks that require excellent reliability rather than speed, necessarily. You will find that reliability of delivery is one of the hallmarks of X.25.

Chapter 19—Remote Access Design One area with which we are all familiar—at least as users—is remote access networking. When designing for the home user, road warrior, or small office, you will find that there are seemingly endless choices and designs available to you. This chapter will help introduce methods with which you may not be proficient. It will also help you learn to design for reliability and speed.

Chapter 20—What Is ATM? Although some in the internetworking world have pronounced ATM dead or limited, it is far from out-of-fashion. Many core networks are designed around ATM and carry voice, video, and data over the backbone. We will cover the role of ATM, the common designs, and the ATM adaptation layers, as well as some issues you may encounter as you work with this technology.

Chapter 21—Overview of WAN Design In order to gain an edge in the ATM realm, Cisco purchased Stratacom—an ATM switch manufacturer. This chapter will cover the different switch models, the appropriate placement of each one and how they help to create a scalable Cisco ATM campus design.

Chapter 22—BGP Design The protocol over which the Internet is routed is *Border Gateway Protocol* (BGP). Every bit as complex as OSPF, BGP requires some skill and careful forethought to each nuance of the design. This chapter will introduce you to BGP, give you the basics (and then some), and show you how to design with this protocol.

Chapter 23—Security Design One of the most important topics in internetworking is security. Most users of Cisco equipment are somewhat familiar with access lists, which are covered in this chapter, but fewer are familiar with other security issues, such as IPSec or VPNs. Also covered are network address translation, firewalls, and the AAA model. While you will not become a security expert from reading this chapter, it will help you understand how to build security into your network design.

Chapter 24—SNA Design Overview The IBM networking system—Systems Network Architecture—is the topic of this chapter that is designed to give you a run-down on the basics of this protocol. Designed for use on mainframes connected to Token Ring, SNA is too complex to be completely discussed within the context of this book. However, we have provided you with the basics, the terminology, the designs, and the major information you need to get started with SNA internetworking.

Finally, the book's appendices will give you some information on multiservice design (including an overview of designing for voice transmission), Cisco hardware, and applications used in these designs and our suggested solutions to the Case Studies contained in most of the chapters.

The authors hope that you find this material helpful to you as you prepare to take your Cisco CID certification exam or as you simply try to expand your knowledge of building scalable Cisco internetworks. Happy networking!

CHAPTER 1

Introduction to Internetwork Design

Overview

As network designers, we rarely get the opportunity to come into a network and build it from the ground up. What we are normally faced with in the course of our careers is a network that has been built like a remodeled house around a rapidly growing family. What began as a rather modest network made up of bridges and a Core router with links to the Internet and perhaps a remote site or two, has become a patched spectrum of devices and protocols, cables and legacy systems.

It is therefore our job to revisit the network design and look for ways to make it better. Perhaps the network requires support for new services such as Voice over IP (VoIP), Quality of Service (QoS), or gigabit Ethernet. Maybe the company has been acquired and needs to be integrated into the corporate infrastructure while considering security, accessibility, and scalability. In all of these cases, it should be our goal to leave the network better than we found it, creating a design that is functional, that performs well under today's load and that scales to suit tomorrow's bandwidth requirements for applications and services. The design must meet user requirements, in other words, while still being at or under budget.

In this chapter we will discuss how to define and set goals for the overall network design. You will learn to spot key issues that will help you in drawing out the design requirements, and you will gather some facts about solid network design methodology.

Design Goals

Networks vary in size and topology, and you never quite know what to expect when you accept a new position or consulting assignment. The wiring closets may be neat and clean, with exceptional cable management and labeling, or you may feel as though you have just walked into the world's largest bowl of Category 5 spaghetti. One thing you can always count on, however, is that a network of any size must make sense to someone. If you are very lucky, that "someone" will be available to help you quickly uncover the network "gotchas" that are unique to each environment. More than likely, you will not be so lucky. You will need a good methodology to help you sort out the issues of the current design.

The best thing to do when you find yourself in an undocumented, unruly bowl of spaghetti is to bear in mind that there are key goals every network architect must follow. A network must be functional for the current applications and number of users it supports. It must also be scalable, to allow for expansion for tomorrow's needs, and adaptable to the applications it may have to handle. A network must also be manageable so that faults can be quickly spotted, isolated, and resolved, preferably before the user realizes that something is wrong. All of these things, however, could easily be built into a network if money was no object, but you must also make the design cost-effective. If you design the Taj Mahal network for a company that has budget enough for an efficiency apartment, then you have not served the customer well.

To recap, here are the design goals we will discuss in greater detail:

- Functionality
- Scalability
- Adaptability
- Manageability
- Cost-effectiveness

Functionality

As we stated earlier, somewhere in the middle of every network is a person who knows exactly how to fix whatever goes wrong. That individual may be the one who created the layers of network cabling and equipment, or he may be the one who has just been there so long that he knows the common problems and where they are most likely to happen. To that person, the network is functional. To management, however, it may be a cause for lost sleep.

A truly functional network must provide a certain level of service, as determined by the customer, to a community of users. The defined level of services may vary from network to network. For example, a college or university might have the following, depending on each department's needs.

- Accounting must be able to reach the financial database in the main building.
- The Math department should easily be able to upload computer-based tests to a server in the Sciences hall.

In its early days, the enterprise network existed to make a user's life easier. Files and resources could be shared and some research databases became available over a very primitive Internet—at least, primitive by today's standards. As the Internet evolved, the network became a faster way for users to get work accomplished, talk with other users around the world, or simply have fun. Businesses in the 1990s discovered the fertile ground of e-commerce, and many "dot-coms" were born. Now that the network spells recreation, productivity, and profit to everyone from the end-user to the carriers, it is your job to create a design that will be truly functional within the guidelines and budget of the customer.

Scalability

Companies tend to grow over time both in personnel and in space. The key to a good network design should be the ability to scale that network—in other words, to grow the network without having it become a patchwork of upgrades that address only a current need or situation. If you design a network taking in *only* today's requirements, you will fall short of this goal. It is up to you to ask questions about projections for the company's growth over 2, 5, or even 10 years and then design a percentage above that. Make recommendations based on what you may have seen or designed at other similar businesses, and based upon what you learn through this guide.

Once you have the corporate vision of the future understood, it is crucial to get a user's perspective. Users are normally looking at a short-term fix to a long-term problem. For example, support personnel want user complaints of slowness to stop. They want to end the trouble tickets they are logging about client timeouts when trying to reach a server. A good design not only fixes the current problems but also is flexible enough to allow future growth.

Adaptability

Keep the future in mind when designing a network. That is not to say that it is wrong to choose a familiar technology such as Fast Ethernet; rather, you should build a design that does not limit customers' ability to change technologies when they find that they simply cannot live without Asyncronous Transfer Mode (ATM). A good network is adaptable enough to allow growth in new directions when and where they become applicable.

Some of the questions to ask when considering adaptability:

- Are the selected routers capable of handling a wide range of routing technologies?

- Is there support for a multiprotocol environment if this is applicable to the network?
- What is the long-range vision for the company as far as growth, staff additions, acquisitions, and moves?
- How flexible is the Access layer design for moves, adds, and changes?

Acquisitions are particularly important considerations when choosing the network design and the devices supporting that design. When a company acquires another company, there may be legacy protocols and network equipment to be integrated into the existing design. It is important that the overall design be able to support the addition of the acquired network with as little disruption as possible to both sets of users. Failure to plan for such scenarios can mean inability to integrate a legacy network or extended network downtime for large segments in the future.

When you take the time to discuss these and other issues with the support staff and users of a network, many headaches associated with major changes can be avoided later.

Manageability

A network should be designed in such a way as to allow for monitoring and management using standard management protocols, such as simple network management protocol (SNMP) and remote network monitoring (RMON), without the tools becoming a part of the problem. Even if a company is not currently using any form of network management, it is important to take this into account for several reasons:

- For future growth
- To avoid redesign
- To add value to the design

First, if the company or user base does continue to grow, the likelihood is that the network will also grow, expanding beyond the level at which the current support staff are accustomed to serving. Network management would allow for more rapid fault isolation and resolution. Secondly, when the company realizes a need for network management, the ability should already have been considered in their new network design so that they don't have to revisit the issue later. Finally, the entire spectrum of network management adds value to a network design by providing a way to avoid problems and to quickly assess and resolve them when they do occur.

If a company has not already considered network management, they have the ability to do so when reviewing the design. If they had considered it but were not ready to implement it, the optimal locations of probes, network management stations (NMS), or analyzers can be shown on the final design. In this manner, the plan is already in place when they are ready. Chances are the subject is already part of the "big picture" for the customer. Usually, when a network redesign has become necessary, a network has experienced many problems that could have been easily spotted through good network management.

Another choice to consider is whether to use centralized or distributed network management. Traditional network management generally uses one network management system that receives all traps, or network management events and messages, that are generated anywhere in the network. This can create problems in many instances, since additional traffic is constantly being fed into an already busy network. Distributed network management, as illustrated in Figure 1-1, places less of a burden on the network by keeping the traffic local between probes or sending devices and their designated SNMP server. Periodic updates are sent from the remote NMS to the "lead" NMS.

As Figure 1-1 shows, it is best to implement distributed network management with periodic updates sent to a Manager-of-Managers (MoM)—where possible—rather than have multiple devices polling more devices across an already congested link. This might mean having RMON probes reporting to

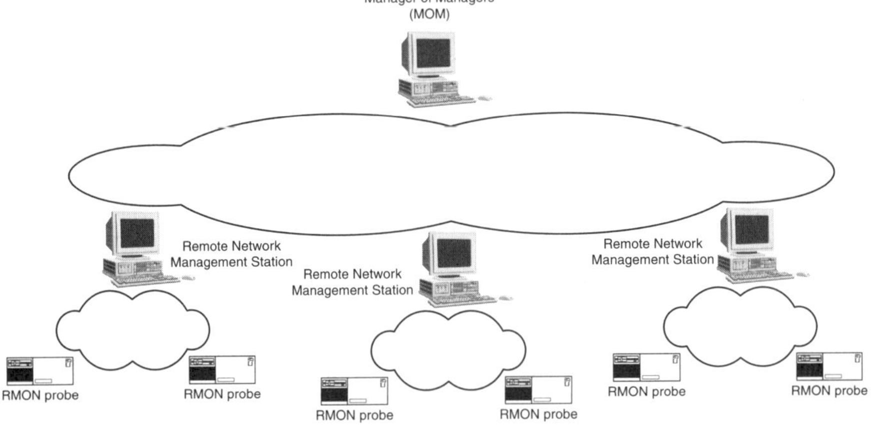

Figure 1-1 Distributed network management

a central NMS, or it might mean further dividing the workload to include a NMS at each remote location, with RMON probes reporting to that station and updates flowing at scheduled intervals back to the main NMS. This is the design shown in Figure 1-1. Each RMON probe reports to a local NMS. That NMS reports to the MOM. Traffic is kept local *most* of the time.

This goal takes you outside the routing and switching area into the entire picture of the customer network. A good network is rarely about having the fastest, most expensive equipment. A good network is usually a result of an excellent eye for details, such as network management and related devices.

Cost-Effectiveness

The best design in the world is worthless if your client cannot afford it. For example, a small business may only have the budget for a basic network, supporting a small number of users and applications. Later, the Core router may need to be upgraded, but if the wiring closets are ready, the cabling is not outdated, and the users are being served adequately, the upgrade should be an easy one. Creation of a good architecture sometimes means taking the requirements and finding the best solution with the least compromise, all within the budget. When you do this, you will earn the trust and loyalty of your customer.

TIP: *Creation of a good architecture means taking the requirements and finding the solution of least compromise—within the budget!*

Design Issues

There is almost always a trade-off in any network design. Some of the factors to keep in mind are fixed costs, recurring costs, and projected longevity of the network design. The network may currently be going through a major upgrade every five years. Even though you have considered the scalability and adaptability of the design, there is still the reality of technological changes that will, at some juncture, mean upgrading certain devices, interface cards, or wiring. If we were to see the issues as an equation, it might look like this:

```
(X + Yn)/n = r
```

Fixed costs (*X*) are a one-time major outlay of funds that can seem to be a great burden if looked at solely on the initial impact. Add this to your recurring costs.

Recurring costs (*Y*) can be something like the monthly cost of the circuit from the service provider or the costs for administration of the systems. Multiply that cost by the number (*n*) of billing periods in the entire projected lifecycle—in this case, 60 months.

Divide the entire cost over the life of the project by the number of billing periods in the lifecycle (*n*). This should yield a resulting monthly cost over the life of the project.

Let's suppose that the fixed costs of a given project are $1,000,000 in equipment, wiring, and installation services. The anticipated lifecycle is 60 months. Recurring costs are $2,500 per month for circuits and $7,500 per month for network management from a consultant. Your equation would be as follows:

```
$1,000,000 + ($10,000 x 60) / 60 = $26,666.66
```

This figure is usually a more digestible sum to the finance department than an initial outlay of 1 million dollars followed by monthly bills totaling at least 10,000 for the next 5 years (assuming no increases in fees).

Another possibility when selling a network design is to consider capital leasing companies. Many smaller or not-for-profit organizations do not have the kind of capital to build the networks that would enable them to grow and be successful. Capital leasing companies can purchase the fixed equipment and lease it to the company for a fee each month. When the lease term ends, the company may then upgrade and start a new lease agreement or may find themselves in a better financial position to purchase equipment outright for the next design.

While financial issues are not always the only hurdle you will encounter in your initial design phase, they are often the most difficult ones to get past, *if you are not prepared.* There are almost always trade-offs in any network design, usually because the best design is the most expensive design. It is incumbent on you, as the network designer, to find the best possible solution for the customer with the fewest trade-offs. Don't sacrifice what you know will be a critical router in the Core for better switches in the wiring closets, for example.

Design Methodology

There is more to designing a good network than selecting the hardware and cabling and coming to a viable trade-off between cost and need. After assessing the requirements, the budget, and the needs of the network, there is the topology consideration, selection of the naming conventions, and the decision of how to address the network entities.

A good methodology gives you a foundation on which to start any project. Cisco recommends a six-step process, shown in Figure 1-2, which is applicable to almost any network plan. Steps 1 through 3 are done sequentially and should only be needed one time, unless the site adopts a new topology at some point. Steps 4 through 6 form a loop that may be repeated at each upgrade or design change in the future of the network. We will go through these steps individually, and then we will dig deeper with some practical examples in figures to follow.

Step 1: Analyze the Requirements

In this step, many questions will be asked and answered before the overall picture of the requirements will begin to emerge. Some of those questions may be as follows:

- How many users exist today?
- Is there a prediction for growth over the target lifecycle?
- What applications are being used in the network?
- Will new applications be deployed in the near future? If so, what are the bandwidth requirements of those applications?
- If a network exists today, where are the bottlenecks and the greatest number of user complaints?
- Are there any available reporting tools, such as a trouble ticketing system, that can be used to gather information?

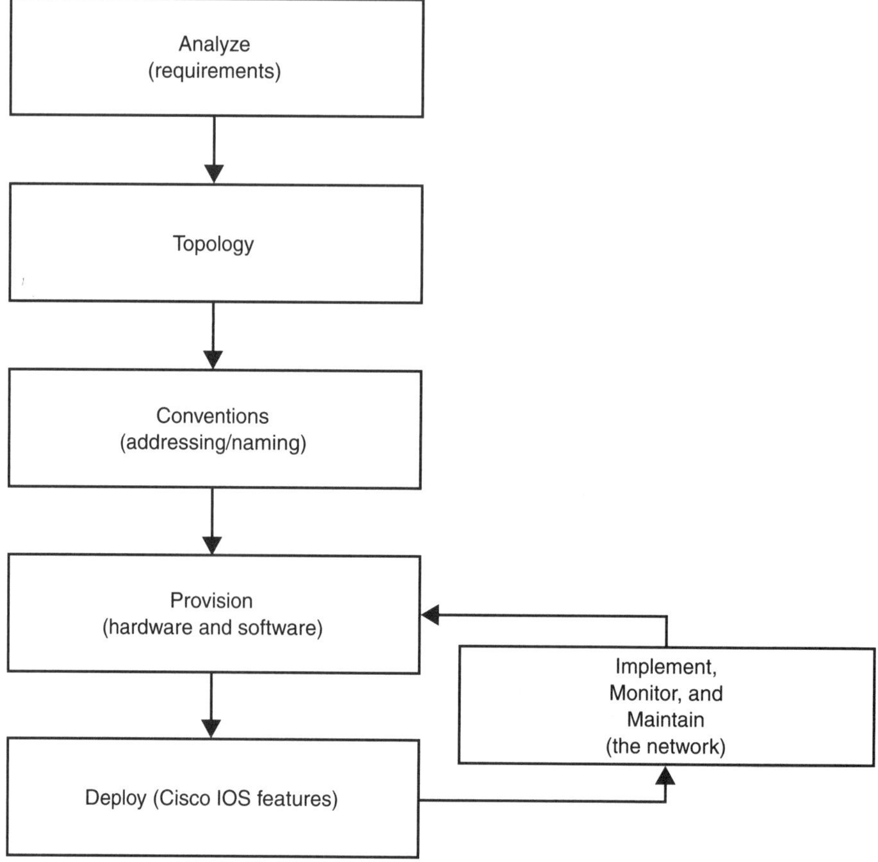

Figure 1-2 Design methodology

- Based upon the business model, what are the applications or technology that would promote the most business growth (video teleconferencing, VoIP, data mining, point-of-sale systems, or Web servers, for example)?
- Are there any new remote sites in the planning stages? If so, what will their bandwidth requirements be? (Will remote clients need to do uploads frequently to a main site server, for example?)
- If there are any network management tools in place, are reports from these systems available to show baselines and trends?

As evidenced here, the list of questions is infinite, depending upon the scope of the project. Careful attention must therefore be paid to not only making the business case for the proposed upgrade or redesign, but to planning for future growth and user needs.

Step 2: Develop the Topology (Internetwork Structure)

In order to design a highly scalable internetwork, the structure of the network must be planned in a hierarchical manner. The Cisco-recommended network design model, the three-tier model, is shown in Figure 1-3. By following this model, you will be able to see the key issues and requirements of each area without becoming overwhelmed by the total network topology and its endless possibilities. These are the three main areas in a network hierarchy.

Core Layer The Core provides the wide-area links between remote sites and "campus" networks that connect to form a WAN. It is where the enterprise network touches the world. At this layer you will find serial links (T1/T3), Frame Relay, and other WAN protocols and Core services. The network backbone exists in the Core area.

Distribution Layer At the Distribution layer, the network begins to take on its personality. Here you will find the campus backbone, firewalls/VPN devices, the beginning of the enterprise naming conventions and number schemes, and the type of network formed, whether Fast Ethernet, FDDI, or ATM. The Distribution layer typically extends the network to the wiring closets.

Access Layer The users enter the network at the Access layer via Fast Ethernet, Ethernet, or Token Ring. The hosts attach to the network in order to reach local and remote applications and network services.

Figure 1-3
The three-tier model

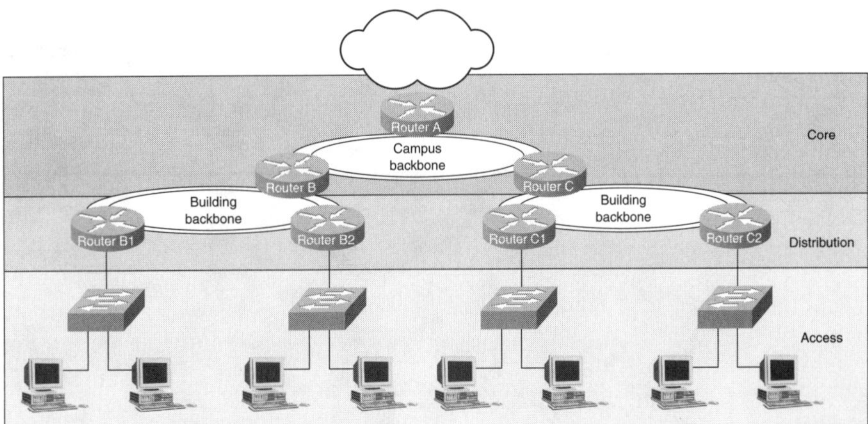

Step 3: Define Naming Conventions and Addressing Strategy

Selecting a good naming convention is more than a way to assign hostnames and to establish a way of communicating with devices (other than by network address); it is a smart way to easily recognize the location and application of a given host. In Figure 1-4, we see an example of what might be a typical campus environment.

For instance, let's assume we have a mixture of Unix and Windows NT servers in the Math department's second-floor server room. To quickly assess a problem with a given Web server running FreeBSD, it is best that the name reflect something unique about the host. Observe the following examples:

Good Choice	Poor Choice
MA2UN4WEB	abacus
2MATHWEB4	webboy

In the first example, MA reflects the building or department, 2 represents the floor, UN represents the operating system in use, and WEB represents the applications. A network manager could quickly determine that Web server 4 in the Math department's second-floor server room was unresponsive. The manager could further deploy a network technician along with the Unix system administrator for that server room. The poor choice,

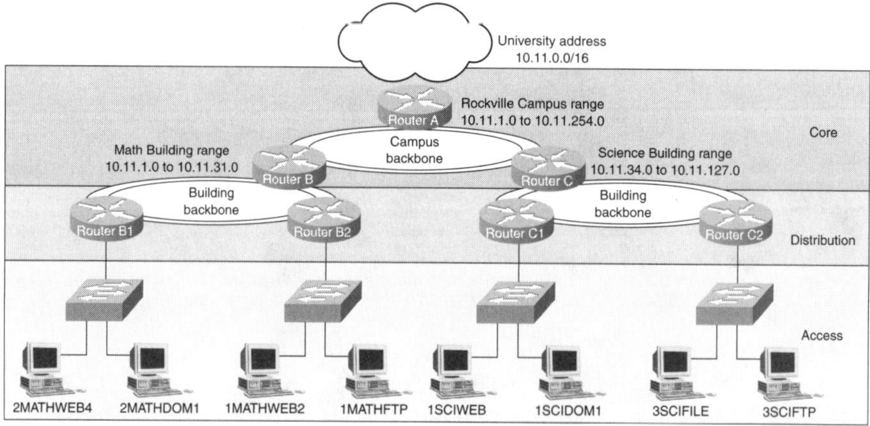

Figure 1-4 Addressing/naming conventions

abacus, may reflect that the unit is in the Math department, but nothing else about the host is revealed. A network technician would have a harder time tracking down the device, perhaps having to resort to knowing the subnet associated with the Math department, in order to track down the offending device.

In the second example, again we have clues that this is Web server 4 on the math department's second floor. The poor choice merely reflects a possible Web server that only the system administrator would recognize.

A good addressing strategy goes hand-in-hand with good naming convention choices. With a good addressing scheme, the groundwork is laid for future growth of the network as well as for good network performance. Network areas should be contiguous, that is, the network should be able to grow in a consecutive block of addresses, even if the block is further subnetted. This simplifies route summarization and routing protocol convergence.

Step 4: Provision the Hardware

There is a lot more to "provisioning the hardware" than just going with whatever is the latest and greatest technology. Many factors have to be taken into consideration when deciding upon the hardware and software to be purchased. You will take into account:

- Cost
- Footprint
- Upgrade path
- Manageability
- Training
- Interface types and port density
- Memory, CPU, and bus requirements
- HVAC/facility requirements

Cost Initial and recurring costs to provision and maintain the hardware and software are always something to be considered in any design plan.

Footprint Is there enough rack space in the computer room or lab? How much rack space will the equipment require? Will the hardware acquired for the new project overflow your area?

Upgrade Path How often are upgrades released for the product, and what is the procedure for obtaining the upgrades? Will each software upgrade also require a memory upgrade? Will entire line cards need to be replaced to upgrade firmware on a piece of equipment? Part of a good overall design should include answers to the questions normally asked either during the install phase or during the operational phase.

Manageability If the site uses network management, are the devices manageable? What version of SNMP are they compliant with? Even a UPS can be managed with SNMP, so if this is an important matter in the selection of equipment or software, be sure to document the answers to these and any other questions on manageability.

Training of Personnel Very important! If you are proposing a design that requires the retraining of all of the network personnel, that also must be taken into account when budgeting. If the design is truly the best solution, find a way to soften the blow by agreeing to package deals or free training from the reseller or vendor.

Interface Types and Port Density Part of the equipment selection is to define the site needs such as number of serial ports (and type) for current and future needs, density required to support the LANs connecting to the equipment, and growth needs. It would be unwise to purchase a five-slot router that will be fully loaded as soon as it is deployed. Leave room for planning.

Memory/CPU/Bus Requirements To support the proposed configuration, purchase RAM in proportions recommended by the vendor. These can usually be found on the Web sites of various manufacturers. In the router realm, CPU power and bus speeds are usually specific to the model.

HVAC/Facility Requirements It is also good practice to run the design by the facilities personnel once the details of the equipment to be ordered are documented. Have the data sheets ready that specify heat output, voltage, and amperage as well as temperature and humidity ranges for a given device. This permits factors such as cooling, humidity control, and power requirements to be addressed before the equipment is purchased.

Step 5: Deploy Cisco IOS Features

During the design process, there will be some idea of the types of traffic that will pass through the network devices—Internet Protocol (IP), Internetwork Packet Exchange (IPX), and Systems Network Architecture (SNA), for example—and as the process goes on, more granularity will be added. Will access lists be employed on the router? If so, what type, and what is the desired outcome? There may also be features such as QoS or Border Gateway Protocol (BGP) communities that are important in the overall traffic management in the design. It is also at this stage that other products may be taken into consideration: firewalls, RADIUS or TACACS1 servers, encryption devices, and configuration management stations. All of these are factors in the final design.

Step 6: Implement, Monitor, and Maintain the Network

Congratulations! Your design has been built, accepted, and is ready for deployment. Whenever possible you will build the network in a lab or demo environment prior to actual deployment into a production network. This step helps to avoid unnecessary downtime and general headaches when the network upgrade takes place. It is a good time to work out the bugs in the plan, to explain each step to the network personnel, and to fine-tune any last-minute requirements that may have been overlooked.

Summary

In this chapter we discovered how to determine and set goals for the network design process and the components that went into those goals. We then covered key design issues common to almost any network structure. Finally, we discussed a design methodology that helps set the course for most network design and redesign projects. You should now have the basic tools to help you get underway with the case studies in this book as well as with "real-life" projects you may be ready to undertake.

In Chapter 2, "Hierarchial Design Model," we'll take a closer look at the three-tier model, at each individual layer, and at the variations and benefits of the model, as well as how to begin using it to build Cisco networks.

Bibliography

Cisco Internetwork Design Course Manual, version 3.0, April 1997, Cisco Systems, Inc.

Cisco Internetwork Design, Cisco Press, 2000, Matthew H. Birkner, Editor

Internet Requests for Comments (RFC) Source, **http://www.cis.ohio-state.edu/hypertext/information/rfc.html**

CHAPTER 2

Hierarchical Design Model

Overview

In Chapter 1, "Introduction to Internetwork Design," we looked at a very broad view of the theory behind the hierarchical network design model and a general view of the network design process. In this chapter we will expand on what you learned in the last chapter, and build on what you have discovered about the three-layered network design model.

In this chapter, we will drill down a little deeper into the hierarchical or three-layer model of network design. By looking at the elements and functions of the Core, Distribution, and Access layers of the design model, we will discover the traffic flow of the network. This is important because in order to understand where to place certain network devices and when to implement policies, for instance, you must understand how the traffic should move through the network for the best efficiency. We will talk about the benefits of using the hierarchical design model and give guidelines for how to design a "real-life" network based on the model. We will also discuss variations on the model that will be important depending on the network in question.

NOTE: *The terms "three-tiered" and "three-layered" are used interchangeably throughout this book. The term "layer" in this context is not to be confused with the layers of the OSI model since we are talking about network design.*

Three-Layer Hierarchical Design Model

Cisco recommends a three-layer model as the basis for designing robust, scalable internetworks. As we discussed in the previous chapter, there are Core, Distribution, and Access layers within this model. This is a very simple, "cookie cutter" method of making networks modular, adaptable, and scalable. It applies not only to the entire enterprise network but can be used to design a campus connecting to that larger network backbone.

But, you may say, every network is different. Every company, university or operation is different. How, then, can we apply a simple model to so many vast possibilities? The model itself, in fact, tends to simplify the process rather than dictate it. Let's take a closer look at this to help us understand how this can be.

Say, for instance, that you are involved in building a doghouse. Before starting to ask any questions about the dimensions, location, or type of dog, you instinctively have a sense about the parts of a doghouse. You will need a foundation, walls, and a roof.

It is the same for networks. There is a point of access for the users, a layer of distribution across buildings via wiring closets and the like, and a core—the heart of the network—which links the entire network together and can be a point of entry to the Internet in some smaller enterprise networks.

It is in this manner that you begin to break down the details of the network design. Once you have completed a number of network designs and implementations, the hierarchy will become instinctive and will enable the details to fall into place much more smoothly. Until you have reached that level of experience, however, the hierarchical model will help you to build a solid network design, step by step, using proven techniques employed by network architects around the world. Here is what you can expect to learn about in this section:

- Hierarchical model benefits
- Goals of the network design
- Design model elements
- Layer functions
- Model variations
- Design guidelines

Hierarchical Model Benefits

What are the benefits of using the three-layered model? Why should you follow the Cisco recommendations? Perhaps you have been designing internetworks for months or years without regard to such a design model. Some of the benefits to be gained are

- Better scalability
- Easier implementation
- Easier troubleshooting
- Predictable traffic patterns
- Protocol support for future applications
- Better manageability

A hierarchical network design also tends to be easier to manage and can provide multiprotocol support for present and future applications. These benefits are discussed in greater detail in this section.

Better Scalability A hierarchical network design model tends to be quite scalable, allowing growth without a total redesign of the network. It is modular in nature, allowing for growth in much the same way a child's building block project can keep growing. The pieces neatly fit together, no matter how large the project may grow.

To fully understand scalability, you must first think of an everyday example such as the telephone number scheme employed by telephone companies. Area codes are assigned to a given geographical area. Years down the road, an area code is exhausted if the population density of the area becomes larger than original growth projections. At that point, a second area code is added, usually for implementation in the densest part of the community.

It is the same for routing. Initial projections for growth are taken into consideration when designing the network. These projections will determine the number of networks that will be needed for a given LAN. Those numbers in turn determine the number of routers and/or switches that will be needed to support the LAN.

The end result of all of this careful planning is that the network is scalable for short- and long-term growth and can be appended to when necessary without a disruption to the rest of the networks in the WAN. Additionally, existing or new campuses are designed in such a way as to be self-contained! In other words, each campus could have a Core, Distribution, and Access layer, thus reducing the traffic flowing to and from the central campus and improving overall network performance.

Ease of Implementation A logical, hierarchical network design model lends itself to a relatively easy implementation. Portions of the network build-out may be undertaken in stages. Additionally, the provisioning of hardware and software is easier when the functions of each layer are clearly spelled out and understood from the outset.

Ease of Troubleshooting A hierarchical network design allows easier isolation of network problems when they occur. Because functions of each layer of the model are known, support staff troubleshooting a network issue can quickly trace problems to their source and can use techniques such as network segmentation to temporarily reduce the scope of the problem.

For instance, if an e-mail server becomes the target of a mail relay bomb (a common security threat), the LAN from which the e-mails are being sent could be cut off from the rest of the Wide Area Network (WAN) by shutting down the point-to-point link. This could also be accomplished by cutting off access to the e-mail servers from the wiring closet.

Predictable Traffic Patterns A hierarchical network tends to exhibit predictable behavior over time. When network management tools are employed, the network behavior can actually be modeled by taking samples of data at different time "slices" and building trends analyses over a period of time. Support staff also begins to learn what problems to expect from different segments of the network. The logical progression of that fact is that problems that are noted in such a way may be addressed appropriately with an upgrade, redesign, or user re-education.

A layered network design is also more predictable for capacity planning, benchmarking, and addressing new networks. For example, if a university's Science department head needs to know whether a network upgrade is justified, it is fairly easy to take measurements of network usage for that segment. The new data is compared to historical data and used to show network growth. In a non-hierarchical network the task would be more difficult, as the team taking the measurements may have to deal with a meshed network where the usage was mixed and the data less cut-and-dried.

Protocol Support for Future Applications If it is important to support multiple protocols within a network, the network designer should take that into account during the planning stages. This will allow for provisioning of the appropriate network equipment to support any protocols that are in use or that may be used in the future. By having a network that is logically organized, providing support for future protocols and applications is easier. Instead of running a protocol such as AppleTalk across the Distribution layer, the traffic (and management) could be kept local to a segment, if servers are collocated with the clients in the original design. We will discuss this more in Chapter 13, "AppleTalk Design."

Better Manageability A network of any size is infinitely more manageable when it is arranged within the hierarchical model. Network Management Stations (NMS) and network management tools, such as RMON probes, are easier to position in a logically designed network. In addition, the predictable behavior of the hierarchical network tends to allow for better modeling of the impact of future applications and protocols.

Goals of the Network Design

We discussed these network design goals in Chapter 1 but we will reiterate them here. You will need to think about your basic goals as you proceed through the rest of this chapter. No matter the size of the network for which you are doing the design, these are common factors that can make your design a credit to your foresight long after you have moved onto new projects. The goals are

- Functionality
- Scalability
- Adaptability
- Manageability
- Cost-effectiveness

Some additional goals that may come up as you talk with your users and management are network performance, reliability, redundancy, and specific application support. With every network design project, you will discover that these and other goals will be on the collective mind of your customer. It is your job to ensure that the final design has adequately addressed the identified goals.

Design Model Elements

There are three distinct parts, or elements, to the hierarchical network design model. These are

- Core
- Distribution
- Access

Each layer has a job to do. If you consider the job of each layer while laying out the design, you can avoid many pitfalls. It becomes easier to see where the pieces fit when considering *only* one layer at a time, rather than always looking at the overall project design.

Certain functionality is appropriate for a certain layer. Different Cisco Internetwork Operating System (IOS) features may work more efficiently at the Distribution layer than at the Core layer. For example, routing policies, such as Access Control Lists (ACLs), belong in the Distribution layer. The core should remain as unencumbered as possible by any configuration element that could slow the flow of traffic. The Core layer should be reserved for rapid transit of bandwidth only. It is important to keep in mind the goals of your design as you start to separate the pieces and features to deploy. Study the ramifications of an action or placement by using modeling software or a test lab, for instance, before committing it to a production environment. We will be discussing modeling later in this chapter.

TIP: *Cisco defines a hierarchical layer as one where an OSI model layer 3 device (typically a router) boundary occurs. The three-layer design model is adequate to suit the needs of most enterprise networks. Even though it is now commonplace to use a Virtual LAN (VLAN) to define a hierarchical boundary, remember that this is the official Cisco answer to this question when taking the tests for your design certification!*

Core Layer The Core layer of the design model provides high-speed, optimized transport between core routers. At this layer we find the WAN taking shape, built from all of the campus networks. Links in this area are usually point-to-point. Generally speaking, there are no hosts in this layer, just core routers and services leased from an Internet Service Provider (ISP) or telecommunications service provider. Important items to note at this layer are path redundancy, load balancing, rapid convergence, and efficient use of bandwidth. We will talk about these later.

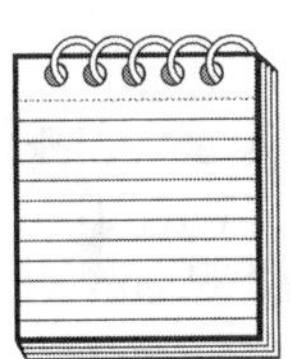

NOTE: *The terminology and technology associated with this layer includes T1/T3, E1/E3, SMDS, DS3, Frame Relay, and X.25.*

Distribution Layer The Distribution layer of the design model should contain routing policies, security, naming conventions, addressing schemes, Internet access, and transport to the core routers. This is generally known as the *campus backbone*.

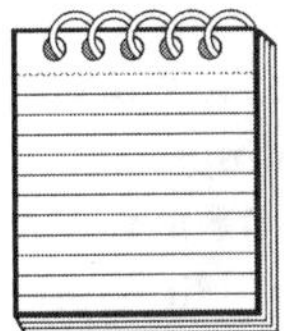

NOTE: *The terminology and technology associated with this layer includes Ethernet, Fast Ethernet, Gigabit Ethernet, ATM, FDDI, and CDDI.*

Access Layer The Access layer of the design model is the LAN or group of LANs. This is where the users or other hosts are linked to network services via hubs, layer 2 or layer 3 switches, or access routers. One school of thought is that this is where the user obtains the link light on the Network Interface Card (NIC) or the connection via the modem.

NOTE: *Terminology associated with this layer includes Ethernet, Fast Ethernet, Token Ring, hubs, switches, bridges, modems, servers, and workstations.*

Layer Functions

Each layer of the design model is best suited to perform certain functions. It is important to understand these functions in order to make the best possible use of the design model.

Core Layer Functions The Core layer of the hierarchical design model, as seen in Figure 2-1, is generally implemented as a WAN. The most important function of this layer is to provide the best service possible between geographically remote locations. In order to provide the best possible service, you must keep hosts and mainframes out of the core. The core routers also should have no routing decisions to make. They are like an assembly line in a factory. They must move things through their area quickly. It is not the function of the core to act as Quality Assurance. Leave that to the Distribution layer. In Figure 2-1, Remote Sites A, B, and C can all reach each other through WAN protocols, such as Frame Relay, Border Gateway Protocol (BGP), or X.25.

Some of the Core layer goals we will discuss are

- Path redundancy and Load balancing/Load sharing
- Rapid convergence
- Efficient bandwidth usage

Path Redundancy Core routers serve the important function of switching packets at high speed. As such, these routers should be connected via multiple paths, or *meshed*, although this can be quite expensive if the network has a large number of core connections. Additionally, small-to-medium enterprise

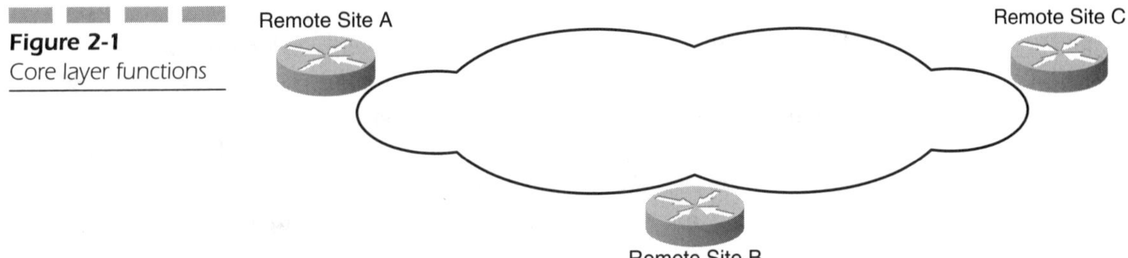

Figure 2-1 Core layer functions

networks may use their core routers to link to the Internet. If this is the case, links may exist to more than one ISP so that if a link to the Internet fails, the other link will take over within a few seconds. This is an especially important consideration in networks where Internet access is mission-critical.

Load Balancing/Load Sharing Links to multiple ISPs, or from core routers to remote sites, may be *load-balanced*, meaning that a routing policy may be implemented to use all available links. This method is used to keep traffic flowing without overloading a single link. Load balancing, also called *load sharing*, can also be used between core routers in large enterprise networks so that the links themselves do not become the bottleneck where large amounts of traffic may be flowing.

Rapid Convergence It is important that *convergence time* be kept to a minimum at the Core layer. Convergence time can be defined as the time required for a new route to be selected when the adjacent routers see a topology change. In the case of a failed serial link, the adjacent router will see the topology change immediately, and the process of selecting a new route will begin right away. Other changes are subtler, like a link that becomes unstable or a router that is reset. If a link to an ISP goes down, a properly configured router should make the change relatively transparent to the users.

WAN routing should be implemented in such a way as to reduce the possibility of route flaps or other problems that could affect the entire network. Since convergence is protocol-dependent, selection of the best protocol for a given network design is crucial to meeting this important Core layer design goal.

Efficient Bandwidth Usage When enterprise networks first began using Internet services and Wide Area Networks, long ago, a very costly 56 Kbps link might have been the network's only Internet connection. At that time, WAN link congestion was primarily managed by selectively allowing users onto the Internet. For example, only high-ranking officers of a company might have access to FTP files or to browsing the Internet.

Today most users have access to Internet services through high-speed links. They expect—in fact, demand!—fast response times when they send e-mail or bring up a browser window. And yet there are more important applications that need to be given a higher priority. By the use of certain Cisco IOS features, such as Quality of Service (QoS) or access lists, traffic can be better managed, without shutting off certain types of access to users altogether.

Distribution Layer Functions The Distribution layer of the hierarchical model is responsible for connecting the campus backbone to all of the remote sites via layer 3 devices, usually routers. As mentioned earlier in the Tip in the "Design Model Elements" section, this is the official Cisco answer. However, in reality we normally use VLAN technology to sort the layers and subnets on boundaries.

TIP: *Although some smaller enterprise networks connect to the Internet from the Core layer, it is far more common—and some would agree, safer—to place your Internet link(s) at the Distribution layer.*

In Figure 2-2 we see three routers connected at the Core layer, with Router B and Router C acting as Distribution layer devices. Router B is distributing services through dial-up or leased lines. Router C is connected via FDDI to a building backbone.

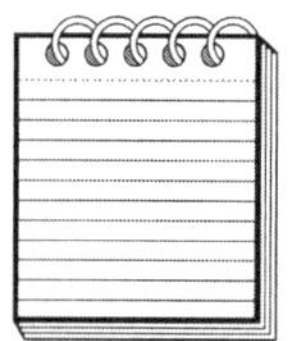

NOTE: *Although most of the figures show an FDDI or CDDI backbone for the campus and building backbones, it is far more common to use some form of Ethernet. Ethernet is less expensive and has a shorter learning curve than FDDI. The connectivity between buildings could also be leased lines or fractional DS3 lines provisioned by the Telcos.*

At the Distribution layer, some of the design goals should be to control access to services offered on the network (including policy implementation), define path metrics, and control various network advertisements.

Implementing Security Through the usage of access lists and network security, users are given access only to the services they need. For network

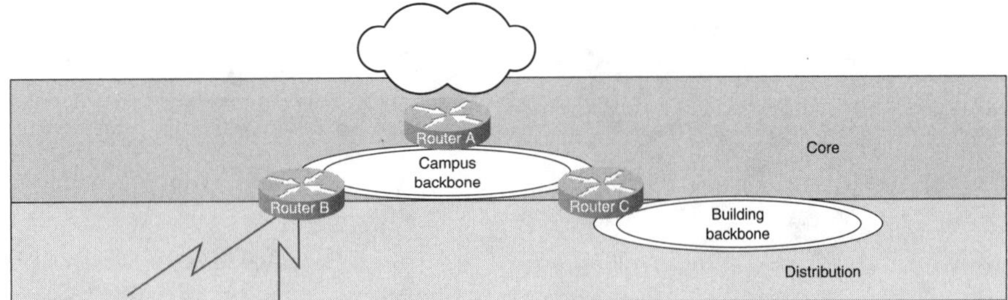

Figure 2-2 Distribution layer functions

access, a TACACS+ or RADIUS server may be put into place, using tokens or login/password combinations to allow secure logons. Access lists that tell the router to accept or reject packets based upon source, destination, or port can be added in order to enforce policies. Firewalls can also be implemented at this layer to provide a more granular level of network security. In fact, it is getting to the point now where a dedicated firewall is becoming commonplace.

Defining Path Metrics Distribution lists, map lists, static routes, and the like can be employed to control the flow of traffic at the Distribution layer. Paths may be weighted to increase the likelihood that the traffic will select one path over another. This can be useful with backup routes, such as dial-on-demand routing (DDR) or in the presence of multiple paths to the same destination.

Control of Routing Updates Network advertisement of routing updates may not be desirable for several reasons. Routing updates consume valuable bandwidth. They can also confuse the selection of the best path for a destination. For instance, in Figure 2-3 Router A has access to the same 65,000 advertised routes as Router B. However, Router B should not advertise those routes to Router A because routing loops could occur. Router A would see a given destination in the routing table advertised from the Internet. Router B would then say, "Hey, I know how to get to these 65,000 destinations!" Router A would favor a route learned from its directly connected neighbor and say, "Okay then, I'll use you as the next hop." With the next routing update from the Internet, it would start all over again.

It would be better in this instance for each router to act as the other's gateway of last resort, with filtered routing updates from each other. If Router A loses its connection to the rest of the network, it will then send outbound traffic through Router B without having conflicting routing information. Routing updates also consume valuable bandwidth.

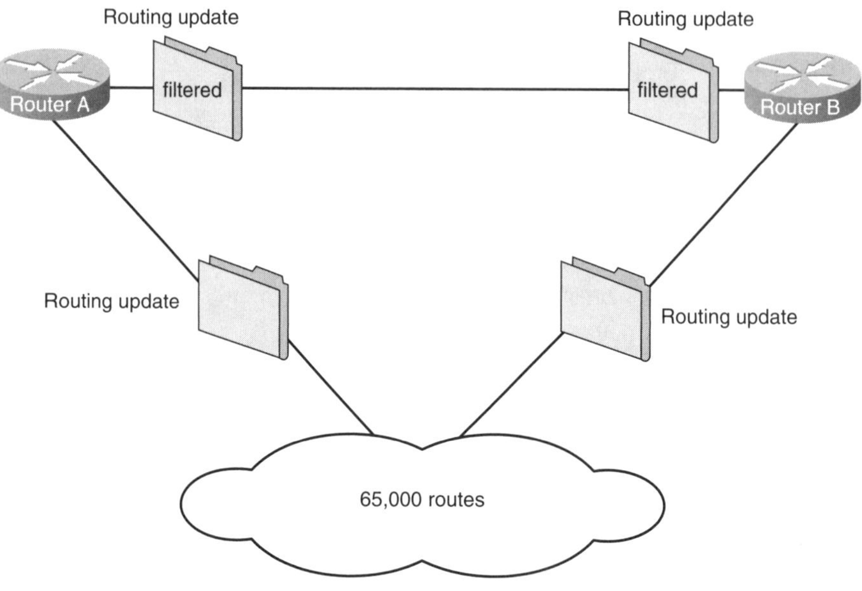

Figure 2-3 Network advertisement control

At the Distribution layer, policies are also built into the configurations. In this case, policy can mean access lists, path metrics, QoS para-meters, addressing schemes, naming conventions, or protocol advertisement control.

The Distribution layer also performs VLAN routing, IP address summarization, routing area aggregation, media transitions, and multicast domain definition. We will go into this in greater detail later.

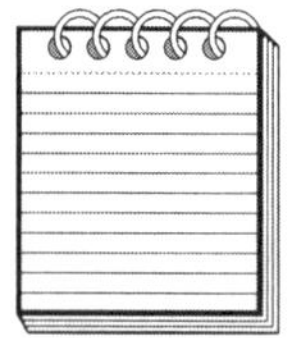

NOTE: *Hosts, including servers, should not be put on the network backbone at the Core or Distribution layers. To do so would reduce the backbone's ability to keep traffic flowing smoothly. Think of a server placed on this layer as the network equivalent of a slow-moving vehicle in the express lane of the highway—isn't that annoying?*

Access Layer Functions The functions of the Access layer, in a nutshell, are logical segmentation of networks, grouping of like users, broadcast isolation, and distribution of services across multiple CPUs.

As mentioned before, the Access layer is the point at which the users first access the network and network services. It is also connects the users to the campus backbone. Servers and workstations, print services, and dial-up services are implemented at the Access layer. Further security and segmentation of the LANs, usually by the use of VLAN technology, also occur at this layer.

In Figure 2-4 you can see that a dial-up user can access network services by connecting to the communications server via a modem. Once the user has been authenticated, the user's traffic proceeds to the router to gain access, if permitted, to services at any point of the rest of the network.

Model Variations

We have talked a lot about the three-layer model of hierarchical network design. How do we decide the number of layers a design has? Typically, it is a matter of how many hops a packet must take to the core of the network. In the designs we have seen so far, we have gone from the user to the Access layer router, or boundary. The next hop is to the Distribution layer boundary. The final hop is to the core router. Three hops: three layers.

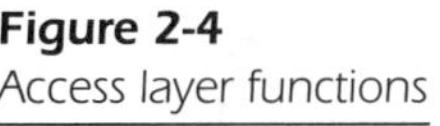

Figure 2-4
Access layer functions

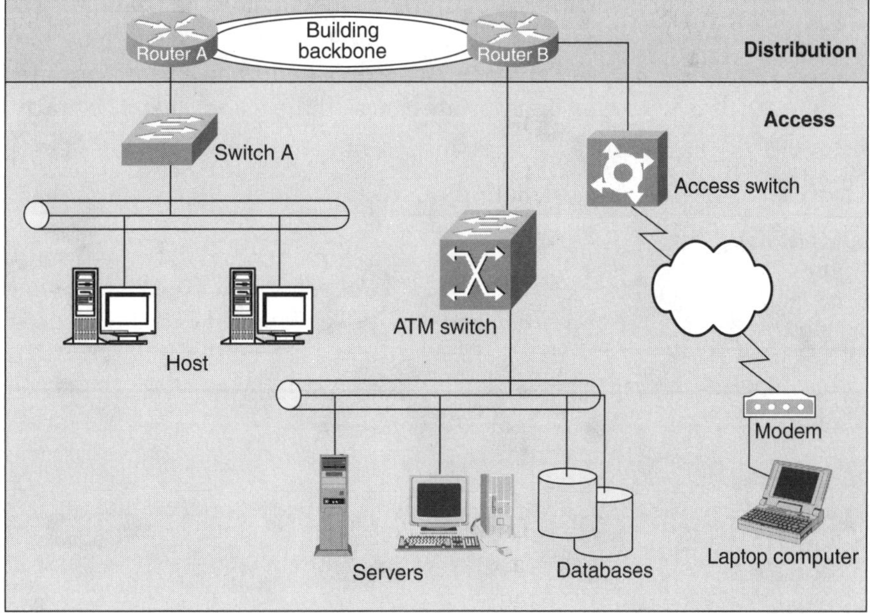

But a three-layered model is not always appropriate for a given network scenario. The selection of a design model is based on individual network requirements including size and type of services. In this section we will talk a little about some of the variations of the three-layered model that may be right for some situations.

Single-Layer Design In Figure 2-5 we see a network with two server farms—one in each location. In this instance, the network has a duplication of services and equipment in two remote locations. As we just discussed, this design is "single layer" because the packet takes one hop (via a layer 2 switch) to the core router.

The advantage of this design is that a great deal of server-based services can be kept local, reducing the load on the core. However, the drawbacks are that the network services become less manageable at a greater financial cost, since two sets of servers must be purchased and maintained.

Figure 2-6 shows a similar single-layer design where the servers and databases are centrally located and accessed via the core. While the servers may be able to take advantage of having higher-bandwidth technology, such as Fast Ethernet, locally, there is a single point of failure in this design. If the link to the server farm fails, the users will be unable to reach the servers for applications or services. This is a disadvantage that should be carefully considered before choosing this design.

Ultimately, the decision will hinge on the size of the network, the amount of usage of the application servers, and the general user population needs. If the servers are only accessed when a user logs onto the domain, this could be an appropriate choice. If the users must constantly access the application

Figure 2-5 Single-layer distributed model

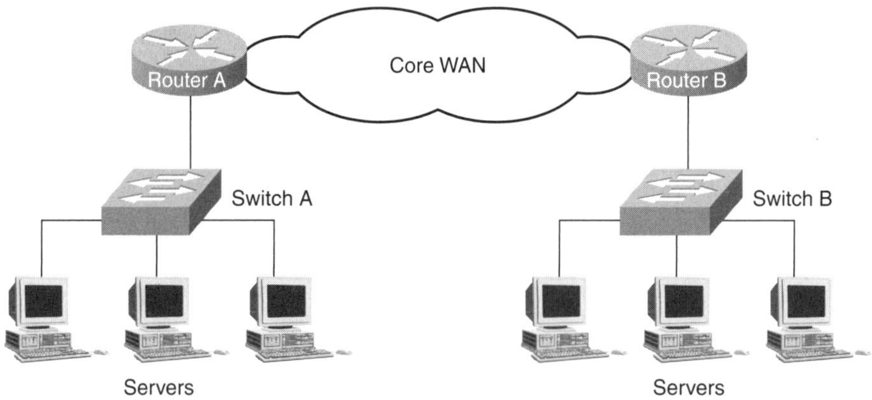

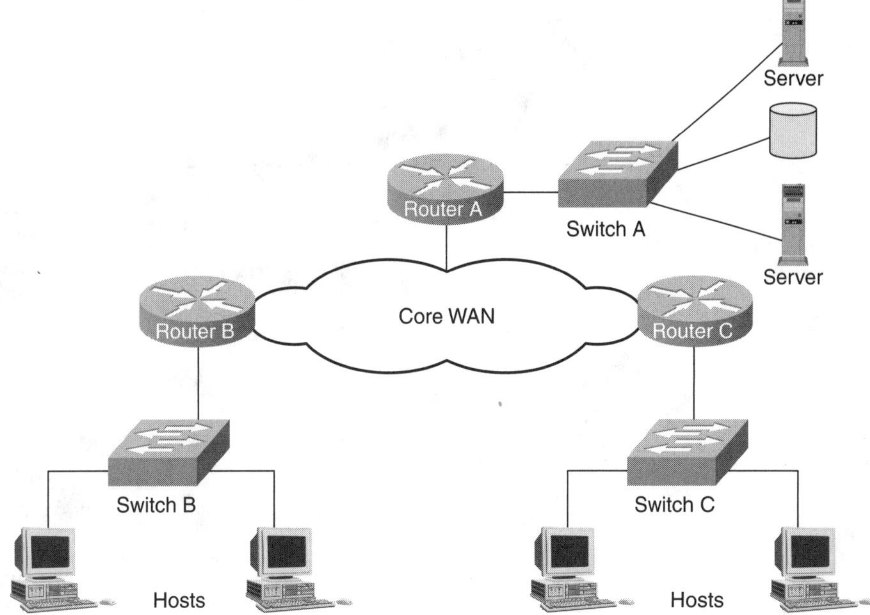

Figure 2-6 Single-layer hub-and-spoke model

servers, as is the case with many accounting databases, it would be inappropriate to recommend this design.

Two-Layer Design In a two-layer design, the campus backbone acts as a bridge between remote locations, serving mostly to connect multiple logical networks or multiple switched networks.

In Figure 2-7 we see three VLANs connected by layer 3 devices on a campus backbone at Remote Site B. It is more likely that you would use Route Switch Modules (RSM) on Cisco Catalyst switches than using routers in the Distribution layer of this design. However, three logical networks have been created on the campus backbone. In the Science and Servers VLANs, the architecture is flat and switched. In the Math building, the workstations are sharing bandwidth over a bridge or hub. All are connected to the building backbone, which then connects to the larger campus WAN.

TIP: *In the design shown in Figure 2-7, you may notice that a packet could be taking more than two hops to the core routers, but for the purposes of Cisco's tests, a hop is only defined as a router hop, not a hop through a layer 3 or 4 switch.*

Figure 2-7 Two-layer model

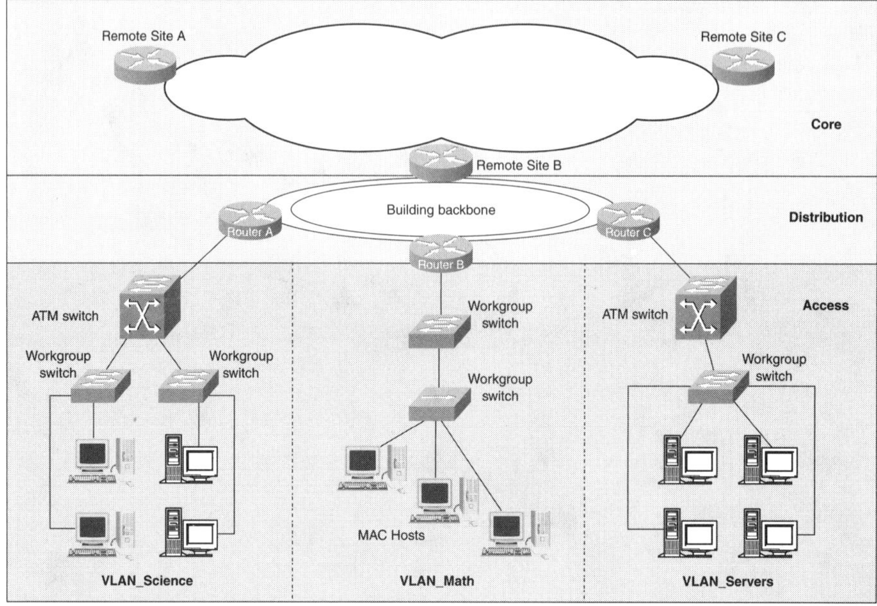

Redundant Two-Layer Design Finally, observe Figure 2-8. The redundancy is built into the design by giving the routers from the remote sites more than one way to access the backbone of the corporate network. For instance, if the router in the Math building loses its T1 line linking it back to the data center, an ISDN link could activate, routing the traffic via an alternate, albeit slower, path. In the design shown in Figure 2-8, traffic will continue to flow even if one of two or more links to the backbone fail.

This design saves money over a period of time by providing for reliability in the network while not incurring the cost of two or more dedicated leased lines for redundancy. However, if a network needed reliability *and* speed on a backup link, multiple leased lines could be employed.

The important thing to note about the model shown in Figure 2-8, however, is that it lacks scalability. Even if using ISDN links through a Frame Relay cloud, the cost to a growing network could blossom into a large amount of money very quickly in the sheer number of ports needed to support multiple termination points.

Design Guidelines

There are a few "rules of thumb" that serve as good advice when designing a network. The point of any good network design is to provide reliable net-

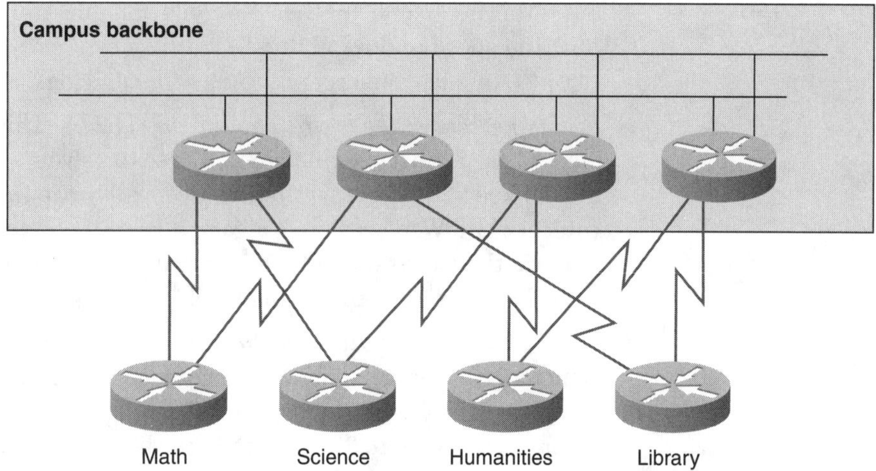

Figure 2-8 Redundant two-layer model

work services to the users and the applications they need to reach. With that in mind, here are a few guidelines for a sensible network design:

- *Bear in mind that a "layer" or "tier" in the hierarchical design model corresponds to a boundary created by a layer 3 (OSI model) device.* Earlier in this chapter we discussed the definition of the layers or tiers of the hierarchical network design model. An OSI layer 3 device, usually a router, generally resides at the boundary of the hierarchical network design layers. Now, this is important for taking the design certification tests, but in "real life" you would probably want to use VLAN technology or layer 3 switches instead of routers. Placement of a router in every closet (or even at every campus) is a somewhat antiquated and expensive idea.
- *Do not completely "mesh" the network.* By this we mean creating haphazard links between Access layer network devices or Distribution layer routers without going through the backbone. Core routers can, however, be meshed for redundancy. Again, while this is important to note for the design certification tests, generally meshing is appropriate for switched environments but not necessarily for routers.
- *Keep end-stations off the backbone.* End-stations belong in the workgroup or Access layer! Putting hosts on the backbone causes a performance hit that no network needs. Remember that the backbone (Core and Distribution layers) should be for routing traffic to and from layer 3 devices at optimal speeds, not for the relative chattiness of

hosts talking to one another. Not only can end-stations on the backbone hurt the speed and reliability of traffic movement, but their presence can also impact convergence and redistribution.

- *Eighty percent of the traffic should stay local.* This is definitely an idea whose time came and went! These days you would be lucky to be able to keep 20 percent of the traffic local! Since the onslaught of the Internet and Web browsing, a good deal of the network traffic will have to leave the local segment. For the purpose of the design certification tests, however, remember this rule.
- *Deploy Cisco IOS features at the appropriate layer.* It is important to remember where to apply the various IOS features. While it may be tempting to set up an access list or two in the core, it can reduce your throughput by up to 30 percent, according to some measurements. It is better to leave the backbone to do its job of rapidly moving the packets to and from the networks within the campus and allow routers at the Distribution layer to employ the filtering and security features.

Study Hints

The study hints contained in this section are designed to give you guidance in preparing to take the CCDA and CCDP certification tests.

1. Remember that Cisco prescribes a three-layer hierarchical design: Core, Distribution, Access.
2. Review the variations on the three-layer design model: single-layer and two-layer variations.
3. Be aware of the functions that belong at each layer of the design model. Associate each layer with a function you know well from your own network experience in order to cement the idea in your mind.
4. Practice what you have learned on your own environment, in a virtual manner, of course. Draw out your current network—or that of a colleague's environment—and find the layers within the design. See if you can find the good and the bad points of the layout. Then try to redesign using the guidelines in this chapter.

CCDP Tips

This section contains an abbreviated list of the topics contained in this chapter. Think of this section as the equivalent of reading Cliff's Notes™ instead of reading an entire book. You will get the general idea of the chapter but will benefit more from reading the chapter in its entirety.

The following are the components of the Cisco Hierarchical Network Design model:

- Core
- Distribution
- Access

The benefits of a Hierarchical Design model include

- Scalability
- Ease of implementation
- Ease of troubleshooting
- Predictability
- Ease of protocol support
- Manageability

The functions of the Core layer are

- Load sharing/load balancing
- Rapid convergence
- Path redundancy
- Efficient bandwidth usage
- Moving the traffic

The functions of the Distribution layer are

- Access control
- Path metrics defined
- Network advertisement control

The functions of the Access layer are

- Logical segmentation
- Workgroups
- Broadcast traffic isolation
- Distributed services

The variations on the three-layer model are

- Single-layer-distributed
- Single-layer-hub-and-spoke
- Two-layer
- Redundant two-layer

Some guidelines to follow include the following:

- Layer 3 devices separate design layers
- Don't mesh the network within a layer
- No hosts on the backbone
- IOS features at the right layer
- Keep traffic local where possible

Summary

In this chapter we went deeper into the three-layer hierarchical design model recommended by Cisco. As we discussed, the framework helps network designers to build networks that work today and scale well for tomorrow. When the appropriate functions are deployed within the appropriate layers, the network is easy to deploy, troubleshoot, and predict. Unnecessary traffic is kept off the backbone and at the workgroup level, where it makes the most sense. Even if we deviate slightly from the three-layer model, using a hub-and-spoke single-layer, for instance, a hierarchy of functionality is still maintained.

Now that you understand more about the elements, functions, and benefits of the hierarchical network design model, including variations on the three-layer model and some guidelines on using the models, we are going to look at the LAN in Chapter 3, "Campus LAN Overview."

Questions

The following review questions have been selected to help you test your knowledge of the subject matter contained in this chapter. You will also find these questions contained in the CD-ROM included with this book. While these are not the questions you will find in the certification exams, knowing the answers to the review questions in this book will help cement the material in your mind as you prepare for the tests.

1. Select one function of the Core layer.
   - a. Access control
   - b. Rapid convergence
   - c. Distributed services
   - d. Security
2. Select one function of the Access layer.
   - a. Distributed services
   - b. Access control
   - c. Network advertisement control
   - d. Security
3. Select one function of the Distribution layer.
   - a. Access control
   - b. Logical segmentation
   - c. Rapid convergence
   - d. MP3 Server
4. What are the three layers of the hierarchical design?
   - a. Edge, Access, Core
   - b. Core, Distribution, Edge
   - c. Core, Access, Distribution
   - d. Distribution, Access, Internet
5. At what hierarchical layer do hosts belong?
   - a. Distribution
   - b. Core
   - c. Access
   - d. Workgroup
6. Identify the terminology associated with the Core layer.
   - a. E1/T1, Frame Relay, X.25
   - b. FDDI, CDDI, Fast Ethernet, ATM
   - c. Token Ring, modem, ISDN, Fast Ethernet, ATM
   - d. Security

7. Identify the terminology associated with the Distribution layer.
   a. E1/T1, Frame Relay, X.25
   b. FDDI, CDDI, Fast Ethernet, ATM
   c. Token Ring, modem, ISDN, Fast Ethernet, ATM
   d. Security
8. Identify the terminology associated with the Access layer.
   a. E1/T1, Frame Relay, X.25
   b. FDDI, CDDI, Fast Ethernet, ATM
   c. Token Ring, modem, ISDN, Fast Ethernet, ATM
   d. Security
9. At which layer of the hierarchical model does VLAN routing appear?
   a. Access
   b. Distribution
   c. Core
   d. Edge
10. At which layer of the hierarchical model does load sharing between ISPs occur?
    a. Access
    b. Distribution
    c. Core
    d. Edge
11. What type of device typically creates the hierarchical boundary?
    a. Hub
    b. Layer 2 switch
    c. Router
    d. Bridge
12. At what layer should access lists be applied?
    a. Access
    b. Distribution
    c. Core
    d. Edge

13. At which layer does the network addressing scheme come into play?
    - a. Access
    - b. Core
    - c. Distribution
    - d. Edge
14. At which layer does the WAN appear?
    - a. Access
    - b. Core
    - c. Distribution
    - d. Edge
15. At what layer should a firewall be placed?
    - a. Distribution
    - b. Access
    - c. Core
    - d. Edge
16. Which statement best represents the term "meshing the network," something you want to avoid?
    - a. Using a variation of the three-layered hierarchical model
    - b. Using a redundant single-layer model
    - c. Using OSPF virtual links
    - d. Connecting two remote sites directly via an alternate route.
17. At which hierarchical layer do dial-up services reside?
    - a. Access
    - b. Core
    - c. Distribution
    - d. Edge
18. What percentage of network traffic should stay local?
    - a. 10
    - b. 20
    - c. 60
    - d. 80

19. Which benefit of the hierarchical model provides for growth in number of users?
    a. Manageability
    b. Ease of troubleshooting
    c. Ease of implementation
    d. Protocol support
    e. Scalability
    f. Predictability
20. Which benefit of the hierarchical model provides for better problem isolation?
    a. Manageability
    b. Ease of troubleshooting
    c. Ease of implementation
    d. Protocol support
    e. Scalability
    f. Predictability

Answers

1. Select one function of the Core layer.
   b. Rapid convergence
   Explanation: Remember that the Core layer exists to provide optimum traffic flow between core routers and Distribution layer devices. Rapid convergence is important in keeping the traffic flowing smoothly with very little interruption in the event of a network link or protocol failure.
2. Select one function of the Access layer.
   a. Distributed services
   Explanation: The Access layer serves the users of the network. Giving users access to network services is part of the Access layer's function.
3. Select one function of the Distribution layer.
   a. Access control
   Explanation: Security services and access lists are best deployed at the Distribution layer. One of the key functions of this layer is to

implement secure control of network services to both external and internal users.

4. What are the three layers of the hierarchical design?
   c. Core, Access, Distribution

5. At what hierarchical layer do hosts belong?
   c. Access
   Explanation: Hosts should be kept off of the network backbone. The Access layer serves the users and is not considered to be part of the backbone.

6. Identify the terminology associated with the Core layer.
   a. E1/T1, Frame Relay, X.25
   Explanation: The Core layer is generally where WAN routing takes place. WAN routing can be accomplished via point-to-point serial links or Frame Relay clouds, for instance.

7. Identify the terminology associated with the Distribution layer.
   b. FDDI, CDDI, Fast Ethernet, ATM
   Explanation: Generally, the Distribution layer uses technologies such as FDDI or CDDI rings, ATM, Ethernet, or Fast Ethernet. These technologies use switches, hubs, bridges, concentrators, or routers.

8. Identify the terminology associated with the Access layer.
   c. Token Ring, modem, ISDN, Fast Ethernet, ATM
   Explanation: The Access layer serves the users. Users can enter the network via dial-up, Token Ring, or traditional LAN technologies such as Ethernet or ATM.

9. At which layer of the hierarchical model does VLAN routing occur?
   b. Distribution
   Explanation: VLAN routing generally takes place on the Route Switch Module (RSM) of a Cisco Catalyst switch or on a traditional layer 3 device of a smaller scale, such as a 2600 router. These devices reside at the Distribution layer.

10. At which layer of the hierarchical model does load sharing between ISPs occur?
    c. Core
    Explanation: If you recall, we discussed load sharing or load balancing as part of the function of the Core layer of the hierarchical network model. This is the layer that connects the WAN together and usually provides the Internet links.

11. What type of device typically creates the hierarchical boundary?
c. Router
Explanation: Remember—Cisco defines the hierarchical layers as those points at which a layer 3 (OSI model) device creates a boundary.

12. At what layer should access lists be applied?
b. Distribution
Explanation: As seen in question 3, IOS features such as access control or access lists should be deployed at the Distribution layer.

13. At which layer does the network addressing scheme come into play?
c. Distribution
Explanation: Addressing and naming conventions are deployed at the Distribution layer. Generally, the ISP assigns the network addresses at the Core layer.

14. At which layer does the WAN appear?
b. Core
Explanation: The Core is the layer at which the remote sites are connected together and are linked to the ISP(s). Functions such as load balancing and rapid traffic routing are found at this layer.

15. At what layer should a firewall be placed?
a. Distribution
Explanation: Again, security and access control services are best deployed at the Distribution layer, so as not to effectively disable the smooth flow of traffic at the core.

16. Which statement best represents the term "meshing the network," something you want to avoid?
d. Connecting two remote sites directly via an alternate route.
Explanation: Remember that the creation of a "backdoor" route between Access layer devices can confuse routing decisions and can create chaos in an otherwise sensible network hierarchy.

17. At which hierarchical layer do dial-up services reside?
a. Access
Explanation: Users access the network at the Access layer. Remembering this simple fact will help you to decide where to place services such as dial-up.

18. What percentage of network traffic should stay local?
d. 80
Explanation: The 80/20 rule of networking says: Keep the traffic local to the segment 80 percent of the time, routing the rest. Switch (locally) where you can; route where you must.

19. Which benefit of the hierarchical model provides for growth in number of users?
e. Scalability
Explanation: We discussed scalability as compared to the area code scheme of the telephone companies. When a segment's address allocation is exhausted, having a scalable design allows smooth growth, without creating discontiguous networks.

20. Which benefit of the hierarchical model provides for better problem isolation?
b. Ease of troubleshooting
Explanation: Remember that one of the benefits we talked about in regards to the hierarchical model was that support staff could easily spot and isolate a network problem. Baselining and trend analysis also allows for the gradual isolation of a problem, for proactive network troubleshooting.

Bibliography

Cisco Internetwork Design Course Manual, version 3.0, April 1997, Cisco Systems, Inc.

Cisco Internetwork Design, Cisco Press, 2000, Matthew H. Birkner, Editor

Internetworking Design Basics, Cisco UniverCD, © 1989-1998

Designing Large-Scale IP Internetworks, Cisco UniverCD, © 1989-1998

CHAPTER 3

Campus LAN Overview

Overview

We have looked at the hierarchical network design model in some detail now, discussing its benefits, some guidelines for its use and a few variations on the accepted model. Now that you have some background from a high-level perspective in how a network should be built, we are going to go a little further into campus Local Area Network (LAN) considerations.

In this chapter, we'll look at how to identify the technical considerations in the campus LAN design, such as types of media, network interface cards, end-station requirements, network management considerations, and types of equipment. We will also talk about the business issues to be considered when designing the campus LAN. To provide a little more background information, we will also look at the evolution of the campus LAN—how we got to where we are today with LAN design.

At the end of this chapter, you will have a good idea of how to identify the problems that need to be solved in a given LAN design and how to solve them in the network design you create.

Design Considerations

In the campus LAN design, there are several issues that must be taken into consideration. We will discuss each of these in detail:

- End-station (client and server)
- Network infrastructure
- Network cabling
- Network management
- Business issues

Take a look at Figure 3-1 where you can see a how a campus LAN might look for a building at a university.

What we see in Figure 3-1 is the Humanities building on an FDDI ring with three routers connecting separate and distinct areas of the building together. In this case the breakout of the network is logical in design, with different departments within the same building running over separate routers. This could conceivably give some autonomy to network managers or LAN support personnel within those areas. It also could permit very fast troubleshooting within a department's area. If a user within the Spanish

Figure 3-1 Traditional campus LAN

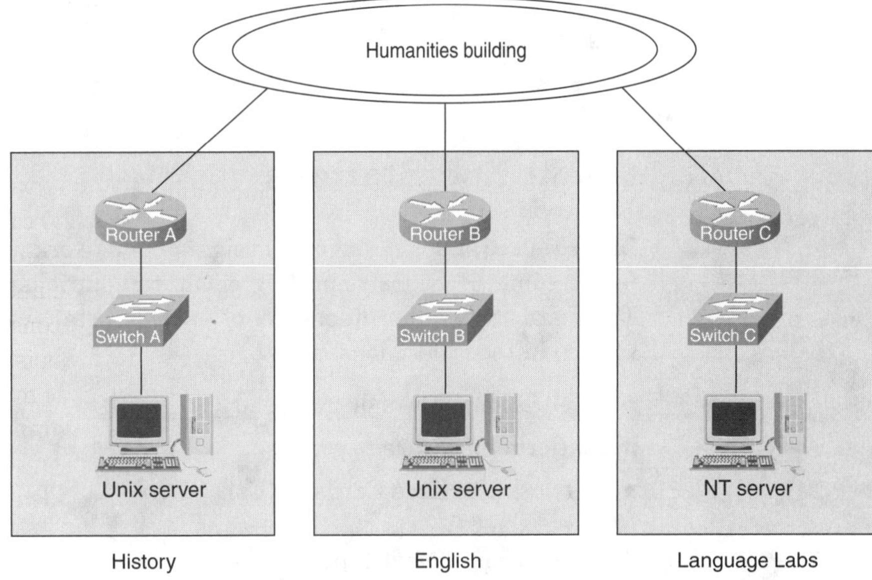

lab reports a problem, isolating the problem would be simple and quick. If we had the LAN distributed in another way, say by floor or wing, it might not be as intuitive, but much of this is up to the preference of the network design staff.

The important item to note about this network design is that the servers have been kept within each department. Traffic from the user PCs in the language labs to the language program server stays within the building, passing through Switch C. The traffic is kept local, per the guidelines discussed in Chapter 2, "Hierarchial Design Model."

Say a user on a PC in the History department needs to access research material contained on the server in the English department. In this case, the traffic will move through Switch A to Router A. Router A will see that the traffic is not destined for any directly connected port. A routing table lookup is performed, and the decision is made to forward the packet to Router B. Router B passes the packets to the final destination through Switch B.

This is by no means the only design we will discuss or recommend, but it should give you a general idea of a typical campus LAN topology and some of the logic behind it. As we mentioned in the last chapter, it is far more likely that you will find some flavor of Ethernet connecting the campus backbone because of its lower cost and ease of use. You would also probably not find each department, or floor, having its own router. It would be more likely to use Virtual Local Area Network (VLAN) technology and layer 3 switches, where inter-VLAN traffic needed to be routed.

Client End-Stations

In the course of designing or redesigning a network, you may find yourself facing some decisions regarding client end-stations, generally user PCs. There are a few different aspects of the client stations that need to be considered in these decisions.

- Applications in use or projected
- Platform hardware upgrades
- Network Interface Cards (NICs)

Applications What kind of applications are the clients running today? What applications will they be running in the near future or in the next few years? What are the bandwidth demands of these applications? These are the kinds of questions that will help determine the kinds of issues that need to be solved in the campus LAN design.

You may find that some users run very low-maintenance applications. Others will need multicast streaming to the desktop or use Voice over IP (VoIP). Applications such as these require special considerations because of their need for dedicated bandwidth. Real-time applications such as these cannot afford to share bandwidth and congestion with bursty applications like FTP or Web browsing. The client end-station must also be a higher-performance machine so that it doesn't become the bottleneck in the transmission.

Platform Upgrades When considering the platform being used for client end-stations, it is important to look at both hardware and software. About every six months, the current PC processor technology becomes obsolete. That is not to say that the PCs in use will become unusable, only that processor development continues to progress at blinding speeds. You also may find that a good number of users in the network have mobility issues—using laptops with docking stations instead of traditional desktop systems—thus, the management team may have already invested a lot in today's technology.

As for software, there are many acceptable operating systems, many of which will have a unique set of requirements from the LAN. In a graphics-heavy shop, you will probably find many Apple Macs, which may run

AppleTalk or MAC IP. (A further discussion of AppleTalk can be found in Chapter 13, "AppleTalk Design.") The users may be thinking of upgrading to Windows 2000 on all of the systems, or they may have a shop divided between Unix and Windows 98. As you will see in Chapter 14, "Windows Networking Design," Windows end-stations have their own set of network issues to be considered.

It is not necessary from a network design perspective to standardize on one operating system, but it is important for you, as the designer, to know what is in the network.

Network Interface Cards When designing the network, it is important to know what kind of NIC is installed in the typical user machine. If there is a mixture of different types of NICs, you will want to establish a count and location of the pockets of these different types of connectors. It will help decide the type of topology and technology needed in that area.

It could be that all users are on Token Ring, which you will find frequently in IBM mainframe environments. Or perhaps only pockets of users are on Token Ring and the rest are on some flavor of Ethernet. Will the choice of NIC remain the same? Considering the cost of maintaining (or upgrading) Token Ring, will the network staff and management really want to continue using Token Ring instead of a cheaper technology like Ethernet? To some users and environments, there is no issue with the use of Token Ring. The attitude may be, "If it isn't broken, don't fix it." However, it is important to discuss those issues in the early design phase.

If all of the users in a given area of the building are running graphics machines with 100 Mbps NICs, you may not want to connect them to the building LAN over a 10 Mbps interface. In some cases, doing so would work with no problems, but for client/server CAD models where the client must transfer large graphics files to and from a server, it could create a bottleneck for that group of users. Likewise, if there are plans to upgrade the hardware on workstations, it is important to note the type of NIC being planned for the platform so that the campus LAN can be designed with those requirements in mind.

In Figure 3-2, you will notice that a user in the Engineering department is connected directly to a switch port in the wiring closet. Because the user is on a VLAN, Engineering, it is irrelevant where the workstation physically resides. Moves, adds, and changes become far easier for the network, because the VLAN is virtual. We are no longer depending on a hard-wire to the wall jack or patching a cable in the closet. A network manager may simply identify the new switch port for the user's new location, when and if the move occurs, by assigning that port to the Engineering VLAN.

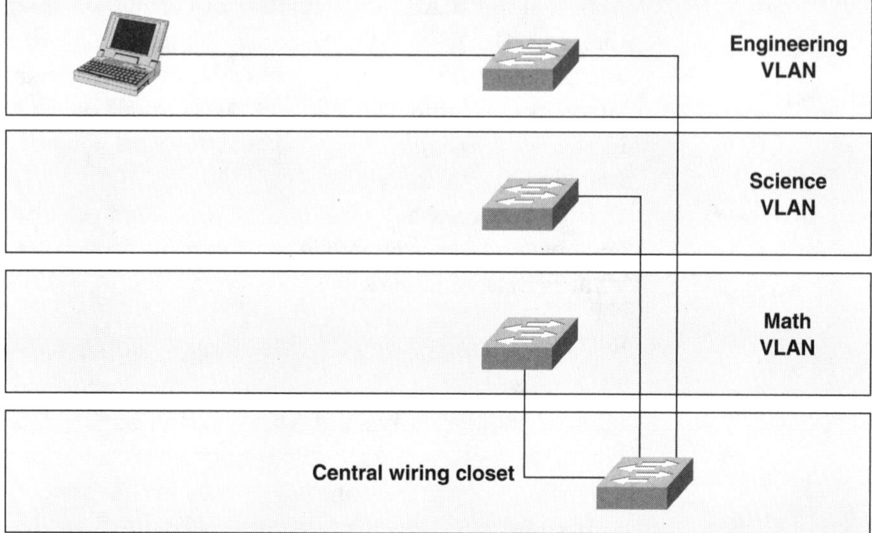

Figure 3-2 Client end-station connectivity

Understanding the needs of today and tomorrow from the client workstation is critical in putting together a workable, scalable campus LAN design.

Server End-Stations

Again, with servers, the considerations are bandwidth requirements, type of NIC, applications in use, and performance requirements. In addition to the questions that are asked about both client and server end-stations, the design needs to address optimal server placement—central or distributed? What type of media will be used?

It is important to address and alleviate as many single points of failure as possible at this stage of the design. Doing so may require upgrades to the servers in existence, either now or in the near future, but to not do so would be irresponsible. The best campus LAN design in the world does not do its job if it allows a power outage at the server farm to halt all productivity in the network.

Figure 3-2 showed you the typical modern connectivity of a client end-station. Servers connect in very much the same way; however, servers will probably need to be given a higher speed port. Where you may give 10 Mbps to a client, you may want to give a 100 Mbps port to a server. It will depend upon the NIC installed in the end-station and the requirements of the network. In some Catalyst switches, you may also assign a priority value of "high" to a switch port if it supports a server. This will improve performance on the port and reduce timeouts that could happen with a busy server. Some applications are very intolerant of delay.

TIP: *Setting port priority to "high" can improve performance on a switch port supporting a server. Not all Catalyst switches provide port priority, however. Consult the product information for your switch selection. A further trick when using client/server applications is to use "portfast," where supported.* Portfast *will allow the port to skip the "listening" mode and will place the port into "forwarding" mode. This reduces the likelihood of timeouts between clients and the server.*

Network Infrastructure

When considering the network infrastructure, there are several strategies and requirements that must be addressed:

- Backbone strategy
- Bandwidth requirements
- Type of technology
- Switching vs. routing

Addressing the backbone design strategy means selecting whether the campus LAN should be distributed or collapsed. A collapsed, or flat, network terminates all segments at a single router, typically. The router backplane performs the Core and Distribution layer functionality in one entity. The router not only becomes the single point of failure but also can experience CPU overload from having to handle all of the traffic for the campus LAN. Figure 3-3 shows an example of a collapsed backbone.

In a distributed backbone, shown in Figure 3-4, the workload is divided across several routers (at the Distribution layer of the hierarchical model), and those routers talk to each other across the Core layer using a high-speed backbone media, such as Fiber Distributed Data Interface (FDDI), Asycronous Transfer Mode (ATM), or Gigabit Ethernet. Each router then has a share of the workload, reducing the stress on the CPU and providing better overall network scalability.

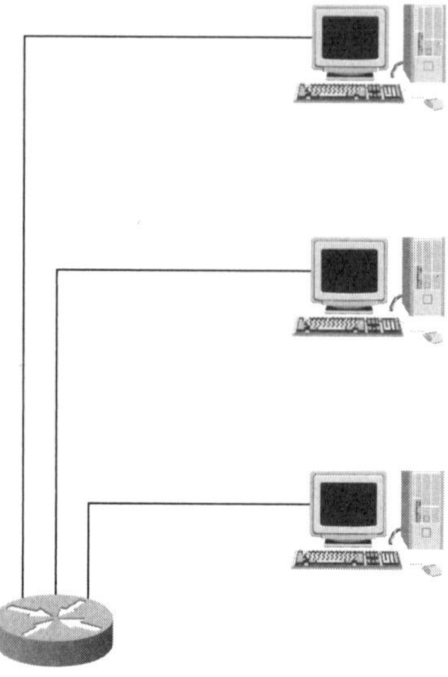

Figure 3-3 Collapsed architecture

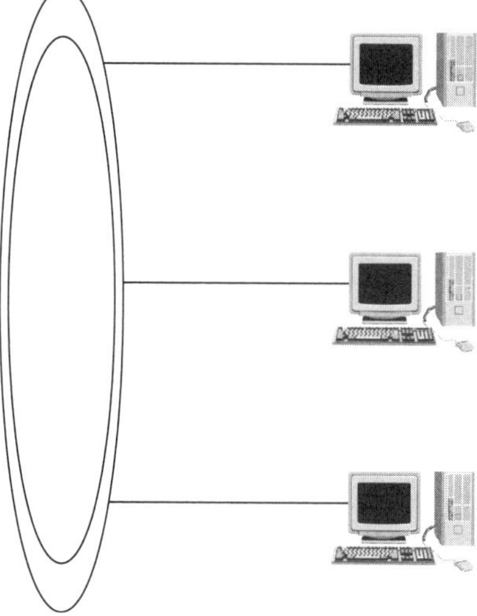

Figure 3-4 Distributed architecture

Bandwidth requirements again take into consideration the type of media being used on the end-stations in the network and the type of LAN bandwidth required for it to act as an optimal transport for the traffic resulting. More networks are seeing a requirement for ATM or Gigabit Ethernet at the Distribution and Core layers, especially when servers and/or client workstations are using Fast Ethernet NICs because this gives them the higher transit bandwidth.

Essentially, the old rules no longer apply to bandwidth requirements. It is no longer possible in most enterprise networks to keep 80 percent of the traffic local to the LAN segment. It is highly unlikely you will be able to keep 20 percent local, in fact. With the advent of Internet access and Web surfing, more and more traffic requires something that the local LAN does not have. Need something? Look it up on the Net!

Designing the LAN bandwidth requirements is usually a "best guess" choice. We will talk more about selecting appropriate bandwidth support in Chapter 4, "Campus LAN Technology."

What types of technology will the campus LAN use? Again, this goes back to the end-stations and the bandwidth requirements. The choices are typically ATM, Ethernet, Fast Ethernet, FDDI, Token Ring or Gigabit Ethernet. FDDI used to be the selection of choice when speed was required, as it supported redundant 100 Mbps pipes. With the introduction of Fast Ethernet, and Gigabit Ethernet now, FDDI is an expensive and unnecessary proposition in most cases. Token Ring is considered to be a legacy technology to many, but with many IBM networks still going strong, the cost of buying and maintaining Token Ring networks is not an issue.

The decision on the type of technology to select not only concerns the media type in use today but also the needs and desires of the business to grow and change. Perhaps the network is currently on Token Ring with Banyan VINES as its Network Operating System (NOS). The network managers may wish to convert to Fast Ethernet with Windows NT on the servers sometime in the next two years. If the campus LAN design is determined without considering these types of future growth issues, it becomes a very shortsighted design.

TERM: *A Network Operating System (NOS) can be defined as any available operating system that defines network parameters within an environment. Operating systems such as Unix, Windows NT, Banyan VINES, Novell NetWare, and others, can all be considered examples of an NOS.*

Finally, switching vs. routing should be considered in the overall design. Some of the things to consider when making this decision are cost-effectiveness, application requirements, and overall benefits to the current and future model. A switch in the wiring closet may be the answer for smaller segments, but a layer 3 switch or a small router may be the best solution for large data centers. This is because a layer 3 device, as you know, can handle multiple VLANs and protocols, as well as multiple media types.

The old network design adage used to be "Route where you can, bridge where you must." Now, however, that has changed to "Switch where you can, route where you must." Consider Figure 3-5. The switch that separates Segment A from Segment B accomplishes a couple of things. First, the switch creates separate collision domains. Second, the switch also increases the physical distance that the overall segment is able to span. In essence, it functions as a repeater in this case. Switches, however, have their limitations. They do not natively understand layer 3 information or network information. They also cannot handle mixed media or multiprotocol environments. A router is needed to accomplish this.

Routers also are a better choice to support broadcast control, security, address summarization, and hierarchical network addressing. If any of these issues appears in a LAN segment, then use of a router is the best choice.

Switches, or bridges, on the other hand, are less costly than routers or layer 3 switches. When a segment requires only single-protocol support, IPX for example, the backbone of that segment may be collapsed—using a bridge or a stack of bridges to all the traffic to flow, and using a router for the uplink to other segments. We will be discussing routing vs. bridging more in Chapter 4.

Figure 3-5
Switches and routers

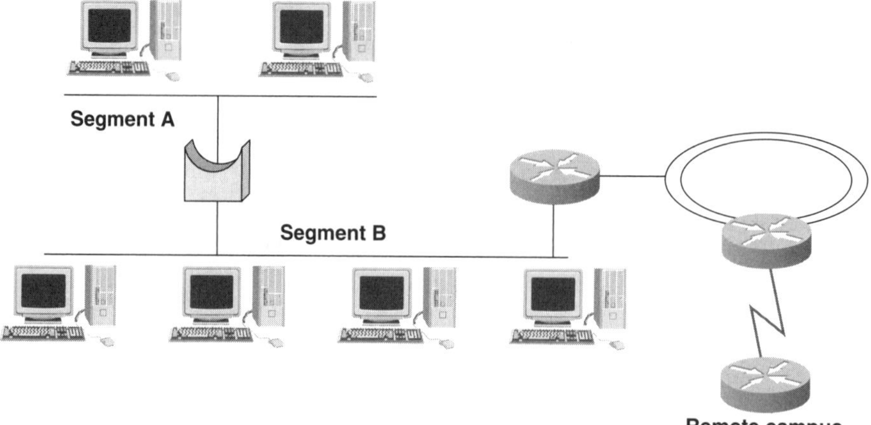

Network Cabling

The choice of type of cable to use in a network design is now more a matter of budget than anything else. For a network that you want to "future-proof," consider putting fiber not only in the risers but also all the way to the wallplate is a great way to do that. More than likely you will put fiber in the risers and use some grade of twisted pair copper in the wiring closets and to the wallplate.

Electrical cable comes in a couple of varieties: coaxial and twisted pair. Coaxial used to be more common than it is now, and if you run across it, it is probably because you will be replacing it. Twisted pair is by far the cable of choice for most networks. It is called twisted pair because it contains four pairs of wires that are twisted together in twos—orange with white and white with orange for one pair, for example. The ends of the cable may be terminated per the standard being used in the building and implementation. Usually, the electrical contractor will handle this requirement. Twisted pair cabling comes in categories 3 through 7, in shielded and unshielded. Generally, category 5 unshielded is found in most buildings, especially to the wallplate. It is relatively inexpensive and robust enough for most applications.

If the budget can support the purchase and installation of fiber (not only in the risers but throughout the network), there are a couple of choices. Both multimode and single-mode fiber is available, depending on the LAN requirements. Single-mode has a distance limitation of 10 to 30 kilometers, much more than most enterprise networks would ever require, and has a strong, single signal beam that is actually laser light. Multimode uses multiple waves of ordinary light, bounced or echoed through the strand to create multiple conversations. Multimode fiber has a distance limitation of 2 kilometers, certainly enough for most network purposes.

Your final wiring decision is based on how the runs from the wallplates to the wiring closet will be made. Will they be home runs, going from the wallplate all the way back to a central wiring closet? Or will they be zoned, hitting intermediate points of termination, with further runs being made from that point to the next wiring closet or data center? Much of the decision will be based on limitations of the cabling type selected. Category 5 twisted pair, for example, has a distance limitation of about 100 meters, or around 300 feet. Going further than that is okay in some cases, but you risk losing signal quality if you push the limits of the standard.

What is the most typical wiring strategy in use today? Generally, multimode fiber is run in the risers, with a patch panel in the basement, or central wiring closet, of the building and in each of the wiring closets throughout the building. Category 5 unshielded twisted pair (UTP) is then run from the closet switches to the wallplates, with Category 5 UTP LAN cables used from the wallplates to the desktop. Sometimes unterminated (dark) single-mode fiber will be run through the risers for future use.

Network Management Strategy

After carefully considering all of the pieces that will be involved in the campus LAN, it is equally as important to address network management issues. In previous chapters we discussed using centralized vs. distributed network management. In other words, your choice is hierarchical network management vs. one single Network Management Station (NMS).

A platform for the NMS will also have to be chosen, from options such as HP OpenView, Tivoli, and Sun Net Manager. HP OpenView is by far the most popular and is available for both Unix and Windows NT platforms. As we discussed before, factors such as size of the network, available bandwidth, and network budget will drive the final decision.

Figure 3-6 shows the unidirectional flow of information from RMON probes in the wiring closets to a central NMS. You must be careful when using Remote Network Monitoring (RMON) in your network, however. Turning on any except the most basic (first four) (RMON) information layers can result in an inordinate amount of traffic in your network. This can cause more problems than it will ever solve!

Other network management issues to consider include the use of VLANs. VLAN technology simplifies moves, adds, and changes that come along with any growing, changing network. VLAN deployment will also need to be considered. How will users be segregated into VLANs? Will they be grouped by job function, location, or application, for example? Certain network management tools, such as CiscoWorks for Switched Internetworks (CWSI), are made to simplify VLAN management even more.

Finally, here are a few last considerations before the final decision is made on network management topology, technology, and tools:

- **Capabilities** What can the tool(s) do? What do you need them to do?
- **Bandwidth Demands** How much traffic for real-time data can your network realistically handle?
- **RMON vs. SNMP** RMON takes far more bandwidth and CPU utilization than does SNMP, but the granularity of the data is finer. This decision is really based upon how much information the network staff needs or wants from a particular segment of the network.

Figure 3-6
Distributed network management

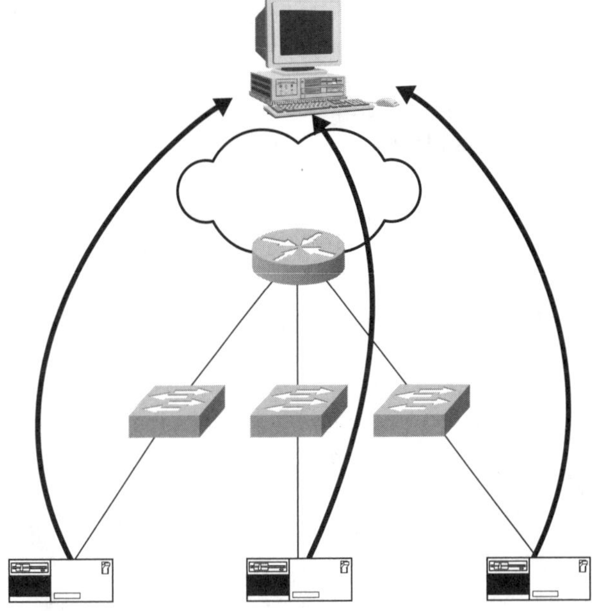

- **Scope of Support** Do you want to manage only the LAN or the entire WAN? Bear in mind that using probes deployed across the WAN can be quite costly both in terms of hardware investment and in terms of bandwidth.

Once these questions have been considered, you will be closer to a final decision on how best to manage the newly designed enterprise network.

Business Considerations

Companies are in business to make money. It is as simple as that. When a network redesign is needed, a great deal of the decision-making process centers on the costs, both short- and long-term. Some of the topics of discussion should be:

- How can the company preserve its current investment?
- What is the total cost of purchase?
- What is the total cost of ownership?

Chances are, the company currently has wiring closets full of networking gear and network cabling. Wherever possible, make use of what is already in the building—upgrade a switch, leave the category 5 UTP cable to the wallplate but run multimode fiber in the riser. Certainly, in some cases this will not be possible, especially in networks that have sorely outdated equipment or category 3 cable. Some equipment and cabling simply have reached end-of-life support or have distance limitations that will not support the new design or future growth. In any case, preservation of current resources will allow for budgeted funds to be used to improve other areas of the network.

We discussed cost factoring in some depth in Chapter 1, so we will only briefly touch on these subjects now. Figuring the total cost of purchase is a matter of factoring in new equipment costs, equipment upgrade costs, replacement of cabling, labor costs, and training costs.

- How much do you really need to buy?
- How much will it cost to own the equipment vs. leasing it?
- Is it possible to buy certain components from cheaper suppliers rather than to buy the whole package from one vendor?
- Have several labor quotes been obtained?
- Have you presented three or more design possibilities? The designer model (most expensive), the off-the-rack model (reasonably priced), and the bargain basement (cheap—and you get what you pay for!).

Cost of ownership includes outsourcing fees, ongoing training, recurring fees, and tariffs for leased lines or circuits and related equipment, and possibly leasing costs for the network equipment itself.

- How much will the equipment cost to lease?
- How much will the equipment cost to own (recurring costs)? This would include software upgrade subscription service, maintenance contracts, and scope of support.
- Are there any pieces on which you can afford *not* to have maintenance?

Another important consideration to most businesses is adherence to corporate and industry standards. If the company has been primarily a 3Com-router shop, it may be difficult to sell them on a Cisco end-to-end solution. Be sure that your design takes the official—or unofficial—company policy into consideration.

Meeting industry standards is sometimes more important to the technical groups within the company than to the executive team. However, with the rapid changes that continue to take place within the technical sectors of the global marketplace, it is becoming important to every corporation to be able to make rapid changes in order to keep up. In order to do that, they must have a network that is not only modern but which is also more in tune with open standards. Be sure that the design will not be self-limiting by the use of outdated wiring specifications, vendor problems, or proprietary issues.

Finally, the design will need to allow for the business to plan for growth. Growth is an extremely subjective topic. Who knows where the industry will go? The best design today may be outdated in six months. The business may actually grow much more rapidly than anyone planned. If you make the network scalable and modular in design, bearing in mind that hierarchical network design model, the growth will be less painful all around.

TIP: *When planning for growth, take your best shot at the design, double or triple it, and it may last two years. It is literally impossible to know what technology will exist beyond that time.*

Campus LAN Evolution

In Figure 3-1 we saw a more traditional campus LAN architecture. How will this change over time? If we consider the applications that were the most bandwidth-intensive in the early 1980s, such as print jobs, we can easily see how far network applications have come. Today Voice over IP is the application against which to plan. How can we predict what will happen in five years? Ten years? Consider Figure 3-7 to see how far applications have progressed in the past 20 years.

As the figure shows, we have moved into areas of network design that we could only have imagined even a few years ago. As recently as the late 1990s, chunky cellular phones were bulky appliances that were neither attractive nor very functional. Now our phones can browse Web sites, allow us to read our e-mail, and carry calls with better clarity. Where will network design go next?

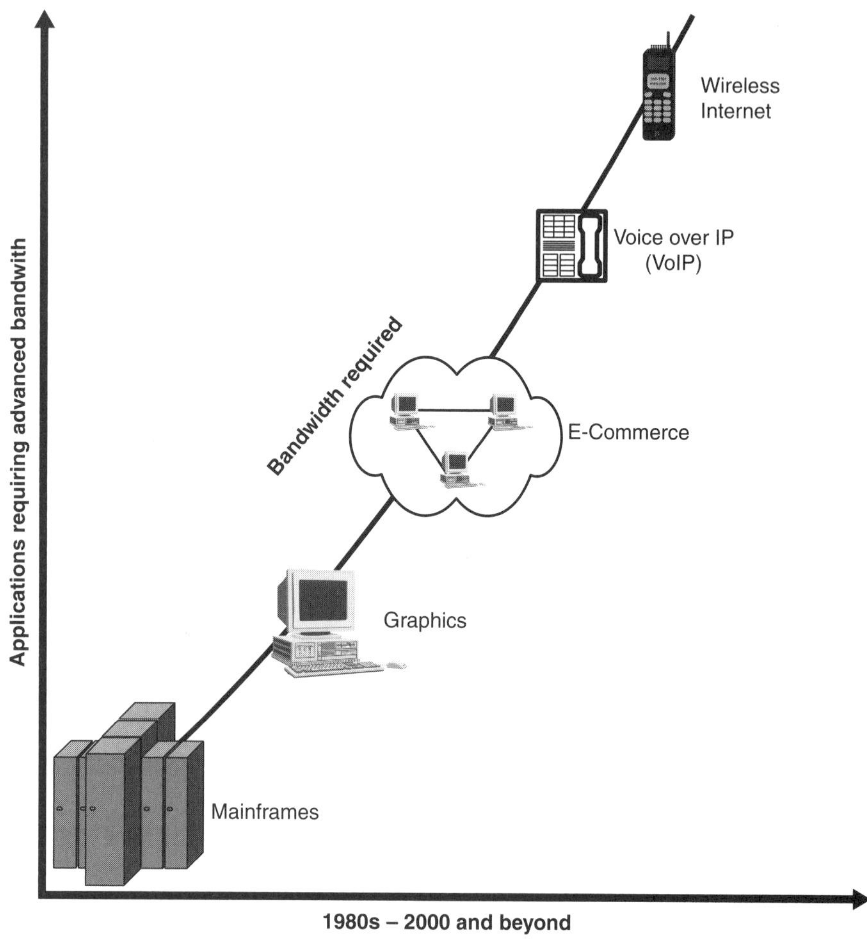

Figure 3-7 Evolution of campus applications

Problem Areas

The real reason for any network design is to solve a problem. The problem may be as simple as a new company in need of a network installation, or it may be as complex as two major corporations merging their operations. Let's look at a few of the problem areas that you may be trying to address:

- Media contention
- Protocols lacking scalability
- New transport needs

In this section, we will explore each of these problem areas, and help you to understand what each of them can mean to a network. A thorough understanding of the problem you are trying to solve for a given network can help you decide what internetworking devices to use and what protocols to deploy.

Media Contention

There is said to be *media contention* on a wire when too many network devices are sharing a single collision domain. This could cause a long wait for the token in Token Ring or FDDI, or it could be seen as excessive collisions on an Ethernet segment.

Ethernet, as you know, is a "polite" protocol. A host sends a packet out onto the wire when it detects no traffic on the wire. If a host further down the wire has also transmitted a packet onto the wire, the packets will very likely meet. A collision will result. All stations on the wire stop talking for a short period of time. Depending on the application, the station will either automatically start sending the traffic again once the wire is quiet or will wait to be asked for a retransmission from the destination host.

While this may sound like a terrible way to do business, it works quite well. When too many hosts are on a single collision domain, however, excessive collisions, retransmissions, and broadcast "storms" can result. A *broadcast storm* is an abnormally high number of broadcasts on a wire, taking up a great deal of the available bandwidth and colliding with unicast traffic that may be trying to use the resources. The broadcasts may be quite valid, advertisements of services or requests for IP addresses, for example. The problem arises when there are too many of these packets in addition to an already heavy network load, causing congestion on the segment.

Protocols Lacking Scalability

Some protocols do not scale as well as others. Some of them, such as Internetwork Packet Exchange (IPX), can create congestion in a segment because of the types of broadcasts they must constantly send. Some of this problem can be solved with appropriate filtering techniques or by ensuring that parameters for protocol usage are set correctly in the routers. In other cases the network can be migrated to a more scalable protocol, like Internet Protocol (IP), with good results and little disruption to users.

New Transport Needs

As we saw in the section "Campus LAN Evolution," new applications are constantly appearing on the horizon. As in the world of personal computers, the topics of speed, power, and appetite are all relative to the present day. What is today's Ferrari will probably be tomorrow's Chevette. Just when you solve the problems of today's bandwidth requirements, new applications come to the market with increased needs for network resources. As we have all learned in the recent past, throwing more bandwidth at a situation is not always the right answer. You must also find ways to make packets move more efficiently through the network, making the first trip count, so to speak. If the first packet makes it to its destination, you avoid the "please-retransmit-okay-here-it-comes-again" phenomenon.

Design Rules

So what are some of the ways you can solve these network problems, now that you know what they are? There are rarely "quick fixes" to the big problems, but there are usually some design rules that work nicely to help get these problems under better control. Let's take a look at a few.

Using LAN Switches to Help Reduce Congestion

By using a method known as *microsegmentation*, or the breaking up of segments into smaller segments, a LAN switch takes a single collision domain and makes it into many. A Cisco Catalyst switch gives each port dedicated bandwidth vs. shared bandwidth in hubs and concentrators. They do not, in and of themselves, separate the collision (or broadcast) domain.

VLANs implemented on switches are the technology actually used to do this. Each VLAN is a separate broadcast domain, regardless of where it is physically deployed. Take a look at Figure 3-8. In these two buildings, there are four departments: Administration, Engineering, Customer Service, and Training. Two of these departments are located across the two buildings. With VLANs you can do something you could never do with bridges or hubs—make the segments appear as though they are co-located. We will see more about VLANs in Chapter 4.

Figure 3-8
Campus research

Switches should be deployed across the network in a hierarchical manner, providing appropriate bandwidth and availability where it is needed. A typical client end-station will probably only need a 10 Mbps port, but an application server will probably require at least a 100 Mbps port. Although it is unlikely that you will use hubs in your network design, they can be useful if you are looking for ways to extend the life of equipment already in the network. Hubs and small switches can be used to expand user workgroups, for instance.

TIP: *Don't trust the auto-sense or auto-negotiate feature of most workgroup switches or NIC cards. The negotiation process is rarely rapid or stable enough to provide the precise support required by most end-stations. Problems with this feature are seen frequently in network troubleshooting, so you would be smart to disable the feature in your network. A good rule of thumb is if you want a connection to be full duplex, —Fast Ethernet, then set it.*

Differentiating Between Collision Domains and Broadcast Domains

Everything associated with a port on a switch is a *collision domain*. In other words, a server plugged into a Fast Ethernet port on a Catalyst switch is in its own collision domain. All end-stations plugged into a mini-hub or concentrator would be on a single, or shared, collision domain. Those devices would all compete for the available bandwidth, whether it was 100 Mbps or only 10. All devices on the hub would see all of the traffic bound for *any* of the devices on that hub. The important factor for scalability for a collision domain is the total traffic occupying the domain.

A *broadcast domain* is generally everything that is associated with a single port, physical or virtual, on a router. This can be a VLAN, a sub-interface, or a physical interface. Routers act as a natural barrier to broadcasts, therefore the buck stops with them, so to speak. Although broadcasts can be quite useful, the only reason they exist is to either advertise something or request something. All CPUs in a broadcast domain listen to all broadcasts on the segment. The important factor for scalability for a broadcast domain is the total broadcast traffic. Thus, reducing broadcasts can greatly extend the life of the segment.

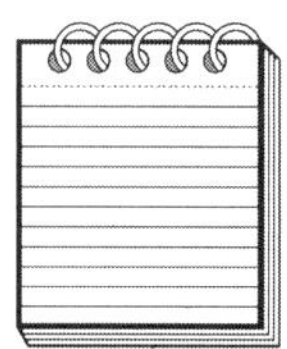

NOTE: *"Bandwidth domain" and "collision domain" are synonymous terms.*

Being Aware of Broadcast Radiation

The term *broadcast radiation* simply refers to the effect of broadcasts and multicasts spreading through a LAN on a flat network. If a network is completely flat and switched, there will be an upper limit on how large the network can grow before it is overwhelmed by broadcast radiation. The use of VLANs, as we have mentioned, can reduce the size of the broadcast domains and the effect of broadcast radiation on a network. Another way to eliminate excess broadcast radiation is to further segment the network with layer 3 devices such as routers or layer 3 switches. Remember that routers are natural broadcast stoppers!

Using Routers to Help Create Scalable Internetworks

The use of a router or layer 3 switch in a network can help provide adequate segmentation and room for growth. Routers not only stop the propagation of broadcasts, they also provide for media conversion between different types, ATM and Fast Ethernet, for example. The media conversion is clean and simple for a router as it opens, discards, and rebuilds the data-link encapsulation on each packet it examines. Where a switch simply passes the traffic based upon the destination MAC address, the router is capable of much more sophisticated functions. Remember that a router is not necessary in every wiring closet, however. Routers require more expertise to configure and maintain and can be inordinately expensive in segments where a switch would suffice.

Using Routers to Impose a Logical Network Structure

In the early days of my career, I found myself in the enviable position of being one of the few "locals" that understood anything about networking or Cisco routers. A nice, challenging position was offered to me in which I would have the opportunity to upgrade a network from Token Ring to Fast Ethernet and deploy Catalyst 5000 switches throughout the building. (At the time, the 5000 was the newest kid on the network block.) On my first day of my new job, I walked into a data center and was led to a few large pallets of equipment. The supervisor said, "It's all yours."

"Great," I replied, "Where's the design?"

He chuckled and walked away. Clearly the design was going to follow the arrival of the equipment—and the job of creating that design was for me to do. I suddenly knew how the miller's daughter in the story of Rumplestiltskin felt! I was standing in front of a load of raw material that my customer wanted to have turned into a golden network.

The moral of this tale, of course, is that the design should *never* follow the equipment! A very good sales rep had apparently convinced the customers that they needed a certain number of routers and switches to be able to support the network cutover. In the end, I was able to create a successful design that used all of the equipment, but in some cases, the switches were overkill for some of the smaller wiring closets. In other cases an excessive amount of redundancy was used because it was what the sales rep had in mind—not because it was necessarily right for the size and complexity of the network.

A router should be used to bring order and structure to a network. It is the decision-maker, the authority on all protocols and subnets that exist in the network, and it is the traffic director, keeping records of all the destinations within its domain. While routers are not appropriate in all parts of a network, they can bring order when they are deployed and configured correctly.

Now you will have a chance to practice what you have learned so far about campus LANs in a short case study.

Case Study

Refer back to Figure 3-8. Campus Research Corporation has two buildings: Headquarters in Detroit and R&D in St. Louis. In Detroit, they have Administration, Engineering, and Customer Service. In St. Louis they have Administration, Engineering, and Training. They are considering adding another location in Milwaukee later in the year, when they hope to acquire the small company that currently does all of their manufacturing of testing and measurement equipment.

The current topology is as follows:

St. Louis	Detroit
The building has three departments in a three-story building.	The building has three major departments spread out over five floors.
On the main floor, there is a reception area and five training rooms. The training servers are housed in the single wiring closet that services the floor.	There is a data center on the first floor along with the reception area and Customer Service. The data center houses a server farm that has to be reached from all departments and from the St. Louis campus.
On the second and third floors, the administration staff for the training center and a small staff of accounting clerks share space with the R&D engineers.	On the second and third floors, Administration has Human Resources, Accounts Payable, Accounts Receivable, and Collections.
There is a server room in the R&D lab on the third floor.	On the fourth and fifth floors, Engineering maintains a staff of 120 engineers along with a testing lab and a separate intranet server.

The company is willing to upgrade the cabling throughout the building to category 5 UTP or better. They currently have a single Cisco router in each building, with hubs and bridges extending their segments to the wiring closets. The network staff has not considered network management or VLANs, but would like to try using LAN switches and possibly routers in the wiring closets instead of hubs. The staff is relatively untrained and needs a lot of help knowing how to get started with their network design.

Network connectivity is Ethernet, a technology the company would like to stay with. Connections between the buildings are established across an ISDN link. Sales personnel dial into their ISP of choice and open a connection to the mail server from their laptops. The IT staff knows that this isn't very secure, but they don't know any other way to allow the traveling staff to get their mail.

We will follow Campus Research Corporation and a few other fictitious companies through the remainder of this book. Your first assignment is to evaluate the current network infrastructure and make recommendations on

- Wiring
- Location of servers
- Technology in the wiring closet (hubs vs. switches, for example)
- The use of routers, where appropriate
- Connectivity recommendations between buildings

Budget is not as much an issue as having a network that can handle the possible new acquisition—and others that may come along. There is no right answer to this case study, but remember all of the tips you have learned so far to help you build a scalable network using the hierarchical network design model. Make the network modular, with redundancy and scalability.

Suggested solutions to the case studies may be found in Appendix C, "Suggested Solutions to Case Studies."

Study Hints

The study hints contained in this section are designed to give you guidance in preparing to take the CCDA and CCDP certification tests.

- Remember that your design considerations include clients and servers, the applications that reside on them, and the NICs that provide connectivity. Also consider any upgrades that are planned for end-stations, such as replacement of the systems altogether or the addition of higher-speed NICs.
- Routers are more expensive than switches. Switch where you can; route where you must. Remember that routers must be used where dissimilar media-types or protocols exist.
- Remember that even though the 80/20 rule is not practical for today's networks, it is still the rule-of-thumb for answering many questions on Cisco design tests.
- Always consider the size of the network when proposing a solution. A design can be modular and scalable without being inappropriately large and complex for the applications and users it supports.
- Design a solid network, then double or triple what it can support by scaling up bandwidth, available ports, and port density.

CCDP Tips

This section contains an abbreviated list of the topics contained in Chapter 3. Think of this section as the equivalent of reading Cliff's Notes™ instead of reading an entire book. You will get the general idea of the chapter but will benefit more from reading the chapter in its entirety.

Design Considerations

These are the items you will need to take into consideration when embarking on the campus LAN design process:

- **End-Station (Client and Server)** Some of the things you need to consider are the applications in use and their effect on the network, the NIC type and speed, and whether the platform is going to be upgraded in the near future. All of these things will have some bearing on your design.
- **Network Infrastructure** You will need to investigate the backbone type, whether distributed or collapsed, and decide if that is still the best strategy based on the current and planned needs of the network. You will also need to calculate bandwidth requirements of current and planned applications. Although it is impossible, and unnecessary, to plan to accommodate a backbone that is 100 percent saturated (packets would begin to be dropped much earlier than that), it is wise to aim high in bandwidth availability. Take a look at the backbone technology currently in use (FDDI, Fast Ethernet, or Token Ring, for example) and help guide the customer towards a decision on whether to stay with that technology or change completely to something more appropriate for the network needs. Finally, in different areas of the network, a decision will need to be made about whether to use switching or routing.
- **Network Cabling** The guideline is generally to buy the best cabling the budget can handle. At the very least there needs to be fiber in the risers to the wiring closets, and at least category 5 UTP to the ports and to the wallplates.
- **Network Management** A good network design should provide for network management whether centralized or distributed. Will the NMS use only SNMP polling or data collected via RMON probes? Will other tools be needed for the management of VLANs? Once the tools

and systems are identified, other factors to be considered are bandwidth impact of the design and tools, and scope of support the tools will address.

- **Business Issues** A business needs to remain profitable, thus the network design should not break the bank. Some of the business issues to be considered are how to preserve the current investment, cost to purchase new equipment and services, and the total cost of ownership, including recurring costs, over a period of time.

Problem Areas

Here are a few problem areas that bear noting before we close this chapter:

- **Media Contention** Are there excessive collisions on the wire? Is the network inordinately slow some or all of the time? Have network analysis tools been used to find some of the problems in the network? Too many packets competing for too little bandwidth will usually result in poor overall network performance.
- **Protocols Lacking Scalability** Some protocols were not meant for large network segments or for the kind of growth a network may be experiencing. The users may see timeouts or decreased performance if there are protocol configuration or scalability issues. It may be time for a change to a more robust and scalable protocol.
- **New Transport Needs** New application deployments could have wide-reaching effects on the network. Whether it is a new client-server model talking across an already busy WAN or a NMS that is polling too frequently, if there is an increased need or new need to transport services across the network, it is a problem to be addressed in the design.

Design Rules

When working with LAN design, there are some rules-of-thumb that you should keep in mind. We have provided a few of the best ones here.

- **Use LAN switches to reduce network congestion.** LAN switches can be used to break large segments into smaller ones and to give dedicated bandwidth to each device. In addition, Cisco Catalyst switches use VLAN technology to separate ports into Virtual LANs across a campus, making moves, adds, and changes inherently easy, especially when used in conjunction with a tool like CWSI.

- **Differentiate between bandwidth domains and broadcast domains.** A bandwidth domain is everything associated with a port on a switch or a shared group of ports on a hub. A broadcast domain is the group of network devices that shares a common collision domain, VLAN, or subnet.
- **Be aware of broadcast radiation.** Broadcast radiation is the effect of broadcasts being propagated throughout a flat, switched network. When layer 3 devices are not used to impose a hierarchical structure, broadcast radiation can impose an upper limit to the growth of the network.
- **Routers can be used to create scalable networks.** Routers act as broadcast firewalls, media-type and protocol translators, and routing decision-makers. Without routers, flat networks would reach an upper growth limit and would have to be alike in type, protocol, and technology.
- **Routers can be used to impose a logical network structure** A router, when properly deployed and configured, brings order to the network. It is a traffic director, decision-maker, and authority on what exists in the network. The design should always come before the decision to place a router or layer 3 switch in any part of the network.

Summary

In this chapter, we saw how to identify the technical considerations in the campus LAN design, such as end-station requirements, different media types, network management considerations, and types of LAN equipment. We also talked about the business issues to be considered when designing the campus LAN. As background information, we explored the evolution of the campus LAN and how we got to where we are today with LAN design.

By now you should have a good idea of how to identify the problems that need to be solved in a given LAN design and how to solve them in the network design you create.

In the next chapter, we will expand on our discussion of LAN topology. Then we will talk about trunking and ATM LAN Emulation (LANE). We will then rejoin our case study, Campus Research Corporation, to continue building upon the network design framework.

Questions

The following review questions have been selected to help you test your knowledge of the subject matter contained in this chapter. You will also find these questions contained in the CD-ROM included with this book. While these are not the questions you will find in the certification exams, knowing the answers to the review questions in this book will help cement the material in your mind as you prepare for the tests.

1. An FDDI backbone is an example of what type of topology?
   - **a.** Token Ring
   - **b.** Distributed
   - **c.** Detached
   - **d.** Collapsed
2. A switched backbone is an example of what type of topology?
   - **a.** Token Ring
   - **b.** Distributed
   - **c.** Detached
   - **d.** Collapsed
3. Which of the following media types has greater distance support?
   - **a.** Single-mode fiber
   - **b.** Category 6 STP
   - **c.** Multimode fiber
   - **d.** Category 5 UTP
4. Which of the following media types uses multiple light waves to carry several parallel conversations?
   - **a.** Single-mode fiber
   - **b.** Category 6 STP
   - **c.** Multimode fiber
   - **d.** Category 5 UTP
5. Which of the following cable types is most likely used from the wiring closet to the wallplates?
   - **a.** Single-mode fiber
   - **b.** Category 6 STP
   - **c.** Multimode fiber
   - **d.** Category 5 UTP

6. A(n) ________________ describes everything associated with a port on a switch or all ports on a hub segment.
   a. Broadcast domain
   b. Uplink
   c. Bandwidth domain
   d. Riser
7. A(n) ________________ describes everything associated with a VLAN or all ports on a subnet.
   a. Broadcast domain
   b. Uplink
   c. Bandwidth domain
   d. Riser
8. A __________ can be used to group like users into a shared broadcast domain.
   a. VLAN
   b. Switch
   c. Router
   d. Wiring closet
9. A layer 2 switch is similar in operation to a ____________.
   a. Router
   b. Bridge
   c. CSU/DSU
   d. Modem
10. A hub is similar in operation to a ____________.
    a. Router
    b. CSU/DSU
    c. Modem
    d. Layer 2 switch
11. This device can be used to limit the effects of broadcast radiation in a network.
    a. Router
    b. Layer 2 switch
    c. Hub
    d. Bridge

12. ______ is an example of a highly scalable protocol.
    a. IP
    b. IPX
    c. AppleTalk
    d. Banyan VINES
13. What is the term for breaking large network segments into smaller, more manageable ones?
    a. Subnetting
    b. Bridging
    c. Microsegmentation
    d. Collision division
14. Which of these terms is part of "cost of ownership?"
    a. Cabling
    b. Leased-line fees
    c. Switches
    d. Reuse of hubs
15. Which of these terms is part of "cost of purchase?"
    a. Cabling
    b. Leased-line fees
    c. Staff training
    d. Reuse of hubs
16. Which of these terms is part of "investment preservation?"
    a. Cabling
    b. Leased-line fees
    c. Staff training
    d. Reuse of hubs
17. What must you install to provide multiprotocol support?
    a. Router
    b. Switch
    c. Bridge
    d. CSU/DSU

18. Distributed network management, using RMON probes, might be appropriate for which of the following?
    a. Small office/home office
    b. Single-layer hub-and-spoke network
    c. Collapsed backbone
    d. Large, hierarchical network
19. These devices can be used to reduce network congestion.
    a. Routers
    b. LAN switches
    c. Bridges
    d. Concentrators
20. Which of the following should be avoided in a campus LAN design at all cost?
    a. Full-mesh
    b. Single points of failure
    c. Multiple VLANs
    d. Service loops in the wiring

Answers

1. An FDDI backbone is an example of what type of topology?
   b. Distributed
   Explanation: With an FDDI backbone, the 100 Mbps is equally shared, or distributed, to the concentrators that access it.
2. A switched backbone is an example of what type of topology?
   d. Collapsed
   Explanation: A fully switched backbone is also known as a collapsed backbone, or flat network. There are typically no routers to impose a hierarchical structure.
3. Which of the following media types has greater distance support?
   a. Single-mode fiber
   Explanation: At 10 to 30 km distance range, single-mode fiber supports longer distances than the other choices.

4. Which of the following media types uses multiple light waves to carry several parallel conversations?
c. Multimode fiber
Explanation: Multimode fiber has a shorter distance support (about 2 km) than single-mode, but it can use multiple light waves to carry multiple, parallel conversations.

5. Which of the following cable types is most likely used from the wiring closet to the wallplates?
d. Category 5 UTP
Explanation: Because of its lower cost, category 5 unshielded twisted pair copper is the most commonly used cable from the wiring closet to the wallplate.

6. A(n) ________________ describes everything associated with a port on a switch or all ports on a hub segment.
c. Bandwidth domain
Explanation: A bandwidth domain is everything that shares bandwidth—a single port on a switch or a group of ports with shared bandwidth.

7. A(n) ________________ describes everything associated with a VLAN or all ports on a subnet.
a. Broadcast domain
Explanation: A broadcast domain is a group of ports associated with a collision domain-VLAN or subnet.

8. A __________ can be used to group like users into a shared broadcast domain.
a. VLAN
Explanation: As we saw in the last question, a VLAN can be used to group ports into a broadcast domain.

9. A layer 2 switch is similar in operation to a __________.
b. Bridge
Explanation: A bridge, like a layer 2 switch, passes traffic based on MAC address.

10. A hub is similar in operation to a __________.
d. Layer 2 switch
Explanation: A hub works like a bridge and like a layer 2 switch, passing traffic without regard to higher-layer information like the network address.

11. This device can be used to limit the effects of broadcast radiation in a network.
a. Router
Explanation: A router is a natural broadcast firewall, dropping broadcasts when they arrive—unless configured to do otherwise.

12. _______ is an example of a highly scalable protocol.
a. IP
Explanation: IP is the most scalable protocol of those listed and is the choice in most large enterprise networks.

13. What is the term for breaking large network segments into smaller, more manageable ones?
c. Microsegmentation
Explanation: Microsegmentation is literally the reduction of segments (into smaller ones).

14. Which of these terms is part of "cost of ownership?"
b. Leased-line fees
Explanation: The cost of ownership includes recurring costs and ongoing maintenance fees. Leased-line fees would be part of this group of costs.

15. Which of these terms is part of "cost of purchase?"
a. Cabling
Explanation: The cost of cabling for the network design is generally a one-time cost paid at the beginning of the implementation and not incurred as an ongoing cost.

16. Which of these terms is part of "investment preservation?"
d. Reuse of hubs
Explanation: Investment preservation is the reuse of what the business already owns. The reuse of hubs in smaller segments would be an example of this.

17. What must you install to provide multiprotocol support in a campus LAN?
a. Router
Explanation: A layer 2 switch cannot translate between protocols. Only a router can do this.

18. Distributed network management, using RMON probes, might be appropriate for which of the following?
d. Large, hierarchical network

Explanation: In smaller networks there is generally no need to go to the expense (in both monetary and bandwidth terms) to deploy probes. This is usually only needed in large to very large networks.

19. These devices can be used to reduce network congestion.
b. LAN switches
Explanation: LAN switches help reduce network congestion by breaking large segments into smaller ones and allowing the creation of VLANs to create smaller collision domains across the campus.

20. Which of the following should be avoided in a campus LAN design at all cost?
b. Single points of failure
Explanation: To create a network design with any major single points of failure would be irresponsible. The idea of a good network design is to create a scalable, robust infrastructure for support of network services and users. Good placement of redundancy can accomplish this goal.

Bibliography

Cisco Internetwork Design, Cisco Press, 2000, Matthew H. Birkner, Editor

Cisco Internetwork Design Course Manual, version 3.0, April 1997, Cisco Systems, Inc.

Internetworking Design Basics, Cisco UniverCD, © 1989-1998

CHAPTER 4

Campus LAN Technology

Overview

We have covered the hierarchical network design model as well as given you an overview of campus LAN design. By now, you should be very familiar with the three-layered model of network design and be able to create simple modular designs for a given case.

In this chapter, we will discuss the various types of technology you may want to implement in a campus network environment. You will also learn about technology that you may see or replace in a LAN. The types of LAN connectivity will be discussed in some detail, with emphasis on bridging types and Virtual LANs (VLANs) used in switching. We will talk about some problem areas you may encounter, give you some tips on how to remember what you have learned, and practice your knowledge in Part Two of your case study on Campus Research—our fictional corporation.

LAN Topology

You may encounter or want to implement several types of topology in a campus network environment. We have discussed most of these in earlier chapters. Ethernet, including Fast Ethernet and Gigabit Ethernet, is one of the better known, most widely used topologies, because it is easy to learn and inexpensive to implement.

You will also find Token Ring in many IBM mainframe-based networks, however, or in networks where Token Ring is preferred because of its reliability. Token Ring is much more expensive to build and maintain than Ethernet, however. Fiber Distributed Data Interface (FDDI) is another ring-based topology, which is similar to Token Ring but runs at 100 Mbps over fiber. Finally, we will look at Asynchronous Transfer Mode (ATM) as another possible topology you will use.

How you connect the campus LAN together will depend on many things, such as the distance between sites, budget, staff and user preference, and segment size requirements. You may want to implement bridging or switching where possible because of the relative cost savings involved. Where mixed media or protocols are in use, however, or where distance is a factor, you may place a Layer 3 switch or a router in the segment. Additionally, VLANs may be appropriate for the network if Cisco Catalyst switches are being used in the wiring closets. Using a VLAN can greatly simplify common network tasks such as user moves, adds, or changes within the campus.

Ethernet

Ethernet (IEEE 802.3 standard) is a "best-effort" delivery protocol and is by far the most popular LAN topology in use today, with an estimated 40 million nodes in use as of 1994. Available in speeds of 10 Mbps (Ethernet), 100 Mbps (Fast Ethernet), and 1000 Mbps (Gigabit Ethernet), Ethernet is vendor-neutral, low-cost, and fairly simple to implement. Additionally, because of its open standard, Ethernet has been widely adapted to many different operating systems, end-stations, and environments. Figure 4-1 shows a typical Ethernet segment.

Ethernet is a Carrier Sense Multiple Access/Collision Detect (CSMA/CD) technology—a "polite" protocol by which the Network Interface Card (NIC) or other Ethernet interface waits to see whether a signal is being sent over the wire before transmitting its own signal. To break it down even further, Carrier Sense means that all stations on the Ethernet segment are listening for a period of quiet, in which they may take a turn to transmit. Multiple Access means that each station is treated equally in Ethernet and that no station takes higher priority on the wire than any other. In other words, a router would not take priority over an end-station. Collision Detect means that if two stations begin to transmit simultaneously, a collision occurs, and the protocol senses this collision, so the two station back off of the wire, using a timing algorithm to wait for a period of quiet before trying to retransmit.

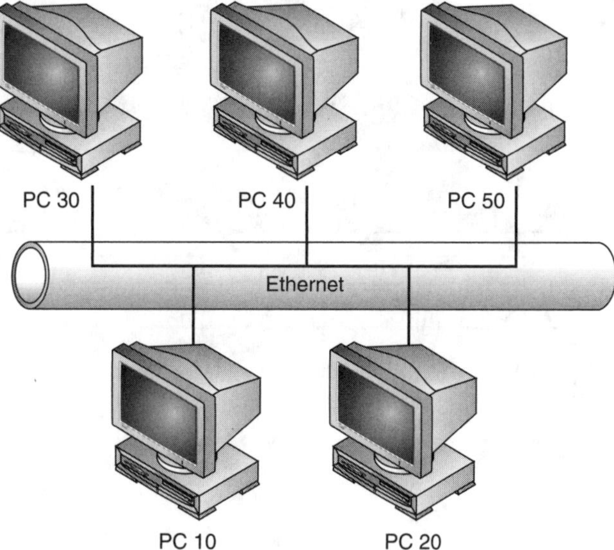

Figure 4-1
Ethernet topology

None of these characteristics serves to avoid collisions entirely, as any user of Ethernet knows. Two end-stations may transmit simultaneously or be so far apart on the wire as not to detect the signal in time to hold transmission. All nodes on a shared Ethernet segment are also sharing the medium, or the physical wire that connects them all together. Therefore, they must take turns speaking, with all nodes having equal access to the wire. The natural occurrence of collisions on a shared Ethernet segment results in an actual available throughput of the segment of only up to about 30 percent of the advertised bandwidth.

A frame transmission may be attempted multiple times in a busy network. Ethernet NICs will expand the timing algorithm exponentially based upon the number of collisions a frame has encountered. This is a way for end-stations to adjust to busy traffic conditions. Collisions are not necessarily a bad thing. Collisions on a network are a fact of life in an Ethernet network and generally mean that all is performing as expected. Figure 4-2 demonstrates a typical Ethernet collision on a segment.

Too many collisions, however, can indicate problems. For example, if a frame transmission has been attempted 16 times, which can happen in a terribly congested network or a segment down situation, the frame is discarded and transmission attempts cease. At this point, higher layer protocols would handle error recovery and may attempt to send the data again.

Figure 4-2
Ethernet collision

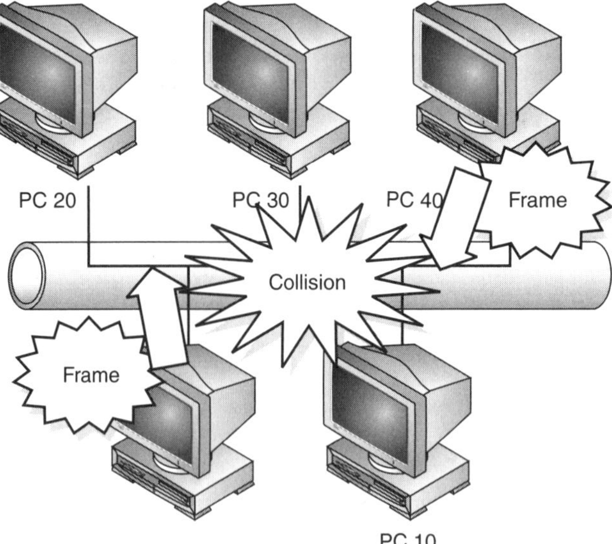

Ethernet is a "bus" topology system, meaning that a single channel carries the signal to all stations on the wire. What this can mean to end-stations is that even if a frame is not destined for its MAC address, it still must stop, listen, and decide whether the frame does or does not belong to it. Figure 4-3 illustrates this reaction to a frame on the wire.

Design recommendations for Ethernet segments can help prevent problems such as timeouts and retransmissions from becoming a problem. Round-trip timing is a way for Ethernet interfaces to expect the amount of time it should take for another interface to respond. When a segment is too large or too congested, for instance, the actual round-trip time of a frame may be longer than what is expected, and the frame may be dropped.

TIP: *Congestion on an Ethernet segment can be defined as link utilization greater than about 30 percent.*

DESIGN TIP: *10BASE-T segment configuration guidelines specify a distance limitation of 100 meters (328 feet) per segment, with a maximum of two Multi-Access Units (MAUs) per segment. Although a MAU usually refers to an end-station, the segment is normally expanded via a hub or switch to handle many more devices, with all devices communicating through the hub or switch.*

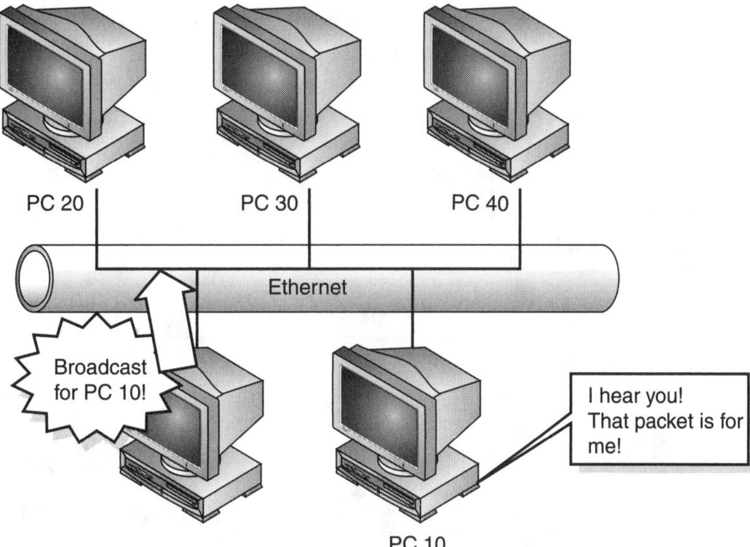

Figure 4-3 CSMA/CD technology

Gigabit Ethernet, 802.3z, has recently experienced an upsurge in usage. Because of the increase in the number of end-stations using Fast Ethernet, it has become necessary to use even faster technology in the wiring closet and backbone and on servers. 802.3z covers the standards for 1000BASE-SX, 1000BASE-LX, and 1000BASE-CX. Gigabit Ethernet over Category 5 Unshielded Twisted Pair (UTP) cabling is covered in standard 802.3ab.

Some differences exist in the IEEE specifications for the various Ethernet standards. Table 4-1 shows these distinctions.

Ethernet Segmentation A single Ethernet collision domain can be divided into two or more smaller collision domains by a process known as *segmentation*. By segmenting the larger collision domain, the impact of collisions on end-station transmissions can be reduced. Because fewer devices are competing for available bandwidth on the wire, naturally fewer collisions will occur. The original, larger collision domain is still a single broadcast domain, however, as illustrated in Figure 4-4. To break up the broadcast domain, you would have to implement VLAN or use a router, as discussed in Chapter 3.

Ethernet Switching With the advent of Ethernet switches, the impact of collisions on end-stations has been eliminated, because every end-station is in its own collision domain. Broadcast domains may either be shared across the switch or broken down using VLANs. This can result in the need for fewer router ports as well, a significant cost savings.

An Ethernet switch gives each port dedicated bandwidth, where the ports would have all shared the bandwidth on a hub—in other words, a 10-

Table 4-1

Ethernet Distance Guidelines

	Ethernet (10 Mbps)	Fast Ethernet	Gigabit Ethernet
Data Rate	10 Mbps	100 Mbps	1000 Mbps (1 gigabit per second)
Category 5 UTP	100 m	100 m	100 m
STP/Coaxial	500 m	100 m	25 m
Multimode Fiber	2 km	412 m (half-duplex) 2 km (full-duplex)	550 m
Single-mode Fiber	25 km	20 km	5 km

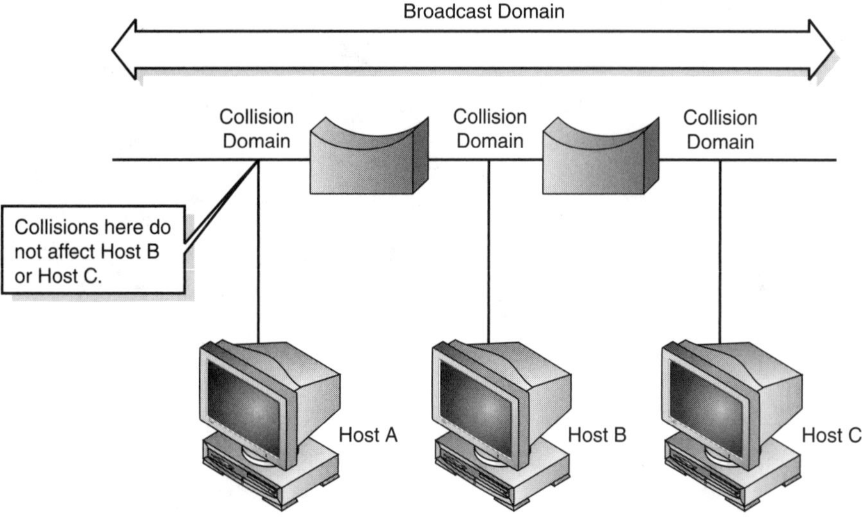

Figure 4-4 Ethernet segmentation

Mbps link to a hub would be shared among all ports. The same ports on a switch would each have 10 Mbps allocated to it. The migration from hubs to switches in a network is infinitely easier because the physical placement is the same.

A switch can be described as *non-blocking* if it supports bandwidth equal to at least the aggregate sum of the bandwidth allocated to the ports. A switch can support either a single end-station per port or an entire segment per port, which is called *segment switching*. Figure 4-5 illustrates the "segment-per-port" method. In the figure, each workgroup switch is connected to a larger switch, thereby aggregating the switch traffic, usually from Fast Ethernet uplinks into a Gigabit-capable switch.

Three types of Ethernet switching can be performed, depending on the switch and/or the configuration:

- Cut-through switching
- Store-and-forward switching
- Dynamic Cyclical Redundancy Check (CRC) threshold switching

Cut-through switching performs no CRC on the frame as it passes through the switch. It simply begins to forward the frame as soon as it has read the first 48 bytes—the destination MAC address in the frame header. This can be a problem, as frames with errors not caught by the switch can

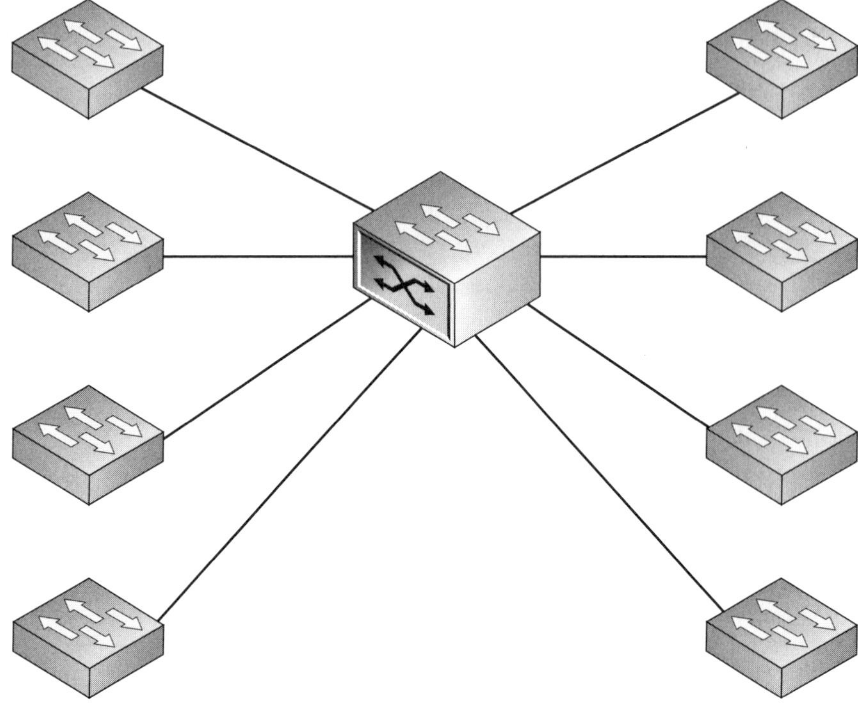

Figure 4-5 Segment switching

continue through the network. Many ICMP retransmit messages can result, wasting both bandwidth and time as another device detects the error later in the network. Another symptom that can be seen when broken frames are being forwarded is an increase in *runt* frames, as the frames can be in the process of being forwarded when a collision or error is detected, further breaking the frame.

Cut-through switching is, however, the fastest method of switching, because the frames do not have to be read in their entirety before they are forwarded toward their destination.

You can alleviate the problems with cut-through switching in a couple of ways. One is to set switch ports to full-duplex. This can eliminate the problem of runts. Another way to deal with the problem is to use a *fragment-free* switching method (available on most Cisco switches). This method waits until at least 64 bytes of a frame are received before beginning the forwarding process. The switch assumes the frame has not been damaged by a collision if 64 bytes have come through cleanly.

Another type of switching is *store-and-forward,* in which the entire frame is buffered and examined for errors before being forwarded to its destination. This is the type of forwarding normally found on a traditional bridge or a router. Although this may sound like a much slower process, the effect of the error checking is actually to use the bandwidth more efficiently. The bandwidth is used more efficiently because fewer error frames are forwarded through the network. This results in fewer retransmissions and more available bandwidth for "normal" transmissions.

Finally, some switches offer dynamic CRC threshold switching that begins by using cut-through switching and then changing to store-and-forward switching when a configurable number of CRCs has been reached.

Token Ring

Token Ring networks work differently than Ethernet in that collisions are avoided altogether. Therefore, no collision domains exist within the Token Ring topology. Token Ring segments are known as *bandwidth domains*. In a Token Ring network, tokens are passed at either 4 Mbps or 16 Mbps. Each time the token passes an end-station, the end-station has the opportunity to transmit data. There is no contention for the bandwidth on the wire, and because of this, there is generally a higher utilization of the bandwidth than in a shared Ethernet network (90 percent or greater utilization).

Usually, the only congestion point in a Token Ring network is at a point where more than one ring comes together. In the past, this might have been accomplished by putting more than one Token Ring NIC in a PC or server, but it is most often accomplished now in the router by using Cisco IOS commands.

Token Ring Switching Token Ring networks tend to be limited in their scalability. Too many devices on a ring can cause timeouts, and congestion can occur at the connection point for rings. Additionally, Token Ring bridges tend to be quite intolerant of delays. The answer to this is Token Ring switching. The switch relieves the backbone ring of having to handle the inter-ring traffic locally within the switch, as shown in Figure 4-6. Token Ring switching can also be configured to act like Ethernet switching, in relation to giving dedicated bandwidth to each port on the switch.

Although this sounds wonderful, data sent to the backbone ring through the switch must still compete for a single token unless early token release is used. Early token release allows a second token to be released onto the

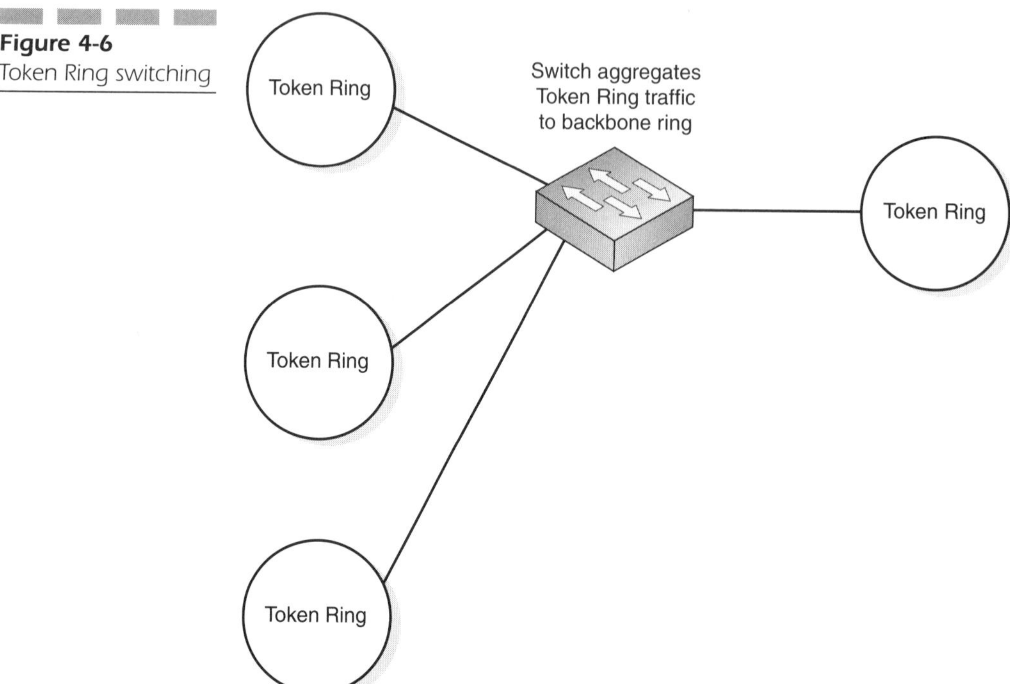

Figure 4-6
Token Ring switching

ring before the first one has made its full round trip. Token Ring line cards in a Catalyst 3500 or 5500 are commonly used to provide switching in a Token Ring environment.

FDDI

Similar to Token Ring in its topology, FDDI is also a logical ring that passes tokens through the network; however, FDDI passes the data at 100 Mbps. FDDI uses dual-ring architecture over fiber-optic cable and is generally very robust and reliable. One ring is called the *primary*, and the other is called the *secondary*. Traffic flows on each ring in opposite directions. This is called *counter-rotating*. When the ring is functioning properly, the primary ring is responsible for data transmission and the secondary ring remains idle. Traffic can also be deployed over copper and would then be referred to as Copper Distributed Data Interface (CDDI).

Although you may encounter FDDI/CDDI in existing networks, it is unlikely that you will be asked to add FDDI into a new network design. FDDI switches tend to be cost-prohibitive, and most networks are now using ATM or, more likely, Gigabit Ethernet in places where higher speeds and reliability are needed.

ATM

ATM is both a hardware and software technology that uses 53-byte fixed-length data units called *cells*. It is media-independent and can operate in very high-speed environments. The main reason that some network managers prefer ATM as a topology is that it is both predictable and flexible. Cells are a fixed length, so bursts of traffic can be handled easily. Data is broken into cells of equal size, so that bandwidth usage is predictable. ATM can also easily handle voice, video, and data as well as traffic prioritization and Quality of Service (QoS) options.

The ATM technology grew out of Time-Division Multiplexing (TDM) and Packet-Switching Data Networks (PSDN). TDM was a fixed-cell technology used to deliver reliable voice traffic on telephone company networks, but because it transmits cells even when no data is being passed, it wastes bandwidth. PSDN uses variable-sized data cells to accommodate bursty traffic patterns, but it cannot accommodate time-sensitive traffic like video. ATM was built on the strength of these two technologies, using the cell framework while improving on it by using the fixed cell length and accommodating time-sensitive traffic. ATM offers improved service over TDM and PSDN in several ways:

- Congestion notification
- Large buffers to guarantee QoS
- Queuing and rate-scheduling on a per-virtual-circuit basis

As a connection-oriented technology, a connection must be established in ATM before data transfer can occur. A signaling request packet is sent from the router requesting the connection to its ATM switch, which is directly connected. This packet will also contain any QoS information as needed. The receiving ATM switch or ATM-enabled router reassembles the packet, examines it, and decides whether it can accommodate the request. If so, the signaling packet is forwarded over a virtual circuit to the next switch until the destination is reached. If any switch along the way cannot accommodate the request, a rejection message is generated back to the source.

ATM offers two different types of virtual circuits: Permanent Virtual Circuits (PVCs) and Switched Virtual Circuits (SVCs). PVCs are statically configured by a network administrator and remain connected but idle when not in use. SVCs are set up when communicating devices require it and are torn down when the communication is complete.

ATM networks should be fully meshed—that is, every router needs to know how to get to every other router. This is because each time a router receives ATM traffic, it must perform Segmentation and Reassembly (SAR). The traffic, when received, is reassembled into the data flow as it was before being broken down into fixed-length cells. If the receiving router is not the final destination, it then breaks the data into cells again and sends it out on the network to the next hop router.

SAR introduces more latency into the data transfer. If all routers know how to reach all others, through full-meshed networks, the data has a better chance of reaching its destination in the fewest hops possible. This is the most important thing to remember about ATM at this stage of your studies. We will explore ATM much more closely in Chapter 20, "What is ATM." ATM in the LAN is generally implemented as LAN Emulation (LANE). We will discuss LANE later in this chapter.

LAN Connection Methods

You can connect your network segments in two ways:

- Switching (formerly known as bridging)
- Routing

Within the framework of switching, however, you can also implement VLANs or LANE technology. It is up to you as the network designer to weigh the benefits and pitfalls of each and make decisions about where to implement a particular connection method.

Switching is a Layer 2 technology that is relatively simple and easy to configure. The architecture is flat. LAN switches work by opening and examining the frames on the network. The switch then builds a table that matches up the source hardware address of the frame with the switch port it was seen on. This way the switch "learns" which devices are physically attached to each port. With this information, the switch can filter frames when forwarding is not necessary or forward frames as needed.

Switches introduce little latency into the network. One major disadvantage to switching, however, is that it is not very scalable, and upper limits exist for the number of end-stations on a flat segment, as we will discuss later in this chapter. Because of the flat address space, switching is limited to a single segment unless VLANs or 802.1Q are implemented.

Routers, on the other hand, maintain tables of Layer 3 (Network layer) addresses, thus making router configuration dependent on the protocol being used. Routing tends to be more difficult to configure than switching and introduces more latency into the network. However, routers create highly scalable networks by allowing the creation of logical address spaces, broadcast filtering, and better administrative control of the network through protocol configuration.

We will now take a closer look at switching, routing, and VLAN usage in respect to your LAN connection method decision.

Switching

A bridge or switch forwards frames on a network from a source to a destination, based on Layer 2 MAC addresses. The MAC addresses of attached end-stations are dynamically learned as traffic moves through the switch. If a destination MAC address is not known, the switch floods the frame to all ports. The end-station with the correct MAC address responds and is added to the table. In Figure 4-7, you will notice that for each end-station, the switch has created an entry in the MAC table that shows the end-station's MAC address along with the associated switch port identifier.

Once the end-station MAC addresses are listed in the table, the switch can make a forwarding decision based upon this information. Referring to Figure 4-7, if a frame enters port 1/1 destined for the MAC address of an end-station on port 1/3, the switch will examine the frame by reading the destination MAC address and by looking up that MAC address in its MAC table. As a result, it will forward the traffic to port 1/3. If the switch sees traffic on port 1/1 destined for another end-station on the same port, it discards the frame. The switch also filters out collision packets on Ethernet segments, but forwards, or floods, broadcast frames to every port.

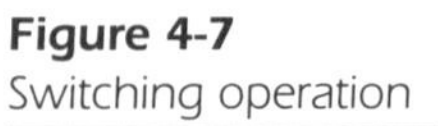

Figure 4-7
Switching operation

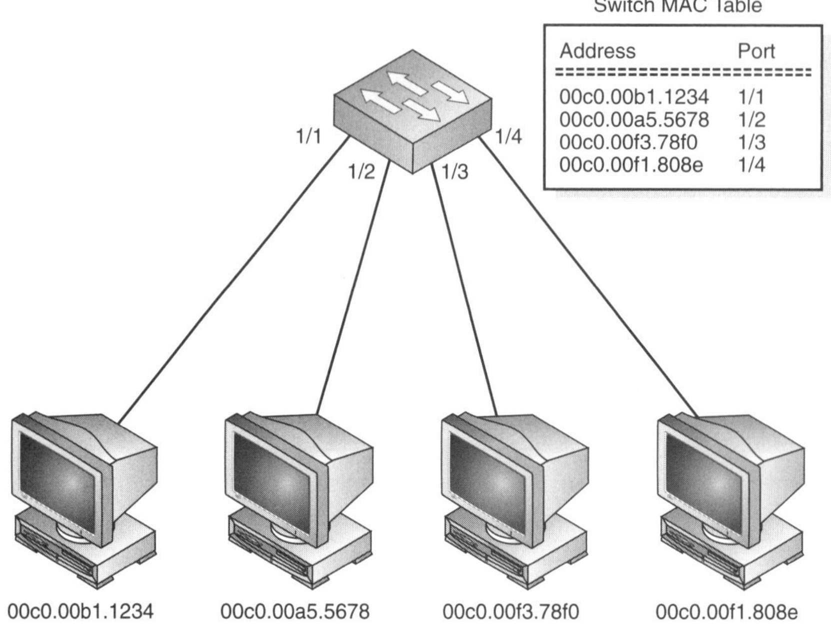

Routing

Routers also build tables of addresses, but unlike switches, routers build tables based upon OSI-model Layer 3 addresses. This enables the router to maintain protocol-specific tables known as *route tables*. A router does not need to build a table containing every end-station address—it depends on the routing protocols to handle the specifics of forwarding. Destination networks are either entered into the router as static routes or entered as part of the routing protocol configuration. The router may also learn of destinations as it exchanges routing information with its neighbors. As shown in Figure 4-8, a router simply keeps a table based upon which network is located on which interface.

Another difference between routers and switches is that while a switch forwards received broadcast frames to every port, a router will discard broadcasts unless a "helper address" has been expressly configured on the router interface. A helper address may be used in conjunction with DHCP, for example, to allow end-stations to broadcast Reverse Address Resolution

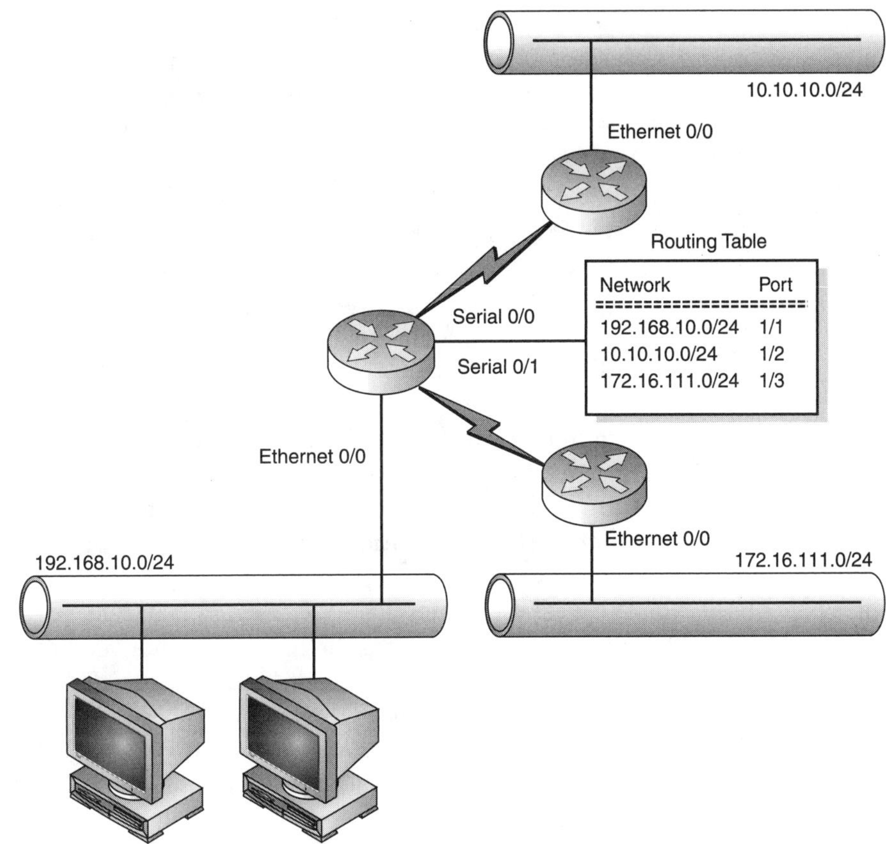

Figure 4-8
Routing operation

Protocol (RARP) packets asking for a network address to map to its MAC address. A properly configured router will forward received broadcasts to the end-station if configured with a helper address.

VLANs

Until the concept of VLANs was introduced, an end-station was tied to the physical segment to which it was attached. For example, if a user in the east wing of a building moved to the south wing, the user's end-station had to be changed to reflect the address of the segment that supported the south wing. Many configuration changes in the end-station had to occur. If the end-station happened to be a server or some other device to which other devices pointed, the problem grew exponentially larger, necessitating changes on many end-stations.

Membership in a VLAN can be based on the MAC address, Network layer address, or physical port configuration, with the latter usually being the case. VLANs are manually configured in the switch, and ports are assigned to a single VLAN. Each VLAN is a separate broadcast domain. Remember also that in a switch, each port is a separate collision domain, but without VLAN implementation, the entire switch is still a single broadcast domain.

Before starting to create VLANs, you will want to decide whether or not to use the VLAN Trunk Protocol (VTP). VTP can help reduce administration in a network by allowing the administrator to make all moves, adds, and changes from a single Catalyst switch, acting as a VTP server. Configuration changes are propagated through the network, negating the need for making the configuration change at each switch when adding a new VLAN, for example.

By default, a Catalyst 5000 switch is in VTP server mode, but is in the "no-management domain" state until a management domain is configured or learned about over a trunk link. VTP basically works as a manager for configuration changes within the VLANs and can help a network administrator avoid potential errors such as duplicate VLAN names and security violations. All of this is done through the use of a Layer 2 messaging protocol, VTP.

Even though the VLAN concept makes user moves, adds, and changes much simpler, a router is still needed in order for VLANs to communicate with each other, as shown in Figure 4-9. A VLAN is simply a virtual subnet. As with any other subnet, the router must make all routing decisions when a source and destination are located in different subnets.

Figure 4-9 shows that switch ports 1/1 through 1/4 belong to VLAN 10.10.10. Ports 2/1 through 2/4 belong to VLAN 192.168.10. Even though both VLANs and all end-stations are on the same switch, because VLANs have been implemented, only a router can forward traffic between the end-station on port 2/4 and the end-station on port 1/3, for example. This is because when a frame reaches the switch, the switch examines the Layer 2 information and compares it to the MAC table of the VLAN in which it was received. If the destination does not match anything in the table, the frame is forwarded to the router or gateway.

The exception to this is Layer 3 or Layer 4 switching. By implementing Multi-Layer Switching (MLS), Cisco has enabled the switch to build a

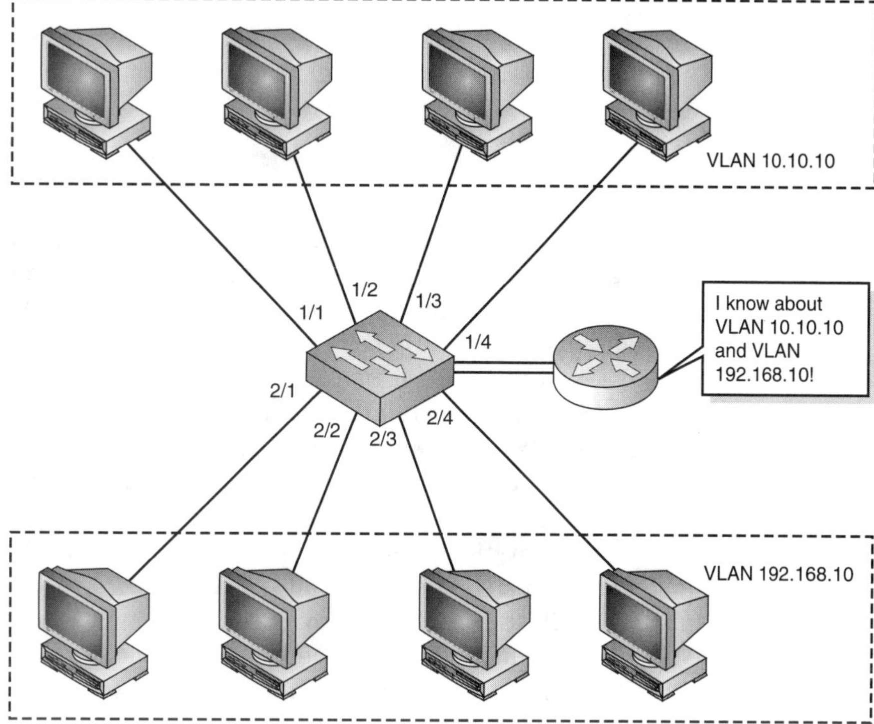

Figure 4-9
VLAN operation

Layer 3 (L3) cache dynamically. An abbreviated routing table is created in a proprietary manner, allowing the switch to make some routing decisions. Although MLS does not make a switch as sophisticated as a router, it does keep more traffic off of the router.

If a frame is received and the Layer 2 destination information does not match anything in the MAC table, the switch does a Layer 3 destination lookup in the MLS cache. If it does not know about the destination address, it reassembles the Layer 2 header and replaces the destination MAC address with that of its gateway—in this case, the router. The router will then dig into the Layer 3 information and forward the packet based upon the Layer 3 destination information. You may also hear the term *flow* associated with the proprietary Cisco process of stripping off the MAC header, examining the destination network address, and reassembling the MAC header.

TIP: *The average timeout of the L3 cache in a Catalyst switch is 256 seconds.*

VLAN Trunking The rule for VLANs is that every switch port can belong to a single VLAN only. This is a problem when multiple VLANs must be carried through multiple switches. Because the frame does not have identifiers to classify it as belonging to one VLAN or another, the network designer faces a problem.

Cisco implements a proprietary modification of the 802.1Q standard that allows a VLAN identifier to be inserted into the frame between the MAC header and the remainder of the packet. It is a two-byte field that is unique to the VLAN. This is also known as *tag switching*. Cisco also provides for the implementation of *trunk ports* that carry multiple VLANs across a single port. Trunk ports are generally used between switches in a network design. This allows VLANs that are on different switches to still be able to communicate as though they were locally connected, as shown in Figure 4-10. VLAN 10.10.10 exists on both switches and, via the trunk port, end-stations on either switch send and receive frames to each other as though they were local, without the need for a router or Layer 3 switch.

Ethernet Trunking VLAN trunking over Fast Ethernet on Cisco switches is done with a proprietary method called Inter-Switch Link (ISL). Notice that we say "over Fast Ethernet," because VLAN trunking for 10-Mbps Ethernet is not supported. Ten-Mbps speeds for trunking are not supported because it is assumed that because you are running VTP across the links, you will need faster speeds, and trunking was never implemented for those lower speeds.

Fast Ethernet trunking works by using a 30-byte field that uses a two-byte VLAN ID. This allows the switch receiving frames over the trunk line to open the frame, discover the VLAN to which the frame belongs, and forward it as needed.

FDDI Trunking For VLANs over FDDI, Cisco switches implement the IEEE 802.10 Secure Bridging field. A 16-byte field is inserted between the MAC and LCC headers, which contain a four-byte VLAN identifier. Cisco switches also support the frame type for 802.1Q, which provides

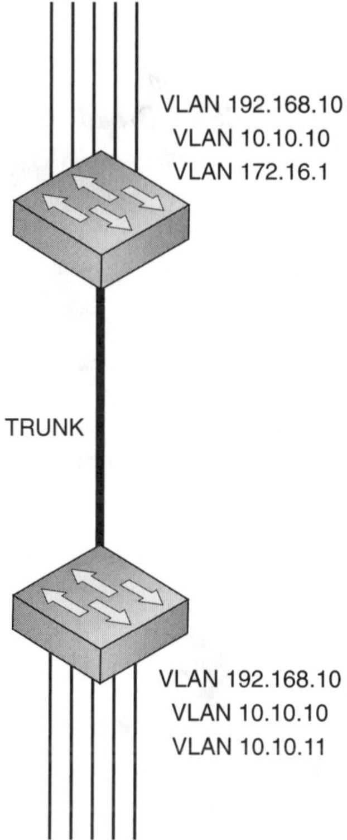

Figure 4-10
VLAN trunking

versatility and ease-of-transition when migrating from FDDI to any type of Ethernet.

ATM LANE

ATM LAN Emulation (LANE) is a standard that allows network design professionals to internetwork their existing topologies, such as Ethernet and Token Ring, into ATM-connected devices. Cisco offers LANE on its switches to emulate a single logical wire, or an Emulated LAN (ELAN) out of multiple physical wires. This also creates a single broadcast domain in which existing end-stations on a LAN can interface with an ATM network. Just like VLANs, ELANs can communicate with each other only over a router.

DESIGN TERM: *An Emulated LAN (ELAN) is a virtual implementation of an Ethernet or Token Ring LAN and contains a LAN Emulation Client (LEC), a LAN Emulation Server (LES), a Broadcast and Unknown Server, and a LAN Emulation Configuration Server (LECS).*

There are four components of an ATM LANE network, shown in Figure 4-11:

- LAN Emulation Client (LEC)
- LAN Emulation Server (LES)
- LAN Emulation Configuration Server (LECS)
- Broadcast and Unknown Server (BUS)

Figure 4-11 Typical LANE configuration

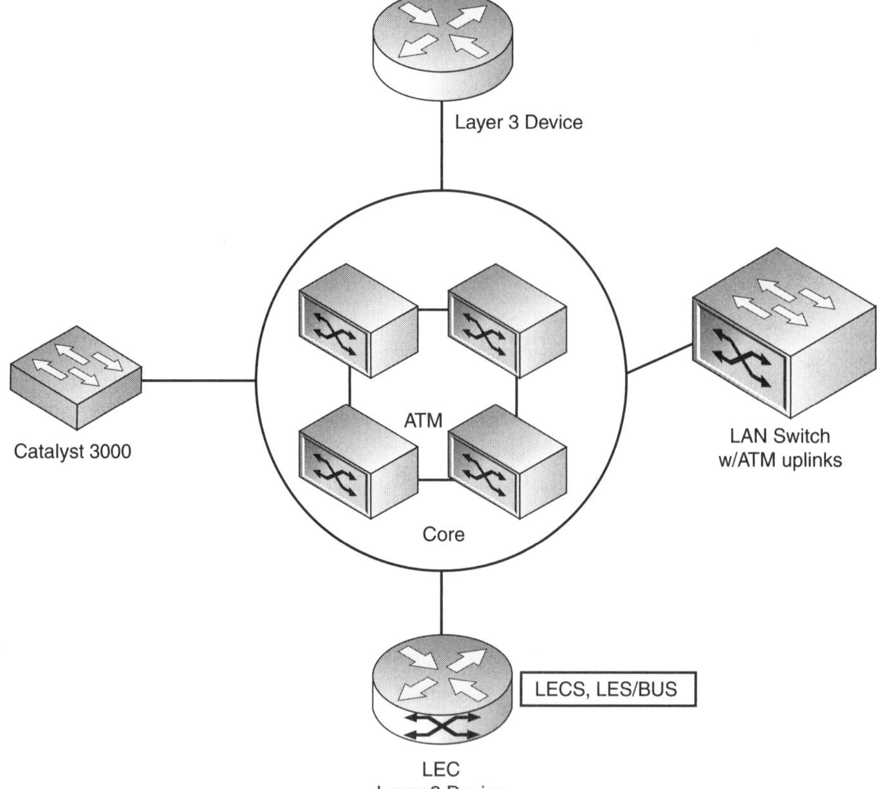

An LEC is an end-station that supports connectivity to LANE. This can be a PC workstation with an NIC, a router with ATM support, or a LAN switch with ATM line cards. The LEC allows a legacy interface to talk to the upper layer protocols through data forwarding, address resolution, and MAC address registration with the LES.

An LES acts as the hub for all LECs. Using special communication channels, the LEC sends registration and control information to the LES. In turn, the LES maintains a point-to-multipoint connection to all LECs over which control information is sent. An LES is specific to an ELAN.

An LECS maintains the database of ELAN identifiers along with the ATM address of the LES that serves that ELAN. The database is maintained manually.

The BUS handles broadcasts and multicasts in the ELAN. Because ATM is a non-broadcast technology and functions in a point-to-point manner, it cannot support the broadcasts that are required for Ethernet, for example. Again, the LECs send registration and control data to the BUS over special communication circuits and receive control information back over a point-to-multipoint circuit from the BUS.

Though LANE is not as popular as it once was, there may still be instances when the design requirements or customer wishes may dictate its implementation or continued use and support. To that end, here are some design considerations of which you should be aware:

- For each ELAN, there is a single LES/BUS pair and any number of LECs.
- There is no provision for LES/BUS redundancy in the current LANE standard.
- The LES/BUS pair must both be defined on the same subinterface and cannot be separated.
- Each network VLAN should be assigned to its own ELAN for the simplification of design.
- A given ELAN should reside only in one subnet per protocol.
- There can be only one LEC per subinterface.
- If several LECs exist on a router and have unique protocol addresses, the routing will occur between the respective ELANs.

LANE will be discussed a little more in Chapter 20.

Recommendations for Scaling Switched Networks

Scaling a switched network is, like many issues in internetworking, more of an art than a science. Many factors can impact the scalability of the network, including the amount of network traffic and the protocols in use.

The protocols that tend to have the most issues are AppleTalk and NetBIOS. An AppleTalk user selects network services by opening a window called a Chooser, which we will discuss more in Chapter 13, "AppleTalk Design." Although the behavior of the Chooser is different depending upon the version of the Macintosh OS in use, typically a succession of multicast packets is generated as soon as a user selects a zone and service. This can become a problem if the user leaves the Chooser window open. Some newer versions of the OS have features built in that will limit this traffic and thus the impact on the network, but some versions do not.

In NetBIOS networks, stations send broadcasts using Source-Route Bridging (SRB) to verify their own names and discover the names of other stations on the network. Because NetBIOS uses the "single route broadcast/all routes broadcast return" SRB option, the response from end-stations takes all possible paths through a network. All end-stations, rings, and segments are affected by this traffic. Each client and server end-station must also process the frames, even if they are not the intended destination.

Because of the inherent problems with AppleTalk and NetBIOS, the number of end-stations on a flat network running these protocols should be limited to 200 or less. In an IP-only or mixed IP and IPX network, you may have up to 500 end-stations without encountering too much trouble. Although you may scale beyond that number, with a well-behaved network, it is generally not advisable.

TIP: *The number of stations on a switched, multiprotocol network should not exceed 500.*

Case Study

We are back with our client, Campus Research, again. In Chapter 3, we asked you to help the client determine cabling, technology in the wiring closet, the location of servers, router placement, and connectivity between buildings.

As a refresher, recall that the client has locations in Detroit and St. Louis, as shown in Figure 4-12. Detroit is home to Headquarters, and St. Louis is home to Research and Development. The connection between the two buildings is an ISDN line. Their technology is 10-Mbps Ethernet. They would like to stay with Ethernet but want to upgrade to faster NICs on the servers. They also would like to increase the bandwidth between the building to a dedicated T1 line or better, perhaps keeping the ISDN line for a backup connectivity method.

The company would like you to come up with a suggested naming convention for the server farm(s) as well as for their network devices. They would also like a plan for handling the increased bandwidth between the buildings through a better LAN connection method.

Your assignment for Chapter 4 is to help the Campus Research network staff decide on the appropriate technology and connection methods between their two buildings and in their server farm. Additionally, you will

Figure 4-12 Campus Research locations

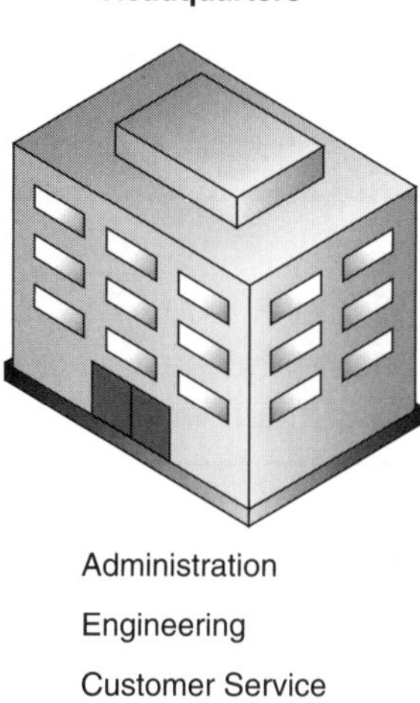

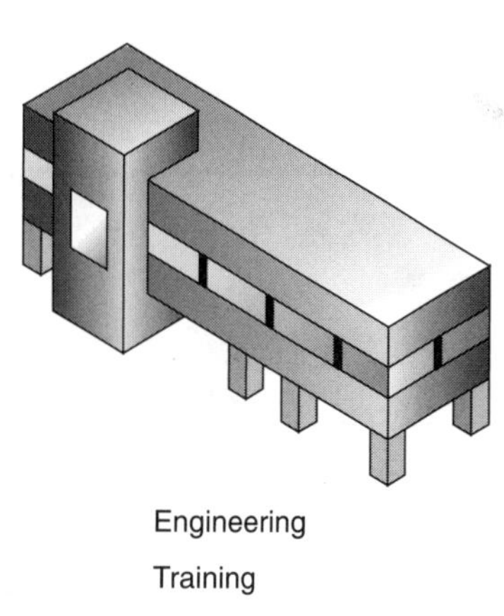

need to create a preliminary design for the server farms in relation to the user end-stations in the network. Here is a recap of what you need to do for this case study:

- Will there be a centralized server farm or a set of servers in each location? How did you address the problem in Chapter 3?
- Define a naming convention for the servers and network devices.
- Define the new connection between buildings. Bear in mind that this may change later, when we explore WAN design. That is expected.
- Make recommendations on LAN topology and the use of VLANs if appropriate.

Build on what you recommended to the client in the previous assignment to create a high-level diagram with LAN connection speeds properly labeled.

Although there is no one right answer in any design scenario, a suggested solution can be found in Appendix C, "Suggested Solutions to Case Studies," of this book.

Study Hints

Although no one who is Cisco-certified is permitted to disclose test items or test content, we can give clues as to what might be valuable to study. For this chapter, a lot of material has been covered from a high yet more detailed level than in Chapter 3. Here are areas that you should review before attempting any Cisco network design certification test:

- Be very familiar with the way Ethernet, ATM, and FDDI work. Be especially aware of standards related to the technology and to the setup and breakdown of communication links.
- Familiarize yourself with not only the purpose of VLAN technology, but also with the particulars of routing between VLANs and 802.1Q and its purpose in the routing and switching world.
- Know every component of LANE. If a technology is still in use anywhere, it is to your benefit to know it, and not just for the purpose of passing a test.
- Understand trunking as fully as possible. Although it may seem like a straightforward concept, many people in the networking world do not truly understand how trunking works.

- Practice as many case studies as you can get your hands on. Use those listed progressively in this book, and search for other Cisco online case studies and books containing network designs. This will not only benefit you for taking the certification tests, but it will also enable you to walk confidently into a customer site and handle almost any situation. The case studies are usually modified versions of what a typical network designer has seen in real life.

CCDP Tips

This section contains an abbreviated list of topics covered in Chapter 4. Think of this section as the equivalent of reading Cliff's Notes™ instead of reading an entire book. Although this provides the general idea of the chapter, you will benefit more from reading the chapter in its entirety.

LAN technology comes in four types:

- Ethernet (10-Mbps, 100-Mbps, 1000-Mbps)
- Token Ring (4-Mbps, 16-Mbps, single-ring, token-passing)
- FDDI (100-Mbps, dual-ring, token-passing)
- ATM (155-Mbps, cell relay)

Four methods for connecting LANs exist:

- Switching (Layer 2)
- Routing (Layer 3)
- VLANs (switch-based)
- ATM LANE (switch-based)

A LAN Emulation (LANE) network has four components:

- LAN Emulation Client (LEC)
- LAN Emulation Server (LES)
- LAN Emulation Configuration Server (LECS)
- Broadcast and Unknown Server (BUS)

The limitations to LAN scalability are as follows:

- Up to 200 end-stations in a flat network for AppleTalk and NetBIOS
- Up to 500 end-stations in a flat network for IP and IPX

Summary

In this chapter, we have explained many of the topologies you might see in a real campus network, such as Ethernet, FDDI, ATM, or Token Ring. It is important to understand each of these various topologies and technologies so that you do not "paint yourself into a corner," so to speak. If you have a favorite type of network design, you are no different than any other network designer, but if you truly understand the common design building blocks, you will be that much more valuable in any situation.

You should now have a better understanding of how these technologies function in a network design and how to implement them. We gave you some guidelines for creating scalability and for interconnecting the LAN segments, including routing between VLANs. LAN Emulation (LANE) was also covered to show you how ATM might be implemented in concert with legacy technologies, such as Token Ring, by using the various components of LANE, like the BUS.

In Chapter 5, "Campus LAN Design Models," we will describe the different campus backbone infrastructures and discover how to implement what you have now learned into a structured design model.

Questions

The following review questions have been selected to help you test your knowledge of the subject matter contained in this chapter. You will also find these questions contained in the CD-ROM included with this book. Although these are not the exact questions that appear in the certification exams, knowing the answers to the review questions in this book will help cement the material in your mind as you prepare for the tests.

1. VLAN technology is based on which Internet standard?

a. 802.3

b. 802.1Q

c. 803.1B

d. RFC 1771

2. If an AppleTalk Chooser window is left open, what is the possible impact on a network?
   a. The router will crash.
   b. The Chooser window will lock up the workstation.
   c. Nothing. The Chooser window does not impact the network, only the client end-station.
   d. Continuing multicasts could be generated, depending on the MAC OS version.
3. If multiple VLANs are housed in a network, what is needed to allow them to communicate?
   a. A router
   b. A VLAN aggregation switch
   c. A zone information server
   d. A firewall
4. The use of a Token Ring switch means that there is no restriction to the number of tokens released on the backbone ring.
   a. True
   b. False
5. Which statement best describes Ethernet technology?
   a. It guarantees delivery.
   b. It is a best-effort delivery method.
   c. It is a token-passing technology.
   d. It always operates at 100 Mbps.
6. What is Cisco's implementation of VLAN over FDDI?
   a. 802.1Q
   b. 802.10
   c. 802.3
   d. 802.5
7. What is one possible problem caused by cut-through switching that can be alleviated by setting a port to full-duplex?
   a. Dropped packets
   b. Runt frames
   c. Giant frames
   d. Late collisions

8. If a switch does not recognize a destination MAC address, how does it handle the frame?
   a. It drops the frame.
   b. It floods the frame to all ports.
   c. It sends the frame to the router.
   d. It sends the frame to the trunk port only.
9. True or False: The cut-through method of switching is likely to generate some runt frames.
   a. True
   b. False
10. True or False: The store-and-forward method of switching must read the first 64 bytes of a packet before forwarding.
    a. True
    b. False
11. The LANE component that provides for broadcasts and multicasts in order to support legacy LAN protocols is
    a. LES
    b. LEC
    c. LECS
    d. BUS
12. The LANE component that acts as the central point for LANE clients is known as the
    a. LES
    b. LEC
    c. LECS
    d. BUS
13. The LANE component that stores a database of all ELANs is the
    a. LES
    b. LEC
    c. LECS
    d. BUS

14. The LES communicates to the LECs in this manner:
    a. Broadcast
    b. PPP
    c. SLIP
    d. Point-to-multipoint
15. True or False: Different ELANs can communicate without a router or Layer 3 device.
    a. True
    b. False
16. What is the function performed by an intermediate router receiving an ATM data transfer?
    a. SAR
    b. Directed broadcast
    c. Cut-through switching
    d. ELAN translation
17. What was the original usage for TDM, one of the technologies from which ATM was spawned?
    a. Data network communication
    b. Postal POS terminals
    c. Clocking on routers
    d. Voice communications
18. CDDI technology is identical to FDDI, except for what?
    a. Media-type
    b. Single-ring versus dual-ring
    c. Multiple allowable tokens on the ring
    d. Clocking
19. At what percentage is it commonly acknowledged that a standard Ethernet segment would begin to drop packets due to congestion?
    a. 80
    b. 70
    c. 40
    d. 30

20. Which LAN topology uses Carrier Sense Multiple Access/Collision Detect?

a. Token Ring

b. Ethernet

c. FDDI

d. ATM

Answers

1. VLAN technology is based on which Internet standard?
   b. 802.1Q
   Explanation: Although VLANs, as discussed in this book, are a Cisco implementation, 802.1Q is a standard that is in draft and that will allow different vendors to intercommunicate using the same type of technology.

2. If an AppleTalk Chooser window is left open, what is the possible impact on the network?
   d. Continuing multicasts could be generated, depending on the MAC OS version.
   Explanation: Although later versions of the MAC OS have addressed this possible problem, it is an important item to be aware of when designing and troubleshooting networks containing the AppleTalk protocol.

3. If multiple VLANs are housed in a network, what is needed to allow them to communicate?
   a. A router
   Explanation: VLANs are a single broadcast domain in and of themselves. As such, they do not "see" traffic outside their broadcast domain. A router can allow the segments to reach each other.

4. True or False: The use of a Token Ring switch means there is no restriction on the number of tokens released on the backbone ring.
   b. False
   Explanation: There can still be only one token on the backbone ring at any given time, unless early token release is employed. This would have nothing to do with the Token Ring switch.

5. Which statement best describes Ethernet technology?
   b. It is a best-effort delivery method.
   Explanation: Although there may be error-checking involved in some implementations of Ethernet, it is not a guarantee that packets will arrive.
6. What is Cisco's implementation of VLAN over FDDI?
   b. 802.10
7. What is one possible problem caused by cut-through switching that can be alleviated by setting a port to full-duplex?
   b. Runt frames
   Explanation: Because the switch is sending the frame through as soon as the destination address is read, errors in the frame may be missed, resulting in a runt frame.
8. If a switch does not recognize a destination MAC address, how does it handle the frame?
   b. It floods the frame to all ports.
   Explanation: This is essentially the same way ARP works. The switch sees the MAC address, compares it to the table, and does not find a match. With an ARP request, the switch would flood a request everywhere on the broadcast domain to find the MAC to match a given Network layer address. In the example given, the switch does not know where to send the frame, so it sends it everywhere, hoping it will arrive at a destination that does know where to send the frame.
9. True or False: The cut-through method of switching is likely to generate some runt frames.
   a. True
   Explanation: Cut-through switching does not do error-checking on the frame. Because part of the frame could be lost in transmission, runt frames can result.
10. True or False: The store-and-forward method of switching must read the first 64 bytes of a frame before forwarding.
    b. False.
    Explanation: Store-and-forward switching waits until the entire frame is received and has passed a CRC before forwarding the frame.
11. The LANE component that provides for broadcasts and multicasts in order to support legacy LAN protocols is
    d. BUS

12. The LANE component that acts as the central point for LANE clients is known as the
a. LES

13. The LANE component that stores a database of all ELANs is the
c. LECS

14. The LES communicates to the LECs in this manner.
c. Point-to-multipoint
Explanation: The LAN Emulation Server must communicate with all LECs assigned to it. Therefore, it is a point-to-multipoint communication.

15. Different ELANs can communicate without a router or Layer 3 device.
b. False
Explanation: Just like VLANs, an ELAN is its own subnet or logical segment. A Layer 3 device must be used to facilitate communication between different logical segments.

16. What is the function performed by an intermediate router receiving an ATM data transfer?
a. SAR
Explanation: Remember—each router that receives the transmission must reassemble the data, examine it, and segment it into cells again before sending it onward.

17. What was the original usage for TDM, one of the technologies from which ATM was spawned?
d. Voice communications

18. CDDI technology is identical to FDDI except for what?
a. Media-type
Explanation: Although FDDI uses fiber-optic cabling, CDDI is the same topology using twisted-pair cabling.

19. At what percentage is it commonly acknowledged that a standard Ethernet segment would begin to drop packets due to congestion?
d. 30
Explanation: Although many schools of thought on this topic exist, Cisco generally states that a standard Ethernet segment will begin to drop packets when it reaches 30 percent saturation.

20. Which LAN topology uses Carrier Sense Multiple Access/Collision Detect?
 b. Ethernet

Bibliography

Charles Spurgeon's Ethernet Web Site, **http://www.ots.utexas.edu/ethernet/ethernet.html**

Gigabit Ethernet Alliance, **http://www.gigabit-ethernet.org/technology/index.shtml**

Cisco's *Designing ATM Networks* Guide, **http://www.cisco.com/univercd/cc/td/doc/cisintwk/idg4/nd2008.htm**

Cisco Internetwork Design Course Manual, version 3.0, April 1997, Cisco Systems, Inc.

Cisco Internetwork Design, Cisco Press, 2000, Matthew H. Birkner, Editor.

CHAPTER 5

Campus LAN Design Models

Overview

In the beginning of this book, we mentioned that a network could sometimes look like a house that has been remodeled over and over to accommodate a growing family inside. In the last four chapters we have gone over many of the campus LAN components. This chapter focuses on the overall campus LAN design model.

As part of the design model, we will examine the typical layout of a building. We will also look at distributed backbones, both at the building and campus levels. Then, we'll describe two of the most common design models you will need in your design toolkit: ATM and VLAN campus design.

Layout

A typical building layout in a campus provides a network infrastructure through which users can access network services and devices. In Figure 5-1 we have five floors, each containing a wiring closet with an equipment rack. The racks may contain hubs, switches, or concentrators. Rarely, routers may be deployed in the wiring closet as well, although it is more common to find a layer 3 switch.

All floors also connect to a building-wide conduit system known as a *riser*. Depending on the size of the building, there may be one wiring closet per floor, or there may be several. Remember that there are limitations to the distance that cable can carry a signal. For category 5 (Cat5) unshielded twisted pair (UTP), the distance limitation is 100 meters, or about 328 feet. If a wing of a building were about 600 feet, you would be wise to have two wiring closets on that floor.

Users and local end-stations on the floors are supported from the wiring closets. In the first floor of the building, there is a data center containing aggregation devices for the other wiring closets as well as support for devices in the data center itself. In some networks the data center is also home to building server farms, high-speed printers or plotters, and mainframe systems. This data center is sometimes referred to as the computer room. Access to the room is typically limited to network staff only. This may be enforced through the use of physical security such as keys, key-coded badges, or security keypads.

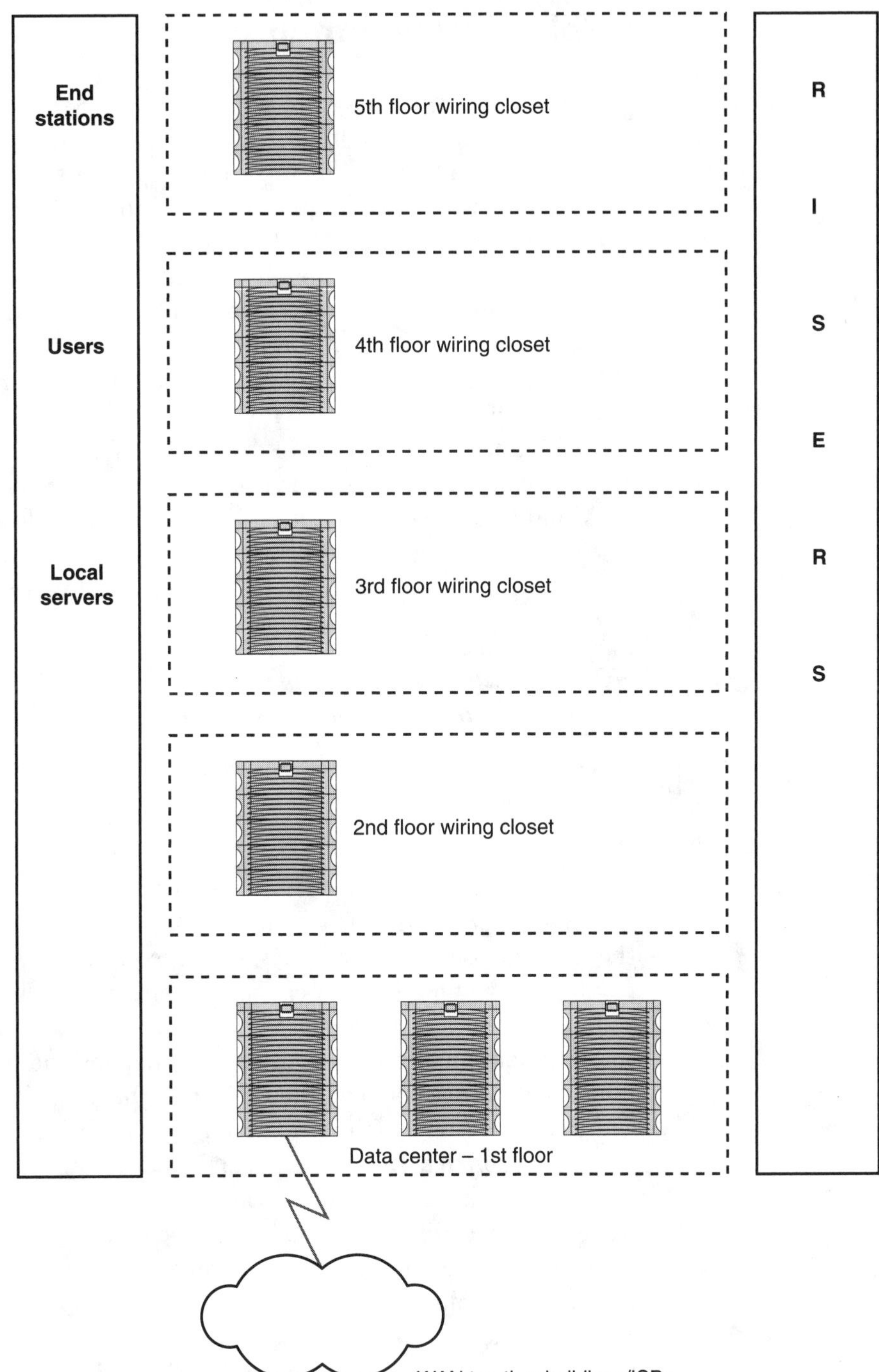

Figure 5-1 Building layout

Cabling Recommendations

The risers in the building are normally connected back to the data center and to each closet by fiber-optic cable, as shown in Figure 5-2. If the building network is a FDDI dual-ring architecture, this is a given. However, fiber in the risers is not just required in an FDDI network. Fiber provides for bandwidth scalability much more so than copper twisted-pair cabling and can carry a signal over a greater distance.

Copper cabling does have its place in the runs from the wiring closets to the wallplates. Even today, with readily available fiber-optic cable, copper is still the most common, because it is cheaper and easier to install and maintain than fiber. If you want to "future-proof" your network, however, fiber to the wallplate is a good way to do that. It is generally accepted that fiber cabling will not degrade over time in the same way that copper cabling does, and therefore will not need to be replaced, unless it is damaged. It is also unlikely that an upgrade would be needed in the foreseeable future for the cabling of a building in which fiber runs to the wallplate are done.

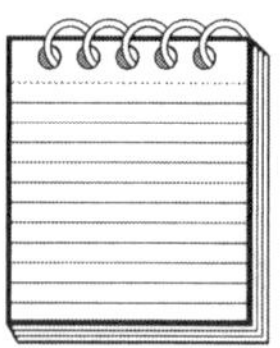

NOTE: *Because of the cost of the switches and NICs to support fiber to the wallplate, this is still a rare occurrence.*

The wallplates serving the end-stations are also known as *network drops*, or *LAN drops*. Each drop corresponds to a port on a patch panel in the wiring closet and ultimately a port on a hub or switch in the closet. A patch panel is an electrical or optical panel in which the cabling between the LAN drop and the closet terminates. Through coded labeling both on the wallplate and on the patch panel, a network administrator can determine connectivity between the closet and the drop.

A *patch cable* is usually a short length of copper UTP cable that connects an end-station to a drop or connects the patch panel to the hub or switch in the wiring closet. Depending upon the type of device being connected, the cable could be referred to as *straight-through* or *crossover*. A straight-through cable has the same pin-out on one end of the cable as on the other. A crossover cable is one in which the pin-out is changed at one end, sometimes completely flipped from the opposite end. Network administrators will frequently choose different colors of cable for straight-through than

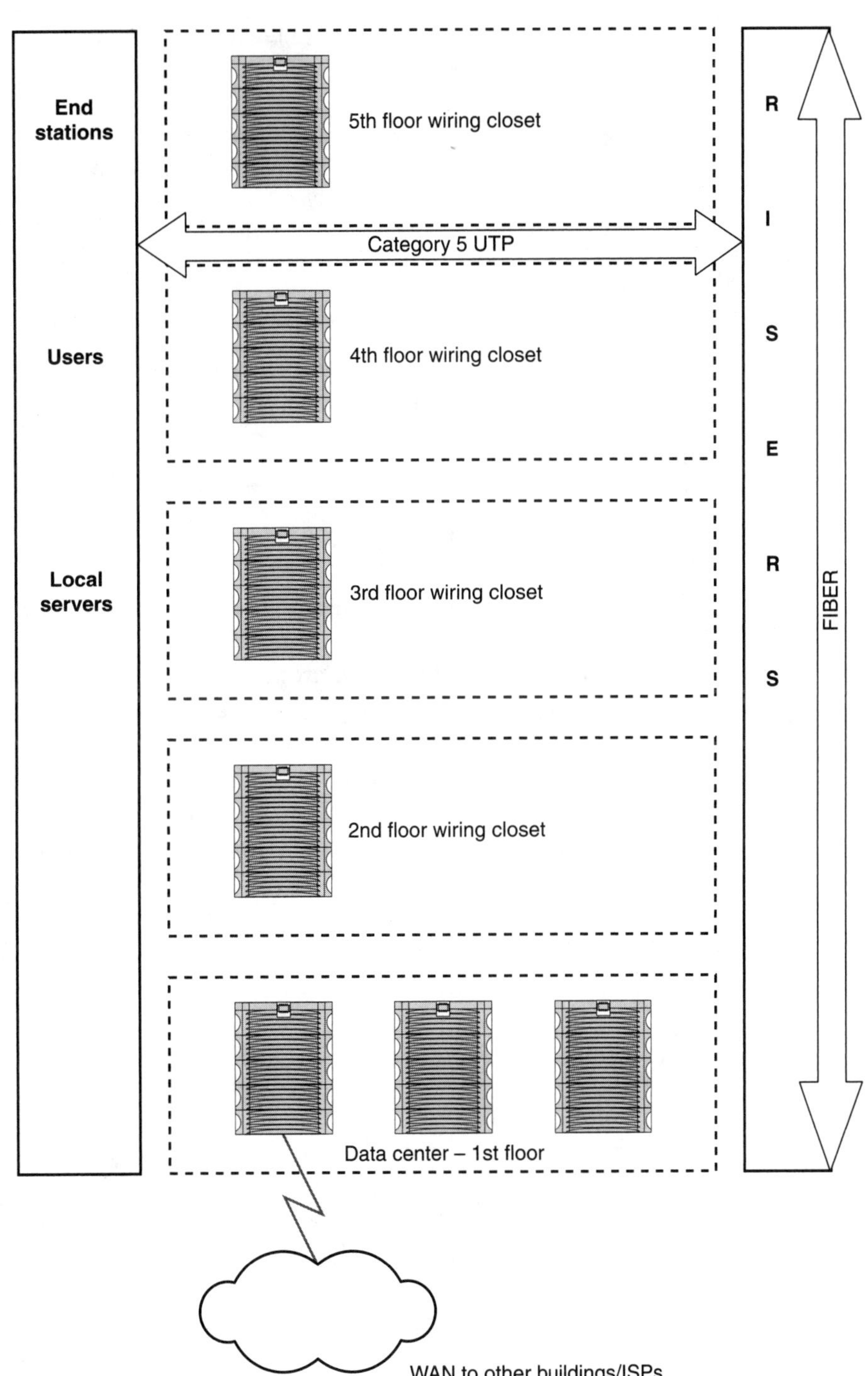

Figure 5-2 Building connectivity

they choose for crossover cables in order to quickly tell them apart. Such shortcuts can be big time-savers in a busy campus network operation.

TIP: A straight-through cable pin-out is usually used between an internetworking device (such as a switch or hub) and an end-station (such as a PC). The crossover cable connects two internetworking devices together.

Now that you have some background on what the building layout might be, we will examine the distributed backbone model of network design.

Distributed Backbones

Whether applied to a campus solution or to a building, a distributed backbone concept allows access to the backbone to be shared equally among several floors or buildings, whatever the case may be. By sharing the backbone, the distribution points all have equal access and equal risk. For instance, in a building in which switches or hubs are daisy-chained together or are linked to a shared switch, as in Figure 5-3, there are several points of failure that could affect many devices. In a distributed backbone, a failure between a switch and the backbone affects no other switches.

Distributed Building Backbone

A distributed backbone is one in which the physical backbone connects to and is shared equally by all wiring closets. In other words, there is a hierarchy in which a router serves the entire building at a core layer and a router or other layer 3 device acts at the Distribution layer. The distributed backbone, as seen in FDDI architecture, is shown in Figure 5-4.

While an FDDI backbone is sometimes the topology of choice for a distributed backbone, and is certainly the most popular design for illustration purposes, Ethernet is by far the more popular of the available topologies. As we discussed in previous chapters, Ethernet is less expensive, more widely used, and easier to learn and implement than many other topologies.

Figure 5-5 shows wiring closets on three floors with two connections each to the backbone. The two routers are configured with the Hot Standby Rout-

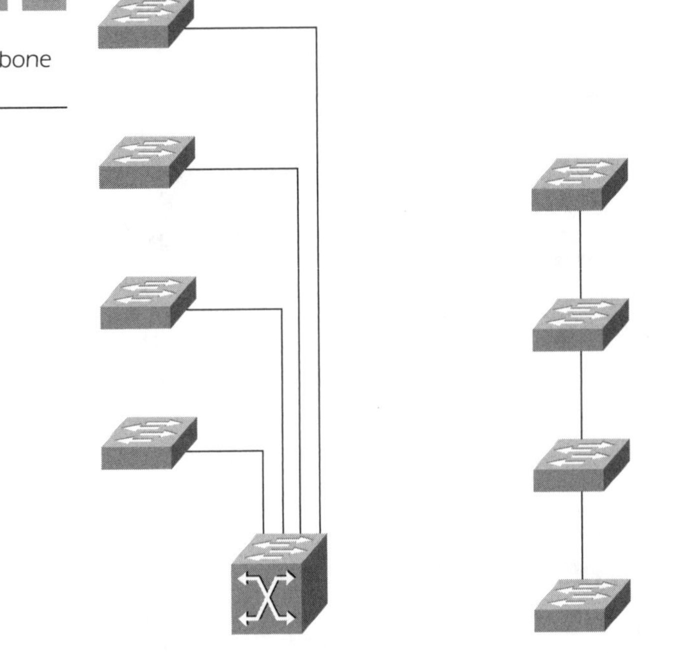

Figure 5-3 Collapsed backbone examples

ing Protocol (HSRP) so that neither is a single point of failure. The design meets the requirement of having all of the wiring closets connected to the backbone, and yet we have not given up the speed or redundancy of the FDDI architecture.

Notice that in Figures 5-4 and 5-5, no user touches the backbone. This is important to note. As we discussed in Chapter 2, "Hierarchial Design Model," the users should be at the Access layer. The backbone or Core layer should be used for optimal transport of network traffic. Therefore, the designs shown in these two figures fit our hierarchical network design model.

However, the models shown so far illustrate a very simple view of a possible distributed backbone design. To provide optimum redundancy and speed for the backbone, a router or layer 3 switch should be deployed at each wiring closet or floor, as shown in Figure 5-6. The main trade-offs in this design are the high cost of such a design and the need for at least one subnet per floor or wiring closet.

Figure 5-4 Distributed backbone-FDDI

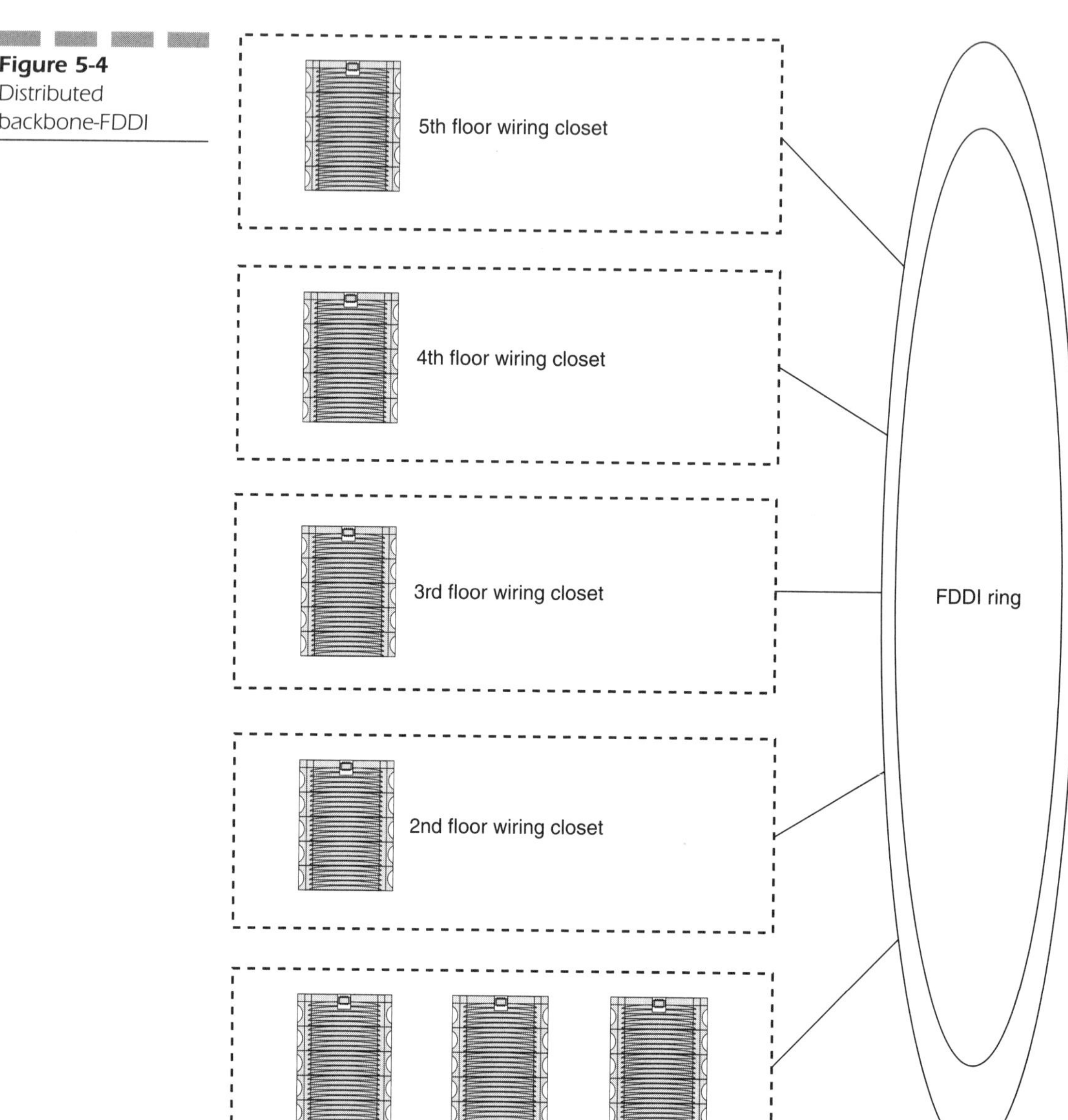

Distributed Campus Backbones

While a distributed backbone at the building level could potentially involve several layer 3 switches or at least two routers, the campus-distributed

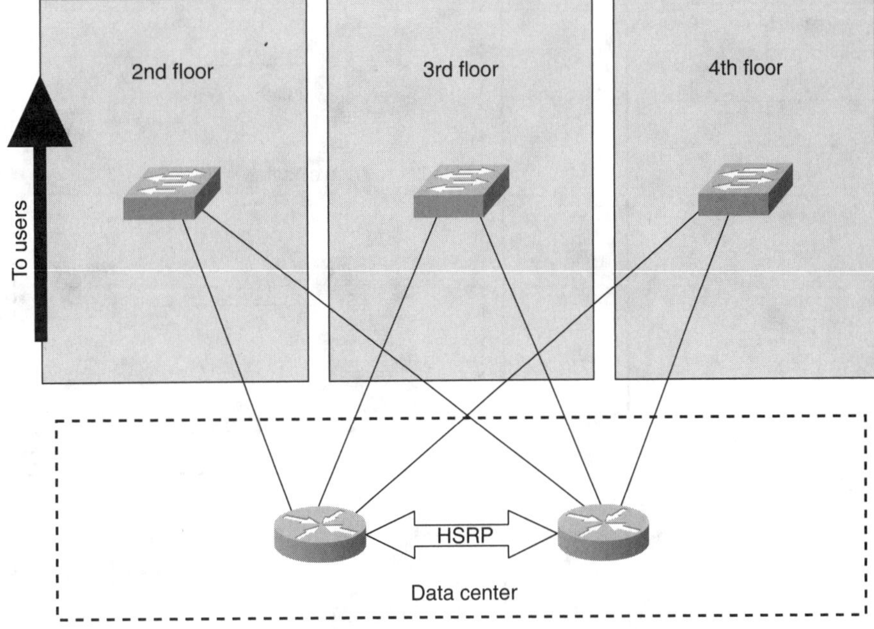

Figure 5-5 Distributed backbone-Ethernet

backbone usually involves one router per building (or two routers, if you run HSRP to eliminate the single point of failure). The distributed backbone at the campus level is much more cost-efficient and allows for fewer IP network numbers deployed in the building. As a result, a user's moves, adds, or changes are more easily accomplished without the need to change the end-station IP address or gateway. The networks behind the building routers shown in Figure 5-7 may be kept flat or collapsed without negating the overall distributed campus structure. We will talk about collapsed backbone structures later in this chapter.

Although FDDI is shown in Figure 5-7 for illustration purposes, you could use almost any LAN topology—Token Ring or Gigabit Ethernet—to connect the buildings. The real drawback to using distributed backbone architecture on the campus is that the design tends to lack flexibility in the way the buildings connect to one another. Once the fiber is run between buildings, your connection is pretty much fixed. You could not, for example, suddenly decide that you want Building A to connect directly to Building B without a great deal of expense incurred.

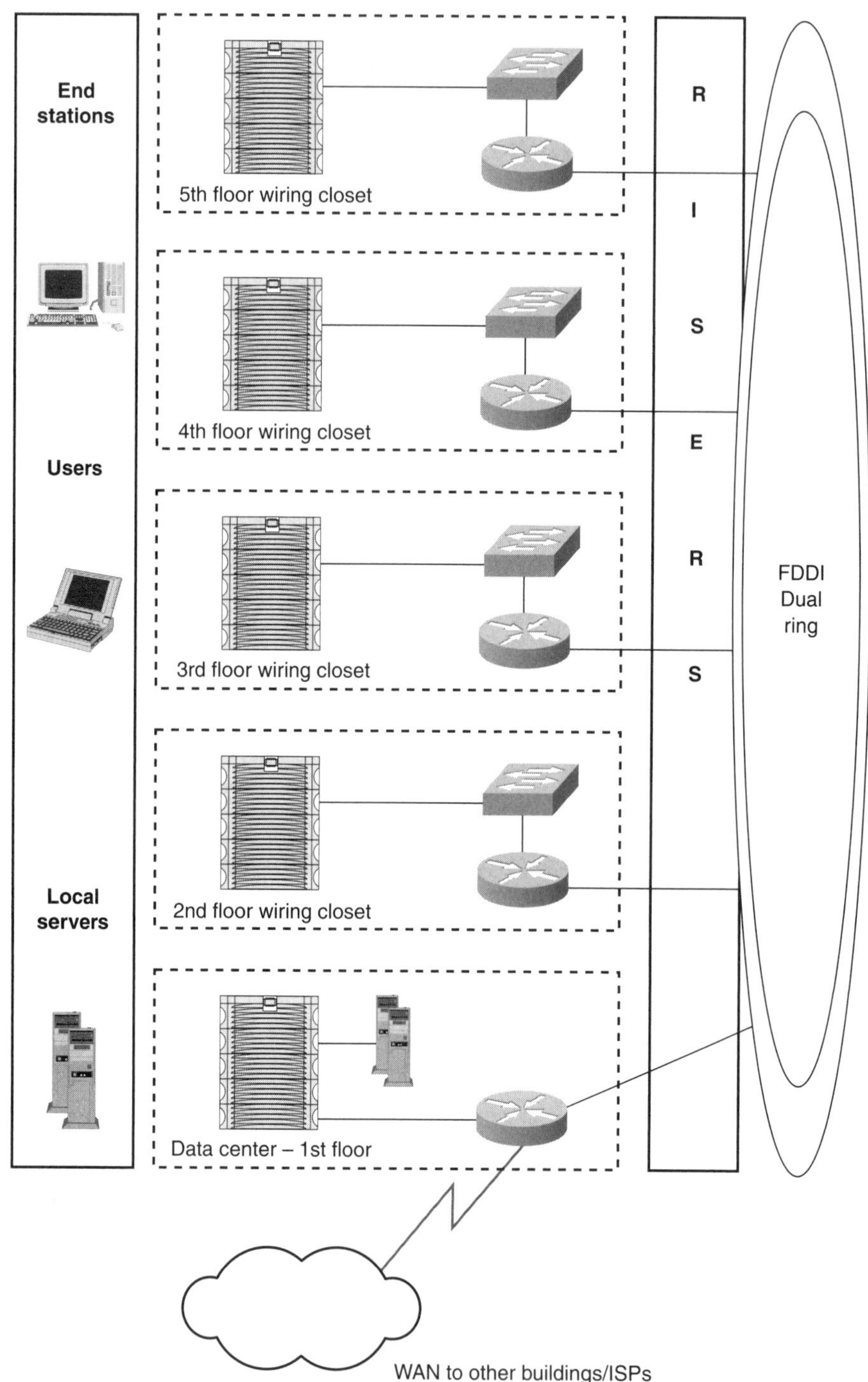

Figure 5-6 Fully distributed backbone

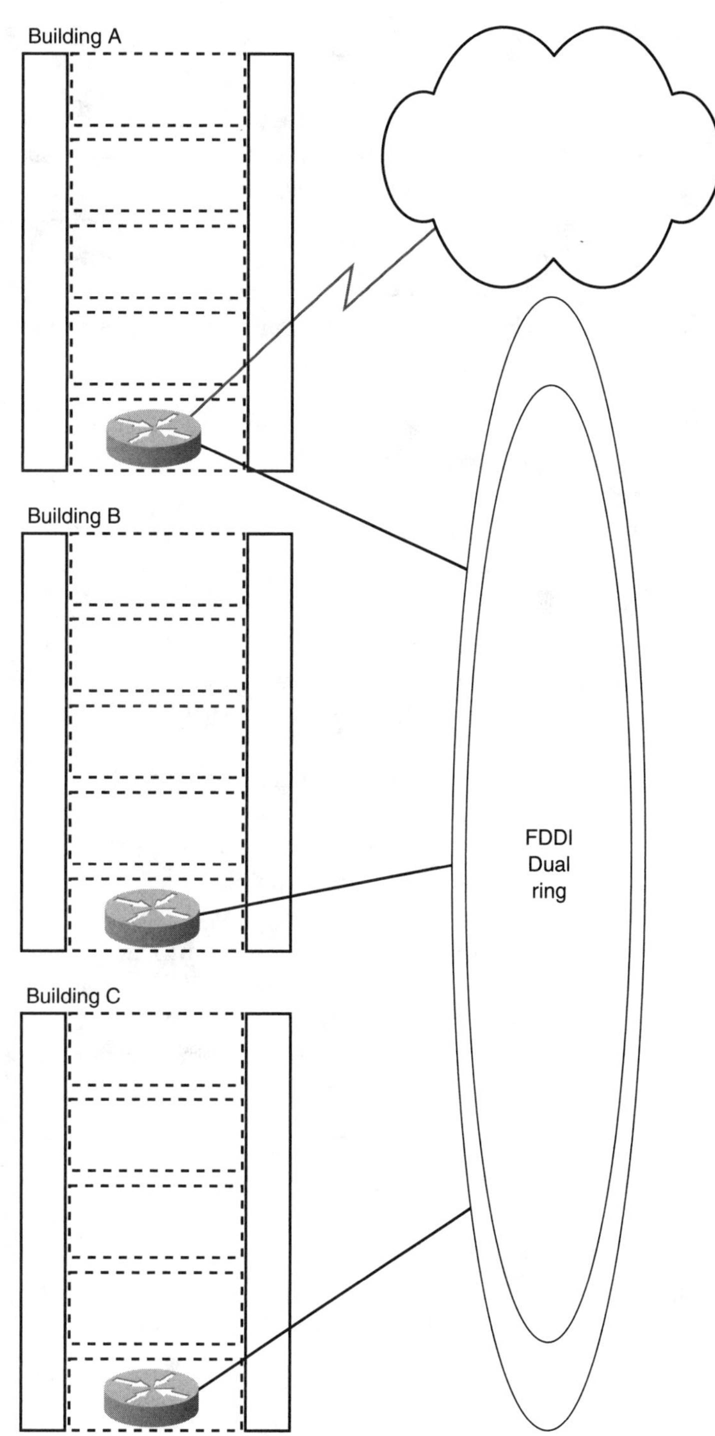

Figure 5-7 Distributed campus backbone

Collapsed Backbones

A *collapsed backbone*, in contrast to a distributed backbone, means that the ring or bus architecture has been reduced to a single switch or router. Rather than having each device or wiring closet connect equally to the backbone, all connections "collapse" into a single device, using its backplane as the network backbone.

We will now investigate several different practical models of the collapsed backbone, at both the building and campus levels, and will discuss ways in which these might be implemented in your network design.

Router and Switch

The application of a collapsed backbone in a building might look something like Figure 5-8. While switches serve the user population attached to a given wiring closet, fiber runs in the risers terminate at a single router. The router in turn handles all of the communication between the IP subnets as well as the communication to the WAN and to the Internet.

There are a couple of problems with this solution. First, the router represents a single point of failure. Placing a second router in the data center and using HSRP to allow for failover can alleviate this problem. Another issue is that VLANs are not understood by the router(s); therefore, user management, in the form of moves, adds, and changes, becomes a problem.

Specifically, a router can understand subnets, but it only understands a single subnet per port. One benefit of VLANs is the capability to have users of a single VLAN spread out in different wings, floors, or buildings. With a network device that can understand VLANs, communication is not a problem. Because a VLAN appears as a subnet to a router, it does not understand the communications arriving from different subnets on the same router port. The next section addresses a way to fix this problem.

TIP: *A VLAN is like a subnet, which represents a broadcast domain. A router acts as a broadcast firewall of sorts and drops the broadcasts it sees. It acts as a boundary to broadcast domains, which is another way to understand why the same VLAN on different switches cannot communicate in this network design model.*

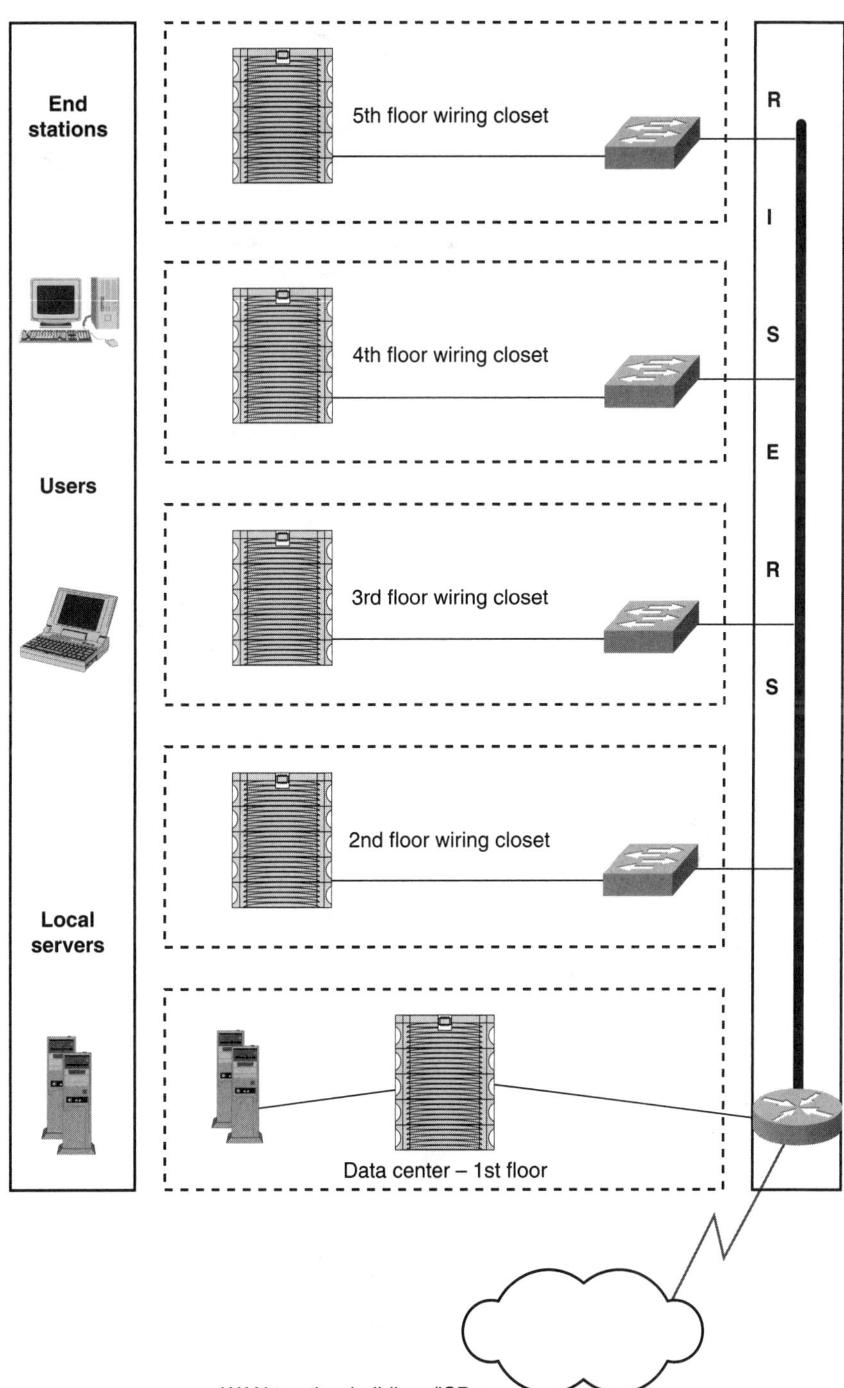

Figure 5-8 Collapsed building backbone-router and switch

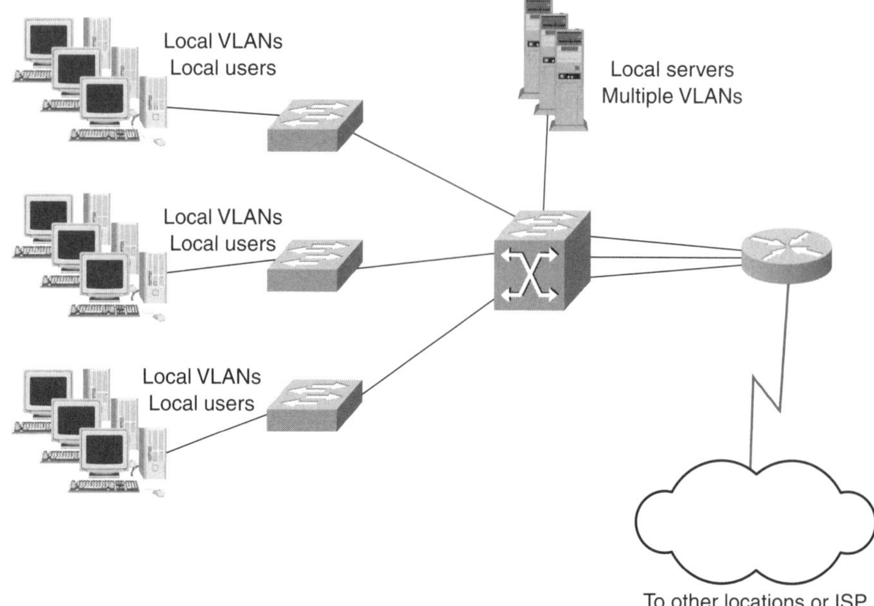

Figure 5-9 Collapsed building backbone-VLAN

Building VLANs

The solution to the problem presented in the last section is to "front-end" the router with a switch. A switch, as you know, can understand the VLANs, can use trunking to allow multiple VLANs to cross the wire between switches, and can use the Inter-Switch Link (ISL) protocol to handle the insertion of a VLAN identifier into the frame. Therefore, the design offered in Figure 5-9 solves the problems of the router and switch design offered in the last section.

Another nice feature of this design model is the capability to leverage most NT servers to house up to four NICs. This means that with an ISL or 802.1Q NIC, the centralized servers can belong to four VLANs at once, each connecting to a single port on the switch. So with this design, you can have users all over the building attached to whatever VLAN makes the most sense, depending on the job function and application needs of each one. The switch handles the inter-VLAN traffic and performs the ISL encapsulation of the frame. Additionally, the router interface can be configured for ISL encapsulation. With the encapsulation, the router could support multiple links between multiple switch trunk ports without caring about the VLANs contained within the frames.

TIP: To maintain the best router performance, use individual ports for each subnet or VLAN. Using subinterfaces or secondary IP addresses can slow down the switching processes in the router.

Campus VLANs

The collapsed backbone concept can be extended to a campus-wide infrastructure by centralizing a switch and server farm in a single building, as shown in Figure 5-10. The switch in the central building acts as the network backbone for the switches in the other buildings. One of the benefits of this design model is the ease with which the aggregate switch and server farm can be administered. It also enables the use of campus-wide VLANs, so users can move between buildings without losing their attachment to a particular VLAN.

There are a couple of drawbacks to the design, however. The flat address space used in a collapsed backbone is usually more appropriate for a single building or a small enterprise network. A ceiling of scalability will eventually be reached with the flat address space that could cause problems down the road for a larger campus. As we mentioned in Chapter 4, "Campus LAN Technology," the upper limit for a multiprotocol flat network should be around 500 end-stations. Limit this to 200 when configuring AppleTalk or NetBIOS.

There are also several single points of failure in this particular design. If the building switch or the aggregate switch fails, the users can no longer reach the servers or the Internet. If the router fails, the entire campus loses its connection to the Internet. If the aggregate switch fails, the inter-building communications are down. The single points of failure can be alleviated with some creative design work, such as using multiple aggregate switches with redundant connections to the buildings, or with two routers in the main data center and possibly two links to the Internet. All of this adds cost to your design, but if cost is not as much of an issue as redundancy, the options are clearly available.

TERM: An aggregate switch is a switch that supports uplinks from other switches in the network.

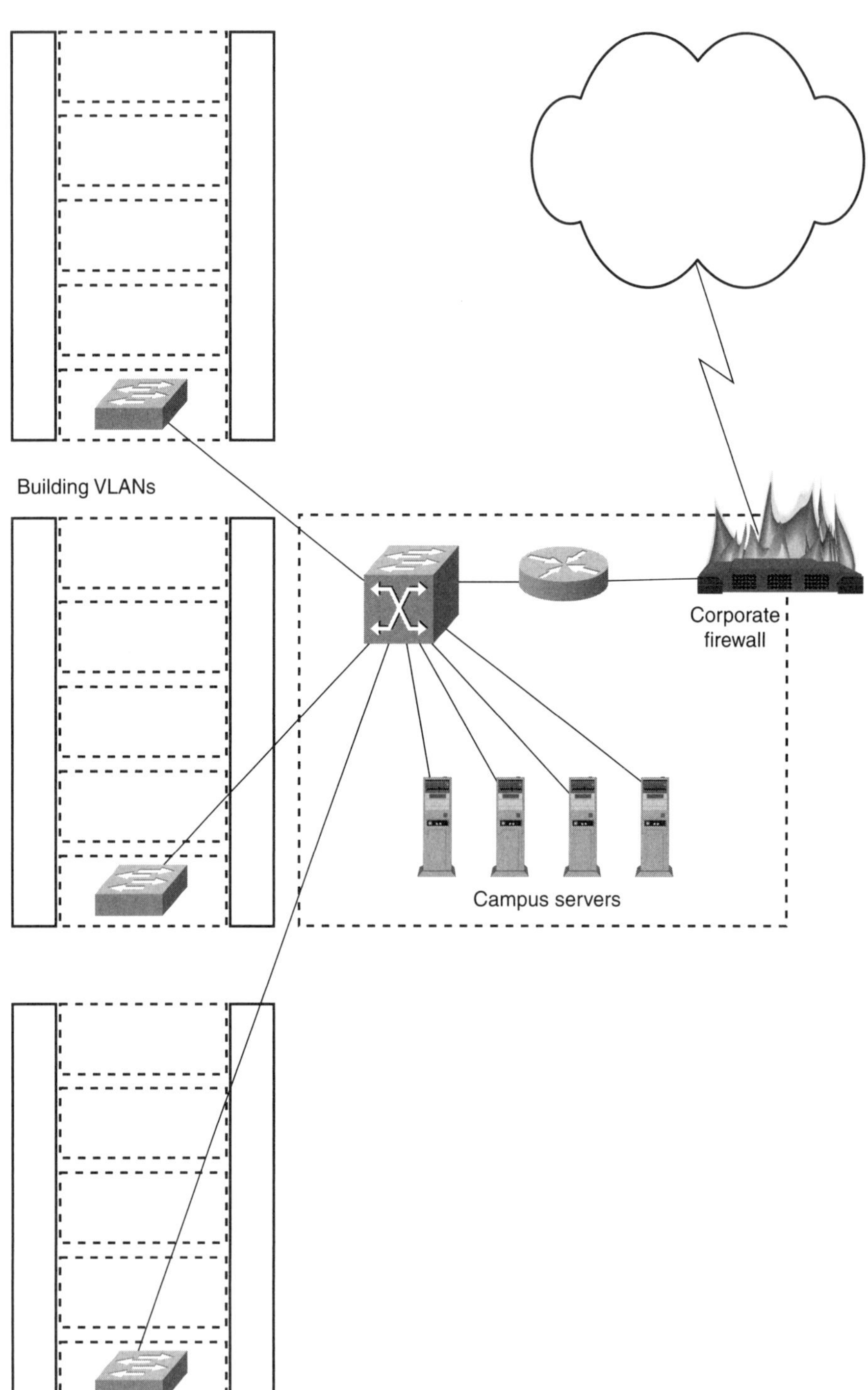

Figure 5-10 Collapsed campus backbone-VLAN

ATM in the Campus

Asynchronous Transfer Mode (ATM) in the campus can also be deployed in either the distributed or collapsed network design model; however, it is not as popular as it was once predicted to be. This is because many network administrators prefer using familiar technologies such as Ethernet. With the growing popularity of Gigabit Ethernet, many companies prefer to use that instead of ATM. ATM is a cell-based technology, as we discussed in Chapter 3, "Campus LAN Overview." It requires a different set of skills and hardware as opposed to Ethernet.

Yet even with the reduced usage of ATM in the United States, it is still a popular technology in some U.S. sectors and in many countries around the world. There are certainly networks where the flexibility of ATM is needed, such as networks carrying mixed traffic types: data, voice, and video. For these types of applications, a company may choose to migrate from FDDI to ATM, for instance, replacing the FDDI ring with at least one ATM switch, as shown in Figure 5-11. Notice that a router is located in each of the campus buildings. A layer 3 switch, depending upon the cost limitations and site requirements, could just as easily represent this. One of the routers carries a connection to the WAN and possibly to an ISP. The ATM switch acts as the network backbone, carrying all types of network traffic.

Another possibility for deploying ATM in the campus is to use LAN Emulation, or LANE. By using LANE, VLANs could be deployed in the network while still using an ATM switch in front of the routers, as illustrated in Figure 5-12, in order to carry mixed traffic types. The router would still be required in order to handle traffic between VLANs. Another point to note is that it is quite difficult to find a server that comes with an ATM NIC installed. When ATM was an "up-and-coming" technology, the NICs were somewhat easier to find.

Case Study

In Chapter 4 you were asked to define naming conventions, select a network topology, decide upon centralized or decentralized server operations and recommend a network link between the buildings of the Campus Research company.

For this case study, you are simply asked to take the recommended network design you have recommended and sketched out so far for the

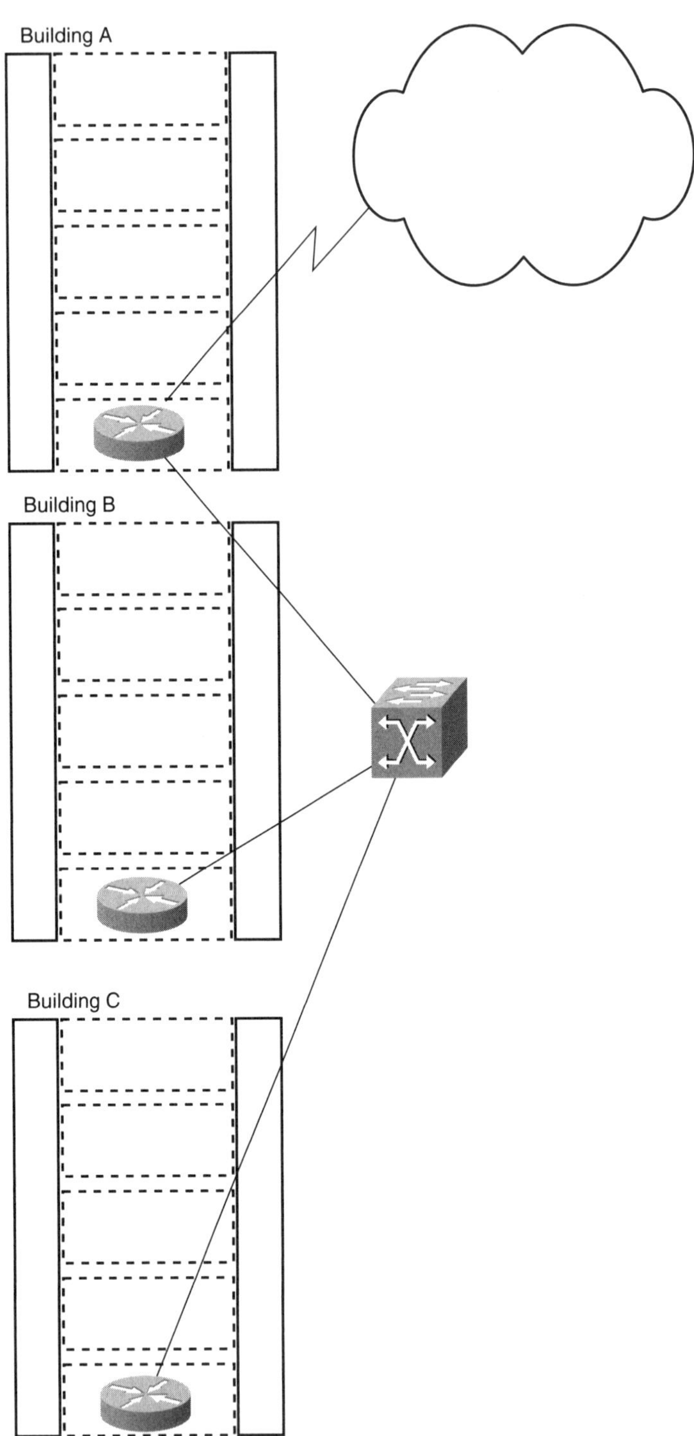

Figure 5-11
ATM distributed backbone

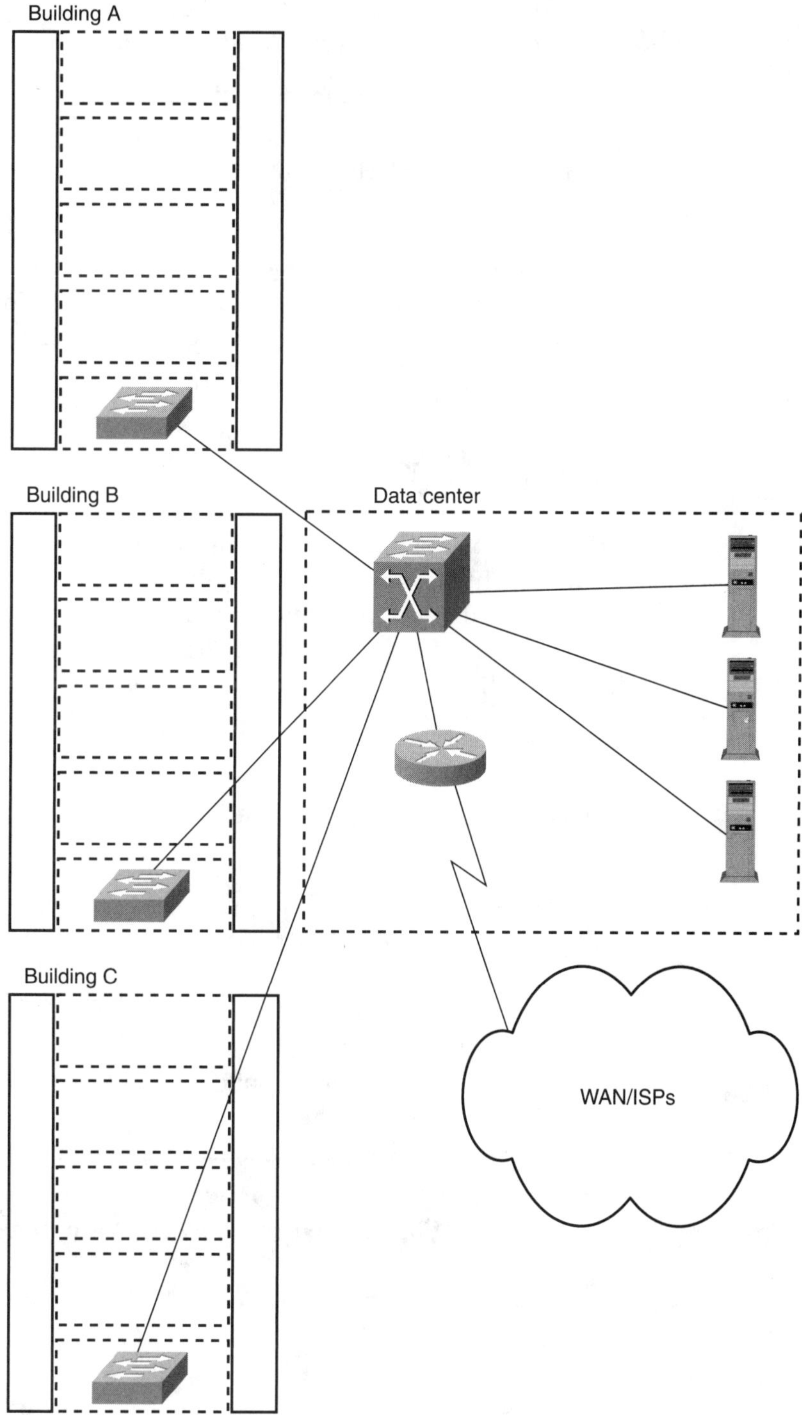

Figure 5-12 ATM collapsed backbone

customer and apply both the distributed backbone model and collapsed backbone model to the overall design. Then answer the following questions:

- Which network design model worked better for your original recommendations?
- What were the drawbacks of each design?
- What were the benefits?

Answering these questions will help you to learn more about the overall process of selection and recommendation when working with an initial network design or network redesign in your professional life.

Study Hints

Although no one can disclose test items or test content, we can give clues as to what might be valuable to study. For this chapter, a lot of material has been covered from a higher and more detailed level than in Chapter 3. Here are areas that you should review before attempting any Cisco network design certification tests.

- A distributed backbone allows all wiring closets equal access to the network backbone.
- A collapsed backbone creates a flat address space that has an upper limit of
  - 500 for an IP or IP and IPX mixed environment.
  - 200 for AppleTalk or NetBIOS.
- The two primary types of collapsed backbone in buildings are router and switch and VLANs.
- It is most common to find a building cabled with fiber in the risers and twisted-pair copper to the LAN drop.
- Centralized servers can be connected to multiple VLANs by the use of multiple NICs that are ISL- or 802.1Q-enabled. Check your operating system limitations to see how many NICs are supported.

CCDP Tips

This section contains an abbreviated list of topics covered in this chapter. Think of this section as the equivalent of reading Cliff's Notes™ instead of reading an entire book. You will get the general idea of the chapter but will benefit more from reading the chapter in its entirety.

A typical building layout consists of

- **Risers** Carrying cable to the wiring closets from a central wiring closet or data center. Risers are usually cabled with fiber-optic cable to the wiring closets.
- **Wiring Closets** Where hubs, switches, or possibly routers serve connectivity to the LAN for local user communities. Wiring closets may also contain patch panels at which the cable runs to the LAN drops terminate.
- **Data Center** (Optional) Where centralized server farms, mainframes, wiring closet termination points, and routing equipment is likely to be housed. Wiring closets may optionally terminate in a central wiring closet, apart from the data center. Also known as a *computer room*.
- **LAN Drops** Also known as wallplates, network drops, or LAN ports. This is the access point for connecting the user to the wiring closet. Cable is run from the drop to the wiring closet—usually with twisted-pair copper.
- **Patch Cables** Short lengths of twisted-pair copper or fiber-optic cable connecting two points together in a network or wiring closet. These can be straight-through or crossover, differentiated by the pin-out on the opposite ends, and can be bought in different colors to help speed up identification of the type of cable in a busy environment.

A distributed backbone has these features:

- All access points from the wiring closet have equal access to the LAN backbone.
- All access points assume equal risk of failure to reach the LAN backbone, with none dependent on the others for access.

- The network is not flat.
- Distributed campus backbones tend to lack flexibility because the runs between buildings can rarely be modified once they are installed.

A collapsed backbones has these features:

- The ring or bus architecture has been collapsed to a single switch or router.
- The backplane of the switch or router acts as the backbone of the collapsed network.
- A building can have a *router and switch* collapsed architecture in which a router handles the backbone for all wiring closet switches. The router becomes the single point of failure unless it is paired with another router and both run HSRP. The router also cannot handle VLAN translation, as it cannot understand a subnet spread among many interfaces.
- The VLAN building design can have a switch act as an aggregate device between the wiring closets and the router. This keeps the VLAN traffic moving and can encapsulate traffic with ISL in order to move multiple VLANs through trunk ports.
- Campus VLAN usage is also popular because all data center activity can easily be centralized into one building, while user connectivity is easily modified anywhere on the campus without losing the user's current VLAN access. A big drawback is the lack of scalability for large campuses. It can also present several single points of failure.

ATM environments have these features:

- Don't tend to be as popular in the United States as in other countries unless a mixed-traffic environment is in use.
- Can be deployed in a distributed manner with a single switch acting as the network backbone and layer 3 switches or routers in the buildings of a campus.
- Can be deployed using LANE, with VLANs in the buildings and a router on the back side of the ATM switch in order to handle inter-VLAN traffic.

Summary

In this chapter we have described the network design models that can be deployed in a campus LAN. In essence, we have pulled together all of the topics from the last three chapters and presented them in a way that should help you to successfully build a campus LAN network, whether distributed or collapsed in architecture.

We discovered that a distributed backbone is shared equally among the interconnecting devices, while a collapsed backbone depends upon a router or switch to handle the building or campus network backbone. Each type of network design model offers strengths and weaknesses. It will depend upon the requirements and needs of the network for which you are creating the design.

In Chapter 6, "TCP/IP Design Overview," we will begin to discuss the addressing and subnetting of IP networks including routing protocols and some of the common pitfalls encountered by network designers in relation to this type of network.

Questions

The following review questions have been selected to help you test your knowledge of the subject matter contained in this chapter. You will also find these questions contained in the CD-ROM included with this book. While these are not the questions you will find in the certification exams, knowing the answers to the review questions in this book will help cement the material in your mind as you prepare for the tests.

1. At what layer of the hierarchical network design is the backbone in a distributed backbone architecture located?
   - **a.** Core
   - **b.** Distribution
   - **c.** Edge
   - **d.** Access
2. What is another name for the wallplate at which the end-station accesses the network?
   - **a.** Outlet
   - **b.** Interface
   - **c.** Telecom port
   - **d.** LAN drop

3. What is the distance limitation for category 5 UTP?
   a. 328 feet
   b. 600 feet
   c. 2 meters
   d. 2 kilometers
4. True or False: Category 5 UTP provides greater bandwidth scalability than fiber-optic cable.
   a. True
   b. False
5. What is the primary difference between a straight-through and a crossover cable?
   a. Color
   b. RJ-11 vs. RJ-45 connector
   c. Speed
   d. Pin-out on the opposite end
6. What type of network device should not touch the backbone?
   a. End-station
   b. FDDI concentrator
   c. Switch
   d. Router
7. What is the maximum number of Windows 98 end-stations running NetBIOS that should exist on a flat network infrastructure?
   a. 200
   b. 500
   c. 100
   d. 600
8. A server can communicate over a trunk port if it has this type of NIC:
   a. 802.3
   b. 802.5
   c. 802.1Q
   d. 802.10

9. Client is to end-station as VLAN is to ______.
   a. Subnet
   b. Secondary interface
   c. Router
   d. Server
10. In a collapsed network backbone that is reduced to a single switch, what part of the switch is the network's logical backbone?
   a. Interface module
   b. Route switch module
   c. Clock module
   d. Backplane
11. Which network device should be placed between a router and the wiring closet switches in order to handle inter-VLAN communication?
   a. Switch
   b. Bridge
   c. Router
   d. Hub
12. Centralized server farms tend be ________.
   a. Easy to register
   b. Easy to administer
   c. Easy to configure
   d. Easy to locate
13. A router can be described as this kind of firewall:
   a. Corporate
   b. Collision
   c. Broadcast
   d. Stateful Inspection
14. True or False: An ATM switch can handle inter-VLAN traffic.
   a. True
   b. False

15. What network technology is sometimes favored over ATM for its familiarity and greater speed?
    a. Fast Ethernet
    b. Token Ring
    c. FDDI
    d. Gigabit Ethernet
16. If both mixed-traffic types and VLANs are required in a campus LAN, what LAN topology should be considered?
    a. LANE
    b. ELAN
    c. FDDI
    d. Ethernet
17. What is one reason that a server might not be able to be connected to an ATM switch in a LANE environment?
    a. The server does not carry mixed-traffic types.
    b. The server does not have an ATM NIC.
    c. The server is using Windows 98.
    d. The server cannot handle multiprotocol environments.
18. In which network would ATM be a better choice?
    a. A network that requires a ring-based topology.
    b. A network that requires a broadcast firewall.
    c. A network that requires video, voice, and data transport.
    d. A network that requires data, IPX, and multiplexing.
19. Which statement best describes a trunk link on a switch?
    a. A link that carries multiple VLANs.
    b. A link that does not carry multiple VLANs.
    c. A link that is faster than the other ports on the switch.
    d. A link that "locks down" access to the router interface to which it connects.
20. What is one effect that the use of secondary IP addresses can have on a router versus using individual interface ports?
    a. Slows down router switching processes.
    b. Increases security on the secondary subnet.

c. Nothing. Secondary addresses are no longer supported.

d. Prevents the application of an access list to that interface.

Answers

1. At what layer of the hierarchical network design is the backbone in a distributed backbone architecture located?
   b. Distribution

2. What is another name for the wallplate at which the end-station accesses the network?
   d. LAN drop

3. What is the distance limitation for category 5 UTP?
   a. 328 feet (or 100 meters)

4. True or False: Category 5 UTP provides greater bandwidth scalability than fiber-optic cable.
   b. False

5. What is the primary difference between a straight-through and a crossover cable?
   d. Pin-out on opposite ends
   Explanation: While we mentioned that most administrators use different color cables to differentiate between straight-through and crossover, that is not an inherent difference. What is different is that in a straight-through cable, the opposite ends are pinned out the same way. In a crossover cable, at least one pair is "flipped" on one end vs. the other.

6. What type of network device should not touch the backbone?
   a. End-station
   Explanation: Hosts, clients, and servers (end-stations) should not be put on the backbone, because the backbone should be reserved for optimal transport of traffic only.

7. What is the maximum number of Windows 98 end-stations running NetBIOS that should exist on a flat network infrastructure?
   a. 200

8. A server can communicate over a trunk port if it has this kind of NIC:
   c. 802.1Q

9. Client is to end-station as VLAN is to _____.
   a. Subnet
   Explanation: A client can also be known as an end-station, because the function is essentially the same. The same can be said of a VLAN. It is essentially a single subnet. While an end-station is not *always* a client, neither is a subnet always a VLAN.

10. In a collapsed network backbone that is reduced to a single switch, what part of the switch is the network's logical backbone?
    d. Backplane
    Explanation: Because all the collapsed network traffic crosses the backplane of the aggregate switch, you could say that the backplane is functioning as the network backbone.

11. What network device should be placed between a router and the wiring closet switches in order to handle inter-VLAN communication?
    a. Switch
    Explanation: See Figure 5-9.

12. Centralized server farms tend to be ________.
    b. Easy to administer
    Explanation: While you could say that the server farm is also easy to configure, the true answer is "easy to administer." Most functions or applications that are centralized mean fewer staff to manage them as well as no geographic limitations or additional trips to remote sites to maintain equipment and software.

13. A router can be described as this kind of firewall:
    c. Broadcast
    Explanation: As we have mentioned several times in the course of the five chapters thus far, a router does not pass broadcasts normally (unless directed broadcasts are expressly permitted by a configuration modification). Therefore, the router could be referred to as a broadcast firewall, since it stops broadcasts and drops them.

14. True or False: An ATM switch can handle inter-VLAN traffic.
    b. False

15. What network technology is sometimes favored over ATM for its familiarity and greater speed?
    d. Gigabit Ethernet

16. If both mixed-traffic types and VLANs are required in a campus LAN, what LAN topology should be considered?
    a. LANE

17. What is one reason that a server might not be able to be connected to an ATM switch in a LANE environment?
    b. The server does not have an ATM NIC.

18. In which network would ATM be a better choice?
    c. A network that requires video, voice, and data transport.

19. Which statement best describes a trunk link on a switch?
    a. A link that carries multiple VLANs.

20. What is one effect that the use of secondary IP addresses can have on a router vs. using individual interface ports?
    a. Slows down router switching processes.

Bibliography

Cisco Internetwork Design, Cisco Press, 2000, Matthew H. Birkner, Editor

Cisco Internetwork Design Course Manual, version 3.0, April 1997, Cisco Systems, Inc.

Cisco's *Designing ATM Networks* Guide, **http://www.cisco.com/univercd/cc/td/doc/cisintwk/idg4/nd2008.htm**.

CHAPTER 6

TCP/IP Design Overview

Overview

Up to this point we have concentrated mainly on becoming familiar with the hierarchical network design model and campus LAN design. For the next few chapters we will focus on the routing protocols and routed protocols that you will use in your design recommendations. In the first of these chapters we will talk about TCP/IP networks and the design concepts that apply to these networks. We will also explain the difference between a physical network and a logical network.

By the end of this rather brief chapter, you should have an understanding of public and private network addressing, limitations of IP version 4 addressing, the purpose of subnetting, and the function of the protocol. We will also touch on TCP/IP security, but we will more thoroughly cover the full aspects of security in your network in Chapter 23, "Security Design."

Physical vs. Logical

When speaking of networks, we tend to generalize, lumping all networks into the same category. In fact, networks can really be divided into two different classifications: physical and logical.

A *physical network* centers on layers 1 and 2 of the OSI model, in other words, the physical and data link layers. At these layers the wiring termination points and the shared media over which the physical network communicates define the network. A physical network also exists as a collision domain for Ethernet networks, or a bandwidth domain for other technologies.

A *logical network* centers on layer 3 of the OSI model, the network layer, which is the OSI model layer most often associated with networks. A logical network always contains a network number that is assigned to the physical network. The type of network numbers assigned depends upon the routed protocol being used.

In Figure 6-1 there are two physical networks and three logical networks. You may wonder how it is possible to have more than one logical network per physical network. The rule is that at least one logical network must be assigned to a physical network in order for routing to take place.

More logical networks may be layered on top. With Ethernet interfaces on a Cisco router, multiple "secondary" addresses may be assigned once the first address has been configured. We will explore this concept more in Chapter 7, "TCP/IP Addressing Design."

Notice that in Figure 6-1, logical network 10.10.10.0 is the only logical network on that physical network. One router interface supports the entire network. Logical networks 10.10.20.0 and 10.10.30.0 share a physical interface on the router as well as a physical network. The router, however, sees them as two logical networks. In other words, data coming from network 10.10.10.0 destined for network 10.10.20.0 does not need to know that any other network (in this case, 10.10.30.0) shares that wire. When the data reaches the router, the router forwards the packets to the physical interface supporting the logical network 10.10.20.0.

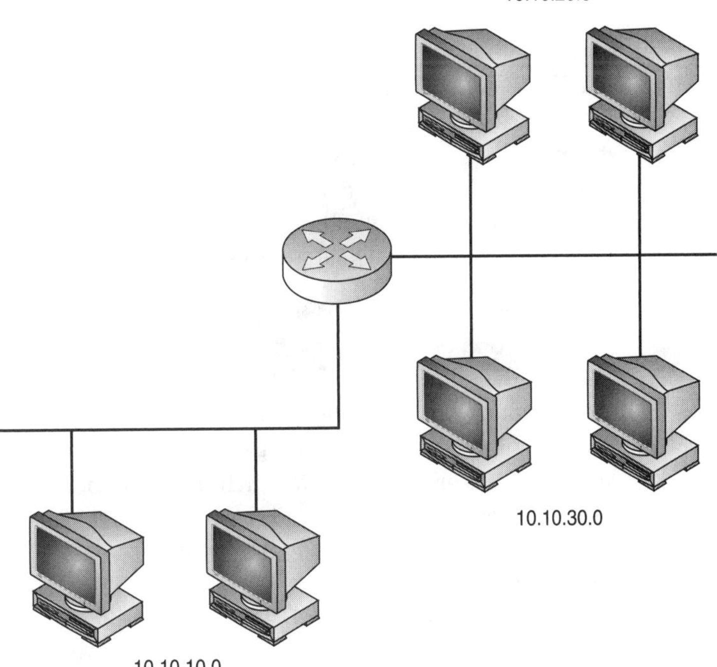

Figure 6-1 Physical vs. logical networks

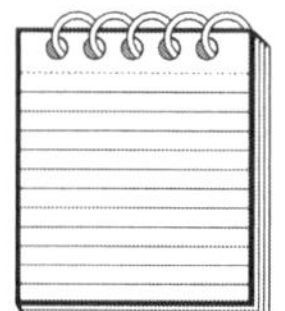

NOTE: Each physical network has to have at least one logical network number assigned in order for other networks and end-stations to find it.

IP: Addressing and Security

This section will introduce you to the concepts of using major IP network numbers and breaking them into smaller networks through subnetting. We will also touch on some simple security methods you can use in your network design to solve some of the security risks inherent in IP networking.

Network Addressing and Subnets

If you have ever experienced an error on your Windows workstation saying that your IP address is already in use, then you are acutely aware that an IP address that is unique to your end-station is necessary for the end-station to communicate on the network. Each IP version 4 address is made up of 4 bytes—or 32 bits. The address could also be said to consist of 4 *octets*. An octet is simply 8 bits, or 1 byte. The notation of an IP address is expressed in a dotted-decimal format, like so:

```
10.10.10.0
```

Each IP address contains two parts: a network portion and a host portion, as shown in Table 6-1. The network portion identifies the logical network to which the host belongs. The host portion is an identifier that is unique to the end-station to which it is assigned. Therefore, the IP address in its entirety is unique. In other words, 10.10.10.1 is a unique address that identifies a single, physical end-station interface within the logical network 10.0.0.0.

The addresses shown in Table 6-1 are known as *classful addresses*, meaning that they obey the rules of the class of IP network to which they are assigned. The first entry, 10.10.10.1, belongs to a Class A address. In a Class A address, the first octet identifies the network portion and the final three octets are uniquely assigned to a single host. We will cover classful and classless addressing more in Chapter 7.

As you may have noticed in Figure 6-1, however, we used 10.10.10.0 on one interface, 10.10.20.0 and 10.10.30.0 on another. The way we were able to divide up portions of the Class A 10.0.0.0 network is by a process called *subnetting*.

Subnetting is simply a way of manipulating the bits that make up the IP address in order to expand the network portion of the address. In other words, you can "borrow" from the host portion in order to make a more specific network number. For example, take a look at Table 6-2 and see how our IP addresses have changed since we saw them in Table 6-1.

Table 6-1

IP Address Structure

IP Address/Netmask	Network Portion	Host Portion
10.10.10.1/8	10.	10.10.1
172.16.21.10/16	172.16.	21.10
192.168.125.97/24	192.168.125.	97

Table 6-2

IP Subnetting

IP Address/Netmask	Network	Host
10.10.10.1/24	10.10.10.	1
172.16.21.10/24	172.16.21.	10
192.168.125.97/28	192.168.125.96	1

The division of the network and host portions may seem fairly clear until you reach the last entry. Why is the network 192.168.125.96? It is that way because we have borrowed 4 bits from the host portion of the address and added it to the network portion. The logical network number for the network containing this host is 192.168.125.96. Within that logical network, .97 is the first host. Therefore, it is host number one.

If your network design needs to support subnets of unequal lengths, using Variable Length Subnet Masks (VLSMs), you will need to carefully plan the address space at the outset. Also, it is important to note that not all routing protocols support VLSM, which we will discuss more as we move into our section on routing protocols. If a protocol does not support VLSM, networks can still be broken into smaller subnets, but they must all be of an equal length.

For instance, *Interior Gateway Routing Protocol* (IGRP), a classful, Cisco-proprietary protocol, can support subnets of equal length. If one subnet uses a 30-bit mask, all masks must be 30-bits. What VLSM does is to allow the subnetting of a network to be variable, meaning that all subnets do not have to use the same number of bits in the mask.

Design Considerations

The task of network and host address assignment in an IP network design may seem daunting the first time you attempt it, but it is important to break the task into smaller decisions.

First of all, you will need to decide whether it is appropriate to use private addresses, as specified in RFC 1918 and RFC 1597, or to use public addresses assigned to the site by the InterNIC, usually through the Internet service provider (ISP) that services the site.

In some respects it is both easier and more secure to use private addresses. It is easier because you can select a range of addresses and place them however you like in your network. If you purchase valid IP addresses from your ISP, you may get one or more contiguous blocks that may not necessarily give you the optimum scalability in your network. It is also expensive to lease these addresses.

Private addresses could also be said to be more secure than public addresses because they are not seen outside your enterprise network. Private addresses are blocks of IP addresses that can be used by any network anywhere in the world. These addresses cannot be routed over the public Internet, however, because the uniqueness of the number cannot be guaranteed. Therefore if any packets with a private source address make it to a router outside your enterprise network, they are dropped. Likewise, packets coming from outside your enterprise network cannot reach destinations inside the enterprise network that are addressed in this manner.

Because of this limitation of the private address spaces, *Network Address Translation* (NAT) is required. NAT provides for the use of valid, publicly assigned addresses to be published in place of the private addresses. This can be in a one-to-one manner or in a many-to-one manner, as illustrated in Table 6-3. By using NAT, the "outside" world sees a false IP address that is mapped in a table within the translating network device (usually a router or firewall) to the actual private address in use on a particular MAC address. Do you see the pattern emerging? The public address maps to (or overlays) the private address. The logical network number maps to (or overlays) the physical network number.

Private addresses, as we hinted earlier in this section, tend to lend greater scalability to a network, in addition to their other benefits. By using private address blocks along with subnetting, it is possible to build scalability into the network design for future network growth.

Another addressing concern is the decision on how to assign addresses to end-stations. For some network end-stations, such as printers, servers and routers, a static address not only makes sense, it is essential to proper operation of the device in the network. It must always be reachable at the same address consistently. For most other end-stations, however, it is preferable to use Dynamic Host Configuration Protocol (DHCP) servers to automatically assign an address to an end-station upon boot-up.

In the past, each end-station had to be manually configured with an address, a subnet mask and a gateway in order to operate on the network. Clearly, this is not as scalable as using DHCP because of the manual intervention required for every network change. As you can imagine, network design changes were terribly labor-intensive with statically addressed end-stations. In some cases, this could be a deciding factor in whether or not to make a change. We will discuss DHCP more in Chapter 7.

Table 6-3

Network Address Translation

Private IP Address	Public IP Address	NAT Method
10.10.10.1	131.152.76.1	One-to-one
10.0.0.0	131.152.76.125	Many-to-one

Security Considerations

An important part of designing a network is to address network security at the outset. This is especially important in a TCP/IP network because of the many exploits that are freely available on the Internet. If there is no current network security policy when the network design is begun, it is important to gather together the decision-makers that can write the policy before trying to design in the network security. These decision-makers can be

- Chief Information Officers (CIOs)
- Security Officers (SOs)
- Network administrators
- Firewall administrators

Other personnel may be involved, based upon the type of business and network with which you are dealing. The network may have certain sectors that need to be more closely guarded than others because of secure servers or sensitive information contained in databases. Access to the network may need to be controlled through the use of *Remote Dial-In User Service* (RADIUS), which provides authentication for and tracking of remote users, or TACACS+, an authentication, authorization, and accounting protocol, for login control.

There are valid concerns about IP security because of its accessibility and popularity. It simply is easier for a savvy programmer with IP knowledge to create extremely malicious executable files that can do a lot of damage to a network. Those files and techniques are shared all over the Internet, where they can be downloaded anonymously by anyone with access to a browser. With very little knowledge, a person can then propagate those files (commonly known as "cracks" or "virii") to innocent users all over the world. The full spectrum of Internet security could fill volumes, so what we will share with you here is a sample of some things you can do to secure your network from the initial design phase.

The need for security ranges from light to extreme, depending upon the resources that need to be protected. Firewall features on Cisco routers in the form of access control lists may be all that the network needs to use, but this can pose a resource issue for the router if the access lists become very large. In networks where security is a greater concern it is usually better to offload the security to a dedicated hardware firewall, such as a Cisco Secure PIX firewall.

The firewall can perform the NAT functions, packet filtering, audit trails, login protection, and applications proxy. By doing so, the router is free to route packets quickly while the firewall takes on the "dirty" job of inspecting the packets for permitted or denied activity as compared to the rules configured in the rule base.

We will discuss security more in Chapter 23, "Security Design."

Routing Protocols

You have a little information now about the difference between physical and logical networks and some security and addressing concerns. Now let's see how different networks exchange information in order to form paths for user traffic.

How do other networks know how to get to their destinations? After all, no single router has information about every network in the world!

Essentially routers are packet-switching devices that work at layer 3 of the OSI model and make decisions on where to send packets based upon the layer 3 logical addresses contained in each packet. Take a look at Figure 6-2. Router A knows about networks 10.10.10.0, 10.10.20.0, and 10.10.30.0. Router B only knows about networks 172.16.10.0, 172.16.11.0, and 172.16.12.0. How would Router B know how to reach a destination on network 10.10.20.0? Router A has shared that knowledge by sending a routing update to Router B.

Every routing protocol has its own way of formatting and sharing this information, and with filters, the contents and destinations of the routing updates can be controlled. This, however, is the basic method by which networks learn about each other. The devices responsible for doing the routing of the packets through a network must send and receive updates that allow them to find either specific routes to certain destinations or a default route to any network that they have not learned about through any method.

We will explain the way each routing protocol handles updates and other functions in detail later in the book, but essentially, we can conclude that routing protocols perform three tasks:

- Determining the best path to a destination
- Internal AS routing
- External AS routing

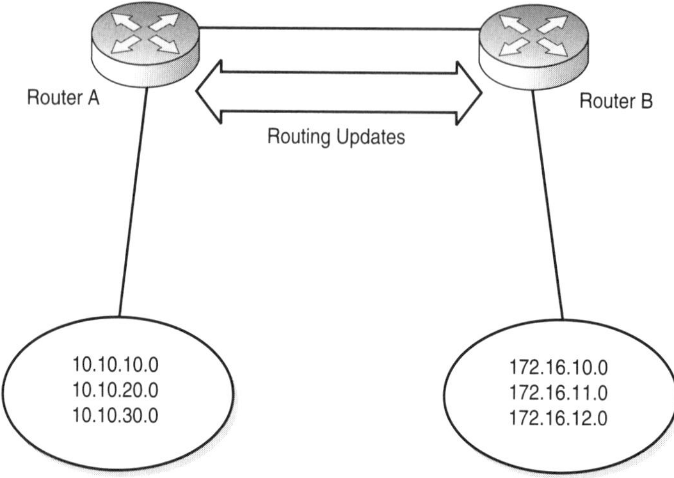

Figure 6-2
Routing updates

By exchanging information with its neighbors, a router can make decisions about the best way to reach a destination. This is a concept we will explore further as we progress to future chapters focusing on specific routing protocols. For now, it is important that you understand that it is part of a routing protocol's "job" to find the best route or path to destination networks.

Let's now look at the types of routing protocols.

Routing protocols can be referred to as either Interior Gateway Protocols (IGP) or Exterior Gateway Protocols (EGP). The difference between the two is whether they are operating to allow updates within the *autonomous system* (AS) or outside of the AS. An AS is a set of networks and end-stations under the same administrative control. Therefore, if two routers are within the same AS, they will talk to each other by using an IGP. If they each belong to a different AS, they will use an EGP to talk.

Routing protocols also perform path determination, meaning that they will make a decision on the best way to reach other networks based upon their particular routing algorithm. There are basically two types of routing protocols in relation to path determination: distance vector and link state. In some earlier documents, Cisco's *Enhanced Interior Gateway Routing Protocol* (EIGRP) was referred to as a "hybrid" protocol, but it is now generally accepted as a distance vector protocol with several improvements.

Distance vector protocols advertise routing information about remote networks based upon information learned from adjacent routers speaking the same "language," or routing protocol. Decisions are based primarily upon the number of hops to reach the destination. Distance vector protocols tend to be bandwidth-intensive, because they send routing updates periodically regardless of the status of the links being advertised.

Link-state protocols have faster convergence than distance vector protocols, because they make rapid decisions based upon the state of the links they know about and within that the cost of the path. They advertise only the links attached to them and only send updates when there is a change in one of those links. Therefore, they are less bandwidth-intensive than distance vector protocols, but they are demanding of the router's CPU and memory resources.

All of the methods of learning routes so far in this section have been based on *dynamic routing*, meaning that the information can change to modify the path if necessary without intervention of an administrator. The other method of path modification is *static routing*.

Static routing simply means that an administrator manually enters a path it wants traffic to take to a given destination or group of destinations. This can work well in small networks or in an emergency situation for troubleshooting purposes, but it should not be seen as a scalable method of routing in general.

The router is unable to override the static route to make a better choice, because the router will usually see the static route as the preferred path to a destination, unless the network administrator sets the *administrative distance* higher on the static route. We will discuss how and why you would do this in Chapter 8, "Routing Protocol Design." Static routing cannot scale well because of the manual intervention needed to allow networks to be added, deleted, and modified. Static routes also require space in the configuration file and routing table for each entry and therefore can sometimes be a burden on router memory.

The best way, by far, of handling routing is to allow the decisions to be made dynamically by the routing protocols. Part of the network design process is the selection of the best protocol to suit the design at hand. Your choice should take into consideration:

- Convergence time
- Bandwidth or router resource consumption

- Flexibility of the addressing scheme
- Proprietary vs. open standard protocol
- Route redistribution

If you have a network that needs to be very stable and adaptable, you will want to consider choosing a protocol that converges quickly. However, if you have lower specification routers with limited resources, the better choice may be to compromise on convergence time in order to preserve precious router resources.

What about standards? Is it important to the network design that an open standard be used? This might be the case when equipment from different vendors is used throughout the network. However, if all Cisco equipment is deployed, the choice may be to go with a proprietary protocol like EIGRP. Much of the decision will be based on network staff preference, unless multivendor use is an issue.

Another option is to use *route redistribution*. When different protocols must be selected in order to support devices on various parts of the network, you may need to perform route redistribution. That is to say, you allow routes learned through one protocol to be shared with another. For instance, if the use of RIP version 2 is necessary to support a large Unix server farm, but the rest of the network is on EIGRP, routes learned from RIP could be redistributed into EIGRP. In this manner, the network is able to support multiple protocols and types of protocols without having to learn about those networks within each and every protocol.

We will discuss routing protocols more in Chapter 8.

CCDP Tips

This section contains an abbreviated list of topics covered in this chapter. Think of this section as the equivalent of reading Cliff's Notes™ instead of reading an entire book. You will get the general idea of the chapter but will benefit more from reading the chapter in its entirety.

Physical vs. Logical Networks

- **Physical network** Describes a network defined at layer 1 and layer 2 of the OSI model. It is the segment contained within a distance and within data link parameters.
- **Logical network** Describes a network defined by layer 3 properties. At least one logical network must be defined on a physical network in order for routing to take place.

  IP version 4 addresses contain two parts:

- **Network Portion** Identifies the part of the 4 bytes, or octets, that make up the network. In a typical Class A, it is the first byte only. In a Class B, it is the first 2 bytes. In a Class C, it is the first 3 bytes.
- **Host Portion** Identifies the unique number of the host. Each host must have a completely unique IP address in order to be routed on an enterprise network, and must have a completely unique public IP address in order to be routed over the Internet.

IP Subnetting

- Allows the network portion of an IP address to "borrow" bits from the host portion in order to create more networks.
- Can be performed using Variable Length Subnet Masks (VLSM) to make the best use of the available addresses. With VLSM, a network doesn't have to be subnetted into equal parts. Some subnets could be 30-bit subnets, others could be 27 bits, all from the same natural network.

Public vs. Private Network Addresses

- **Public network addresses** Assigned by the InterNIC and are usually purchased or leased from your Internet service provider (ISP). These addresses are publicly routable and unique to your network.
- **Private addresses** Defined by RFC 1918 and RFC 1597. These are blocks of IP networks that may be used by any network in the world. The caveat is that they may not be routed over public networks because they are not unique. Therefore, when private addresses are used in the network, provisions must be made to do Network Address Translation (NAT) so that hosts inside the network can reach the Internet.

A router or firewall can perform Network Address Translation (NAT), which is implemented in either of these two fashions:

- **One-to-One** One valid address is assigned to one private address. This is usually static in nature.
- **Many-to-One** All internal private addresses appear as one address to the outside world.

Security

- The security policy should come before the security design and should be an official corporate document.
- Packet filtering can be performed on the router or a firewall device.
- Private addressing adds a layer of security to an IP network.

Routing Protocol Choice Guidelines

- Routing protocols are used to determine gateways or paths to other networks.
- Routing can be dynamic or static.
- Static routing is not scalable and is manually labor-intensive.
- Either an Interior Gateway Protocol (IGP) or an Exterior Gateway Protocol (EGP) can perform dynamic routing.
- An autonomous system (AS) is a group of networks within a single administration.
- An EGP is designed to route between different autonomous systems.
- An IGP is designed to route within a single AS.
- A routing protocol can be either distance vector or link-state.
- A distance vector protocol advertises networks it learned about through other routers. It makes routing decisions primarily based upon hop-count and can be bandwidth-intensive because of periodic updates.
- A link-state protocol advertises only the networks it knows about directly. It makes routing decisions primarily based on the availability and administrative cost of a path and can be CPU- and memory-intensive on a router. Convergence, however, is faster than in a distance vector protocol.

- Some routing protocols support VLSM; some do not. If VLSM is important, make your choice accordingly.
- Some routing protocols are proprietary to a vendor. When designing a multivendor network, use protocols that are "open standard," meaning that all router manufacturers usually support them in an accepted, prescribed manner.
- Choose a protocol that fits the design requirements. With each choice there are trade-offs, like those mentioned above.

Summary

You should now have a basic understanding of the concepts of IP addressing as it applies to network design. We compared physical networks to logical networks and illustrated how multiple logical networks could be applied to a single physical network. We also explained a little about private vs. public addressing and how private addressing can add a layer of security as well as great scalability to your network design. You also were given some information about addressing and security considerations as well as a short explanation of IP subnetting.

Finally we touched on the topic of routing protocols—different types and different methods used by routers to make path decisions. In Chapter 7, "TCP/IP Addressing Design," we will give you the information needed to select an addressing scheme, identify problems, manage the addresses, and implement some basic TCP/IP security. You will then have a chance to practice what you learned in a case study.

This chapter has no case study because the information presented was meant to server only as an introduction to the next few chapters. You will have plenty of opportunity to practice what you have learned.

Frequently Asked Questions (FAQs)

There are questions that typically come up in class or in the workplace about TCP/IP that we have chosen to enter here along with some explanations. We hope you find it helpful.

1. *Why should I subnet a "classful" network number?*

   Typically, the answer to this question is "to save IP addresses." Years ago, it was not as common to use private addresses when numbering a network. In the early days of networking, the network numbers had typically already been purchased and assigned before consultants were brought on-site. This was the case most often with government facilities, where the decisions were made far above the networking or consulting echelons. The greatest difficulty was in the scalability. Six Class-C addresses, for instance, to serve a core facility and eight satellites was not enough without subnetting the Class-C addresses for point-to-point links and smaller network segments. The problem then became, of course, discontiguous networks. But that is for another chapter.

2. *What is the purpose of using VLSM?*

   As in the last question, the answer is really to save IP addresses. You could use a full Class C address to assign to a point-to-point link, but why? Since you only need two host addresses, you could elect to use 30 bits of subnetting in order to have a network number, two host numbers, and a broadcast address for the subnet. The remaining IP addresses in the Class C network are still available to be used and subnetted as needed.

3. *Why is it that some routing protocols can't use VLSM?*

   If a routing protocol does not understand or use the subnet mask, it is said to be a classful routing protocol. RIP version 1 and IGRP are examples of classful routing protocols. They assume a natural mask on the incoming address or configured network and route accordingly. In other words, if network 192.168.10.0 was configured in RIP version 1 routing, the routing protocol would assume that all hosts in that Class C network, from 1 through 254, would be routed through the same interface. It would not understand if you broke the network up into smaller subnets and scattered them about into different interfaces. Note that RIP version 1 does not allow you to enter a subnet mask along with the network number in the configuration.

4. *If a router will allow me to use packet filters, why do I need a firewall?*

   As we mentioned in this chapter, access lists use router resources such as CPU cycles and memory space. In a very "beefy" router with absolutely no problems and light traffic, using it as a firewall would be no problem, theoretically. However, it is almost always better to use a firewall to do your security work. Let the router do the job of routing. There are other benefits to using a firewall, of course, other than just saving your router's processing power. Firewalls are uniquely designed to do things such as maintaining state tables so that connections are not lost in a failover scenario or offloading mail attachments to content servers for further processing. A router was never designed to handle complex network security tasks.

5. *What good is a security policy?*

   A security policy gives you a "leg to stand on" when implementing policy in the network design. If, for instance, you must create access lists to disallow the FTP traffic from the user networks into a server farm, the security policy backs you up as having the right to do this. It also forces the decision-makers to have to think about what is and is not acceptable use of the network resources. A good security policy is like a good network design. It creates a solid infrastructure in which to work, but it should be adapted as necessary as the network grows and changes.

Bibliography

Cisco Internetwork Design, Cisco Press, 2000, Matthew H. Birkner, Editor

Cisco Internetwork Design Course Manual, version 3.0, April 1997, Cisco Systems, Inc.

Internet RFC Source, **http://www.cis.ohio-state.edu/hypertext/information/rfc.html**

CHAPTER 7

TCP/IP Addressing Design

Overview

In the last chapter we introduced you to the overall aspect of TCP/IP addressing as it relates to network design. Now we will show you how to choose an IP addressing scheme that is appropriate for the network you are designing. You will also be given some common IP addressing problems and the strategies for solving them. Finally, you will learn a few ways to implement security features in your TCP/IP design along with address management tools to keep things running smoothly.

By the end of this chapter you should have a good basis on which to proceed in creating a TCP/IP addressing scheme and design for our continuing case study and any "real-life" network designs on which you may work.

IP Addressing

In this section we will look at various aspects of IP addressing. We will talk about the arrangement of addresses into a hierarchical tree that permits easy transition into the more complex phases of TCP/IP routing. You will see how failure to arrange IP addresses in this manner can create discontiguous subnets, with problems of their own. You will learn about prefix routing and how routers look at the bits in the network portion of an IP address in order to find the routing table entry that most closely matches the destination IP address in a given packet.

Address bit manipulation that allows you to *subnet* a network into smaller address groups or *supernet* addresses into groups of networks will also be explained in this section. Finally, we will take a look at how the use of a secondary address on router interfaces can help solve some design problems, on a temporary basis.

Hierarchical Addressing

TCP/IP addresses should be arranged in a hierarchical manner, like a reversed "tree" (shown in Figure 7-1) of addresses stemming from one "root," or link, and giving way to many "branches" of subnets. Notice that the major network of 10.0.0.0, a Class A address, breaks down into three subnets, which further breaks down into more subnets. Of course, there are many more subnets possible, but this is just an example. Overall, you only

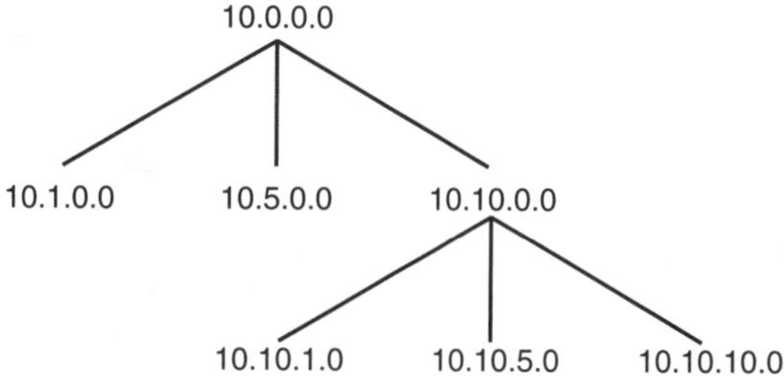

Figure 7-1
Tree hierarchy

need to know about the major network number in order to know that the rest of the subnets fall beneath the 10.0.0.0 entry. If you were a router needing to reach any of the 10.x.x.x subnets, you would only need to know how to get to the major network of 10.0.0.0 *if* the designer used hierarchical addressing.

This is one of the best ways to arrange your addresses, in fact, because it works well for all routing protocols and prevents problems caused by *discontiguous networks*. A discontiguous network is simply one that is separated from its main group (tree) of addresses, a subnet that exists in another part of the network from the rest of the major network number.

The concept of hierarchical addressing is fairly logical. Stated simply, one router does not need to know how to get to every network device in a given network; it only needs to know how to get to the major network number. This is one of the reasons that the use of discontiguous subnets can be a problem. A discontiguous subnet cannot support some concepts such as address summarization, which we will discuss a little later, because it may only contain portions of different major networks.

For example, in Figure 7-2, Router A knows how to reach any subnet, or branch, of major network 10.0.0.0 (the main tree). It does this by forwarding all traffic bound for network 10.0.0.0 out of Serial 0/1 to Router B. Router B is advertising only the major network number, rather than all of the subnets behind it.

In Figure 7-3, however, network 10.10.20.0 is found through a different interface than network 10.10.30.0. Router A has to store an entry for each in its routing table. Neither Router B nor Router C can advertise the entire major network of 10.0.0.0 to Router A, because if they do, routing problems can occur. Note that the routers, if they are classful or are using any autosummary features, may, by default, try to advertise the entire major network number of 10.0.0.0. Router A learns that the entire network is found

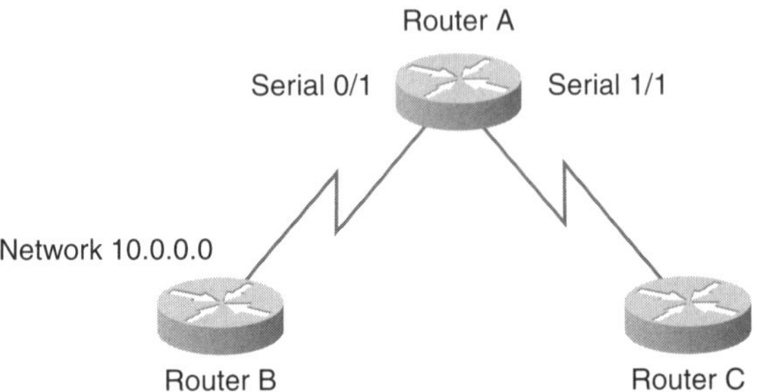

Figure 7-2 Hierarchical addressing

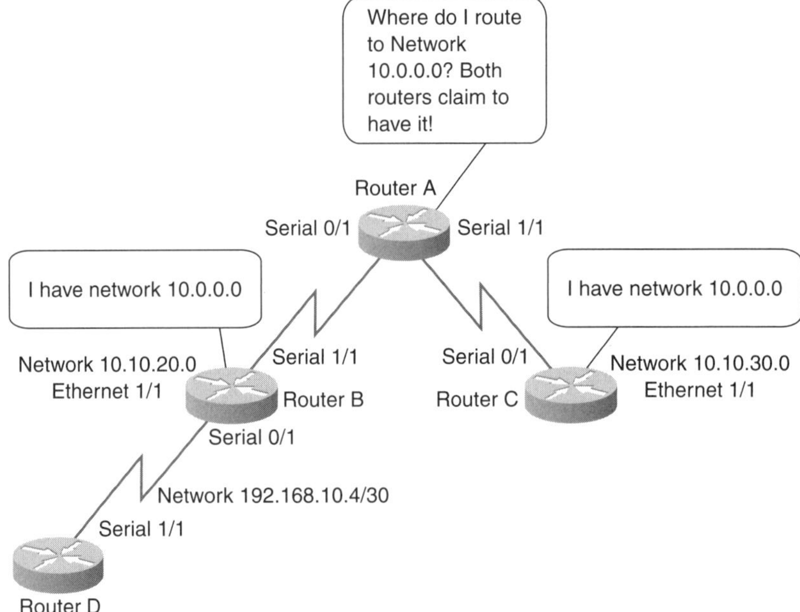

Figure 7-3 Discontiguous subnets

through Router B. Then it receives a routing protocol update from Router C saying that *it* has the entire network of 10.0.0.0. It is easy to see how this would create problems in your network.

Let's look at one final example that shows hierarchical addressing put to its best use. Figure 7-4 illustrates Router A finding the entire 10.0.0.0 network through Router B. Router B knows that the network is subnetted. It knows that it can reach 10.10.10.0 through its Serial 1/1 interface and can

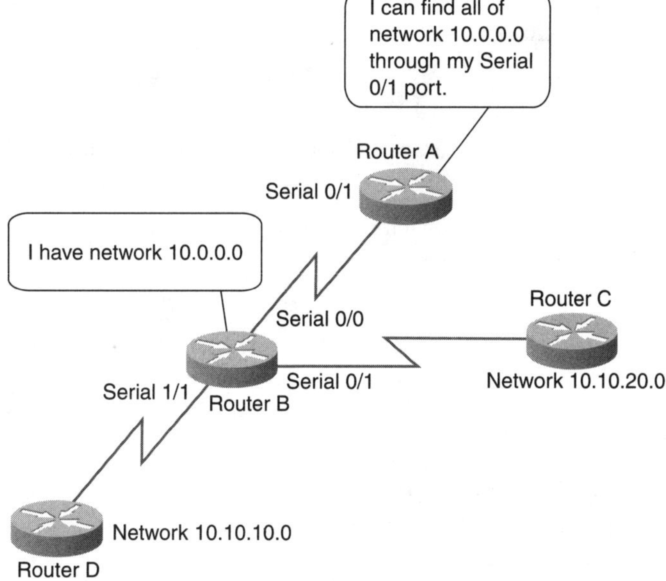

Figure 7-4
Complex hierarchical addressing

reach the 10.10.20.0 network through its Serial 0/1 interface. 10.10.20.0 is further subnetted on Router D to different Ethernet ports on the router. Router A does not have to have all of this information stored; it simply needs to know to route packets bound for a 10.*x.x.x* destination through Router B. Router B will then handle the routing to the different subnets from there.

Prefix Routing

Prefix routing enables the router to decide where to route packets based upon a match on the prefix field (similar to the netmask) of a packet, which identifies the network portion of the IP address that represents the subnet number. The host field, identifying which bits belong to the host address, then follows the prefix field. In the original IP specification, RFC 760, there was no concept of *classful* or *classless* networks or protocols. That concept was introduced in RFC 791, which is now considered to be the accepted IP-v4 standard specification.

Classful Networks There are some basic rules of prefixes as they relate to classful networks:

- Class A addresses have a prefix length of 8 bits and always begin with a "0" bit pattern.
- Class B addresses have a prefix length of 16 bits and always begin with a "10" bit pattern.
- Class C addresses have a prefix length of 24 bits and always begin with a "110" bit pattern.

Subnetting, as we discussed in Chapter 6, is a way of allowing the network, or prefix, portion of an address to borrow bits from the host field. If a router is configured to use a classful routing protocol, it only accepts the prefix lengths specified in RFC 791 and listed above.

Classless Networks If a router is configured to use a classless routing protocol, it can accept any prefix length, which would be carried along with the IP address as a subnet mask or netmask. Networks would not then use the same rules as with classful networks or routing protocols. Classless routing protocols allow for flexibility that can assist the network designer in the task of saving addresses, and thus saving money, or using creativity in the design of the network.

Some of the characteristics of using classless routing protocols and prefix routing are

- Routing tables can be smaller because fewer statements are needed in order to advertise the same number of overall destination networks.
- Router performance can be faster because the router has less information to parse in order to make its routing decision.
- Overall routing protocol traffic is reduced.

Take another look at Figure 7-3. Although designing a network with discontiguous subnets is never a good idea, from a routing point of view, it is not really a problem for classless routing protocols such as Open Shortest Path First (OSPF), Enhanced Interior Gateway Routing Protocol (EIGRP), and Intermediate System-to-Intermediate System (ISIS).

TIP: *The one caveat regarding discontiguous subnets when used with EIGRP is that the auto-summary feature is turned on by default. In order for EIGRP to handle discontiguous subnets, the auto-summary feature would need to be manually disabled in the configuration.*

It is important to understand that when we say "prefix routing" we mean that routers will make decisions based upon the longest prefix match. In other words, multiple entries may exist in the routing table that *could* match a given destination, but only one can be chosen. The one with the greatest number of bits matching (from the left) will be selected. In the list below, a router trying to send data to a destination address of 192.168.10.6 will select the entry that is the most specific, which is how it will find 192.168.10.6/32, where all 32 bits of the entry match the destination.

- 192.168.l0.6/32 is the host.
- 192.168.10.4/30 is the subnet.
- 192.168.10.0/24 is the network.
- 192.168.10.0/22 is the block of networks.
- 0.0.0.0/0 is the default route.

It is unlikely, even undesirable, to have 32-bit matches for every host in the network residing in the routing table. One of your goals as a network designer should be to keep the routing tables as small as possible in order to keep routing as efficient as possible.

As we move now into a discussion of Variable Length Subnet Masks (VLSM) and route summarization, keep prefix routing in mind. Prefix routing allows the router to be able to take full advantage of these address manipulation techniques.

Variable Length Subnet Mask (VLSM)

In the past, IP only understood classful network addresses with traditional default class masks. Routers knew that a Class A network used an 8-bit mask, a Class B network used a 16-bit mask, and a Class C network used a 24-bit mask. Then subnetting was introduced, allowing for the number of network, or prefix, bits to be extended to the right. This allowed the use of part of what were traditionally the bits for the host in order to create *sub*networks, or *subnets*. In this manner, better use of IP addresses was allowed. In networks where the IP addresses had to be valid (public) and had to be purchased, such as in many government networks, it was extremely costly to use an entire Class C network for a point-to-point link, for example, so the ability to subnet represented real cost savings.

NOTE: Remember, a network mask reserves the network portion of the 32 bits used by the IP address, or blocks the bits from being used for host addressing. Only the host portion is then available and used to find unique hosts.

In Figure 7-2, notice that network 192.168.10.4/30 is a point-to-point link to Router D from Router B. Remember that we can subnet the Class C address to make the best use of all IP addresses. A 30-bit subnet is perfect for point-to-point links.

But let's say that Router C has a point-to-point link to another router using network 192.168.10.8/30. Is this another example of discontiguous networks? Yes. Can this be done? Yes, but it is not as efficient as it could be. It does create additional entries in the routing tables along with negating any summarization that could be done. However, there are times when discontiguous networks are part of a legacy network design or may be supported because of business network acquisitions and the like. In those cases, you may need to support discontiguous networks, even though they are not an optimal design element.

A better choice might be to use the rest of the subnets within 192.168.10.0/24 to serve the end-user population at the remote site. In this manner, the routing table only needs to know where to send all traffic for that major network.

In Figure 7-5, we have a Class C address in which we have borrowed one bit of the host field in order to create two subnets within the network, each containing 127 hosts. The two networks created are 192.16.148.0 and 192.16.148.129, both with a mask of 255.255.255.128.

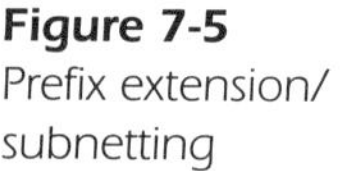

Figure 7-5
Prefix extension/ subnetting

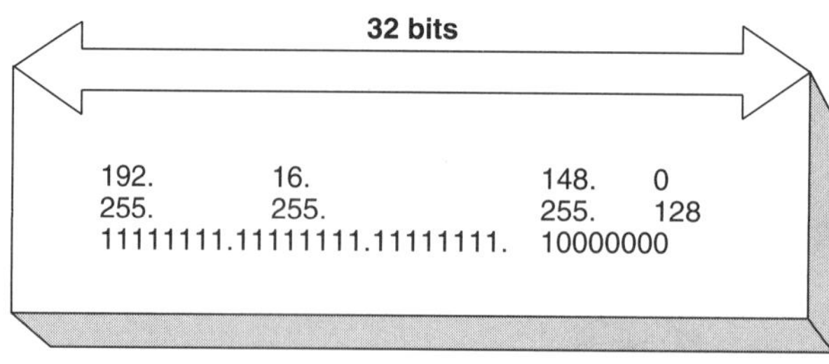

NOTE: Some older texts will tell you that you cannot use all 1's or all 0's (binary) in the subnetwork number, but this was due to the limitations of some older IP hosts and under some special circumstances they can be used.

Classful routing protocols, such as Routing Information Protocol version 1 (RIPv1) or Interior Gateway Routing Protocol (IGRP) do not understand VLSM because no prefix length information is carried by these protocols. However, the addresses can still be subnetted, as long as they are consistently using the same mask throughout the network. For instance, in the example given in Figure 7-4, all networks using the RIPv1 protocol would have to use the 1-bit subnet.

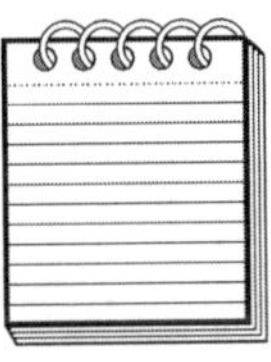

NOTE: It is very important to keep the networks contiguous when subnetting RIPv1 and IGRP, which are classful protocols. If subnets are discontiguous, routers in the network will be confused as to where to send the packets. Although tunneling and secondary addressing can be used to patch the networks together, this is an inefficient and temporary way to rectify the situation and should not be seen as a permanent solution.

Table 7-1 provides you with an easy reference for use when selecting a subnet mask. You can easily see not only which decimal mask to use, but also how the 8 bits normally given to the host field are now divided between the host

Table 7-1

Subnet Reference

Decimal Mask	# of Networks	Bits to Subnet	Bits to Host	# of Hosts
.252	64	6	2	2
.248	32	5	3	6
.240	16	4	4	14
.224	8	3	5	30
.192	4	2	6	62
.128	2	1	7	127

and network fields. Notice that if you add 252 (the decimal mask) to 2 (the resulting number of hosts), you only get 254. Since there are 256 numbers between 0 and 255, you may wonder where the other two went! The other two are allocated to the network and broadcast numbers in each subnet.

Route Summarization and CIDR

Route summarization, also known as *aggregation* or *supernetting*, is another way of using the flexibility of mask bits in order to manipulate the result. Described in RFC 1518, route summarization allows multiple networks or subnets to be collectively advertised as a single IP network. The main difference between summarization and subnetting is that subnetting generally refers to the splitting up of networks for better utilization of IP addresses. Another difference is that in manipulating the bits for subnetting, the bits expand to the right. In summarization, the bits collapse to the left. Summarization groups networks together for better utilization of the routing processes.

In Figure 7-6, notice that Router A learns about four networks through a single advertisement from Router B and learns about thirty-two networks through a single advertisement from Router C.

Figure 7-6 Summarization

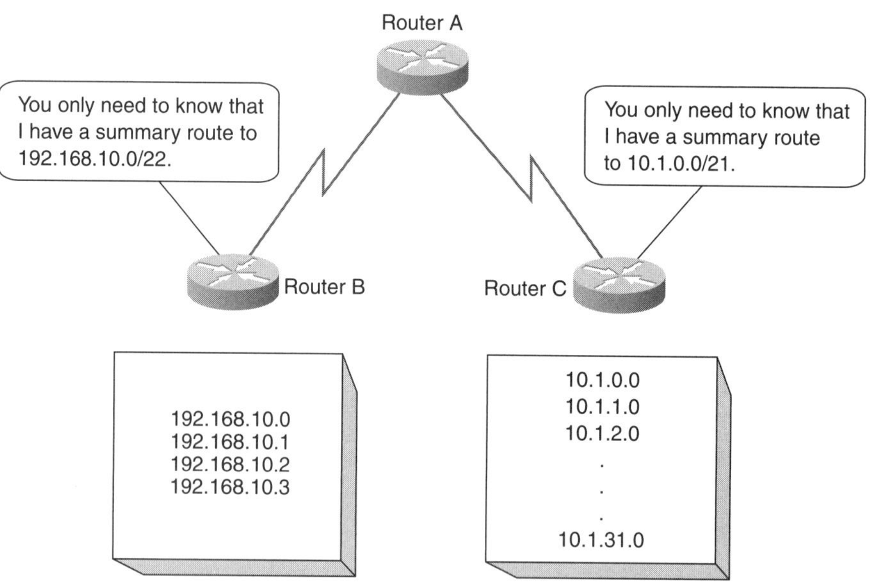

According to the specifications set forth in RFC 1518, the following requirements have to be met in order for summarization to work:

- The routing protocol must carry the prefix length in a separate field along with the full 32-bit IP address.
- The multiple addresses being summarized must all carry the same high-order bits.
- The routing protocols and routing tables must base their decision on the full 32-bit IP address and the prefix length, which can be up to 32 bits long.

TIP: *For every bit collapsed to the left, you get a power of 2 summarization. For example, if 2 bits were borrowed for summarization, you would have* 2^2 *networks summarized, or four networks. This formula will work for every example except the 0-bit summarization.*

Classful routing protocols, such as RIPv1 and IGRP, can only summarize based on major network number, using the natural mask as dictated by the class of network number. As you learned earlier in this section, these protocols cannot carry prefix length information, so summarization requirements, as outlined in the RFC, are not met.

Classless Inter-Domain Routing (CIDR—pronounced *CIDER*) is used by BGP4 as one way to apply route summarization. CIDR is primarily used to summarize or aggregate networks into a single route advertisement in order to reduce the number of routes advertised over the Internet. BGPv4 is the most common Exterior Gateway Protocol (EGP) in use by major Internet service providers. EIGRP and OSPF, which are Interior Gateway Protocols (IGP), can also support prefix routing, allowing for summarization to be used.

Another difference between VLSM and summarization that you will notice in Table 7-2 is that you can add the decimal mask to the resulting number of networks and get a total of 256. This is different from VLSM in that you do not have to subtract a broadcast and network number from 256 for each network.

TIP: *In most Cisco texts, you will still see 2 subtracted from these numbers, even though it is not applicable to summarization. Therefore, you will probably want to keep this in mind when reading Cisco texts or taking the tests.*

Table 7-2 Summarization Reference

Decimal Mask	# Potential Networks	Bits to Network	Bits to Host	Nets Advertised
.255	256	8	0	1
.254	128	7	1	2
.252	64	6	2	4
.248	32	5	3	8
.240	16	4	4	16
.224	8	3	5	32
.192	4	2	6	64
.128	2	1	7	128

Secondary Addresses

Cisco routers support secondary IP address assignment on router interfaces. The term "secondary address" may sound a little misleading, as though you can only put two addresses per interface. You can, in fact, put multiple secondary addresses on an interface, but it is generally not a good policy, as it slows down the routing processes. There are typically three reasons to use secondary addresses:

- Support for a switched network
- Support for discontiguous networks
- Extending the life of the current investment

Secondary addresses come in handy when designing a switched network in which many switches supporting multiple subnets may uplink to a common router port. Take the example in Figure 7-7. Both the 192.168.10.0 subnet and the 192.168.20.0 subnets connect to the network backbone through a common switch to a single router interface. In order to allow the backbone to route to both subnets, a secondary address is used on the router interface.

Secondary addresses are also useful in connecting a discontiguous subnet to the network backbone. In Figure 7-8, Router A and Router B each have a subnet of 192.168.1.0 supporting end users. The two routers are con-

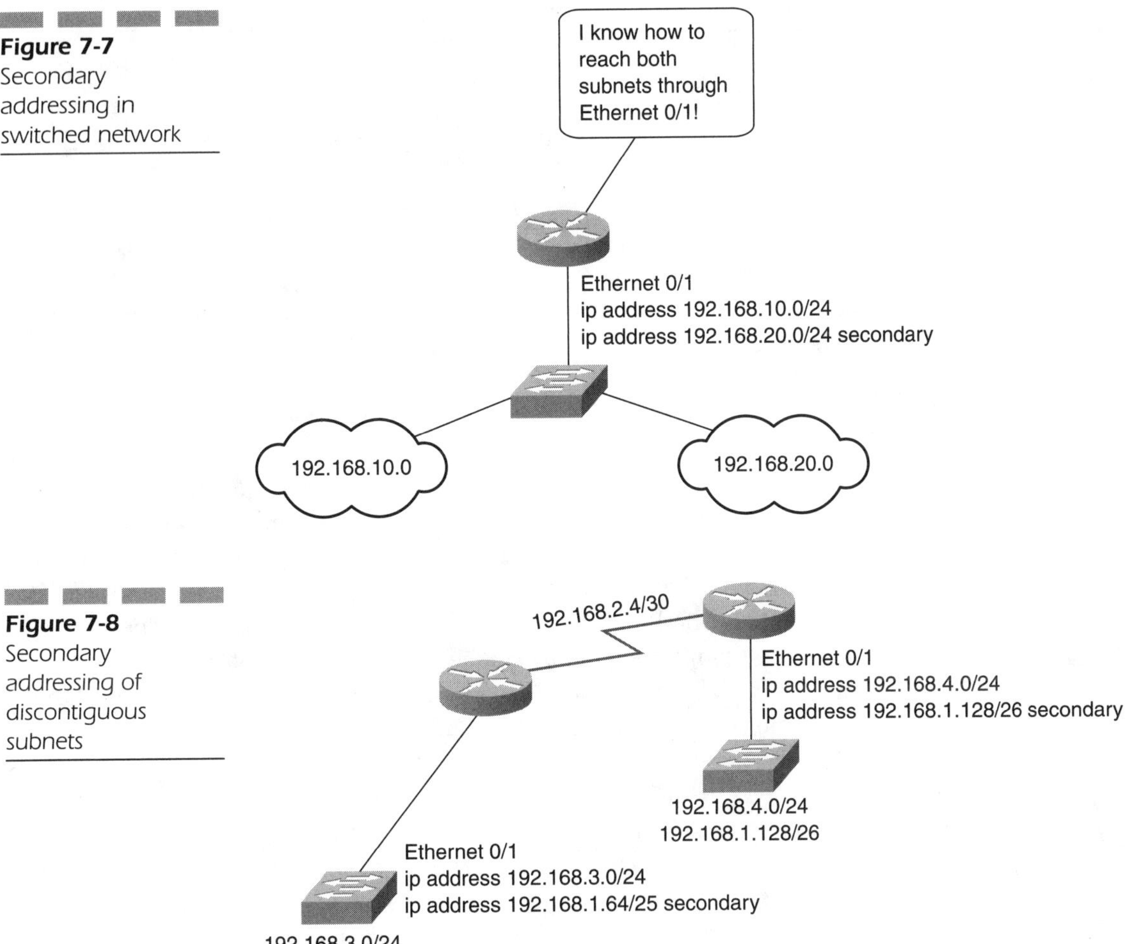

Figure 7-7 Secondary addressing in switched network

Figure 7-8 Secondary addressing of discontiguous subnets

nected, however, by a point-to-point subnet—192.168.2.4/30. By placing a secondary address on the Ethernet interface of each router, the routing protocols may advertise the subnets to their neighbors.

Another use of secondary addressing is to extend the use of a current router interface instead of upgrading equipment to add more interfaces. In other words, instead of having three router interfaces, a network administrator may choose to have three networks on a single interface. It is sometimes done in order to preserve the current investment. This is generally not advisable unless it is for a "short-term" fix. It should never be done for long-term addressing needs.

IP Address Management

All of the IP addresses that may be contained in a network have to be managed either manually or automatically. This can be done statically or dynamically.

In the past, each end-station in an enterprise network had a statically assigned IP address. When networks were small, this made sense and was relatively easy to manage. However, static addresses are as administratively cumbersome as static routes in a router. Each time an end-station needs to make a change, a network administrator must update the system and make changes to network records.

At one facility where I worked, I was the unfortunate keeper of the IP address spreadsheets. This was before the availability of dynamic address management. What started out easily enough became a daunting task that kept my pager going off all day long, as each new workstation was added to the network. Not only did I have to deal with tracking the information about the workstations (such as serial number, domain name server, and the like), I also had to assign an address, mask, and gateway. Then I had to remember to update my spreadsheets and hope that no one "stole" an address by picking one out of thin air when it was needed. DHCP automates that which I once did all by hand.

As networks have evolved from mainframes and virtual terminals to PCs that all need to have IP addresses, it has become necessary to use dynamic addressing tools to allow hosts to get an IP address from the network when they boot-up. This greatly reduces the number of tasks necessary for each end-station. Of course, some end-stations such as router interfaces, servers, and printers, will still have static IP address assignments and are not configured to use dynamic address management.

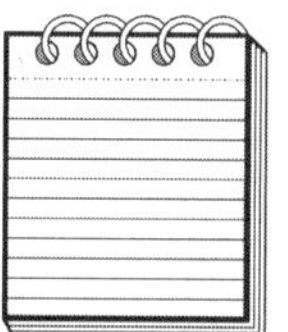

NOTE: *Sometimes renumbering end-stations is required in order to create a better design strategy, by eliminating discontiguous networks, for example. Remember to weigh the benefits against the short-term administrative labor. When using dynamic address management, the long-term benefits are immeasurable.*

Dynamic Host Configuration Protocol (DHCP)

DHCP is a method that allows end-station clients to ask for their IP configuration information from a server residing on the network when they boot up or when their current IP address expires. DHCP differs from the bootstrap protocol (BOOTP) in that it can "lease" an IP address for a period of time and reclaim it for reuse later. It can also allow other configuration parameters, such as the subnet mask, to be assigned to a client.

Basically, DHCP works by allowing a client to broadcast a request for an address upon boot-up. DHCP servers on the network then respond. Although more than one DHCP server may offer an IP address, the client generally takes the first offer.

The configuration of DHCP varies, depending upon the needs of the individual network. Some of the configuration tasks may include setting up:

- Scopes
- Relay agent
- Optional client configuration (per RFC1533)

Scopes Scopes are simply ranges of addresses eligible to be assigned for networks supported by the DHCP server. Some addresses that may be removed from a scope are the addresses on a network that are permanently assigned to routers, servers, and printers. A DHCP server may contain a single scope, when only one network is supported, and may reside on the network with the clients. This is not usually the case, however. Normally, a DHCP server provides address assignment to multiple networks within an enterprise and resides on a single subnet within the enterprise. When this is the case, DHCP relay must be configured.

Relay Agent DHCP relay agent allows clients to find the DHCP server, which may not be sitting on the same network as they are. Typically a router will be configured to act as the agent for the DHCP requests. This can be done by turning on an IP helper address, which enables many IP broadcast types to be forwarded to the helper address, or by selectively allowing different protocols to be forwarded. Cisco IOS configuration is not within the scope of this document. For further information, please consult the Cisco Web site.

Optional Client Configuration Some optional information may be configured on the client in addition to the IP address. These optional configuration parameters are specified in RFC 1533, although the exact setup is application-specific. The additional options are

- Subnet mask
- Router (gateway)
- Domain
- Domain Name System (DNS)

Details on how to configure these options are available through the application vendor.

DNS/DHCP Manager and Network Registrar

Cisco provides two different methods for configuring DHCP services on your network:

- Cisco Network Registrar
- Cisco DNS/DHCP Manager

Cisco Network Registrar Cisco Network Registrar is intended to be a scalable dynamic naming and addressing application for both enterprise and service provider networks. It is meant to act as an upgrade or replacement to Cisco DNS/DHCP Manager.

Network Registrar works well with some of the newer demands on networks, particularly service provider networks supporting cable modem access and the like. Able to assign up to 1800 leases per second, Network Registrar can classify devices based upon MAC address, device type, user class, vendor class, or other criteria. This permits easier configuration of Quality of Service (QoS) parameters based on device type or the use of private IP address spaces for remote access users.

Cisco DNS/DHCP Manager Cisco DNS/DHCP Manager is an earlier, IOS-based application that permitted the router to run a process that assigned IP addresses and other device configuration parameters to clients on the network.

Although still supported, DNS/DHCP Manager should be considered only when cost is a factor in the network design. The preferred choice should be Cisco Network Registrar. Remember, whenever possible, to offload tasks from the router in order to maximize the router's performance.

IP Multicast

Traditional IP routing did not provide efficient support for some of the newer multimedia applications that began cropping up in the 1990s. Unicast datagrams only understand one source and one destination address. Broadcasts provide for communication from a single source to all destinations within a broadcast domain. IP multicasting came about to meet the requirement of a single or multiple sources to send to a single or multiple destinations, selectively. Applications such as video teleconferencing to the desktop, movie viewing "on demand," and other multimedia presentations are becoming more commonplace, requiring support for multicast in many networks.

Multicast destinations are addressed using Class D IP addresses. A router supporting multicast has to be able to efficiently route to many networks at once, but all end-stations receiving the multicast only need to know about one "group" address. The group address acts as the entity that joins the sender(s) and the receiver(s) together.

The Internet Assigned Number Authority (IANA) owns a block of addresses used for multicast.

- IANA owns 01:00:5e:00:00:00 through 01:00:5e:7f:ff:ff for multicast.
- The high-order bits, 1110, identify an address as a multicast address.
- The next five bits do not participate in the mapping to an Ethernet address.
- The low-order 23 bits are copied to the Ethernet multicast address or the lower three bits of the MAC address to make it unique.

In other words, the first octet (first byte) and the highest bit of the next octet (most significant bit) do not change or take place in the mapping of the layer 3 address to a layer 2 address. The first four bits are always 1110, which translates to 224 in decimal. Because the next five bits also do not participate in the mapping, the result is that 32 different multicast group IDs can map to the same Ethernet address. For this reason, the drivers or IP modules perform filtering that determines whether or not the traffic being received is something in which the group members are interested.

Joining Groups

In order to receive multicast traffic, an end-station must join the multicast group. In other words, multicasting can exist on a network with no end-stations actually receiving any traffic from it. Hosts join the group using Internet Group Management Protocol (IGMP), a standard described in RFC 1112. Hosts use IGMP to tell the routers to which they are directly attached which multicast group(s) they wish to join or leave. In turn, the router uses IGMP to discover if members of those multicast groups are located on networks to which the router is attached. If other members are found, the multicast-enabled router can then join the group and begin forwarding the multicast traffic to the hosts who wished to join the groups.

Periodically, the routers using IGMPv2 will send out queries to find out which groups are active or inactive and will listen to messages coming from other IGMP routers.

Best Path for Multicasting

There are three routing protocols that build the route distribution tree necessary to allow for multicast routing:

- Distance Vector Multicast Routing Protocol (DVMRP)
- Multicast Open Shortest Path First (MOSPF)
- Protocol-Independent Multicast (PIM)

DVMRP is defined in RFC 1075. It is the protocol that is the basis for the Internet's Multicast Backbone (MBONE). DVMRP uses a reverse path-flooding technique, which means that the router sends a copy of a packet to all paths, except the path on which it received the packet. If a router is attached to a LAN that does not wish to receive the multicast traffic, the router will send a prune message back to the source, asking it not to send the traffic to that LAN. DVMRP uses its own unicast protocol to determine the interface leading back to the source, rather than using the protocols already in use. DVMRP has some scalability issues and can cause problems with the flooding and reflooding mechanisms, especially in older versions in which pruning was not supported.

We include MOSPF here because you may encounter it in network design, but MOSPF is not supported by Cisco Systems. It is described in RFC 1584 and has been implemented by some router manufacturers.

MOSPF tends not to be very scalable, because it must be turned on for every OSPF router in the network and runs the Dijkstra algorithm (the algorithm used by OSPF) for every multicast source and group within the network. This can, as you can imagine, cause excessive strain on all of the routers in a large network using MOSPF. MOSPF works by including multicast information in OSPF link-state advertisements and by ensuring that every MOSPF router learns which multicast groups are active on the connected LANs. It also builds a distribution tree for every source/group pair. It is the size of the network, the number of source/group pairs, and the volatility of the network that can cause problems with running MOSPF.

Cisco first implemented PIM in IOS version 10.2. PIM can operate in sparse or dense mode, depending upon the size of the group, small or large, respectively, being supported. PIM sparse mode is generally used when there are many data streams but few LANs to be supported. Dense mode uses a reverse path-flooding mechanism similar to DVMRP, but the difference is that PIM uses whatever routing protocol is already in use to determine the source interface for a multicast stream, which is an improvement over DVMRP. PIM operates by allowing the sender of data to have its first-hop router send data to a rendezvous point. Receivers interested in receiving data register with the rendezvous point via their last-hop router (the interface closest to the receiver).

TIP: *An important design note is that PIM can interoperate with routers running DVMRP.*

PIM is the most likely choice in relation to your network design goals, especially for a network that is heavily Cisco-centric.

TCP/IP Security

Because it is so popular and widely used, TCP/IP also has become the target of many network security threats and exploits. It is important, therefore, to build network security into the design from the beginning. This section will introduce you to the concepts of TCP/IP security, but network security will be further discussed in Chapter 23, "Security Design." While the content of this book is not intended to address all security needs and concerns, it should give you an ample introduction to the topic.

Requirements

Cisco defines the phases of securing an IP network, and keeping it secure, as follows:

- Establish a security policy.
- Implement network security technologies.
- Audit the network.

One of the first tasks that must be attended to when designing and building a network is the documentation of a security policy. A company's security policy is a living document that commits to paper the company's official stance toward various internal and external threats to the security, privacy, and integrity of the network devices, users, and data. If no policy exists, it is extremely difficult to design the right security solution. It would be equivalent to putting policemen on the streets with no written laws to enforce. The determination of right and wrong would forever be under debate and no valid enforcement would be possible.

A few good "rules of thumb" to bear in mind with relation to the security policy are as follows:

- Let a security specialist do the security work. If the company does not have such an individual, recommend that they hire or contract someone who specializes in the field to make recommendations.
- Keep the business in mind when writing the policy. Do not build a Fort Knox fortress for a log cabin LAN.
- Determine what data must be available to the outside world or the public. Find a way to allow the access to that data without opening the gates to the entire network.
- Keep the security costs balanced with the needs of the network.
- Keep it simple!

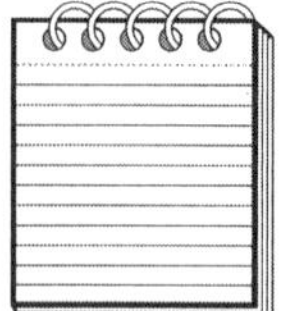

NOTE: *The security policy should dictate the security technology choices to be implemented.*

Once the company's security policy is written, it must be enforced. The best and most administratively sound method of doing this is to put technologies in place to continually monitor network activity for violations of the policy. This can mean the use of Access Control Lists (ACL), firewalls, network probes, and access management applications. It can also mean finding ways to secure, or "lock down," applications and platforms so that known vulnerabilities are ruled out before the start.

Finally, it is important to continually update the security policy and to audit the network periodically to ensure that the latest threats are addressed immediately. Often a network or host vulnerability is so new or so infrequently seen that it is not adequately protected against. Many vulnerabilities have been spotted by tools or sharp-eyed administrators who notice an anomaly in network activity. Security administration can be likened to detective work. One "bust" does not mean that crime is forever off the street. The job of network security should be seen as an ongoing battle.

Firewalls, Access Management, and Host Security

In the last section we mentioned that technologies should be put into place to enforce policy. Here we will discuss a few of the products, tools, or methods that can be used to do just that.

The Cisco Secure PIX Firewall is one way of enforcing the security policy. The PIX firewall is a network appliance that runs on an embedded non-Unix OS. It is a simple, easy-to-implement part of a total network security solution. By examining packets coming into and leaving the network, the firewall can apply the security policy dynamically.

The Cisco Secure Policy Manager allows for up to 500 firewalls to be centrally managed and ruled by a single network security policy. The PIX firewall is highly scalable and can also be used to implement IPSec encryption and *Virtual Private Networks* (VPNs). A VPN creates a secure tunnel between two hosts over an unsecured medium.

Access to the network resources can be controlled both inside and outside the network by using everything from simple username/password pairs to complex access servers. Dial-up users can be required to use VPNs, RADIUS authentication, TACACS+ authentication, or a token-based authentication method using a credit card-sized device along with a Personal Identification Number (PIN) to generate a one-time password.

Any of these authentication methods accomplishes a single task-determining if you are who you say you are. Once that is determined, the security policy dictates whether or not you are authorized to access whatever resources you are trying to access. Again, it is important to guard against overkill when selecting an access authentication method for a network. Keep it simple, but keep it relative to the type and strength of security needed in the network design on which you are working. If security were paramount, stronger methods would be warranted. Cost would probably not be as much of a factor as it would be in a smaller, less private network.

It can be said of a network that it is only as secure as its weakest link. That link could be a router, server, or client. Router security can be addressed via the use of ACLs, which will be further discussed in Chapter 23. Host-based security on clients and servers is dependent on several factors such as

- Operating system
- Physical security
- Services that are enabled
- IP spoofing vulnerability

First, it is important to know your operating system. There are a number of sites and search engines on the Internet that can assist you with finding the known vulnerabilities of the operating system in use on the end-stations. There are also many commercially available tools that can greatly automate the task of "locking down" an end-station. Whatever the method of choice, it is important to ensure that all end-stations on the network are as invulnerable as possible while still being available and useful to the users who need them.

Next, think about physical security. Access to servers and databases should be limited to those who need to administer and maintain the devices. It would be foolish to secure the applications and operating systems, only to leave the doors open for intruders to physically access the machines themselves. Many business travelers have been the unfortunate victims of laptop theft. Unsecured data on those systems may have fallen into the wrong hands. Even a company's home office should not be considered safe, however. As many facilities managers can tell you, theft inside the building does exist. A weekend cleaning crew could easily be infiltrated by someone who knows the value of your systems and data, or could simply have someone on staff who sees a computer for the taking.

Another way to avoid malicious activity on the network is to deny any services that are not absolutely necessary. If Trivial File Transfer Protocol (TFTP) is never used in your network, make sure it isn't allowed over the routers and isn't running on the hosts. Restrict telnet access to only those users who have to have it. Turn off daemons running services like Network Time Protocol (NTP), Remote Procedure Call (RPC), and others that may be running by default on hosts. Streamline the operations of the hosts and network overall.

IP spoofing is another activity that should be closely guarded against. Spoofing is a method by which intruders gain access to network resources by pretending to be an IP address that exists inside the network. An easy way to stop this activity is to deny packets coming into an external router interface that claim to be from a subnet residing on an internal router interface.

There are many network security tips and tricks than we can put in this section, but now you have a few more tools in your toolbag to use when tackling a good network security design.

Private Addresses

As mentioned in Chapter 6, the use of private (RFC 1918) addresses is one way to add a layer of security to a good TCP/IP network design. Because RFC 1918 addresses are not permitted to route over the public Internet, it is highly unlikely that intruders could manage to masquerade as a host with a private IP address. If you were using private addresses inside your network, IP spoofing, which we discussed in the last section, would be highly unlikely to happen to the network.

One thing to consider when using private IP addressing, however, is that privately addressed hosts cannot access resources external to the enterprise network unless Network Address Translation (NAT) is used. NAT allows for a privately addressed host to masquerade with a valid IP address in order to access external networks. The external networks are prevented from learning the private address of the source. A map detailing valid addresses to private addresses is either stored dynamically or statically in the firewall, router, or other device providing NAT service to the hosts.

Case Study

We now return to Campus Research, the company we have been following through the last several chapters. In this case study, you will have a chance to apply what you have learned about TCP/IP addressing and design.

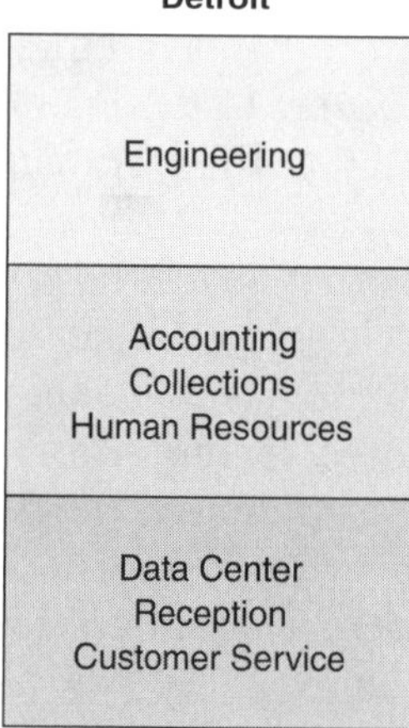

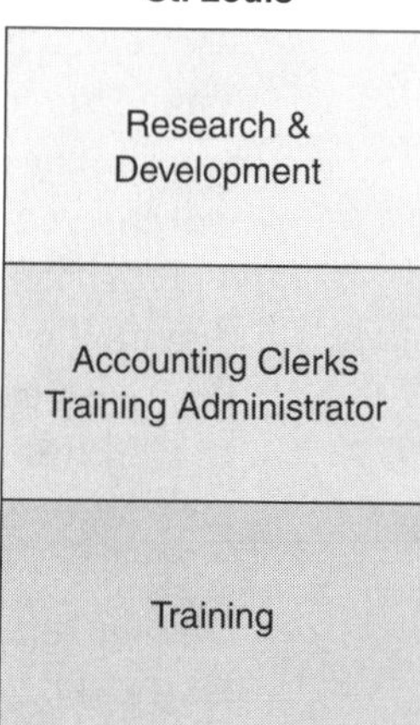

Figure 7-9 Campus research locations

As illustrated in Figure 7-9, we have buildings in St. Louis and Detroit, with various departments in each one.

For the purposes of this case study, certain assumptions will be made in order to permit you to try your hand at a thorough TCP/IP design. Those assumptions are

- A single router at each building provides routing within the building and connectivity via a T-1 link between locations.
- A switch has been deployed on each of the five floors at the Detroit location and on each of the three floors at the St. Louis location. Wiring has been upgraded to Category 5 UTP between the closets and LAN drops, with multimode fiber in the risers.
- Server farms have been centralized in the Detroit Data Center and the St. Louis R&D center.
- Accounting clerks in St. Louis need to be able to FTP files at the end of each day to the servers in Detroit.
- Engineering needs to be able to reach the R&D server farm to browse Web pages, download files (via FTP), and update code (via TFTP).
- Data Center personnel need to be able to use Telnet and TFTP in order to manage network devices in both locations. They also need to be able to manage servers.

The resulting layout looks something like Figure 7-10.

Campus Research currently leases six Class C network numbers from their ISP, but they are interested in saving the thousands of dollars a year

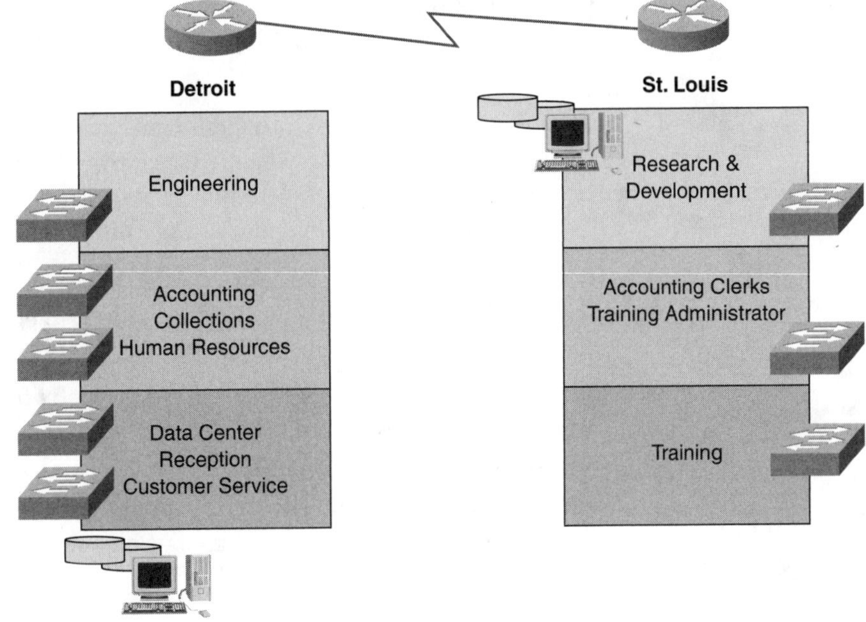

Figure 7-10 Campus research connectivity

now spent on the leases, if you can show them a better method of addressing. They are willing to consider using private address space. The ISP would then assign a subnet to the T-1 link.

Some of the questions you will need to answer with the design will be

- If RFC 1918 addresses are used, what device will handle network address translation?
- Will firewalls be needed at both locations?
- Will a DHCP server be placed at both locations? If placed at only one location, how will traffic between buildings be affected?
- How will authentication be handled in order to verify personnel that are managing network devices and servers?
- What services need to be allowed to pass between buildings?
- What addresses will you select for the networks and departments contained within the locations?

Although there are no absolute answers to any given network design scenario, suggested solutions can be found in Appendix C, "Suggested Solutions to Case Studies."

CCDP Tips

This section contains an abbreviated list of topics covered in Chapter 7. Think of this section as the equivalent of reading Cliff's Notes™ instead of reading an entire book. You will get the general idea of the chapter but will benefit more from reading the chapter in its entirety.

Keep in mind the following addressing guidelines:

- Hierarchical addressing provides for one major network to be advertised, using a single network statement to effectively advertise all subnets that fall within it.
- Prefix routing allows a packet to carry the prefix field identifying the number of bits representing the network portion of the address.
- Subnetting allows the network portion of an address to borrow bits from the host portion in order to create many networks out of one. Classful protocols allow subnetting, but all subnet masks must be the same.
- Variable Length Subnet Masking (VLSM) allows for subnets to be customized within the same major network, creating subnets of varying sizes to match the needs of a LAN. Only classless routing protocols can permit VLSM.
- Route summarization permits multiple contiguous networks to be advertised in one statement.
- Classless Inter-Domain Routing (CIDR) is a method of route aggregation employed by BGPv4.
- Secondary addresses can be used to bridge the gap with discontiguous subnets and to provide for routing in a flat switched network. It does, however, slow the performance on a router and should not be seen as a permanent design choice.
- Manual administrative tasks associated with addressing end-stations on a LAN can be greatly reduced by the use of Dynamic Host Configuration Protocol (DHCP). Cisco provides for DHCP through its DNS/DHCP Manager or Network Registrar products.
- DHCP uses scopes to identify address ranges that can be leased out to end-stations and uses relay when the DHCP server does not reside on the same LAN as the end-stations being served.
- DHCP provides for subnet mask and default gateway assignments, services not provided by BOOTP.

- Routers and end-stations use the Internet Group Management Protocol to find and join groups.
- Three multicast protocols exist to build the distribution trees, which define the best path for multicast traffic: MOSPF, DVMRP, and PIM (sparse or dense mode).
- The three phases of securing a network are: 1) establish a security policy, 2) implement network security technologies, and 3) audit the network.
- Access management requires user identification validation for remote or local users.
- A firewall enforces the security policy established by a network.
- End-station security must be considered, particularly regarding operating system vulnerabilities, physical security, and services that are running by default.
- IP spoofing allows intruders to masquerade with an internal address. Using RFC 1918 addresses reduces the likelihood of this being effective.
- Keep routing tables small! Routing tables can be smaller when using route summarization, because fewer statements are needed in order to advertise the same number of overall destination networks.
- Let the routers move traffic efficiently. Switching performance can be faster when using route summarization, because the router has less information to parse in order to make its routing decision.
- Keep traffic on the network concise. Overall routing protocol traffic is reduced when using route summarization.

Summary

This chapter has introduced you to a deeper understanding of issues relating to the design of a TCP/IP network. By now you should have a better grasp of IP addressing, subnetting, and summarization concepts, as well as an understanding of why the reduction or aggregation of networks might be useful.

You have also had an introduction to IP multicast routing and IP security, two topics that will be discussed again, further along in the book. Finally, we explained the use of DHCP and the tools related to streamlining menial network administration tasks.

As the use of TCP/IP has become more widespread, it is important for network designers to have a good, basic understanding of all of the concerns related to the protocol.

Questions

The following review questions have been selected to help you test your knowledge of the subject matter contained in this chapter. You will also find these questions contained in the CD-ROM included with this book. While these are not the questions you will find in the certification exams, knowing the answers to the review questions in this book will help cement the material in your mind as you prepare for the tests.

1. VLSM stands for ____________.
   a. Variable Length Subnet Mask
   b. Variable Logical Subnet Mask
   c. Visible Length Subnet Mask
2. CIDR is address summarization used in this routing protocol.
   a. RIPv2
   b. OSPF
   c. IGRP
   d. BGPv4
3. What part of a security infrastructure enforces the company's security policy?
   a. Network Registrar
   b. PIX Firewall
   c. TACACS+ Server
4. DHCP stands for ________.
   a. Dynamic Host Control Protocol
   b. Dynamic Host Configuration Parameters
   c. Dynamic Host Control Parameters
   d. Dynamic Host Configuration Protocol

5. Which RFC provides for private address spaces?
   a. RFC 791
   b. RFC 1918
   c. RFC 1518
   d. RFC 760
6. How many bits are allocated to a Class A address network portion?
   a. 8
   b. 16
   c. 24
   d. 30
7. How many bits are allocated to a Class C address host portion?
   a. 8
   b. 16
   c. 24
   d. 2
8. A secondary address can be used to provide support for which two situations? (Select two.)
   a. Discontiguous subnets
   b. Point-to-point links
   c. VPNs
   d. Flat, switched network
9. What information must a classless routing protocol carry in order to define the number of bits used in the network portion of an address?
   a. Prefix length
   b. Suffix length
   c. Host ID
   d. Router ID
10. Which multicast protocol is not supported by Cisco?
    a. PIM
    b. DVMRP
    c. MOSPF

11. PIM sparse mode works well in which of these situations?
    a. Many LANs with many data streams
    b. Few LANs with many data streams
    c. Few LANs with few data streams
12. Which method is employed by DVMRP in order to build the multicast distribution tree?
    a. Directed broadcast
    b. Reverse path-flooding
    c. Link-state advertisements
13. Which netmask is best applied to point-to-point network links?
    a. 255.255.255.252
    b. 255.255.255.248
    c. 255.255.255.240
    d. 255.255.255.224
14. What function must be used when a DHCP server is on a LAN other than that on which some of the clients reside?
    a. Scopes
    b. Relay agent
    c. Gateway
    d. Secondary address
15. If you needed to split a Class C network address into eight subnets, which is the best choice of subnet mask?
    a. 255.255.255.252
    b. 255.255.255.248
    c. 255.255.255.240
    d. 255.255.255.224
16. Given the following statement, how many networks are being summarized in the advertisement?
    Network 192.168.0.0 255.255.252.0
    a. 8
    b. 4
    c. 6
    d. 2

17. When using private addressing, a network design must also provide for this, if hosts are to reach the public Internet.
    a. Network Address Translation (NAT)
    b. Firewall
    c. RFC 1918 addresses
    d. TFTP
18. Which statement does not describe something you should do when designing network security?
    a. Hire a security specialist
    b. Allow open access to the database servers
    c. Encourage the company to document the security policy
    d. Implement a firewall
19. What network address class is used for multicast addressing?
    a. Class A
    b. Class B
    c. Class C
    d. Class D
20. A major goal of a good TCP/IP network design should be to keep __________ small.
    a. The firewall
    b. The routing table
    c. Switches
    d. Multicast groups

Answers

1. VLSM stands for ___________.
   a. Variable Length Subnet Mask
2. CIDR is address summarization used in this routing protocol.
   d. BGPv4

3. What part of a security infrastructure enforces the company's security policy?
   b. PIX Firewall
   Explanation: Remember that the security policy comes first. The firewall enforces the policy.

4. DHCP stands for ________.
   d. Dynamic Host Configuration Protocol

5. Which RFC provides for private address spaces?
   b. RFC 1918

6. How many bits are allocated to a Class A address network portion?
   a. 8

7. How many bits are allocated to a Class C address host portion?
   a. 8

8. A secondary address can be used to provide support for which two situations? (Select two.)
   a. Discontiguous subnets
   d. Flat, switched network

9. What information must a classless routing protocol carry in order to define the number of bits used in the network portion of an address?
   a. Prefix length
   Explanation: If no prefix bits are carried, then the routing protocol has no idea which bits are allocated to the network portion. In that case, it would default to the use of the natural mask for the class of address it is seeing.

10. Which multicast protocol is not supported by Cisco?
    c. MOSPF

11. PIM sparse mode works well in which of these situations?
    b. Few LANs with many data streams
    Explanation: An easy way to remember this one is to remember that sparse means few, and dense means many. If you remember the terms in relation to the number of LANs, it will make sense.

12. Which method is employed by DVMRP in order to build the multicast distribution tree?
    b. Reverse path-flooding

13. Which netmask is best applied to point-to-point network links?
a. 255.255.255.252
Explanation: A point-to-point link can only use two addresses. This mask only provides two usable addresses, with the other two addresses allocated to the network number and the broadcast address.

14. What function must be used when a DHCP server is on a LAN other than that on which some of the clients reside?
b. Relay agent
Explanation: A relay agent helps the hosts "find" their server. A Cisco router can act as a relay agent.

15. If you needed to split a network into eight subnets, which is the best choice of subnet mask?
d. 255.255.255.224

16. Given the following statement, how many networks are being summarized in the advertisement?
Network 192.168.0.0 255.255.252.0
b. 4

17. When using private addressing, a network design must also provide for this, if hosts are to reach the public Internet.
a. Network Address Translation (NAT)
Explanation: Because the RFC 1918 addresses are set aside for everyone to use, there is no way to insure the uniqueness of the address. Therefore, these addresses are not allowed to route outside enterprise networks.

18. Which statement does not describe something you should do when designing network security?
b. Allow open access to the database servers
Explanation: Open access to the databases would be the equivalent of leaving your house unlocked, the keys in your car, and a sign outside your house advertising everything that you own. While it doesn't guarantee that anything will be stolen, it makes it far too easy for someone to do so.

19. What network address class is used for multicast addressing?
d. Class D

20. A major goal of a good TCP/IP network design should be to keep __________ small.
b. The routing table
Explanation: The smaller the routing table, the less bandwidth routing updates will take. Small routing tables can also produce better performance in the router itself.

Bibliography

Cisco Internetwork Design, Cisco Press, 2000, Matthew H. Birkner, Editor

Cisco Internetwork Design Course Manual, version 3.0, April 1997, Cisco Systems, Inc.

Cisco IOS DNS/DHCP Server, **http://www.cisco.com/univercd/cc/td/doc/product/software/ios120/120newft/120t/120t1/easyip2.htm**

Cisco Multicast Routing and Switching, McGraw-Hill Technical Series, 1999, William R. Parkhurst, PhD, CCIE #2969

Cisco Network Registrar 5.0 Data Sheet, **http://www.cisco.com/warp/public/cc/pd/nemnsw/nerr/prodlit/cnr30_ds.htm**

Cisco Windows Networking Design Implementation Guide, **http://www.cisco.com/warp/public/473/winnt_dg.htm**

Designing and Implementing an OSPF Network, **http://www.cisco.com/cpress.cc/td/cpress/design/ospf/on0407.htm**

Increasing Security on IP Networks, **http://www.cisco.com/univercd/cc/td/doc/cisintwk/ics/cs003.htm**

Internet RFC Source, **http://www.cis.ohio-state.edu/hypertext/information/rfc.html**

RFC 760

RFC 791

RFC 1075

RFC 1112

RFC 1518

RFC 1533

RFC 1584

RFC 1918

RFC 2131

Security Overview, **http://www.cisco.com/univercd/dd/td/doc/product/software/ios113ed/113ed_cr/secur_c/scoverv.htm**

Understanding DHCP, **http://www.cisco.com/warp/public/779/smbiz/service/knowledge/tcpip/dhcp.htm**

CHAPTER 8

Routing Protocol Design

Overview

In this chapter, and the next few that follow, we are going to look at the various routing protocols available for use in today's complex internetworks. We will focus primarily on the aspects of the decision process in this chapter. There are business requirements to be analyzed, technology requirements to be supported, and the preferences and expertise of the network staff to consider.

We will cover the categorization of routing protocols and briefly summarize the benefits and drawbacks of each one. By the time you finish this chapter, you will have a better idea of how to select a routing protocol. Then in the chapters that follow, you will have a chance to practice each protocol in a case study.

Analyzing Requirements

As with most of the major decisions in creating or modifying a network design, the needs of the environment must be carefully considered. Part of this step is to educate the decision-makers. Of course, there will be some environments in which the routing protocol selection is straightforward, and in many cases, the current protocol in use may be the one the staff wishes to continue to use. However, a discussion of the available choices is usually a wise move. Often it gives the engineering support staff an opportunity to air differences of opinion, discuss new or future requirements, and reaffirm their current choice or decide to move in a new direction.

Business Needs

Some of the questions that may need to be answered during this phase of the design process are

- Is the network 100 percent Cisco equipment?
- How likely is it that the business will acquire another company?
- What is the growth projection over the next 5 to 10 years?

In a network that contains only Cisco routers, it would be possible to stay with a Cisco proprietary routing protocol such as Interior Gateway Routing

Protocol (IGRP) or Enhanced IGRP (EIGRP). However, if there is currently a requirement—or if there may be one in the future—to connect to non-Cisco routers, it would be a better choice to go with an open standard protocol such as Open Shortest Path First (OSPF) or Intermediate System to Intermediate System (ISIS).

NOTE: *By "open standards" protocol, we mean one that is freely available to be implemented within any vendor's router equipment.*

If the company tends to acquire other companies or if they have any plans to do so, it would be better to stay with an open standards protocol. If the company is small, closely held, or not-for-profit, the chances of their acquiring other companies are small. If they were to be acquired, there would be little effect on their particular choice of protocol, as the acquiring company would probably decide that.

Finally, the projected growth of the business over the next five to ten years should play a part in the final routing protocol decision. Some routing protocols are more scalable than others and will support large networks with ease.

Technical Needs

When examining the needs of the business, you will find that the engineering support staff probably has strong feelings about the routing protocol currently in use, if applicable. It is the role of the network designer to point out the items to be considered before a final decision is made. In some cases you will bring to light issues the staff never considered, such as

- Will the current network have to communicate with other autonomous systems (ASs)? This is normally the case when communicating with an ISP or in a carrier-level environment.
- Is support for Variable Length Subnet Masking (VLSM) important?
- What protocols must be used to support existing legacy systems and routers?

- How well is the network handling the traffic created by the current routing protocol, if applicable? Of course, if you were bringing up a new network, this question would not apply.
- How quickly can the current routing protocol, if applicable, adapt to changes in the network?

Often you will find that an engineering support staff has had no need to worry about an Exterior Gateway Protocol (EGP), because that is something their Internet service provider (ISP) handles for them. In such a situation, the only routing protocol choice they need to make is to select an Interior Gateway Protocol (IGP), or one that will handle the routing of traffic inside their AS. If, however, you are designing a network for a carrier-class company or ISP, you will need to consider the way inter-AS traffic will be handled.

Something else to consider is the way the network addresses will be subnetted. If VLSM will need to be supported, it will affect the choice of routing protocol. As you may recall from our previous chapters, RIP version 1 and IGRP do not support VLSM.

Hosts and network devices within the network also must be considered, because they may require certain protocols. There may be Unix hosts, such as servers, in the network that can only run RIP and need to send or receive RIP updates. Then you will need to design a network with RIP support on certain networks. If hosts need RIP, and it is not the primary protocol in use, redistribution can be used so that multiple routing protocols can share information. We will discuss redistribution later in this chapter.

At this point, an analysis of current network traffic in the case of an existing network is quite valuable. If a "chatty" protocol like RIP is in use, you may be able to predict how growth over the short and long term can further bog down the network with even more routing protocol traffic. The analysis will give you a realistic insight into what is actually crossing the network and help document and predict traffic patterns. Often the process will add tremendous insight and value to the overall network design.

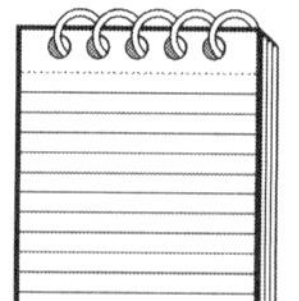

NOTE: *RIP is considered to be "chatty" because RIP sends many types of communications on a regular basis to its neighbors.*

You will probably find that there is nothing quite like the look on a network manager's face when he or she realizes that a host is sending RIP advertisements or that a 4:00 P.M. game of MechWarrior is running over the network. Many times none of the engineering support staff has any idea that these types of traffic are the source of network slowdowns, unless good network management tools are already in use.

After the analysis you will also be able to discuss the way in which the different routing protocols behave, that is, how often they send routing updates, what is contained in those updates, and how flexible the protocol is in allowing filtering of the updates. By explaining the protocols and applications, then showing the customer the traces, you will build a stronger partnership and trust relationship. Generally, customers feel more secure when you are forthcoming with background information and when you involve them in every part of the process.

Concepts

When traffic enters a router, the router must perform two basic tasks in order for the traffic to continue along its route:

- Switching
- Path determination

The basic process of switching is shown in Figure 8-1. You will notice that it is a five-step process that encompasses the decisions made by the router as it receives and processes a packet for forwarding. There are alternate methods of packet switching within a Cisco router that vary somewhat from this representation. We will discuss those in the section called "Basic Switching Types," later in this chapter.

Pretty simple, right? The process of *path determination* is not quite as simple as the switching process, however. Path determination actually puts overhead on the overall routing process. By exchanging information with other routers, running routing algorithms, and converging when a change occurs, the router makes a rather complex decision based upon metrics, availability, and such. We will discuss the various parameters used by different routing protocols later in this and the next few chapters.

Note that path determination is not a real-time activity. Most of the work is actually done when the routing algorithm for the protocol is run. This does not happen with each packet that comes into the router. All of this will be discussed in greater detail later in the chapter.

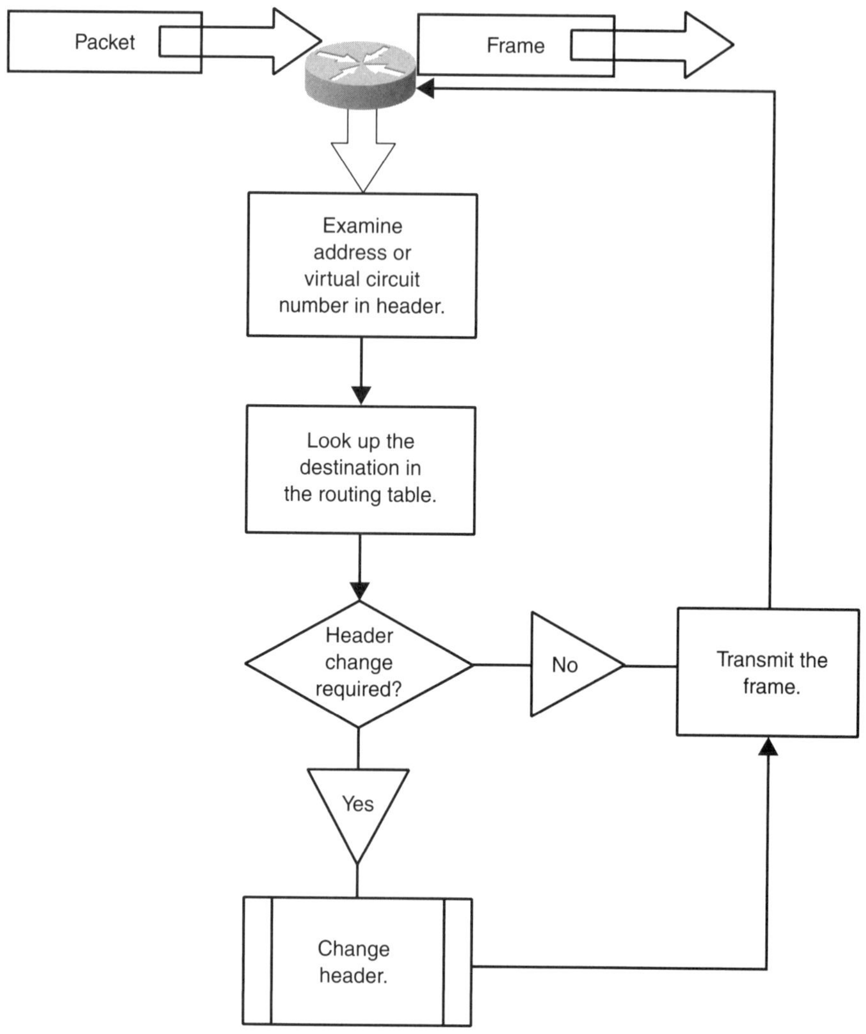

Figure 8-1 How a router forwards packets

Switching

How a packet is switched, or relayed, through a router is dependent upon the type of switching in use. A Cisco router can support up to six equal-cost switching paths to a destination to do concurrent load balancing. This is a limit set in Cisco IOS, but certain IGPs have limitations of their own. IGRP and EIGRP, for example, only permit load balancing to four equal-cost paths.

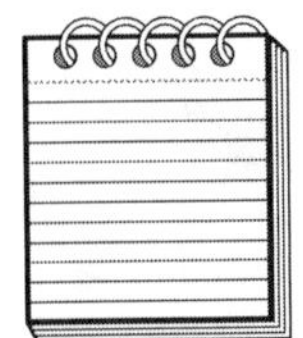

NOTE: *For more information on Cisco IOS load balancing, refer to this link:* **http://www.cisco.com/warp/public/105/46.html**

The type of switching determines the method in which this is done. It could be packet-by-packet, performing a routing table lookup with each new packet received, or it could be destination-by-destinations, switching all packets to and from the same source/destination pair through a single path. The path used for the same source/destination pair in the next conversation may be different, however.

We will discuss the types of switching paths and methods available a little later.

Path Determination

In order to create the routing table, the router derives information from several sources:

- Static routing entries
- Configuration and operational state of local interfaces
- Dynamic routing protocols and routing metrics
- ARP and inverse ARP
- Redistributed routes between routing protocols
- Applied routing policies

In Figure 8-2, Router A is looking for the best path to host 172.16.214.25, in this case a host on network 172.16.214.0/24. You see that there is a connected route via its Serial 1/0 interface. It may learn about the connected routes of its neighbor, Router B, through the point-to-point link. It is also being told about the existence of the network through RIP and OSPF.

Each of these, in this case, is going to take a different route. The administrative distances of each type of source will determine the best path to that host or network. The *administrative distance* (AD) of a route is essentially the internal cost of using a route.

Static vs. Dynamic Network engineers can force the router to use a certain path to a destination by using a *static route*. Static routes are fixed

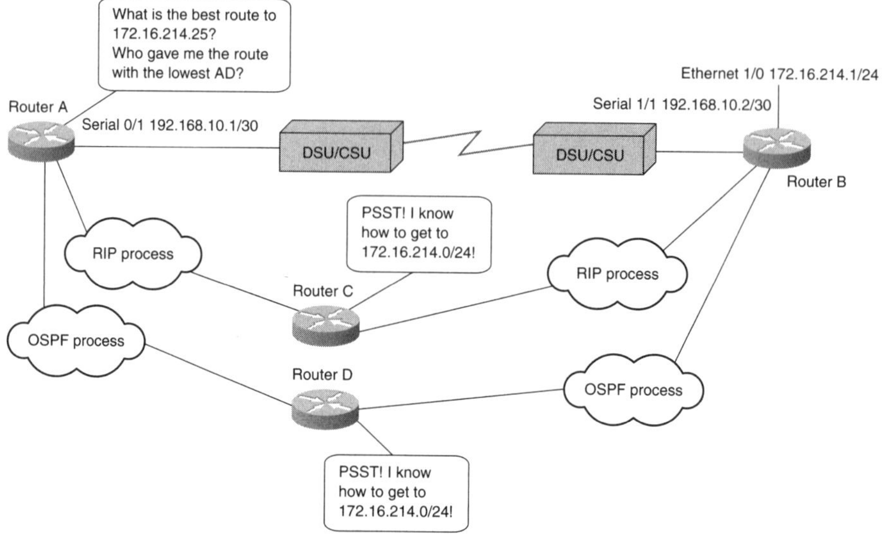

Figure 8-2 Path determination

statements in router configurations that are manually put there by an administrator. They are generally preferred to routes learned through a dynamic routing protocol because of their lower AD. A connected route has an AD of 0. A static route has an AD of 1. Therefore, only the connected routes will be preferred over static routes.

Later in this section you will see how the administrative distance of a static route can be changed, as well as why you would want to do that.

A static route entry may look like this:

```
ip route 192.168.10.0 255.255.255.0 172.16.101.2
```

In the example, the router has been configured to find the entire 254-host range of 192.168.10.0 through a neighbor at 172.16.101.2. This is an example of a static route with an AD of 1.

Another way to write the static route so that it has an AD of 0, is to do this:

```
ip route 192.168.10.0 255.255.255.0 serial 0/1
```

In this example, the administrator uses its own connected interface to forward packets to the distant end of the Serial0/1 connection. The *distant end* is simply the other end of a point-to-point link. Another example of a static route is the use of a default route, like this one:

```
ip route 0.0.0.0 0.0.0.0 serial 0/1
```

In this example, all traffic bound for any destination other than known destination networks contained in the routing table or on connected interfaces would be sent out of interface Serial0/1. This is a handy configuration when you have an isolated area, such as a *stub network* in OSPF. We will discuss stub networks more in Chapter 9, "OSPF Network Design," but generally speaking a stub network does not know of any routes outside its own area. It depends upon the default route to find anything that it doesn't know about locally.

That is static routing, and as we have said, a connected route is preferred over a static route, if the connected route is up and available. What about dynamically learned routes?

Once a router has determined that it has no connected or static routes to a destination, it begins path selection based upon *dynamic* routing protocols. Table 8-1 shows the AD of common routing protocols.

Routers will always prefer the least-cost path, meaning the path with the lowest administrative distance (path cost). The default AD values, as shown in Table 1, can be manipulated with the **distance** IOS command to an integer up to 255 so that one type of route might be favored over another.

Table 8-1

Administrative Distance

Routing Protocol or Method	Administrative Distance
Connected	0
Static to a layer 3 address	1
Static to a connected interface	0
External BGP	20
Internal BGP	200
EIGRP	90
IGRP	100
OSPF	110
RIP	120

TIP: When making a transition from one routing protocol to another, give the less-preferred protocol a higher administrative distance than the preferred protocol. The routing table will begin to change to use the preferred protocol.

Floating Static Routes Remember that we said in the last part of this section that you could manipulate the cost of a static route? The case in which you might want to do this is when you want to create a "fall-back" plan in case of link failure. By making the AD of a static route higher than that of the protocols in use on your router, you will ensure that the static route will only be used in case of an emergency. This is referred to as a *floating static route.* In most cases, setting the AD to 201 on a floating static route is sufficient.

Take the example in Figure 8-3. If the link between Router A and Router B fails, the traffic will begin to route through the ISDN backup link. Admittedly, this will be a slower path than the T-1 link, but at least the network traffic will still flow instead of coming to a screeching halt.

Cisco Routing and Switching Processes

In this section we will look at the types of routing and switching processes that the Cisco router uses to make its forwarding decisions.

Routing

As we discussed in the beginning of this chapter, "routing" is really a switching process performed by the router. What you may traditionally think of as

Figure 8-3
Floating static route

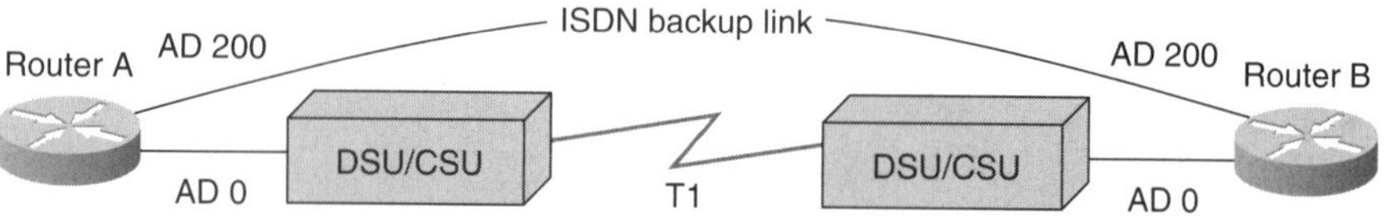

routing is the path determination made by the use of routing algorithms. In this section we will examine the categories of routing protocols and how these categories are important to the selection of the protocol for your network design.

Categorizing Routing Protocols There are many special types of protocols that allow hosts and network devices to communicate and find each other in a network environment. It is important to understand why and where these are needed in order to make your design work. The three basic categories of routing protocols are

- Host routing protocols
- Interior Gateway Protocols (IGP)
- Exterior Gateway Protocols (EGP)

Host Routing Protocols (Host to Router) A host generally finds its gateway router through the static configuration of the default gateway address in its initial setup. The problem with this method is that if the configured gateway fails or changes, each host must be changed or re-routed. There are a couple of alternative methods that may work better, especially in environments where downtime is absolutely unacceptable.

The most popular method of avoiding downtime is the use of *Hot Standby Router Protocol* (HSRP). This protocol allows two or more routers to advertise one address, thus allowing hosts to have a "fall-back" gateway without a configuration change. As long as one of the routers is still up, the host can communicate with it. A lesser-used option is to run Gateway Discovery Protocol (GDP) or ICMP Router Discovery Protocol (IRDP) on a host, allowing it to find a default gateway dynamically.

There are a couple of other options that are rather outdated but which still bear mentioning, because you may come across these issues in your design process.

Hosts can be configured with no default gateway. This essentially means that the host will have to use Address Resolution Protocol (ARP) before communicating with a destination. If a router has that destination in its routing table, it responds with a proxy ARP reply, saying, "Send it to me." The problem is that the router does not know if the destination host is up and reachable when it sends the reply to the source host, therefore the sending device could be sending a steady stream of traffic to a host that is non-responsive.

A final option is to have hosts listening to RIP updates. This is sometimes the case with Unix hosts running the routing daemon or "routed" (pronounced "route D"). This is not necessarily the best way to handle host-to-router communication. For one thing, it means additional overhead for the host, and it also means that if a routing protocol other than RIP is used elsewhere in the network, redistribution into RIP will be necessary in order for the host to accurately find the destinations in the network.

Interior Gateway Protocols *Interior Gateway Protocols* (IGP) are routing protocols that are used to route packets within an *autonomous system* (AS). An AS is a network or group of networks that are all within the same administrative control. An AS is a registered network entity, much like a public IP address.

The types of IGPs are as follows:

- Routing Information Protocol (RIP)
- Interior Gateway Routing Protocol (IGRP)
- Enhanced IGRP (EIGRP)
- Intermediate System-to-Intermediate System (ISIS)
- Open Shortest Path First (OSPF)

Each of these routing protocols will be discussed in detail in future chapters, but the information in Table 8-2 should give you an idea of the differences that exist within this category. Some use *hello packets* to establish the state of their neighbors. Some send routing updates containing route information; some send only link state information. Some protocols are classful but use the prefix in routing updates and tables; others do not. This type of information will be helpful in making the protocol selection for your design.

Table 8-2
Categorizing IGPs

Protocol	Classful?	Uses Hellos?	Topology Update Type	Uses Prefix?
RIPv1	Yes	No	Routes	No
RIPv2	Yes	No	Routes	Yes
IGRP	Yes	No	Routes	No
EIGRP	No	Yes	Routes	Yes
OSPF	No	Yes	Links	Yes
IS-IS	No	Yes	Links	Yes

Exterior Gateway Protocols *Exterior Gateway Protocols* (EGP) are routing protocols that allow different ASs to route traffic to each other. Typically the only EGP you will encounter is Border Gateway Protocol (BGP). In the early 1990s there was another EGP, which was called EGP (same acronym). Because of its lack of scalability, this protocol quickly disappeared in favor of BGP.

The categories of routing protocols are shown in Figure 8-4.

Switching

It is important to understand the types of switching employed by Cisco routers so that you can make the right decision for the network environment. In some cases you will not necessarily want the fastest kind of switching enabled. Take, for example, a situation where data is coming from many very fast interfaces and leaving on a slower interface. Having the fastest kind of switching enabled on the router could cause buffer overflows and overruns. Let's take a closer look at each kind of switching process.

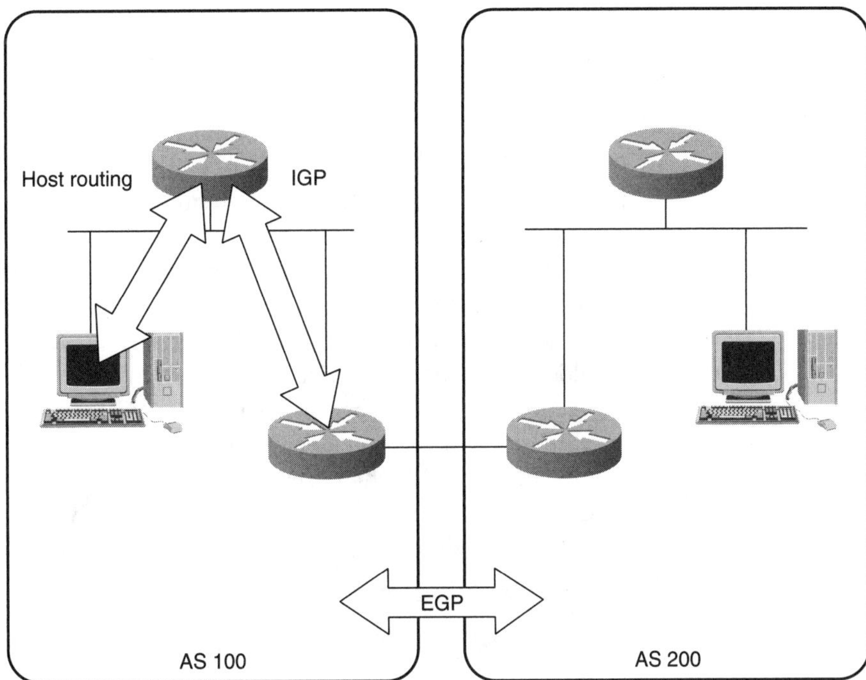

Figure 8-4 Routing protocol categories

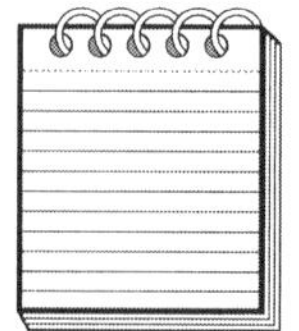

NOTE: Switching is performed on egress (outbound) ports, not ingress (inbound) ports.

Process Switching Process switching is the slowest type of switching process in the router. It can switch traffic by doing packet-by-packet load balancing. For each packet received by the router, a lookup must be performed in the routing table, CPU cycles are spent to do so. The entire overhead takes place in the "brains" of the router, thus slowing down the overall performance.

When process switching is used, access lists configured on a router cause the router performance to decrease dramatically, sometimes by 30 percent or more. Additionally, although load balancing can be performed when the router is using process-switching mode, it is done on a packet-by-packet basis.

As we mentioned in the introduction to this section, there are times when you will want to use a slower switching method such as this. Two examples are

- When moving traffic from a LAN port to a firewall
- When moving traffic from a fast port to a slower port (100 Mbps down to 10 Mbps, for instance)

In moving traffic from the LAN to a firewall, the speed could differ tremendously, and the firewall also must examine the packets closely as it performs its duties. If you are running Gigabit Ethernet in your LAN and connecting to the 100 Mbps port on a firewall, you could experience problems with congestion. The exception would be a firewall between the LAN and the Internet in which a moderate portion of your overall LAN traffic would not be constantly hitting the firewall.

In moving traffic from a fast port—for instance, one that connects to a server farm—to a slower port, such as on a client LAN, you could also experience congestion. If the percentage of overall LAN traffic crossing the link is small, you may have no problems at all. However, we point this out as something to watch out for as you are designing the network. Remember that the network is only as fast as its slowest link.

Fast Switching An improved switching method is fast switching. Fast switching is enabled by default for most protocols on Cisco routers. It load-balances on a destination-by-destination basis, whereas process switching does so on a packet-by-packet basis. Once the first packet to a destination is examined, the remaining packets are "fast-switched" to the destination over the same switching path. The routing table stored in the *Route Switch Processor* (RSP) must be consulted only once, which saves CPU cycles and improves router performance. This switching method is illustrated in Figure 8-5.

Notice that in Figure 8-5 the fast cache learns about how to switch the packet from the process of the RSP writing a copy of the frame header to the fast cache. Once this entry is in the cache, it uses the same header (and information contained within) over and over for the remaining packets in the transmission.

There are three optional fast-switching methods available on various models of Cisco routers. These are

- Autonomous switching
- Silicon switching
- Optimum switching

Autonomous switching is available on 7000 Series routers. It uses a different kind of switching cache—the autonomous-switching cache, appropriately named—to have the packets switched by the CiscoBus controller. Incoming packets do not interrupt system processes.

Silicon switching is similar to autonomous switching, but it uses a *Silicon Switch Processor* (SSP) that contains a silicon-switching cache. Again, system processes are not interrupted. The cache buffers the packets as they come in.

Optimum switching uses an enhanced fast-caching algorithm and the optimum-switching cache, instead of the fast-switching cache model. This feature is available only on routers containing an RSP.

Distributed Switching Distributed switching refers to the method of "off-loading" the packet switching process to the Versatile Interface Processors (VIPs) available on some Cisco routers. Essentially, a subset of the Cisco IOS is running on each of the VIP cards. Each added VIP enhances the router's ability to provide throughput by adding the total switching capacity of the router. The way distributed switching works, as shown in Figure 8-6, is by running the routing algorithm on the RSP only when a new destination is encountered.

One way that distributed switching can work is with Distributed Cisco Express Forwarding (dCEF). With dCEF the *Route Switch Processor* (RSP) dynamically updates the VIPs anytime a change occurs in the routing table.

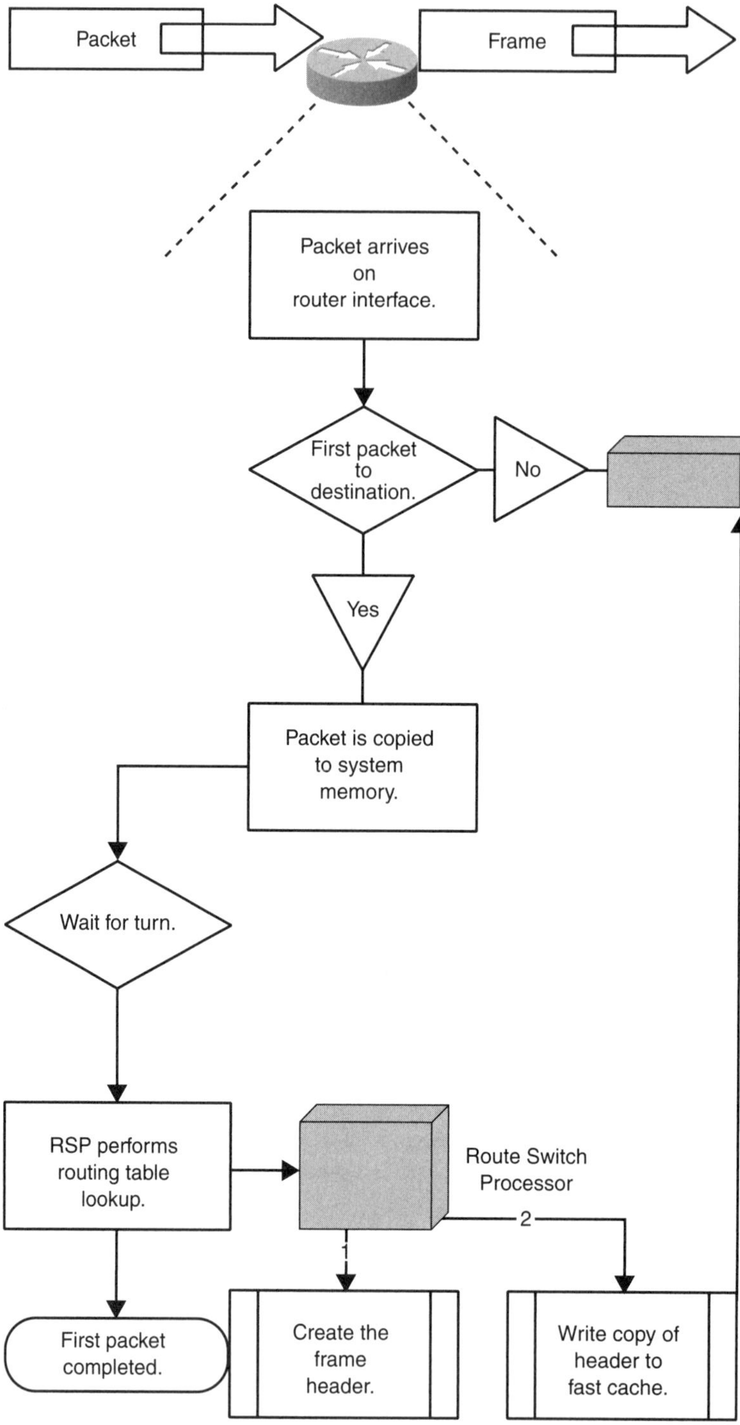

Figure 8-5
Fast switching

Packet

Frame

Packet arrives on router interface.

First packet to destination.

No

Fast cache

Yes

Packet is copied to system memory.

Wait for turn.

RSP performs routing table lookup.

Route Switch Processor

1

2

First packet completed.

Create the frame header.

Write copy of header to fast cache.

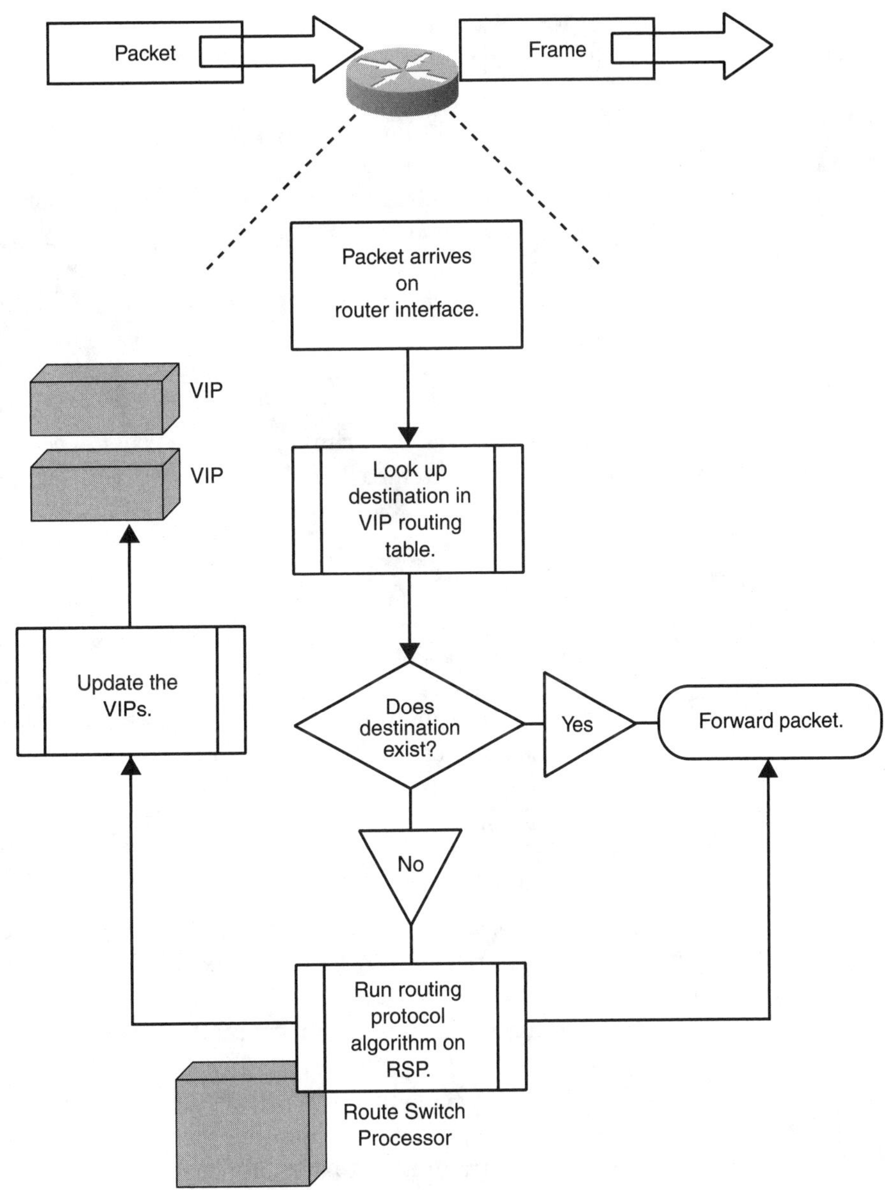

Figure 8-6
Distributed switching

Therefore, the VIP is allowed to do its own layer 3 switching rather than having it done by the RSP. The closer to the port the lookup is done, the less latency there will be in the data transfer. By providing this service, dCEF separates the tasks occurring on the RSP (that is, router control processes) from the tasks (that is, packet switching) that occur on the VIP and port adapters.

NetFlow Switching NetFlow switching is one of the newer types of switching available in Cisco routers. It is generally implemented at the point where the enterprise network meets the Internet, or the Distribution layer of the design, in order to apply services such as security, Quality of Service (QoS), and accounting to packets.

This type of switching creates a "flow," which is something like a reserved space, between a source and destination pair and rapidly switches packets through while applying the policies (security and so on) to the content of the flow. In addition to creating an efficient switching path, NetFlow switching gives the network manager a way to capture bandwidth usage that can later be used in trend analysis, billing, or capacity planning, for example.

NetFlow switching is usually not the best choice for the Core layer of a network design, as the primary function is not necessarily speed. There are faster ways to switch packets in the core, such as Distributed Cisco Express Forwarding.

Routing Overhead

Each type of routing protocol requires a certain amount of router resources in order to function. All of the resources consumed add to the overhead burden of the router. When designing a network, it is very important to examine each possible routing protocol choice in order to make the best selection for your network design.

You will want to find out how the routing updates are transmitted by the protocol. Is a timer used? In other words, are periodic updates sent out? Or are updates triggered by a network event, such as a router failure?

Each routing protocol differs also in the content of the routing updates. Some will send the entire routing table at each update. Some will send only the changes that have occurred since the last update. As you can imagine, the bandwidth consumed by each type of update can vary greatly.

Another issue is to which routers the updates are sent. It is possible that the updates are limited to an autonomous system or a particular area. Or the updates could go to all neighboring routers. Again, the amount of bandwidth and router resources consumed will vary with each protocol.

When we look at the routing protocols in detail during the following chapters, you will have a chance to get to know the behavior of each protocol along with the type of update traffic it generates.

The Routing Table

What types of decisions must a router make when populating the routing table? There are many factors that go into this decision, some of which were covered when we talked about static routes and floating static routes. This section of the chapter focuses on how the dynamic routing protocols add entries to the table.

Metrics and Administrative Distance

Each routing protocol has a type of *metric* that it uses to calculate the best route to a destination. The metric is different for each protocol and its primary function is to differentiate between the paths within a protocol. For instance, if you have several routes to a destination, all learned through RIP, they would all have the same administrative distance, would they not? But are all of the paths equal in cost? They can be. If you remember, the switching process could then perform load balancing over the equal-cost paths.

If the paths are not equal, the routing metric helps decide a hierarchy of best possible paths to a destination. In Figure 8-7, Router A has three unequal paths to Router B. The preferred path would be through the connected serial link with an AD of 0. If that route fails, will the floating static route we configured take over in this instance?

In this case, the answer is probably no. We set the AD high on the floating static route. A value of 201 is a good rule of thumb for a "last resort"

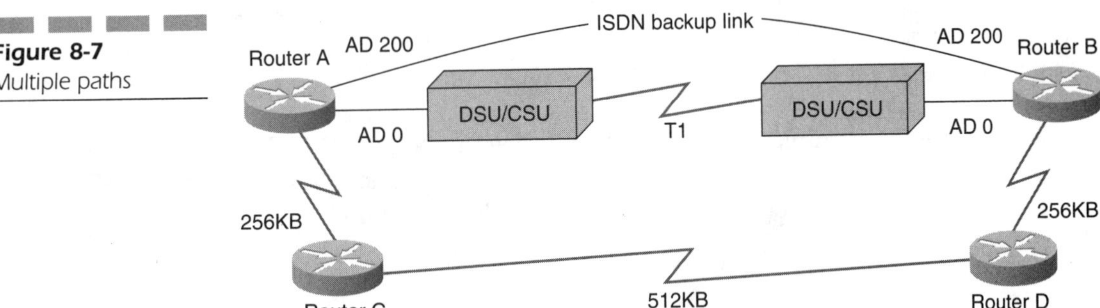

Figure 8-7 Multiple paths

route—one that should have an AD higher than any other possible route. Thus if the dynamic routing protocol should fail, the static route will be used. If we were to apply RIP routing to Figure 8-7, we would see that RIP uses a hop count to determine the best path to Router B from Router A. In addition to having the lowest AD over the serial link, it is only one router *hop*. A hop is counted as the number of routers that traffic must touch in order to get to a destination. In this case, the router touches one more router to reach its destination. If the path were through Routers C and D, however, the hop count would be three, with the RIP administrative distance of 120. It is only if this route goes down that the ISDN backup link will be used.

Scalability and Convergence

Of the work that goes into all of the selections for a network design, planning for scalability and rapid convergence rank toward the top as far as importance is concerned. Some older protocols like RIP and IGRP are not scalable because of the inherent limitations in their protocol design.

For instance, RIP uses a 32-bit hop count for its metric. That would lead you to believe that it can support 2^{32} hops, right? Wrong. RIP can only support 15 hops. After that, a destination is considered unreachable (value of 16). This greatly limits the diameter to which a RIP network can grow. IGRP is slightly more sophisticated. It uses a 24-bit metric that is based on bandwidth and delay on a path.

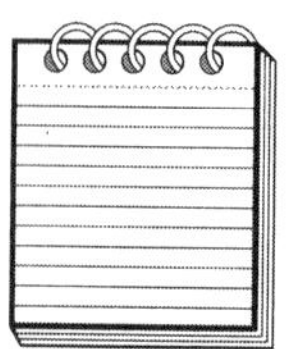

NOTE: *To disable an RIP-learned route, you can set the hop count to 16, which equates to "count to infinity" in the protocol's terms. The destination would be considered unreachable through that path.*

Link state protocols will need to be looked at in a little different way. Take the example in Figure 8-8, for instance. When designing OSPF areas, it will be important bear a few things in mind:

- How many areas?
- How many routers per area?
- How many networks in an area?

Figure 8-8
Link state design

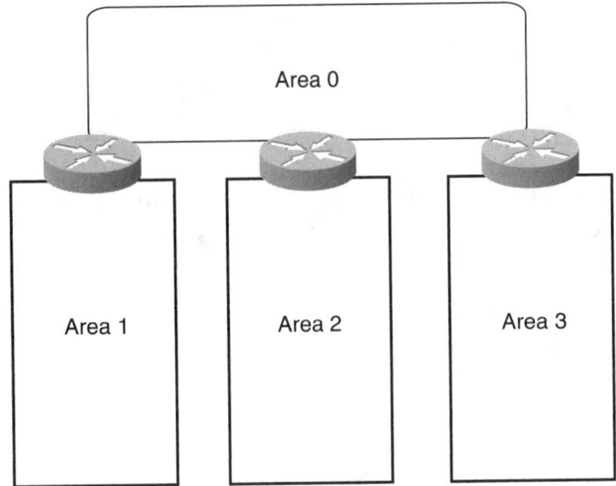

- How is the address space going to be mapped?
- How stable are the links?

The term *convergence* refers to the amount of time it takes for all routers (communicating over a certain protocol) to come to agreement on network reachability. This really takes into account a couple of factors: network diameter and network complexity. The entire autonomous system must converge so that routers know where to send packets. This is one of the reasons why a volatile network or one with a link that is fluctuating between an up and down state (also known as a *route flap*) can become bogged down so quickly. The routers are constantly forced to run the routing algorithms and send updates. Soon, all available router resources and bandwidth are being consumed just by trying to come to agreement on reachability.

Route Summarization

All protocols require efficient use of route summarization. In some ways you are already accustomed to thinking of summarization, probably without knowing it. When you see a host IP address, you know that it is part of a subnet and that it has a gateway within that subnet. The gateway is usually to a router (or other routing device, like a firewall) that knows about the subnet or subnets attached to that interface. That is simple summarization. The gateway knows one route to multiple destinations—in this case, hosts. If this kind of summarization did not already exist, the gateway would have to have an entry in its table for *every single host in that subnet!* Can you imagine how large the table would have to grow? Can you imagine how much memory the gateway would have to have just to be able to reference all those entries?

That is a good place to start when thinking about summarization on a more expanded level. Figure 8-9 shows how each piece fits into a larger part of the puzzle. Keeping summarization consolidated means fewer total entries in the routing table, which reduces its overall size. This lends itself well to rapid convergence.

Figure 8-9 Summarization hierarchy

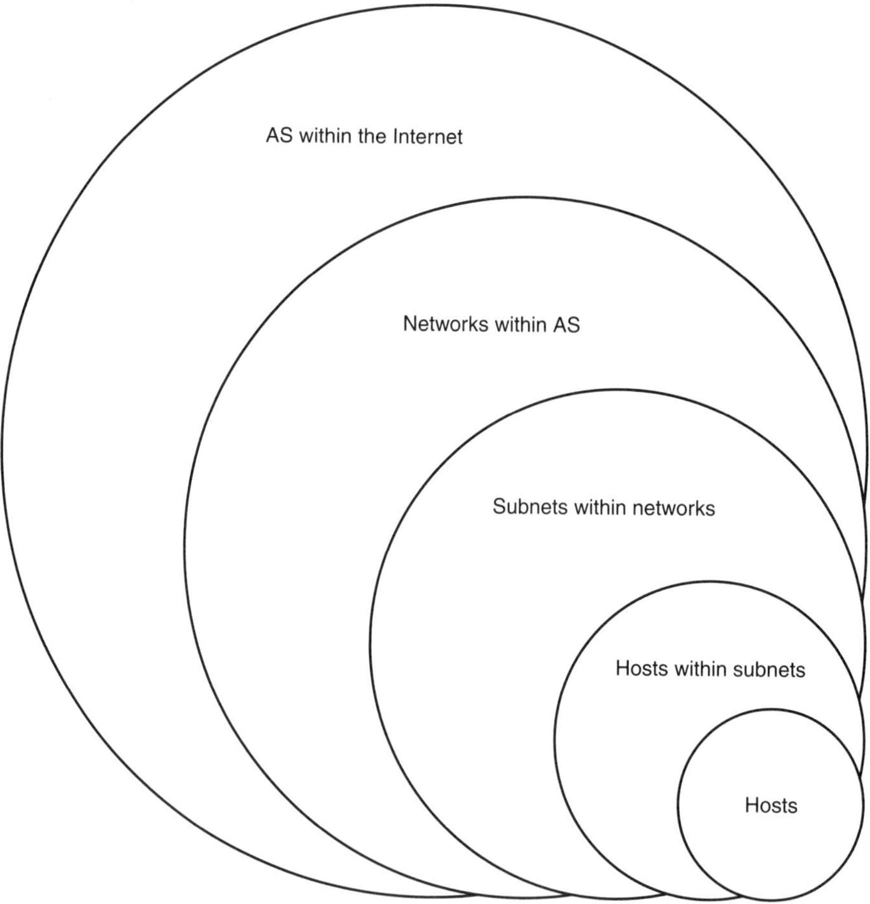

Convergence

As we said earlier in this chapter, convergence is the amount of time it takes for all routers to agree on network reachability. Summarization of routes aids this process by keeping the routing tables small.

Another way to understand convergence is that it is the time that passes until a router starts using a new route either after a failure or when a new route is introduced. During that time, all routers within an autonomous system will be coming to an understanding of the new network topology. They do this by exchanging information with other routers, running routing algorithms, and updating their own routing table and databases, if applicable. During this convergence period, packets may not reliably reach their destination and applications have to wait to continue sending and receiving information. It is likely that the network users will begin to complain if this process takes too long.

Fault Detection

A fault must first be detected in the network before routers must re-converge. How long it takes to determine a link failure and how this is detected depend upon the topology in use. The following conditions are required to trigger the actions needed to find a new route:

- Serial Lines
  - Carrier detection is lost, *or*
  - Two to three keepalives are missed (keepalives are at 10-second intervals by default)
- Ring-Based
  - Once a ring has a problem, the end-stations start beaconing, which signals a failure
- Ethernet
  - Two or three keepalives are missed, *or*
  - Local or transceiver failure (immediate)
- Routing Protocol Hellos
  - Missed hello packets take precedence over missed keepalive packets if the hello timer period is shorter than the keepalive timer

Distance Vector Protocols A distance vector protocol uses update timers to determine how often updates should be sent (and received) from adjacent routers. Therefore, if a link failure occurs, the router will not notify other routers until the update timer has expired—or in some cases, multiple update periods must pass before a failure is assumed! Another factor in distance vector network convergence is the total diameter, in hops, of the network. These two factors are key.

The best way to ensure faster convergence in a distance vector network is to use equal-cost multiple paths. In Figure 8-10 we can see that three equal-cost paths (all are three hops) from Router A to Router E exist. If

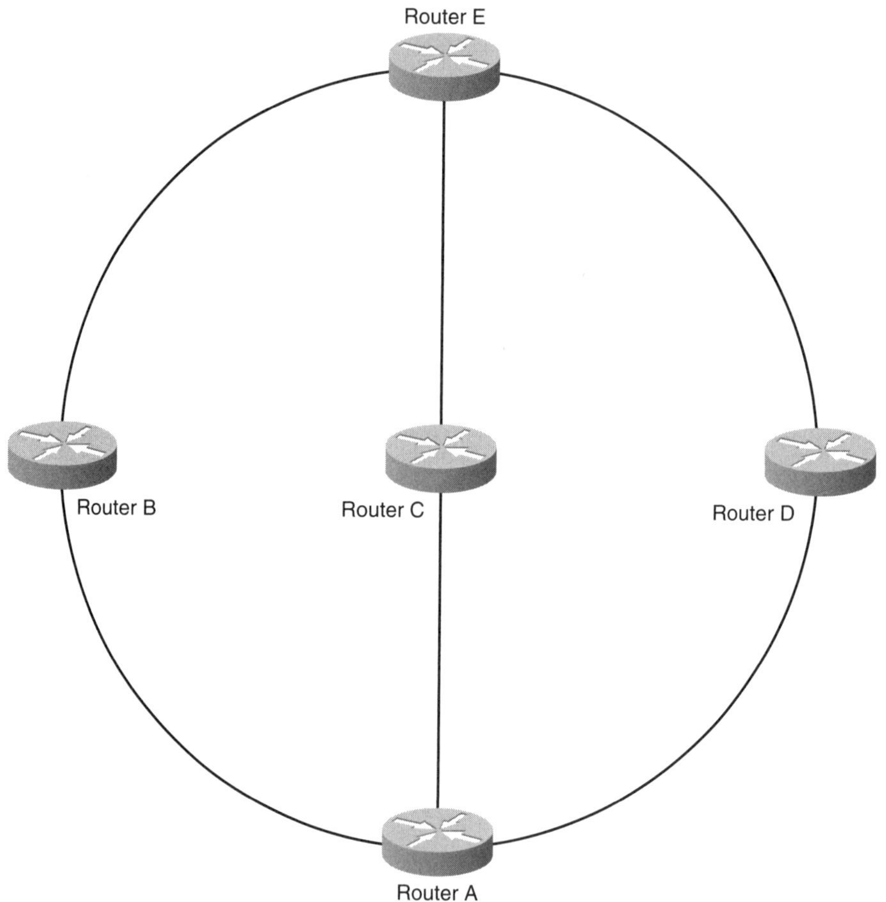

Figure 8-10 Distance vector convergence

Router A is primarily going through Router B to get to Router E and the link to Router B fails, there are two other paths that are ready to go. The traffic can be re-routed immediately.

TIP: Implement equal-cost multiple paths in your distance vector designs to reduce the impact of a link failure.

Link-State Protocols Link-state protocols do not wait for an update timer to expire before they notify their neighbors that a link is down. They do it right away. You can think of it as your own neighborhood. In one house a neighbor looks out the window and sees smoke coming from the house across the street. That neighbor tries to call the owners of the house. Then he tries knocking on their door. Then he tries to call again. After all of these attempts with no response, the neighbor calls 911.

In the house next door, another neighbor has spotted the smoke. He calls 911 right away. This allows the fire trucks to arrive more quickly. Perhaps that is overly simplistic, but you get the general idea. The smoke triggered a reaction in both neighbors, but the reaction was different.

The link-state neighbor is the one who called 911 right away, or in the case of networking, he sent a Link-State Advertisement (LSA) right away to all of his neighbors and to the backbone area routers. Those neighbors then had reactions of their own. They all ran routing algorithms to build a new routing table of their own. The entire process takes seconds instead of minutes.

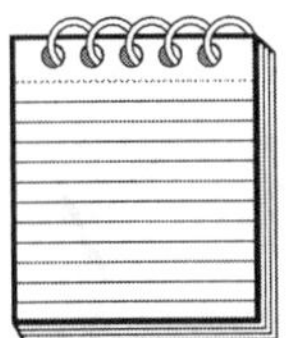

NOTE: Link-state protocols will also converge faster if you implement equal-cost multiple paths between them.

Routing Loops

A routing loop is a disagreement between routers about the path to a destination. This can be humanly caused by a mistake in the router configuration, or it can be caused because the routing algorithm has not converged. Most routing loops, if due to topology changes, will usually work themselves out. Manually caused routing loops will not.

In Figure 8-11, a routing loop has occurred that is probably caused due to the link failures seen between Routers B and D to Router E. Because not all routers have updated their tables, they are sending the packets in a round-robin fashion. IP datagrams can keep going through up to 255 nodes, so there is a chance that the packets will finally reach Router E, if convergence occurs soon in this network.

Distance vector protocols can use holddown timers, split horizon, and poison reverse as methods to prevent routing loops. These terms will be explained in further detail in the following section.

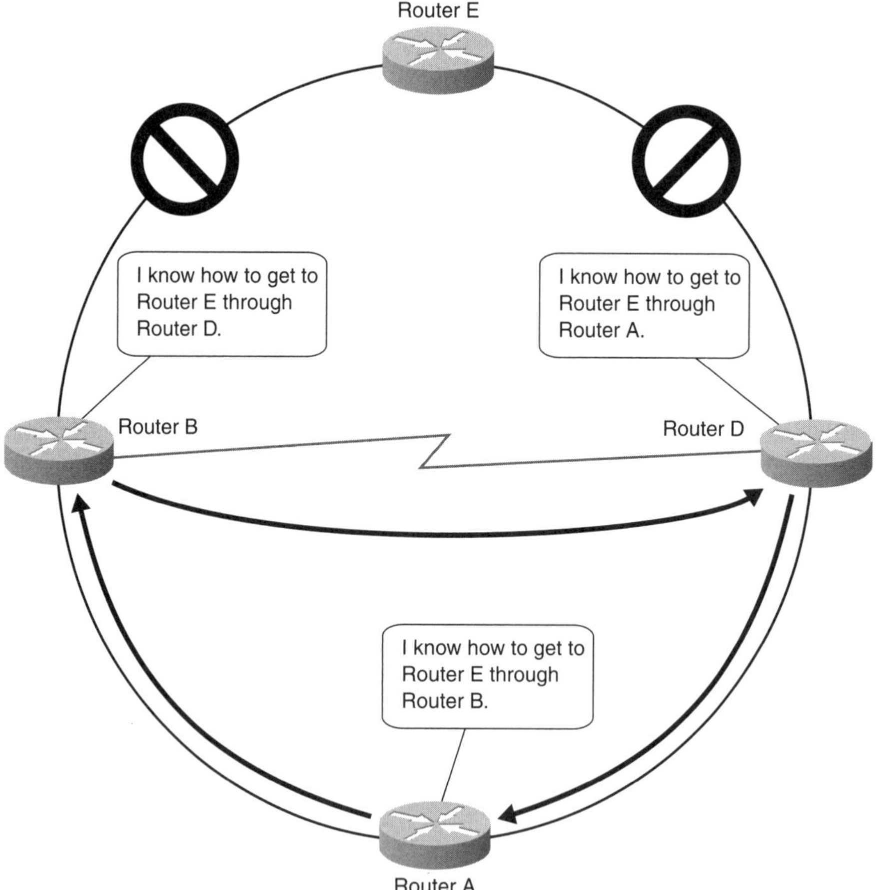
Router E
I know how to get to
Router E through
Router D.
I know how to get to
Router E through
Router A.
Router B
Router D
I know how to get to
Router E through
Router B.
Router A

Figure 8-11 Routing loop

Link-state protocols tend to converge more quickly than distance vector protocols and provide reliable link-state updates in order to help prevent routing loops.

A routing loop caused by static or default routes that were manually entered will continue until an administrator discovers the problem and corrects it in the router configuration. This is a good reason not to use manual routing methods unless it is absolutely necessary.

Preventing Routing Loops

Distance vector protocols, as stated above, can use several methods to help prevent or short-circuit a routing loop.

Split Horizon Split horizon is a way of preventing a router from advertising a route to the same neighbor from which it learned the route. This helps prevent the two routers from becoming confused and routing the same packets back and forth to each other, which is called a "straight-line" routing loop, as shown in Figure 8-12. This simply means that two routers are passing the traffic back and forth between themselves, each with a routing table entry that says, "Send traffic to this destination through that router." Router A advertises its routing table containing the path to *destination x*. Router B now adds that entry to its routing table. Without split horizon configured, Router B will mistakenly advertise that it knows a path to *destination x*. Router A could end up sending that traffic to Router B. Router B would in turn send it back to Router A (from where it learned about the path).

Figure 8-12 Routing without split horizon

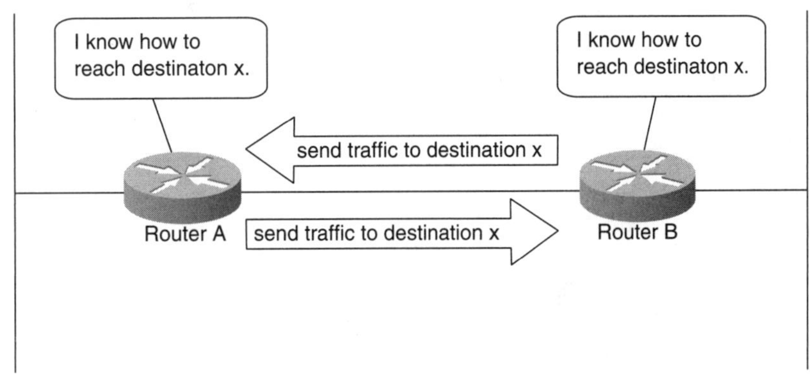
I know how to
reach destinaton x.
I know how to
reach destinaton x.
destination x
send traffic to destination x
Router A
send traffic to destination x
Router B

Split horizon is configured to prevent the router from advertising a route back to its original source. In other words, if Router A advertises that it knows how to reach *destination x,* then Router B won't advertise to Router A that it (Router B) *also* knows how to get to *destination x*-unless it is through a path other than Router A.

Holddown Timers Larger, more general, routing loops can be prevented with the use of holddowns. A holddown occurs when a route fails. A router will place the route into a holddown state, and a timer will start-the holddown timer. During the timed period, the router will ignore all advertised paths to the route it knows to be down. This period of time is usually long enough to allow the changed route information to propagate to all routers in the autonomous system. Convergence time will be at least as long as the holddown time.

In Figure 8-13 Router C has noticed that the route to *destination x* has failed. If Router C listens to advertisements about that network from any of

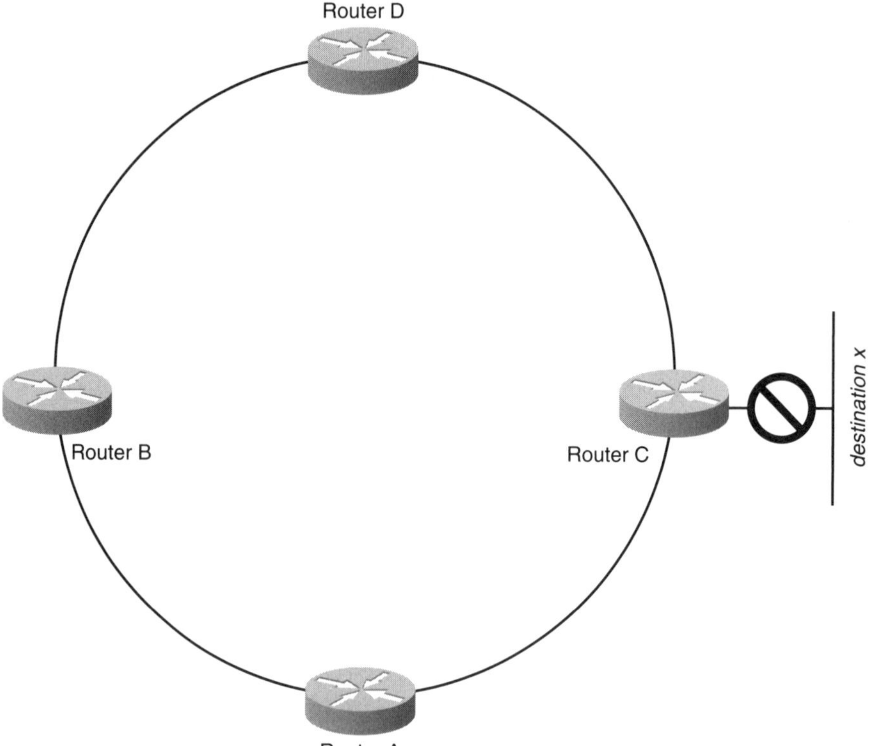

Figure 8-13 Holddowns

its neighboring routers, it might believe that the link is really still up. There is a possibility of a routing loop.

In the case of Figure 8-13, Router C will stop listening to any of its neighbors advertising routes to *destination x* for the period of time when the holddown is active.

NOTE: *Setting the holddown timer to a lower value can decrease convergence times but risks an increase in the possibility of temporary routing loops.*

Poison Reverse In addition to the use of holddowns, the routing protocol can have poison reverse enabled. Simply put, *poison reverse* says to see a route as unreachable and advertise it as unreachable, rather than just ignoring it. It does this by setting a *poison metric*, which is a maximum reachability value. This helps prevent routing loops of a broader nature.

Route Redistribution

Redistribution takes place in the router software. It allows the exchange of routing information between different protocols, sometimes within the same major network. You may also want to use redistribution for an environment where hosts are running RIP and the rest of the network is running another protocol, like OSPF, for instance. There are some pitfalls you will need to watch for, and we will discuss those at the end of this section.

Between Protocols

In redistribution between protocols, one router is a participant in two (or more) separate routing processes. An internal process running in the IOS takes routes learned through one protocol and shares them with the other. In Figure 8-14 the router is participating in and learning routes from both RIP and OSPF. Redistribution shares the routes between the two protocols.

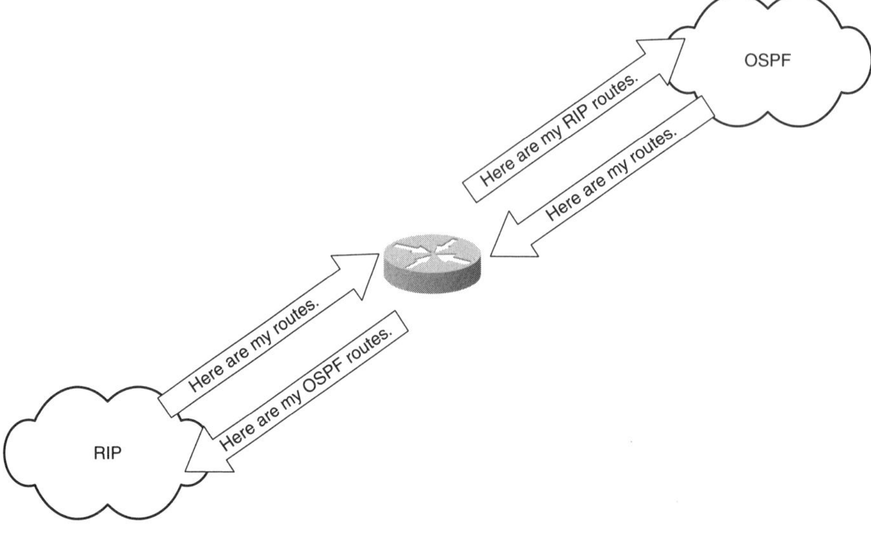

Figure 8-14 Redistribution between protocols

Within the Same Network

When more than one routing protocol is running within the same major network number, you may want to block advertisements between the protocols while still redistributing subnet information. In Figure 8-15, you will notice that the same networks exist in the RIP and OSPF processes. By using the **passive-interface type | slot/port** command in the router, you can prevent the routes learned from RIP from being redistributed into OSPF and vice versa.

Subnet information should be redistributed within the same major network number, but in some instances you will need to force it. This can happen in the example used in Figure 8-15, when redistributing between RIP and OSPF. In this instance, you would need to use the **subnets** keyword in the redistribution statement, as shown here:

```
router ospf x
redistribute rip subnets
```

The *subnets* keyword in OSPF tells the process to redistribute all subnet routes. The default behavior would be to redistribute only unsubnetted routes.

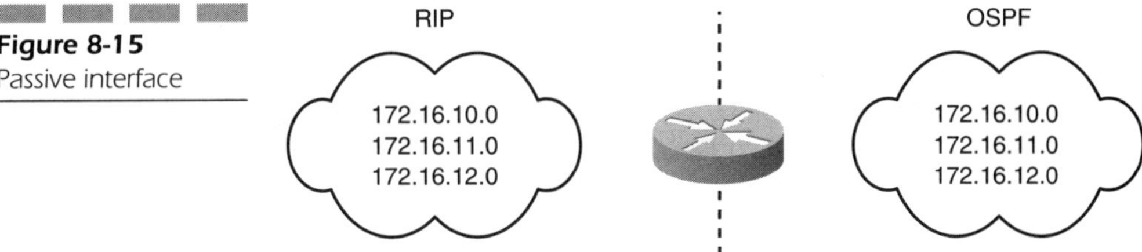

Figure 8-15 Passive interface

RIP for Hosts

When Unix workstations in the network need to receive RIP routing updates in order to build their own routing table, routes learned from other protocols will need to be redistributed into RIP. This would work the same way as illustrated in Figure 8-14 if Unix workstations in the RIP cloud are running **routed -q**. The -q qualifier puts the Unix host interface into passive, or listening-only, mode.

NOTE: *Make sure that the Unix workstations are not advertising routes which can then be redistributed into other routing processes. The passive mode of routed can accomplish this. Another way to block any possible advertisements caused by workstation misconfiguration is to put filters on received routing updates.*

Inconsistencies During Redistribution

Care must be taken during the configuration of redistribution to take into account differences between routing protocols. One such difference is the way default routes are handled. For instance, RIP understands that a route to 0.0.0.0 is a default route, or a route that is to be used if no more specific route exists. IGRP, on the other hand, can use different networks for candidate default routes. In Figure 8-16, the IGRP routing process has two different candidate default routes. When the IGRP routes are redistributed into RIP, the default route should translate to 0.0.0.0. If not, then a default route can be manually configured.

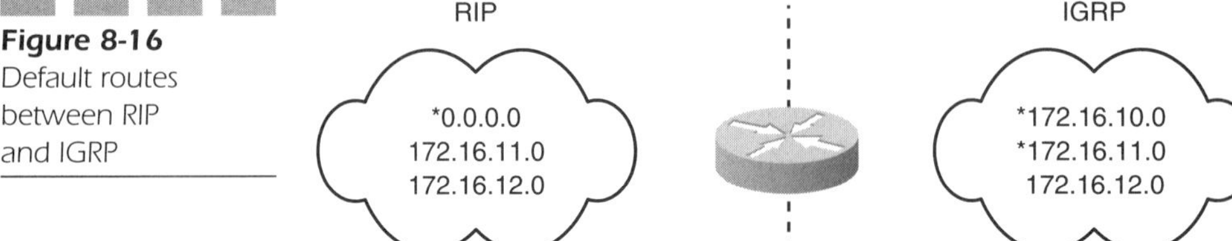

Figure 8-16 Default routes between RIP and IGRP

Avoiding Redistribution Feedback

Another problem when redistributing between different protocols is that each protocol uses a different metric for routing decisions. You must set a value for the default-metric in RIP so that all redistributed routes will use that metric. In the example shown in Figure 8-16, IGRP routes redistributed into RIP will be given a hop count of one, unless the value for the default-metric is changed.

Problems can also occur when protocols are performing mutual redistribution. In such a case, it is prudent to use filters on the routing updates in order to prevent routes originating in one protocol to be advertised back into the same protocol. The original metric information is lost, which could cause problems, and as we saw earlier in this chapter, routing loops can occur. By imposing split horizon, route filters, or route maps, the protocols will be selective about what they send and receive. Take a look at Figure 8-17. Several routers are listening to RIP and IGRP processes. RIP is filtering its updates to exclude a route it learned from IGRP from being readvertised to IGRP. Likewise, IGRP is filtering out routes learned from RIP. This is another way to help prevent "feedback" from occurring.

In addition to or instead of using the methods of split horizon and update filters, you may also use access lists to change the administrative distance on a route that is coming back into a protocol. In this way, if RIP tells IGRP that it knows a route to 172.16.11.0 (which IGRP already knows about), access lists can set the administrative distance high—to, say, 200—in order to have a possible alternate path, but only in the rarest of cases.

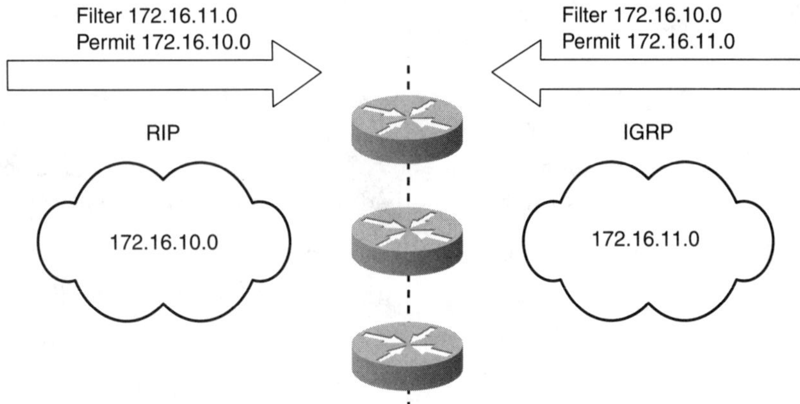

Figure 8-17 Mutual redistribution

Study Hints

A lot of material has been covered in this chapter. Here are areas that you should review before attempting any Cisco network design certification tests:

- **Switching Processes** Study each type of switching to determine how the flow of the packets is different. Learn the ways that each type of switching affects load balancing.
- **Differences Between Protocols** Each protocol has different categories and characteristics that affect the way it behaves both alone and with other routing protocols.
- **Route Redistribution** Too many individuals attempting the tests do not fully understand how to redistribute routes, including how to apply metrics and prevent feedback.
- **Practice Labs** When possible, gain access to online practice labs and hands-on practical labs in order to further understand how processes work in a "live" network. If possible, use a modeling tool like Cisco NetSys to artificially cause routing problems. This is a great way to see what effect a routing loop would have, for instance, or to simulate a failure. Theory is great, but practice makes perfect!

CCDP Tips

This section contains an abbreviated list of topics covered in this chapter. Think of this section as the equivalent of reading Cliff's Notes™ instead of reading an entire book. You will get the general idea of the chapter but will benefit more from reading the chapter in its entirety.

- Analyzing Requirements
  - Is the network 100 percent Cisco equipment?
  - How likely is it that the business will acquire another company?
  - What is the growth projection over the next five to ten years?
  - Will the current network have to communicate with other autonomous systems (AS)?
  - Is support for Variable Length Subnet Masking (VLSM) important?
  - What protocols must be used to support existing legacy systems and routers?
  - How well is the network handling the traffic created by the current routing protocol, if applicable?
  - How quickly can the current routing protocol, if applicable, adapt to changes in the network?
- Router Processes
  - Switching packets
  - Path determination through:
  - Static routing entries
  - Configuration and state of local interfaces
  - Dynamic routing protocols and routing metrics
  - ARP and Inverse ARP
  - Redistributed routes between routing protocols
  - Applied routing policies
- Ways to Populate the Routing Table
  - Static route
  - Floating static route
  - Dynamic routing protocols

- Categories of Routing Protocols
  - Host routing protocols (host-to-gateway)
  - Interior Gateway Protocols (IGPs) (gateway-to-gateway, internal-to-one autonomous system [AS])
  - Exterior Gateway Protocols (EGPs) (gateway-to-gateway, between autonomous systems [ASs])
- Ways to Switch Packets
  - Process switching
  - Fast switching (autonomous, silicon, optimum)
  - Distributed
  - NetFlow
- Sources of Routing Overhead
  - Type of updates
  - Frequency of updates
  - Content of updates
  - Audience of updates
- Factors that Affect Dynamic Routing Table Entries
  - cMetric and administrative distance
  - Scalability and convergence
  - Route summarization
- Factors Affecting Convergence
  - Fault detection
  - Routing loops
  - Route redistribution

Summary

This chapter has given you a solid base of information about the categories and characteristics of routing protocols we will study in the next few focal chapters. We also introduced you to some of the concepts you could encounter when a network design fails to address certain key issues related to the protocols. Additionally, we covered some of the decision-making that surrounds selection of a protocol.

In the following chapters, we will dig deeper into the individual routing protocols so that you will gain an even better understanding of which one may be right for your network design.

Bibliography

Configuring IP Routing Protocols—Cisco Systems CCO Online, **http://www.cisco.com/univercd/cc/td/doc/product/software/ios11/cbook/ciproute.htm**

RIP and OSPF Redistribution—Cisco Systems CCO Online **http://www.cisco.com/univercd/cc/td/doc/cisintwk/ics/cs001.htm**

CHAPTER 9

OSPF Network Design

Overview

The first of the dynamic routing protocols that will we address is Open Shortest Path First (OSPF). In addition to breaking it down to its basic components, we will explore the functions of OSPF, the benefits of its use, and the ways in which it is applied in network design. By the end of the chapter, you will have a better idea of how and when to use OSPF, and of the types of issues you may face when implementing it.

OSPF Protocol

OSPF is a hierarchical, link-state routing protocol that uses cost as its metric. It is said to be a link-state protocol because it bases its reachability information on whether or not a link is in an "up" state. The OSPF protocol is documented in RFC 2178.

First introduced in the late 1980s, OSPF addressed many of the shortfalls of the popular Routing Information Protocol (RIP), such as:

- Exceeding the 15-hop distance limit imposed by RIP
- Providing support for Variable Length Subnet Masking (VLSM) to make better use of address space.
- Speeding up network convergence times
- Reduction of wasted bandwidth used by periodic broadcasts of the routing tables

OSPF is a complex, link-state routing protocol that uses a rather simple *area* concept in its design. Routers are grouped into areas that, either directly or indirectly, attach to the backbone area. The backbone is universally accepted as being Area 0. In Figure 9-1, we have Area 0, to which all of the routers are attached, and Areas 1 through 3, which are segregated from each other. By keeping the areas separate, each area can maintain its own rather small topology and link-state database, as compared to Area 0, which must keep tabs on the entire network.

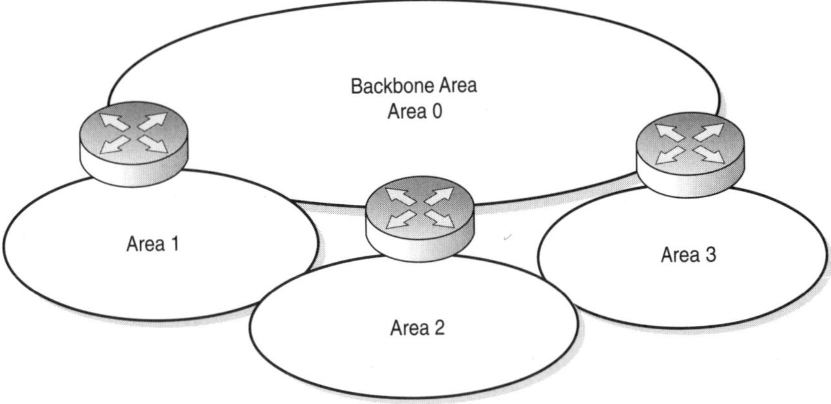

Figure 9-1
OSPF areas

DESIGN RULE: *Keep the number of routers in an area to no more than 50 to 100—on the smaller end for the backbone area. By keeping the number of routers low, you can reduce the overhead and router database size within the area. Reduced overhead and database size helps ensure efficient routing and fast convergence.*

Part of the function of the protocol itself is contained within its name. "Shortest Path First" is a statement that not only describes the path that the protocol will prefer but also refers to the algorithm that is used for path calculations. The Dijkstra algorithm, also known as the Shortest Path First (SPF) algorithm, calculates the shortest path known to the router based on the information it has. We will discuss this process again later in this section when talking about link-state advertisements.

In this section we will introduce the network types that can be used with OSPF. Certain router types are also part of the terminology of OSPF. Their names, you will find, describe their unique function within the network design. These will be discussed and shown within a design.

OSPF Path Cost

OSPF uses *cost* as its routing metric. No discussion of OSPF is complete without an explanation of how path cost is calculated. Cost is really a way to describe the amount of overhead that will be incurred when trying to send data over a link. The amount of effort required to send data over a 56 Kbps link, for example, is greater than over a T1 (1.544 Mbps) link. The cost of an interface is almost always based on bandwidth, although cost is also manually configurable. The formula for calculating the cost is

10^8/bandwidth in bps = cost

An example would be 1000000000 / 15440000= 64 for a T1 line cost. For a 56 Kbps line, on the other hand, the formula would be 1000000000 / 56000, which would equal a cost of 17857. OSPF prefers the lowest cost route when making a routing decision. As you will see later in this chapter, there are ways to modify the cost of a link by modifying the bandwidth on which OSPF bases its calculation.

Network Types

There are several types of network connections that work well for OSPF. You will see these used throughout this chapter and your internetworking career. They are

- Point-to-Point
- Broadcast Multi-Access
- Non-Broadcast Multi-Access

The Point-to-Point network connection, shown in Figure 9-2, is a simple concept. The router says, "Hey, it's just me, you, and the wire!" One router knows about the other as its only other neighbor on that path, although both can communicate independently with other OSPF routers to which they are connected by other interfaces.

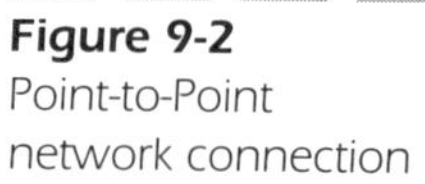

Figure 9-2 Point-to-Point network connection

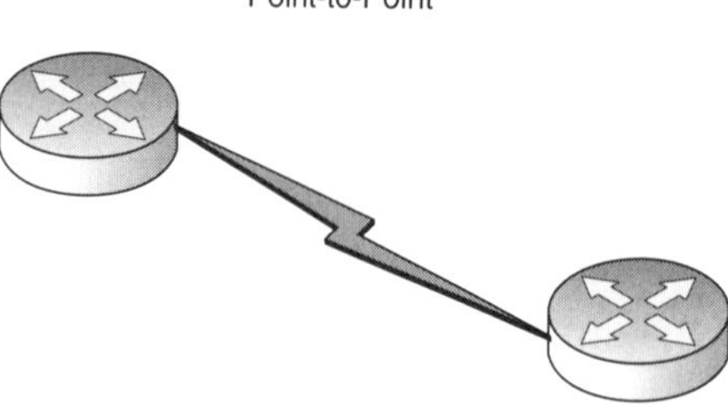

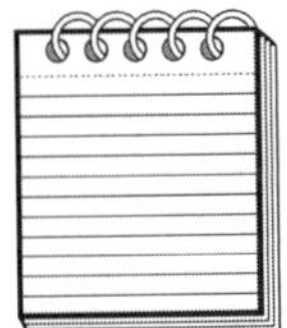

NOTE: In OSPF networks, a neighbor can be defined as one of any number of routers sharing a common OSPF area.

In a Broadcast Multi-Access network, like the one shown in Figure 9-3, the network elects a king, so to speak—the *Designated Router* (DR). The DR is the spokesperson for the network, establishing communication with other networks and speaking on behalf of the other routers within the immediate network. The neighbors in this type of network learn about each other through multicast communications with the DR.

NOTE: There are two Class D addresses reserved for use in OSPF router communication. All OSPF-speaking routers must be able to send and receive on 224.0.0.5. All DRs and BDRs use 224.0.0.6 for their "private" communication.

In a *Non-Broadcast Multi-Access* (NBMA) network (such as through a Frame Relay cloud), neighbors cannot use broadcast or multicast to learn about each other. They must learn about each other through static configuration of the network. A typical NBMA network is shown in Figure 9-4.

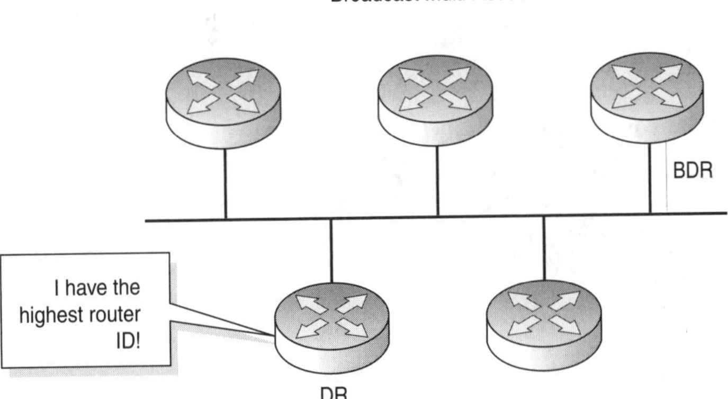

Figure 9-3 Broadcast Multi-Access network connection

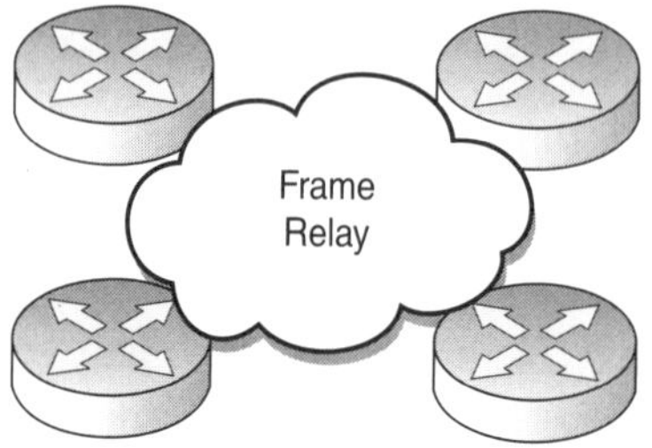

Figure 9-4 NBMA

OSPF Router Types

OSPF also has a certain, specialized router terminology that is used to describe the function and classification of "router types" within an OSPF routing domain (that is, the AS). Bear in mind that these can be any kind of Cisco router. What we mean by "router type" is not that the router has to be a certain model, but that the router has a certain function within the OSPF hierarchy. Figure 9-5 shows a sample OSPF design and the router types as they are contained within.

The simplest classification of OSPF router is the *internal router*. This classification simply describes a router that exists within an area and which has all of its interfaces within the same area. An internal OSPF router will have a single link-state database for the area in which it belongs.

An *Area Border Router* (ABR) is a router that has interfaces in multiple areas. The ABR is also treated as an internal router to the areas of which it is a member. The ABR will have a link-state database and topology database for each of these areas. Therefore, Cisco recommends that you should not have an ABR participating in more than three areas. Even the most robust routers would be overburdened with more than three.

A *backbone router* is any router (including internal routers and ABRs) that has an interface connected to the backbone area (Area 0). Note that a router that has all of its interfaces within the backbone area is an internal router to Area 0.

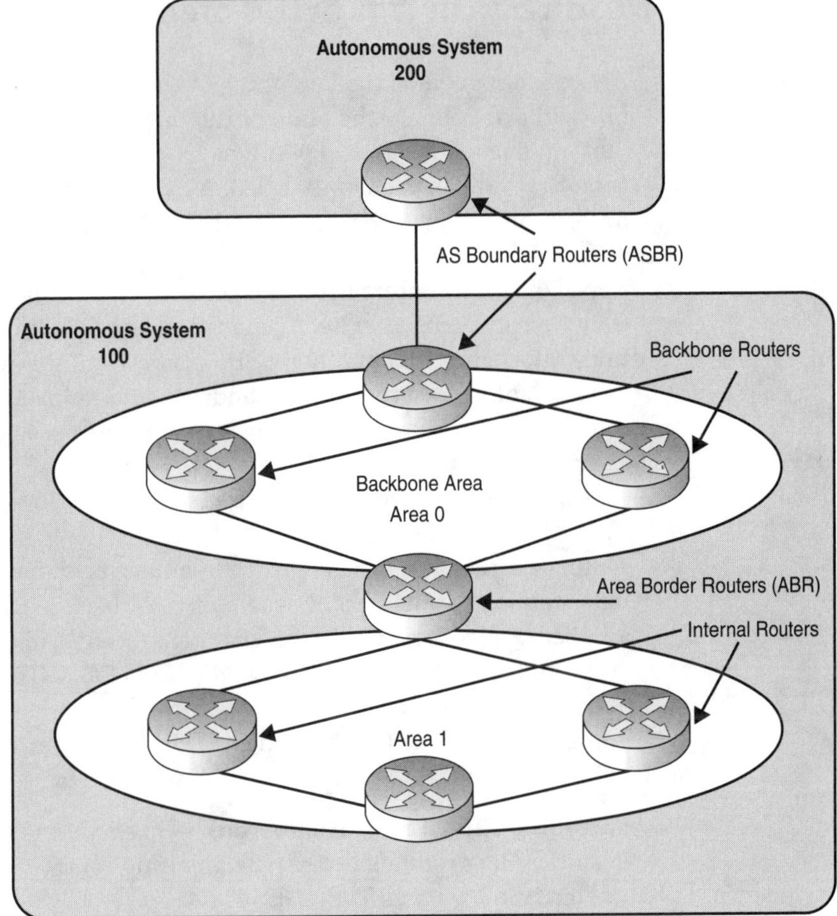

Figure 9-5
OSPF router types

Finally, the autonomous system boundary router (ASBR) is a router that exchanges routing information between different autonomous systems. This router type can also be called a *redistribution router*, because in such case it acts as an ASBR between OSPF and other protocols, such as EIGRP or RIP.

Link-State Advertisements (LSA)

As we mentioned at the beginning of this section, OSPF bases its reachability information on the state of the links in each area. It uses link information shared with it by other OSPF routers that is contained in Link-State Advertisements (LSA). As you will learn in this section, LSAs are specialized packets that communicate information about the status of different types of links.

Neighboring routers flood an LSA to all of their neighbors in order when they first initialize or when a change occurs to a link state. The LSA contains information about other OSPF routers and the links being advertised, such as interface type, the IP address and subnet mask, and the other routers that it knows about. An LSA from a router contains information about all of its interfaces.

When a router receives an LSA, it stores the information in its own *link-state database* and forwards an LSA to its neighbors. This goes on until all routers participating in an OSPF area have been notified of the link-state information. At that point, the network becomes free of LSAs unless another change is noted. The information received in the LSA also helps the OSPF process to build a *topology database* of all of the neighboring routers and interfaces it knows about. This topology database is like a map of the autonomous system (AS) for which OSPF is the routing protocol.

The types of LSAs that a router may receive are

- **Router Link LSA (Intra-Area)** This LSA has information about the sending router's links to neighboring routers within the same area. This is known as a Type 1 LSA.
- **Network Link LSA (Generated by the Designated Router)** This LSA lists routers connected within a segment of the network. This is known as a Type 2 LSA.
- **Summary Link LSA (Forwarded by ABR)** This LSA provides information on routes to networks that are reachable beyond the current area (Type 3 LSA) and can be used in route aggregation. The ABR also propagates information about routes to the ASBR (Type 4 LSA). This helps routers within an area learn about external AS destinations.
- **External Link LSA** This LSA describes links from another AS or routing protocol. An external link LSA is usually originated by an

ASBR. This is known as a Type 5 LSA and is flooded everywhere except stub areas. We will discuss stub areas later in this chapter.

As you can see in Figure 9-6, OSPF routers are given information that originates from various sources. Each time any LSA is received, the process of updating the link-state database happens all over again. It is because of this behavior that OSPF convergence is costly in terms of CPU utilization on the participating routers as well as bandwidth utilization in the entire OSPF network.

Figure 9-6 Link-State Advertisements

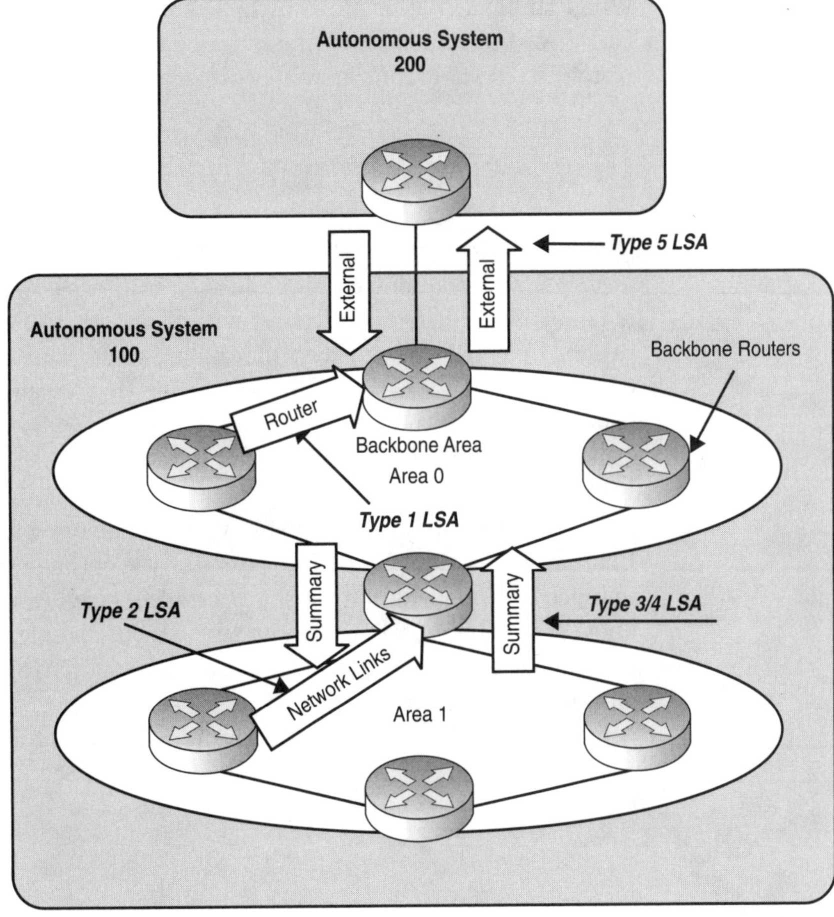

NOTE: *An interface that is having problems, such as a route flap condition, can have a catastrophic effect on an OSPF network. The repeated LSAs would cause routers to continually have to recompute their routing table and possibly never converge. To address this issue, the* **spf holdtime** *command was added. By default, routers are prevented from recalculating the routing table more often than every ten seconds. The* **spf holddown timer** *is a configurable timer.*

Once the routers have updated the link-state database, they calculate the shortest path to each known destination in the network by running the Dijkstra algorithm, also known as the Shortest Path First (SPF) algorithm. When this calculation is run, the resulting information is placed in the OSPF routing table. The link-state update process is shown in Figure 9-7. Note that the new routing table overwrites the old routing table.

Designated and Backup Designated Routers

Designated Routers (DRs) are elected through the use of the hello protocol (over multicast) and are unique to the multi-access environment, as there is no use for a designated router within a Point-to-Point network configuration. In OSPF multi-access networks, every network has a DR and a backup DR (BDR). As we stated earlier in this chapter, the DR is the spokesperson for the network, meaning that it sends LSAs on behalf of the other routers in the network. It also acts as a consolidation point for other LSAs.

Every router in an area must have an adjacency to the DR and the BDR. In other words, like political representatives of the other routers, they have to touch in some way so that the DR and BDR know everything there is to know about the routers they represent. (If only politicians were so well connected to their constituents!) As you can see in Figure 9-8, the DR keeps the adjacency relationship open by the use of hello packets exchanged, by default, every 10 seconds with adjacent routers.

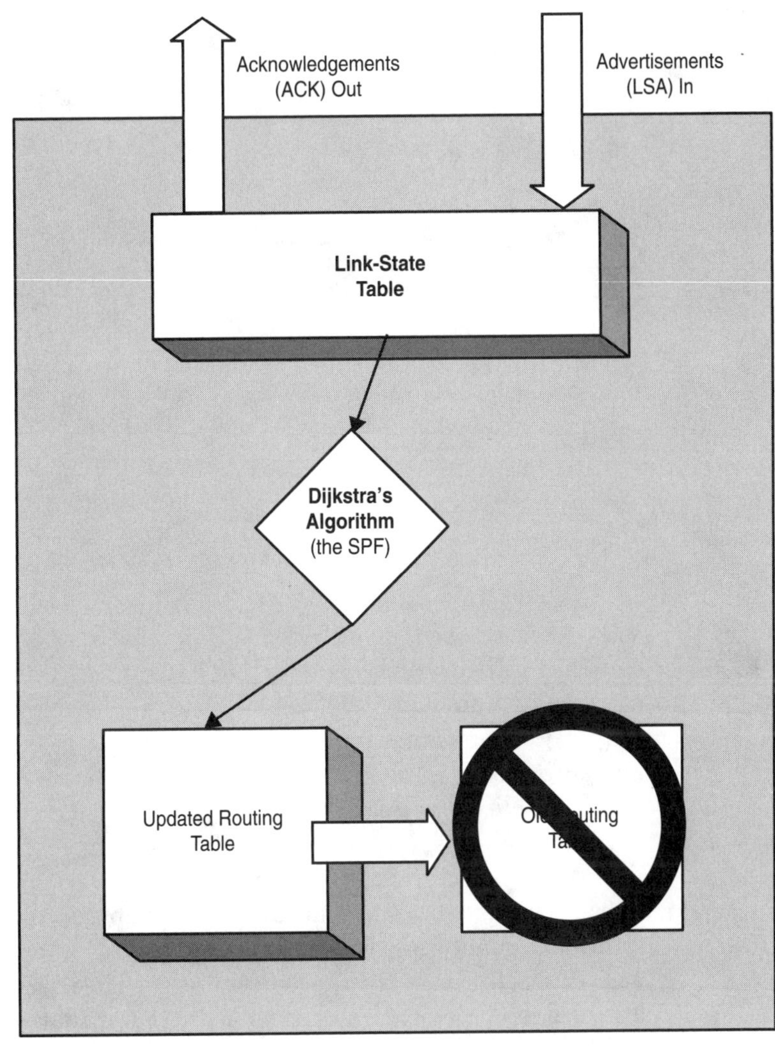

Figure 9-7
Link-state update process

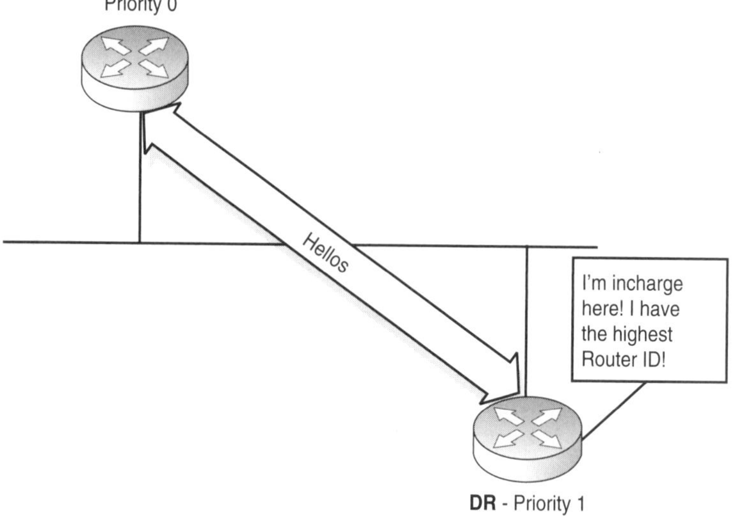
Priority 0
Hellos
I'm incharge here! I have the highest Router ID!
DR - Priority 1

Figure 9-8 DR on a multi-access connection

TIP: *A word about neighbors and adjacencies! OSPF neighbors are classified as two or more routers that have at least one interface in a common network area. Adjacencies are formed between neighbors so that they can exchange information on routes. In general, an adjacency will be formed if either of the routers in question is a DR or BDR, or if connectivity between the two neighbors is via a virtual or point-to-point link.*

The DR remains "in charge" of the communications to and from the multi-access network. A DR can be any router in an area that is up and operational first (usually the fastest router). The BDR is the next router up. The election process then begins for the router that will be next in line for the BDR throne, so to speak. This is provided the routers in question not have a *priority* of 0! Any router with a priority of 0 is ineligible to be a DR or BDR.

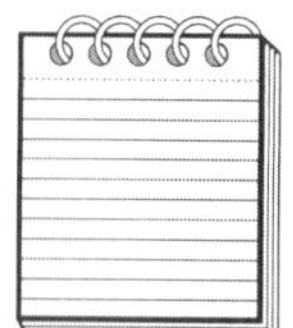

DESIGN RULE: *Be sure to have multiple eligible routers in your areas!*

You must have at least one eligible router in your OSPF network or OSPF cannot function. If multiple routers exist in the networks and all have a priority greater than 0, the router with the highest router ID wins the election. Priority for a router is set by the use of the following command:

```
ip ospf priority
```

DESIGN RULE: *In order to ensure a static router ID (one that cannot go into a "down" state), it is best to configure the loopback address on every router. To further manipulate the DR election process, use the highest numbered loopback address of all loopback addresses in use in the area, on your most robust router. This will guarantee that it is chosen as the DR.*

Once a router is the DR, it can only lose its position through a reboot. It is also possible to shut down the interface in use as the router ID to cause the DR to lose its status, but this can take about 40 seconds to take effect. A reboot is the fastest way to take a DR out of the running.

Hierarchy in OSPF

One of the hallmarks of the OSPF routing protocol is its hierarchical nature. By using the area structure and by keeping as much of the routing protocol traffic localized to an area as possible, one can design a network that is both scalable and reliable. As we have repeated several times in this chapter, the backbone area is known as Area 0. Using this concept globally, it makes it far easier for network architects to create logical designs wherever they may go.

When naming the areas, as we have done in Figure 9-9, it is a matter of preference in how you select the area numbers. Most network designers have a method to their naming conventions. For instance, one school of thought is to use the subnet number to name the area, in order to make troubleshooting more intuitive. If Area 1 in our figure were comprised of network 192.168.10.0, for example, we could call it Area 192.168.10.0. There is really nothing wrong with that approach. Most designers choose a single number, as we have done here, rather than use a subnet number. One could even use building numbers in the naming scheme. Whatever convention works well for the network engineering staff will be the best choice.

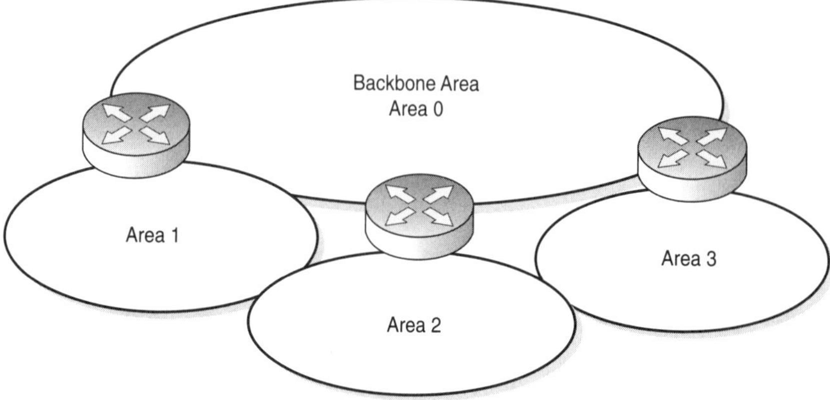

Figure 9-9 OSPF adjacent areas

The best rule of thumb in creating the network areas, however, is to keep the areas adjacent to the backbone. In Figure 9-9, ABRs connect Areas 1 through 3 to Area 0. Another possibility is for more than one ABR to attach an area to the network backbone. In that instance, the area would have more than one way to reach the network backbone. As you will see when we discuss virtual links, it is possible to statically connect areas to the backbone if they are not adjacent, but it is not the best design decision.

Another benefit of the hierarchical area design for OSPF is that by the use of network summarization, routing between areas can be handled much more efficiently. Hierarchy and network summarization are themes you will see recurring throughout this chapter and this book. Those two concepts are the keys to a scalable design.

OSPF Areas

The basic OSPF design we have used throughout this chapter, shown in Figure 9-10, can be used to discuss the way LSAs are propagated throughout the OSPF network. The ABR between Area 0 and Area 1 will, by default, forward all LSAs from the backbone.

The types of LSAs that could come from Area 0 might include

- Specific-link LSAs from within Area 0 or from other areas
- Specific or summary external links from an ASBR
- Summary-link LSAs from within Area 0 or from other areas

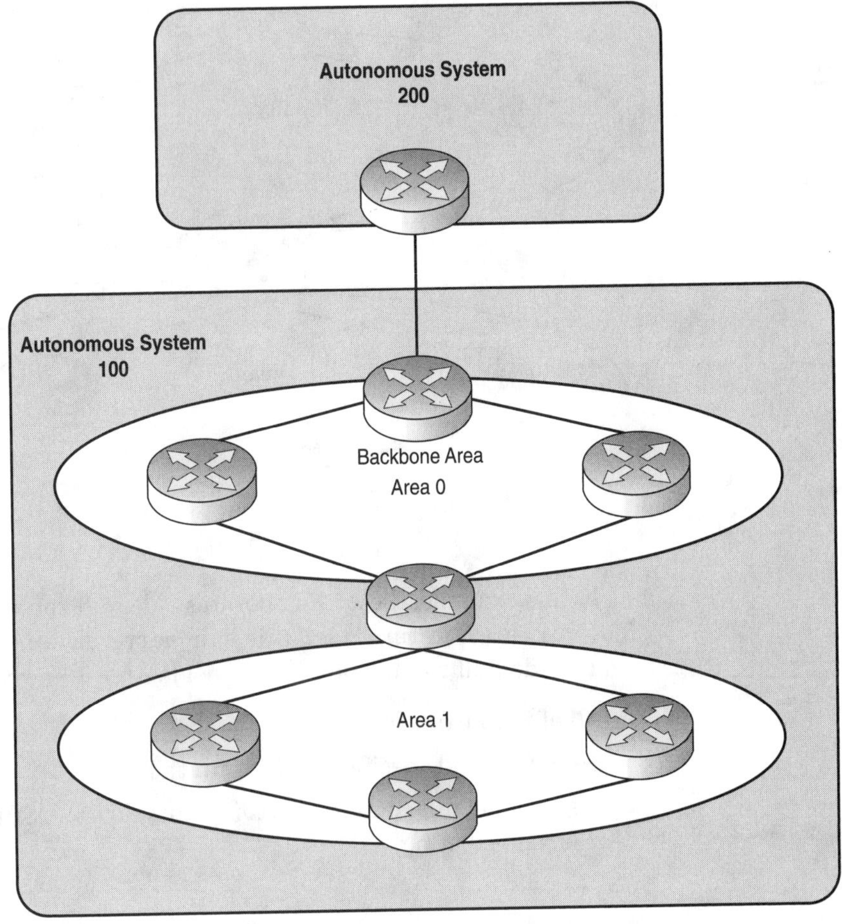

Figure 9-10
OSPF areas

In this section of the chapter, we will discuss different ways to configure OSPF areas in order to control the propagation of LSAs.

Stub Areas

A *stub area* is a special kind of area within OSPF networks. A stub area consolidates all external LSAs—that is, those originating outside the AS—as one default route. It does, however, see all summary-link and specific-link LSAs within the AS. In Figure 9-11, Area 1 can be considered a stub area. The backbone area can *never* be a stub area!

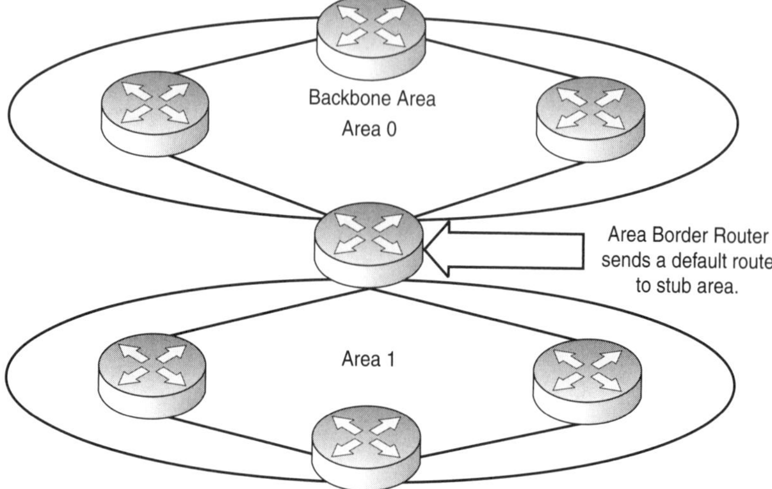
Backbone Area
Area 0
Area Border Router sends a default route to stub area.
Area 1

Figure 9-11
Stub area

In this example, the ABR generates a default route to inject into Area 1. The stub area, in turn, forwards summary-link LSAs, specific-link LSAs, and the default route. The routers inside Area 1 know about

- All of the intra-area routes
- Summary and specific links within the AS
- A single default route to anything outside the OSPF process in which it is participating

TIP: *By definition, a stub area does not accept any external routes.*

It is important to note that a stub area cannot be used as a transit area for a virtual link. In other words, an area is not a stub if another area must use a virtual link across it to connect to the backbone area. Another fact that would prevent an area from being a stub is if an ASBR is internal to that area. This is because an ASBR must learn and forward external routes, by definition.

TIP: With a stub area, the basic rule is "All exits end up at the backbone!"

In our example in Figure 9-11, all routers within Area 1 must be configured as stub routers. This will set the *E-bit* to 0 in all hello packets. To configure a router as a stub, use the following command:

```
area <area-id> stub
```

Totally Stubby Areas

Another kind of stub area is called a *totally stubby area*. This is configured with the stub area command plus the no-summary extension, as shown here:

```
area <area-id> stub no-summary
```

A totally stubby area is even more limited in its information than a stub area. All it will learn is a default route and its own intra-area routes. Specific- and summary-link LSAs between areas, as well as external routes, are blocked. In Figure 9-12, Area 1 will only know how to reach intra-area routes (within Area 1) and will know to use the ABR for anything else (as a default route).

Not-So-Stubby Area (NSSA)

Another type of stub area is the not-so-stubby area (NSSA). The NSSA uses a special kind of LSA, called a type 7 LSA. The ASBR within the NSSA generates the type 7 LSA, and it is translated into an LSA that can be understood within the OSPF domain (type 5 LSA).

Take a look at the example shown in Figure 9-13. Area 1 is an NSSA. Because it is a stub area, the incoming routes—whether from an external AS or another routing protocol—cannot be passed to the OSPF backbone area. With an NSSA, however, the external routes can be repackaged into a

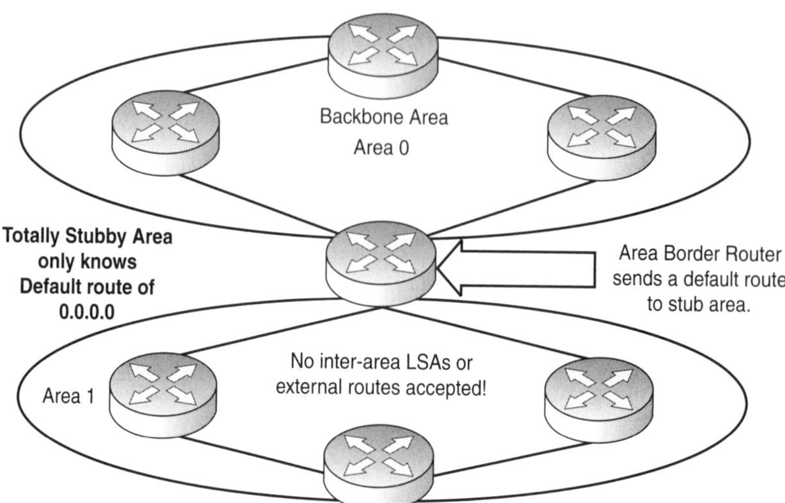
Backbone Area
Area 0
Totally Stubby Area
only knows
Default route of
0.0.0.0
Area Border Router
sends a default route
to stub area.
No inter-area LSAs or
external routes accepted!
Area 1

Figure 9-12
Totally stubby area

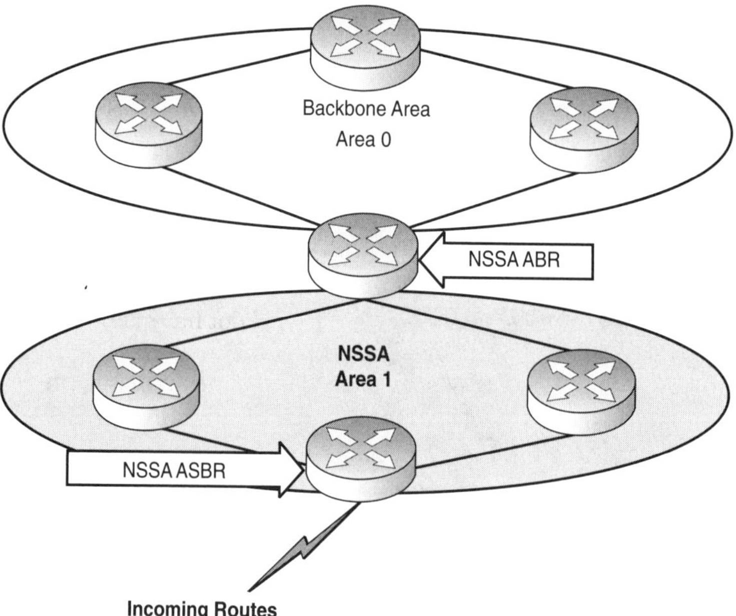
Backbone Area
Area 0
NSSA ABR
NSSA
Area 1
NSSA ASBR
Incoming Routes

Figure 9-13
NSSA

type 7 LSA, which passes through Area 1 and is translated at the ABR into something the rest of the OSPF network can understand.

The following command can be used to make an area into an NSSA:

```
area <area-id> nssa
```

Each router within Area 1 would need to have this command entered within the OSPF configuration in order for the NSSA concept to work. If you want the NSSA to also be a totally stubbed area, it is important that you also use this command on the ABR so that type 3 and type 4 LSAs (inter-area and external) are not injected into the area:

```
area <area-id> nssa no-summary
```

OSPF Backbone Design

The first rule for designing a good OSPF backbone is to keep it simple. Use your most robust routers in the backbone. Stay away from using a complex mesh. Instead, use a simple "one-hop" LAN design, like the one shown in Figure 9-14.

When possible, isolate the routers from the rest of the network equipment by keeping them in a secure closet. While many businesses do this, it is not always practical because of limited space and resources.

Bear in mind, too, that you should keep your backbone logically segregated, as well. This means that unless you have an extremely small OSPF network, keep your workgroups out of the backbone area! Early in the days of OSPF, a site I was on was forced to put everything into Area 0, simply because the design engineer did not have enough experience to properly set up the areas. Don't let this happen to any network with which you are involved. Network performance was poor, as was convergence. A route flap would have been a disaster.

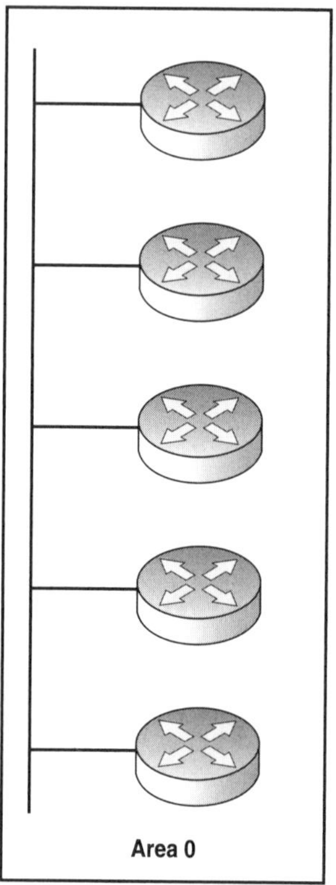

Figure 9-14 Simple OSPF backbone

OSPF and Scalability Design Rules

As with most internetworking matters, it is best to keep things as simple as possible. When you do so, you create designs that are easy to grow, modify, and troubleshoot. There are some easy-to-follow design guidelines when it comes to OSPF that will help you create a scalable network.

- Keep your topology simple. To do this, use logical area structures, and *do not* "daisy-chain" your areas. Think "top (Area 0) down" for your design.
- Keep the number of areas relatively small.
- Use fewer than 100 routers per area.
- When possible, use totally stubby areas.
- Make the most of summarization at the ASBRs and ABRs.

OSPF Convergence, Load Balancing, and Resource Utilization

Convergence, as you may recall from our last chapter, is the amount of time it takes for routing updates to propagate—and thus, for the network to stabilize after a change. OSPF, in particular, has three components that affect convergence. They are

- Time to detect a link failure
- Time for OSPF to propagate LSAs and run the Dijkstra algorithm
- The SPF delay timer

The amount of time it takes for a link failure to be detected depends upon the link type. For FDDI, Token Ring, or Carrier Detect (CD) link types, the OSPF process senses the failure immediately. For Ethernet or serial lines, it depends upon the setting of the keepalive timers. It is usually two to three times the keepalive timer setting before a link is considered to be "down." Finally, the OSPF dead timer will be used to determine that a link is down, if the OSPF hello timer is less than the interface keepalive timer.

The time it takes for OSPF to propagate LSAs and compute the Dijkstra algorithm is less than 1 second. The SPF delay timer is set to 5 seconds, by default, but can be modified as needed. If you have high-speed links (OC3 and above), you may want to adjust this timer as low as 0.

To wrap it all up—the final time for OSPF to converge can be from 6 seconds (for links such as FDDI, Token Ring, or CD) to 46 seconds. That is,

- Instant link failure detection (0 seconds)
- Plus time for OSPF to propagate the change and run the calculations (1 second)
- Plus the SPF delay timer (5 seconds)

For different types of links, the process can take longer than 6 seconds, depending on the link type, timer settings, and network size. The worst-case scenario is when the OSPF dead timer (40 seconds) is used to determine when the SPF is recomputed.

Load Balancing

Part of creating a robust network design for any routing protocol is making the best use of alternate routes. Think of it as a map for your vacation or daily commute. If you know multiple ways to get to your destination, you will still be able to get there—even if the path you end up using is not the optimal path. With OSPF, keeping several entries in the "map," or routing table, means that in the event of a link failure, the traffic can keep moving along another route.

Cisco routers running OSPF support up to four equal-cost routes to a destination. If multiple equal-cost paths to a destination exist, OSPF will automatically load balance over those paths. This load balancing behavior will be, by default, on a per-destination basis, when fast switching is enabled. If fast switching is disabled, by the use of the **no ip route-cache** command, the load balancing will be on a per-packet basis. When links are 56 Kbps or greater, Cisco's recommendation is that you should leave fast switching enabled. This prevents the relatively costly per-packet switching behavior. When dealing with slower link speeds, it is a particularly important consideration.

As we discussed early in this chapter, OSPF cost is based upon the bandwidth of the interface. The cost is determined by dividing 100,000,000 by the configured bandwidth of the interface. The cost can also be manually configured, if you want to create the illusion of equal-cost paths. Here are some tips about OSPF cost:

- Cost must be a whole number greater than 1.
- The default cost for a 100 Mbps link is 1.
- If you do the calculations for a Gigabit Ethernet port, your cost would be the same as for a Fast Ethernet port, so you may want to adjust the *reference bandwidth* (see instructions below).

To adjust how OSPF calculates the cost on an interface, use this command in OSPF configuration mode:

```
reference-bandwidth ref-bw
```

Because the default reference bandwidth is 100, there is no difference between a Gigabit Ethernet port, a Fast Ethernet port, and a FDDI interface, for instance. If you use a reference bandwidth of 1000, however, a

FDDI interface would have a cost of 10 and the Gigabit Ethernet would have a cost of 1. This is much more realistic in terms of traffic handling.

DESIGN RULE: *If you are modifying the reference bandwidth on one OSPF router, you must do so on all OSPF routers within the same OSPF process!*

Resource Utilization

When considering the layout of the OSPF design, there are a few important facts that you need to keep in mind about how the processes work. You already know that OSPF routers only exchange the entire routing table when there is a change in link-state. That is one of the benefits of using a link-state routing protocol. What about overhead?

The biggest source of overhead in an OSPF network is the exchange of hello packets. This happens, by default, every 10 seconds between routers and their DR and BDR. A hello packet is sent, and an ACK packet is received in reply. Your DR and BDR will be doing the most work in this process, so it works best when the fastest, most robust routers are the DR and BDR.

The next biggest source of overhead is the link-state table updates, which happen every 30 minutes. This is just a way of keeping information fresh in the tables and ensuring that nothing is amiss with link states.

Another way to minimize the resource consumption in an OSPF network is to maximize your use of summarization. This greatly reduces the amount of work that the routers have to do and keeps the work localized to an area as much as possible. Note that each entry in the OSPF routing table will consume between 200 and 280 bytes of memory plus 44 bytes per extra path. Each LSA will consume 100 bytes of overhead, plus the size of the LSA, which could be another 60 to 100 bytes.

TIP: *If you want to know exactly how much memory your OSPF process is consuming, use the* **`show memory`** *command with and without OSPF enabled.*

Virtual Links

One of the questions I always ask prospective employees during a technical interview is how he or she would connect an OSPF area to the backbone if the backbone should "break" or lose connectivity to a given area. If the candidate cannot answer that question, they usually don't come to work for the company. As with any internetworking task, it isn't always a matter of what is best for the network. Sometimes it's a matter of what you have to do to keep things running until the bigger problem is solved.

Rather than just memorizing the fact that you would need to use a virtual link between the separated area and the backbone, it is important to understand when and why you would apply this temporary solution. The problem shown in Figure 9-15 is a good example. Area 2 is not adjacent to the backbone, either through design or through loss of connectivity through an ABR.

A virtual link is simply a way to connect one non-backbone area through another non-backbone area to the nearest ABR. A virtual link keeps the non-backbone area connected to the backbone through a tunnel, of sorts. Performance will be worse than through a normal adjacency and adds

Figure 9-15
OSPF virtual link

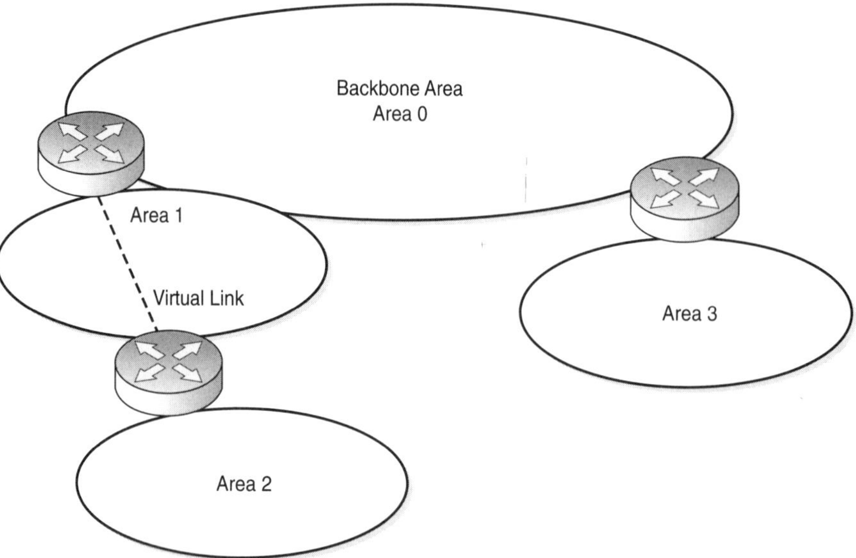

another layer of complexity and manual configuration to an OSPF design. A virtual link should be treated as a temporary Band-Aid® solution, rather than part of a good overall design.

OSPF Summarization

This section will address all sorts of topics related to summarization within an OSPF network design. Address assignment and summarization go hand-in-hand and simply make OSPF work properly. In this section you will see why that is so. We will also discuss how to deal with discontiguous subnets, how to use Variable Length Subnet Masking, and how to create area address ranges with a little trick called *bit splitting*.

Address Space

All of the possible network nodes within an area will perform better, as will the area as a whole, if the address space is logically laid out in a block pattern. Figure 9-16 shows that our three non-backbone areas each have a block of IP addresses assigned from the 10.0.0.0 major network RFC 1918 numbers. By looking at the design, we know nothing more than that to find an address that matches 10.10.0.0/16 or more specific, we must go through the ABR into Area 1. That is as simple as it gets.

Figure 9-16 Address allocation

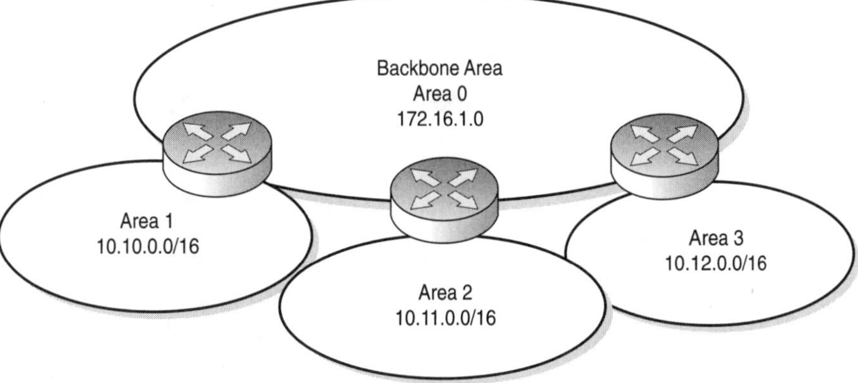

If, however, we were to have a mixture of some other IP addresses within each area, arranged in an illogical manner, it would be much more difficult for the router. Remember, each subnet (or host, in some cases) must have an entry in the routing table. Using address summarization, however, allows many entries to be consolidated into one. This not only makes routing more efficient, it cuts down on CPU and memory utilization in the routers and makes performance much better.

DESIGN RULE: *Configure your addresses so that, within an area, they are contiguous.*

An area that is using summarization can have any of these characteristics:

- One or more major network numbers
- One or more fixed-mask subnets
- A mixed bag of major networks and subnets from other major network numbers
- An assortment of major networks, subnets from other major networks, single hosts, and variable subnets

TIP: *You can allocate a block of addresses in powers of two so that they can be represented by a single link advertisement. Make the blocks as large as possible. Contiguous groups of address blocks can then be summarized using the* **area** *area-id* **range** *address mask command. Use bit splitting to allocate bits to area.*

Bit Splitting

There is a technique that can be used to divide a major network number for use in more than one area. It is called *bit splitting*. Bit splitting allows you to borrow subnet bits for use in designating an area.

For example, if you want to split a network into two areas, split 1 bit. To use 16 areas, split 4 bits. This is how the 16-area concept would work:

1. Use a range mask of 255.255.240.0. Four bits are allocated to the area.
2. Use a subnet mask of 255.255.255.0 to specify 8 subnet bits, 4 leftover bits, and 16 subnets per area.
3. The result is that the subnet bits look like this:

- 11111111.11111111.11110000.00000000 (advertised to the network)
- 00000000.00000000.00001111.11111111 (within the area)

Figure 9-17 shows how the first three areas might look in such a design.

VLSM

Variable Length Subnet Masking (VLSM) is used with routing protocols that support it (OSPF, RIPv2, ISIS, and EIGRP) to make efficient use of IP address space. VLSM helps to accomplish this by allowing the network address administrator to allocate smaller subnets to networks with fewer hosts and allocating large subnets to networks with a greater number of hosts.

TIP: *Cisco has a binary-to-decimal conversion chart for use with VLSM on its Web site at* **http://www.cisco.com/warp/public/104/4.html#21.0**.

Figure 9-17
Bit splitting

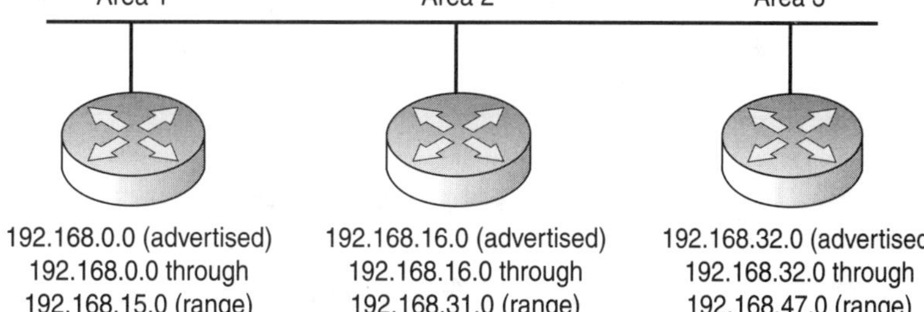

Before VLSM support was added to routing protocols, the older protocols recognized only major network boundaries or a single mask for subnets. I once worked on a network design that used IGRP. Because it was a government institution, the decision had been made higher up that the subnets would come from a Class B address space and would use 11 bits of subnet masking. This made the design phase difficult, but the end result was still successful.

With OSPF, you can use VLSM to create small, two-host areas for dedicated lines. Within the same major network number, you could create a subnet with 14 hosts and another with 60 hosts. Of course, you will want to keep the design logical and simple. This will make it easier for you and for those who manage the network after you move on to your next design.

DESIGN RULE: *Allow adequate space within a subnet for growth. Allow for adequate growth within contiguous subnets in an area, as well.*

For more information on address design tips and VLSM, refer back to Chapter 7, "TCP/IP Addrssing Design."

Discontiguous Subnets

A subnet that is separated from its major network number by at least one other major network number is said to be discontiguous. Figure 9-18 shows that the backbone area, which is of a different major network number, separates the subnets contained within Areas 1 through 3. Therefore the subnets in Areas 1 through 3 are discontiguous. OSPF supports discontiguous areas because it uses subnet masks as part of the link-state database. Therefore, our design will work, whether or not summarization is in use. In this design, we can use summary LSAs between the areas and the backbone.

Summarization on ABRs

Part of the summarization done within OSPF happens between areas. The *Area Border Router* (ABR) can provide a summary statement that consists of a single line to the backbone (or other adjacent areas). In Figure 9-19, the

Figure 9-18
Discontiguous subnets

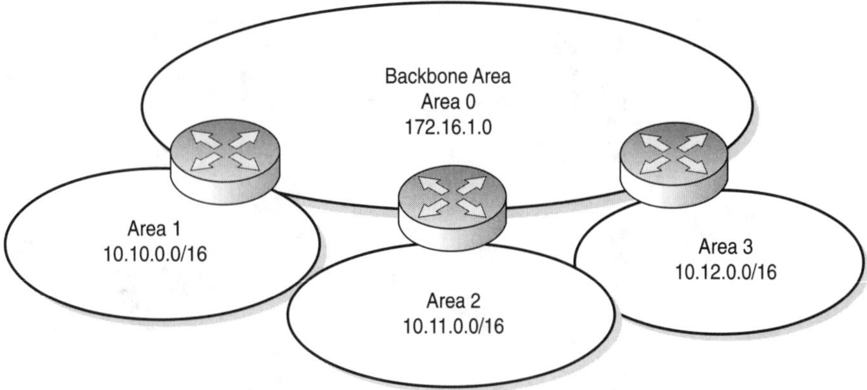

ABR will send a summary advertisement to Area 0 from Area 1 that will say, "I have 192.168.0.0 with 16 subnets (per the subnet mask)." To get to any of those subnets, the backbone area only needs to know that one line.

When summarization is not used on the ABR, information about every link will go to the backbone. If our example in Figure 9-19 did not use the area range, the backbone area would receive an LSA for 192.168.1.0, 192.168.2.0, and so on. If one of the links begins to have problems such as route flapping, the continuous bombardment of the backbone with these specific-link LSAs will cause every OSPF router that receives the LSA to recompute its SPF algorithm over and over.

As you can imagine, the toll this would take on the network would be tremendous. The **spf-holdtime** command will, by default, limit the routers to running the SPF algorithm no more often than every 10 seconds. This helps somewhat, and can be configured, but summarization is still the best policy in an OSPF network.

With summarization in use by the ABRs, link-state changes within a summarized area will not propagate to the backbone. A route flap, for instance, would remain an area problem and would not affect the rest of the network through the backbone. This is a key to creating a stable OSPF design.

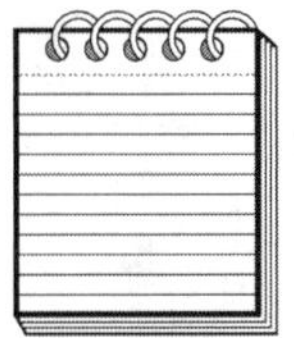

DESIGN RULE: *Use summarization at the Area Border Routers to create a stable OSPF network.*

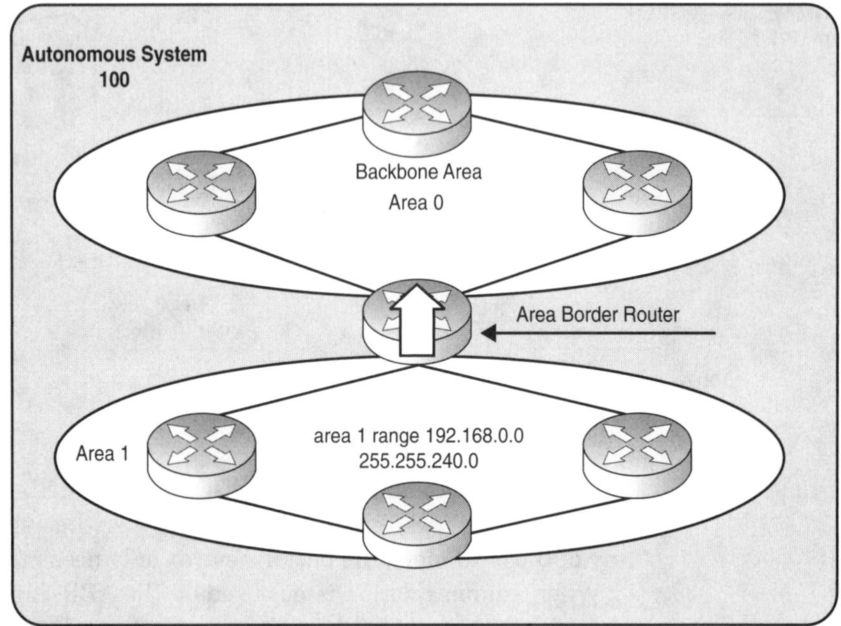

Figure 9-19
ABR summarization

Summarization on ASBRs

The *autonomous system boundary router* (ASBR) is best defined as a router that injects or redistributes routes into an OSPF domain. The ASBR performs some summarization of those external links. Depending upon the policies set up by the service provider, the ASBR may inject only a default external link of 0.0.0.0 into the autonomous system. In the example shown in Figure 9-20, this would direct the router on the customer side (AS 100) to send any traffic for which it did not have a route to the router on the service provider side (AS 200).

If an autonomous system is connected to more than one service provider, and therefore has more than one ASBR, you can use the **default-information originate** command to reduce the external routing information that is injected into the AS. This command will inject a default route into the OSPF routing process. Routers inside the AS will use whatever ASBR is closest, because the information it knows about external routes is very limited.

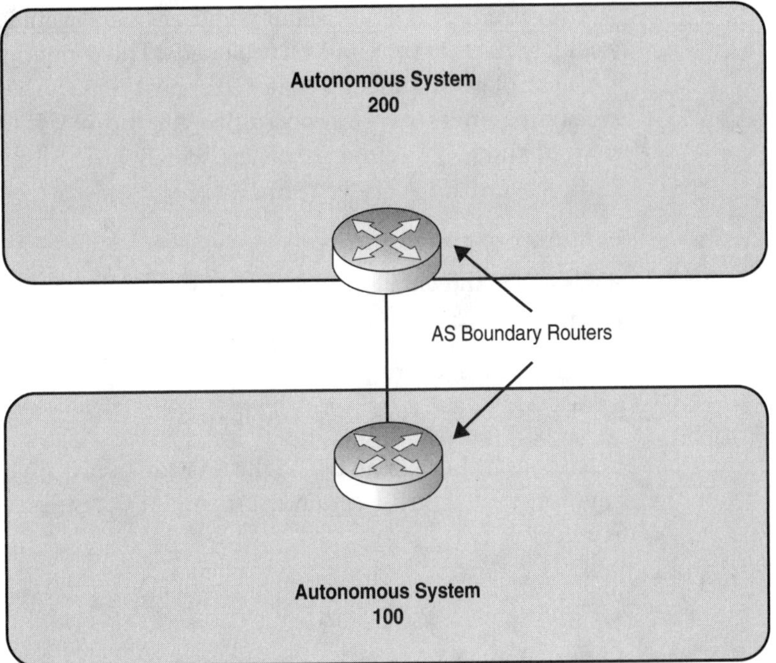

Figure 9-20
ASBR summarization

Case Study

Calabash Shipping Company has a network infrastructure that has outgrown the RIP routing protocol, which it has used for many years. A 300 percent increase in business over the last 2 years has allowed the company to open four regional offices in Denver, Boise, Columbus, and Raleigh. These regional offices will need to connect back to the headquarters for Calabash in Detroit.

The company has funds allocated for a network upgrade this year and has already had the network cabling upgraded from the backbone to the desktop in their headquarters building. The four new locations are housed in completely new accommodations. Robust core routers have been purchased for the backbone, with the smaller routers that are currently at HQ moving out to the regional offices. Each of the regional locations will connect over a T3 to the main building. Even though this allows for a lot of bandwidth, the network engineering staff is concerned about protocol traffic using too much of that bandwidth. They also recognize that RIP cannot scale to the kind of growth they are expecting in the next 5 years.

They are ready to talk about whether OSPF would be a good routing protocol for their current and future needs. The company has hired you to create a simple OSPF design that will show them the best way to organize the areas for minimum protocol traffic over the WAN. They have a small network at the HQ building, however, which will still need to run RIP for the Unix servers. Here are your main objectives:

- Minimize protocol traffic.
- Use RIP and OSPF together.
- Allow for scalability.
- Summarize where possible.
- Identify your areas in a simple design.

Although there is no one right answer to any given design problem, we have suggested one solution in Appendix C, "Suggested Solutions to Case Studies."

Study Hints

Although no one can disclose test items or test content, we can give hints as to what might be valuable to study. For this chapter, there are key facts that need to be reviewed and remembered.

Design Rules

- Keep the number of routers in an area no higher than 50 to 100—on the smaller end for the backbone area. By keeping the number of routers low, you can reduce the overhead and router database size within the area.
- If you are modifying the reference bandwidth on one OSPF router, you must do so on all OSPF routers within the same OSPF process!
- In order to ensure a static router ID (one that cannot go into a "down" state), it is best to configure the loopback address on every router. If you want to further manipulate the election process, use the highest IP address out of the loopback addresses in use on your most robust and reliable router.

- Be sure to have multiple DR/BDR eligible routers in your areas!
- Configure your addresses so that, within an area, they are contiguous. Allow ample room for growth.
- Keep areas stubby.
- Don't "daisy-chain" your areas. Keep each area one hop away from the backbone.
- Use summarization at the Area Border Routers to create a stable OSPF network.

Tips

- An interface that is having problems, such as a route flap condition, can have a catastrophic effect on an OSPF network. The repeated LSAs would cause routers to continually have to recompute their routing table and possibly never converge. To address this issue, the **spf holdtime** command was added. By default, routers are prevented from recalculating the routing table more often than every ten seconds. The **spf holddown timer** is a configurable timer.
- The formula to calculate cost is

  10^8/bandwidth in bps=cost

- You can allocate a block of addresses in powers of two so that they can be represented by a single link advertisement. Make the blocks as large as possible. Contiguous groups of address blocks can then be summarized using the **area** *area-id* **range** *address mask* command. Use bit splitting to allocate bits to area.
- If an autonomous system is connected to more than one service provider, and therefore has more than one ASBR, you can use the **default-information originate** command to reduce the external routing information that is injected into the AS.
- If you want to know exactly how much memory your OSPF process is consuming, use the **show memory** command with and without OSPF enabled.

CCDP Tips

This section contains an abbreviated list of topics covered in Chapter 9. Think of this section as the equivalent of reading Cliff's Notes™ instead of reading an entire book. You will get the general idea of the chapter but will benefit more from reading the chapter in its entirety.

OSPF Network Types

- Point-to-Point is "Just me, you, and the wire."
- Broadcast Multi-Access elects a "king" (the DR) and an "heir to the throne" (the BDR) that learn all about the interfaces and routers in the area where they "reign."
- Non-Broadcast Multi-Access must use static configuration to learn about its neighbors.

OSPF Router Types

- Internal routers have all of their interfaces in a single area and have a single link-state database.
- Area Border Routers (ABRs) connect two areas together and have more than one link-state database (one for each area of which they are a member).
- An autonomous system boundary router (ASBR) connects another autonomous system to the one of which it is a member or connects another routing protocol to OSPF. It can also be called a redistribution router.
- Backbone routers (also called internal routers) have all interfaces in the backbone area (Area 0).

LSA Types

- **Network Link LSA** Sent by the DR advertising all routers within its area.
- **Summary Link LSA** Sent to advertise networks that are reachable within other areas.
- **Router Link LSA** Sent only to routers within one area, advertising the link-state of the neighboring interfaces.
- **External Link LSA** Usually sent by the ASBR to advertise routes external to the OSPF domain. Flooded to all but stub areas.

OSPF Adjacencies

- Formed between the DR or BDR and intra-area routers.
- Formed between routers who have a point-to-point or virtual link connection.

OSPF Summarization

- Keep addresses contiguous within an area.
- Use VLSM to efficiently use address space.
- Use bit splitting to summarize areas.
- Summarize at ABR.

Virtual Links

- A *virtual link* is a static route used to connect an area through another area to the backbone when it has become disconnected from the backbone.

Designated Router/Backup Designated Router

- The *Designated Router* is usually the fastest router to come up and only loses its place if it is rebooted or its router ID goes down.
- The *Backup Designated Router* is the second faster router to come up and assumes the role of DR if the DR should fail.
- DR/BDR cannot be configured with a *priority of 0*.
- You should have multiple eligible routers within an area for redundancy.

OSPF Area Types

- **Stub Area** Knows a default route to its ABR, all of the routes internal to its area, and summary and specific links within the AS.
- **Totally Stubby Area** Only knows the default route to its ABR. Knows no other routes outside its area.
- **Not-So-Stubby Area** Can have an ASBR into other routing protocols and act as a conduit to the OSPF backbone by using a type 7 LSA that can pass to its ABR, where it is translated into a type 5 LSA that appears to be coming from the ABR (and not a stub area).

Backbone Design

- The backbone should be logically and physically secure, when possible.
- The backbone should contain fewer than 100 routers per area.
- Keep the areas stubby, for simplicity.
- The backbone should be one hop away from any other area.
- All areas should be adjacent to the backbone.

Summary

Now that you have been given a solid introduction to OSPF, you should feel confident that you would be able to begin designing your own scalable networks. You should have a good understanding of the benefits and pitfalls of creating an OSPF design, and you have had a chance to practice with our case study. The next chapter will introduce you to Cisco's proprietary routing protocols—Interior Gateway Routing Protocol (IGRP) and Enhanced Interior Gateway Routing Protocol (EIGRP).

Questions

The following review questions have been selected to help you test your knowledge of the subject matter contained in this chapter. You will also find these questions contained in the CD-ROM included with this book. While these are not the questions you will find in the certification exams, knowing the answers to the review questions in this book will help cement the material in your mind as you prepare for the tests.

1. Select the definition of DR.
   - **a.** Designated Route
   - **b.** Designated Router
   - **c.** Default Route
   - **d.** Default Router
2. True or False: An area must have both a DR and a BDR.
   - **a.** True
   - **b.** False

3. What is the table that is distributed every 30 minutes by default in an OSPF network?
   a. Routing table
   b. Topology table
   c. Link-state table
   d. Neighbor table
4. What is the default hello interval in OSPF?
   a. Every 5 seconds
   b. Every 10 seconds
   c. Every 30 seconds
   d. Every 60 seconds
5. What is the length of the OSPF dead timer?
   a. 10 seconds
   b. 30 seconds
   c. 40 seconds
   d. 60 seconds
6. A router which has all of its interfaces in a single area is called what?
   a. Backbone router
   b. Internal router
   c. Area border router
   d. AS boundary router
7. Which type of LSA lists the routers within a given segment of the network?
   a. Network link LSA
   b. Summary link LSA
   c. External link LSA
   d. Router link LSA
8. Which method is the best choice for reducing the size of the OSPF routing table?
   a. Keep the number of areas small.
   b. Use robust routers in the backbone.
   c. Prevent discontiguous networks.
   d. Configure summarization.

9. What type of router generates a network summary (type 2) LSA?
   a. DR
   b. BDR
   c. ABR
   d. ASBR
10. True or False: Any router within an OSPF area can form an adjacency with any other router.
   a. True
   b. False
11. Over how many equal-cost paths can OSPF load balance?
   a. 1
   b. 2
   c. 3
   d. 4
12. An autonomous system boundary router can also be called a redistribution router. Why is this?
   a. It can be used to perform redistribution between autonomous systems.
   b. It can be used to perform redistribution between other protocols and OSPF.
   c. It can be used to perform redistribution between areas.
13. The Shortest Path First algorithm, used to calculate the best path to a destination, is also called what?
   a. SPF tree
   b. Dijkstra algorithm
   c. OSPF algorithm
14. Which type of stub area will only know a single default route and no other external routes?
   a. Not-So-Stubby area
   b. Totally stubby area
   c. Stub area

15. Which type of stub area can act as a transit for another protocol to reach the backbone?
    a. Not-so-stubby area
    b. Totally stubby area
    c. Stub area
16. What is the default setting for the SPF holddown timer?
    a. 5 seconds
    b. 10 seconds
    c. 30 seconds
    d. 60 seconds
17. How long does OSPF take to detect that an FDDI interface is in a "down" state?
    a. 0 seconds
    b. 5 seconds
    c. 30 seconds
    d. 40 seconds
18. If you want to manipulate the cost calculation for interfaces, what command should you use?
    a. **interface** *<interface-id>* **cost** *<cost>*
    b. **reference-bandwidth** *<ref-bw>*
    c. **ospf cost** *<value>*
19. The highest numbered IP address on a router's interfaces will be used as the router ID for OSPF. If that interface fails or begins to "flap," the router will leave and join the OSPF process as its router ID fails and comes back. What is the best way to configure a stable router ID?
    a. Configure a loopback interface.
    b. Configure the highest IP address on your most stable interface.
    c. Use the command **router ID** *<IP address>* **static** in OSPF configuration mode.
20. True or False: In a stub area, only the DR and BDR must be configured as stub routers.
    a. True
    b. False

Answers

1. Select the definition of DR.
   b. Designated Router

2. True or False: An area must have both a DR and a BDR.
   a. True
   Explanation: By the rules of OSPF, in order for routing to function properly, there must be both a DR and a BDR.

3. What is the table that is distributed every 30 minutes by default in an OSPF network?
   b. Link-state table
   Explanation: The link-state table is flooded every 30 minutes to keep the information fresh. This is one of the sources of OSPF overhead.

4. What is the default hello interval in OSPF?
   b. Every 10 seconds

5. What is the length of the OSPF dead timer?
   c. 40 seconds

6. A router which has all of its interfaces in a single area is called what?
   b. Internal router
   Explanation: A backbone router, which has all of its interfaces in Area 0, can also be considered an internal router.

7. Which type of LSA lists the routers within a given segment of the network?
   a. Network link LSA
   Explanation: A type 2 LSA (network link LSA) advertises the link-state of the connected routers within a network segment. The DR of the area sends it.

8. Which method is the best choice for reducing the size of the OSPF routing table?
   d. Configure summarization.
   Explanation: Although there are arguably many ways to reduce the size of a routing table, the most efficient way is through the use of summarization.

9. What type of router generates a network link (type 2) LSA?
   a. DR
   Explanation: The DR is responsible for sending network link LSAs.
10. True or False: Any router within an OSPF area can form an adjacency with any other router.
    b. False
    Explanation: Only the DR and BDR routers can form adjacencies within an area, unless the router in question has a virtual or point-to-point link to another router.
11. Over how many equal-cost paths can OSPF load balance?
    d. 4
12. An autonomous system boundary router can also be called a redistribution router. Why is this?
    b. It can be used to perform redistribution between other protocols and OSPF.
    Explanation: An ASBR can be used to act as a boundary between autonomous systems or between OSPF and any other routing protocol.
13. The Shortest Path First algorithm, used to calculate the best path to a destination, is also called what?
    b. Dijkstra algorithm
14. Which type of stub area will only know a single default route and no other external routes?
    b. Totally stubby area
    Explanation: A totally stubby area has no connection to anything outside its area other than through a default route to the ABR.
15. Which type of stub area can act as a transit for another protocol to reach the backbone?
    a. Not-so-stubby area
    Explanation: A not-so-stubby area can act as a transit area for any other routing protocol to reach the OSPF backbone. This means that the router with interfaces in both the NSSA for OSPF and in the other routing protocol is acting as a redistribution router or ASBR.
16. What is the default setting for the SPF holddown timer?
    b. 10 seconds

17. How long does OSPF take to detect that an FDDI interface is in a "down" state?
    a. 0 seconds
    Explanation: A "down" state is detected immediately in the case of FDDI, Token Ring, or Carrier Detect (CD) link types.
18. If you want to manipulate the cost calculation for interfaces, what command should you use?
    b. reference-bandwidth *<ref-bw>*
    Explanation: One can also use the auto-cost qualifier on this command in order to allow the router to auto-sense and auto-configure the proper interface cost based on actual bandwidth.
19. The highest numbered IP address on a router's interfaces will be used as the router ID for OSPF. If that interface fails or begins to "flap," the router will leave and join the OSPF process as its router ID fails and comes back. What is the best way to configure a stable router ID?
    a. Configure a loopback interface.
    Explanation: A loopback interface cannot go into a "down" state, and therefore is the most stable way to configure the router ID.
20. True or False: In a stub area, only the DR and BDR must be configured as stub routers.
    b. False
    Explanation: In a stub area, all participating routers in the area must be configured as stub routers.

Frequently Asked Questions (FAQs)

1. *Loopback interfaces show up in the routing table with a /32 subnet mask. Why is that?*

   A loopback interface is considered to be a host route, rather than a network route. Therefore, it is a completely specific destination and is reflected as such with a 32-bit mask.

2. *How does OSPF send its LSAs and other communication? Through broadcast?*

   No. OSPF uses multicast to send communications between routers. This *does not* mean that you have to configure multicast on your router, however! OSPF uses reserved Class D addresses in the following manner:

   - **224.0.0.5** All OSPF routers can listen and send on this address.
   - **224.0.0.6** Only DR and BDR routers can listen and send on this address.

   For more information, please refer to the Cisco Web page at **http://www.cisco.com/warp/public/104/4.html#20.0**.

Bibliography

ARIN RFC Index, **http://www.arin.net/rfc/**

Cisco Internetwork Design, *Cisco Press, 2000, Birkner*

Cisco Internetwork Design Course Manual, version 3.0, April 1997, Cisco Systems, Inc.

OSPF Design Guide, **http://www.cisco.com/warp/public/104/1.html**

OSPF Design Guide—Section 2, **http://www.cisco.com/warp/public/104/3.html**

OSPF Network Design Solutions, Cisco Press, 1998, Thomas

OSPF Not-So-Stubby Area (NSSA), **http://www.cisco.com/warp/public/104/nssa.html**

RFC 1583

RFC 2178

CHAPTER 10

IGRP-EIGRP Design

Overview

In the last chapter, we discussed OSPF, a link state protocol that is somewhat difficult to grasp until you have had a lot of practical experience with it. Now we are going to look at the two most commonly used distance vector protocols, both of which are Cisco proprietary. What this means is that in a network using vendor equipment other than Cisco, you will probably see RIPv2 in use where appropriate, because IGRP and EIGRP are not interoperable with other vendors.

IGRP Routing

The Interior Gateway Routing Protocol (IGRP) was introduced with the earliest versions of Cisco IOS software as an improvement over the then popular RIPv1 protocol. Although it has some limitations based on hop count, you will probably still find it in use in small- to medium-sized networks. The reason for this is fairly straightforward; it is a simple protocol to implement and troubleshoot.

IGRP uses a 24-bit metric to find the best path to a destination network. It can also use several default gateways, advertise them, and choose from them the best one to use. It is also quite tolerant of nonhierarchical, haphazard networks that have resulted from poor planning or rapid growth.

Split Horizon

As with many of the distance vector protocols, IGRP uses split horizon by default to prevent routing loops in the network. In Figure 10-1, you can see that Router B will advertise all routes it knows about to Router A, *except* the ones it learned about from Router A. Even though Router B has routes to Networks 3 and 4 in its table, it will not tell Router A. If it did, it is likely that Router A might try to send packets to those networks through Router B. Router B could in turn say, "I learned that Router A has a path to those networks; I'll send these to him!" That is a routing loop.

In a Frame Relay or Switched Multimegabit Data Service network over a WAN or ATM, topics to be covered in Chapters 17, "Frame Relay Design," and 20, "What is ATM," IGRP will automatically disable split horizon. It does this because those types of networks need to be able to send routing

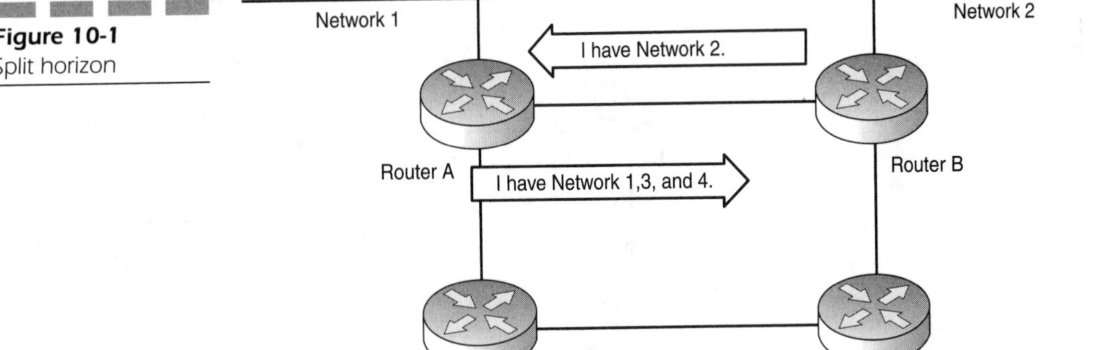

Figure 10-1
Split horizon

updates back out of the same physical interface on which they were received. Multiple virtual circuits may all share the same physical interface, and each circuit is like a unique interface unto itself. Therefore, Frame Relay in particular would have problems with split horizon.

Split horizon is only disabled for physical and multipoint sub-interfaces. Point-to-point sub-interfaces running Frame Relay, ATM, or SMDS preserve the split-horizon attribute.

Unequal-Cost Load Balancing

IGRP can load balance packets over several different unequal paths. As you can see in Figure 10-2, Router B knows how to get to Network 3 over two different paths. One path is a T1 line. The other path is a 128-Kbps line. Router B can send a two-to-one ratio of packets over the T1 line versus what it sends over the 128-Kbps line. You can control the ratio of packets sent with the *variance* factor.

The variance factor is a number by which a route's distance is divided. If it is less than or equal to the best metric to a destination, it is entered into the routing table. In Figure 10-2, if the best metric from Router B to Network 4 were 100 and the variance factor were 2, then paths with a metric of 200 would be eligible for load balancing (200/2 = 100), as would paths with a metric of 180 (180/2 = 90).

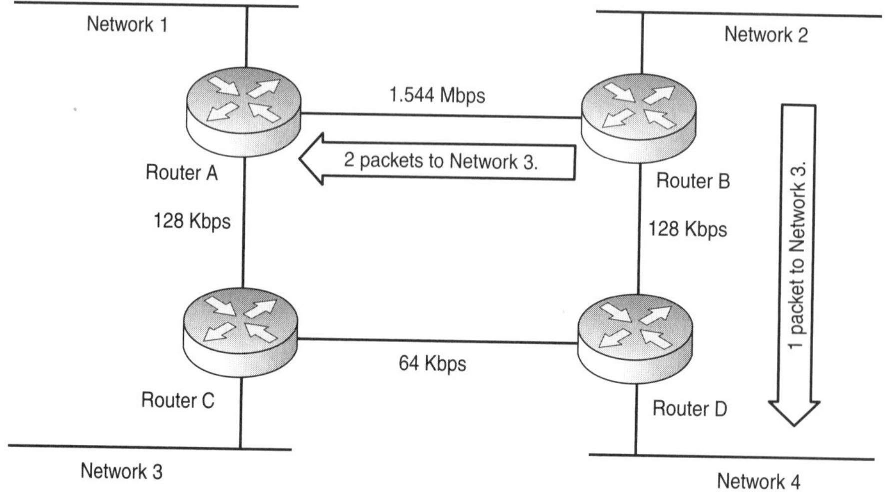

Figure 10-2
IGRP load balancing

The variance in IGRP is set to 1 by default. This will result in load balancing over equal-cost paths, because all paths must be equal in metric. If you are using fast or autonomous switching, you should leave the variance factor at 1. Cisco makes this recommendation because with the faster switching methods that use a cache function, packets via the slower path could be cached, resulting in congestion. It is appropriate to set the variance to 2 for process switching over WAN links, however.

Routing Metrics

IGRP uses a combination of bandwidth and delay as its routing metric, but it also considers several other elements in its decision:

- **Bandwidth** This metric is measured as the smallest of the links between the source and the destination. In other words, in a multiple-hop environment, an intervening 56-Kbps link would be the bandwidth that would be used for calculation. This is a static value.
- **Delay** This metric is a value based on the types of interfaces encountered along the path to the destination. Each type of interface has a different delay value. The sum of all these values results in the delay value used in the calculation. This is a static value.

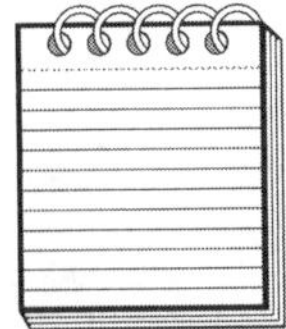

NOTE: *The delay value is inversely proportionate to the bandwidth of a link. In other words, the higher the bandwidth, the lower the delay. However, Cisco routers set the delay on serial links regardless of the bandwidth as though they were all T1 connections. This can be a problem if several serial links are crossed in one path that are actually higher in delay than their reported values.*

- **Loading** This metric is based on a measurement of the load between the source and destination. The heaviest load encountered (in bits per second) will be used in the calculation. This is a dynamic measurement and, as such, may change at each calculation.
- **Reliability** This metric is based on keepalives. The measurement taken at the point of worst reliability is what will be used in the calculations. This is a dynamic value.
- **Maximum Transmission Unit (MTU)** This metric is a measurement of the smallest MTU size restriction encountered between source and destination. Although this is not factored into the calculation, it will prevent problems for frames that may be too large to reach their destination with the IP "don't fragment" bit set. This is a static value.
- **Hops** This metric is the value of the total hop count from source to destination. Hop count is only important as a preventive measure to avoid the count to infinity problem. Hop count is a static value but is not part of the calculation.

Convergence

IGRP sends routing updates in the following two ways:

- Normal, full routing tables at scheduled intervals
- Triggered, or flash, updates

Like RIP, IGRP sends the full routing table at scheduled intervals—in this case, every 90 seconds. However, when a link fails or is reported as being in a down state, IGRP can also send a triggered update, shown in Figure 10-3, that contains only the changes. This provides for better overall convergence, because not only is the update sent right away, rather than at

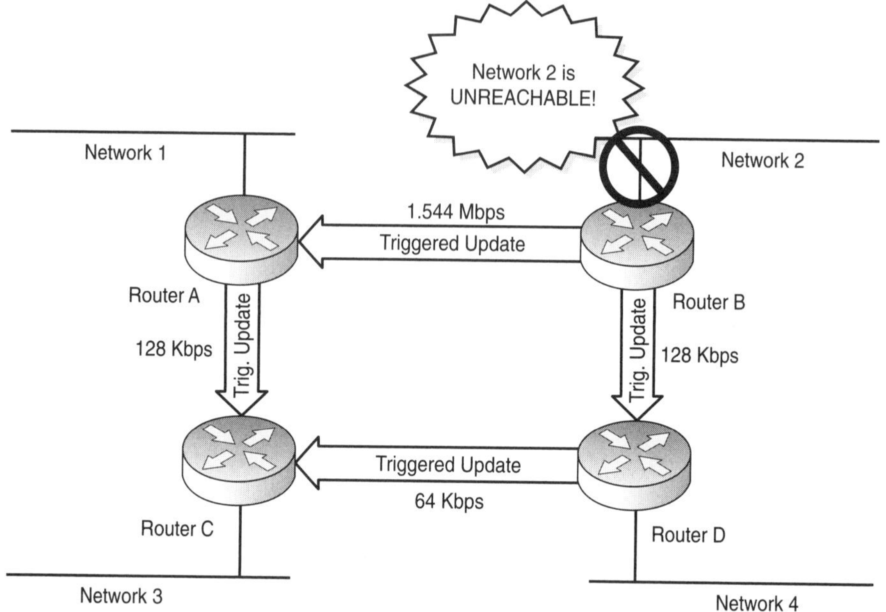

Figure 10-3
Triggered update

the next interval, but it is sent in a smaller form that communicates only the necessary changes. Here is how it works.

First, the link failure is detected. For FDDI or Token Ring, or in the event of a carrier loss, the update is instantly sent. In other cases, two to three hello packets must be missed from the link before an update is triggered.

Next, the router sends a triggered update to all its adjacent routers with the information that a network has become unreachable. The adjacent routers, in turn, send triggered updates to their adjacent neighbors, and so on.

Finally, the routers continue sending their regularly scheduled routing updates. In some instances, the triggered updates are still propagating through the network when the link that was down returns to normal. To allow the network to stabilize, holddown timers prevent the router from sending updates about the previously unreachable link for a period of time.

Timers

Timers are an integral part of how IGRP works. Timers control intervals of everything from routing updates to purges of the routing table. As we talked about in the last section, timers can even help enhance convergence. This section provides information about each kind of timer used by IGRP.

Update Interval The default interval at which the routing update is broadcast —in this case, the full routing table—is every 90 seconds. You can modify this timer if you want to speed convergence. For instance, it may make sense to send updates every 30 seconds over a fast WAN link.

NOTE: *When modifying timers, you do so for the entire autonomous system. The only way to use differing values is to have more than one IGRP process running and redistribute between them.*

Invalid Timer The invalid timer dictates that if you don't receive any information about a route to a destination network in this period of time, consider it timed out. If all routes to that destination time out, the destination is considered unreachable. This value is, by default, three times the value of the update interval. By allowing for a longer period of time, you allow for update packets that may have been dropped in the network.

Holddown Timer The holddown timer helps prevent routing loops by telling a router not to accept routing updates about a destination while that destination is in a holddown state. This is shown in Figure 10-4. The default holddown time is 280 seconds, which is three times the default update period plus 10 seconds. Although you may modify this timer, it is recommended that it remain larger than the update timer. Unless a network is very large, this should allow ample time for the triggered updates to reach the farthest routers in the network.

A route that is in a holddown state is also advertised as being unreachable. This is referred to as *route poisoning*. The only way a route can be removed from a poisoned state is for the holddown timer to expire or for a route to the destination with a *lower* administrative distance to be received.

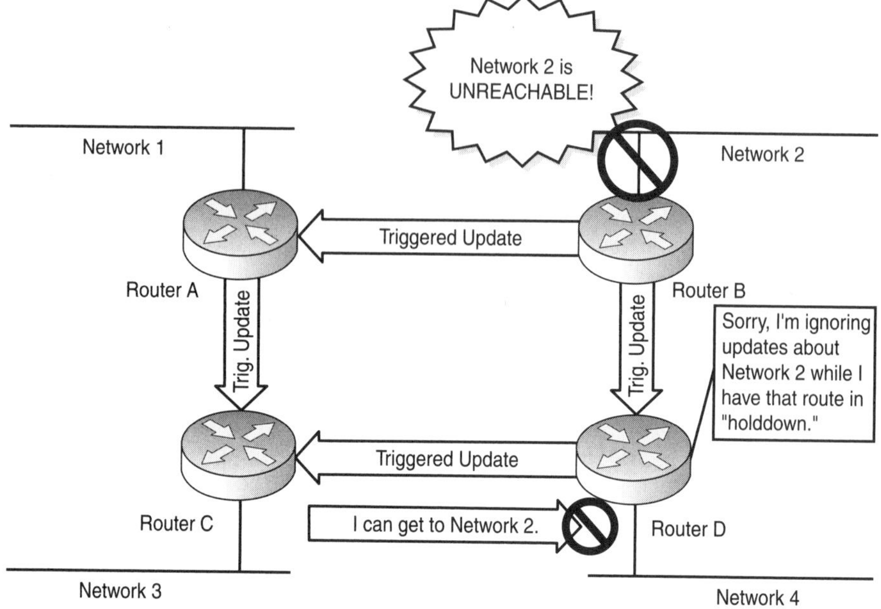

Figure 10-4 Holddown timers prevent routing loops.

If you want to trade fast convergence for possible routing loops, you may reduce or eliminate the holddown timer altogether. To turn off holddown, use the command *no metric holddown.* This enables routers to begin using any route received in update messages right away, as long as the route does not have a larger hop count than the original route.

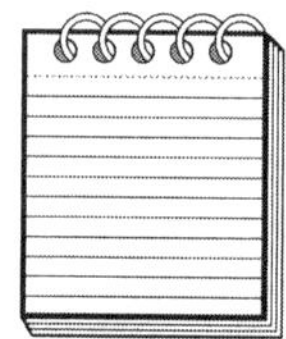

NOTE: *If the hop count is larger than the original and there is no holddown timer, the route is poisoned immediately.*

Flush Timer The flush timer is similar to the invalid timer with one critical difference. When the invalid timer expires for a route, the destination network is *not* removed from the database. If the network were to be removed, there would be no way to enforce a holddown against it. When the flush timer expires, however, the destination is "flushed" from the database. The value for this timer should be slightly more than the total of the hold-down timer plus the invalid timer. The default is seven times the update timer, or 630 seconds, by default.

Bandwidth Consumption for Updates

As we have discussed, IGRP is similar to RIP in that it sends the entire routing table in its update packets. IGRP sends these packets every 90 seconds. RIP, on the other hand, uses 30-second intervals.

To calculate the amount of bandwidth that will be consumed by the updates in IGRP, you need to know the total number of routes in the advertisement and divide it by the number of routes that an update packet can hold, which is about 104 routes in a 1500-byte packet. In very large networks, you may see many routing updates crossing the network. Say you have 1040 routes. Every 90 seconds, you will have about 10 updates crossing the wire. Each update is about 1500 bytes in size. Conceivably, you could use a lot of bandwidth this way.

If bandwidth is scarce, you may want to tune the update interval to send the routing table less frequently. Bear in mind, however, that the tradeoff for this is slower convergence.

EIGRP Routing

Cisco introduced Enhanced IGRP to be a step up from IGRP. Although still a distance vector protocol based on IGRP, EIGRP uses a more sophisticated, 32-bit routing metric, and can scale well for even the largest networks.

EIGRP differs from IGRP significantly in how it handles routing. Here are some of the differences:

- EIGRP does not send out regular routing updates, whereas IGRP does this every 90 seconds. EIGRP merely sends hello packets every 5 seconds to assure its neighbors that it is still alive. In turn, it receives hellos from its neighbors to indicate that they are still alive.
- EIGRP updates are sent only when a change occurs in the network topology, such as a link-down state, for instance. Then EIGRP only sends the necessary information to the neighbors who need to know

about it. It is also careful about the pace of the updates. These factors help keep the network from being overwhelmed and keep convergence very fast.

- EIGRP also supports classless addressing, so subnets can be planned using variable-length subnet masks (VLSM).

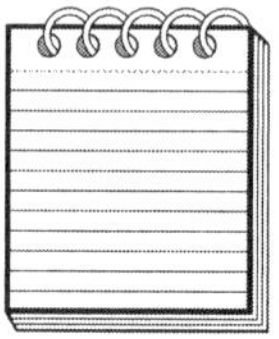

NOTE: *EIGRP uses hello packets every 5 seconds on Ethernet, Token Ring, FDDI, ATM point-to-point, point-to-point leased lines, and circuits higher than T1 speed. Multipoint or circuits of T1 or slower bandwidth have 60-second hello intervals.*

As shown in Figure 10-5, each protocol in EIGRP has separate tables. For IP, routing tables, a topology database, and the neighbor database are maintained separately from anything having to do with AppleTalk or IPX. EIGRP is considered to be a "ships-in-the-night" routing protocol, because each protocol is handled individually. Although they all reside in the same process, they have their own timers, hellos, and metrics. The one thing they all have in common is the use of the protocol engine, which provides the routing algorithm (DUAL), reliable transport, and neighbor discovery.

As you will see in more detail when we come to the section of this book on desktop protocols, EIGRP works very well in the WAN for protocols such as AppleTalk and IPX, which normally do not scale very well. Consider the example in Figure 10-6. With EIGRP running in the WAN, protocol-specific updates for AppleTalk and IPX remain in the LAN. These can be carried over EIGRP, but the hop count or ticks will not increase as a result. This allows for greater scalability.

EIGRP does not rely solely on the routing table for its routing decisions and all other information. Conversely, it builds a topology table first and then uses what it has learned to build a routing table. The topology table is built from what EIGRP learns through listening to hello packets and information sent by neighboring routers. It learns about networks that the neighbors know of, along with the distance from the neighbors to the destination networks.

EIGRP then calculates metrics to find the best path to a destination. The metrics it uses are lowest bandwidth, total delay, load, reliability, and MTU:

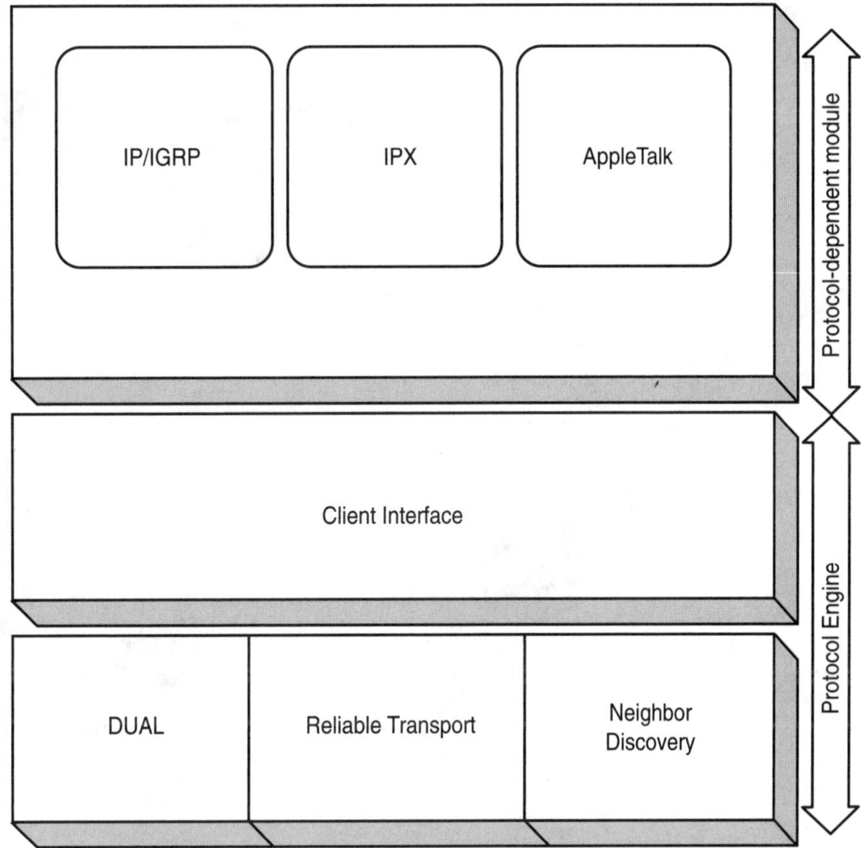

Figure 10-5
EIGRP tables

- Lowest bandwidth is based on the least bandwidth to a destination. *Required.*
- Total delay is the total of all delays to the destination (AB + BC + CD = AD total delay). *Required.*
- Load is measured by the congestion on the egress link.
- Reliability is based on the reliability of the path to the destination. This works similarly to IGRP.
- The Maximum Transmission Unit (MTU) of the egress interface is not used by default in the metric.

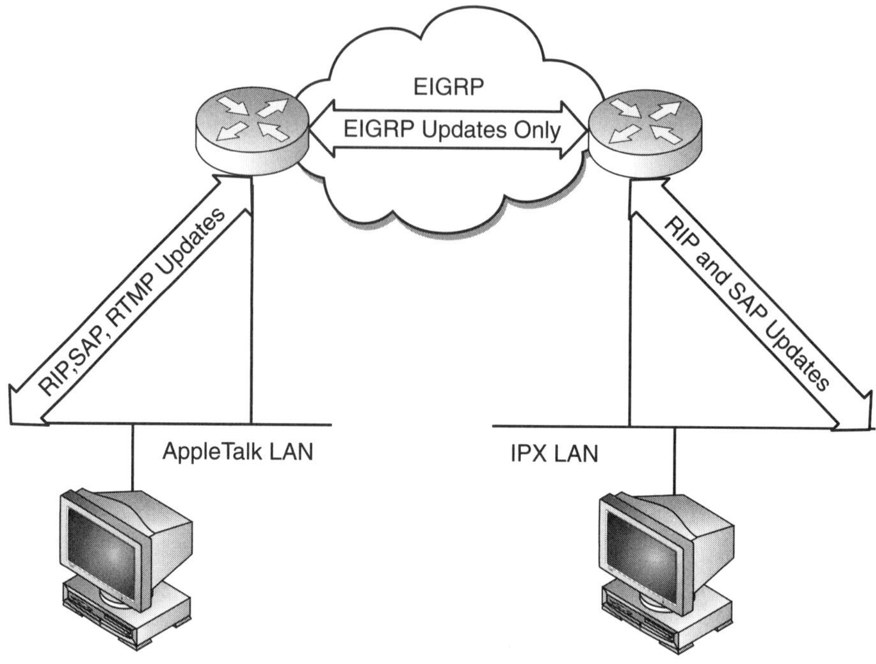

Figure 10-6
EIGRP in the WAN

Route Summarization

Like IGRP, EIGRP summarizes on major network boundaries by default. This can be turned off with the use of the command *no auto-summary*. The reason you would want to do this is if you are planning to use VLSM or have discontiguous networks. Bear in mind that you can *still* use VLSM if your network design is well planned, but if you have discontiguous networks or have networks that require manual summarization for any other reason, you will want to disable auto-summary.

A network like the one shown in Figure 10-7 can easily use prefix summarization because the subnets were well planned ahead of time. By advertising a single subnet—10.11.0.0/16—to its neighbors, this network has effectively reduced the size of its routing tables and updates.

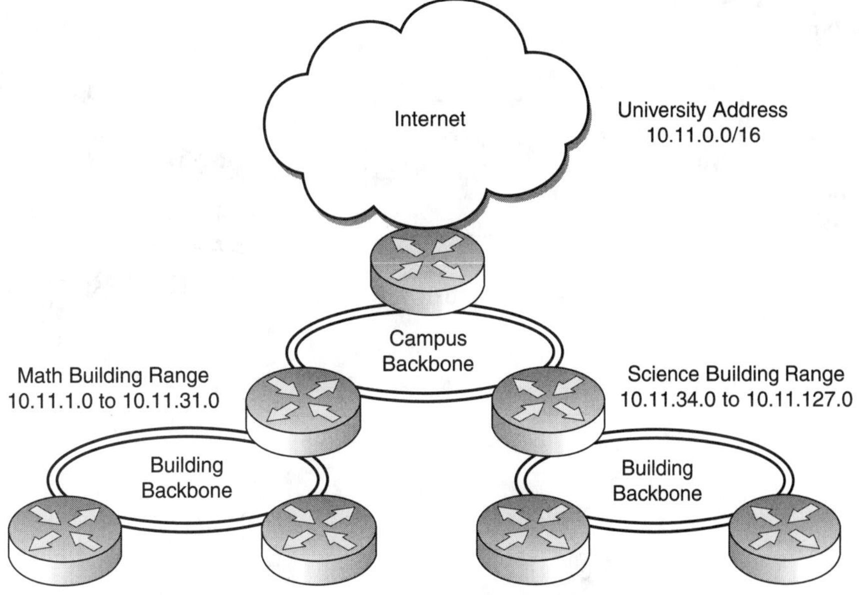

Figure 10-7 Prefix route summarization

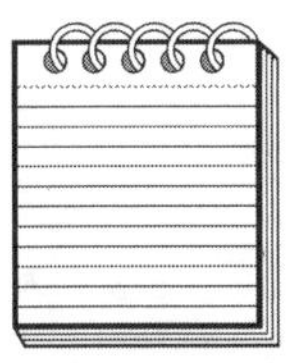

NOTE: *To manually summarize a network on a bit boundary, use this command:*

ip summary-address eigrp *autonomous-system summary address mask*

Mobile Hosts

EIGRP, like other major routing protocols, can use exception routing to enable hosts to move around within the same major network boundary. Take a look at Figure 10-8. A host has moved away from its primary LAN but is still within the same major network. EIGRP can use the most specific route to a host or a prefix match, whichever is best. This is a better alternative than using bridging in the network, but it is not as scalable as using classful routing.

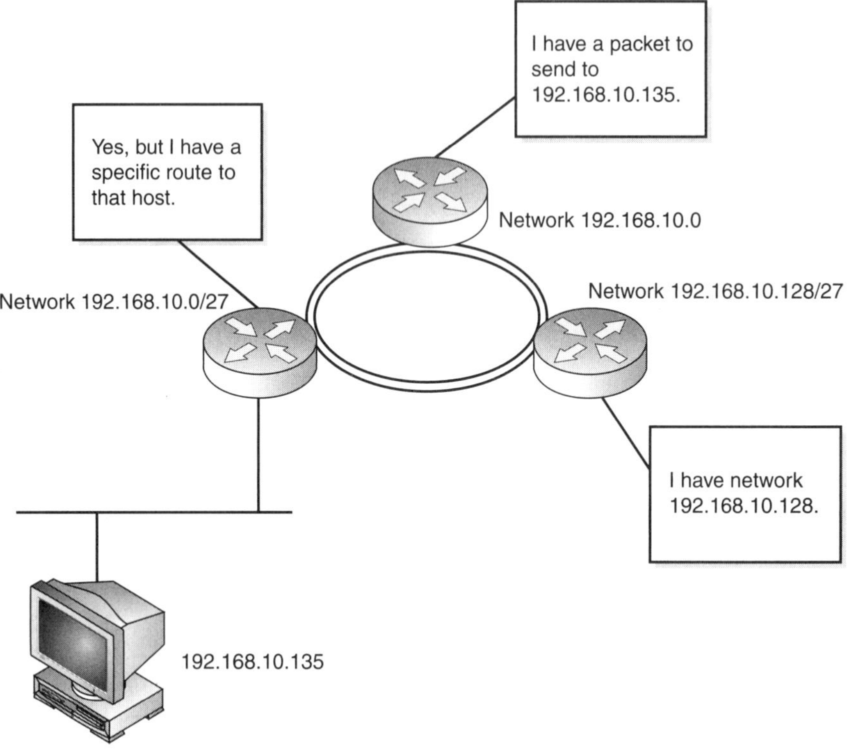
I have a packet to send to 192.168.10.135.
Yes, but I have a specific route to that host.
Network 192.168.10.0
Network 192.168.10.0/27
Network 192.168.10.128/27
I have network 192.168.10.128.
192.168.10.135

Figure 10-8
Exception routing

Discontiguous Subnets

As stated in the beginning of this section, the auto-summary feature of EIGRP works well for networks that have been planned along major network boundaries. The network shown in Figure 10-9, however, has a dedicated line linking two parts of major network 192.168.10.0 over a subnet that is not contiguous with that network. In this instance, you would turn off the auto-summary feature and manually configure the subnet advertisements.

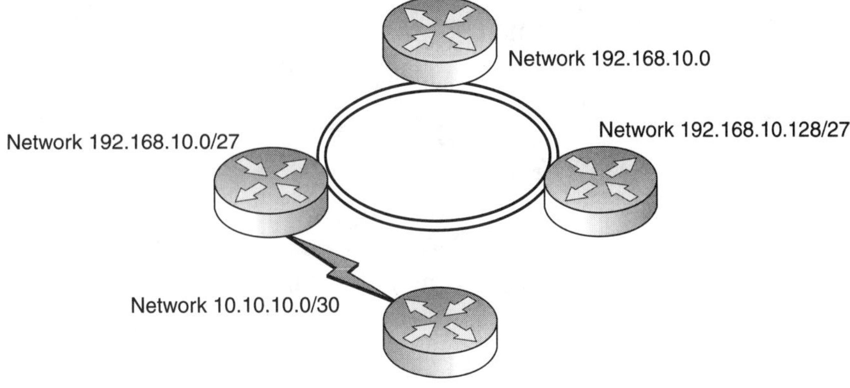

Figure 10-9 Discontiguous subnets

Enhanced Convergence

EIGRP converges very quickly, usually within 1 second of a failure. It determines what the fault is and then finds a workaround. Here is how the process works:

1. A local interface is down. If the carrier detect has failed or this is a beaconing Token Ring environment, this happens immediately. For other types of links, it is generally three times the 5-second hello timer.
2. The router searches its routing table for an alternate path to the destination.
3. If an alternate path is found, the router begins using it.
4. If no alternate path is found, the router queries its neighbors for another route. The queries propagate until an alternate route is found.
5. All routers that are affected update their routing tables.

The worst-case scenario for failover time is about 16 seconds. That is the equivalent of three missed hello packets from a down node plus 1 second to converge. In any case, the convergence is terribly fast.

DUAL

What is the DUAL algorithm? The acronym stands for Diffusing Update Algorithm. It is an algorithm that is used by EIGRP to ensure loop-free routing with update-only type routing updates. It is part of the DUAL finite-state machine. Here are the characteristics of DUAL:

- It permits rapid (1-second) convergence after link failures.
- It can perform route filtering at any node.
- The hello protocol helps prevent black holes. A *black hole* in a network is a destination to which traffic is being forwarded but which is unreachable.
- Because EIGRP is a reliable delivery protocol, DUAL provides for sequenced and acknowledged packets between nodes in order to guarantee convergence.
- Finally, routing information only goes to affected nodes, and then only the information that has changed.

The route that is found to have the best metric to a destination network is known as the *successor*. The way that EIGRP figures the routing metric is a little complex but is based on a formula applied to the minimum bandwidth and the delay of the link. The resulting value of the path with the best metric is known as the *feasible distance.* The paths with higher metrics to the same destination are known as *feasible successors.* Note that this only applies to loop-free paths.

One of the ways that DUAL keeps convergence time to a minimum is by not only having its own local routing table to work with, but also having a copy of the routing tables of all its neighbors. This allows it to calculate *ahead of time* a feasible successor for a least-cost path to any given destination. This greatly shortens the process of finding a route to a destination when the primary route fails. In a way, it allows the router to make an educated guess about what will happen if a route fails.

Load Balancing

Enhanced IGRP uses the same rules and functions for load balancing as its predecessor, IGRP. It can load balance over as many as four equal-cost paths. Using the variance command allows support for unequal-cost load balancing.

The variance in EIGRP is set to 1 by default. This will result in load balancing over equal-cost paths. With fast or autonomous switching, Cisco recommends that you leave the variance factor at 1. It is acceptable to set the variance to 2 for process switching over WAN links, however.

For more information on how unequal-path load balancing and variance work in both IGRP and EIGRP, go to Cisco's Web site at www.cisco.com/warp/public/103/19.html.

Problem Areas

A few problems can occur in both IGRP and EIGRP, but most of these are related to troubleshooting, which is outside the scope of this book. However, there is a redistribution issue that bears mentioning.

Redistribution is automatic between IGRP and EIGRP when both are configured with the same autonomous systems (AS) number. As a refresher, Table 10-1 shows the administrative distances for IGRP and EIGRP, as mentioned in Chapter 8, "Routing Protocol Design."

Table 10-1 Administrative Distances

Protocol	Administrative Distance (AD)
Internal EIGRP	90
External EIGRP	170
IGRP	100

What if Router C, in Figure 10-10, needs to reach Router A? It has both IGRP-derived routes as well as EIGRP-derived routes, assuming that redistribution is configured. You would think that the path through Router B would be preferred, because of the higher bandwidth and presumably lower delay. The configuration of Router C is shown here:

```
hostname Router C
!
router eigrp 100
 redistribute igrp 110
 network Router A
!
router igrp 110
 redistribute eigrp 100
 network Router A
!
```

However, the path through Router B will not be preferred. Note that the AD of internal EIGRP is higher than that of IGRP. According to Cisco, the

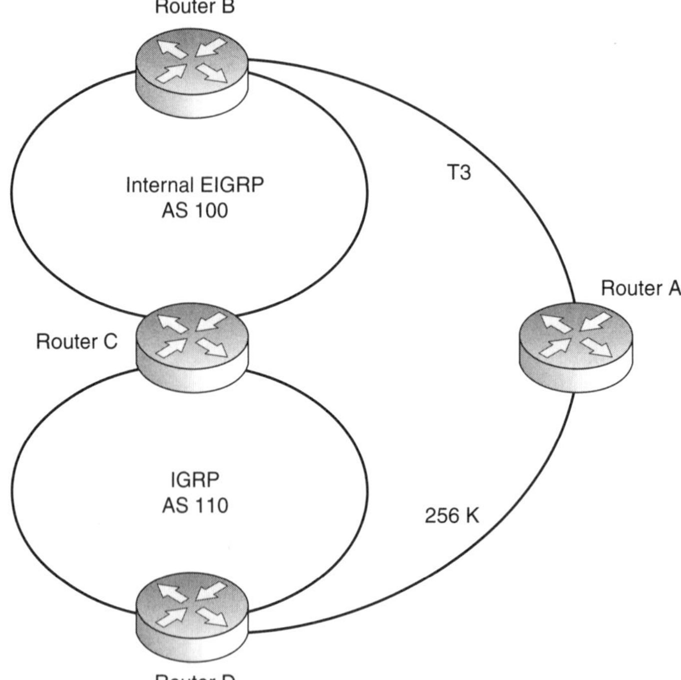

Figure 10-10 EIGRP/IGRP Redistribution

path through the routing protocol with the lowest AD will be selected and entered into the routing table.

A very simple fix to this problem is to use the same AS number for both routing protocols. This will cause the router to ignore the AD for the routing protocols and use the best metric for the path:

```
hostname Router C
!
router eigrp 100
 redistribute igrp 100
 network Router A
!
router igrp 100
 redistribute eigrp 100
 network Router A
!
```

Case Study

The WAN that supports communications for Tesla Oil Company is based in Texas and has three major locations: Houston, Austin, and Dallas, as shown in Figure 10-11. The Houston office was actually acquired from Armadillo Oil recently and is now about to be merged into the overall core network. From Houston to Austin, a T1 line has been installed, and likewise from Houston to Dallas. Between Dallas and Austin, however, there is a T3 line. This is because most of the bandwidth-intensive traffic will continue to be between those two sites.

The network in Houston was built using IGRP as the routing protocol and using a portion of the private address 172.16.0.0. Dallas is also using a portion of that private address space. Dallas and Austin, however, are using EIGRP. The network engineering staff in Houston does not want to transition to EIGRP. You have been hired to negotiate the overall design of the combined networks as well as to address any problems that may come up.

Here are the questions and concerns you will need to address:

- How will redistribution occur between EIGRP autonomous system 200, in Dallas and Austin, and IGRP autonomous system 110, in Houston?
- How will the discontiguous major network that is split between Houston and Dallas be resolved by EIGRP?

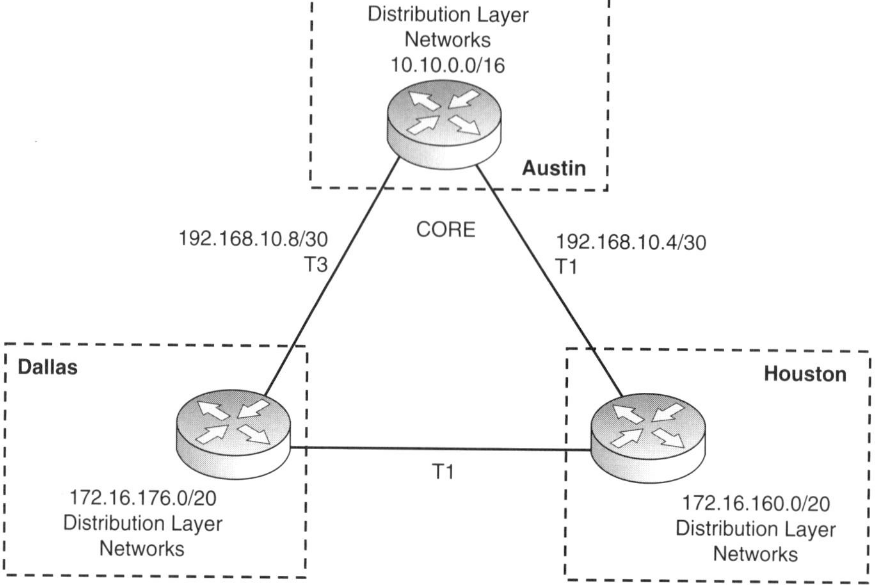

Figure 10-11 Tesla Oil Company

- The serial links also contain discontiguous network numbers. How will these be handled by EIGRP? Will they need to be renumbered?
- Will Houston be able to load balance between the direct T1 to Austin and the route through Dallas? If so, how will this be accomplished?

Although there is no one right answer to any given design problem, one possible solution appears in Appendix C, "Suggested Solutions to Case Studies."

Study Hints

Although no one can disclose test items or test content, we can give hints as to what might be valuable to study. For this chapter, some key facts need to be reviewed and remembered:

- Know your protocol facts about IGRP and EIGRP, although this applies to the other routing protocols as well.
- Understand what is meant by hierarchical design and how it impacts summarization.

- Review the facts about the timers and what they do.
- Understand how load balancing is performed and the impact of a change in the variance factor.

CCDP Tips

This section contains an abbreviated list of topics covered in this chapter. Think of this section as the equivalent of reading Cliff's Notes™ instead of reading an entire book. You will get the general idea of the chapter but will benefit more from reading the chapter in its entirety.

- **IGRP Routing** The Interior Gateway Routing Protocol is a protocol that works within a single autonomous system. It uses a sophisticated 24-bit metric that is based on bandwidth and delay but also takes other factors into account when finding the best path. It is a Cisco-proprietary protocol.
- **Split Horizon** Split horizon is enabled by default on IGRP (as well as EIGRP) but will disable when crossing a Frame Relay or SMDS WAN. A routing protocol using split horizon will not allow the advertisements of a route through a physical interface from which it learned that route.
- **Load Balancing** IGRP and EIGRP can load balance over as many as four paths, equal or not. If the variance factor is set to 1 (a recommendation when autonomous or fast switching is being used), the routing protocols can only load balance on equal-cost paths. A variance factor of 2 is usually appropriate for WAN links.
- **Routing Metric** The IGRP routing metric is a 24-bit value based on bandwidth and delay. Other factors involved in the selection of the best path include reliability, load, hops, and MTU.
- **Convergence** IGRP convergence is based on the use of triggered updates that are sent to other routers in the autonomous system when a link-down state occurs. A triggered update contains only the information needed, making it smaller than the 90-second-interval routing updates, and causes the other routers to place the route in a holddown state. Routers will then not "listen" to routing updates about that route until a timer has expired, making the route eligible for updates once again.

- **Timers**
  - Update interval: 90 seconds, by default
  - Invalid timer: 270 seconds, by default
  - Holddown timer: 280 seconds, by default (three times the update interval plus 10 seconds)
  - Flush timer: 630 seconds, or seven times the update interval, by default
- **EIGRP Routing**: EIGRP tables determine how each protocol will be handled over EIGRP. Each protocol type has its own module, which determines routing metric, times, and so on, but each protocol shares a common client interface to the protocol engine. The protocol engine calculates the next-hop router and feasible successor(s), provides reliable delivery of traffic, and discovers EIGRP neighbors. Each protocol module contains the following components:
  - Protocol-dependent modules (IP/IGRP, IPX, AppleTalk)
  - Client interface
  - Protocol engine (DUAL, reliable transport, neighbor discovery)
- **Route Summarization**: By default, EIGRP summarizes at major network boundaries. This is fine if you are using a hierarchical design. To support discontiguous networks, turn off the auto-summary feature of EIGRP.
- **Enhanced Convergence** EIGRP provides enhanced convergence over a typical distance vector protocol by calculating feasible successors, or the router that traffic to a destination will most likely use in the event that the primary path fails. This keeps convergence down to as little as 1 second. In the event that a link will not be considered down until three hellos have been missed, the convergence time will be 16 seconds (three missed 5-second hellos plus 1 second).
- **Diffusing Update Algorithm** DUAL performs the routing calculation and update functions in EIGRP. It is part of the DUAL finite-state machine and has the following characteristics:
  - Permits rapid convergence after link failures.
  - Performs route filtering at any node.

- Uses a hello protocol to prevent black holes.
- Provides for sequenced and acknowledged packets between nodes in order to guarantee convergence.
- Routing information only goes to affected nodes, and then only the information that has changed.

Summary

Enhanced IGRP is probably the most commonly used distance vector protocol in use in all-Cisco networks. It is robust, scales well for large internetworks, and has the versatility needed in many complex network designs. Its predecessor, IGRP, also provides scalability and critical features such as load balancing over unequal paths, but it does not offer some of the needs of today's modern networks, such as VLSM and multiprotocol support.

In the next few chapters, we'll be looking at AppleTalk, IPX, and Windows Networking—the desktop protocols. You will see how EIGRP can enhance what you can offer to your enterprise network users.

Questions

The following review questions have been selected to help you test your knowledge of the subject matter contained in this chapter. You will also find these questions contained in the CD-ROM included with this book. Although these are not the questions you will find in the certification exams, knowing the answers to the review questions in this book will help cement the material in your mind as you prepare for the tests.

1. Of the factors used by IGRP to determine the best path, which two comprise the routing metric? (Select two.)
   - a. Bandwidth
   - b. Delay
   - c. Hops
   - d. Reliability

2. Which statement best describes the function of the variance factor?
   a. A multiple that the router uses to determine the number of packets to send to each equal-cost path
   b. A multiple that the router uses to determine the number of paths over which it can load balance
   c. A multiple that the router uses to determine the number of keepalives to send to each unequal-cost path
3. What type of network model do you think works best with EIGRP?
   a. Nonhierarchical
   b. Hierarchical
4. In a worst-case scenario, what is the maximum convergence time for EIGRP?
   a. 1 second
   b. 15 seconds
   c. 27 seconds
   d. 16 seconds
5. True or False: IGRP will automatically enable split horizon over a Frame Relay WAN.
   a. True
   b. False
6. What is the optimum variance factor for a router using autonomous switching?
   a. 1
   b. 2
   c. 3
   d. 4
7. True or False: Delay is higher when the speed of the link is faster.
   a. True
   b. False
8. Which timer prevents regular routing updates from overtaking triggered updates?
   a. Flush timer
   b. Holddown timer
   c. Invalid timer
   d. Update timer

9. The update interval for IGRP is every ___ seconds.
   a. 30
   b. 60
   c. 90
   d. 180
10. Which statement best describes the function of the invalid timer?
    a. The invalid timer determines the time during which, if a route has not been heard about, it will become timed out.
    b. The invalid timer determines the time during which, if a route has not been heard about, it will be flagged as unreachable.
    c. The invalid timer determines the time at which, if a route has not been heard about, it will be removed from the database.
11. The next-hop router to which a given router will forward packets in the event of a primary path failure is called (a) ______________.
    a. Designated router
    b. Feasible successor
    c. Backup designated router
    d. Router A
12. True or false: The DUAL finite-state engine will send triggered updates to all adjacent neighbors in the event of a path failure.
    a. True
    b. False
13. What function of EIGRP should be modified if the network contains discontiguous subnets?
    a. Variance factor
    b. Keepalive timer
    c. Update interval
    d. Auto-summary
14. For EIGRP, which statement best describes the function of the protocol-dependent module?
    a. The protocol-dependent module is responsible for talking to DUAL.
    b. The protocol-dependent module is responsible for individual protocol behavior.
    c. The protocol-dependent module is responsible for reliable transport.

15. IGRP routing updates contain up to _____ entries in a _____-byte packet.
    a. 100, 1500
    b. 25, 1040
    c. 104, 1040
    d. 104, 1500
16. If the update interval for EIGRP were set to 180, what should the value of the flush timer be set to?
    a. 630
    b. 1260
    c. 760
    d. 540
17. Which statement best describes why IGRP cannot support VLSM?
    a. Because it does not carry the prefix in the header
    b. Because it does not understand subnet masks
    c. Because it does not support auto-summary
18. EIGRP can support mobile hosts by the use of what type of routing?
    a. Shortest path routing
    b. Exception routing
    c. Variance routing
    d. DHCP
19. For IGRP, what is the value of reliability based on?
    a. Hellos
    b. Keepalives
    c. Static values
    d. Dropped packets
20. True or False: EIGRP cannot be used in a WAN between two AppleTalk LANs that must see each other's Routing Table Maintenance Protocol (RTMP) updates.
    a. True
    b. False

Answers

1. Of the factors used by IGRP to determine the best path, which two comprise the routing metric? (Select two.)
   a. Bandwidth
   b. Delay
   Explanation: Although many factors are taken into account when a path is selected, only bandwidth and delay are part of the true routing metric for IGRP.

2. Which statement best describes the function of the variance factor?
   b. A multiple that the router uses to determine the number of paths over which it can load balance.
   Explanation: Although this is the best of the answer choices, even more specifically, variance of 1, which is the default, still load balances. It just does so over equal-cost paths only.

3. What type of network model do you think works best with EIGRP?
   b. Hierarchical
   Explanation: Most protocols do function better with a hierarchical structure. EIGRP, with its auto-summary feature, tends to like hierarchical models best.

4. In a worst-case scenario, what is the maximum convergence time for EIGRP?
   d. 16 seconds
   Explanation: Maximum convergence time is three missed hellos (5 seconds each) plus 1 second for DUAL to reconverge.

5. True or False: IGRP will automatically enable split horizon over a Frame Relay WAN.
   b. False
   Explanation: Although split horizon is enabled by default on IGRP, it is disabled automatically for traffic that is traversing a Frame Relay or SMDS WAN link.

6. What is the optimum variance factor for a router using autonomous switching?
   a. 1
   Explanation: A variance factor of 1, the default, helps prevent routes from being inadvertently cached when paths are of unequal speeds. This could cause what Cisco refers to as pinhole congestion.

7. True or False: Delay is higher when the speed of the link is faster.
   b. False
   Explanation: Delay is actually lower on faster links. It is inversely proportionate to the speed of the link.

8. Which timer prevents regular routing updates from overtaking triggered updates?
   b. Holddown timer
   Explanation: The holddown timer prevents routers from learning about a network that it has in a holddown state until the timer expires. This gives the network a chance to propagate the triggered updates and helps prevent routing loops caused by conflicting information.

9. The update interval for IGRP is every ___ seconds.
   c. 90 seconds

10. Which statement best describes the function of the invalid timer?
    a. The invalid timer determines the time during which, if a route has not been heard about, it will become timed out.
    Explanation: Remember the invalid timer only marks when the route times out. The route must still remain in the database in order for the holddown timer to enforce any holddown of the route. It is the flush timer that will eventually purge all knowledge of the route.

11. The next-hop router to which a given router will forward packets in the event of a primary path failure is called ________________.
    b. Feasible successor
    Explanation: DUAL can calculate ahead of time, based on the information in its databases, the path most likely to be the next-best path in case of a primary path failure. This choice is known as the *feasible successor*.

12. True or False: The DUAL finite-state engine will send triggered updates to all adjacent neighbors in the event of a path failure.
    b. False
    Explanation: Although DUAL will send updates in the event of a failure, it will not send them to neighboring routers that do not need the information.

13. What function of EIGRP should be modified if the network contains discontiguous subnets?
    d. Auto-summary
    Explanation: If EIGRP is using its auto-summary feature, it will be unable to route to certain networks that are not contiguous.

14. For EIGRP, which statement best describes the function of the protocol-dependent module?
    b. The protocol-dependent module is responsible for individual protocol behavior.
    Explanation: Although it is true that all the protocol-dependent modules talk to the DUAL finite-state engine, it is more specific to say that they are responsible for the behavior—timers, hellos, and metrics—of their individual protocol.

15. IGRP routing updates contain up to _____ entries in a _____ byte packet.
    d. 104,1500

16. If the update interval for EIGRP were set to 180, what should the value of the flush timer be set to?
    b. 1260
    Explanation: The rule of thumb is to make the flush timer seven times the value of the update interval, which in this case would be 1260.

17. Which statement best describes why IGRP cannot support VLSM?
    a. Because it does not carry the prefix in the header.
    Explanation: IGRP can, in fact, use subnets, but because the prefix is not carried in the header, it cannot use *variable* subnetting. All subnets that are advertised by IGRP or RIP must be equal. If the protocol compares the subnet mask before sending the update and finds that it does not match what is configured for that protocol in the router, it drops the route advertisement. For more information, see Cisco's Web site at www.cisco.com/warp/public/105/53.html.

18. EIGRP can support mobile hosts by the use of what type of routing?
    b. Exception routing
    Explanation: Exception routing enables EIGRP to use the most specific path to a destination, even if it doesn't agree with the prefixes advertised.

19. For IGRP, what is the value of reliability based on?
    b. Keepalives
    Explanation: The measurement of reliability is taken by determining the reliability at which keepalives are received. The point of worst reliability is used as the factor in the equation.

20. True or False: EIGRP cannot be used in a WAN between two AppleTalk LANs that must see each other's RTMP updates.
    b. False
    Explanation: In fact, EIGRP works well between two AppleTalk LANs. It can carry AppleTalk between the two without adding to the hop count.

Frequently Asked Questions (FAQs)

1. *Is EIGRP difficult to configure?*

   If you can configure IGRP, you can configure EIGRP. They are quite similar, but EIGRP gives you a lot more versatility.

2. *How is EIGRP different from OSPF?*

   For one thing, EIGRP doesn't use the area concept that is integral to OSPF operation. It is also a distance vector protocol, rather than a link-state protocol. It offers similar scalability as well as VLSM, the same as OSPF, without many of the complexities.

3. *What is Fast IGRP?*

   Fast IGRP is a modified IGRP configuration that prevents routes from going into a holddown state when a route is lost. This can be detrimental, so Fast IGRP should only be configured on the advice of a Cisco TAC expert. For more information, refer to **www.cisco.com/warp/public/103/8.html**.

Bibliography

An Introduction to IGRP, Cisco Systems, Inc., **www.cisco.com/warp /public/103/5.html**.

An Introduction to EIGRP, Cisco Systems, Inc., **www.cisco.com/warp/ public/103/1 .html**.

Cisco Internetwork Design Course Manual, Version 3.0, April 1997, Cisco Systems, Inc.

EIGRP, Cisco Systems, Inc., **www.cisco.com/pcgi-bin/Support/PSP/ psp_view.pl?p5Internetworking:EIGRP**.

Retana, Alvaro, Don Slice, and Russ White. *CCIE Professional Development: Advanced IP Network Design*. Cisco Press, 1999.

CHAPTER 11

Desktop Design Overview

Overview

Over the last few chapters we have talked about routing protocols and how to design networks based on them. Now we are going to introduce you to the protocols that work at the desktop level. These are the protocols that allow clients to talk to servers and vice versa. AppleTalk, Novell's Internetwork Packet eXchange (IPX), and Microsoft Windows products will be briefly explored before we move on to focus on each type of client/server design in the next few chapters.

Desktop Protocols

Desktop protocols, in general, are the *routed* (routable), network layer protocols in the network design—with the exception of NetBIOS and NetBEUI (NetBIOS over LLC2), which are non-routable protocols. In the last few chapters we have been discussing *routing* protocols that set the rules for communication over routers in the enterprise or Wide Area Network (WAN). Routed protocols are carried along the network path by routing protocols to allow clients and servers to talk to one another over a LAN.

With routable protocols, all of the nodes, or physical devices, in a network are subdivided into smaller, logical groups. These groups are usually network segments, such as Ethernet segments or the like. Each logical group has a unique network number within the greater enterprise network. If two nodes within a logical group need to pass traffic to each other, they do not need the network number, as they are on the same network. They find each other by using the layer 2 address of each other's NIC through a bridge, switch, or hub.

If the nodes must talk to a device on another logical group, they must send the traffic through a router, which knows the location of all of the logical groups by unique network number. If the network number were not unique, the router would not know to which logical group it should forward the packet. This is also the best explanation of why RFC 1918 private addresses cannot be used over the Internet. The network numbers are not unique to a given logical group. Many groups all over the world use the same numbers.

The desktop protocols we are going to discuss were created to allow LANs with multiple hosts to operate as a single broadcast domain, linking clients to servers that deliver content and services over the network. From a design standpoint, you must create a functional environment with sufficient bandwidth to handle the broadcasts to and from the end-stations as well as the content to be carried. Since the desktop protocols rely on broadcasts for clients and servers to find one another, there is a lot of overhead that needs to be considered.

As seen in Chapter 1, clients can be found at the Access layer of the three-layer network design model. Since this is where you will find the clients, this is also where you will find the protocols that support those clients, as shown in Figure 11-1.

Designed to communicate over the LAN architecture on layers 1 and 2 of the OSI model, desktop protocols are based on layers 3 and above, as seen in Figure 11-2. Remember that the routing protocols operate at layer 3, but some routed protocols can also operate at layer 3. AppleTalk and IPX are routable and can be routed across a campus backbone, but it is not normally considered to be appropriate to do so.

Windows desktop protocols, such as NetBIOS and NetBEUI, are non-routable and require bridging in order to communicate with other end-stations over a campus backbone. Bridging, which works at layer 2, extends the broadcast domain over multiple network segments. This is not usually recommended, as it is almost always detrimental to overall network performance. Routers, as you recall, are natural broadcast limiters. To negate this positive trait is to flood your entire network with broadcasts, which creates a lot of unnecessary network overhead.

Figure 11-1 Desktop protocols in the design

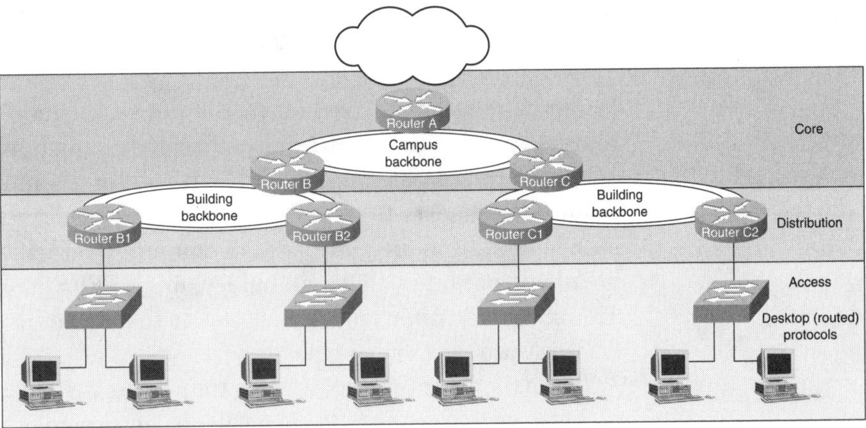

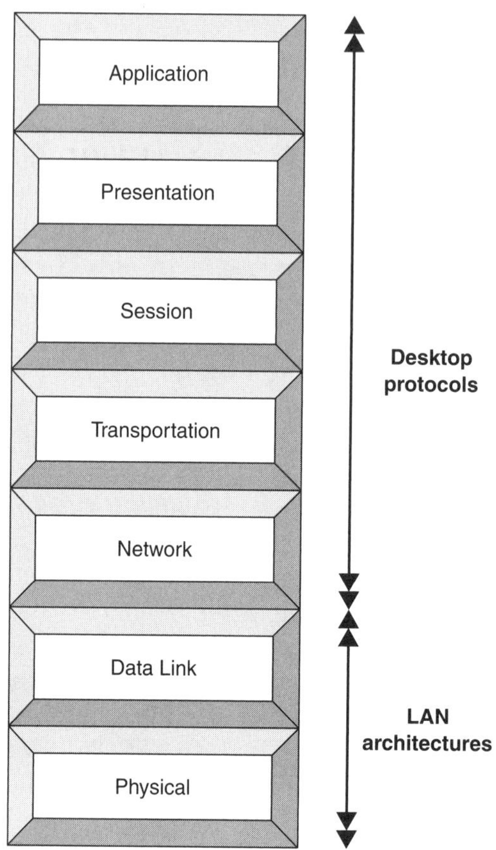

Figure 11-2 Desktop protocols in the OSI model

Broadcast Design

In our discussions of routing in the network thus far, we have seen that routers function as a natural broadcast limiting device, creating a barrier between broadcast domains. Client/server communications, however, require broadcasts to be able to function. Broadcast packets are heard by each end-station in a broadcast domain. The destination address in a broadcast packet is all 1's (in binary) or FFFFFF-FFFFFF in hexadecimal. This special destination address serves to make sure that every host on the network processes the packet.

In the client/server architecture, the servers may broadcast announcements of the services they have to offer. Clients, in turn, may broadcast a request for a service. If a client requires print services or an IP address, for example, it broadcasts on the LAN for these resources, as shown in Figure 11-3.

Wide Area Network (WAN) Considerations

As you can probably imagine, any kind of broadcast traffic creates a lot of overhead for the LAN or WAN, especially if the network design is not well planned in order to limit the need for many broadcasts or the number of hosts in a broadcast domain. In a high-speed LAN environment, the network performance may not suffer very much from the overhead, but in a lower-speed environment, such as over a dial-up line, the network may slow down greatly because so much bandwidth is being consumed by the broadcast traffic.

Another reason you may want to consider limiting broadcast traffic is that unnecessary traffic may activate a dial-on-demand link, thus incurring charges for "uninteresting" traffic. In Figure 11-4, the same LAN we saw in Figure 11-3 is now connected by a 256Kbps (fractional T1) link to the WAN through a router.

The router could be configured to forward *all* broadcasts, by enabling bridging on the interface, or could be allowed to drop all broadcasts as they arrive. In some instances you may want to allow certain broadcasts to be

Figure 11-3 Client/server broadcasts

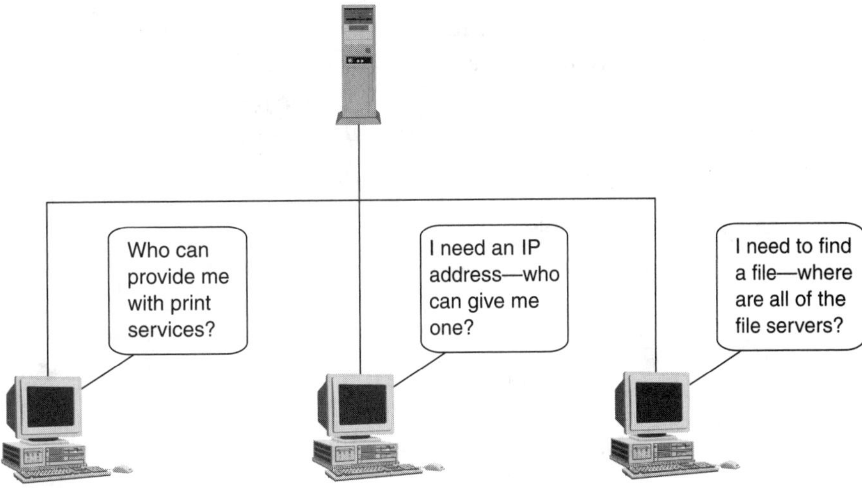

Who can provide me with print services?
I need an IP address—who can give me one?
I need to find a file—where are all of the file servers?

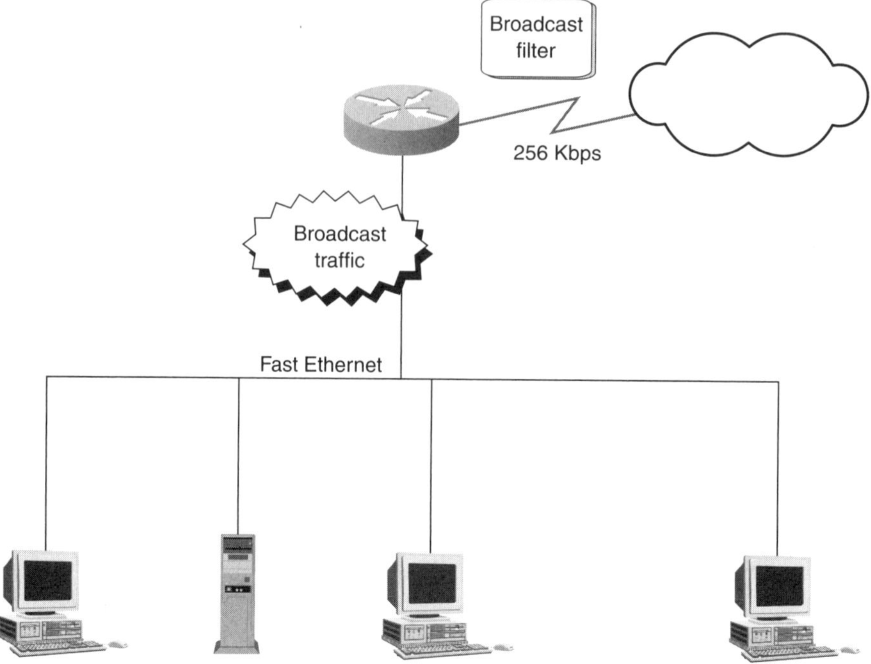

Figure 11-4
Broadcast filters

forwarded, selectively, by the router. If this requirement is part of your network design, be sure that all other options are carefully considered first. Things such as moving the servers to the same broadcast domain with the clients, allowing clients to use a local server for resources, or eliminating the need for the resources being requested over the WAN, can all help you to avoid the need to forward broadcasts.

Of the many types of client/server protocols used over the last two decades, the ones that have remained the most common are

- Novell Internetwork Packet eXchange
- AppleTalk
- Windows NetBIOS/NetBEUI

Novell Internetwork Packet eXchange (IPX)

Novell IPX was created by Novell, Inc., in the 1980s. Based on Xerox Network Systems (XNS), a product of Xerox Corp., IPX is a protocol that runs on the NetWare networking software suite. We will discuss IPX in more detail in Chapter 12, but for now we will look at the types of broadcasts seen in a network using IPX and some methods to control them.

The types of broadcasts used in Novell Networks' IPX protocol are

- Routing Information Protocol (RIP)
- Service Advertisement Protocol (SAP)
- NetBIOS over IPX (NWLink)

RIP is the protocol used to send and receive routing updates, a process that normally takes place every 60 seconds on an IPX network. These updates can carry up to 50 network advertisements per packet.

SAP is the protocol used by the IPX servers to advertise the services that they are offering to IPX clients. SAP updates are also broadcast every 60 seconds and can contain up to seven SAPs per update.

Broadcasts for NetBIOS are *only* seen when NetBIOS emulation is in use on the IPX network. Filtering strategies should be used in an IPX network in order to control the numbers and scope of the broadcasts, as in Figure 11-5. LAN A is able to send and receive the required broadcasts to operate the client/server network without disrupting LAN B, when filtering is appropriately applied.

When the three-layer hierarchical network design model is applied, filtering the broadcasts is relatively straightforward. The LANs shown in Figure 11-5 are operating at the Access layer of the design, while the router could also be in the Access layer but is more likely in the Distribution layer of the design.

Another design strategy for IPX networks is to use an advanced routing protocol, such as Enhanced Interior Gateway Router Protocol (EIGRP) or NetWare Link Services Protocol (NLSP), a Novell proprietary hierarchical link-state protocol similar to OSI's Intermediate System-to-Intermediate System (ISIS).

AppleTalk

Apple Corporation developed AppleTalk for its Macintosh computer line in the 1980s. As with all of the desktop protocols, it enables clients to find servers that are offering the files, printers, users, and other resources that they need. A Cisco router connected to an AppleTalk network is considered a *node* or a *port,* while the physical segment itself is considered to be the *network*, which is identified by a unique 16-bit number. AppleTalk users are grouped into *zones*, which are logical groups of one or more networks.

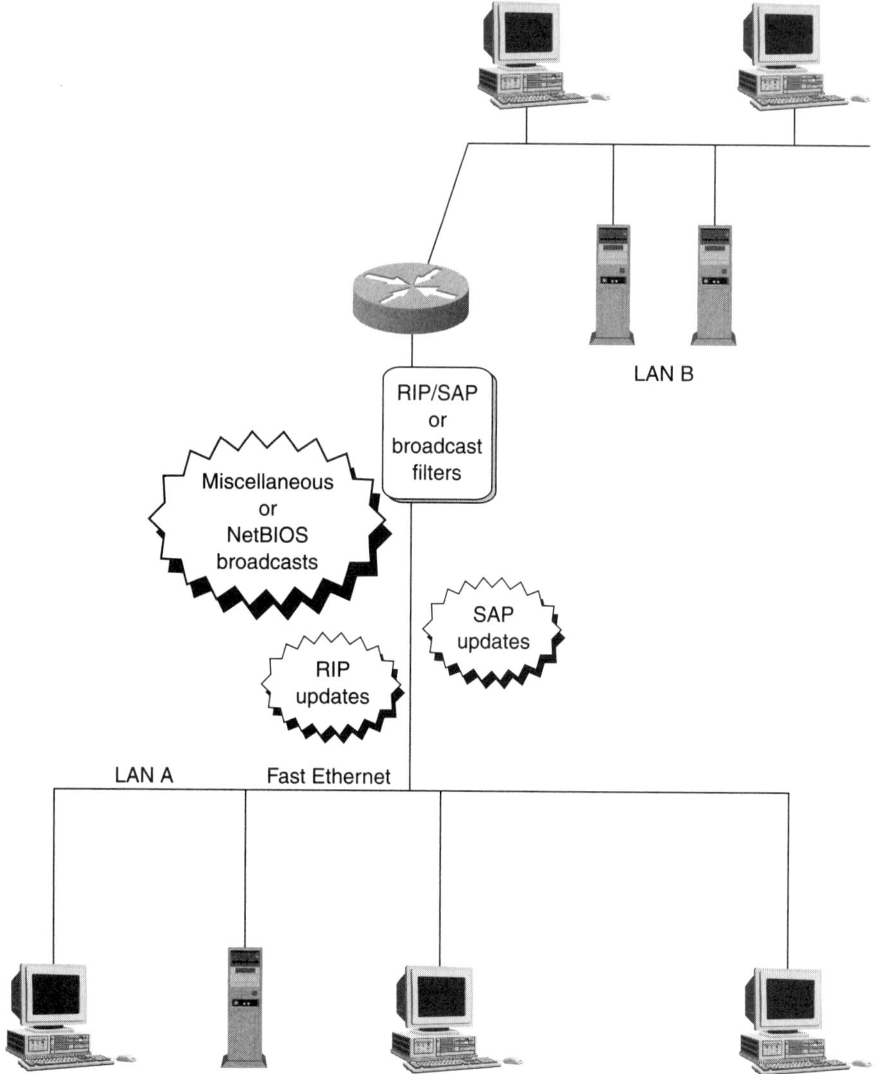

Figure 11-5 Filtering IPX broadcast traffic

In Cisco routers, AppleTalk is supported over FDDI, Ethernet, synchronous serial, and X.25 interfaces, as well as over bridging. It can be routed by using any of these three routing protocols:

- Enhanced IGRP
- Routing Table Maintenance Protocol (RTMP)
- AppleTalk Update Routing Protocol (AURP)

We will be discussing AppleTalk at a deeper level in Chapter 13, but what we will concentrate on for now is the type of broadcast traffic that you will see coming from AppleTalk in the network environment and how to control that.

The types of broadcasts seen in an AppleTalk environment are

- Routing Table Maintenance Protocol (RTMP)
- Zone Information Protocol (ZIP)
- Name Binding Protocol (NBP)

RTMP is very similar to RIP in its functionality. It is a distance vector protocol that sends the entire routing table every 10 seconds and is limited to 15 hops. RTMP follows split-horizon rules in sending its updates.

When an AppleTalk client is booted up, it starts sending broadcasts to request zone, address, and name information. An AppleTalk zone is the broadcast domain in which the clients and servers are operating. But, similar to a VLAN, a zone can reside across multiple AppleTalk networks. The clients and servers communicate and share this information by using ZIP to provide the zone information and NBP to bind the name and address to the client's MAC address.

To control the broadcast traffic on an AppleTalk LAN, the network designer can use filters, the hierarchical network design and well-planned AppleTalk zones. Advanced routing protocols can also be used to reduce the size of zones and thus the size of the broadcast domain.

Windows Networks

Client/server networks using Windows software communicate over a Session layer protocol called NetBIOS, with the exception of Windows 2000 implementations, which only uses NetBIOS for backward compatibility. NetBIOS can run on any of the following transport protocols:

- NetBEUI (which is NetBIOS over LLC2)
- NWLink (which is NetBIOS over IPX)
- NetBIOS over TCP (NBT)

The NetBIOS protocol is used in a similar fashion to other desktop protocols—for file sharing, printer sharing, messaging, and name resolution. Windows desktops can browse other desktops in the same subnet by broadcasting queries by name. The name-to-address mapping can either be accomplished through a host file called LMHOSTS that resides on the client or through browsing listings contained on the master browser of the domain.

When using this type of name resolution in a network, the only way that clients from different subnets could find each other was if bridging were enabled over the router interfaces. This is not recommended, because it allows all types of protocols to flow freely between interfaces and slows performance on the router. A better choice is to use Windows Internet Name Service (WINS), which acts as a registration point, to put it simply, for clients and servers, regardless of subnet affiliation.

In the network design, the two best options for avoiding broadcast problems are to use either NBT, which allows NetBIOS to run via the TCP stack, or NWLink, which allows NetBIOS to run over the IPX protocol. Since both protocols are routable, this helps to solve the problems inherent in a non-routable protocol, such as standard NetBIOS.

Problem Areas

The primary problem in designing the desktop portion of the network is the need to contain broadcasts in small segments of the WAN. Since broadcasting over a WAN environment can lead to poor overall network performance, it is critical to lay out the network design carefully, so that clients are contained within the subnet in which the resources they need (on servers) reside. This is the best way to control broadcast traffic.

The second way to control the traffic is to use a routable protocol to route the broadcasts over the WAN only when necessary. Controlling the broadcast traffic in this scenario involves the use of filtering or caching techniques. We will discuss how to do this in future chapters.

Study Hints

In this chapter, a lot of material has been covered. Here are areas that you should review before attempting any Cisco network design certification tests.

- *Understand the difference between routed and routing protocols.* A routed protocol is one that can be routed over a network—a routable protocol, in other words. Examples are IPX, AppleTalk, and NWLink (NetBIOS over IPX). A routing protocol sets the rules for how traffic moves through a network, including path determination and routing table updates.
- *Know what makes a protocol non-routable.* A protocol is non-routable if it does not use a unique network numbering system. Examples of non-routable protocols are DEC LAT and standard NetBIOS.
- *Understand the effect of broadcasts on a WAN and how to control this detrimental behavior.* Broadcasts tend to lead to poor performance on a WAN because of the unnecessary overhead they create. Remember that the WAN is generally the Core layer of the network design, where the movement of traffic at optimal speeds and efficiency is of utmost importance. Broadcasts can also keep lines such as ISDN links active, even if they are primarily for backup use. This can be costly. The control of broadcast traffic is usually performed by allowing the default behavior of the router (a natural broadcast firewall), employing filtering or caching techniques, and avoiding bridging traffic.
- *Know the appropriate location of the desktop protocols in the three-layer network design model.* Desktop protocols are normally found at the Access layer of the three-layer network design model. Remember that hosts (including clients and servers) should be kept out of the Core layer. The Distribution layer generally provides for Internet connectivity and the movement of traffic to and from the core.

CCDP Tips

This section contains an abbreviated list of topics covered in Chapter 11. Think of this section as the equivalent of reading Cliff's Notes™ instead of reading an entire book. You will get the general idea of the chapter but will benefit more from reading the chapter in its entirety.

- Commonly used desktop protocols for client/server communications are
  - AppleTalk
  - Internetwork Packet eXchange (IPX)
  - NetBIOS/NetBEUI (Windows)
- Desktop protocols are the routed protocols versus the routing protocols, which we have been discussing.
- Desktop protocols are normally found at the Access layer of the three-layer network design model.
- Clients and servers communicate by using broadcasts for resources. Since routers are natural broadcast firewalls, you may route the IPX or AppleTalk traffic when needed.
- NetBIOS and NetBEUI are non-routable and must be bridged in order to communicate across separate broadcast domains, but *this is not recommended!*
- Novell's IPX protocol uses the following three types of broadcasts:
  - Routing Information Protocol (RIP)
  - Service Advertisement Protocol (SAP)
  - NetBIOS
- Apple's AppleTalk protocol uses the following three types of broadcasts:
  - Routing Table Maintenance Protocol (RTMP)
  - Zone Information Protocol (ZIP)
  - Name Binding Protocol (NBP)
- Windows networking uses the following methods of client/server communications:
  - NetBIOS
  - NetBIOS over TCP (NBT)
  - NetBIOS over IPX (NWLink)

- Broadcast control can be accomplished by the following:
  - Default router behavior
  - Filtering
  - Caching
  - Avoiding bridging

Summary

As we have shown you, the most commonly deployed protocols for client/server communications are Novell's IPX, Windows NetBIOS, and Apple Corporation's AppleTalk protocols. Each type uses its own special broadcast packets to advertise and find network resources. The focus of designing for desktop protocols should be the containment of this broadcast traffic to small, specific areas so that it does not become a drain on overall network performance.

In Chapter 12 we will take a more in-depth look at designing for Novell IPX networking.

Questions

1. Select the broadcast type IPX uses to advertise print services.
   a. RIP
   b. SAP
   c. NetBIOS
   d. PRT
2. Which protocol is non-routable?
   a. AppleTalk
   b. IPX
   c. NetBIOS

3. At which network design layer are desktop protocols found?
   a. Core
   b. Access
   c. Distribution
4. Select the broadcast type AppleTalk uses to share routing updates.
   a. AURP
   b. RIP
   c. RTMP
   d. ZIP
5. True or False: SAP updates cannot be filtered.
   a. True
   b. False
6. How often are SAP updates broadcast?
   a. Every 10 seconds
   b. Every 30 seconds
   c. Every 90 seconds
   d. Every 60 seconds
7. True or False: AppleTalk Update Routing Protocol (AURP) is an open standard protocol.
   a. True
   b. False
8. True or False: Broadcast filters must be enabled on a router in order to block broadcast radiation across a WAN.
   a. True
   b. False
9. In which case will NetBIOS broadcasts be seen on a broadcast domain?
   a. When NetBIOS over IPX is enabled
   b. When Windows workstations are on the same broadcast domain
   c. When Raw Ethernet is in use
   d. When a user enables the TCP/IP stack in the Novell workstation

10. At which layer of the OSI model will you find desktop protocols?
    a. Session
    b. Network
    c. Transport
    d. All of the above

Answers

1. Select the broadcast type IPX uses to advertise print services.
   b. SAP
2. Which protocol is non-routable?
   c. NetBIOS
3. At which network design layer are desktop protocols found?
   b. Access
4. Select the broadcast type AppleTalk uses to share routing updates.
   c. RTMP
5. True or False: SAP updates cannot be filtered.
   b. False
6. How often are SAP updates broadcast?
   d. Every 60 seconds
7. True or False: AppleTalk Update Routing Protocol (AURP) is an open standard protocol.
   a. True
8. True or False: Broadcast filters must be enabled on a router in order to block broadcast radiation across a WAN.
   b. False
9. In which case will NetBIOS broadcasts be seen on a broadcast domain?
   a. When NetBIOS over IPX is enabled
10. At which layer of the OSI model will you find desktop protocols?
    d. All of the above

Bibliography

Cisco Connection Online-Routing Protocols: AppleTalk **http://www.cisco.com/warp/public/cc/techno/dety/alty/tech/aptlk_pc.htm**

Cisco Internetwork Design, Cisco Press, 2000, Matthew H. Birkner, Editor

Cisco Internetwork Design Course Manual, version 3.0, April 1997, Cisco Systems, Inc.

Thomas Concise Telecom and Networking Dictionary, McGraw-Hill, 2000, Thomas M. Thomas II, Editor

CHAPTER 12

IPX Design

Overview

What desktop protocol should you choose for the enterprise network? The answer to that question may depend more on client or staff preference than on anything else, or, in some cases, it may depend on your particular area of expertise. You may find that you are more comfortable with one protocol than another. Some network architects make their living designing only Windows networks; others prefer AppleTalk or IPX. In this first of three desktop protocol chapters, we are going to examine Novell's Internetwork Packet eXchange (IPX) protocol and related-design topics.

History

Novell's IPX is a routed protocol based on Xerox Network Systems (XNS), an earlier network-layer software. IPX was created to be the Network Operating System (NOS) for the once very popular Novell NetWare client/server system. Novell was one of the first companies to introduce the idea of print and file services—and the related cost savings—to the PC user world. It also had great flexibility, because it could support many different types of access methods—Token Ring, FDDI, Ethernet—and a variety of NICs. Although it was designed primarily with DOS-based PCs in mind, it also supported SNA, Apple, Unix, and OS/2 environments.

What Novell created was a protocol that allowed users on different types of workstations to all use the same resources and to share files with each other. One user might be on an Apple Macintosh while another might be on a Unix workstation. By placing a native IPX router in the middle of the segments, Novell allowed for the "bridging" of the access methods. What Novell called *bridging* was actually *routing*, but the terminology was different in Novell's original documentation (prior to version 3.x).

Novell Network Protocols

Novell supports several different processes and protocols that closely correspond to the OSI model, as shown in Table 12-1. It is because of the extensive support at all layers of the OSI model that Novell was able to offer

Table 12-1

OSI Model vs. Novell Protocols

OSI Layer	Novell Protocols
Presentation Application	NetWare Core Protocol (NCP), Remote Procedure Call (RPC) and related applications, Service Advertisement Protocol (SAP), Routing Information Protocol (RIP)
Session	NetBIOS emulation, NetWare shell
Transport	SPX
Network	IPX
Data Link Physical	Access protocols/wiring techniques, Ethernet, Token Ring, FDDI, PPP

support to so many types of access methods and user communities. For a period of time, Novell held a very large market share and enjoyed great popularity.

Novell Encapsulations

The type of encapsulation used for your IPX network will depend largely on what type of topology will be used. If you are using Ethernet, you have several choices. FDDI and Token Ring users have a couple of choices. This decision also depends on whether you will be bridging or routing IPX. When bridging, you must design the network to support *all* encapsulation types. When you're routing, the router can handle different encapsulations on different interfaces. It is important to stick with a single encapsulation per interface, however.

Ethernet

Four types of encapsulation are available for IPX over Ethernet, as listed in Table 12-2.

Table 12-2
Ethernet Encapsulations

Cisco Term	Novell Term	Encapsulation
novell-ether	ETHERNET_802.3	802.3 with FFFF
SNAP	ETHERNET_SNAP	802.2 SNAP with 8137
sap or iso1	ETHERNET_802.2	802.2 with E0E0 sap
ARPA	ETHERNET_II	arpa with 8137 type

You may have heard the term *raw Ethernet* in conjunction with IPX networks. This is an older Novell term that referred to ETHERNET_802.3. This term is now no longer in use, but you may run across it in some texts and therefore in some tests. Remember that now it is called *novell-ether*, by Cisco. Basically, novell-ether is an IEEE 802.3 encapsulation with a Destination Service Access Point (DSAP) and Source Service Access Point (SSAP) value of FFFF, with no Logical Link Control (LLC) layer. This was once the default encapsulation for IPX.

With the Novell NetWare 4.x release, the default is now ETHERNET_802.2, which places a value of E0E0 in both the DSAP and SSAP. This would either be configured as *sap* or *iso1* on a Cisco router.

Token Ring and FDDI

Because the router can tell the difference between the different encapsulations, IPX networks can use a variety of media, including FDDI and Token Ring. For FDDI, both snap and 802.2 are supported, as is FDDI_RAW, which is used on bridges and switches in some Novell implementations. FDDI_RAW can then be routed to other media using one of the other two FDDI encapsulations. Encapsulation types support for Token Ring and FDDI are shown in Table 12-3.

Table 12-3

Token Ring and FDDI Encapsulations

Cisco Term	Novell Term	Encapsulation
snap	FDDI_SNAP	802.2 SNAP with 8137
sap or iso1	FDDI_802.2	802.2 with E0E0 saps
novell-tr	TOKEN-RING	802.2 with E0E0 saps
Snap	TOKEN-RING_SNAP	802.2 SNAP with 8137

Multiple Encapsulations on a Single Interface

Because a router strips off the frame that encapsulates the data, it can convert encapsulation between different sub-interfaces on the same LAN and connect networks together that use different encapsulation types. In Figure 12-1 you can see that three sub-interfaces have been configured, each with a different IPX network number and encapsulation type. Although all three IPX networks connect to a single-physical interface, the use of sub-interfaces permits the different frame types to be used.

This is not an optimal design. The preference would be to stick with a single encapsulation type per physical interface. Using the router as a relay introduces latency into what could be a single network, single frame type environment. It also introduces a "middle man" (the router) where there need not be one.

TIP: *To enable IPX fast switching on the interface shown in Figure 12-1, use the command* **ipx route-cache same-interface**.

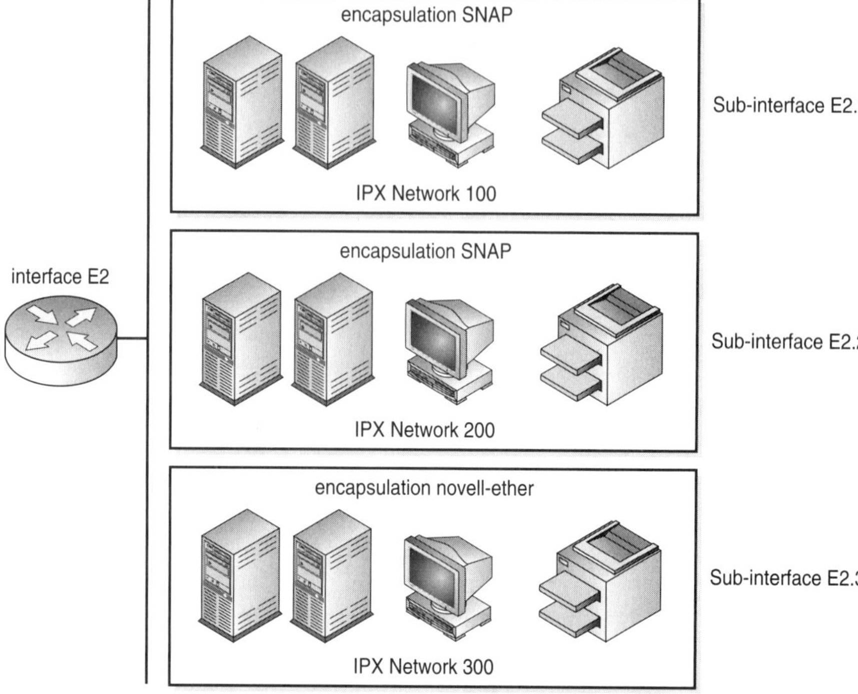

Figure 12-1 IPX sub-interfaces and multiple encapsulations

Novell Routing

Novell uses a routing protocol similar to IP Routing Information Protocol (RIP). This protocol, called IPX RIP, sends routing updates every 60 seconds, with a 180-second interval to flush the route cache. IPX RIP also uses split horizon to avoid the "count-to-infinity" problem. You cannot disable split horizon on IPX RIP, however, so there can be a problem with some Non-Broadcast Multi-Access (NBMA) packet-switched WAN configurations. Connectivity for IPX RIP is limited to directly connected peers.

In addition to split horizon, IPX RIP uses the *lost route algorithm* to find an alternate route if a route fails. When a route fails, as shown in Figure 12-2, an update is triggered that flags the network as unreachable. The router then waits for a count of 10 ticks—putting the network into hold-down—before checking for an alternate route. A tick is defined as approximately 1/18th of one second, or 55 msecs. (There are 18.21 ticks per second on a personal computer.) The lost route algorithm is then run only if there is not a suitable alternate route already in the table.

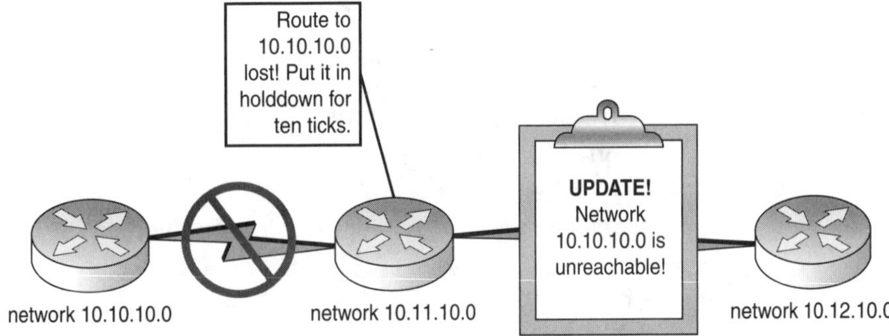

Figure 12-2
IPX RIP route failure

The routing metric used for IPX RIP is *delay*, as measured in hop count and ticks. A LAN port counts as one tick. A WAN port counts as six ticks. You can see an example of this in Figure 12-3. How is the best route chosen, you may ask, when all counts are equal?

If the tick count to a destination is equal in more than one path, the router will then consider hop count. Hop count will break the tie, so to speak. In the unlikely event that even the hop count is equal and the number of routes in the routing table has reached the value of the **ipx maximum-paths** command, the final decision rests on the interface delay. We will further discuss the **ipx maximum-paths** parameter in the IPX Switching Modes/Load Balancing section later in this chapter.

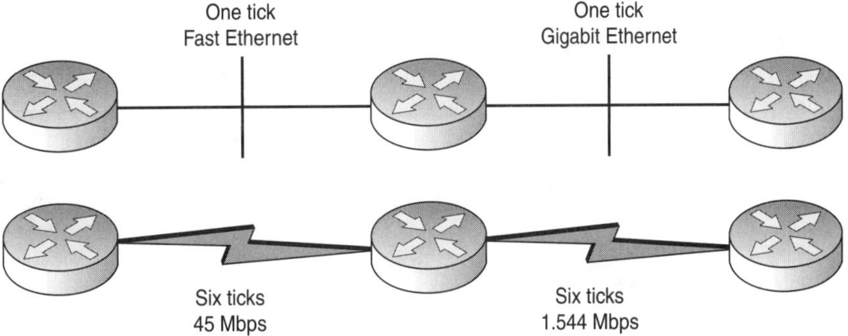

Figure 12-3
IPX routing metrics

Transport Protocol

NetWare uses the Sequenced Packet eXchange (SPX) protocol at the transport layer. SPX is a connection-oriented protocol, derived from XNS Sequenced Packet Protocol (SPP), that complements the service provided by IPX. When using the TCP/IP stack, however, you would use UDP as the transport protocol for communication over a TCP/IP network.

IPXWAN

IPXWAN is a Novell serial link encapsulation protocol—defined in RFC 1634—that allows for the link setup and negotiation packets over a point-to-point, Frame Relay or X.25 link. IPXWAN is supported on all Cisco routers. It is required in order to interoperate with the Novell NetWare Multiprotocol Router (MPR), which is a software-based router that runs on a server. IPXWAN can use the NetWare Link Services Protocol (NLSP) routing protocol over the serial connection.

A point-to-point WAN using IPXWAN is shown in Figure 12-4. IPXWAN is very similar to IPX RIP, in that each uses a combination of ticks and hop counts as the default-routing metric.

IPXWAN supports both IP and IPX over PPP between Novell servers and Cisco routers. When you're connecting two Cisco routers, IPXWAN over High-Level Data Link Control (HDLC) is supported.

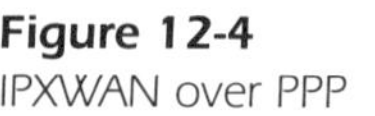

Figure 12-4 IPXWAN over PPP

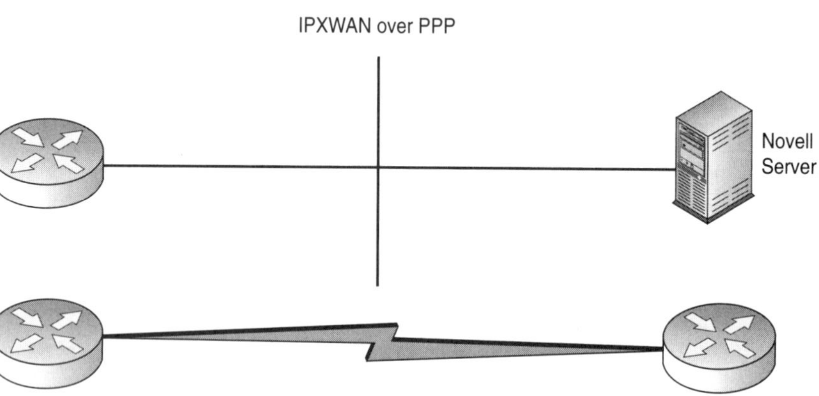

As discussed in the last section, a tick equals 1/18th of one second. When a WAN link comes up, IPXWAN determines the tick count, or *metric*. Alternatively, you can set this value manually for an interface, if you wish, by using the **ipx delay** command. Cisco and Novell recommend using the values shown in Table 12-4, which are based on the formula used in IPXWAN 2.0.

IPX Switching Modes/Load Balancing

Switching for IPX is a little different from switching for IP on the router because of the data structure differences with IPX packets. Three kinds of switching can be done for IPX:

- *Process switching* is a form of load balancing that operates on a per-packet basis. This is also the way IP process switching works.
- *Fast switching* in IPX also works on a packet-by-packet basis, which is different from the way it works in IP, where it is by destination.
- *Autonomous* or *silicon switching* is the method in IPX that load-balances on a per-destination basis.

Table 12-4

Suggested Delay Values

WAN Connection Bandwidth	Tick Count
2.04 Mbps	6
1.544 Mbps	6
256 Kbps	6
128 Kbps	12
56 Kbps	18
38.4 Kbps	24
19.2 Kbps	60
9600 Bps	108

NOTE: You must have a Cisco 7500 series router (or better) in order to perform autonomous / silicon switching.

Even though you will notice that fast switching uses the same method as process switching, they do differ in one important aspect. The fast switching method will build a fastswitch cache that keeps track of the paths to a given destination. If load balancing is not enabled, the fastswitch cache will only contain one entry per destination. If more than one equal-cost entry exists to the destination, the router will send the packets in a round-robin fashion to the destination via different paths.

The type of switching enabled *plus* the number of available paths is what enables load balancing in an IPX environment. The default is no load balancing. Unless you have a "beefy" router (that is, a series 7500 or better with more than the default amount of memory), it is probably not a good idea to turn on load balancing.

The next section describes the two types of IPX routing that can affect load balancing.

Single-Path IPX Routing By saying the default in IPX routing is "no load balancing," we mean that the maximum path value is 1. This effectively disables multipath routing, or load balancing. Figure 12-5 shows an example of a typical network in which the command **ipx maximum-paths** 1 is in use.

Multipath IPX Routing To configure load balancing, you must first increase the value for maximum paths. The values can range from two to four maximum paths. Here's an example:

```
ipx max-paths 2
```

By using load balancing, you can enable faster convergence in an IPX network. Rather than having to run an algorithm to find an alternate path, the router can simply continue to forward packets through an equal-cost path to the same destination network. Therefore, in addition to increasing the value for maximum paths, you need to build in redundancy to the network where it is needed most. In Figure 12-6, you can see the result of the change to the configuration, when the two paths to Router D are equal in cost.

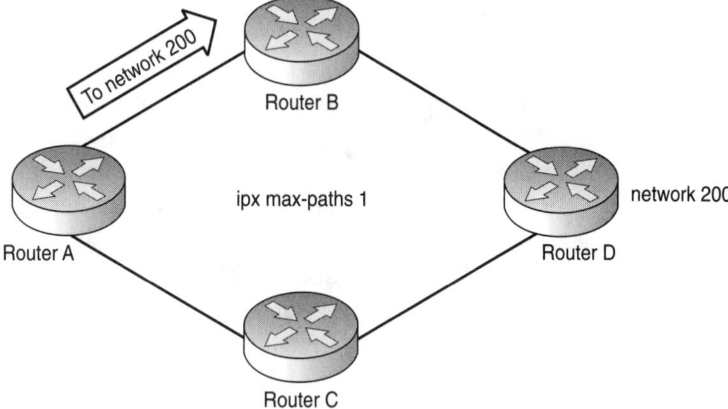

Figure 12-5 Single-path IPX routing

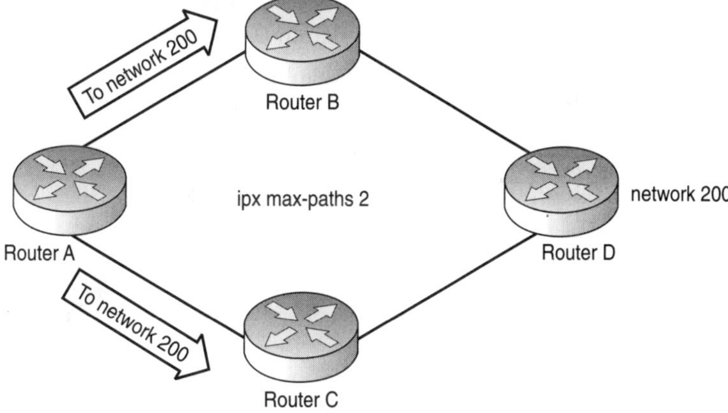

Figure 12-6 IPX load balancing on equal-cost paths

NetWare Link Services Protocol (NLSP)

Up until this point, we have only talked about RIP as a routing protocol for IPX networks. RIP is a somewhat limited, distance-vector protocol. Starting with the release of NetWare 3.11, Novell introduced a link-state protocol based on OSI IS-IS, called NetWare Link Services Protocol (NLSP). As of release 11.1 of the IOS, Cisco now supports up to 28 separate NLSP areas.

NLSP is an improvement over RIP in its ability to send only incremental routing updates when needed, rather than full routing tables every 60 seconds. NLSP, like other link-state protocols, also converges faster than RIP. Because it runs the Dijkstra Shortest Path First (SPF) algorithm when a link state changes, however, NLSP is quite a bit more CPU intensive than RIP and should not be configured on lower-end routers.

An NLSP area should not contain more than 400 routers, per Cisco recommendations. As with other link-state protocols, each router will keep a copy of the link-state database. NLSP uses three databases: adjacency, link-state, and forwarding. Hello packets from connected routers build adjacencies. The Link-State Packets (LSPs) from other routers running NLSP help build the link-state database. LSPs contain lists of adjacencies that are refreshed every two hours or when a state changes. The forwarding database is built when the SPF calculation is made based on the entries in the other two databases.

NLSP uses cost as its routing metric. The cost on an interface can be a number from 1 to 63. Maximum hops for an NLSP network is 1,023.

A couple of issues arise when NLSP is used. One of these is that even though the router is configured to use NLSP, the clients in the Novell environment must still use RIP and SAP to communicate. This means that the maximum number of hops supported is still only 15 because RIP becomes the limiting factor in this environment. The problem can clearly be seen in Figure 12-7, where clients on Network A and clients on Network B must communicate across an NLSP process.

Figure 12-7 NLSP and RIP in the network

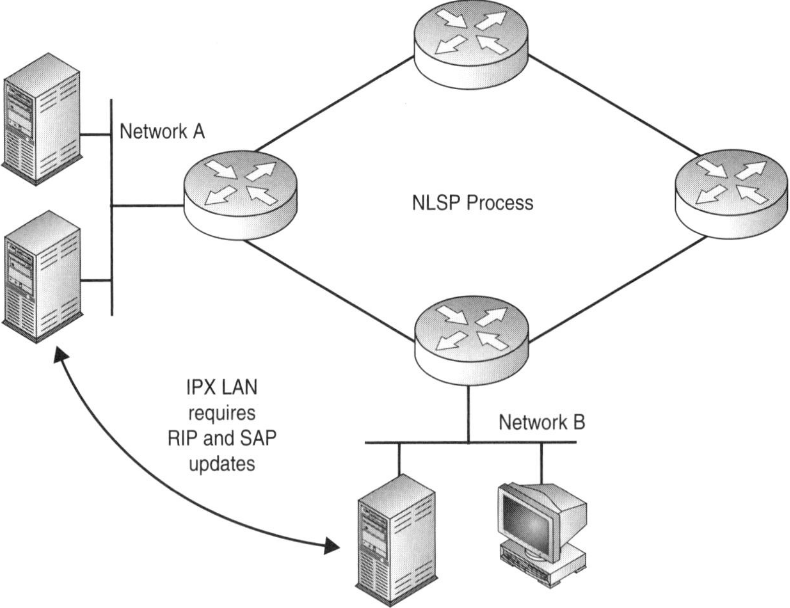

Redistribution is handled a little differently by NLSP. It is not necessary in a mixed NLSP/RIP environment to manually enable redistribution because it is performed automatically. NLSP runs an algorithm to ensure that the topology remains loop free, although this may result in less-than-optimal route selections.

Cisco now supports NLSP route aggregation for creating larger, more scalable NLSP implementations. Much like route aggregation for IP, networks can be designed in a hierarchical manner in order to reduce the size of the routing table.

As mentioned earlier in this section, up to 28 areas are supported, which differs from earlier IOS releases that only supported a single area. With single-area support, IPX RIP had to be run between the areas in order to carry routing information. Now the routers can even support multiple instances of NLSP running on a single router. Information is shared (called "leaking") between the areas.

IPX EIGRP

A much better way to create a large, scalable IPX network is to use IPX EIGRP, shown in Figure 12-8. As you know, EIGRP is a modified distance vector protocol that sends incremental routing updates, much like a link-state protocol. This conserves bandwidth by reducing unnecessary information on the wire. Specifically, the IPX EIGRP process will send the incremental updates of reliable information to other routers in the WAN while performing redistribution automatically to RIP and SAP. In turn, RIP and SAP will run on the LAN by default and will redistribute to EIGRP.

Although EIGRP can be run in the LAN as well as in the WAN, many times network designers will choose it specifically for the WAN in order to leverage the fast convergence and low bandwidth consumption that are hallmarks of this routing protocol.

The IPX RIP metric is ticks, as you remember, combined with hops. EIGRP treats this metric as an *external metric*. What happens to the tick count is that as it passes through the EIGRP cloud at the WAN, it does not increment. The EIGRP cloud appears to be zero ticks to the IPX RIP and SAP processes. The hop count, however, is incremented by two—one as it enters and one as it leaves the EIGRP process—regardless of how many hops may actually be in the EIGRP cloud.

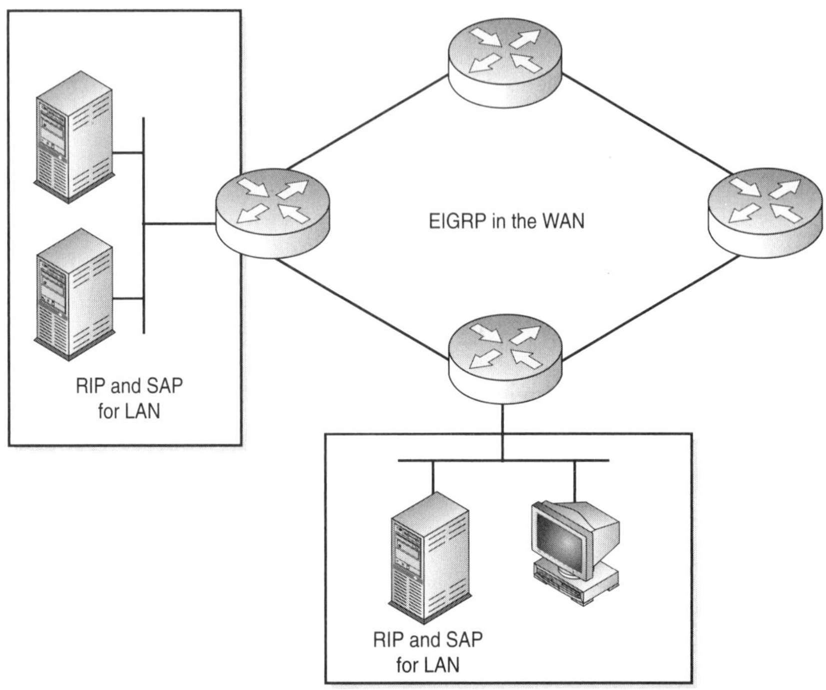

Figure 12-8
EIGRP in the WAN

If a route originates in the EIGRP cloud, it is treated a little differently. Because IPX RIP requires a tick count, and EIGRP does not use ticks as part of its metric, IPX RIP assigns a tick count based on the interface delay. This tick count is then redistributed, as the route metric to all routers running IPX RIP.

For more good information on the EIGRP process as related to IPX, refer to **http://www.cisco.com/warp/public473/57.html**.

Get Nearest Server (GNS) Queries

When an IPX client boots up, it sends a GNS query to search for a server. Without a server, the client is unable to use network resources. Some networks have local servers, as shown in Figure 12-9, where you see that the clients can easily reach Server XYZ on the LAN.

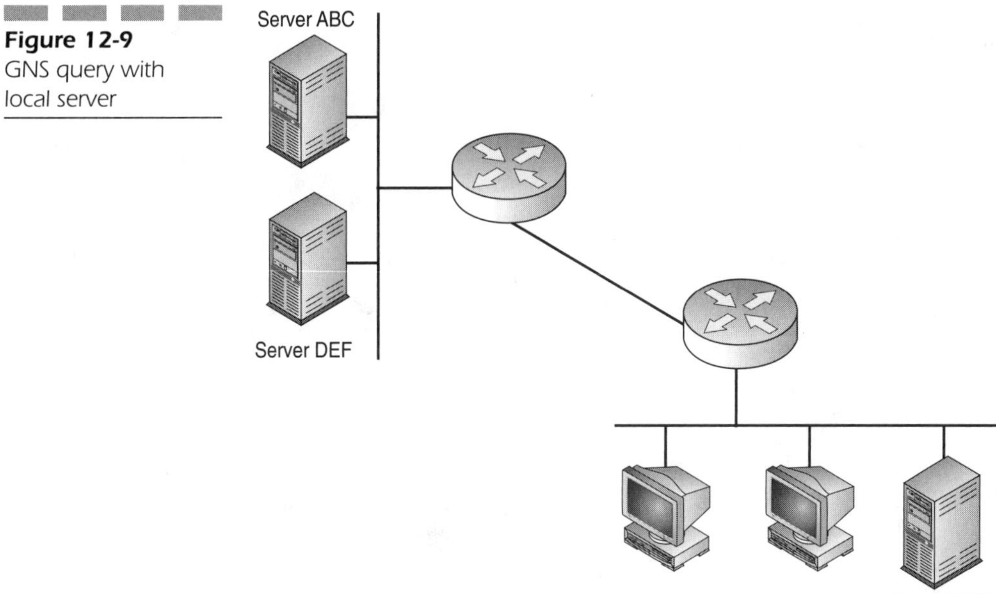

Figure 12-9 GNS query with local server

In some instances, the nearest server will be on another LAN, as shown in Figure 12-10. In this case, the Cisco router will perform a lookup in the SAP table to find the nearest server and will respond to the client with the name of the nearest server (usually the one with the lowest route metric for a given service). The client then sends a request for the internal network number of the server. The router responds with the hops and ticks required to reach the network on which the server resides. The client is then able to open an NetWare Core Protocol (NCP) session with the server.

When the router responds to a GNS query, it does so with zero delay. For some slower clients, this could be a problem. If you encounter problems with the client receiving the response, you can adjust the delay in the router configuration. Cisco routers also work with the Novell *preferred server* implementation, in which a certain service can use a particular server instead of other alternatives. In this instance, the client will send a *bindery* lookup to the nearest server via NCP in order to find the preferred server. If a preferred server is found, the client will disconnect from the nearest server and connect to the preferred server. Cisco routers will handle the routing of the NCP packets for this process, but they do no respond to bindery lookups.

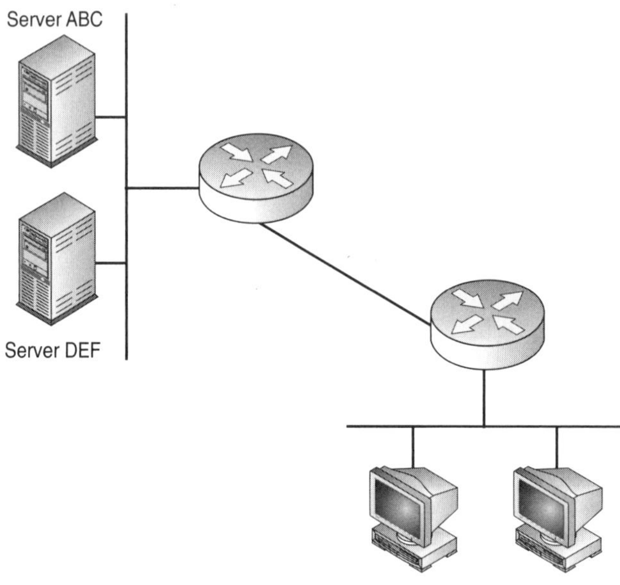

Figure 12-10 GNS query with no local server

IPX and NetBIOS

In order for clients using NetBIOS to function on an IPX network, a type of broadcast known as an *IPX type 20 broadcast* must be flooded out of all router ports on which an IPX network is configured. This process, shown in Figure 12-11, allows the NetBIOS clients to find their servers by name while not allowing other types of IPX broadcasts to flood through the network. Anytime broadcasts are used as part of an implementation, however, it can cause problems with performance, bandwidth usage, and scalability.

Cisco router software supports filtering by name for NetBIOS over IPX. This is one way that broadcasts can be controlled in this instance. For the example shown in Figure 12-12, either input or output filters can block broadcasts that concern the MATH domain from entering routers that do not handle that domain. This can increase the efficiency and scalability of an IPX network that must carry NetBIOS traffic. More information on how to configure these filters can be found at **http://www.cisco.com/univercd/cc/td/doc/product/software/ios11/cbook/cipx.htm#xtocid2894284**.

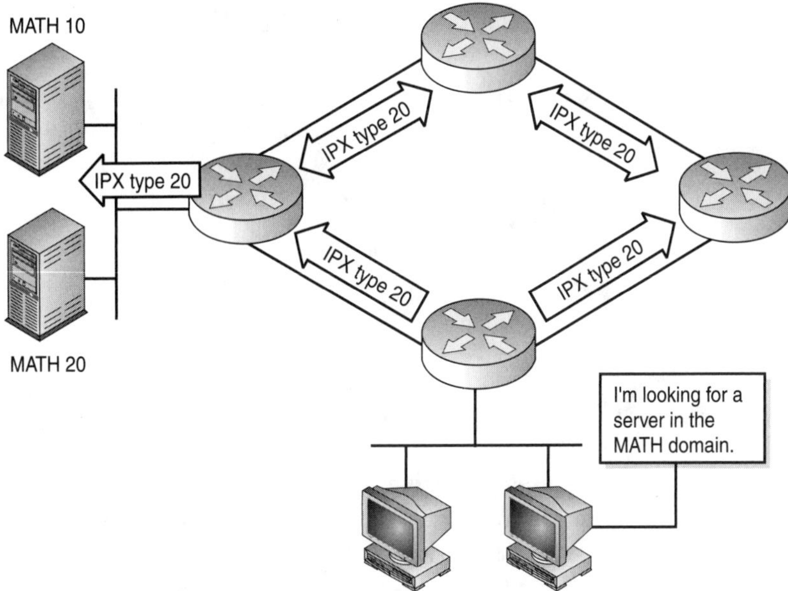
MATH 10
MATH 20
IPX type 20
IPX type 20
IPX type 20
IPX type 20
IPX type 20
I'm looking for a server in the MATH domain.

Figure 12-11
NetBIOS over IPX

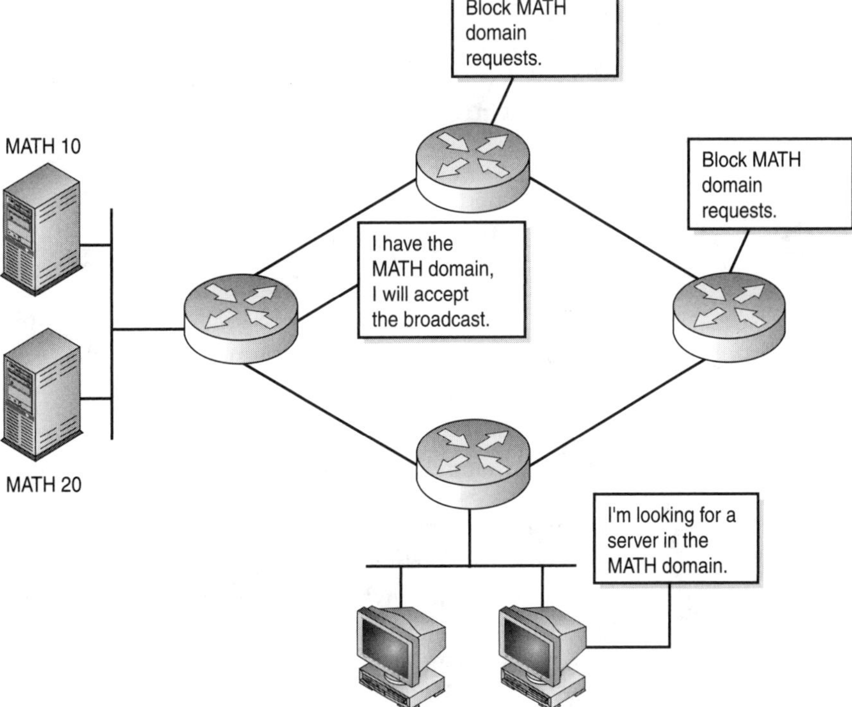
Block MATH domain requests.
MATH 10
Block MATH domain requests.
I have the MATH domain, I will accept the broadcast.
MATH 20
I'm looking for a server in the MATH domain.

Figure 12-12
Filtering NetBIOS by name

IPX/IP Gateways

Because IPX is primarily a LAN protocol, special concerns arise when a client needs to be configured to reach an IP network or the Internet, or to use traditional IP services such as FTP, Web browsing, or telnet. There are really two ways to implement a gateway:

- Load a TCP/IP stack on each client.
- Use a TCP/IP gateway in a central location.

If you choose to load a TCP/IP stack on every client, you will be running two protocol stacks on each client, which could hurt performance of the clients themselves. You will also have the administrative task of IP address assignment.

As an alternative, you can set up an IPeXchange Gateway. This is a software product that utilizes a client product, which is loaded on a Windows-based PC, and a server product, which is loaded on a Windows NT server. As shown in Figure 12-13, the client communicates with the server, which then communicates to the Internet for the client. In a pure-IPX environment, the gateway also serves as a firewall, so it is important that the server running the gateway is as robust as possible so that it doesn't become a bottleneck.

For more information on the IPeXchange Gateway, please refer to **http://www.cisco.com/univercd/cc/td/doc/product/iaabu/ipx/ipechng/ijintro.htm.**

Problem Areas

Designing an effective, scalable IPX network requires adequate planning for trouble spots. Here are a couple of areas that deserve special attention.

RIP and SAP Updates

As you can imagine, any process that requires large amounts of data to be broadcast regularly is going to impact performance. This is especially true in an environment where not only does the information need to be passed to the LAN but to the WAN as well. Let's take a look at the two types of packets that IPX needs to send on a recurring basis.

Figure 12-13
IPeXchange Gateway

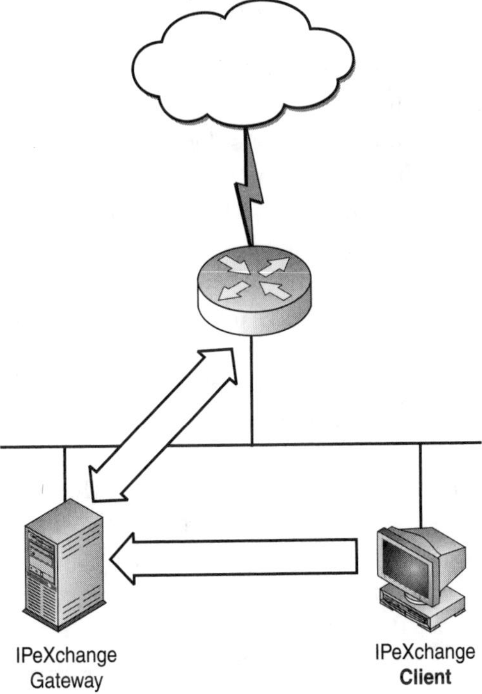

The SAP update tells all other members of the IPX network about services that are available—print services, file services, etc. Without these updates, the IPX network would cease to function, which is why the router must forward them—*even though they are broadcasts*. The knowledge of these services is an inherent part of how IPX works. An SAP update packet can contain up to seven SAPs per packet every 60 seconds for a packet size of 480 bytes. Because there can be much more than seven services available, there can be multiple SAPs sent constantly. Part of your calculation will be based on the total number of SAPs in the LAN.

RIP, on the other hand, can send updates for up to 50 networks per 432-byte packet every 60 seconds. You will probably not see as much RIP traffic as SAP traffic on an IPX LAN or WAN as a result. So, we can now do some calculations based on what we know about the packets.

You will need to know the total number of networks advertised in your RIP process and the total number of SAPs advertised in the IPX network. Divide the number of RIP routes by 50 and the number of SAPs by 7. This will tell you how many packets must be generated every 60 seconds.

Multiply the size of the RIP packet (432 bytes) times the number of RIP packets that will be sent every 60 seconds. Now multiply the number of SAP updates required times the size of the SAP packet (480 bytes). You now can see how much traffic will be crossing the LAN and/or WAN every minute. This can consume a considerable amount of bandwidth. So how do we fix this potential problem before it impacts our users?

One way to do this is by the use of IPX access lists. You can use either a standard or extended list. The standard list uses a number range from 800 to 899 and can filter based on source, destination, and wildcards. The extended list uses a number range from 900 to 999, and is a little more granular, allowing additional filtering down to the port and socket of a packet. It is better to filter at the distribution layer. Remember our three-layer model? The distribution layer contains fewer routers, normally, than the access layer and is the layer at which filtering or policy enforcement belongs. If you move the access lists down to the access layer, you risk slowing performance by reducing the effectiveness of the switching process.

Although it is not normally recommended to use access lists at the access layer, the one exception is when trying to control SAPs. Because the route processor and not the switching process handles SAP packets, performance of the switching process is not affected. You can use three types of filters with SAPs:

- input-sap-filter
- output-sap-filter
- router-sap-filter

Input and *output* refer to whether the SAPs are incoming or outgoing advertisements. The *router-sap-filter*, however, is used to filter SAPs at the source. A good rule to use when creating SAP filters is to filter by network number rather than by host address. This is because the host address is based on the MAC address. If the NIC has to be replaced, the MAC address changes. Because the host address on an IPX host is subject to change, you would have to modify your access list if a host address changes. Modifying access lists is usually not a simple task, nor would it be easy to remember to modify an access list every time host information changes. Use the network number instead.

For more information on configuring SAP filters, refer to **http://www.cisco.com/univercd/cc/td/doc/cisintwk/ics/cs005.htm.**

For more information on Cisco recommendations for controlling SAPs on slower lines on in the WAN, refer to **http://www.cisco.com/warp/public/701/34.html.**

Routing IPX on Dial-on-Demand Routing (DDR) Links

Novell clients and servers keep their line of communication open by the use of keepalive packets, sent every five minutes. This can be an expensive proposition for a DDR link that charges for usage. The keepalives will appear to be "interesting" traffic and will keep the link up all the time. A better way to design for DDR links with an IPX network is by the use of spoofing.

When using IPX, you can enable *watchdog spoofing* on the Cisco router, which allows it to answer the keepalives locally for the client, thus keeping the session alive without keeping the DDR-link alive. The router at the server end can do the same thing.

For some applications, such as SAA and rconsole, that use SPX, the router can provide SPX spoofing. An application running over SPX sends an unsolicited ACK packet (the same ACK and sequence number it used when it received the last data) to keep the session alive. In turn, it waits for an ACK from the other end. With SPX spoofing, the Cisco router will send the ACK in order to keep this traffic off of the DDR link.

For an excellent Cisco white paper on the challenges of designing IPX networks with DDR links, refer to **http://www.cisco.com/warp/public/cc/techno/dety/nvty/tech/ddr_wp.htm.**

Tunneling IPX

Another way to introduce greater scalability into the IPX network is to use Generic Router Encapsulation (GRE) tunneling to connect two IPX LANs together. The tunnel acts just like any other interface, so you can use access lists and filters on the traffic as with other interfaces. Additionally, the IPX network sees the tunnel as a single hop, regardless of the number of actual routers being traversed. This means that in addition to creating scalability in an enterprise network, tunneling can also allow IPX to pass through the Internet without requiring a gateway. Bear in mind that this does *not* mean that the IPX clients can use IP services with the use of a tunnel.

Case Study

As you may recall, Campus Research Corporation has two buildings—Headquarters in Detroit and R & D in St. Louis. At Headquarters, it has Administration, Engineering, and Customer Service. In St. Louis they have Administration, Engineering, and Training. The company has completed the acquisition of a small manufacturing company in Milwaukee that uses Novell NetWare throughout its LAN with an IPX stack running on the end-stations.

There are 40 Novell servers running a variety of services for the 200 clients in the network. Approximately 400 SAPs are being advertised in the network, which causes some slowness at times. There is a concern that when a small division of the group moves to the Headquarters building in Detroit, the users will be unable to reach their servers without a great deal of delay. The network engineering staff in Detroit wants to get rid of Novell and IPX altogether, but there is understandably a good deal of resistance from the newly acquired staff in Milwaukee.

For this case study, you need to design a network that will allow the users in Milwaukee to continue using Novell for their NOS, and will allow the division that is moving to Detroit to remain on a Novell NetWare platform. In order to do this, you must come up with a plan that will not impact the relatively stable IP environment in the existing buildings or the performance of the WAN greatly. You will need to specify a high-level design that meets the needs of the company without discounting the needs of the users.

Suggested solutions to the case studies may be found in Appendix C, "Suggested Case Study Solutions."

Study Hints

Although no one can disclose test items or test content, we can give hints as to what might be valuable to study. For this chapter, the following key facts need to be reviewed and remembered:

- IPX uses RIP and SAP broadcasts to communicate.
- RIP updates contain up to 50 networks per packet and are sent every 60 seconds.

- SAP updates contain up to seven SAPs per packet and are sent every 60 seconds.
- Ticks are the route metric for IPX RIP. LANs are one tick; WANs are six ticks (configurable).
- A tick is 1/18th of 1 second.
- Switching methods for IPX are similar to other protocols, except for fast switching, which switches packet by packet, rather than by destination.
- Encapsulation for Ethernet, Token Ring, and FDDI is supported.
- A Cisco router can respond to GNS queries on a serverless network, introducing zero delay.
- EIGRP and IPXWAN can handle WAN communications.
- NLSP is Novell's link-state protocol, similar to IS-IS.
- Watchdog spoofing can be used to limit the kind of traffic that will keep a DDR link up.
- NetBIOS requires IPX type 20 propagation through the network.

CCDP Tips

This section contains an abbreviated list of topics covered in this chapter. Think of this section as the equivalent of reading Cliff's Notes™ instead of reading an entire book. You will get the general idea of the chapter, but you will benefit more from reading the chapter in its entirety.

History

- IPX is based on Xerox Network System (XNS).
- Novell once referred to the process of routing between LANs as "bridging."

Novell Network Protocols

- IPX works at the network layer.
- SPX works at the transport layer.
- The Novell protocol stack loosely corresponds to the OSI model.

Novell Encapsulations

- For Ethernet: Novell-ether, snap, iso1/sap, arpa
- For Token Ring: Novell-tr, snap
- For FDDI: snap, iso1/sap

For different encapsulations on the same interface, use sub-interfaces. To enable fast switching on an interface, use **ipx route-cache same-interface**.

Novell Routing

- Novell uses an implementation of RIP called IPX RIP.
    - Primary metric is ticks. Hop count is secondary, as a tiebreaker.
    - Hop count still limited to 15.
    - Full routing updates every 60 seconds.
    - A LAN link is equal to one tick (1/18th of 1 second).
    - A WAN link is equal to six ticks.
- For WAN implementations, use IPX WAN, based on PPP.
- Though WAN links equal six ticks, this can be adjusted for slower links using **ipx delay** to manually set the tick count.

IPX Switching Methods

- *Process switching* is a form of load balancing that operates on a per-packet basis. This is also the way IP process switching works.
- *Fast switching* in IPX also works on a packet-by-packet basis, which is different from the way it works in IP, where it is by destination.
- *Autonomous* or *silicon switching* is the method in IPX that load-balances on a per-destination basis.
- Load-balancing is disabled by default in IPX networks. To enable load-balancing, use **ipx max-paths** <2-4>.

NetWare Link State Protocol (NLSP)

- NLSP is based on the IS-IS protocol.
- NLSP uses Link-State Packets (LSPs) to update neighbors.
- NLSP runs the Dijkstra SPF algorithm.
- Cisco can support up to 28 NLSP areas.
- Cost is the primary routing metric, using a value of 1 to 63.
- Though hop count can extend to 1,023. IPX RIP still limits the implementation to 15 hops.

IPX EIGRP

- Can be used in the WAN to create a more scalable network
- Introduces zero ticks to the count as traffic passes through from one LAN to another
- Adds only two hop counts to the traffic
- Uses redistribution automatically with IPX RIP
- Treats ticks as an external metric

Get Nearest Server (GNS) Communications

- For clients on a LAN with a server, GNS queries stay local.
- For clients on a serverless LAN, the Cisco router responds to the query for the nearest server and network number before setting up the communication.
- Novell's preferred server process is done via NCP once the client and server communication is established. The router does not need to participate.

IPX and NetBIOS

- Because NetBIOS requires name queries, IPX type-20 packets must be flooded through the network.
- To limit the impact of the type-20 packets, filtering can be used based on name and wildcards.

IPX-to-IP Gateway

- Because IPX cannot communicate to the Internet or to IP network devices, you can either load a TCP/IP stack on the end-station (running dual-network stacks) or implement an IPeXchange Gateway software product.

IPX over DDR Links

- To prevent IPX keepalive packets from keeping a link up with "uninteresting" traffic, use the Cisco router to perform IPX-watchdog spoofing.
- To prevent SPX unsolicited ACKs from keeping a link up with "uninteresting" traffic, use the Cisco router to perform SPX-watchdog spoofing.

- To decrease the impact of the SAPs on the network, use SAP-filtering techniques to limit the type and number of SAPs that cross the network.

Summary

While not enjoying the popularity it once did as the premier LAN protocol of choice, Novell's NetWare still has its following. It supports many platforms, technologies, and a variety of encapsulations. Novell has also made it easier with later versions to run a TCP/IP stack on its systems while still using its basic client/server model. Another place you will see IPX in use is in network gaming, where many of today's most popular games use IPX to communicate in small, networked environments.

It is important to remember that IPX, while requiring broadcasts to operate, can be easily managed with filtering, the use of alternate protocols (such as EIGRP), and adequate planning. In the next chapter, we will examine another desktop protocol—AppleTalk.

Questions

The following review questions have been selected to help you test your knowledge of the subject matter contained in this chapter. You will also find these questions contained in the CD-ROM included with this book. Although these are not the questions you will find in the certification exams, knowing the answers to the review questions in this book will help cement the material in your mind as you prepare for the tests.

1. In a DDR environment where IPX is in use, what is the process that will answer keepalives locally?
   a. NLSP hello packets
   b. Automatic pings from the interface
   c. SPX-watchdog spoofing
   d. IPX-watchdog spoofing

2. What will a client send upon bootup in order to find a server?
   a. GNS query
   b. GNS ACK
   c. GNS request
   d. GNS ping
3. In a DDR environment where SPX in is use, what is the process that will send an unsolicited ACK to keep communications open to rconsole, for example?
   a. NLSP hello packets
   b. Automatic pings from the interface
   c. SPX-watchdog spoofing
   d. IPX-watchdog spoofing
4. Which routing protocol works well in the WAN, making an IPX network more scalable?
   a. NLSP
   b. EIGRP
   c. IPX RIP
   d. IS-IS
5. Which packet-type must be enabled in order for NetBIOS workstations to find their servers?
   a. GNS query
   b. IPX-watchdog packets
   c. IPX-helper address
   d. IPX-type 20
6. What is the primary routing metric for IPX RIP?
   a. Cost
   b. Ticks
   c. Hops
   d. Delay

7. SAP filters should filter traffic by ________________.
    a. host address
    b. network number
    c. SAP type
    d. socket number
8. RIP updates can handle how many networks per packet?
    a. 10
    b. 30
    c. 50
    d. 70
9. SAP updates can carry how many SAPs per packet?
    a. 3
    b. 7
    c. 15
    d. 25
10. When responding to a GNS query, how much delay will a Cisco router introduce to the process?
    a. Zero ticks
    b. One tick
    c. Two ticks
    c. Three ticks
11. What is the protocol used by Novell clients and servers for primary communication?
    a. IPX
    b. SPX
    c. IPX RIP
    d. NCP
12. Which task can a client perform on the nearest server in order to find a preferred server?
    a. GNS query
    b. Bindery lookup
    c. NCP call
    d. RCONSOLE

13. True or False: The tick count increments by one when passing through an EIGRP cloud.
    a. True
    b. False
14. True or False: The hop count increments by two when passing through an EIGRP cloud.
    a. True
    b. False
15. In order to use load balancing, which IPX value must be set to a value greater than 1?
    a. IPX Maximum Hops
    b. IPX Maximum Paths
    c. IPX Load Balance Enable
    d. IPX Networks
16. What is the tick count for a T1 WAN connection?
    a. Zero
    b. Two
    c. Four
    d. Six
17. What is the maximum number of hops allowable in an NLSP environment?
    a. 6
    b. 15
    c. 255
    d. 1,023
18. What is the transport protocol used by Novell networks?
    a. IPX
    b. IPX RIP
    c. NCP
    d. SPX

19. If you wish to use raw Ethernet in an IPX environment, which encapsulation method should you choose?

a. arpa

b. novell-ether

c. iso1

d. snap

20. Fast switching in IPX differs from fast switching in IP in what way?

a. Fast switching in IPX does not perform load balancing.

b. Fast switching in IPX is on a per-packet basis.

c. Fast switching in IPX is on a per-destination basis.

d. Fast switching in IPX is performed in the route processor.

Answers

1. In a DDR environment where IPX is in use, what is the process that will answer keepalives locally?
d. IPX watchdog spoofing
Explanation: The router will send keepalives on behalf of the distant server or client when IPX-watchdog spoofing is enabled.

2. What will a client send upon bootup in order to find a server?
a. GNS query
Explanation: A Get Nearest Server query must be made when a Novell client is first booted.

3. In a DDR environment where SPX in is use, what is the process that will send an unsolicited ACK to keep communications open to RCONSOLE, for example?
c. SPX-watchdog spoofing
Explanation: When enabled, SPX spoofing sends the unsolicited ACK in the format of the previous ACK and sequence number.

4. Which routing protocol works well in the WAN, making an IPX network more scalable?
b. EIGRP

5. Which packet type must be enabled in order for NetBIOS workstations to find their servers?
   d. IPX type 20

6. What is the primary routing metric for IPX RIP?
   b. Ticks
   Explanation: Even though the RIP process can further use hops and even delay in its choice of route, the primary metric is ticks.

7. SAP filter should filter traffic by ________________.
   b. network number
   Explanation: The network number will not change. The host address could change if a NIC is replaced, because it is based on MAC address.

8. RIP updates can handle how many networks per packet?
   c. 50

9. SAP updates can carry how many SAPs per packet?
   b. 7

10. When responding to a GNS query, how much delay will a Cisco router introduce to the process?
    a. Zero ticks
    Explanation: Remember, a Cisco router will not introduce delay for GNS responses. This is configurable, however, to accommodate slower clients.

11. What is the protocol used by Novell clients and servers for primary communication?
    d. NCP
    Explanation: Even though the other protocols are part of the total IPX implementation, the client and server communicate by using NCP.

12. Which task can a client perform on the nearest server in order to find a preferred server?
    a. Bindery lookup
    Explanation: A bindery lookup on the server that responded to the GNS query would provide a list of preferred servers for given services.

13. True or False: The tick count increments by one when passing through an EIGRP cloud.
a. False
Explanation: The EIGRP process adds zero ticks to the count.

14. True or False: The hop count increments by two when passing through an EIGRP cloud.
a. True
Explanation: Regardless of the true number of hops in the cloud, EIGRP will only add a count of two to the total hop count, effectively extending the scalability greatly.

15. In order to use load balancing, which IPX value must be set to a value greater than 1?
a. IPX Maximum Paths
Explanation: A value between 2 and 4 will enable load balancing.

16. What is the tick count for a T1 WAN connection?
a. 6
Explanation: WAN connections are equivalent to 6 ticks.

17. What is the maximum number of hops allowable in an NLSP environment?
b. 15
Explanation: Because IPX RIP is still the limiting factor in any Novell environment, NLSP usage does not increase this limit.

18. What is the transport protocol used by Novell networks?
a. SPX
Explanation: Refer to the comparison to the OSI model. SPX is at the transport layer.

19. If you wish to use raw Ethernet in an IPX environment, which encapsulation method should you choose?
b. novell-ether
Explanation: Novell-ether was formerly referred to as *raw Ethernet*.

20. Fast switching in IPX differs from fast switching in IP in what way?
b. Fast switching in IPX is on a per-packet basis.
Explanation: Fast switching in IP is on a per-destination basis. This is where IPX differs.

Bibliography

Cisco Internetwork Design Course Manual, version 3.0, April 1997, Cisco Systems, Inc.

Cisco Internetwork Design, Cisco Press, 2000, Matthew H. Birkner, Editor

Thomas Concise Telecom and Networking Dictionary, McGraw-Hill, 2000, Thomas M. Thomas II

Network Protocol Handbook, McGraw-Hill, 1994, Matthew G. Naugle

Cisco: IPX: **http://www.cisco.com/warp/public/458/32.html**

Cisco IOS Solutions for Novell NetWare Networks: **http://www.cisco.com/warp/public/732/Novell/novl_pc.htm**

CHAPTER 13

AppleTalk Design

Overview

In this second of three chapters on desktop protocols, we are going to take a look at the design issues related to AppleTalk. Although many networks that contain Apple computers are using them over TCP/IP today—for both simplicity and consolidation of administration—there are still plenty of networks that do use AppleTalk to its fullest.

By the end of this chapter you will have a better picture of what AppleTalk is, how it works, and how to design for it. At the end of the chapter there will be a short case study that will allow you to use what you have learned.

History

Apple Computer Corporation developed one of the first distributed client/server network models early in the 1980s, when they introduced AppleTalk. AppleTalk was developed to address the new business need for shared resources, specifically for their Macintosh computers running Mac OS. AppleTalk was designed to be easy to use and administer. The problem, of course, was that the first version (AppleTalk Phase 1) was not as flexible and extensible as it would need to be in order to meet future network needs. Therefore, we will be discussing primarily Phase 2 of AppleTalk in this chapter.

AppleTalk Protocol Suite

AppleTalk can be carried on a variety of media: Ethernet, Token Ring, and FDDI. While primarily a LAN protocol, it can be routed over the WAN. As we break the protocol down into its basic parts, you will begin to see where the strengths and pitfalls of this protocol lie.

The AppleTalk protocol suite has four basic components:

- Nodes
- Sockets
- Networks
- Zones

A *node* is what you might imagine it to be—an end-station on a network. It could be anything from a laptop to a line printer. Each node can contain up to 254 *socket* numbers. The sockets are conduits that exist between the upper-layer applications (known as *socket clients*) and the network layer process—Datagram Delivery Protocol (DDP)—that we will discuss later in this chapter. This conduit allows the upper layers and network layer to pass data.

An AppleTalk *network* is defined as a single, logical cable, meaning that it is not necessarily one long physical run, including the multiple nodes that can be connected to it. The two types of networks in AppleTalk are nonextended and extended. A *nonextended network* is one that is identified with a single network number and from 1 to 1,024 uniquely named nodes. A nonextended network can also not be contained in more than one AppleTalk zone. An *extended network* can have devices belonging to multiple AppleTalk zones and can have multiple, contiguous network numbers associated with it. The group of network numbers associated with an extended network is known as a *cable range*. This is a term we will spend more time on in this chapter.

An AppleTalk *zone* is a logical group of nodes that belong together administratively. In other words, these devices do not have to be physically co-located, nor do they have to be in the same network number or cable range.

AppleTalk Addressing

As with other network protocols, AppleTalk must provide a way to uniquely identify and address each node in the network. An AppleTalk address consists of a 16-bit network number, an 8-bit node number, and an 8-bit socket number. These are usually represented in a dotted-decimal format, similar to IP. In the following example, 100 is the network number, 10 is the node number, and 250 is the socket number:

```
100.10.250
```

AppleTalk nodes are dynamically addressed, which makes administering addresses very simple. When the node first boots up, it receives a temporary network address selected from the *startup range*, with a randomly selected node number. The startup range is a reserved range of network numbers from 65,280 to 65,534. Once the node is communicating by way of the Zone Information Protocol (ZIP), which we will discuss further in this chapter, it negotiates with the router for a valid network number and node number.

AppleTalk and the OSI Model

AppleTalk has at least one protocol corresponding to every layer of the OSI model. The only protocol which does not fit "neatly" into the model is AppleTalk Filing Protocol (AFP), which can be categorized as both an application layer and presentation layer protocol, as shown in Figure 13-1.

AppleTalk Protocol Components

Now that you have some idea of how the AppleTalk protocol is constructed, we are going to introduce you to how packets find their way around the network. As you saw in Figure 13-1, AppleTalk has many protocols corresponding to the layers of the OSI model. This section will give you a sense of what these different protocols do and how they work together to move data through the network.

AppleTalk Address Resolution Protocol

AppleTalk, like TCP/IP, uses an address resolution protocol to find the hardware address that corresponds to network addresses it hears on the wire. *AppleTalk Address Resolution Protocol* (AARP) was developed to meet this need. AARP keeps a table of network addresses and hardware addresses that it learns in a table called an address mapping table (AMT).

Each time an address is learned, the entry is placed in the table (if it does not already exist in the table) and a timer is set. Because of the potential for addresses in an AppleTalk network to become invalid over time, the timer allows the addresses to expire and be deleted from the AMT. When a packet is received that updates the entry, the change is made, if necessary, in the AMT and the timer is reset. Each AppleTalk node keeps its own AMT. Therefore, when a node needs to send data to a destination, it first consults its own AMT before generating an AARP request for the destination's hardware address.

If the address is not in the local node's AMT or in the router's AMT, an AARP broadcast is sent asking for the hardware address of the node using the given network address. Once the node using the network address responds, the AMT in the router is updated and an AARP reply is sent to

Figure 13-1
AppleTalk Protocol model

AppleTalk

Application	AppleTalk Filing Protocol (AFP)
Presentation	
Session	• AppleTalk Data Stream Protocol (ADSP) • Zone Information Protocol (ZIP) • Apple Talk Session • Protocol (ASP) • Printer Access Protocol (PAP)
Transport	**• Routing Table Maintenance Protocol (RTMP)** **• AppleTalk Update-Based Routing Protocol (AURP)** **• Name Binding Protocol (NBP)** **• AppleTalk Transaction Protocol (ATP)** **• AppleTalk Echo Protocol (AEP)**
Network	• Datagram Delivery Protocol (DDP) • AppleTalk Address Resolution Protocol (AARP)
Data Link	• EtherTalk Link Access Protocol (ELAP) • LocalTalk Link Access Protocol (LLAP) • TokenTalk Link Access Protocol (TLAP) • FDDITalk Link Access Protocol (FLAP)
Physical	• IEEE 802.3 Hardware • LocalTalk Hardware • Token Ring 802.5 • FDDI Hardware

the sending node. It, in turn, updates its AMT and sends the data to the destination. As you can imagine, all of this can create unnecessary traffic on a network. Because broadcasts are employed, all nodes on a cable have to process these broadcasts and performance can suffer.

Datagram Delivery Protocol

Not all AppleTalk implementations use AARP for learning addresses. Some use node information contained in received DDP packets in order to populate the AMT. This is called *address gleaning* and is not typically used—but can help reduce the number of broadcasts in the network. There is more to DDP than just address mapping, however.

DDP is a connectionless, best-effort network layer protocol. It doesn't care if the data gets there or not. The upper-layer protocols in AppleTalk, like ADSP, which we will discuss later in this chapter, handle retransmission, if needed. DDP handles the transmission and receipt of packets only.

DDP receives the data from the socket client (the application) and places a DDP header on the data containing the destination address. It then passes the data to the data link layer. When DDP receives a packet, it opens the header to find the destination socket before passing the data to the appropriate socket. DDP also maintains a mapping of every node in the cable range of which it is a member.

Notice that we said that DDP maintains a mapping of every node *in its cable range*. What happens if the node is *not* in the same cable range, which is often the case? If the destination node is not on the same cable range as the source node, DDP will not have a mapping of the network to hardware address for the destination. When this happens, DDP places a header on the packet directing it to the router for processing. Routers can then forward the packet until it reaches the router closest to the final network address destination for proper handling.

Name Binding Protocol

The *AppleTalk Name Binding Protocol* (NBP) provides a way for network numbers to be mapped to node names. This requires an introduction to a new AppleTalk term—*Network Visible Entity* (NVE). An NVE is simply an addressable network resource, such as a file server or print server. The NVE is addressed by an entity name and has a zone and other attributes, known as *entity types*.

An entity name works in much the same way as NetBIOS names in Windows networks, which we will discuss in Chapter 14, "Windows Networking Design." It gives the user community an easy-to-remember and easy-to-use way to talk to other user nodes. It eliminates having to remember complex numeric addresses or other lower-layer functions. The entity name also is not subject to change, as is the network address.

NBP works by broadcasting queries containing two of three components and asking the responder to fill in the blank. The three fields of an NBP broadcast are

- Object name
- Zone
- Type

It is important to note here that the end user of an AppleTalk network, while unaware of NBP or its functions, nevertheless has direct interaction with NBP. The user opens a window called a *Chooser* in order to find network resources. An NBP query from the Chooser would contain the user's zone and the type of resource for which they are browsing. NBP lookups, using a responder daemon, produce a listing of available resources in the user's zone and display them in the Chooser screen. The user then selects a resource from the choices presented.

NOTE: *A problem can arise when users are on any OS older than System 7.0 of Mac OS. Earlier versions caused NBP packets to continue being generated if a user forgot to close the Chooser. System 7.0 uses an exponential timing delay that reduces the frequency of the NBP broadcasts based upon how long the Chooser has been open.*

NBP provides four functions:

- Lookup
- Registration
- Confirmation
- Deletion

By performing these functions, NBP learns the name-to-address mappings in a network and keeps them current. *Lookup* is the process of verifying the mapping of an NVE ahead of time (before services are used). *Registration* allows a node to create its entry in the NBP table. *Confirmation* permits NBP to validate that a mapping is still accurate, and *deletion* is performed when a node is powered off or is otherwise inaccessible.

Zone Information Protocol (ZIP) and AppleTalk Data Stream Protocol (ADSP)

We mentioned AppleTalk zones earlier in this chapter. Zones are logical groups of AppleTalk nodes. *Zone Information Protocol* (ZIP) is a way for AppleTalk routers to maintain a map of these zones. When a node first comes online, it is ZIP that allows it to find its zone. Take the example in Figure 13-2, for instance. We have a Math zone, a History zone, and a Science zone. ZIP would maintain the mapping of the various nodes inside these zones in a *zone information table*. ZIP works at the session layer of the OSI model, as seen in Figure 13-1.

AppleTalk Data Stream Protocol (ADSP) is another session layer protocol that runs on DDP to provide for full-duplex communications between sockets. It provides some reliability in the transmission, using flow control to speed up or slow down the flow of traffic when needed. It also handles keeping the packets in sequence and preventing errors such as packet duplication and drops. If a transmission were to contain errors, it is ADSP that would request the retransmission of the data.

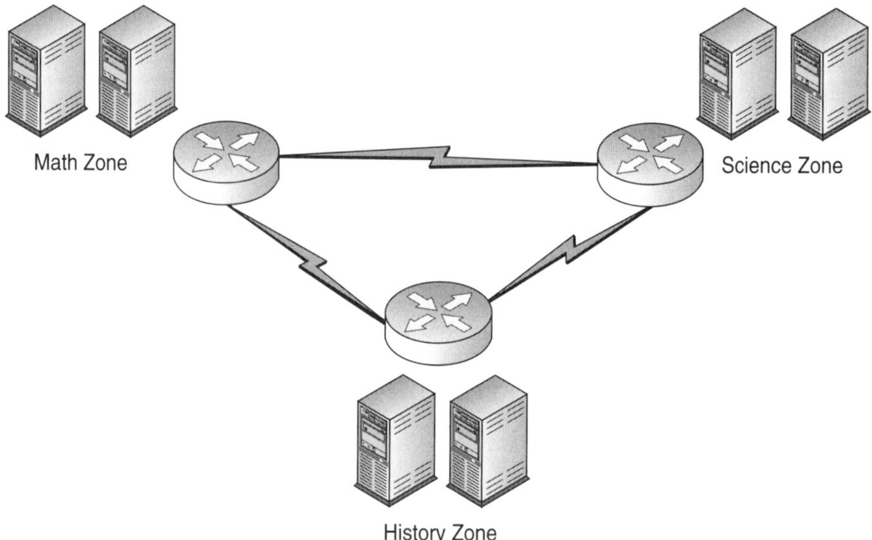

Figure 13-2 Zones in the AppleTalk network

AppleTalk Routing

In this section we will discuss the routing protocol used in AppleTalk LANs and provide you with options for routing AppleTalk in the WAN.

LAN: Routing Table Maintenance Protocol

Used primarily in the LAN, Routing Table Maintenance Protocol (RTMP) is similar in function to RIP. It uses a hop count as its metric, with a maximum hop count of 15. RTMP sends the full route table every 10 seconds. RTMP uses split horizon, as well, to limit connectivity when used in partially meshed, packet-switched WAN networks. We will discuss the effect of split horizon in a WAN environment more in Chapter 17, "Frame Relay Design."

RTMP sends routing packets that contain *tuples*, which is a combination of hop count and the cable range. In the same way that a RIP routing update may contain a network and the path, the RTMP update identifies the number of hops needed to reach a destination cable range. Because it uses split horizon, it will not advertise a cable range back out of the same interface on which it was learned.

For every cable range, RTMP generates one routing tuple. Each RTMP packet can contain between 100 and 200 tuples. The packets are up to 600 bytes long, with no fragmentation. Since the full routing table is generated every 10 seconds, you can calculate the amount of overhead by

- Determining the number of cable ranges
- Dividing by 200 (maximum tuples per packet)
- Multiplying the resulting number of packets by 600 bytes to find how much traffic is generated every 10 seconds by RTMP

This can be a devastating amount of overhead for a WAN in larger AppleTalk networks. Fortunately, there are alternatives to using RTMP in the WAN—AppleTalk Update Routing Protocol or Enhanced IGRP.

WAN: AppleTalk Update Routing Protocol

AppleTalk allows multiple networks to be connected together across a WAN through a virtual link, of sorts. AURP uses both *exterior routers* and *tunnels* to accomplish its task. The exterior routers exist at either end of an AURP tunnel and serve to connect the local AppleTalk network to the tunnel. AURP provides several benefits to an AppleTalk implementation:

- Reduces the total hop count from network to network
- Provides some security, which AppleTalk alone does not provide
- Allows AppleTalk to be tunneled through other protocols
- Reduces routing traffic because it sends only routing updates instead of full tables

AURP will send updates to other routers when a network is added or removed from its routing table, when the distance to a neighboring network is changed or when a path to a network changes. The path change is usually because the router now has to access a network locally rather than through the tunnel, or vice versa.

In order to move the traffic across the tunnel from the local networks, AURP exterior routers must receive the traffic from local protocols, such as RTMP, and encapsulate it into AURP packets. It does this by adding a UDP header, which then allows the traffic to move through a TCP/IP network, for example. At the other end of the tunnel, the exterior router receives the traffic, strips off the UDP header and passes it to the local area protocol.

AURP tunnels can be point-to-point or multipoint, meaning that they can have multiple termination points. The tunnel can be *partially connected*, meaning that not all of the exterior routers are aware of all the others, or *fully connected*, meaning that all routers know about all other routers. The difference, of course, would be that in a partially-connected environment, less routing update traffic would be passed through the tunnel because not all routers would be eligible for the updates.

For more on AURP, please refer to **http://www.cisco.com/univercd/cc/td/doc/cisintwk/itg_v1/tr1909.htm**.

WAN: Enhanced IGRP

Another alternative to using RTMP in the WAN is to use Enhanced Interior Gateway Routing Protocol (EIGRP), a Cisco-proprietary protocol. As we saw in Chapter 12, "IPX Design," with IPX, EIGRP can be used to create scalability in an otherwise limited network model.

Let's review a couple of the benefits of EIGRP. First of all, it sends only the routing updates when there is a reason to do so. RTMP sends everything every 10 seconds! EIGRP also converges quickly, usually within 1 second of a route failure. RTMP must recalculate the tuples and send the full routing table to every router—and then continue to do so every 10 seconds. Finally, EIGRP will automatically perform redistribution with RTMP, and vice versa, as we saw also with IPX in Chapter 12.

When EIGRP is used in the WAN, the RTMP process (which is still running in the LANs) does not have its hop count affected. Router A, in Figure 13-3, believes that it is two hops to Router B. As the traffic passes

Figure 13-3
EIGRP in the WAN

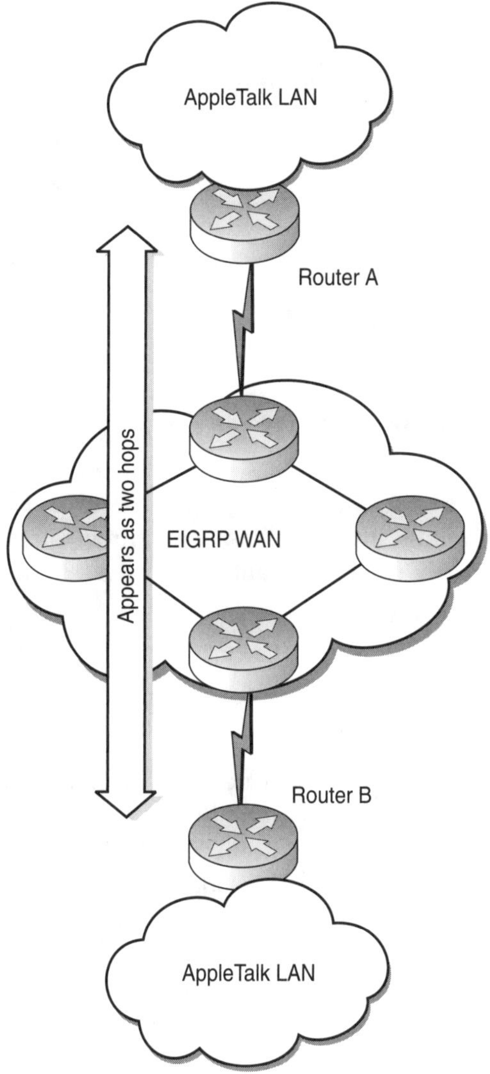

through the EIGRP cloud, there could be 50 routers, but Router A will still only see the distance as two hops.

EIGRP, on the other hand, needs to convert the hop count metric to something it can understand and use. Here is what it does to the RTMP hop count:

- Multiplies the number of hops by 25,652,400
- Views each RTMP hop like a 9,600-bps link

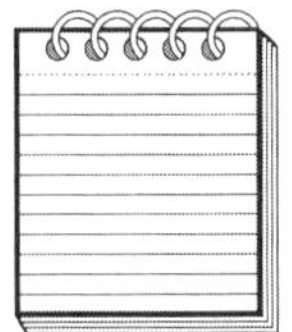

NOTE: *A benefit of using EIGRP for WAN networks that are carried over Frame Relay is that you can disable split horizon when using EIGRP with the command* **no appletalk eigrp-splithorizon**.

For more information on EIGRP in an AppleTalk network, please refer to **http://www.cisco.com/univercd/cc/td/doc/product/software/ios100/eigrp/36539.htm**.

AppleTalk Administrative Choices

As with any network design, certain choices must be made about naming conventions, numbering of networks, and fault tolerance. This section will present you with some tips and options on how to create a winning AppleTalk design.

AppleTalk Network Number Allocation

Part of designing an AppleTalk network involves the selection of network numbers that create logical scalability for the network. The network number is a 16-bit integer that creates over 64,000 available network numbers —similar to a Class B IP network address.

If you are redesigning a network, try to maintain cable ranges that are already in use. Find the logic in the cable range layout, and try to establish the scalability needed in order for the network to grow. If this is not possible, renumbering the networks is always a somewhat labor-intensive option.

In a new network design, build in scalability to the ranges. Try to use numbering conventions that will make growth and configuration easy for the network engineering staff. For instance, you may want to use cable range 1100 to 1199 for Building 11. Within that cable range, you may want to break it out further by floor, using 1100 to 1150 for the first floor, and so on.

As long as the cable range is unique within the AppleTalk design and does not overlap any other cable range, your administrative choices are strictly up to you and to the staff.

Floating Static Routes

As you have seen with other protocols, such as TCP/IP, the use of a floating static route can create an alternate path for traffic to use if the primary route should fail. AppleTalk networks are no exception. A *static route* is a manually configured path that would normally have an administrative distance (AD) of 1. When creating a floating static route, use an AD that is higher than any other in use on the network. Using a number greater than 200 is a good rule of thumb, as it is higher than any AD learned from any other routing protocol. Table 13-1 shows the AD for various routing protocols.

Table 13-1

Administrative Distances

Route Type	AD
Connected	0
Static	1
IBGP/EBGP	200/20
EIGRP (internal/external)	90/170
IGRP	100
OSPF	110
RIP	120
Floating Static	>200

NVE Naming Conventions

As we saw in the section on NBP, an NVE is an addressable entity on the network that is known by entity name and categorized by entity type. The entity name is a 32-character configurable string that contains

- Object
- Type
- Zone

By using a naming convention that is logical and descriptive of the entity, you create an easy-to-use network for the real customer—the end user. Say, for instance, that you have a color laser printer in the Science department for use by the Botany zone. The entity in its final form might look like this:

```
ColorPrinter:LaserJet@Botany
```

This is how it would appear to the user in the Chooser screen. Make the names unique and sensible so users will be able to quickly find the resource they need.

AppleTalk Zones

A *zone* is a logical group of network resources. The zone names should be descriptive of the geographical and functional aspect of the zone. For instance, in the example used for NVE naming conventions, the zone for the Botany department could either be "Botany" or "Science Botany," describing both levels of the zone. Using only "Science" as the zone name might be too restrictive, if there are divided resources and different physical locations for subdepartments within the Science department.

It is also useful to keep the names short, however, so "Science Botany" may be a little lengthy in appearance to a user who is scanning quickly through a Chooser screen in search of a zone. In that case, "Botany" may be descriptive enough, or perhaps something like "SciBot," as long as it would make sense to the users.

Another way to manage zones is to keep them small. In Figure 13-4 we can see how client/server traffic in a zone works. The fact that every server and router in a zone must process the NBP traffic clearly shows how large zones —especially those that are geographically diverse—can impact performance. By keeping the zones small, NBT traffic is kept localized and to a minimum.

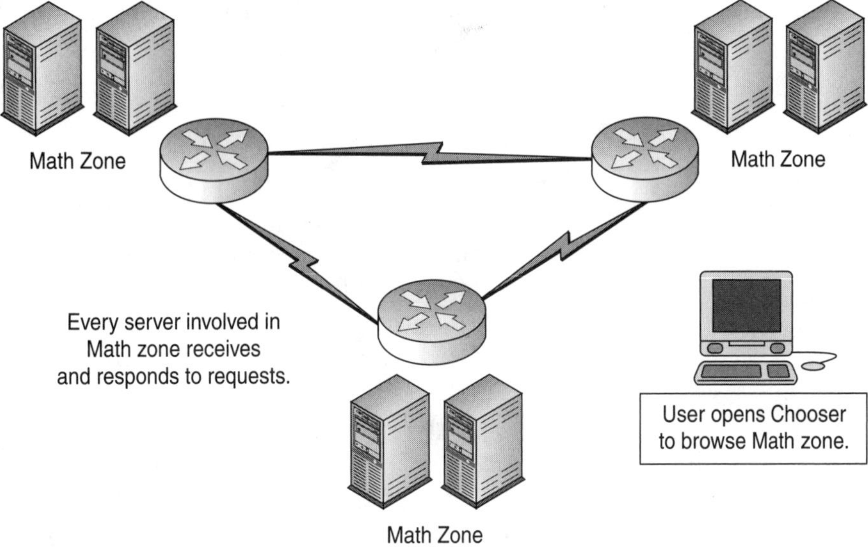
Math Zone
Math Zone
Every server involved in
Math zone receives
and responds to requests.
User opens Chooser
to browse Math zone.
Math Zone

Figure 13-4 Large zones

If you are routing AppleTalk over a WAN, create a zone just for the WAN interfaces, without permitting the WAN interfaces to participate in the LAN zones. Use a naming convention for this zone that begins with a "Z" so that it appears at the bottom of the Chooser screen. There is usually no reason for users to need these resources. You can omit these from appearing in the Chooser at all with filtering, which we will discuss in the next section.

Zones can be distributed across the WAN. This can be useful when several departments—organized as zones—need to access the same resources. Rather than have separate resources for each zone, zones can be allowed to share them. Be careful when implementing this, however, as excess NBP traffic across the WAN links can cause performance problems and can keep DDR links active unnecessarily.

AppleTalk Filtering Options

As with most desktop protocols, it is important to be sensible about the overall design and to keep broadcast traffic to a minimum on the network. To allow broadcasts to propagate through the network is to detract from optimal network performance. In this section, we will examine a few types of AppleTalk filters that will help curb the amount of broadcast traffic your AppleTalk network will see.

GetZoneList Filters

When a user opens the Chooser window, the end-station sends out a GetZoneList (GZL) request over the ZIP protocol. The response will be a list of zones from the router for which the end-station can use resources. *GetZoneList filters* work by filtering the ZIP reply that the router sends back to the end-station, thereby reducing the number of zones the user actually sees in the Chooser.

In order for the GZL filter to be effective, it must be identical on each Cisco router. As you can imagine, this does not scale well, because a manual process must take place on each router to configure this filtering. Additionally, if non-Cisco routers are in use on the network, the results of the GZL filter can be somewhat unpredictable. When either non-Cisco routers or inconsistently configured routers are in use, the list of zones in the Chooser window will be different depending on which router responds to the request. This can cause confusion and frustration for users and network engineering staff alike.

NBP Filters

NBP filtering provides a method that is configured much like an access list to control the forwarding of NBP packets and to hide services. This can help control excessive NBP packets on a LAN segment. An *NBP filter* is defined based on the NBP packet type, class of an NBP entity, individual NBP entity, or entities in a given zone. NBP filters are then applied to an interface.

ZIP Reply Filters

In order to hide zone information between networks, a *ZIP reply filter* can be used. The primary benefit of using a ZIP reply filter is when routers connect two separate AppleTalk administrative domains. In the example shown in Figure 13-5, Router A shares all of its RTMP information with Router B. When Router B requests zone information, however, through the

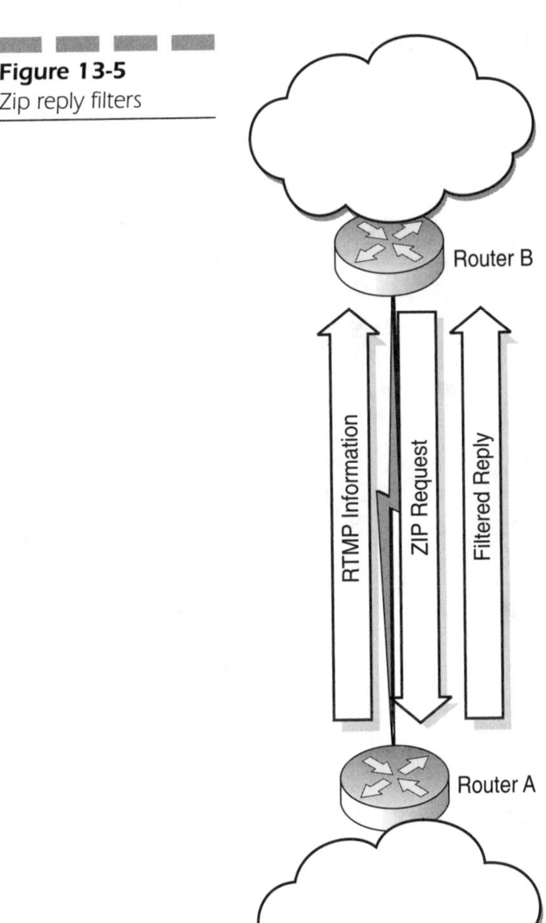

Figure 13-5
Zip reply filters

use of a ZIP request, Router A provides a filtered list of zones. This effectively makes some zones "invisible" from Router B and its neighbors.

Distribute Lists

A *distribute list* is used in an AppleTalk network the same way it might be used in any other kind of network—to control routing update packets.

Specifically, this distribute list will control RTMP broadcasts from router to router in order to hide cable ranges. It is important to note that using a distribute list will not filter out entire networks, or hide them from other networks. It will only prevent a route for that network from being added to the routing table of the receiving router.

Partial-Zone Filters

You should note that when a network number, as part of a cable range, is hidden, the zone(s) containing that network are denied as well. This could result in restricting zones unintentionally. The solution to this is to use *partial-zone filters*. There are some negative effects on the AppleTalk network, however, such as inconsistencies in NBP behavior and in outgoing routing updates. For more information, please refer to **http://www.cisco.com/univercd/cc/td/doc/product/software/ios113ed/113ed_cr/np2_c/2capple.htm#xtocid1711950**.

AppleTalk and IP

The fastest way to route AppleTalk traffic through the network is to allow native DDP to handle the network layer functions. This may not be the preferred way in a large IP network, however, for several reasons. Many large networks have "IP-only" backbones with routers that do not handle multiple protocols. Some networks may find that running native DDP through the network slows overall network performance. Whatever the reason, you may find a need to tunnel AppleTalk through IP rather than running native DDP.

There are two ways to tunnel AppleTalk through an IP network:

- AURP tunnel
- Generic Router Encapsulation (GRE) tunnel

AURP tunneling was mentioned in our section on AURP, earlier in this chapter. GRE tunneling is a Cisco-proprietary method that allows point-to-point tunneling from one Cisco router to another. For more information on configuring these tunnels, please refer to **http://www.cisco.com/univercd/cc/td/doc/product/software/ios113ed/113ed_cr/np2_c/2capple.htm#xtocid1711958**.

Problem Areas

AppleTalk has a few issues that bear mentioning before we close on this topic. One of these is security. AppleTalk has no built-in security as designed. The best way to address security in an AppleTalk network is by tunneling the traffic when crossing the WAN and by using basic network security as outlined in Chapter 23, "Security Design."

AppleTalk also creates a lot of overhead in the network, with its many broadcast types. A few steps you can take to reduce the overhead are listed below:

- Ensure that users are on Mac OS 7.0 or better. Older OSs may generate excess NBP traffic when the Chooser is left open.
- Be sure that the network components are using AppleTalk Phase 2, for greater scalability.
- Use AURP or EIGRP across the WAN. By doing so, you eliminate the 10-second RTMP updates from being carried across what may be your core routers.
- Keep network numbers hierarchical in nature for scalability.
- Use filtering techniques to reduce the GZL and ZIP traffic on the network. Filter routes by using distribute lists.
- Keep your zones small in order to reduce the distance traffic has to travel for intrazone communications.

Case Study

Campus Research Corporation has brought on a small design consulting group as part of its quest for new business. This group will work out of the office in St. Louis and will communicate with the new manufacturing unit in Milwaukee in order to design new components. This group was a small, independent agency before being purchased outright by Campus Research. They were accustomed to using a small AppleTalk Phase 1 LAN with Macintosh computers running Mac OS 6.0.

The network engineering staff at CRC has no experience with running AppleTalk, but they have been unable to talk the design group out of using their Macintosh computers. Because the group has to be able to communicate between St. Louis and Milwaukee, the company has enlisted your help to find a quick and easy solution to the problem. What steps would you take in order to create a design that will work for everyone in this situation?

Suggested solutions to the case studies may be found in Appendix C, "Suggested Case Study Solutions."

Study Hints

Although no one can disclose test items or test content, we can give hints as to what might be valuable to study. For this chapter, there are key facts that need to be reviewed and remembered:

- A *zone* is a logical group of AppleTalk nodes.
- A *node* is any device on an AppleTalk network.
- A *socket* is any one of 254 ports on a node that allow socket clients (applications) to talk to the DDP protocol.
- A *cable range* is a group of consecutive AppleTalk networks.
- Using EIGRP in the WAN, you can use the command **no appletalk eigrp-splithorizon** to disable split horizon for partially meshed Frame Relay WANs.
- An open Chooser window in Mac OS 6.0 and older can generate excessive NBP broadcasts.
- An AppleTalk node gets its temporary address from a startup range, which is a reserved block of numbers between 64,280 and 65,534.

CCDP Tips

This section contains an abbreviated list of topics covered in this chapter. Think of this section as the equivalent of reading Cliff's Notes™ instead of reading an entire book. You will get the general idea of the chapter but will benefit more from reading the chapter in its entirety.

The AppleTalk protocol suite has four basic components:

- **Nodes** Any device on an AppleTalk network
- **Sockets** Conduits between an application and DDP
- **Networks** A single logical cable with any number of nodes
- **Zones** A logical group of AppleTalk nodes

An AppleTalk address contains a(n)

- 16-bit network number
- 8-bit node number
- 8-bit socket number

Name Binding Protocol (NBP) is a broadcast-based protocol that binds a network address to a friendly name for a Network Visible Entity (NVE), which is an entity that can be communicated with on the network. It works by broadcasting queries containing two of three components and asking the responder to fill in the blank. The three fields of an NBP broadcast are

- Object name
- Zone
- Type

NBP provides four functions:

- Lookup
- Registration
- Confirmation
- Deletion

The NVE entity name is a 32-character configurable string that contains

- Object
- Type
- Zone

The format of an entity name looks like this:

```
ColorPrinter:LaserJet@Botany
```

AppleTalk Address Resolution Protocol (AARP) is a broadcast-based request and reply protocol that allows a node to find the hardware address corresponding to the network address it hears on the wire. The addresses are then stored in the node's Address Maintenance Table (AMT).

Datagram Delivery Protocol (DDP) is a connectionless, network layer protocol that provides best-effort delivery for AppleTalk. Other nodes can glean address information by reading the DDP headers in addition to or instead of using AARP.

Zone Information Protocol (ZIP) is a broadcast-based, session layer protocol that allows nodes to learn their zone, find other nodes within their zone—through the Zone Information Table—and find an address to replace the temporary address assigned to them when they first boot.

AppleTalk Data Stream Protocol (ADSP) is another session layer protocol that AppleTalk uses to provide flow control and error checking over full-duplex communications between nodes. ADSP runs on top of DDP.

AppleTalk routing in the LAN is performed by Routing Table Maintenance Protocol (RTMP), which is closely patterned after RIP. It sends the full routing table every 10 seconds in packets known as *tuples*. Each tuple contains a network or cable range and a hop count. Between 100 and 200 tuples are carried in each RTMP packet, which can be up to 600 bytes in size. By knowing the number of networks to be advertised, you can calculate the impact of RTMP on the network. It is not advisable to use this routing protocol in the WAN.

For the WAN, Apple created AppleTalk Update Routing Protocol (AURP), an update-based routing protocol that greatly reduces routing traffic on the network. It uses exterior routers and tunnels to create point-to-point or multipoint tunnels between endpoints. AURP adds some security to the network and can be used to tunnel AppleTalk through other protocols.

Another option for routing AppleTalk through the WAN is to use EIGRP. Redistribution between EIGRP and RTMP is automatic and does not add to the hop count from LAN to LAN. EIGRP is an update-based routing protocol, like AURP, and can be used when running AppleTalk between two or more Cisco routers.

Cable ranges should be planned for scalability and organized logically—by building, for instance. Zones should also be carefully thought out, with descriptive, unique names. Zones should also be relatively small in size.

Filtering AppleTalk can keep overhead to a minimum. There are several types of filters that can be used on the network:

- **NBP filter** To selectively hide services from nodes
- **Distribute list** To reduce the routing protocol traffic on the network

- **GetZoneList filter** To filter the zones that a node will receive in response to a GZL request
- **ZIP reply filter** To filter the advertised zones between networks

Summary

We have presented the AppleTalk basics to you, from the components to the routing issues, and have given you a chance to practice with a case study. Although AppleTalk is not enjoying the same popularity it once did, you will still encounter it in schools, government networks, graphics shops, and the like. As a network designer, you should know how to make any desktop protocol function at its best in your design. Remember to keep the components of the network hierarchical in order to create scalability.

In Chapter 14, "Windows Networking Design," we will show you how to design around the popular Windows operating system in a networked environment.

Questions

The following review questions have been selected to help you test your knowledge of the subject matter contained in this chapter. You will also find these questions contained in the CD-ROM included with this book. While these are not the questions you will find in the certification exams, knowing the answers to the review questions in this book will help cement the material in your mind as you prepare for the tests.

1. When an AppleTalk client boots up, what is the protocol it uses to broadcast for its node number?

   a. ZIP

   b. DDP

   c. AARP

   d. GZL

2. A tuple contains which two components? (Select two.)
   a. ZIP replies
   b. Hop count
   c. Cable range
   d. RTMP updates
3. AURP stands for:
   a. AppleTalk Update Routing Protocol
   b. Address Update Routing Protocol
   c. AppleTalk Uplink Routing Protocol
   d. Address Uplink Routing Protocol
4. At which layer of the OSI model does DDP operate?
   a. Data Link
   b. Network
   c. Transport
   d. Session
5. Which protocol provides for flow control of communication between clients?
   a. AURP
   b. ZIP
   c. ADSP
   d. NBP
6. What are two tunnel types that can be used to carry AppleTalk through an IP backbone? (Select two.)
   a. AURP
   b. GZL
   c. EIGRP
   d. GRE
7. Choose the statement that best describes an AppleTalk zone.
   a. A logical group of socket clients
   b. A logical group of AppleTalk networks
   c. A physical group of socket clients
   d. A logical group of AppleTalk nodes

8. Select the filtering method that will reduce RTMP traffic between routers.
   a. GetZoneList filtering
   b. Distribute list
   c. NBP filtering
   d. ZIP reply filtering
9. Choose the item that shows a correctly-formatted NVE name.
   a. FileServer:NTServer
   b. FileServer@NTServer
   c. FileServer@NTServer:Math
   d. FileServer:NTServer:Math
10. Select the methods by which a client can learn the addresses of other nodes. (Select two.)
    a. ZIP
    b. DDP
    c. AURP
    d. AARP
11. Which statement correctly defines the *startup range*?
    a. A reserved block of number between 64,280 and 65,534.
    b. The temporary address given to a node when it first boots.
    c. A reserved address for an AppleTalk router.
    d. A cable range from 1000 to 1100.
12. When an AppleTalk node learns the address of another node, where does it store the information?
    a. ZIP
    b. AMT
    c. GZL
    d. AARP
13. What is the maximum number of tuples per RTMP packet?
    a. 100
    b. 200
    c. 300
    d. 600

14. What filtering method will reduce the number of zones seen in the Chooser?
    a. ZIP reply filtering
    b. Distribute list
    c. GetZoneList filtering
    d. NBP filtering
15. What filtering method will hide services from a user?
    a. ZIP reply filtering
    b. Distribute list
    c. GetZoneList filtering
    d. NBP filtering
16. The available number of AppleTalk network numbers roughly corresponds to this IP address class.
    a. A
    b. B
    c. C
    d. D
17. Which upper-layer protocol would request retransmission of packets in the event of errors?
    a. AARP
    b. DDP
    c. ADSP
    d. ZIP
18. Select one way in which security can be provided on an AppleTalk network.
    a. Tunneling
    b. Careful cable range numbering
    c. Unplugging sockets
    d. Using ambiguous node names
19. True or False: GRE tunnels work with any vendor's router for tunneling AppleTalk.
    a. True
    b. False

20. True or False: The use of a floating static route will allow for a backup route for AppleTalk networks.

    a. True

    b. False

Answers

1. When an AppleTalk client boots up, what is the protocol it uses to broadcast for its node number?
   a. ZIP
   Explanation: The node will first broadcast for its zone, then negotiate for a valid node address via ZIP.
2. A tuple contains which two components? (Select two.)
   c. Hop count

   d. Cable range
3. AURP stands for:
   a. AppleTalk Update Routing Protocol
4. At which layer of the OSI model does DDP operate?
   b. Network
5. Which protocol provides for flow control of communication between clients?
   c. ADSP
   Explanation: ADSP can request a flow to be increased or decreased depending on congestion.
6. What are two tunnel types that can be used to carry AppleTalk through an IP backbone? (Select two.)
   a. AURP
   d. GRE
   Explanation: Although there is a third type listed in Cisco documentation—Cayman tunneling—this is for use with a specific vendor's (Cayman) product for interoperability.
7. Choose the statement that best describes an AppleTalk zone.
   d. A logical group of AppleTalk nodes

8. Select the filtering method that will reduce RTMP traffic between routers.
   b. Distribute list
   Explanation: By using a distribute list to hide cable ranges from other routers, a router reduces the size of the routing table that is sent through RTMP. Fewer entries eqfuals fewer tuples. Fewer tuples means fewer RTMP packets.

9. Choose the item that shows a correctly formatted NVE name.
   a. FileServer:NTServer

10. Select the methods by which a client can learn the addresses of other nodes. (Select two.)
    b. DDP
    d. AARP
    Explanation: An AppleTalk node may either send an AARP request for a node's hardware address or may learn this through looking at the header information in a DDP packet.

11. Which statement correctly defines the *startup range*?
    a. A reserved block of number between 64,280 and 65,534.
    Explanation: The startup range is used for providing temporary node addresses to AppleTalk clients so they can communicate before receiving their "official" node address.

12. When an AppleTalk node learns the address of another node, where does it store the information?
    b. AMT
    Explanation: As we saw in this chapter, each AppleTalk client stores known destinations in its address maintenance table.

13. What is the maximum number of tuples per RTMP packet?
    b. 200

14. What filtering method will reduce the number of zones seen in the Chooser?
    d. GetZoneList filtering
    Explanation: By filtering at the router on GZL, zones sent in reply to the user's request for available zones will be reduced.

15. What filtering method will hide services from a user?
    d. NBP filtering
    Explanation: Because it filters on NVE name, it can effectively be used to hide services from users.

16. The available number of AppleTalk network numbers roughly corresponds to this IP address class.
    b. B
17. Which upper-layer protocol would request retransmission of packets in the event of errors?
    c. ADSP
    Explanation: Because ADSP handles flow control and sequencing, it can request a retransmission if packets are corrupted or received out of sequence.
18. Select one way in which security can be provided on an AppleTalk network.
    a. Tunneling
    Explanation: Tunneling is a way to move traffic through a network, particularly a WAN, so that it cannot be intercepted (such as with a sniffer) without breaking down the communications altogether.
19. True or False: GRE tunnels work with any vendor's router for tunneling AppleTalk.
    b. False
    Explanation: GRE is a Cisco-proprietary technology.
20. True or False: The use of a floating static route will allow for a backup route for AppleTalk networks.
    a. True
    Explanation: Using a floating static route—that is, a static route with an administrative distance greater than 200—will allow for an alternate path to become active if the primary route should fail.

Frequently Asked Questions (FAQs)

1. *Does Cisco support AppleTalk over a Frame Relay network?*

AppleTalk, like IPX, is supported over the WAN. The one caveat with Frame Relay is that because AppleTalk routing uses split horizon, the Frame Relay network must be fully meshed. Note that you can overcome this limitation by using EIGRP in your WAN.

2. *Why do I see an entry for "martians" when I use the command "***show apple traffic***?"*

   Cisco logs packets from unknown sources (those for which there is no route in the routing table) as "martians." The fact that the source is unknown could either be because a device has recently been moved or because a device is misconfigured in the network.

Bibliography

AppleTalk—Cisco, **http://www.cisco.com/cpress/cc/td/cpress/fund/ith2nd/ it2427.htm**

Cisco Internetwork Design, Cisco Press, 2000, Matthew H. Birkner, Editor

Cisco Internetwork Design Course Manual, version 3.0, April 1997, Cisco Systems, Inc.

Configuring AppleTalk—Cisco, **http://www.cisco.com/univercd/cc/ td/doc/product/software/ios113ed/113ed_cr/np2_c/2capple.htm**

CHAPTER 14

Windows Networking Design

Overview

You may be tempted to skip this chapter—but don't! If there's one type of networking in which everyone thinks he is an expert, it's Windows networking. This could be because most of us use Windows end-stations in our everyday home and work life and have, at one time or another, had to troubleshoot the connectivity or some other aspect of the network stack. Or it could be because every radio station is constantly advertising "boot camps" that will make you an instant expert in Microsoft products, including networking.

Once you have finished reading this chapter, you will understand a little more about the design issues you could encounter related to Windows networking as well as some of the "behind the scenes" inner workings of the NetBIOS and NetBEUI protocol stack and operation. Although this will not make you an "expert," it will equip you to deal with the issues commonly found in Windows networking—from the design process to implementation. You will have a chance to practice what you have learned from this chapter with a short case study followed by some review questions.

Windows Networking

Here's what Windows networking is: a way for clients and servers that are using a Windows operating system (OS) to communicate and share resources. Here's what Windows networking is not: a true network-layer protocol stack allowing for logical addressing and traditional inter-LAN communication.

Windows networking is a general term referring to the framework and network software that is part of these Microsoft products:

- LAN Manager
- MS-DOS with LAN Manager client
- Windows for Workgroups
- Windows 95, 98, and Millennium Edition (ME)
- Windows NT and 2000

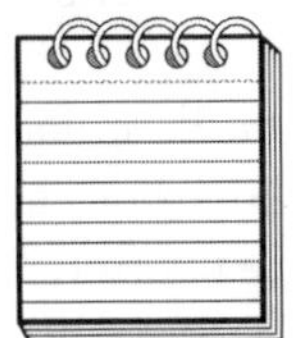

NOTE: This chapter does not cover design material related to LAN Manager, MS-DOS with LAN Manager client, or Windows for Workgroups, as these products are considered to be outdated.

By allowing for users, printers, file servers, and the like to be grouped into sets that will allow for the sharing of resources, the networking software in these products bridged the gap that once existed in the workplace. Microsoft took the common practice of saving information to a floppy diskette and handing it off to another user for saving, editing, or printing, and turned it into a virtual workplace where Jane, in Figure 14-1, could print to a printer on Bob's machine. This is a simplistic view of the Windows networking setup and process, but as we move on through this chapter, you will see the components, such as the NetBIOS protocol, which allows for the virtual workplace to function.

Figure 14-1
Windows networking

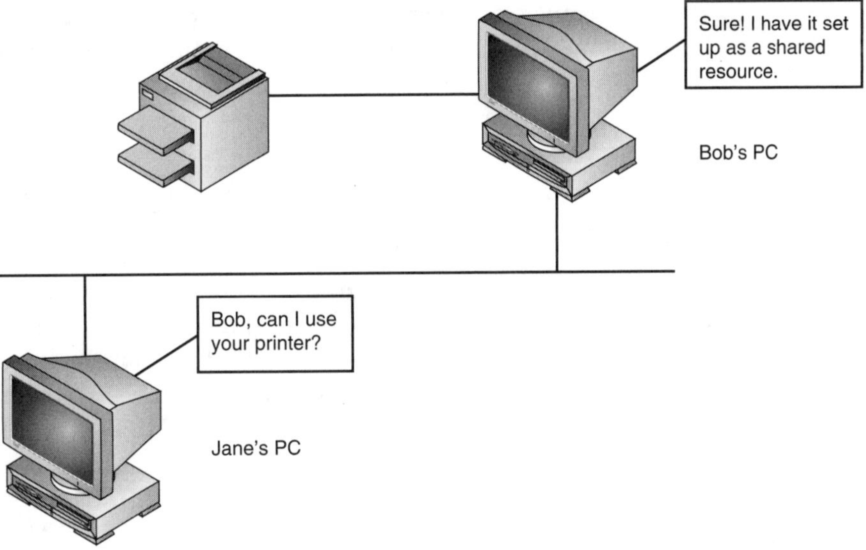
Sure! I have it set up as a shared resource.
Bob's PC
Bob, can I use your printer?
Jane's PC

When Microsoft introduced Windows for Workgroups, a specialized version of the relatively new Windows GUI, the form and function of the workplace began to change rapidly. Windows resources could suddenly be grouped into blocks of centrally managed resources. Instead of each user having to have a printer, several users could share a single printer. The cost savings quickly added up.

Of course, some operating systems, which were designed for mainframe use, were already using this concept. VAX VMS users, for example, were managed by a system administrator, could send print jobs to line printers, and could use messaging protocols to send e-mail and "instant" messages to other terminals and consoles. While this worked well for mainframe users, the popularity of the PC was growing both in the workplace and in the home.

Over time the look and feel of the Windows OS have evolved to great popularity, but little has changed about the structure and underlying concepts that drive the networked environment.

Domains vs. Workgroups

In order for users to talk to each other and share resources, they must be joined into logical groups. These groups can be viewed through a network browser called the Network Neighborhood.

There are two types of groups within a Windows networked environment:

- Domains
- Workgroups

The important distinction is the amount of administrative control that exists over the group. Let's first talk about domains. A *domain* is a formal collection of network resources that is administratively controlled by a Primary Domain Controller (PDC), which is sometimes backed up by a standby Backup Domain Controller (BDC). The PDC/BDC resides on a Windows NT or 2000 server.

NOTE: *The "domain" under discussion here has nothing to do with the Domain Name System (DNS) used for Internet domain structures.*

TIP: *Having a BDC is a good measure for providing redundancy and fault-tolerance in a domain.*

As shown in Figure 14-2, the PDC/BDC contains information about individual user IDs, collections of users into groups, and other network resources such as print servers, file servers, printers, and so on. The administrator of these domain controllers has the ability to manage users,

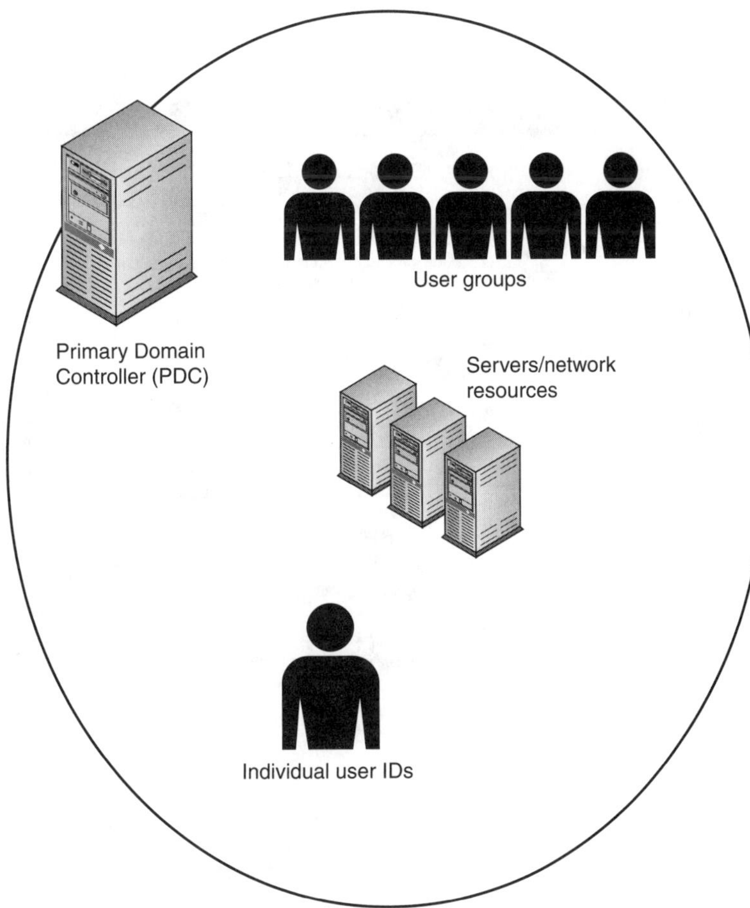

Figure 14-2
Windows domain

resource security, and group resources in a logical manner. This is something that is not a characteristic of workgroups.

With Windows 2000, a new type of domain hierarchy has been introduced, called Active Directory Hierarchy. It allows for the collection of domains into parent-child relationships that enable several new features, including easier searching through multiple domains with a single query.

A Windows workgroup is also a collection of resources, but it is very informal. Anyone can set up a new workgroup simply by creating a new workgroup name. In Figure 14-3 we see the Network dialog box where a new workgroup can be created. The system will allow me to put in anything I want as my workgroup. It is easy to set up a simple home network, when all equipment is connected to a common hub or switch, by creating a workgroup on one PC, and then setting up all of the PCs in the house on the

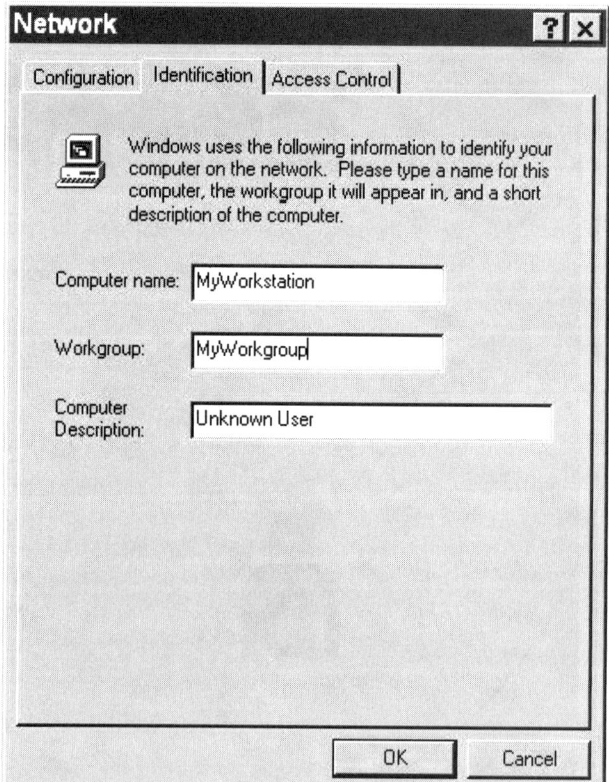

Figure 14-3 Creating a workgroup

same workgroup. There is no administrative control over these workgroups. Essentially, everyone can be on their own workgroup, if they like.

So you can see how different a workgroup is from a domain. Although these terms are easily confused, if you remember these facts about Windows networking domains, you will successfully be able to differentiate between the two:

- A domain is centrally administered.
- A domain is a formal collection of network resources.
- Domains can provide security and resource management that is not available with workgroups.
- A domain must have at least one Windows NT or 2000 server acting as a PDC.

NetBIOS Protocol

Although Windows 2000 brings some changes to the protocol setup for Windows networking, we will first address how products prior to Windows 2000 behaved. NetBIOS is the first protocol we will discuss.

The NetBIOS protocol operates at the session layer of the seven-layer OSI model. As you recall from working with that model, this layer handles the way end-stations communicate. In other words, it establishes the "ground rules" for how they will talk to each other. Much like a business meeting or forum, if there is no agenda and no set of rules, you can end up with a lot of noise and confusion—with nothing accomplished. Figure 14-4 demonstrates the relationship between the NetBIOS protocol stack and the seven-layer OSI model.

NetBIOS is used for file and printer sharing, Windows messaging, authentication (CHAP and PAP), and name resolution. By providing an Application Program Interface (API) and a naming service, NetBIOS provides for every type of Windows networking operation from browsing servers by name to printing to a networked printer.

Instead of having to know an address, such as an IP address, for a network resource, one can simply perform a Name Query broadcast (generated when the user browses for the resources), as shown in Figure 14-5. Bob may wish to connect to the print server in the Math department, so that he can then have access to add one of the department's printers for use from his PC. By opening a browser window, he generates a broadcast requesting the

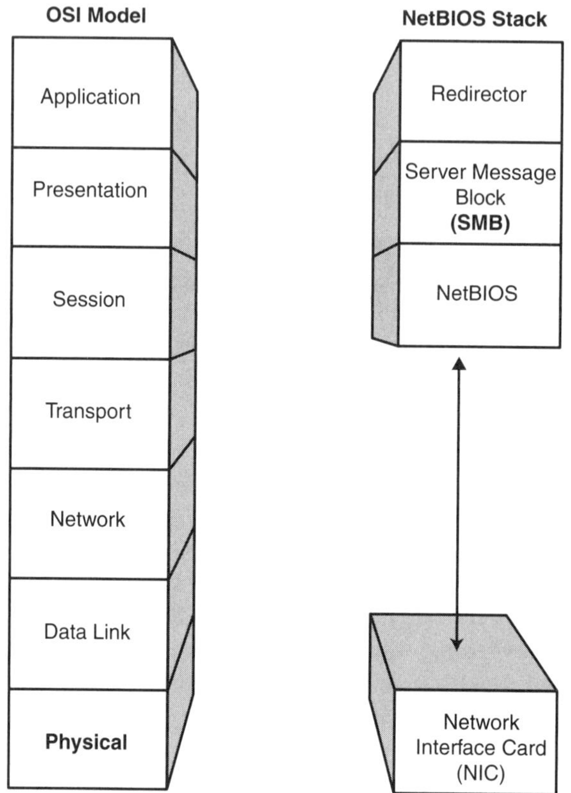

Figure 14-4 The NetBIOS protocol stack

names of all available NetBIOS resources in the LAN. He will then be able to select a resource from the results.

Because this is a session-layer protocol, however, other software is required at the transport layer to carry the data. We will discuss this a little more in the next section.

Since it was designed in the very early days of networking, NetBIOS does not provide for network-layer logical addressing and routing. It was intended to be an extension of the input/output (I/O) operation of a PC, to permit each PC to be able to communicate with other PCs on the same LAN. At that time, there was not really a broad concept of how explosive the networking world would become. Remember, at that time, even Bill Gates thought there would never be a need for more than 64 KB of memory in a PC. Can you imagine trying to run a system today with that memory sizing?

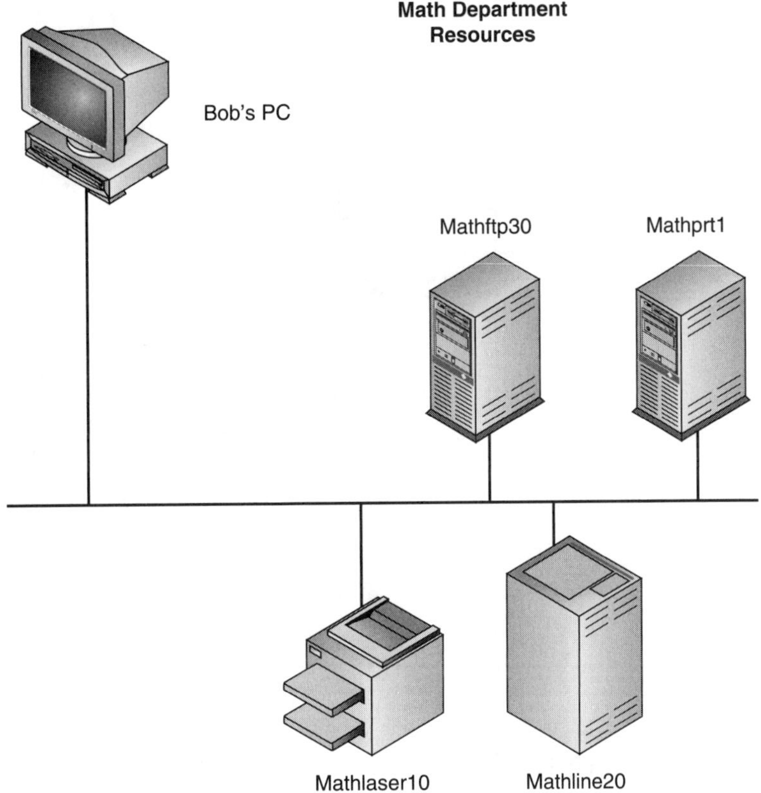

Figure 14-5 Network resource browsing

Transport Protocols

As we said earlier in the chapter, NetBIOS requires a transport mechanism, represented by the trains in Figure 14-6, to carry it across the network. There are, of course, two ways to move information over a network: bridging and routing.

Windows networking has three methods available for transporting NetBIOS:

- NetBEUI (bridged)
- NWLink (routed)
- NBT (routed)

Figure 14-6 Transporting NetBIOS

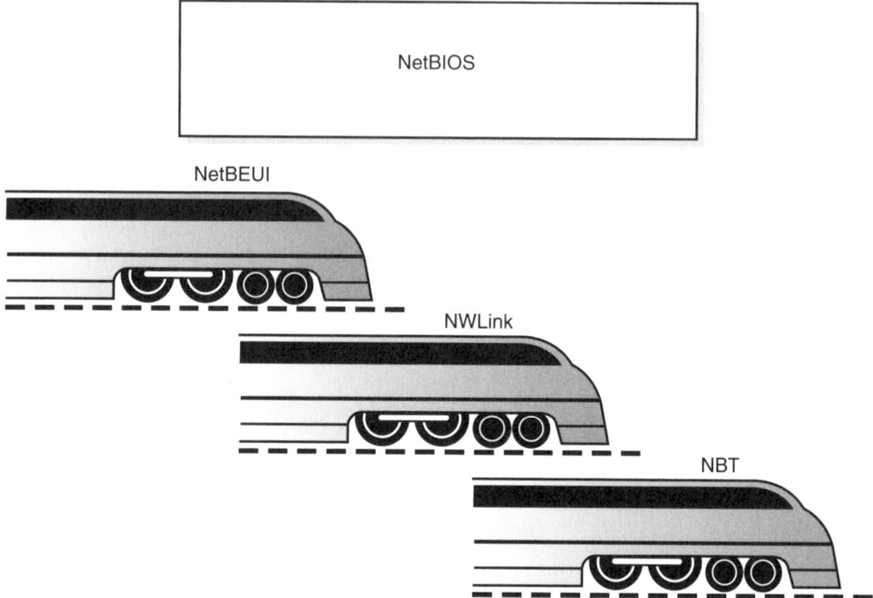

NetBIOS over LLC2 (NetBEUI)

NetBEUI, short for NetBIOS Extended User Interface, is a variation on the NetBIOS protocol that allows it to run on the Windows OS. It uses the Logical Link Control (LLC) 2 specification, which implements a connection-oriented sublayer of the data link layer. NetBEUI also provides functions corresponding to the transport and network layers of the OSI model, as shown in Figure 14-7. NetBEUI is the protocol that, when enabled, can cause the greatest performance hit on your network, because it must be bridged. It requires a flat topology and broadcasts in order to function. This in turn does not scale well and causes excess traffic to consume valuable bandwidth on the network. There is no explicit workstation address configuration involved in using NetBEUI.

The workstations communicating using NetBEUI are grouped into *bridge groups*. Although there is no "hard" limit to the number of workstations in a bridge group, the "soft" limit is a drop in performance beginning somewhere around the 50th workstation. Because NetBEUI was created with older technologies such as LAN Manager and Windows for Work-

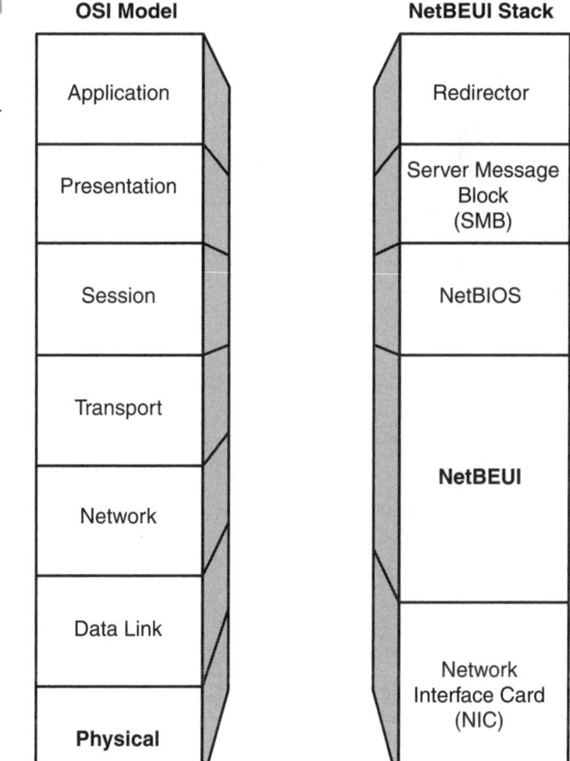

Figure 14-7 NetBEUI protocol stack

groups in mind, it is unlikely that you will encounter a design where NetBEUI is still the protocol of choice. If you do, then it is up to you to find a more scalable solution for the Windows network.

NetBIOS over Internetwork Packet eXchange (NWLink)

When designing for a small- to medium-sized network that is using older versions of the Novell networking protocol, Internetwork Packet eXchange (IPX), you will need to use NWLink, seen in Figure 14-8. As with NetBEUI, no address configuration is required on the client workstation, but IPX must already be in use on the network for NWLink to work.

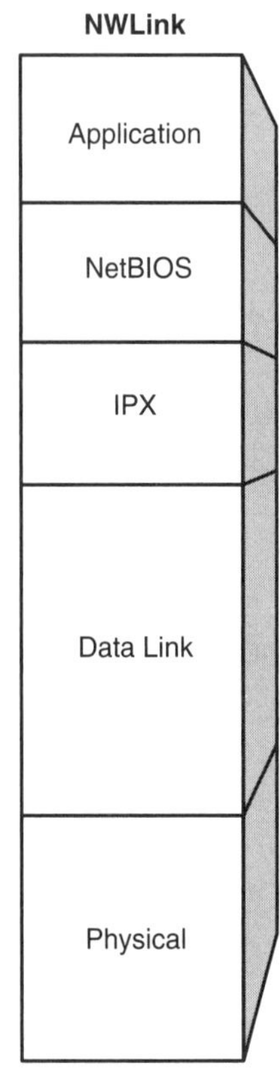

Figure 14-8
NWLink

To use NWLink, each Cisco router in the network must be configured to forward type-20 IPX packets across the network. This must be configured for each interface of each router. It is recommended that you use NWLink *only* when you cannot upgrade the Novell clients to a version that will permit the use of TCP/IP to communicate.

NetBIOS over TCP (NBT)

In most medium- to large-sized designs, Cisco recommends that you use NBT, shown in Figure 14-9, which runs over the TCP transport protocol. This is especially important in most modern networks, which are part of a

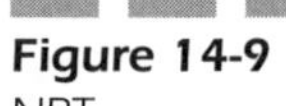

Figure 14-9
NBT

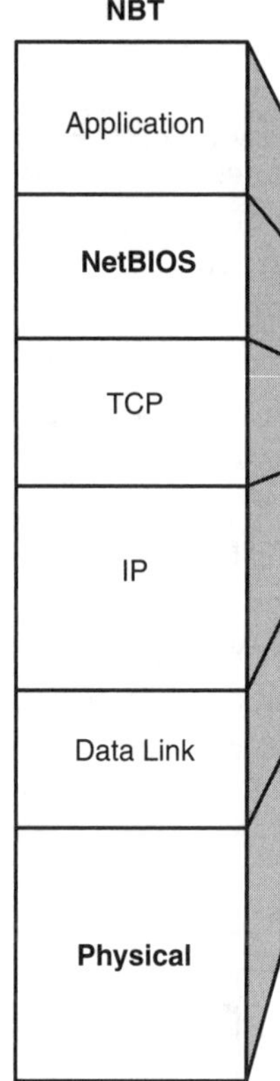

WAN design. When using NBT, each client workstation must be configured with either a static or dynamically assigned IP address that is unique to the workstation. Addresses can be assigned dynamically through the use of the Dynamic Host Configuration Protocol (DHCP), which permits a client workstation to request an IP address for a single sign-on or a leased period of time. A DHCP server administers the addresses, eliminating the need for manual intervention in most cases.

Because NBT uses unique workstation addresses and the TCP protocol, optimum network performance can be achieved by avoiding bridging or unnecessary broadcasting on the network. Using DHCP in conjunction with NBT also provides for easier administration and client workstation setup.

Browser Service

Now that you have a session-layer protocol (NetBIOS) being carried through the network by one of the transport-layer protocols we mentioned in the last section, you have established connectivity for the clients and servers on the Windows network. Now the clients and servers need to be able to find each other quickly and easily.

This was easy enough in the beginning of Windows networks, when it was assumed that all of the workstations would be on a small to medium shared LAN. Workstations would broadcast an advertisement with their name, and all other workstations would process that broadcast and remember that workstation. Things become a little more complex when there are a larger number of workstations, or multiple LANs.

Microsoft designed the LAN Services Browser to address the need for many workstations to register their addresses and to quickly gather a list of other workstations in the network. Figure 14-10 depicts how worksta-

Figure 14-10
LAN Services Browser

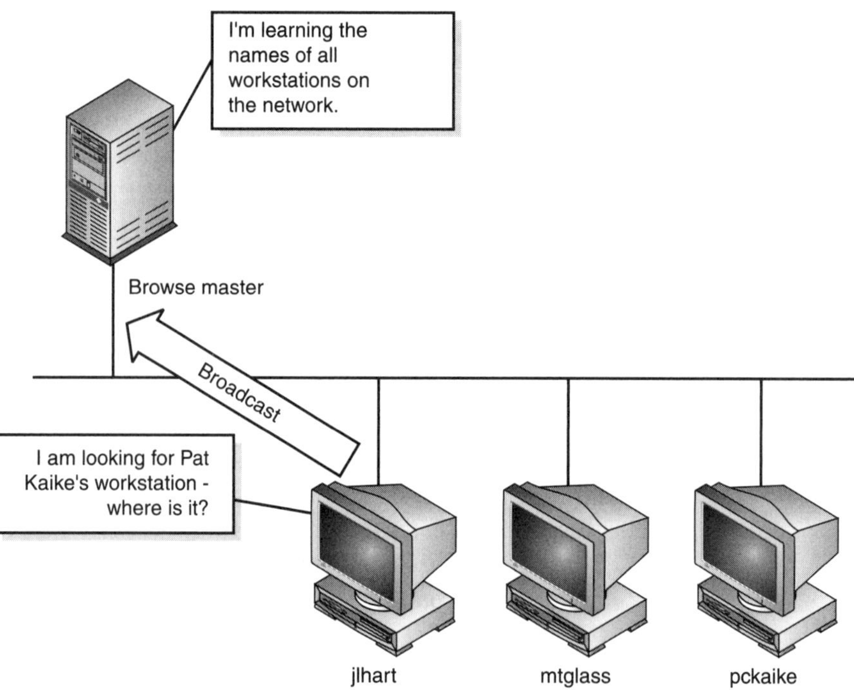
I'm learning the names of all workstations on the network.
Browse master
Broadcast
I am looking for Pat Kaike's workstation - where is it?
jlhart
mtglass
pckaike

tions broadcast to elect the browse master. The browse master learns all of the workstations on the network and will respond to broadcast requests from clients.

There are usually backup browse masters in a network, so that an outage on a single browse master does not effectively shut down browsing on the LAN.

Name Resolution

Name resolution is somewhat different from the browser service offered in Windows networking, although it also uses a NetBIOS workstation name. In this case, relating a "friendly" name, such as BobsPC, to the workstation's unique IP address, such as 172.16.10.187, provides name resolution. There are several ways to accomplish name resolution. The types discussed here are current as of the release of Windows 2000.

- Broadcasts
- LMHOSTS
- NetBIOS name cache
- WINS
- Internet DNS

Broadcasts

One method of name resolution is the use of broadcasts, which can be seen in Figure 14-11. As you know, a workstation receiving a broadcast must process that broadcast, and a broadcast sent out on a given subnet will be received by all workstations on that subnet. In Windows networking each subnet can have a browse master and backup browse masters that listen for the clients and servers on the LAN to broadcast their NetBIOS names. The browse master then keeps a master list of all of the clients and servers on the LAN.

Using broadcasts is not a scalable method of name resolution and consumes valuable bandwidth on the subnet. The broadcast method was originally created with flat, bridged subnets in mind. Remember—a router acts as a natural broadcast barrier and does not forward broadcasts by default. To allow a broadcast technology to scale into multiple subnets, the router

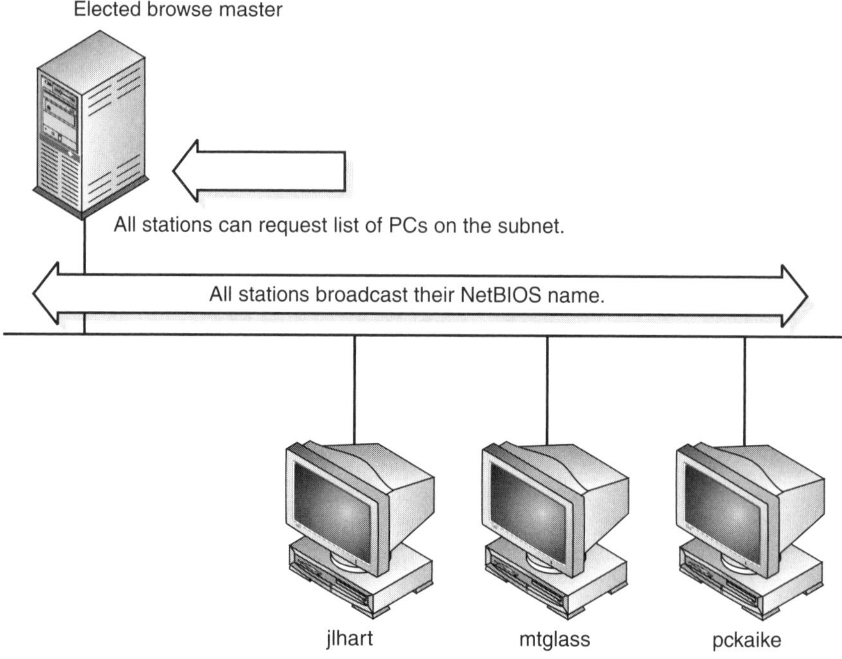
Elected browse master
All stations can request list of PCs on the subnet.
All stations broadcast their NetBIOS name.
jlhart
mtglass
pckaike

Figure 14-11 Subnet broadcasts

would have to be directed to forward broadcasts or bridge all protocols. If the router does not forward the broadcasts, then services may not be visible to users of other networks. This does not mesh with today's requirement for robust, scalable designs that usually include WANs. This method of name resolution is therefore not recommended.

For more information on some of the problems that can be encountered in the broadcast name resolution method, see the "Problem Areas" section of this chapter.

LMHOSTS vs. HOSTS

There are two types of manually configured files on Windows workstations for address resolution:

- HOSTS
- LMHOSTS

The HOSTS file is used primarily when the TCP/IP stack is implemented. It contains a network layer address and the registered host name address in a text-based file. The Windows LMHOSTS file is a file of name-to-address mappings that is used normally when the WINS name resolution method or NetBIOS over TCP/IP is used. The LMHOSTS file also permits some special configurations, such as directing the workstation to load the file entries into the name cache at bootup (see the next section for this information). If LMHOSTS will be used in the network, the recommended configuration is to have an LMHOSTS file on the PDC that contains all of the static name-to-address mappings that exist in the network, as well as the names and addresses of all other PDCs in the network. Obviously, this will not apply to any workstation that receives its address dynamically.

The LMHOST file on the individual client workstations, in this hierarchical scenario, only needs to contain the name-to-address map for their PDC and a path leading them to the master LMHOSTS file on the PDC.

NetBIOS Name Cache The NetBIOS name cache is related to the LMHOSTS method of name resolution. As the workstation resolves names during daily usage, a cache of these names is stored for quick reference. Depending on configuration, there may be a limit to the number of names that can be stored in the cache or a limited period of time for which they are stored. Consult your OS manual or **http://www.microsoft.com** for more information.

If there is a need to have a pre-configured set of quick name-to-address mappings that loads up into the cache at system startup, these can be added to the LMHOSTS file with a **#PRE** tag appended to the beginning of the line.

Windows Internet Name Service (WINS)

To address the need for name resolution across multiple subnets, Microsoft introduced WINS. End-stations are configured to send unicast packets to the WINS server. This is accomplished by enabling WINS resolution and entering one or more WINS server addresses in a designated search order, usually based upon proximity to the end-station itself. The process is shown in Figure 14-12.

The WINS name resolution method is highly recommended, because it effectively reduces broadcasts on a network. This improves the overall

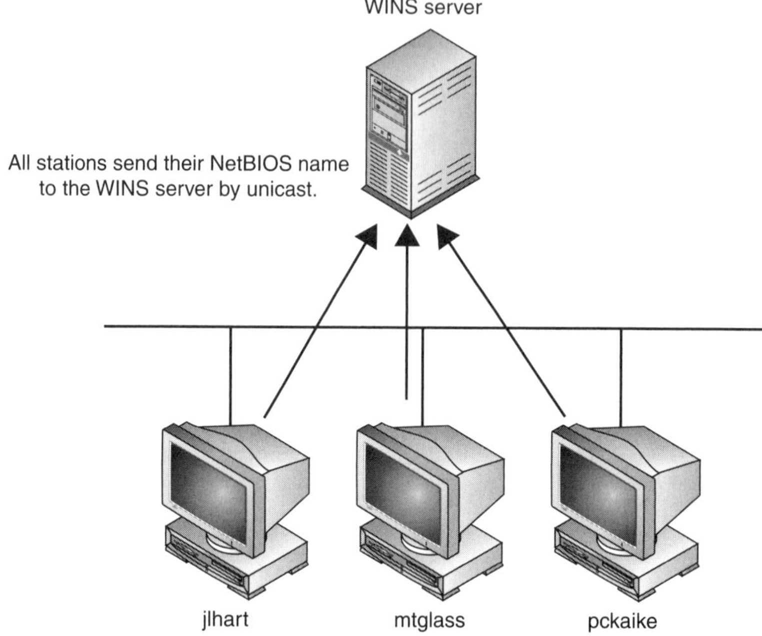
WINS server
All stations send their NetBIOS name to the WINS server by unicast.
jlhart
mtglass
pckaike

Figure 14-12 WINS server

performance of the LAN and allows for end-stations on different LANs to find each other by name without enabling bridging on the routers.

NOTE: *When end-stations using older versions of the Windows OS exist in the LAN, it may still be necessary to leave the broadcast method enabled on all* end-stations.

NetBIOS Node Types There are four node types used in conjunction with NetBIOS:

- Broadcast (b)
- Peer-to-peer (p)

- Mixed (m)
- Hybrid (h)

A *b-node* type uses broadcasts for name registration and resolution. The biggest problem is that routers do not forward the broadcasts by default, and when the router is directed to forward the broadcasts, network performance suffers.

A *p-node* type uses a NetBIOS Name Server (NBNS), like WINS, to register and resolve node names. All systems must be configured with the IP address of the NBNS in order for this to work.

An *m-node* type is a mixture of type b and type p. What this means is that by default it will function as a b node. If it fails to resolve the name by broadcast (which would be the case in a multiple network environment), it will then use the p-node method of resolution.

An *h-node* type is also a combination of type b and type p. The key difference is that it tries first to resolve as a p-node, going to an NBNS, and resorting to broadcast only as a last resort.

A workstation's node type can be set via DHCP as part of the configuration.

Internet DNS

One final method of name resolution that can be used to streamline end-station configuration is the use of the DNS server to resolve name-to-address mappings within the network. This is easy enough to do with statically addressed end-stations, such as servers, but it can also be used with the WINS server.

To configure with statically addressed end-stations, the administrator simply enters the name-to-address mappings into the DNS. Then all end-stations on the network are configured to resolve names at the DNS server, while registering their names with the WINS server. The DNS server consults the WINS server in the background for resolving any names not in its static configuration. This process is shown in Figure 14-13.

As of the Windows 2000 OS release, a dynamic DNS server can also be configured to work with the DHCP servers and clients. With the use of this configuration, all components work together to keep the DNS name-to-address mapping current. For end-stations not using the Windows 2000 OS, the DHCP server provides the information to the DNS server.

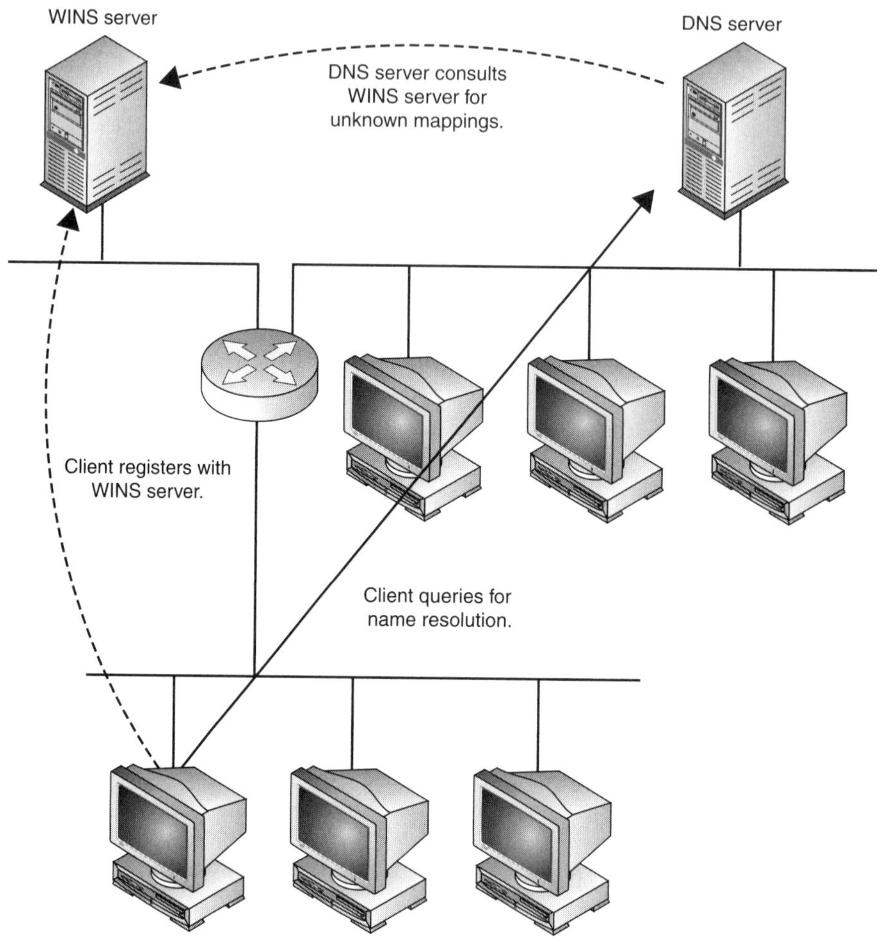

Figure 14-13 DNS name resolution

Name Lookup Order

The default lookup order for Windows networking is as follows:

- NetBIOS name cache.
- Broadcast query or WINS query.
- Check LMHOSTS file.
- Check HOSTS file—only if "Resolve Using DNS" is checked.
- Send a query to the DNS server—only if "Resolve Using DNS" is checked.

There are several different NetBIOS node types. Different types have different default behavior that will override the order listed above. For more information, see Cisco's Web site (**http://www.cisco.com/warp/public/473/winnt_dg.htm**), consult your operating system manual, or Microsoft.

Domain Models

When creating the domain infrastructure of the network, you can take advantage of trust relationships between domains to eliminate the need to manage users individually. By "trust relationship" we mean that one domain trusts the user authentication of another. This is a point-to-point relationship only. In other words, if there are more than two domains, any two can trust each other, but one cannot trust a domain through a third party. By using trust relationships, you can administratively grant access to domains or allow users to gain access by the leverage of the trust relationships. A user will authenticate to the first domain they log into. Any domain trusting the authenticating domain will also grant the privileges that were granted by the authenticating domain.

There are four common domain models that can be used:

- Single domain
- Global domain
- Master domain
- Multiple master domains

The *single domain* is appropriate for a small- to medium-sized network with simple administrative needs. As the name implies, there is one domain for all users. For situations in which an open trust relationship will exist among all domains, the *global domain* model is appropriate. Regardless of the number of domains, each domain will have full access to all others. This is an easy-to-comprehend but complex to control model, usually well suited to networks in which there is no IT staff to handle the administration.

With the *master domain* model, the master domain is the leader, trusted by all. The master domain, however, trusts no one. The individual domains and related resources can be controlled locally, but all domain authentication could take place at the master domain.

Finally, the *multiple master domain* model, shown in Figure 14-14, is an extension of the master domain model for larger-sized networks. In this

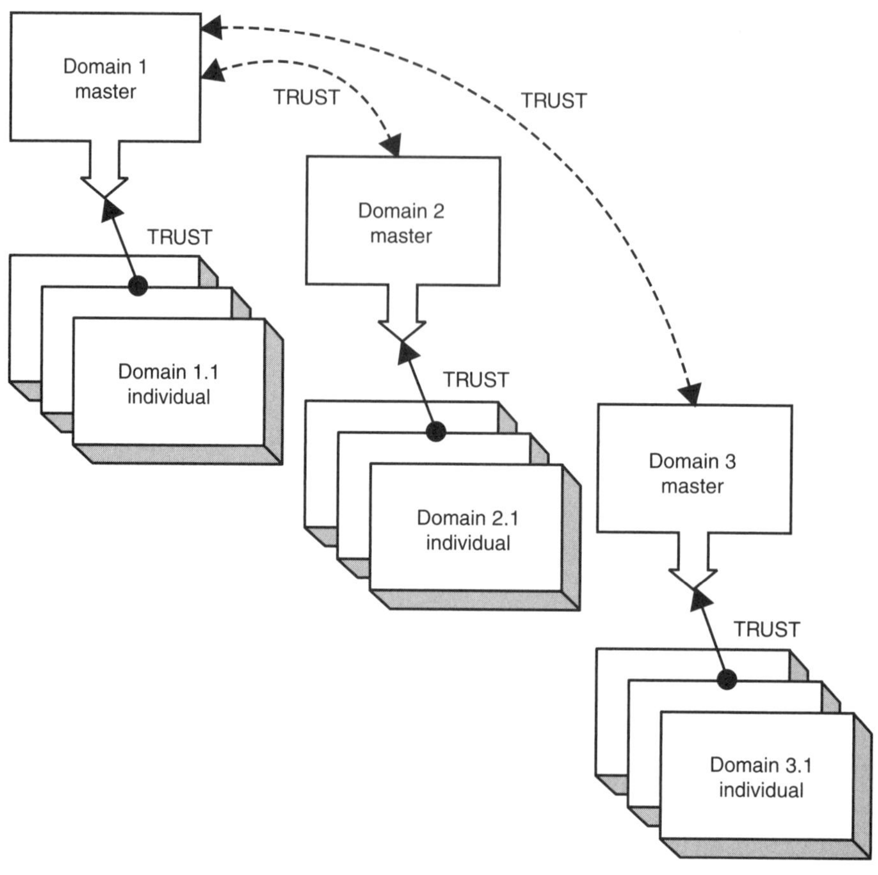

Figure 14-14 Multiple master domain model

model, each master domain trusts the other master domains. The individual domains that fall under the master trust only their master domain. Master domains do not trust individual sub-domains.

Remote Access Servers (RASs)

Both Windows NT and Windows 2000 have bundled software that provides for remote access, called Remote Access Server (RAS). The software is based on the Point-to-Point Protocol (PPP) and works well for smaller networks. Where larger dial-in services are required, however, you will probably want to consider Cisco access servers to provide better performance. We will discuss remote access more in Chapter 19.

The Windows products, as well as Cisco IOS after release 11.1, support TCP/IP, IPX, and NetBEUI for dial-up. The related control protocols are

- TCP/IP—IP Control Protocol (IPCP)
- IPX—IPX Control Protocol (IPXCP)
- NetBEUI—NetBIOS Frames Control Protocol (NBFCP)

Problem Areas

In this section we will provide you with a few quick tips on things to watch out for in a Windows networking environment. These are issues that could adversely affect the performance and efficiency of your network design, if improperly handled.

Rogue Browse Masters

Windows 95/98 workstations are unable to serve as browse masters in a Windows NT environment. They are incapable of handling Windows NT server and domain information. By default, however, they will attempt to become a browse master, which can slow browsing for all computers on the network. The slowing of performance happens because clients try to use another client, essentially, for browsing. The client normally does not have the horsepower to handle a task that should be a server's job. The priority for the browse master election is as follows:

- PDC
- BDC
- NT Server
- NT Workstation
- Windows 95/98 PC

By virtue of the order of priority for the election, the problem of having a "rogue," or unauthorized, browse master *should* never happen. In the event that performance indicates that a rogue browse master exists, the use of a utility called BROWSTAT, from the Windows NT 4.0 Server Resource Kit, will help identify any rogue browse masters on the network.

Browser Updates on a Slow Link

In the event that browse masters and domain masters are separated by a slow or charge-per-packet link, you may want to adjust your Registry settings on the master browser and backup master browsers. Here is how to do that:

1. Open the following Registry key:

```
hkey_local_machine\system\currentcontrolset\services\browser\
parameters
```

2. Ensure that MaintainServerList is set to Yes and that IsDomainMaster is set to False.
3. Change the setting on MasterPeriodicity to a value (in seconds) that corresponds to the length of time you wish to configure between browse list queries to the domain master. You may want to set this to an hour or more, in cases of very slow links.

Disabling Broadcast Name Resolution

If file and printer sharing are enabled on a Windows 95/98 workstation, check the network settings in the Control Panel (see Figure 14-15). Be sure that the value for Browse Master is disabled. If using DHCP, ensure that node types are set to either "p-node" or "h-node." This will ensure that either broadcast is not used at all or is used only as a last resort.

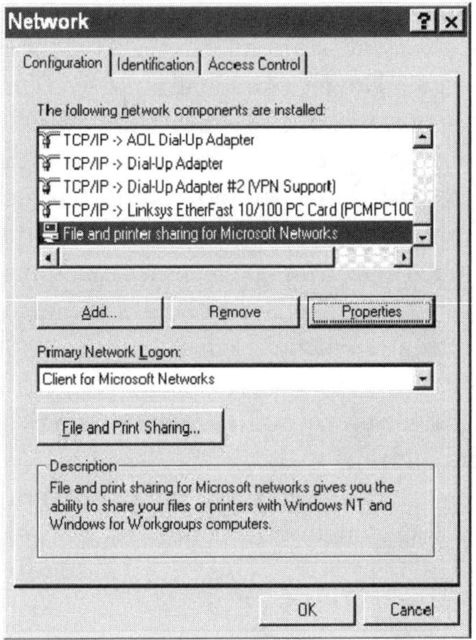

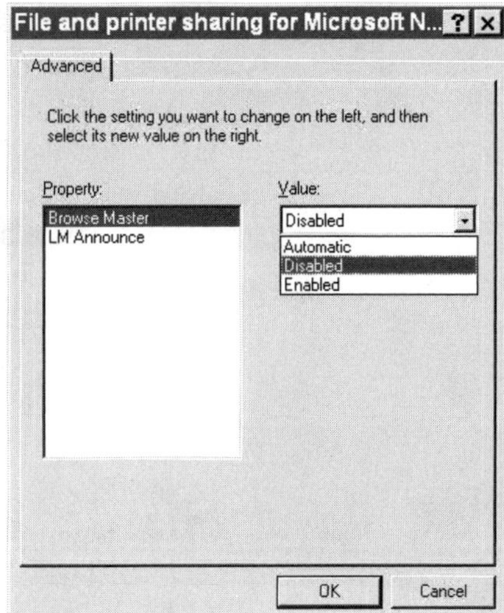

Figure 14-15 Disabling broadcast name resolution

Case Study

Valley Manufacturing wants to incorporate all of its departments into a Windows networked environment. It has the following departments, each with unique administrative needs:

- Operations
- Engineering
- Finance
- Marketing
- Information Technology (IT)
- Human Resources

The Human Resources department is using an older Novell OS but is open to upgrading the workstations if necessary. The department does, however, wish to stay with Novell as its operating system, even though the rest of the company is going to begin using Windows 98. The department has custom applications that require Novell in order to run.

The IT department will install and maintain a centralized Windows NT server farm in a physically secure location in the building. IT needs to provide simple dial-up services for the Engineering department without going to the expense of installing dedicated access servers in the network.

Your task is to create a domain infrastructure, recommend a name resolution method, and draw out a simple design. In addition, you must address the need for Engineering to dial-in from outside the network. Keep the design simple and logical.

Although there are always multiple right answers for any case study, an example solution is provided in Appendix C, "Suggested Solutions to Case Studies."

Study Hints

Although no one can disclose test items or test content, we can give hints as to what might be valuable to study. For this chapter, there are key facts that need to be reviewed and remembered.

- *Each domain must have at least one PDC.* Remember that a Primary Domain Controller (PDC) is the entity through which the domain is administered.
- *When using Novell OS without TCP/IP, you must enable IPX type-20 propagation on the routers.* Type-20 packets must be forwarded in order for Novell type-20 NetBIOS traffic to be passed.
- *A rogue browse master can wreak havoc with a Windows network.* The browse master setting should be disabled in all end-stations that will not be used to store browse lists. Generally, only the servers in a network should have this ability.

CCDP Tips

This section contains an abbreviated list of topics covered in Chapter 14. Think of this section as the equivalent of reading Cliff's Notes™ instead of reading an entire book. You will get the general idea of the chapter but will benefit more from reading the chapter in its entirety.

Windows Networking—Defined Windows networking is a general term referring to the network software that is part of these Microsoft products:

- LAN Manager
- MS-DOS with LAN Manager client
- Windows for Workgroups
- Windows 95, 98, and Millennium Edition (ME)
- Windows NT and 2000

Domains vs. Workgroups Windows networking uses two major group types: domains and workgroups. Their functions are different, as outlined here:

- A workgroup can be created by anyone and does not need to be administered.
- A workgroup is an informal entity.
- A domain is centrally administered.
- A domain is a formal collection of network resources.
- Domains can provide security and resource management that is not available with workgroups.
- A domain must have at least one Windows NT or 2000 server acting as a PDC.

NetBIOS The NetBIOS protocol operates at the session layer of the seven-layer OSI model. NetBIOS is used for file and printer sharing, Windows messaging, authentication (CHAP and PAP), and name resolution. By providing an Application Program Interface (API) and a naming service, NetBIOS provides for every type of Windows networking operation from browsing servers by name to printing to a networked printer.

Transporting NetBIOS NetBIOS requires a transport mechanism to carry it across the network. There are, of course, two ways to move information over a network: bridging and routing. Here are the different transport protocols available for NetBIOS.

- NetBIOS over LLC2—NetBEUI (bridged)
- NetBIOS over IPX—NWLink (routed)
- NetBIOS over TCP—NBT (routed)

Windows Browser Services Microsoft designed the LAN Services Browser to address the need for many workstations to register their addresses and to quickly gather a list of other workstations in the network. Many workstations broadcast to elect the browse master. The browse master learns all of the workstations on the network and will respond to broadcast requests from clients.

Name-to-Address Resolution There are several ways to accomplish name resolution. The types discussed here are current as of the release of Windows 2000.

- Broadcasts
- LMHOSTS
- NetBIOS name cache
- WINS
- Internet DNS

Name Lookup Order The default lookup order for Windows networking is as follows:

- NetBIOS name cache
- Broadcast query or WINS query
- Check LMHOSTS file
- Check HOSTS file—only if "Resolve Using DNS" is checked
- Send a query to the DNS server—only if "Resolve Using DNS" is checked

Domain Models There are four common domain models that can be used:

- **Single Domain** All users belong to this one domain.
- **Global Domain** Multiple domains, all domains trust all others.
- **Master Domain** One domain acts as master to subordinate domains. All subordinates trust the master, but the master trusts no one.
- **Multiple Master Domains** All masters trust all other masters. Subordinate domains trust their master. Masters trust no subordinates.

Remote Access Server (RAS) Both Windows NT and Windows 2000 have bundled software that provides for remote access, called Remote Access Server (RAS). The software is based on the Point-to-Point protocol (PPP). Related control protocols are as follows:

- TCP/IP—IP Control Protocol (IPCP)
- IPX—IPX Control Protocol (IPXCP)
- NetBEUI—NetBIOS Frames Control Protocol (NBFCP)

Summary

By now you should be able to tell a domain from a workgroup and a browse master from a domain master. There are quite a few terms and hidden pitfalls you will encounter when implementing Windows networks that you may not have ever seen before. It is important to be as educated as possible about the way these concepts and components work, as you will certainly need to understand them in order to design a scalable solution that will work well for the users of the network.

Questions

The following review questions have been selected to help you test your knowledge of the subject matter contained in this chapter. You will also find these questions contained in the CD-ROM included with this book. While these are not the questions you will find in the certification exams, knowing the answers to the review questions in this book will help cement the material in your mind as you prepare for the tests.

1. Domain or workgroup? Any user can create it.
   a. Domain
   b. Workgroup
2. Domain or workgroup? This entity can have administratively controlled security.
   a. Domain
   b. Workgroup
3. True or False: The domain requires at least one PDC in order to function.
   a. True
   b. False
4. True or False: Each PDC must have a BDC.
   a. True
   b. False
5. Which protocol provides for transport of NetBIOS over IPX?
   a. NetBEUI
   b. NWLink
   c. NBT
   d. TCP
6. Which protocol provides for transport of NetBIOS over TCP?
   a. NetBEUI
   b. NWLink
   c. NBT
   d. TCP
7. Of these three transport protocols, which is *not* routable?
   a. NetBEUI
   b. NWLink
   c. NBT
8. Which of these name resolution methods employs unicast between the client and the server?
   a. NetBIOS name cache
   b. LMHOST
   c. WINS

9. Which of these methods is employed in order to elect a browse master?
   a. Broadcast
   b. Multicast
   c. Unicast
10. In a multiple master domain model, which of the following is a true statement?
   a. All domains trust all other domains.
   b. All master domains trust all other master domains.
   c. All individual domains trust all other individual domains.
   d. The master domains trust only the individual domains reporting to them.
11. True or False: In the master domain model, the master domain controller trusts the individual domains.
   a. True
   b. False
12. Which of these domain models permits all domains to trust all others?
   a. Single domain
   b. Global domain
   c. Master domain
   d. Multiple master domain
13. To which layer of the OSI model does the NetBIOS protocol correspond?
   a. Transport
   b. Network
   c. Session
   d. Application
14. True or False: When a DNS server is used for name resolution, a WINS server is unnecessary.
   a. True
   b. False

15. Slow performance when browsing could indicate that
    a. You are using NetBEUI for your transport protocol.
    b. Your workstation's Browse Master setting is disabled.
    c. You need to reboot the PDC.
    d. You may have a rogue browse master on the network.
16. What is the number of workstations in a bridge group at which performance begins to degrade?
    a. 10
    b. 50
    c. 100
    d. 250
17. If the LMHOSTS method of name resolution is used, where is the master LMHOSTS file normally stored?
    a. PDC
    b. BDC
    c. DNS server
    d. WINS server
18. True or False: When configuring Windows networking with Novell clients, you must use NWLink.
    a. True
    b. False
19. Which of the following is true when using NWLink as the transport protocol?
    a. Cisco routers must be configured to bridge IPX.
    b. Cisco routers must be set for directed broadcasts to a Novell server.
    c. Cisco routers must have bridging turned off.
    d. Cisco routers must be configured to forward type-20 packets.
20. Which Windows OS can use a Dynamic DNS server?
    a. Windows NT
    b. Windows ME
    c. Windows 2000
    d. Windows 98

Answers

1. Domain or workgroup? Any user can create it.
b. Workgroup

2. Domain or workgroup? This entity can have administratively controlled security.
a. Domain

3. True or False: The domain requires at least one PDC in order to function.
a. True
Explanation: By definition a domain must have a domain controller through which administration of the domain is performed.

4. True or False: Each PDC must have a BDC.
b. False
Explanation: Although it is recommended, it is not necessary, operationally, to have a BDC.

5. Which protocol provides for transport of NetBIOS over IPX?
b. NWLink

6. Which protocol provides for transport of NetBIOS over TCP?
c. NBT

7. Of these three transport protocols, which is *not* routable?
a. NetBEUI
Explanation: Because NetBEUI does not use a network addressing scheme that provides each end-station with a unique address, it is not a routable protocol and therefore must be bridged.

8. Which of these name resolution methods employs unicast between the client and the server?
c. WINS
Explanation: Remember—the client registers itself with the WINS server, which is a well-known address configured in the client's network settings.

9. Which of these methods is employed in order to elect a browse master?
a. Broadcast
Explanation: All end-stations broadcast on the network to elect a browse master, which is normally the PDC.

10. In a multiple master domain model, which of the following is a true statement?
b. All master domains trust all other master domains.

11. True or False: In the master domain model, the master domain controller trusts the individual domains.
b. False

12. Which of these domain models permits all domains to trust all others?
b. Global domain

13. To which layer of the OSI model does the NetBIOS protocol correspond?
c. Session

14. True or False: When a DNS server is used for name resolution, a WINS server is unnecessary.
b. False
Explanation: The DNS server must consult the WINS server for name-to-address mappings.

15. Slow performance when browsing could indicate that
d. You may have a rogue browse master on the network.
Explanation: While poor performance on a network in general can cause slow browsing, the correct selection of these choices is "d." A rogue browse master may not be able to handle the demand of many end-stations polling it for browse lists. This can, in turn, slow all network browsing.

16. What is the number of workstations in a bridge group at which performance begins to degrade?
b. 50
Explanation: Somewhere *between* 50 and 100, performance begins falling off in a bridge group, so the correct answer here would be 50.

17. If the LMHOSTS method of name resolution is used, where is the master LMHOSTS file normally stored?
a. PDC

18. True or False: When configuring Windows networking with Novell clients, you must use NWLink.
b. False
Explanation: NWLink is only *necessary* when older Novell versions are in use. For older versions that do not support TCP/IP, you will have to use NWLink. Otherwise, use TCP/IP.

19. Which of the following is true when using NWLink as the transport protocol?
    d. Cisco routers must be configured to forward type-20 packets.

20. Which Windows OS can use a Dynamic DNS server?
    c. Windows 2000

Frequently Asked Questions (FAQs)

1. *What kind of bridging is used on the router for passing NetBEUI traffic?*

   Cisco routers can use transparent or Source-Route Bridging (SRB) when NetBEUI traffic needs to be passed. Additionally, you can configure Data Link Switching (DLSw) or Remote Source-Route Bridging (RSRB) in conjunction with these.

2. *Do I need to configure anything special on the router if I'm going to use WINS for name resolution?*

   No. Because WINS uses Native IP, there is nothing special that needs to be configured on the routers.

3. *If I have IPX clients that need to dial in, do they need to hear Service Advertisement Protocol (SAP) advertisements?*

   No. Dial-in clients do not need to hear the SAPs. Turn them off by using

```
ipx sap-interval 0
```

Bibliography

Cisco Internetwork Design, Cisco Press, 2000, Matthew H. Birkner, Editor

Cisco Internetwork Design Course Manual, version 3.0, April 1997, Cisco Systems, Inc.

Cisco Windows Network Design Implementation Guide, Cisco Systems, Inc. **http://www.cisco.com/warp/public/473/winnt_dg.htm**

Thomas Concise Telecom and Networking Dictionary, McGraw-Hill, 2000, Thomas M. Thomas II

CHAPTER 15

WAN Design Overview

Overview

For the next several chapters we will be exploring the topic of Wide Area Network (WAN) design and issues related to the choices that need to be made. Some of the items covered in this chapter, intended to introduce you to the overall WAN design structure, are customer concerns, desires versus needs, and ways to help the customer distinguish between the two. We will also look at the design needs for core connectivity that will help make the best use of network resources and provide the maximum availability of those resources.

WAN Design Issues

Over the past decade, the face of network support has changed quite a bit. In the past it was common to have support shops that were segregated for desktop, Local Area Network (LAN), and WAN support. Each part of the shop focused upon a specific portion of the network services. Today this model has changed to a single Information Technology (IT) support organization that handles all network services, "from soup to nuts," as they say. This means not only an increased workload but also a need for a simpler, more robust WAN design.

Some of the most common design issues are the following:

- Cost of WAN resources
- Latency
- Reliability
- Amount of traffic
- Multiprotocol support
- Support for legacy systems
- Difficulty of configuration
- Remote office support

As always, the cost of the WAN design must be considered. What is the budget for the overall design? What are the recurring costs to keep the proposed links up on a monthly basis?

After budgetary considerations, the most important issues are link latency and reliability. Of all the individual network parts, the WAN is probably the one area that has the potential to affect the most users. If a desktop system is down, normally only one user is affected. If a LAN segment is down, only a certain group of users is affected. If a WAN link fails, however, the cost can be measured in large groups of users as well as in actual dollars lost, if the link is supporting publicly available servers and revenue-generating resources. Therefore, it is imperative that the types of links chosen can support the resource requirements with as little "soft" downtime (latency) and "hard" downtime (outages) as possible.

It is also important to assess the amount of traffic that will cross the WAN links by using baseline and historical data, measurements taken over a period of time with various available network measurement tools, or by using a modeling program such as Cisco's Netsys Baseliner™ product. By determining ahead of time the peak periods, peak rates, and maximum necessary bandwidth, it becomes easier to create a design that can not only support current needs, but future needs, as well.

Will multiple protocols be routed over the WAN links or will they be tunneled across an "IP-only" backbone? Will protocols other than IP consume more bandwidth because of the inherent broadcasts needed for their operation? As we will discuss later in this chapter there are other reasons you may want to explore using an "IP-only" option, other than just from a cost perspective. There may be legacy systems across the WAN that require protocols other than IP to be used, and in some situations, this may become cost-prohibitive. In a situation such as that, it may require the network engineering staff to make a decision on whether to retain the legacy resources or to increase the budget for the WAN links needed to support those resources.

Another issue that will probably arise is the type of equipment needed to support the various WAN design options. The network engineering staff may have expertise in Frame Relay and no competency in ISDN, for instance. It is important to select components in the WAN design that will require a very short, if any, learning curve for the staff.

Finally, support for remote offices must be considered. What types of protocols will be needed? What are the distances, and therefore the associated costs, for the point-to-point links? How many users will be supported, and will there be any servers or other shared resources at that remote location?

As you can now see, building the WAN design involves many small decisions, each dependent on the other for the final picture. It is important at this juncture of the design process, as in all other steps, to keep a good line of communication open with all of the key players in the decision-making process.

WAN Technology Options

There are typically two major options available for the WAN design:

- Dedicated (leased) lines
- Switched connections

As shown in Figure 15-1, there are a variety of selections available, once you know the technology option that will be best for the WAN design in question. If a network or a portion therein requires a dedicated line, there are fractional T1/E1 lines that can deliver a fraction of the bandwidth that would be provided with a full T1/E1 line. In this manner, the network must bear the cost of only the portion of the bandwidth that is needed. Likewise, if more bandwidth is required, a full T1/E1 or even T3/E3 line can be leased.

If a switched connection will be more appropriate for the network, there are choices between circuit-switched or packet/cell-switched connections. We will explore these options in the section that follows.

Dedicated Lines

The benefits of choosing a dedicated line for a WAN connection include the full-time, guaranteed network connectivity it provides as well as its ability to carry voice, data, and video traffic over customizable links. Commonly these dedicated, or leased, lines are used between different geographical locations or between major LAN segments. The most often used bandwidth is the T1 (or E1, in European networks), which provides 1.544 Mbps between points (or 2.048 Mbps in Europe).

Not all network connections will require this much bandwidth, however, so these lines may also be purchased as fractional T1/E1 connections in increments of 64 Kbps. For networks requiring more bandwidth than a single T1/E1 line can provide, a T3 (or E3) line may be leased that can provide up to 45 Mbps of bandwidth. Another option is to bundle multiple T1 lines and use multiplexers to aggregate the bandwidth. This will be discussed further in Chapter 16, "Dedicated Lines."

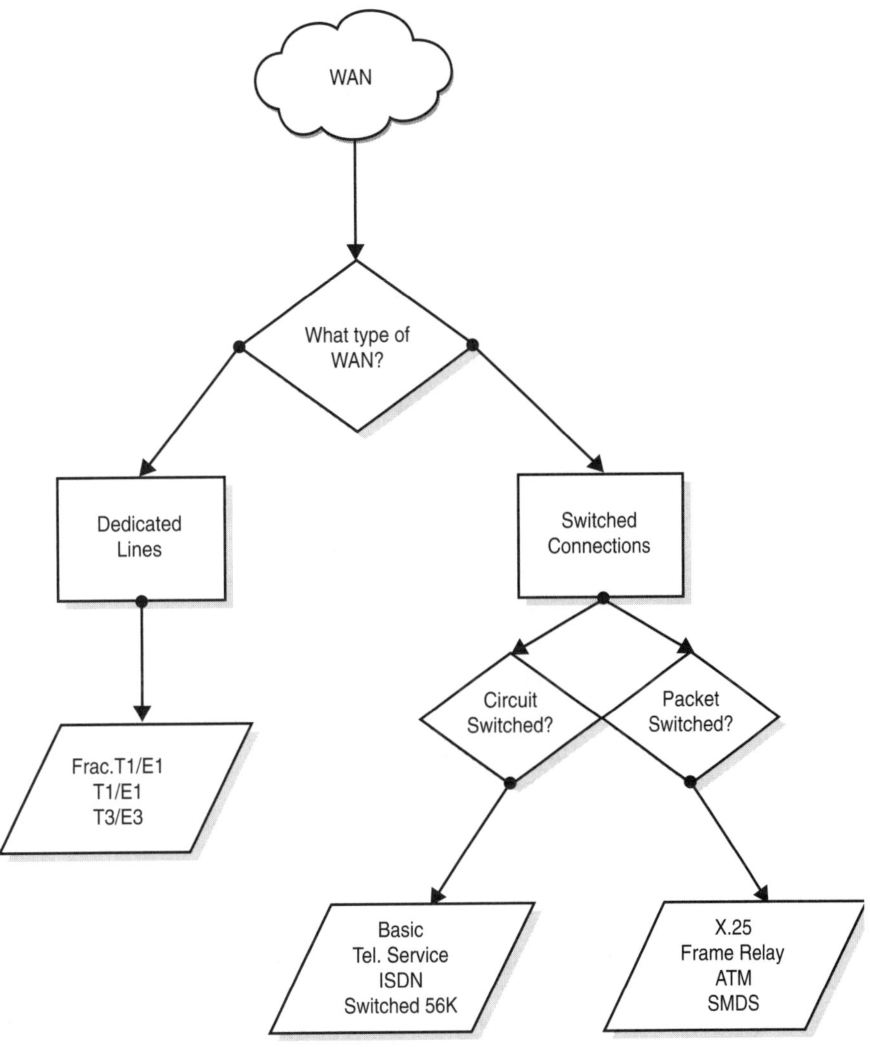

Figure 15-1 WAN technology options

Switched Connections

When choosing a switched connection for WAN links, there are two basic types available with a variety of options within each:

- Packet- or cell-switched connection
- Circuit-switched connection

Packet- or cell-switched connection A *packet-* or *cell-switched connection* is one that is generally reliable and available, more so than the circuit-switched type of connection. Packet-switched network types include

- Frame Relay
- X.25
- ATM/SMDS

Frame Relay is a commonly used WAN connectivity choice that works well for connections between LAN segments and for remote access from smaller sites to a headquarters site, for example. Frame Relay can provide up to T1 speeds over a Permanent Virtual Circuit (PVC) that is streamlined, with very little error checking. Frame Relay circuits are requisitioned on the basis of the amount of Committed Information Rate (CIR) needed. Generally the CIR will be at or slightly less than the maximum bandwidth needed for the link. Bursts above the CIR are not guaranteed, but are usually handled by the circuit. This is known as *oversubscription* of the link. If it happens on a regular basis, your service provider will probably require that you increase the CIR for the circuit.

X.25 is provisioned on either a PVC or Switched Virtual Circuit (SVC) basis. The SVC only becomes active when it is needed and is usually a good, cost-effective choice for links that are used less and do not require constant up-time. X.25 uses extensive error-checking, unlike Frame Relay, and therefore has a lot of network overhead involved. X.25 is a good choice for links needing the reliability it can provide; however, it is not available in speeds over T1. If higher bandwidths are needed, it is a good idea to go with another technology.

Asynchronous Transfer Mode (ATM) and Switched Multi-megabit Data Service (SMDS) are cell-switched technologies that are not as widely used or available as some other options. While there was a trend at one time to deploy ATM in WAN design, it is becoming less common today.

Nevertheless, ATM can be used to deploy core connectivity between sites at speeds of T1/E1, T3/E3, OC-3, and greater, depending upon the availability of the appropriate hardware to support the configuration. It can be used to support clients that use LANE, provide LAN-to-LAN connections, and provide connections between large sites carrying data, voice, and video. ATM can be configured in point-to-point or multipoint configurations and can handle Class of Service (CoS) and Quality of Service (QoS) configurations.

SMDS is similar to ATM but supports only point-to-point configurations and does not handle CoS or QoS configurations. SMDS, where available, is normally used only for data traffic. It is unlikely that you will see voice and video being transmitted across SMDS links.

Circuit-switched connection A *circuit-switched connection* is one that is enabled "on demand" and works well for low-bandwidth, low-usage link needs. Examples of a circuit-switched connection are ISDN lines and basic telephone service lines that provide up to 56 Kbps of non-compressed bandwidth. Generally, you will find these types of connections for Small Office/Home Office (SOHO) users connecting to the corporate network or service provider, mobile users, and Remote Office/Branch Office (ROBO) users. However, ISDN lines are very popular for use as backup links for Frame Relay circuits. In the event of a failure on the PVC, the ISDN circuit would become active and remain so until the primary link failure could be resolved. Whereas the bandwidth available is frequently less than that of the primary line, the ISDN circuit can help avoid a total network outage for users depending on that link.

Whatever technology is chosen, it must be scalable, reliable, and appropriate for the type of traffic it will support.

Optimizing Availability

As we have already mentioned, the WAN is a critical network resource that provides service to many users. If the WAN fails, not only can users be affected, but the bottom line (revenue) for the business can be affected as well. So how do you ensure that the WAN is up and available all of the time?

First of all, select the right tools for the job. That means choosing equipment that can handle the tasks at hand. Don't select a router that is barely capable of handling the type of traffic it needs to handle. Buy the router with the future in mind. Buy all the memory and processing power your budget can handle, within reason.

Next, build fault-tolerance into the WAN design. Use redundant fans, power supplies, and routers in the network design. When using multiple power supplies, place them on separate circuits within the computer room. That way, if one circuit fails, the other one may not, which means that the router can keep working once the failover has taken place. Also, provide for redundant links, using ISDN dial-backup, for example, to back up a primary Frame Relay link with a source for routing traffic in case of a link failure. Redundant links should terminate at different routers, when possible, so that a router outage does not mean a complete outage for the link itself.

Consider having "cold spares" for your major network components. It is a good idea to have a backup to your backup, so to speak, especially in the case of line cards or port adapters supporting important, revenue-generating WAN links. Some organizations may not wish to provide the budget or storage space for spares, but in some cases the Cisco reseller can do this for the organization. It is a very valuable recommendation to make.

Other tips can be found online at Choosing Internetworking Reliability Options: **http://www.cisco.com/univercd/cc/td/doc/cisintwk/idg4/nd2002.htm#35741**

Optimizing Performance

So you have made the WAN available, striving for a 100-percent network up-time ratio. The next most important factor is WAN performance. Some of the goals relative to optimizing WAN performance are

- Achieving maximum throughput
- Minimizing overhead and delay on the WAN link

"Great," you say, "but how do I do this?" The most obvious way is to tune some of the applications that will be sending data over the WAN. In some cases you may be able to do this and in others, you will have little control. A lot of the control you are able to exert over the applications depends upon the applications themselves and upon the structure of the application support team. You may encounter resistance if the group supporting network applications is reluctant to make changes to a set of resources that appears to be working "just fine." Approach the topic gently, knowledgeably, and with several solutions in mind.

When approaching application support staff about making changes, here are some hints that will help you to be successful:

- Do your homework so that you know all that you can about the application and parameters you wish to tune.
- Find out if there have been any problems with the applications or changes to them in the past. This will help you avoid such problems with your proposed changes.
- Find out who you need to convince and work up a proposal written with that person's concerns in mind.

- Present several workable solutions, if possible, so that it is not a "go/no-go" type of decision. This helps the staff feel that the solution was really their decision.
- Be prepared to lose the battle. If you are prepared to lose, you will be more likely to have several contingency plans in mind. There should always be a "Plan B."

Besides tuning the applications, another way to improve performance is to tune the Cisco IOS to handle such tasks as filtering excess broadcast traffic, using QoS to share the bandwidth based on traffic type, and using an IP-only backbone whenever possible. The objective is to get the packet out of the router as quickly as possible so that the router can go on to processing other packets. How the router is behaving can greatly impact overall WAN performance.

Here are a few configuration parameters and tuning methods to investigate in order to improve performance:

- Type of switching. Try to ensure that the router is not using process switching as a general rule. Use faster switching methods, when possible.
- Take a close look at what is happening in the process table. Troubleshoot anything causing excess process utilization. For more help, check out Troubleshooting High CPU Utilization on Cisco Routers at **http://www.cisco.com/warp/public/63/highcpu.html.**
- Remember that larger packet sizes equal more efficient links. By using larger packet sizes, you increase the ratio of payload to overhead in your WAN transmissions.
- Some reliable transport protocols allow for adjustments to window size in response to congestion. If this applies to the network that you are designing, investigate any parameters relative to allowing the router to handle window size adjustments automatically.
- Use an efficient routing protocol, such as EIGRP, which can result in less routing traffic because it does not send full routing table updates periodically.
- Use priority queuing methods in the configuration in order to ensure delivery of the most important traffic first.

NOTE: Remember that bandwidth consumption by routing protocols involves three factors: when, what, and where. When are routing table updates sent (how often)? What is sent (full or update only) to the other routers? Where are the updates sent (flooding to all routers consumes considerably more overall bandwidth)? Once you know the answers to these questions, you will be more educated about the impact of the selected routing protocol on your WAN design.

Whatever methods you use to enhance WAN performance, remember to implement a single change at a time unless you are using modeling software such as Cisco NetSys Baseliner to view the impact in a simulated environment first. By implementing a single change at a time, you reduce the possibility of unforeseen catastrophic impact and provide for quick problem resolution. Backing out a single change is much easier than trying to figure out which change caused a problem.

Backbone Routing Protocols

When selecting a routing protocol for use in the WAN, it is important to choose a protocol that can "intelligently" choose a route based upon more than just hop count. Where the WAN is concerned, many factors—such as delay—can negatively impact the delivery of traffic. In Figure 15-2, for example, LAN users trying to reach the same destination router may be routed over either a T1 link or over a fractional T1 at 128 Kbps. Whereas some protocols would select the higher bandwidth link every time, a more intelligent protocol, such as EIGRP, which also takes link delay into consideration, may react to congestion on the T1 link and re-route traffic over the fractional T1.

Tunneling over IP Whereas some WAN designs will require support for more than one desktop protocol, the WAN is inherently easier to manage and predict when an IP-only solution is used. There are several reasons for this:

- Single protocol support
- Greater IP competence in most staffs
- IP has less router overhead than other protocols
- Native IP packets consume less bandwidth than encapsulated (tunneled) datagrams

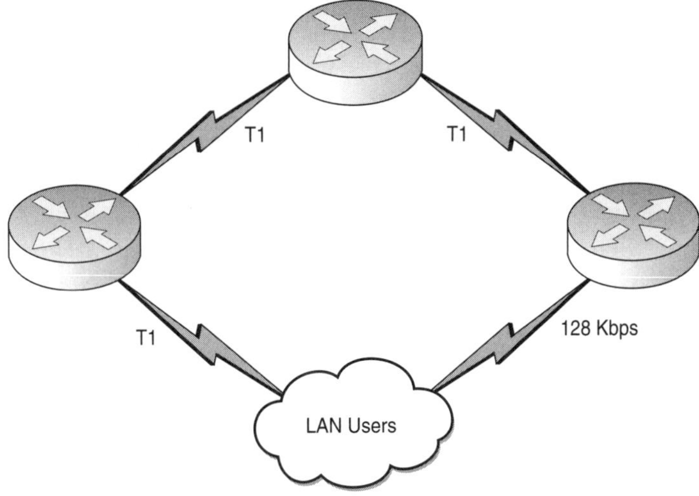

Figure 15-2 Multiple paths over WAN

It is always easier to support one protocol than many. This is because, whether troubleshooting or configuring for the first time, most network engineering staffs have a greater amount of competency and experience regarding IP configuration than in, say, AppleTalk. This generally results in a staff that is more comfortable with being able to implement and support any WAN design that is agreed upon.

When protocols other than IP are used across a WAN link, it is likely that they will be tunneled, or encapsulated, in IP packets. Doing so increases the amount of overhead and CPU processor power that is used at both ends of the WAN link. This can, in turn, hurt overall performance and efficiency of the WAN link.

The resulting encapsulated datagrams also consume more bandwidth as they cross the link. This is caused from the additional headers in which the original datagram is "wrapped." Remember that part of increasing WAN performance is to reduce such overhead.

Problem Areas

When designing the WAN, some of the common problems that are encountered include budgetary constraints, political issues, and lack of trained personnel. We mention these because, unlike technical problems to which you may find a quick resolution, the human factors are more likely to have a greater impact on the WAN design issues.

Budgetary constraints that can impact the design include a lack of education on the part of the financial department on how expenses such as those incurred for a leased line can quickly mount. Router upgrades that may be needed for the type of links required may also be an issue. Remember that you may have to trade some redundancy—typically one of the higher WAN expenses—for the proper memory sizing and bandwidth. It is highly unusual that the "perfect" WAN design will be approved. Be ready to compromise by preparing three solutions: high-cost/high-redundancy, medium-cost/less-redundancy, and low-cost/minimum-redundancy. In this manner, you give the decision-makers a choice in how and where they want to compromise.

Political issues range from lack of communication within the organization to reluctance of a network engineering staff to embrace a new protocol or technology that may be a better fit for their WAN needs. Handle issues such as this with kid gloves, and remember that it is only your task to be the network designer, offering a wide variation of solutions to the technical, not the human resource, needs.

Finally, it is important, as we have mentioned several times throughout this book, to gauge the technical competency of the network engineering staff and try to stick as closely to that as possible in your network design. By doing so, you increase the likelihood of quick acceptance and implementation of the design solution and decrease the chance of political or financial issues becoming a problem. If the staff must all be retrained in a new technology to support the WAN design, there is not only a financial impact (training and travel costs) but also a staffing impact (personnel away for a week or more for training) as each member is retrained. This can cause delay or rejection of the WAN design implementation.

Summary

We have shown you a few of the overall design issues you will encounter as you begin to look at the WAN design task. You will have several choices in the type of technology to use in the WAN, as well as some control over how efficient these choices will be. Remember that you will need to fully understand the requirements and constraints of the task at hand as you create a few possible solutions to creating highly-scalable and available WAN designs.

Now that we have introduced you to some of the design issues facing the network architect related to the design of the WAN, we will go in depth into each type of WAN technology over the next few chapters.

Questions

The following review questions have been selected to help you test your knowledge of the subject matter contained in this chapter. You will also find these questions contained in the CD-ROM included with this book. While these are not the questions you will find in the certification exams, knowing the answers to the review questions in this book will help cement the material in your mind as you prepare for the tests.

1. A circuit-switched network can be described with which one of these statements?

  a. It is a network that is activated "on-demand."

  b. It is a network that is active all of the time.

  c. It is a dial-backup technology.

  d. It is not available in all areas.

2. A packet-switched network can be described with which one of these statements?

  a. It is a network that is activated "on-demand."

  b. It is a network that is active all of the time.

  c. It is a dial-backup technology.

  d. It is not available in all areas.

3. Which of the following best describes the impact of tunneling over a WAN link?

  a. There is no increase in overhead.

  b. There is no increase in router CPU usage at either end.

  c. There is a delay in the frequency at which packets are sent.

  d. There is an increase in traffic overhead and router CPU usage at both ends of the link.

4. Which statement is true regarding link redundancy?
   a. Redundant links should be terminated on different routers.
   b. Redundant links should not exceed two miles in distance between end points.
   c. Redundant links must be on different circuits.
   d. Redundant links are not applicable to Frame Relay networks.
5. Which of the following WAN technologies has increased overhead with greater reliability at speeds no more than T1 (1.544 Mbps)?
   a. Frame Relay
   b. ATM/SMDS
   c. X.25
   d. Dedicated lines
6. What are the two major technology choices for WAN connectivity? (Select Two.)
   a. Frame Relay
   b. Dedicated lines
   c. Packet-switched networks
   d. Switched connections
7. As a general rule-of-thumb, how many WAN design solutions should you prepare before presenting them to the decision-makers?
   a. 1
   b. 2
   c. 3
   d. 4
8. Which of the following is true in regards to IP-only WAN solutions?
   a. There is an increased latency over the WAN links.
   b. There is a reduced administration burden.
   c. There is an increased administration burden.
   d. There is an unusually steep learning curve.
9. True or False: Cisco NetSys is a product that can be used to model new networks *and* simulate the impact of changes on an existing network.
   a. True
   b. False

10. True or False: An outage in the WAN has the least impact of any type of network outage.
    a. True
    b. False

Answers

1. A circuit-switched network can be described with which one of these statements?
   a. It is a network that is activated "on-demand."
2. A packet-switched network can be described with which one of these statements?
   b. It is a network that is active all of the time.
3. Which of the following best describes the impact of tunneling over a WAN link?
   d. There is an increase in traffic overhead and router CPU usage at both ends of the link.
   Explanation: Tunneling adds more headers to the datagram, increasing the overhead and therefore the bandwidth required by the packets. The router must examine and strip off additional headers, causing more CPU cycles to be used for each packet.
4. Which statement is true regarding link redundancy?
   a. Redundant links should be terminated on different routers.
   Explanation: Terminating the backup link through different endpoint routers decreases the likelihood of total network outages by giving the backup link different termination points altogether.
5. Which of the following WAN technologies has increased overhead with greater reliability at speeds no more than T1 (1.544 Mbps)?
   c. X.25
   Explanation: Remember that X.25 does extensive error-checking. This increases the overhead but also increases reliability of traffic delivery.
6. What are the two major technology choices for WAN connectivity? (Select Two.)
   b. Dedicated lines
   d. Switched connections

7. As a general rule-of-thumb, how many WAN design solutions should you prepare before presenting them to the decision-makers?
   c. 3
8. Which of the following is true in regards to IP-only WAN solutions?
   b. There is a reduced administration burden.
   Explanation: When only one protocol must be supported across a link, troubleshooting is simplified and the network engineering staff does not have to be proficient in many protocols and their pros/cons.
9. True or False: Cisco NetSys is a product that can be used to model new networks *and* simulate the impact of changes on an existing network.
   a. True
10. True or False: An outage in the WAN has the least impact of any type of network outage.
    b. False
    Explanation: Remember that the WAN is the connection point for many network users and can be a link for the general public to access revenue-generating network resources.

Frequently Asked Questions (FAQs)

1. *Is it likely that ATM will become a more popular WAN solution anywhere in the world?*

This is highly unlikely because of the complexity and expense of using ATM instead of dedicated lines or Frame Relay connections. Although ATM still enjoys global popularity, this is still more in the LAN rather than the WAN sector.

2. *I've heard that tunneling can create routing problems — is this true?*

It depends on what you mean by "routing problems." Using Cisco's Generic Routing Encapsulation (GRE) to provide an IP-only ride for traffic through the WAN can simplify configuration on the one hand, but on the other hand, there are some other routing considerations that bear note:

- A tunnel can appear to some protocols as the best path to a destination, if the protocol is looking at hop count only. In truth, the tunnel may cross links that are much slower than other possible paths. Bear this in mind when setting up tunneling.

- Traffic crossing a tunnel is switched at about half the speed of traffic across a native IP link. Appropriate filtering should be in place on both ends of the link so that the link does not become saturated by broadcast traffic.
- One additional note is that traffic entering a tunnel will not be subjected to scrutiny by protocol-based traffic filters that may be part of the site's security infrastructure. Therefore, unchecked traffic may be allowed to pass. Ensure that only "acceptable" tunnels are permitted, terminate the tunnel outside the secure network, or filter the traffic as it enters the destination network.

The following table should help you sort out other benefits and drawbacks of using GRE tunneling:

Pro	Con
One protocol to configure	Higher bandwidth consumption and administer
Ability to use QoS	Some CPU utilization impact at end-point routers
Ability to use faster switching methods on end-point routers	
Permits desktop protocols to take advantage of enhanced IP route selection capabilities	
Can be used to bridge invalid or discontiguous networks to establish reachability	

Bibliography

Cisco Internetwork Design, Cisco Press, 2000, Matthew H. Birkner, Editor

Cisco Internetwork Design Course Manual, version 3.0, April 1997, Cisco Systems, Inc.

Cisco Performance Tuning Basics, **http://www.cisco.com/warp/public/63/tuning.html**

Network Design and Case Studies, Cisco Press, 1998

CHAPTER 16

Dedicated Lines

Overview

In this chapter we will cover the components of dedicated lines and how they relate to your network design. In addition to showing you the overall architecture used with dedicated lines, we will also compare a few different types of dedicated lines you can use and the encapsulation techniques that are related to them.

When selecting dedicated lines for your network design, you should consider your overall architecture and need for redundancy. You will also need to gather information about the bandwidth requirements for the traffic expected between locations. This information includes types of traffic, peak periods, types of applications, and the number of users. It also can include measurement data from analyzers, probes, or network management stations. In addition to the present data, future applications and growth that will affect the link should be considered.

Wide Area Architecture

When considering the selection of a dedicated line type, you will be taking a broader look at the character and scope of the Wide Area Network (WAN). That is sometimes difficult to bear in mind when working on the design for one link at a time. It is a good rule of thumb that you carefully map out all of the WAN during this phase, as you go, so that you don't miss any important requirements. It also helps you to avoid making any design mistakes such as creating single points of failure or rolling a high-bandwidth link into a much smaller one. The latter can sometimes be sufficient if the traffic rolling up to the lower-bandwidth link is bursty or is a fraction of the traffic on the higher-bandwidth link. Considering all possibilities while discussing the dedicated lines to be provisioned at this phase is still a very good design guideline, however.

What exactly is a dedicated line? Simply put, it is a point-to-point frame or cell-based Non-Broadcast Multi-Access (NBMA) circuit through which voice, data, and video can travel. More to the point, the circuit is an end-to-end connection between a customer and a service provider, for which the customer pays a recurring lease rate agreed upon in advance. Part of the terms of the agreement include the bandwidth required, the length of the initial (or subsequent) lease, and the payment terms. A dedicated line connection consists of several individual components:

- Router interface
- Channel Service Unit/Data Service Unit (CSU/DSU)
- Circuit

The router interface is part of the Customer Premises Equipment (CPE), meaning that it resides at the customer end of the dedicated line, rather than at the service provider end. The service provider end is known as the Central Office (CO). In between are miles of cable. A frequent misconception about dedicated lines is that the lines are point-to-point, dedicated lines. This is simply not true.

What actually exists from the CPE to the CO is a variety of links through telecom equipment and providers. Although you will see one router hop reported if you use a troubleshooting tool like *traceroute*, the physical layer of the connection is generally not one hop.

The CSU/DSU is a "black box" device that resides at the customer end. It performs a variety of tasks, such as setting up clocking (or timing) and frame type, depending upon the configuration dictated by your service provider. Its primary task, however, is to condition the line so that traffic passes from end to end with as little delay, jitter, or framing errors as possible.

The circuit itself is a virtual end-to-end connection between the customer and the provider, in the case of Internet connectivity, or customer to customer, through service providers for which the customer pays a recurring lease rate agreed upon in advance.

Usage of Dedicated Lines in the WAN

Typically, dedicated lines are seen in the WAN at the Core layer, although these lines can also enter the network at the Distribution layer, especially when connecting to the Internet. Fees for dedicated lines can be greatly increased depending on the distance between the two points, so generally it is wise to use dedicated lines for shorter distances.

TIP: *Use Frame Relay, when possible, for longer distances, because the cost tends to be less than for longer-distance dedicated lines.*

In Figure 16-1 we have a typical small WAN with a "main" site connecting to three remote sites through dedicated lines. These lines could be T1s, fractional T1s or any combination thereof. We will talk about the bandwidth of different types of dedicated lines a little later in the chapter.

In Figure 16-2 the remote sites also have dedicated line connections to each other, which adds some flexibility to the WAN. If the link from Site A to Site B fails, for example, Site A can then use its link to Site C in order to reach Site B. While this network is not "fully meshed" (meaning every router does not have at least one connection to every other router), it is as close as you normally want to get with a dedicated line. To increase the mesh in this example would probably be prohibitively expensive.

Although a full-mesh is great for failover, it is expensive. There are ways to plan redundancy in the core WAN without breaking the bank. In Figure

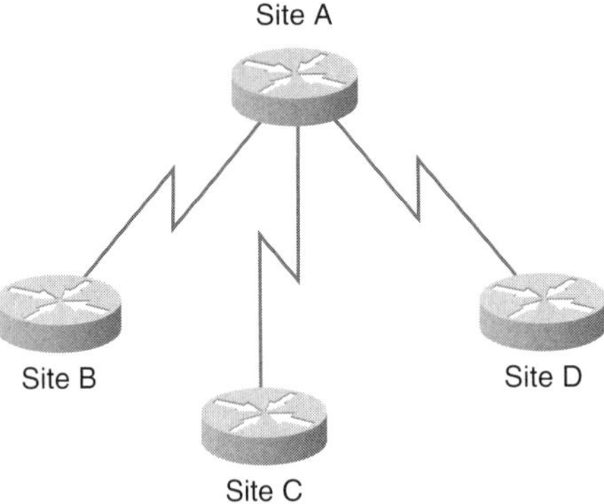

Figure 16-1 Small WAN, dedicated lines

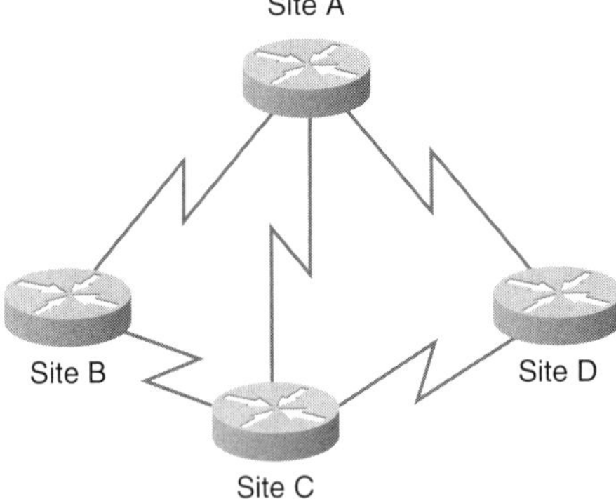

Figure 16-2 Small WAN, dedicated line redundancy

16-3 we have created multiple paths through the core with two routers at each site and a partially meshed WAN. If the dedicated lines are of equivalent bandwidth and the interfaces are of equivalent speed, the routing protocols can be configured to use equal cost paths for load balancing.

A more likely possibility for a redundant WAN is shown in Figure 16-4. Site A is load balancing between two core routers. Each router has a link to each of the remote sites. If one router fails, traffic from the remote site can still find its way to Site A through the other dedicated line. It is important to note that the link speeds should be kept the same so that traffic does not "bog down" in the event of a link failure.

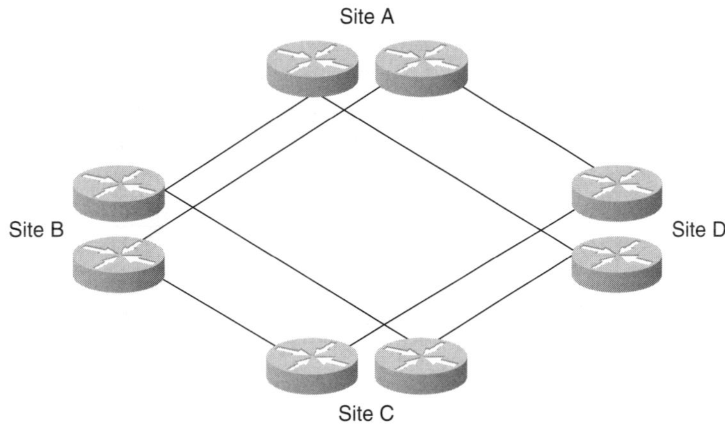

Figure 16-3 Multiple paths through core

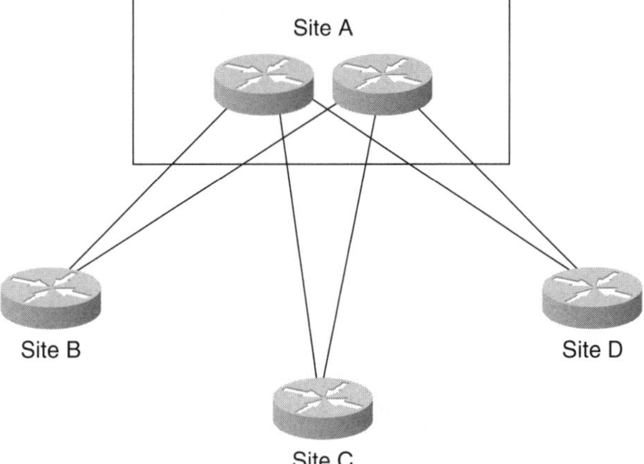

Figure 16-4 Redundant WAN

Remember our three-layer network design model from our early chapters? Site A, in this example, represents the Core layer. It is at this layer that the traffic is moving (and should continue to move) very quickly and efficiently. The three remote sites represent the Distribution layer. The Access layer, where the users enter the network, is not illustrated here. Redundancy could be further carried to that layer, however, by having redundant links to the Distribution layer routers.

Dedicated Line Bandwidth

At what speed will your WAN devices communicate? The type and amount of traffic traversing the wire dictate how much bandwidth is required. Low bandwidth-intensive traffic requires less bandwidth, and thus lower cost, since the cost of provisioning the lower bandwidth results in a total cost savings. The core of a carrier network, however, will need robust network links with the capacity for higher throughput. In this section you will be introduced to some of the selections available.

Please note that in this section we will be dealing with synchronous links rather than asynchronous links. The term *asynchronous link* normally applies to dial-up connections, which have no clocking provided from either side of the link. With *synchronous links*, however, the carrier side of the link or the CSU/DSU normally provides clocking.

Digital Dedicated Lines

Several types of dedicated lines available through service providers can carry voice and data traffic over multiplexed digital signals. The bandwidth and a description of the most common types are listed here:

- **T1** A T1 line is actually an aggregate of 24 channels of 64 Kbps each. Typically a North American designation, T1s can be leased in the "full" T1 bandwidth of 1.544 Mbps or fractions thereof. It is not uncommon for businesses to lease fractional T1 lines for small offices. For instance, a business may only need 12 channels of a T1, resulting in an aggregate bandwidth of 512 Kbps.
- **T3** A T3 line, usually referred to as DS3, is able to carry voice and data at 44.736 Mbps, the equivalent of 28 T1s. Also a North American

designation, a T3 line consists of 672 channels of 64 Kbps each. By the use of an inverse multiplexer, a business leasing a T3 line can break out the signal into individual channels to create new point-to-point T1s or fractional T1s inside the WAN.

- **E1** European businesses use the E1 lines, which operate in a similar manner to T1s. The E1 consists of 32 channels of 64 Kbps each and can carry a total bandwidth of 2.048 Mbps.
- **E3** The big brother of the E1, the E3 consists of 512 channels of 64 Kbps each, carrying a total bandwidth of 34.368 Mbps (or the equivalent of 16 E1s).

Synchronous Optical Network/Synchronous Digital Hierarchy (SONET/SDH)

Synchronous Optical Network (SONET) is a multiplexing technology used over fiber-optic cable in very large core networks, usually an ISP. It is appropriate for the high-speed data transmission requirements of any size network, however.

The basic interface rate of a SONET port is 51.84 Mbps, usually just noted as 51 Mbps or referred to a Synchronous Transport Signal level 1 (STS-1). It is used primarily to multiplex the lower-speed North American data rates, such as T1 (~1.5 Mbps) and DS3 (~45Mbps). In the European market, SDH (which supports a subset of SONET) is used to multiplex E1 (~2 Mbps) and E3 (~35 Mbps).

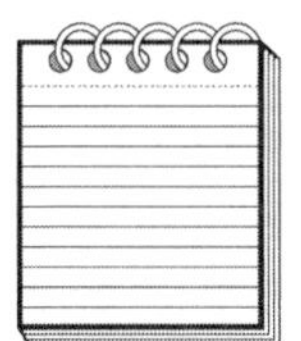

NOTE: *The STS level indicator terminology is used infrequently. Optical Carrier (OC) designation is the preferred designation.*

To find the line rate supported by North American designations, you must use the following formula:

```
n x 51 Mbps = line rate
```

In this case, *n* refers to the Optical Carrier (OC) multiple. In other words, if you have an OC-3 interface, you would multiply 3 times 51 Mbps to find the total speed of the interface. The basic interface rate for SDH, however, is 155 Mbps. The line speed is found for SDH using this formula:

```
n x 155 Mbps = line rate
```

For SDH, n is the multiple defined by the Synchronous Transport Module (STM) rate. So an STM-1 interface has a line rate of 155 Mbps, which would equate to an OC-3 interface. It can be confusing, so refer to Table 16-1 for a clearer picture of how the terms and speeds all relate to each other.

Out of the need for higher-capacity throughput in large networks and WANs, a new type of technology emerged that could use SONET/SDH-Packet over SONET (PoS). PoS allows native IP packets to be carried over SONET/SDH framing.

Table 16-1

SONET/SDH Line Rates

SONET N. America STS Level	SONET N. America STS Level	SDH European STM Level	Both Line Rates (Mbps)
STS-1	OC-1	N/A	51.84
STS-3	OC-3	STM-1	155.52
STS-12	OC-12	STM-4	622.08
STS-48	OC-48	STM-16	2,488.32
STS-192	OC-192	STM-64	9,953.28

Encapsulation of Dedicated Line Traffic

Encapsulation refers to the agreed-upon framing method by which the packets crossing between two points in a dedicated line will comply. All forms of encapsulation are found at the Data-Link layer of the OSI model (layer 2). The types of encapsulation we will discuss here include

- SDLC
- HDLC
- PPP
- LAPB

SDLC

Synchronous Data Link Control (SDLC) is a bit-oriented communications protocol developed by IBM and primarily used when SNA traffic is to be carried. SDLC can be used for point-to-point or multipoint WAN links and is flexible enough to support half- or full-duplex and circuit- or packet-switched networks.

HDLC

High-Level Data Link Control (HDLC) was developed by the International Organization for Standardization (ISO) and is used worldwide for serial line encapsulation. It is an efficient encapsulation method that can operate with a higher Maximum Transmission Unit (MTU) than most other types of encapsulation. The average frame is about 150 bytes, making excellent use of bandwidth. Because of the inherent overhead of a frame, the more data it can carry, the less overhead the line must carry.

Cisco uses HDLC as its default encapsulation for serial lines, but like most vendors, it has not adopted the full protocol standard. Therefore, Cisco HDLC is usually not interoperable with other vendors' equipment. First we will look at the strictest interpretation of the HDLC format.

Standards-Based HDLC Pure HDLC supports full- or half-duplex lines and point-to-point and multipoint networks. Because HDLC uses specific control information that is always located in the same position, it greatly reduces the chance of errors in transmission. The HDLC frame structure is shown below in Figure 16-5.

The Flag field and Closing Flag field are the control sequences used in HDLC to keep the link active and signal the beginning and ending of a frame. The flag sequence consists of 8 bits (or an octet) that look like this: 01111110. Stations on an HDLC link must constantly listen for a flag sequence, so it is important that something is always being transmitted in order to keep the link "up."

Figure 16-5 HDLC frame

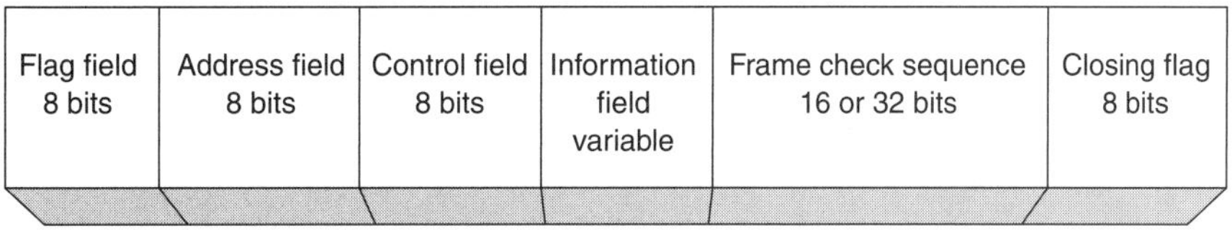

Flag field 8 bits	Address field 8 bits	Control field 8 bits	Information field variable	Frame check sequence 16 or 32 bits	Closing flag 8 bits

Two other bit sequences are important to HDLC. The abort signal—containing at least seven but less than 15 1s—tells the stations listening on the link that the link has a problem. Conversely, an idle signal—containing 15 or more 1s—indicates a link that is in an idle state. In normal operation, flag sequences are generated constantly in the time between transmissions.

The HDLC protocol also manages the flow or pacing at which data is sent and supports several modes of operation, including a simple sliding window mode for reliable delivery. HDLC is an ISO standard developed from the Synchronous Data Link Control (SDLC) standard proposed by IBM in the 1970s and documented in ISO 3309. For any HDLC communications session, one station is designated primary and the other secondary. A session can use one of the following connection modes, which determine how the primary and secondary stations interact:

- **Asynchronous Response Mode** This mode permits the secondary station to initiate communication (used by X.25 LAP protocol).
- **Asynchronous Balanced Mode** This mode permits any node to communicate with any other node, without having to obtain permission from the primary (used by the X.25 LAPB protocol).

Cisco HDLC Cisco HDLC, a proprietary form of HDLC, differs from the ISO standard in several ways. First, it does not support multipoint configurations, only point-to-point. Second, it does not use windowing or flow control, thereby streamlining the transmission. Third, the bits in the Address field are always set to all 1's. Finally, Cisco uses a proprietary 2-byte field after the Control field, which identifies type. This 2-byte Type field is the primary reason that Cisco HDLC differs enough from other HDLC encapsulation methods to render it unable to interoperate with a different vendor's router on the other end of the link.

TIP: *HDLC does not support any type of authentication.*

NOTE: *When using Cisco HDLC, you can also use the auto-install feature supported by Cisco, which allows a new router coming online to receive its configuration from the other end of the point-to-point connection.*

PPP

The Point-to-Point Protocol (PPP) is defined in RFC1661 and works well for both synchronous and asynchronous connections. It is a layered protocol that provides

- Link monitoring
- Multiprotocol support
- Authentication
- Address notification

A link-level echo that periodically checks the status and operation of the link provides link monitoring.

Multiprotocol support means that more than one protocol can share a PPP link. IP and IPX can both use the link, provided that additional Network Control Packets (NCP) are running.

Optional authentication, as specified in RFC1334, is available over a PPP link in the form of either the Password Authentication Protocol (PAP) or the Challenge-Handshake Authentication Protocol (CHAP), either of which can provide additional security to the traffic on the link.

PPP address notification allows a client to communicate with a server to request an IP address as well as to have a fallback configuration in the event of an error. In the past, when using Serial Line IP (SLIP), a client had to be manually configured with an IP address and other configuration parameters. The PPP standard does away with that problem.

Cisco's implementation of PPP adheres to the open standards, meaning that there is nothing proprietary about it. It can also use a multilink/multichassis PPP, which can make many links appear as one across the wire.

LAPB

When media reliability is a problem, Link Access Procedure Balanced (LAPB) is recommended. LAPB provides reliability by sending a frame back to the source each time it successfully reaches another hop during its transmission. This creates a lot of overhead that is not needed in many cases.

Most types of media, such as fiber-optic, are very reliable, so it is redundant and wasteful to have the encapsulation method compensate for something for which no compensation is needed. You will most often find a need for LAPB in X.25 networks or over satellite links where quick error detection and recovery is a must. LAPB is also appropriate over analog lines.

Case Study

Campus Research has acquired several smaller manufacturing companies in the Detroit area; therefore, they need to link these campuses to the main building in Detroit. Although all of the buildings are in the Detroit metropolitan area, they are of varying distances from the main campus, as shown in Figure 16-6. Your assignment is to develop a plan for connectivity between the main campus in Detroit and the three new buildings, within the requirements stated by the company.

The following is known about the buildings:

- Chip Components has a Cisco 2611 router in their wiring closet and was running over a T1 line to an ISP locally.
- Michigan Fiber-Optics has two Cisco 7513 routers in their main computer center, which will connect to Campus Research.
- Argyle Industries has a different vendor's router in the wiring closet.

The company has given you the following requirements:

- Actual bandwidth consumption is not known, of course, but several experts in the applications and networking departments have estimated the requirement for today's applications. Take the current estimated bandwidth consumption, shown in Table 16-2, and allow for bursty traffic exceeding that amount.
- Take into consideration that Michigan Fiber-Optics will be critical to daily business at Campus Research. The company cannot afford for the

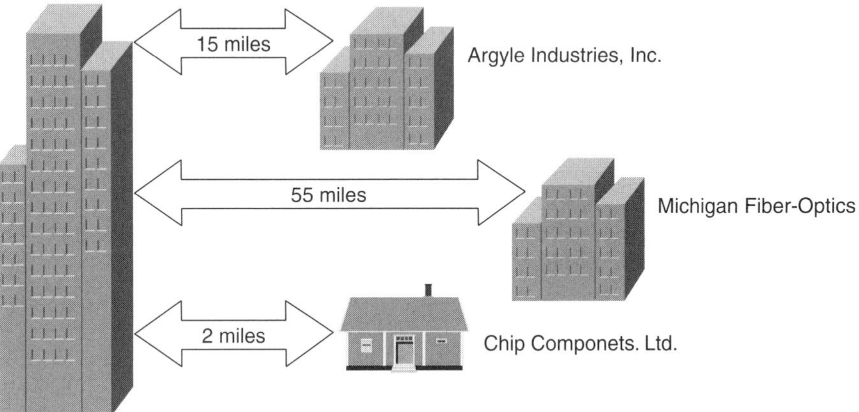

Figure 16-6 Detroit acquisitions

link to be down, so provide dial backup or mesh in your design for fault tolerance.

- Cost is of no concern to Michigan Fiber-Optics, but the other two campuses need to have costs kept to a minimum. Refer to Table 16-3 for costs associated with the dedicated lines.
- No new routers will be purchased for the Argyle Industries or Chip Components buildings.

Reference Tables 16-2 and 16-3 for your final design.

Now that you have the basic information, you should be able to draw up a simple design of what the WAN for Campus Research needs to look like in order to support the proper amount of traffic that is estimated to cross between buildings. Be sure to build in proper scalability and redundancy where you can. Finally, think about the encapsulation that can be used and supported over the lines. In your final design, note the distance, cost, encapsulation, and line type for each connection. Always be confident in the design you present to the customer so that you can defend that design, even

Table 16-2 Bandwidth Required

Location	Bandwidth Needed (in Mbps)
Michigan Fiber-Optics Corp.	30
Argyle Industries, Inc.	8
Chip Components, Ltd.	61

Table 16-3 Cost of Connectivity

Type of Connection	Base Monthly Cost	Monthly Cost per Mile
T-3/DS-3	$1750	$50
T-1	$1500	$50
512 Kbps	$1300	$50
256 Kbps	$1000	$50
64 Kbps	$350	$50
ISDN (backup line)	$159	N/A

if it involves trade-offs in cost or other factors. A suggested solution to this case study can be found in Appendix C, "Suggested Solutions to Case Studies."

Study Hints

Although no one can disclose test items or test content, we can give hints as to what might be valuable to study. For this chapter, certain key facts need to be reviewed and remembered.

- Study the bandwidth of each type of line. It is good to know these facts, because you will need to reference them over and over again.
- Know your encapsulation! Each method has its own benefits, and each one is designed to support a different network need.

CCDP Tips

This section contains an abbreviated list of topics covered in Chapter 16. Think of this section as the equivalent of reading Cliff's Notes™ instead of reading an entire book. You will get the general idea of the chapter but will benefit more from reading the chapter in its entirety.

- WAN Architecture
  - Dedicated lines are most often found at the Core layer of the WAN design.
  - Three components of a dedicated line are the router interface, the CSU/DSU, and the circuit.
  - Customer Premises Equipment (CPE) is at the customer end. The Central Office (CO) is at the provider end.
  - The CSU/DSU provides line conditioning for the dedicated line. The service provider provides the circuit and the parameters under which the circuit will operate.
  - Lease as much bandwidth as you can afford without having it become "overkill." By this, we mean that you should plan for extra bandwidth, usually about 30 percent more than you think you will need during peak periods.

- Dedicated Line Bandwidth
  - Each channel in a digital line is 64 Kbps.
  - Channels can be aggregated or "bundled" to form a higher-bandwidth link.
  - T1 lines have about 1.5 Mbps bandwidth.
  - T3 or DS3 lines have about 45 Mbps bandwidth and can be inverse-multiplexed to split off into multiple channels or groups of channels to form T1 or fractional T1 links.
  - Refer to Table 16-1 for bandwidth facts about SONET/SDH rates.
- Dedicated Line Encapsulation
  - **SDLC** Developed by IBM. Most often appropriate for SNA networks. Supports point-to-point or multipoint, half- or full-duplex, and circuit- or packet-switched WANs.
  - **Cisco HDLC** Differs from pure HDLC in that there is a 2-byte Type field inserted after the Control field. Not interoperable with other vendor equipment. Point-to-point only. No windowing or flow control. Enabled by default on Cisco's routers.
  - **PPP** Point-to-point only, synchronous or asynchronous connections. PPP offers PAP or CHAP authentication, link monitoring, multiprotocol support, and address notification, which supports dynamic address assignment for remote clients.
  - **LAPB** High-overhead, reliable encapsulation that replies back to the source as each new point toward the destination is reached. Used with analog and X.25 lines and when media reliability is a problem.

Summary

As you have seen in this chapter, there are a variety of ways to link together the routers in the WAN. The decision on the bandwidth and type of the dedicated line will depend upon the geographical location and bandwidth needs of the network. The encapsulation type you select will depend on requirements such as authentication, media reliability, the type of routers in use, and the type of traffic to be supported.

Frequently Asked Questions (FAQs)

1. *Do I have to create the configuration for the CSU/DSU when a dedicated line is installed?*
   Because the service provider has very specific conditions for the dedicated line, the service provider will normally provide you with both the CSU/DSU and the configuration parameters that it requires to keep the link operational.
2. *Why wouldn't I want to create a fully meshed network for my dedicated line connections?*
   This comes down to a question of expense. Having a fully meshed network based on dedicated lines means having many router interfaces to support those lines (especially if you have a "hub" site) and many circuits incurring cost (even if they may never be used). It is better to go with Dial-on-Demand Routing (DDR) or an ISDN link to back up a circuit. In this way you will provide redundancy, but you won't be paying for a full circuit that will only be used in emergencies.
3. *I just installed a Cisco router that is connected by dedicated line to another vendor's router. I have tried everything, but the link will not come up. What could my problem be?*
   Remember that Cisco routers have default encapsulation set to Cisco HDLC. This encapsulation method is not interoperable with any other vendor's router. Set the encapsulation on the interface to PPP (on both ends) and try again.

Questions

The following review questions have been selected to help you test your knowledge of the subject matter contained in this chapter. You will also find these questions contained in the CD-ROM included with this book. Although these are not the questions you will find in the certification exams, knowing the answers to the review questions in this book will help cement the material in your mind as you prepare for the tests.

1. What is the bandwidth, in Mbps, of an OC-3 link?
   a. ~52 Kbps
   b. ~64 Kbps
   c. ~1.5 Mbps
   d. ~155 Mbps
2. What is the bandwidth, in Mbps, of an OC-192 link?
   a. ~1.5 Mbps
   b. ~155 Mbps
   c. ~10 Gbps
   d. ~622 Mbps
3. True or False: Cisco HDLC is interoperable with most vendor equipment.
   a. True
   b. False
4. Which type of encapsulation supports CHAP?
   a. PPP
   b. HDLC
   c. Cisco HDLC
   c. LAPB
5. At which WAN layer do dedicated lines usually reside?
   a. Core
   b. Distribution
   c. Access
   d. Data Link
6. What is the speed of each channel in a T3 line?
   a. ~64 Kbps
   b. ~128 Kbps
   c. ~256 Kbps
   d. ~512 Kbps

7. True or False: It is always a good idea to create a full mesh for redundancy.
   a. True
   b. False
8. What is the primary responsibility of the CSU/DSU?
   a. Clocking
   b. Line conditioning
   c. Termination of the circuit
   d. Encapsulation
9. True or False: The CPE is the customer end of a dedicated line.
   a. True
   b. False
10. A dedicated line is an example of what type of cost for a network?
    a. Fixed
    b. Recurring
    b. Aggregate
    d. Tax-exempt

Answers

1. What is the bandwidth, in Mbps, of an OC-3 link?
   d. ~155 Mbps
2. What is the bandwidth, in Mbps, of an OC-192 link?
   c. ~10 Gbps
3. True or False: Cisco HDLC is interoperable with most vendor equipment.
   b. False
4. Which type of encapsulation supports CHAP?
   a. PPP
5. At which WAN layer do dedicated lines usually reside?
   a. Core

6. What is the speed of each channel in a T3 line?
   a. ~64 Kbps
7. True or False: It is always a good idea to create a full mesh for redundancy.
   b. False
8. What is the primary responsibility of the CSU/DSU?
   b. Line conditioning
9. True or False: The CPE is the customer end of a dedicated line.
   a. True
10. A dedicated line is an example of what type of cost for a network?
    b. Recurring

Bibliography

Cisco Internetwork Design, Cisco Press, 2000, Matthew H. Birkner, Editor

Cisco Internetwork Design Course Manual, version 3.0, April 1997, Cisco Systems, Inc.

Internet RFC Source: **http://www.cis.ohio-state.edu/hypertext/information/rfc.html**

RFC 1334

RFC 1661

Thomas Concise Telecom and Networking Dictionary, McGraw-Hill, 2000, Thomas M. Thomas II, Editor

CHAPTER 17

Frame Relay Design

Overview

We covered the design of a WAN using dedicated lines in Chapter 16, "Dedicated Lines." Now we are going to talk about a less expensive alternative —Frame Relay. Not only will we cover the terminology and design models associated with a Frame Relay WAN, but we will also talk about some of the pitfalls and problems encountered in putting the network together.

Frame Relay is a packet-switched WAN architecture that is available in a variety of bandwidths—typically 56 Kbps, 64 Kbps, and 1.544 Mbps. It is a more inexpensive method of creating a redundant, efficient network versus using point-to-point links through leased lines, for instance. Leased lines represent a circuit-switching method that works very well for steady-stream applications such as voice and video. For data traffic, which tends to be bursty in nature, Frame Relay provides a high-performance alternative.

Figure 17-1 shows a number of routers between Detroit and Washington, DC that are connected by multiple T1 lines. The resulting, partial-mesh topology is costly in terms of the number of links, the number of router ports in use, and the latency incurred by the traffic as it moves through multiple hops. Note that you would not normally see a full-mesh leased line network because the number of lines needed would be the square of the total number of routers. For instance, 12 routers would need 144 lines.

By contrast, Figure 17-2 shows Frame Relay circuits used in a full-mesh topology. The hops between Detroit and Washington, DC have been reduced

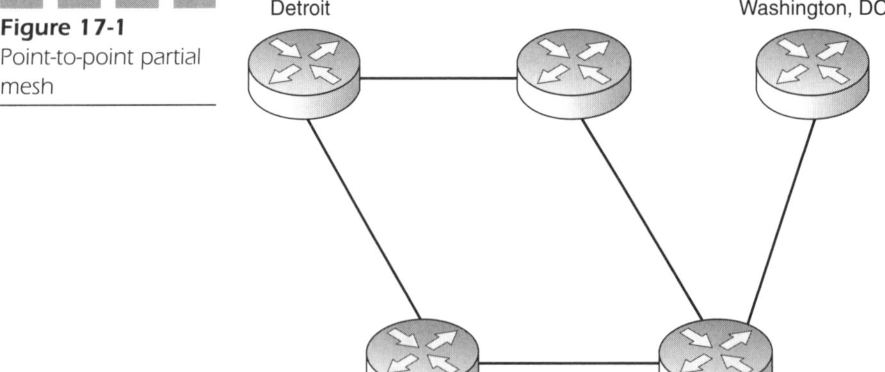

Figure 17-1 Point-to-point partial mesh

Figure 17-2 Frame Relay full-mesh topology

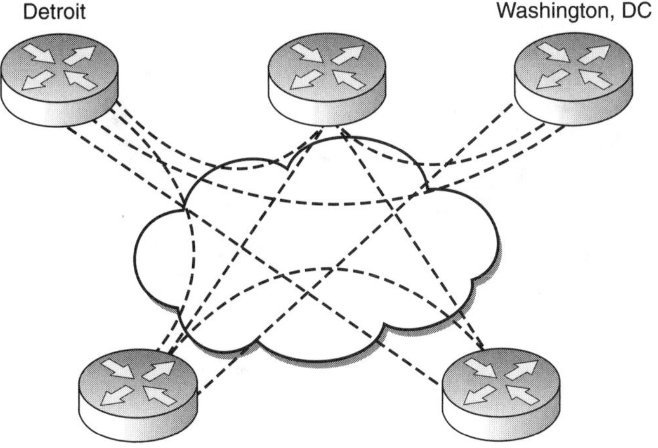

to a single logical hop by the use of virtual circuits. Also, the number of ports in use has been reduced to one.

TIP: *To find the number of virtual circuits needed to create a full-mesh topology, use the following formula:*
$(x \times x - 1)/2 = y$
In this formula, x is the total number of routers in use.

Although it is typically a carrier network that uses Frame Relay, you may also see Frame Relay in use for large, geographically diverse non-carrier networks. Additionally, we should mention that the latency actually incurred depends largely on the infrastructure between the two virtual points.

Frame Relay is similar to X.25 in that it uses Data Terminal Equipment (DTE)—usually a router, a Frame Relay Access Device (FRAD), or an IBM front-end processor (FEP)—at the customer end, and Data Circuit Equipment (DCE)—usually a Frame Relay switch—at the carrier end. These data-link layer devices define the connections between the two endpoints, as shown in Figure 17-3. Frame Relay differs from X.25 in that it does not provide the hop-by-hop reliability features that create the vast amount of overhead on X.25. It depends instead on the reliability of the physical layer, typically fiber-optic cabling, as well as on the upper-layer protocols to retransmit if necessary.

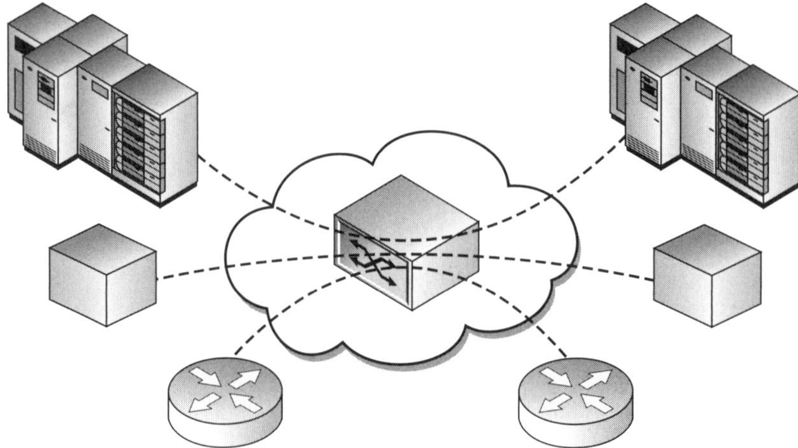

Figure 17-3
Frame Relay access

DLCI

The most commonly used circuits in Frame Relay are called permanent virtual circuits (PVCs). A PVC represents a point-to-point virtual link that is configured on each end of the circuit. It is identified with a locally significant, 10-bit number known as a Data-Link Connection Identifier (DLCI). A DLCI is said to be locally significant because it, along with the circuit information, identifies the local address. The port reference will change as it moves from switch to switch. It only needs to be unique between the DTE and DCE. The DLCI is an integer between 0 and 1023 that identifies and points to the local switch. The local switch, in turn, is mapped for a destination.

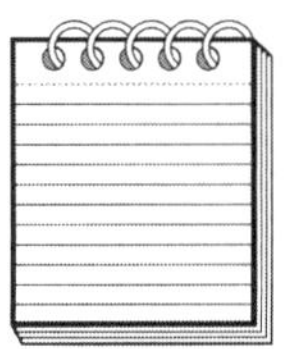

NOTE: *Cisco recommends that no more than 200 to 300 DLCIs be configured on any given serial interface. That recommendation drops to 30 to 50, if you are broadcasting. Although the serial port can theoretically support all 1,000 possible DLCIs, to preserve performance, follow these guidelines.*

You can think of a DLCI as a first name. If your name is David, there may be many other people named David around you, but there is only one with your first, middle, and last name. This is not a perfect analogy, because there could be more than one person in the world with the same name as you. However, you get the general idea.

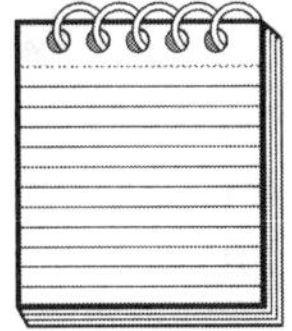

NOTE: Although DLCIs are locally significant, some rules must be applied. A DLCI of 0 is reserved for local management interface (LMI) signaling. Additionally, 1–15 and 1008–1022 are reserved, and 1023 and 992–1007 are for management functions. That leaves 16–991 for use by networks. Because some DLCI numbers are reserved, they can be said to be "globally significant."

The circuit between the DTE and DCE is referred to as a *local loop* and carries an agreed-upon amount of traffic at a Committed Information Rate (CIR). This is a theoretical guarantee made between the service provider and the network. The CIR is the rate at which the carrier agrees to accept the data over the virtual circuit. In Figure 17-4, you can see the components of a Frame Relay network and how they work together.

Because traffic can be bursty, however, it is likely that traffic rates may exceed the CIR from time to time. This is known as *oversubscription*. It is like betting on the fact that not all circuits will be in full use at all times. Service providers usually oversell their bandwidth, counting on the fact that there is usually more than enough bandwidth to go around. If traffic

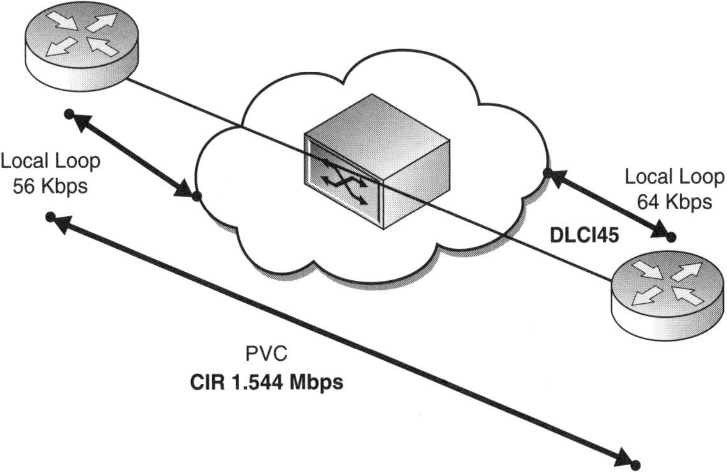

Figure 17-4
Frame Relay circuits

exceeds the CIR, there is no guarantee by the carrier that the frames will not be dropped.

A Frame Relay switch has a table that maps its ports based on incoming and outgoing DLCIs. The DLCI of an incoming packet is contained in the Frame Relay header of the packet, along with other information. It is compared to the switching table for the incoming port. If a packet were received on port 2 of a switch, for instance, the switching table might look something like Table 17-1. The switch would compare the incoming DLCI to the DLCI representing the next hop in the virtual circuit. It would know to send your traffic out of port 7/DLCI 225, if you were coming from DLCI 450. This is a manually configured map that directs the traffic in a simple manner.

NOTE: A DLCI is locally significant, but the number can be the same at both ends, as shown in Table 17-1.

LMI

The customer end of a Frame Relay circuit needs to be able to query the network for information about its link. It needs to know the status of the virtual circuits, the status of the link (or local loop) to the carrier switch, and it needs to be able to get some configuration information. In order to do this, the customer uses signaling; specifically, it uses a signaling technique known as a local management interface (LMI). Although the standards bod-

Table 17-1

Switching Table

IN_Port	IN_DLCI	OUT_Port	OUT_DLCI
P2	450	P7	225
P2	110	P1	50
P2	250	P3	150
P2	100	P4	100

ies, mentioned later, consider the LMI to be optional, it is generally implemented everywhere. The basic functions of the LMI are as follows:

- Learn about the virtual circuits that are configured and whether they are active or inactive.
- Learn about any new virtual circuits that were created since the last poll.
- Make sure that the link to the switch is alive.
- Set up switched virtual circuits as needed.

Three Cisco-supported LMI types exist:

- Frame Relay Forum
- ANSI T1.617 Annex D
- ITU-T Q.933 Annex A

The Frame Relay Forum is an international group of vendors, carriers, and users that share a common interest in the standards and application of Frame Relay.

The American National Standards Institute (ANSI) is a non-profit, non-governmental agency that serves to create voluntary standards internationally. Its standards can be recognized by T1, followed by a period, followed by a number. For example, T1.617 Annex D is commonly known as *ANSI LMI* or *LMI Annex D*. It uses DLCI 0 for all its circuits.

The International Telecommunications Union-Telecommunication (ITU-T) is a part of the ITU (formerly known as the Consultative Committee on International Telegraphy and Telephony, or CCITT), a United Nations agency based in Geneva, Switzerland. The standards put forth by ITU-T are always represented by a letter, followed by a period, followed by a number, such as X.25. The letter I represents ISDN standards. The letter X is for digital packet networking standards, and the letter V represents digital transmission over analog facilities (for example, V.35). The letter Q represents most Frame Relay standards, although some can be ISDN (I) standards as well. ITU-T Q.933 Annex A is commonly referred to as *LMI Annex A*.

Frame Relay Forum is the default LMI type for Cisco routers, but it's a first-generation LMI and, as such, is somewhat outdated. In 11.2 and greater versions of the Cisco IOS, the LMI type of the Frame Relay switch is auto-sensed. A good rule of thumb is to configure whatever type the provider's Frame Relay switch is using. Most modern routers of any brand do auto-sense the LMI and lock onto it.

RFC 1490/2427

In order to provide for the use of multiple protocols over Frame Relay, RFC 1490 defines an encapsulation method capable of various types of datagrams. This also allows for nonroutable protocols, such as SNA and LAT, to be carried through a PVC in the same manner as routable traffic. It also permits for the efficient usage of a PVC, because multiple types of traffic can use the circuit. RFC 1490 also standardizes the encapsulation method as an "open" standard, that is, one that can be implemented across vendor platforms in a uniform manner.

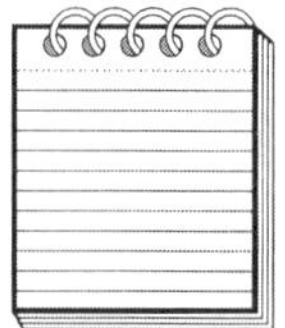

NOTE: *To use RFC 1490 encapsulation, use the following command:*

```
encap frame ietf
```

A header is added to the frame in which a Network Level Protocol ID (NLPID) is included. The NLPID tells the network what kind of protocol is being encapsulated in the frame: an IP, a Connectionless Network Protocol (CLNP), or an IEEE Subnetwork Access Protocol (SNAP). Because of the limited number of NLPIDs available, not all protocols have a unique ID. For those cases, a special NLPID (80) is used that signifies that a SNAP header is to follow. The header of a frame encapsulated with RFC 1490 specifications differs from a normal encapsulation. In a normal encapsulation, you would have a Frame Relay header, the datagram, and the Frame Check Sequence (FCS). Figure 17-5 shows an RFC 1490 header.

Figure 17-5
RFC 1490 header

Frame Relay Header 2 octets
Control Field (for ISDN) 03 hex
NLPID CC hex
IP Datagram
Frame Check Sequence 2 octets

RFC 1490 also specifies protocol address resolution. A sending station can use standard ARP by sending the ARP (or RARP) request over the PVC in a SNAP-encapsulated Frame Relay frame. Another alternative is to send the same ARP request through all the PVCs. This is similar to multicasting. When the DLCI is known, another process, called *inverse ARP*, can be used. We will discuss inverse ARP, or InARP, later in this chapter.

Router Interaction

A router needs to be able to have a map of the network, regardless of the protocol or technology in use. It creates this picture through the use of topology databases, routing tables, and other mapping techniques. With Frame Relay, it is important that the router be able to match network-layer information, such as an IP address of a next-hop router, with a DLCI and a PVC. In this section, we will discuss some of the methods the router has at its disposal to help with these tasks.

Frame Relay Maps

A router has to be able to associate a next-hop router address with a DLCI. As you know, the router already has a routing table that contains a list of destination networks, along with next-hop addresses and interfaces. With physical interfaces or point-to-multipoint interfaces, the router also has a Frame Relay Map entry that identifies the next-hop router for a particular DLCI. This can be manually configured or can be dynamically populated through inverse ARP.

Inverse ARP

For multipoint and physical interfaces, Frame Relay inverse ARP is enabled by default, and split horizon is disabled. Inverse ARP reduces the manual configuration of the router by allowing the router to build its own map of the Frame Relay network—dynamically. As the router talks to the Frame Relay switch via the LMI exchange (with an explorer frame), it learns about the DLCIs that are being used (from the switch's port table). Once the information is received, it sends an inverse ARP request to each

DLCI using a protocol supported and enabled on that interface. The reply information is then used to build the map.

For point-to-point interfaces, manual configuration of the mapping is implemented through the following command:

```
frame-relay interface-dlci dlci
```

This command is normally used to configure point-to-point subinterfaces or physical interfaces. Point-to-multipoint interfaces typically rely on inverse ARP to create their Frame Relay Map entries.

Routing Protocols

It is important when designing Frame Relay networks to take into account how different routing protocols will behave within a Frame Relay environment. Figure 17-6 shows a typical Frame Relay network with multiple PVCs. Each router has two PVCs originating from the same interface (S0). As you learned in the chapters on routing protocols, distance vector protocols use split horizon to prevent routing updates from being advertised out of the same interface on which they were received. This is a valuable tool to help prevent routing loops, but in a Frame Relay network, split horizon can cause problems.

In Figure 17-6, Detroit is receiving routing updates from Boston and Washington, DC over different PVCs via the same physical interface. If it learns about network 172.16.58.0 from Boston, it needs to advertise that to Washington, DC. Otherwise, Washington, DC might not be able to reach

Figure 17-6
Frame Relay routing

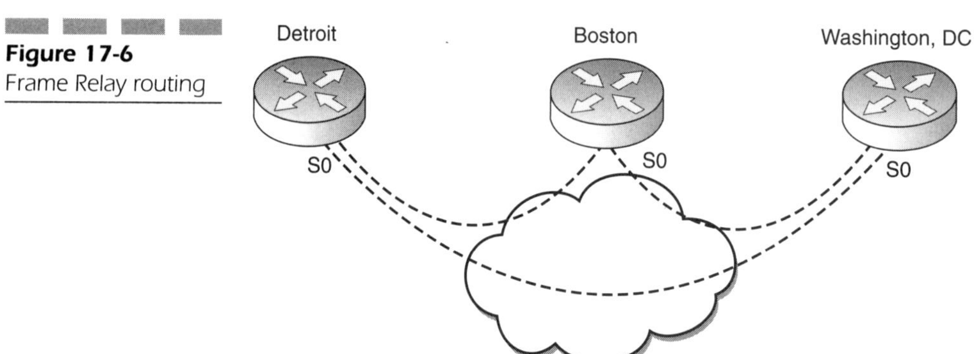

Boston, were the network not fully meshed. There are two ways to resolve this issue:

- *Disable split horizon.* This is probably the least preferred solution because split horizon helps prevent routing loops.
- *Configure static routes or default routes.* This is somewhat better, but it is laborious. Use point-to-point sub-interfaces. The router will treat each sub-interface as a separate entity and will allow the routes to be advertised.

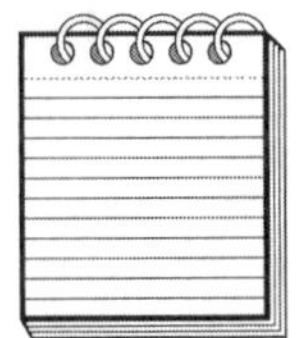

NOTE: *Remember that multipoint and physical interfaces have split horizon disabled by default.*

In Figure 17-7, you can see that even though serial 0 is still the physical interface, the sub-interfaces are separate virtual interfaces that correspond to the PVCs. Each sub-interface has its own number and subnet associated with it.

Non-Broadcast Multi-Access (NBMA)

Another way to avoid split horizon problems is by using a full-mesh Frame Relay NBMA design. Although Frame Relay is inherently non-broadcast,

Figure 17-7
Sub-interfaces avoid split horizon problem

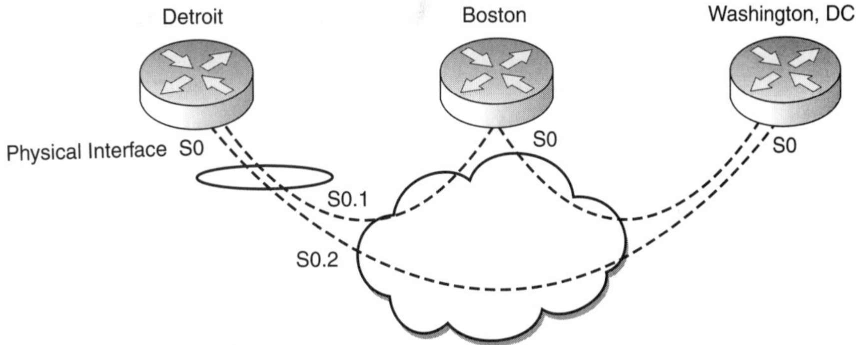

it does allow for multicast transmissions. If a network is fully meshed, meaning that each router has a connection to every other router in the network, all multicast transmissions (routing tables, SAP updates, and so on) are forwarded to all other routers in the network. A full-mesh Frame Relay network is expensive, however, because of the number of PVCs that must be used for the connections. This also creates overhead for the router because it must replicate each transmission for each PVC. Not only does the router have to process and send the same multicast out of multiple PVCs, it also has to receive the replies from all PVCs that may reside on a single physical interface.

This can cause quite a performance hit, which is why this is not the preferred method of handling the split horizon problem. This method can work for a smaller network, however, with a small number of PVCs.

Topology Options

A Frame Relay network can be designed in a few different ways. The primary goals are the same as they have been with other types of networks. You want to build in redundancy, resiliency, usability, and scalability—all while keeping your costs down. Here are a few ways to do that.

NBMA

We just discussed, in the previous section, how a full-mesh NBMA model can help prevent problems with split horizon. Creating a full-mesh Frame Relay network, however, can be quite expensive. It also does not scale well because of the number of PVCs to be configured and managed in this type of environment. Although the example in Figure 17-7 is fully meshed, imagine what would happen if the network were to grow beyond the three routers shown. The interface will support multiple PVCs but just a single subnet.

Sub-interfaces Using Full Mesh

Figure 17-8 shows a full-mesh Frame Relay network using sub-interfaces. All routers have a PVC to all other routers. As we discussed before, a full-

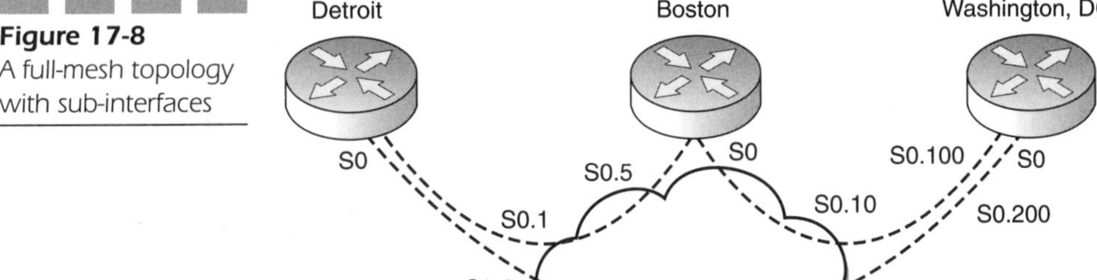

Figure 17-8
A full-mesh topology with sub-interfaces

mesh environment requires a great number of circuits, creating more expense and management responsibility for each router and for the network as a whole. Although this is somewhat scalable (if you are willing to handle the increased cost), it is not the best solution for large network designs. It does work well for creating fault-tolerant small networks, however.

Remember the formula for finding the number of PVCs required for a full-mesh network? In the example shown, you would multiply 3 (routers) by 3, subtract 1, and then divide by 2. That equates to three PVCs in this case. What if you had 15 routers? That would be 105 PVCs! Now you can see why this could be a problem administratively. That's a lot of PVCs to manage for only 15 routers.

Sub-interfaces Using Hub and Spoke

Perhaps a more palatable approach (and certainly a less expensive approach) for most businesses is the hub-and-spoke model using sub-interfaces. In Figure 17-9, you can see that we are able to remove a PVC from the previous example. By making Boston the hub site, Washington, DC and Detroit can still reach each other, as long as the traffic passes through Boston first. This reduces the number of PVCs needed.

Rather than being a partial-mesh environment, you create several virtual point-to-point connections from a single physical interface, thus reducing both cost and management. The drawbacks are that the router in

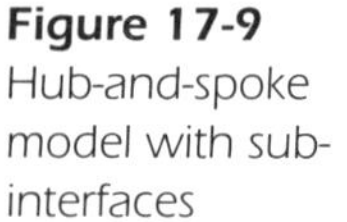

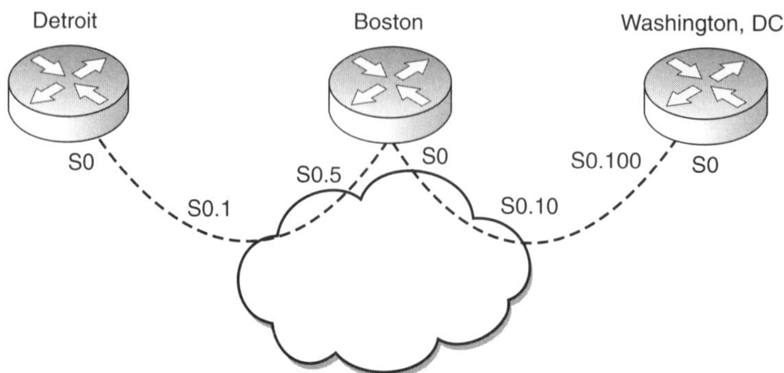

Figure 17-9 Hub-and-spoke model with sub-interfaces

Boston becomes a single point of failure for the Frame Relay network. It also takes on a great deal of overhead, because it must process as though it has multiple interfaces.

The formula to use to figure out the number of PVCs needed to create this design is to multiply the number of hub sites (if you create more than one) by the number of remote sites that will talk to the hub sites.

DDR for Backup

When designing fault-tolerant Frame Relay networks, you need to consider designing a backup strategy, especially when using a model such as the hub-and-spoke model. What if Boston goes down? How will Detroit and Washington, DC continue to do business? A commonly used method is to employ dial-on-demand routing (DDR) as a backup.

As we have discussed in other chapters, one method is to use a floating static route—that is, one with an administrative distance higher than any protocol in use on the network—to enable the route only when all other routes have failed. The traffic going from Detroit to Washington, DC, in Figure 17-10, will trigger and bring up the ISDN link between devices, should traffic try to reroute over that link.

Another possibility is to use a backup interface for point-to-point or multipoint sub-interfaces. Rather than waiting for an entire physical interface to fail, this will create a backup for a failure of a single PVC on a sub-interface. Note that this cannot be brought up based on line load only, but rather on total sub-interface failure.

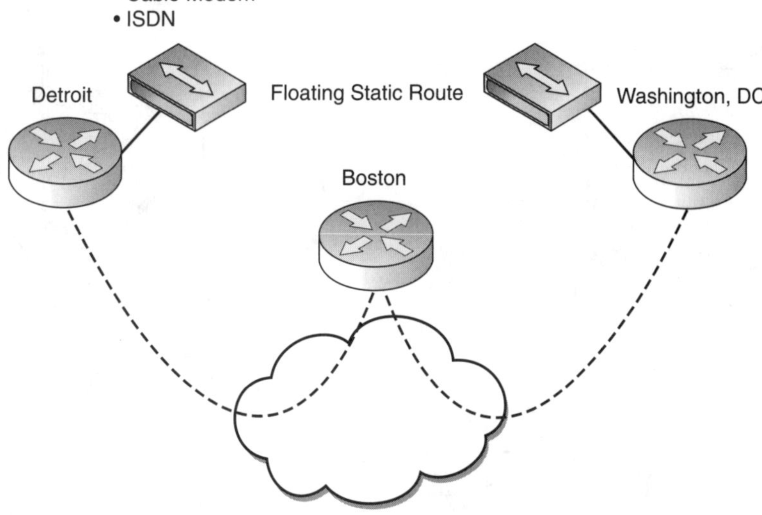

Figure 17-10 DDR for fault-tolerance

For more information on this topic, please visit Cisco's Web site: **http://www.cisco.com/univercd/cc/td/doc/product/software/ios121/121cgcr/wan_c/wcdfrely.htm#xtocid1553148**.

TIP: *Because both backup interfaces and static routes are valid fault-tolerance configurations, they can show up on Cisco tests. You would be advised to be familiar with both.*

Case Study

Campus Research is in a quandary about the type of topology to use for their WAN. Currently, they have three sites: St. Louis, Detroit, and Milwaukee. Between the three sites, they have established connectivity through the use of dedicated lines, as shown in Figure 17-11.

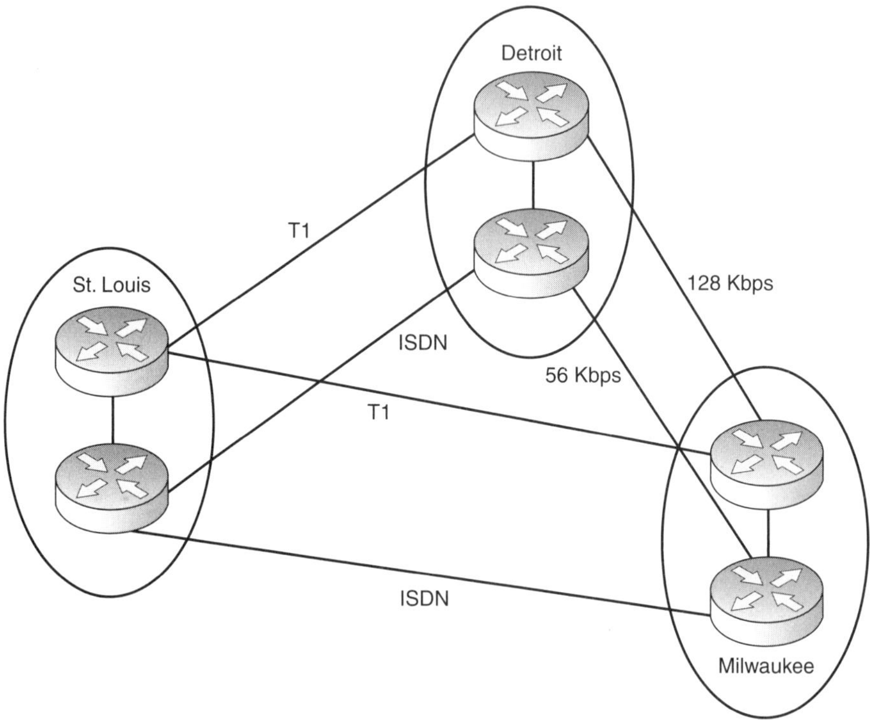

Figure 17-11 Campus Research's WAN topology

The problem they are encountering is the cost of keeping these dedicated lines, especially the lines between Detroit and St. Louis. They are being charged a basic provisioning fee for each T1 of $1,500 per month, and 25 cents per mile for the 500-mile distance. They feel they must have both T1 lines for fault tolerance. The routing protocol currently in use is IGRP. They are willing to change protocols, as long as it doesn't involve a great amount of retraining of the network engineering staff.

The studies they have performed show that the primary T1 from St. Louis to Detroit can burst as high as 512 Kbps during peak hours between 1:00 P.M. and 3:00 P.M. The remainder of the time, usage is about half of that. Traffic between Milwaukee and the two original Campus Research sites remains very light for now, but it is growing as they add staff and migrate applications.

Your task is to determine whether Frame Relay would work well for connectivity of these sites. If so, you must recommend a routing protocol that will scale better than IGRP. Watch out for problems with split horizon! Determine which topology model works best for the business and draw out a simple diagram.

Although there is no one right answer to any given design problem, one solution is suggested in Appendix C, "Suggested Solutions for Case Studies."

Study Hints

Although no one can disclose test items or test content, we can give hints as to what might be valuable to study. For this chapter, "Frame Relay Design," certain key facts need to be reviewed and remembered:

- **Formulas to use**
  - To find the number of PVCs required to create a full-mesh Frame Relay network, where *x* is the number of routers and *y* is the number of PVCs needed, use the following formula:

    $(x \times x - 1)/2 = y$
  - To find the number of dedicated lines required to create a full-mesh WAN, where *x* is the number of routers and *y* is the number of dedicated lines needed, use the following formula:

    $x^2 = y$
- **Split horizon** Remember that split horizon creates a problem for Frame Relay, because multiple virtual circuits may terminate at a single physical interface. Because split horizon dictates that it will not advertise a path it learned through a physical interface back out the *same* physical interface, the result could be that the other routers talking to PVCs on that interface may not learn about all routes.
- **Reserved DLCIs**
  - 0 is for LMI.
  - 1–15 and 1008–1022 are reserved.
  - 1023 and 992–1007 are for management functions.
- **Special NLPIDs**
  - CC is for the IP protocol.
  - 81 is for ISO CLNP.
  - 80 indicates that a SNAP header will follow.

- **NBMA** A Non-Broadcast Multi-Access model works well for small networks with a single subnet and very few PVCs. Because it simulates a one-to-many model and copies the broadcasts to every router in its full-mesh environment, it avoids the split horizon problem. It does, however, create a great deal of overhead in the network and impacts the performance of the router.
- **CIR** The Committed Information Rate is the rate at which the service provider guarantees throughput on a Frame Relay circuit. Traffic may burst periodically over the CIR but is subject to discard if it does. Frequent oversubscription of the line can result in the service provider requiring that the CIR be raised, and therefore the cost as well.

CCDP Tips

This section contains an abbreviated list of topics covered in this chapter. Think of this section as the equivalent of reading Cliff's Notes™ instead of reading an entire book. You will get the general idea of the chapter but will benefit more from reading the chapter in its entirety.

- **Benefits of Frame Relay over other WAN topologies** A Frame Relay circuit is frequently less expensive than dedicated lines. It is also less costly to create a full-mesh network in Frame Relay than it is with dedicated lines. Frame Relay also works better than dedicated lines for bursty traffic, such as data, rather than for voice and video, which require more error-checking and guarantee of service.
- **Virtual circuits** Frame Relay works by using virtual circuits. There can be multiple virtual circuits from a single physical interface, resulting in a cost savings. The circuits can be switched or permanent. Switched virtual circuits (SVCs) are less common because of the difficulty in setting them up, from a user perspective, and in handling the setup/breakdown of the connection by the router. SVCs are billed on a usage basis, however, and could result in a significant cost savings. Permanent virtual circuits are billed at a set rate for a set amount of the CIR. Because they require manual configuration, however, they can be initially cumbersome to administer.

- **Partial-mesh networks versus full-mesh networks**
    - Partial-mesh works well in most situations, when it is not critical to have each router have a path to every other router. It is less costly and easier to maintain.
    - Full-mesh is required in designs requiring complete fault-tolerance and in NBMA networks.
- **DLCIs and the switching table**
    - Each DLCI is locally significant, meaning that it identifies the circuit to the local router.
    - The Frame Relay switch at the provider end matches an ingress DLCI and port to the switching table for that port. It then looks up the egress port and DLCI to which it should send the traffic.
- **LMI functions**
    - Learn about the virtual circuits that are configured and whether they are active or inactive.
    - Learn about any new virtual circuits that were created since the last poll.
    - Make sure that the link to the switch is alive.
    - Set up switched virtual circuits as needed.
- **LMI types**
    - The Frame Relay Forum is the oldest specified LMI type and is the default LMI for Cisco routers.
    - ANSI T1.617 Annex D, also known as LMI Annex D, is the current ANSI specification for encapsulation.
    - ITU-T Q.933 Annex A is commonly referred to as LMI Annex A.
- **RFC 1490/2427**
    - Allows for the encapsulation of multiple protocols, including nonroutable protocols, over a Frame Relay circuit by adding a special header.
    - Allows for address resolution over Frame Relay.
    - The header contains an NLPID that identifies the protocol being encapsulated. It can additionally add a SNAP header if there is no specific NLPID for the protocol.

- **Frame Relay maps** A Frame Relay map is similar to the Frame Relay switch's switching table. It tracks the ingress DLCI and port to an egress DLCI and port for forwarding decisions.
- **Inverse ARP** Inverse ARP is a method of address resolution that is used when only the DLCI is known.
- **Topology options**
  - NBMA uses a single subnet, one-to-many broadcast method to keep all routers informed of routes and circuits on the network. It works well for small networks with very few PVCs.
  - Sub-interfaces using full-mesh work well in small-to-medium networks. It permits several virtual interfaces to be created on a single physical interface. Each router has a PVC to every other router. This can be administratively costly in larger networks.
  - Sub-interfaces using the hub-and-spoke design work well for large networks. Again, several virtual interfaces are created on a single physical interface. The difference is that a hub site is established. Most satellite, or spoke, locations must go through the hub site to reach other spokes of the network. Although this is not as fault-tolerant as a full-mesh environment, it is practical and less expensive for most large network designs.
- ***Fault tolerance***
  - Full-mesh Frame Relay networks are the most fault-tolerant design.
  - In partial-mesh environments, use dial-on-demand routing (DDR) or backup interfaces to create a "fallback" plan for circuit failure.

Summary

Frame Relay is a cost-effective method of routing WAN traffic. Avoiding the usage of dedicated lines for large networks and using virtual circuits and sub-interfaces can result in savings recognized in the number of router interfaces, the cost of leased lines, and the ability to support bursty traffic. With RFC 1490 to provide for multiprotocol support and encapsulation, most networks can use and benefit from a Frame Relay WAN design. In the next chapter, we will explore the X.25 design.

Questions

The following review questions have been selected to help you test your knowledge of the subject matter contained in this chapter. You will also find these questions contained in the CD-ROM included with this book. Although these are not the questions you will find on the certification exams, knowing the answers to the review questions in this book will help cement the material in your mind as you prepare for the tests.

1. What are the three most common CIRs of a Frame Relay circuit?
   - **a.** 56 Kbps, 64 Kbps, and 128 Kbps
   - **b.** 56 Kbps, 64 Mbps, and 1.544 Mbps
   - **c.** 56 Mbps, 64 Kbps, and 1.544 Mbps
   - **d.** 56 Kbps, 64 Kbps, and 1.544 Mbps
2. What does PVC stand for?
   - **a.** Permanent Virtual Circuit
   - **b.** Permanent Virtual Channel
   - **c.** Permanent Visual Circuit
3. What type of switched network is Frame Relay?
   - **a.** Circuit switched
   - **b.** Packet switched
   - **c.** Relay switched
4. Which formula best describes how many routers it would take to create a full-mesh WAN with dedicated lines?
   - **a.** $(x \times x + 1)/2 = y$
   - **b.** $(x \times x - 1)/2 = y$
   - **c.** $x^2 = y$
   - **d.** $(x^2 \times x - 1)/2 = y$
5. Which formula best describes the number of Frame Relay circuits it would take to create a full-mesh Frame Relay WAN?
   - **a.** $(x \times x + 1)/2 = y$
   - **b.** $(x \times x - 1)/2 = y$
   - **c.** $x^2 = y$
   - **d.** $(x^2 \times x - 1)/2 = y$

6. A router is an example of what?
   a. DTE
   b. DCE
7. A FRAD is an example of what?
   a. DTE
   b. DCE
8. Frame Relay is patterned after what WAN technology?
   a. SNA
   b. X.21
   c. X.25
   d. V.35
9. Which DLCI is reserved for LMI signaling?
   a. 0
   b. 80
   c. 1023
   d. 15
10. True or False: The CIR is a hard limit that does not allow for oversubscription.
    a. True
    b. False
11. True or False: Each port in a Frame Relay switch has its own switching table.
    a. True
    b. False
12. Cisco uses which Frame Relay encapsulation as the default?
    a. ANSI LMI
    b. LMI Annex D
    c. Frame Relay Forum
13. Inverse ARP is used when what is known?
    a. DLCI
    b. LMI
    c. MAC address
    d. Network address

14. Because more than one virtual circuit can be created on each physical router interface, which routing protocol characteristic can be problematic?
    a. Hop count
    b. Split horizon
    c. Poison reverse
15. True or False: A sub-interface is treated like a separate physical interface by the routing protocols.
    a. True
    b. False
16. Based on what you have learned in this chapter, what type of specification do you think V.90 represents?
    a. ISDN
    b. Digital transmission over analog facilities
    c. Digital packet networking
17. Refer to Table 17-1. If a packet were received on DLCI 110, what will the switch do with it?
    a. Send it out port 1.
    b. Change the header and send it to DLCI 1.
    c. Send it to port 2 and change the DLCI to 50.
18. What would an NLPID value of 80 represent?
    a. A frame error has occurred.
    b. A SNAP header is to follow.
    c. LMI signaling is set to LMI Annex D.
19. If a Frame Relay switch tracks the DLCI and circuit on its switching table, what does the router at the customer end use?
    a. A similar switching table
    b. The routing table, with DLCIs appended
    c. A route switch processor
    d. A Frame Relay map
20. True or False: PVCs can be dynamically created.
    a. True
    b. False

Answers

1. What are the three most common CIRs of a Frame Relay circuit?

   d. 56 Kbps, 64 Kbps, and 1.544 Mbps

2. What does PVC stand for?

   a. Permanent Virtual Circuit

3. What type of switched network is Frame Relay?

   b. Packet switched

4. Which formula best describes how many routers it would take to create a full-mesh WAN with dedicated lines?

   c. $x^2 = y$

5. Which formula best describes the number of Frame Relay circuits it would take to create a full-mesh Frame Relay WAN?

   b. $(x \times x - 1)/2 = y$

6. A router is an example of what?

   a. DTE

7. A FRAD is an example of what?

   a. DTE

8. Frame Relay is patterned after what WAN technology?

   c. X.25

9. Which DLCI is reserved for LMI signaling?

   a. 0

10. True or False: The CIR is a hard limit that does not allow for oversubscription.

    b. False.
    Explanation: The Committed Information Rate is a maximum rate at which the service provider has guaranteed throughput. Anything exceeding that rate will be permitted if there is available bandwidth. However, if the traffic constantly exceeds the CIR, the provider will likely require an increase in the amount of CIR for which the customer is paying.

11. True or False: Each port in a Frame Relay switch has its own switching table.

    a. True.
    Explanation: Each port has a map of the DLCIs with which it is associated and instructions on how to handle packets coming from those DLCIs.

12. Cisco uses which Frame Relay encapsulation as the default?

    c. Frame Relay Forum

13. Inverse ARP is used when this is known.

    a. DLCI
    Explanation: If a switch is aware of the DLCI, it can send an ARP request asking for information about the interface associated with that DLCI.

14. Because more than one virtual circuit can be created on each physical router interface, which routing protocol characteristic can be problematic?

    b. Split horizon
    Explanation: Because split horizon says that it will not advertise a route through the same interface by which it learned the route, it does not function well with multiple virtual circuits on the same physical interface. The result is that not all networks will learn about each other.

15. True or False: A sub-interface is treated like a separate physical interface by the routing protocols.

    a. True
    Explanation: The creation of a sub-interface allows the router to treat packets to and from the sub-interface as though they were from an entirely different physical interface. This helps solve the split horizon problem.

16. Based on what you have learned in this chapter, what type of specification do you think V.90 represents?

    b. Digital transmission over analog facilities
    Explanation: Refer back to the section on LMI encapsulation methods, particularly regarding the ITU-T specifications for more information.

17. Refer to Table 17-1. If a packet were received on DLCI 110, what will the switch do with it?

    a. Send it out port 1.

    Explanation: By looking at the switching table, you can see that packets arriving through port 2 with a DLCI of 110 need to be sent out port 1 to DLCI 50.

18. What would an NLPID value of 80 represent?

    b. A SNAP header is to follow.

    Explanation: Because of the limited number of values available for protocols through NLPID, the value of 80 was set aside to indicate that a SNAP header will carry more information.

19. If a Frame Relay switch tracks the DLCI and circuit on its switching table, what does the router at the customer end use?

    d. A Frame Relay map

    Explanation: The router has a Frame Relay map that contains information similar to the provider equipment's switching table.

20. True or False: PVCs can be dynamically created.

    b. False

    Explanation: Dynamically created virtual circuits are known as *switched virtual circuits.* PVCs require manual creation and management.

Frequently Asked Questions (FAQs)

1. *What is RED or WRED?*

   Random Early Detection (RED) or Weighted Random Early Detection (WRED) allows a router—which normally does not do flow control on Frame Relay traffic and can easily send enough traffic to overload a Frame Relay switch—to detect congestion and randomly discard packets. The benefit is that TCP performs some complex flow control at the router end and can avoid discarded packets at the service provider end. It allows for some adaptive measures to be applied at the customer end—dynamically.

2. *What is traffic shaping?*

   Traffic shaping is a method by which routers can scale back the maximum burst rate of packets forwarded to the Frame Relay switch. This can help avoid congestion and packet discards at the service provider end.

3. *What is an SVC, and why would I use one?*

   Switched virtual circuits (SVCs) are still not very popular because of the difficulty in setting them up from a user perspective and in handling the setup/breakdown of the connection by the router. An SVC differs from a PVC in that it is dynamically created as needed by the router. The benefit is that it may be on a circuit that is not needed often. Because the consumer is charged for the SVC on a usage basis, this can represent a significant cost savings for the consumer. The biggest drawback is that if the router is forwarding Layer 3 packets over a Frame Relay network, it must do a route recalculation every time a circuit is set up or torn down. As you can imagine, if a network has to reconverge every time a circuit is needed, the network could be crippled.

Bibliography

Black, Ulysses. *Frame Relay Networks: Second Edition*, McGraw-Hill Series on Computer Communications, 1996.

Buckwalter, Jeff T. *Frame Relay: Technology and Practice*, Addison Wesley Longman, Inc., 2000.

Cisco Internetwork Design Course Manual, Version 3.0, Cisco Systems, April 1997.

Configuring ISDN Dial-Backup for Frame Relay Networks, Cisco Systems, **http://www.cisco.com/warp/public/125/fr_isdn_backup.html.**

Designing Packet Service Internetworks, Cisco Systems, **http://www.cisco.com/univercd/cc/td/doc/cisintwk/idg4/nd2009.htm#xtocid1346012.**

Frame Relay, Cisco Systems, **http://www.cisco.com/cpress/cc/td/cpress/fund/ith2nd/it2410.htm.**

Frame Relay Forum, **http://www.frforum.com.**

ANSI, **http://ansi.org.**

ITU-T, **http://www.itu.ch.**

CHAPTER 18

X.25 Design

Overview

In the last chapter, we explored Frame Relay design, which is more popular than X.25, the subject of the chapter at hand. The Consultative Committee for International Telegraph and Telephone (CCITT), which is now the International Telecommunications Union-Telecommunication Standardization Section (ITU-T), defined a standard for communication between data circuit-terminating equipment (DCE) and data terminal equipment (DTE) over public switched telephone networks (PSTNs), meaning that it was one of the earliest methods of sending data over telephone lines. This chapter will show you some basics about X.25 and how it relates to today's internetwork designs.

Service Fundamentals

Like Frame Relay, which is based on X.25 technology, X.25 networks are packet switched. It is available in most countries and can therefore be encountered whenever international communication links are being established. X.25 networks can be private, but most of the networks are public, known as public data networks (PDNs).

The keyword for X.25 is *reliable.* It is a connection-oriented protocol that uses reliable protocols at both the network and data-link layers of the OSI model. X.25 uses the Layer 2 Link Access Procedure Balanced (LAPB) reliable data-delivery method as well as the X.25 Packet-Level Protocol (PLP) to provide reliable virtual circuits. Both LAPB and PLP use sliding windows to provide for flow control. As you can imagine, this means extensive error checking, resulting in lower throughput and higher latency than with Frame Relay.

TIP: *The default encapsulation for a Cisco serial interface is the High-Level Data Link Control (HDLC). In order to use X.25, you must manually set the encapsulation using the following command:*

```
encapsulation x25
```

X.25 uses two basic communication components: the X.25 switch (which is usually a Cisco router configured as an X.25 switch) and the Packet

Assembler/Disassembler (PAD), which buffers, disassembles, and assembles the packets. As shown in Figure 18-1, the data-link layer handles the flow control between communication components. At the network layer, PLP handles error checking for the entire logical channel established between endpoints.

As you can see in Figure 18-2, the DTE end of the link is normally a Cisco router configured as an X.25 DTE. At the service provider end, the DCE is normally a concentrator or an X.25 switch. Between the two endpoints of a connection is a virtual circuit. This could conceivably be configured as a permanent data-link structure, but that would probably be overkill, considering the amount of error checking that is already in place for X.25.

Normally, the two endpoint routers would use switched virtual circuits (SVCs) to dynamically establish a link when needed. The router could reach the other end by mapping the X.121 address of the neighboring routers to their network layer address. You will learn a little more about X.121 addresses later in this section.

Figure 18-1 Reliable delivery

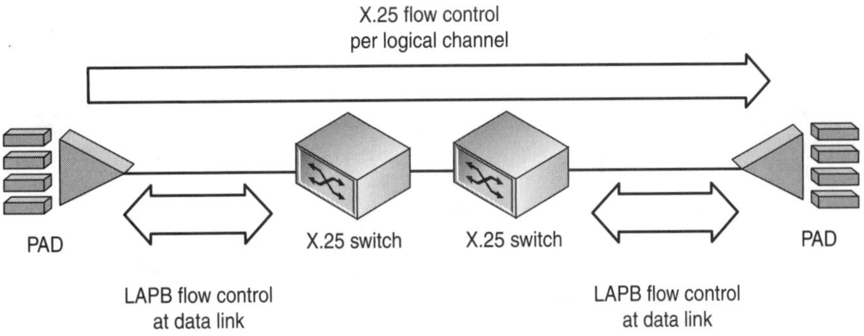

X.25 flow control
per logical channel
PAD
X.25 switch
X.25 switch
PAD
LAPB flow control
at data link
LAPB flow control
at data link

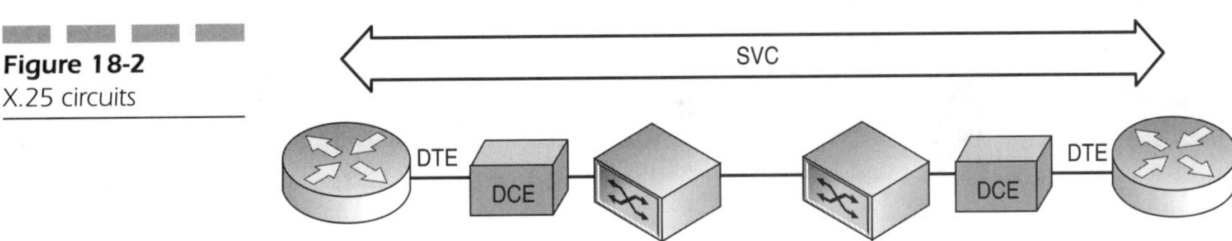

Figure 18-2 X.25 circuits

TIP: *Use an SVC when traffic is intermittent. Use a permanent virtual circuit (PVC) when more frequent data transmission is needed to conserve the bandwidth normally used in the setup and teardown process for an SVC.*

It is important to note that whereas Frame Relay addresses (DLCIs) are *locally significant*, meaning that the numbers are meaningful to the origination point, X.25 addresses are *globally significant*. You can think of this like the telephone system. You would not dial your own number if you wanted to call your friend Janet. You would dial Janet's number. Many people know Janet's number and can call her. Her number therefore is globally significant and unique to her telephone line within the entire world.

X.25 Protocol Suite

X.25 uses a basic three-layer model of communication that roughly corresponds to the first three layers of the OSI model. The X.25 model is shown in Figure 18-3.

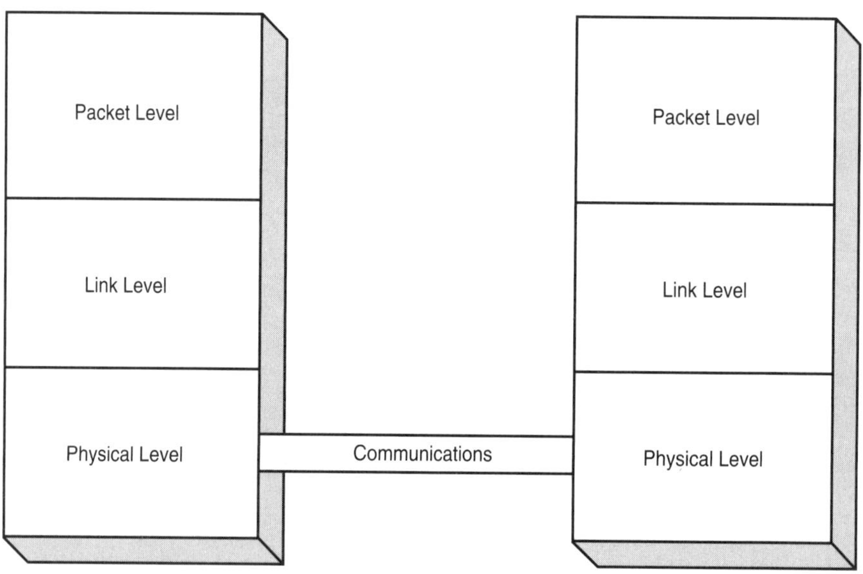

Figure 18-3
X.25 model

At the physical level, one of three physical layer recommendations can be used: X.21, X.21bis, or V.24. Each of these formats is an ITU-T recommendation for DTE operating over an analog line. X.21 is the most commonly used format in Europe and Japan. In the United States, X.21bis is normally used. It enables the DTE to communicate with the DCE by using a certain format for setting up and clearing calls on a channel.

X.21bis is very similar to EIA/TIA-232 (formerly referred to as *RS-232*). It is simply a physical specification that defines how the electrical signals will use the physical medium. It allows for the physical communication for X.25.

At the link level, some guarantees of reliable data transfer exist. The devices at both ends of the link are synchronized. The packets are sequenced and transferred efficiently, and errors are detected and recovered from. Finally, errors are identified and reported to the upper-layer protocols in order for a recovery or retransmission to take place. The data-link protocol used by X.25, as mentioned earlier in this chapter, is LAPB. The LAPB frame format is shown in Figure 18-4.

Three kinds of LAPB frames can be transmitted:

- **Information** This frame type actually contains the data being transmitted, including the frame sequence number in the control field.
- **Supervisory** This frame type either acknowledges that a frame was received in sequence so that the next frame can be sent, negative-acknowledges a frame if there were errors, or asks that the sender slow or stop transmission due to difficulties other than bad or out-of-sequence frames.
- **Unnumbered** This frame type is only used as a control frame.

At the network layer, PLP handles all services related to establishing and clearing virtual circuits and the creation of datagrams (or *packets*). PLP has five modes of communication:

- **Call setup** This is the first step in setting up an SVC. On a per-circuit basis, PLP begins the process of establishing the link by using X.121 addresses to start the call.

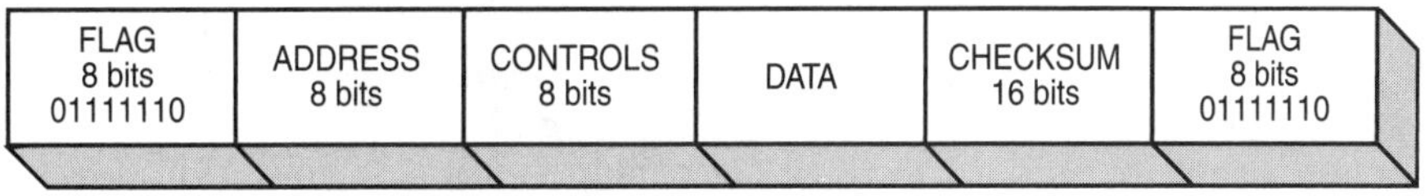

Figure 18-4
LAPB frame format

FLAG 8 bits 01111110	ADDRESS 8 bits	CONTROLS 8 bits	DATA	CHECKSUM 16 bits	FLAG 8 bits 01111110

- **Data transfer** This is, of course, the mode in which data crosses either a PVC or an SVC. Bit stuffing, assembly, and flow control are handled in this mode. Like the Call Setup mode, Data Transfer mode is handled on a per-circuit basis, meaning that many PVCs or SVCs can be handled simultaneously, all in different modes.
- **Idle** This mode is for SVCs only. In this mode, the SVC is still active, but no data is currently being transferred.
- **Call clearing** This mode is for SVCs when the call is over. It is the "teardown" part of the session and is handled on a per-circuit basis.
- **Restarting** This mode affects all circuits at once. It is like a reboot of a personal computer. The DTE and DCE must resynchronize with each other in order to establish communication. In the event that this causes instability in a network, it can be disabled.

X.121 Address Format

The X.121 address is used by PLP (the network layer protocol) when setting up the call for an SVC and has a maximum of 15 digits. It is a method for addressing the equipment on either end of the virtual circuit. It functions in much the same way as any other network layer address; it permits packets to go from a given source to a given destination. In the setup of a PVC, where each end of the virtual circuit is statically configured, it is not necessary to have X.121 addresses. The address permits a call setup for an SVC to find the destination DTE for the circuit.

TIP: *Think of the PVC as having an unlisted number, as you may have with your personal telephone number. The routers know to route the calls between source and destination. An SVC has no static mapping. It can be between any source and destination. The source has to look up the "411" on the destination to know how to call it, as you would do when calling for information on a person's phone number.*

An X.121 address is applied to a router interface using the following command in interface configuration mode:

```
# x25 address x.121-address
```

Figure 18-5 shows the format of an X.121 address.

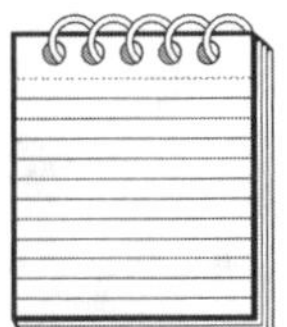

NOTE: *Although the X.121 address can be zero digits in length, a null X.121 address causes the Cisco router to act as the destination (rather than some connected DTE) for these packets.*

An X.121 address is also sometimes referred to as an *International Data Number* (IDN). The IDN is made up of the Data Network Identification Code (DNIC), which is an optional field. The DNIC is the identifier for the packet switched network (PSN) of the destination DTE (usually not necessary if the call is within the same PSN). The subfields of the DNIC are the actual PSN identifier (one digit) and the country identifier (three digits). These two fields make up the DNIC.

The National Terminal Number (NTN) is an assigned number that identifies the DTE in the PSN. It is unique within the PSN and can be a variable-length number, up to 10 digits long.

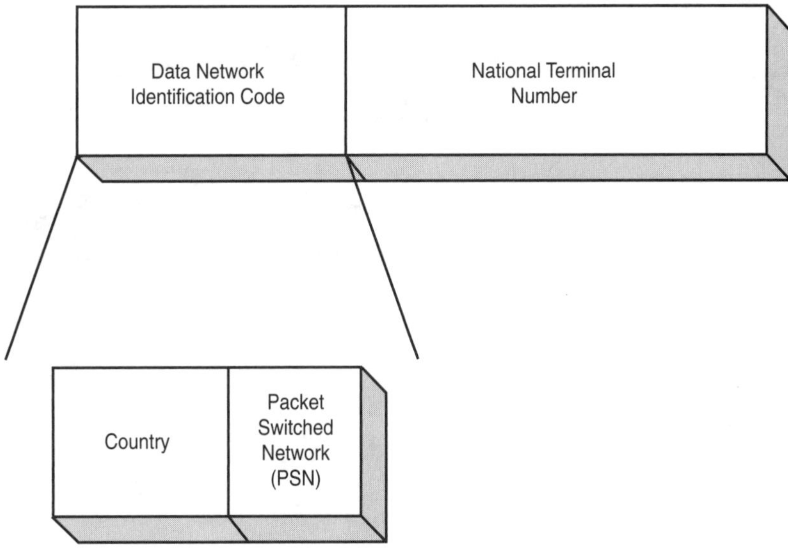

Figure 18-5
X.121 address

Non-Broadcast Multi-Access (NBMA)

X.25, like Frame Relay, has traditionally been treated as an NBMA protocol. This means that to create a robust, fault-tolerant network design, the network must be fully meshed, as shown in Figure 18-6. Every router has a connection to every other router. Traffic can almost always find a way to the destination.

A more practical approach is to use a partially meshed network in a hub-and-spoke configuration, as shown in Figure 18-7. This reduces the cost associated with having many interfaces and circuits, each with its own cost and tariffs.

With this partial-mesh design, fewer interface and circuits are necessary, but the hub router becomes a single point of failure. Some X.25 designs use a combination of full and partial mesh to create fault tolerance where absolutely necessary but to save money in areas of the network that can weather a potential outage.

Today, many of the issues of NBMA have been solved with the use of sub-interfaces in the network design.

Figure 18-6
Full-mesh NBMA

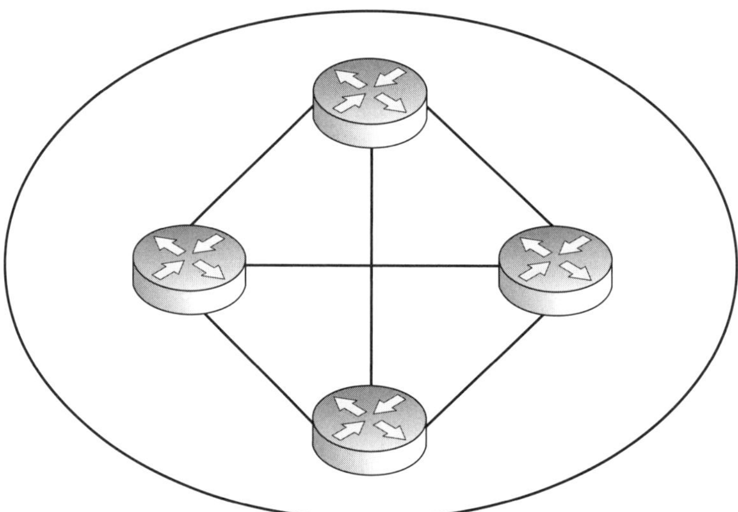

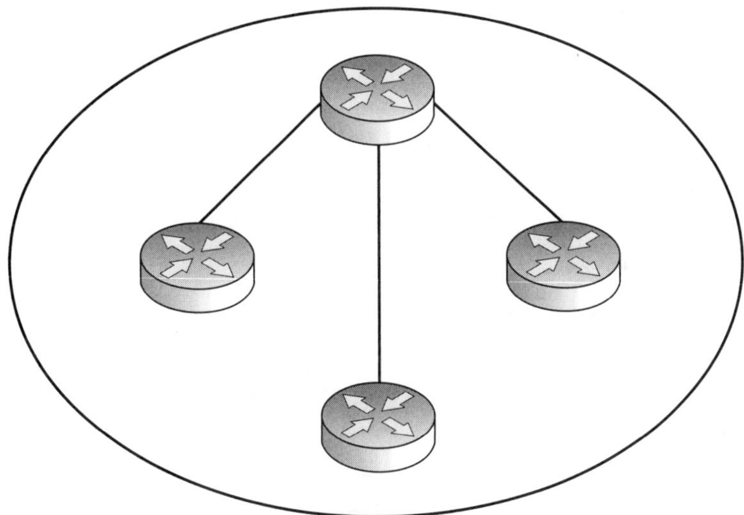

Figure 18-7
Partial-mesh NBMA

Sub-Interfaces

As with Frame Relay, you can configure sub-interfaces, as shown in Figure 18-8, on a single physical interface in order to prevent problems with split horizon and to extend the capacity of the router without purchasing more physical serial interfaces.

Split horizon, as you may remember, is a principle by which routes are not advertised out of the same interface on which they were received. This can be a problem for Frame Relay and other connection-oriented WAN protocols. Split horizon is enabled by default on X.25.

X.25 can be used on both point-to-point and multipoint sub-interfaces. Note that a sub-interface is inherently multipoint unless otherwise specified. Point-to-point sub-interfaces are used when encapsulating one or more protocols between two hosts. Multipoint interfaces are used to encapsulate one protocol to one or more hosts.

For more information on configuring sub-interfaces for X.25, refer to the Cisco Web site at **www.cisco.com/univercd/cc/td/doc/product/software/ios11/cbook/cx25.htm#41145**.

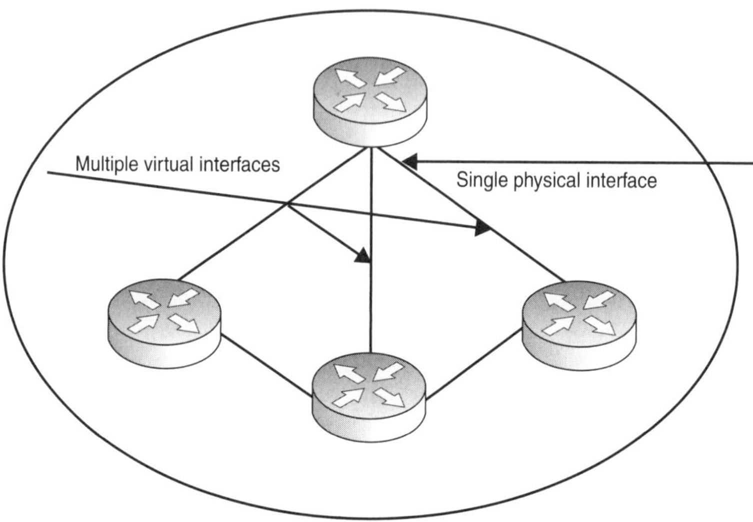

Figure 18-8
Sub-interfaces in X.25

Switching

Local X.25 switching between serial interfaces is supported on Cisco routers for both PVCs and SVCs. In Figure 18-9, you can see that a single router, acting as an X.25 switch, is enabling the connection of two X.25 clouds. It does this by using the software to forward an incoming call from one serial interface to another.

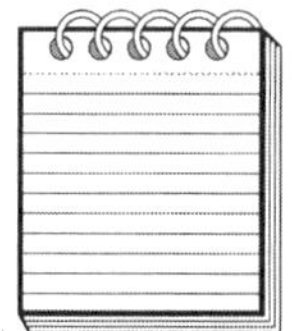

NOTE: *Cisco routers can be configured to act as an X.25 switch. Likewise, they may be configured to act as a Frame Relay switch.*

In Figure 18-9, Router A receives a call from a connected PAD. It forwards the call through a second serial interface to Router B, which then forwards the call to the destination DTE. The router interface can be configured to act as a DTE or DCE, but the software will handle the rout-

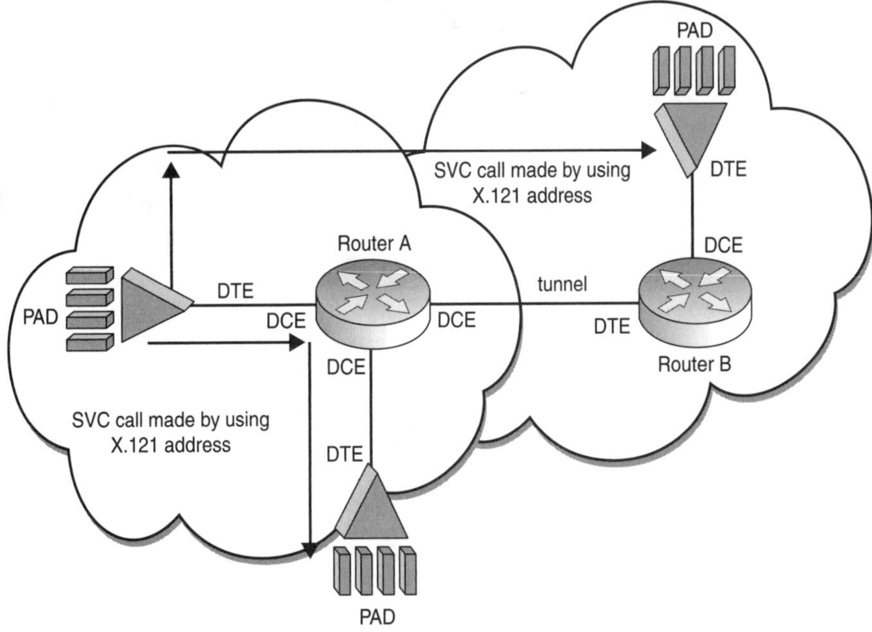

Figure 18-9 Local X.25 switching

ing of calls. To enable this feature, use this command in the global configuration mode:

```
x25 routing
```

Cisco also supports remote X.25 switching, which enables the routers to establish a TCP connection between the source and destination DTEs. This data stream will enable reliable communication between the two devices.

The router requires some mapping in order to know how and where to route the packets. The X.25 switching map must be configured manually and is read in a top-down fashion by the router, so the order of entry is significant.

If you need more specific information on how to set up the mapping for X.25, consult the Cisco Web site at **www.cisco.com/univercd/cc/td/doc/product/software/ssr83/rpc_r/48377.htm#xtocid382827**.

Problem Areas

One problem with X.25 is that you may need to configure static routing between endpoints. X.25 typically reroutes in the event of a failure due to its reliable nature, so the use of a dynamic routing protocol is somewhat redundant. It can also be costly because many PDNs charge per packet. Imagine the cost escalation for frequent routing protocol updates and broadcasts! Although it is somewhat manually intensive to configure static routes, it is usually the best solution to this X.25 problem.

Case Study

Campus Research is considering using X.25 in the WAN because of the fault-tolerance required, especially for two new locations in Michigan. These new locations, in Trent and Lansing, will be communicating frequently with the network in Detroit. The data must be sent in a reliable manner.

The company is quite interested in establishing the utmost fault tolerance in Michigan, but for connections to St. Louis and Milwaukee, they are not as concerned. They know that because they will pay based on usage, it is less important for them to have constant connectivity at those sites.

Your task is to find a workable solution for an X.25 network that will address the company's concerns with the lowest cost possible. Although there is no one right answer to any given design problem, one possible solution is provided in Appendix C, "Suggested Solutions to Case Studies."

Study Hints

Although no one can disclose test items or test content, we can give hints as to what might be valuable to study. For this chapter, certain key facts need to be reviewed and remembered:

- X.25 is a *packet-switched* WAN protocol.
- X.25 is an *ITU-T standard* that defines the way data communications will be carried between a DTE and a DCE over a PSTN.

- When X.25 is used for a public network, the network is referred to as a packet data network (PDN).
- The command to enable X.25 on a Cisco router is *encapsulation x25*.
- The layers of the X.25 protocol closely correspond to the first three layers of the OSI model: *physical, data link,* and *network*.
- X.25 is a *connection-oriented, reliable protocol* that provides sliding window flow control at the data-link and network layers.
- X.25 uses *X.21bis* as its physical layer protocol.
- X.25 uses *X.121 addressing* for DTEs. These addresses can also be referred to as IDNs. Addresses used in X.25 are globally significant.
- *LAPB* is used at the data-link layer to provide a reliable transmission of frames.
- *PLP* is used at the network layer to provide a reliable transmission of packets.
- *Call management* functions are used in X.25 when SVCs are used. PVCs are permanent and do not require setup or teardown of the virtual circuit.
- X.25 networks can be set up in a traditional *full- or partial-mesh NBMA manner* or with *sub-interfaces* to add flexibility and do away with the split horizon problems of a traditional NBMA network.
- Cisco routers support *local and remote X.25 switching,* permitting the router to function as an X.25 (or Frame Relay) switch. This requires manual mapping of the DTEs.

CCDP Tips

This section contains an abbreviated list of topics covered in this chapter. Think of this section as the equivalent of reading *Cliff's Notes* instead of reading an entire book. You will get the general idea of the chapter but will benefit more from reading the chapter in its entirety.

- **Overview** X.25 is the packet-switched WAN protocol on which Frame Relay was based. It was defined by the CCITT (now called the ITU-T) in order to allow for data communications over traditional phone lines (POTS) and public phone networks (PSTN).

- **X.25 Fundamentals** X.25 is a connection-oriented, reliable WAN protocol that corresponds to the first three layers of the OSI model: physical, data link, and network. It provides encapsulation of the data over telephone networks between DTEs and DCEs with reliability built in at the data-link and network layers. Through the use of X.25 switches and PADs, the data is encapsulated into a frame and is sent to the destination DTE, which is an addressable device.
- **Protocol basics** Physical-layer services are provided by X.21bis (X.21 in Europe and Japan), which is a physical communication specification that is very similar to EIA/TIA-232. It allows for the formatting of the transmission across the wire. X.25 uses LAPB at the data-link layer. Error checking is performed at this layer as well as sliding window flow control. At the network layer, PLP handles all services related to establishing and clearing virtual circuits (PVCs and SVCs) and the creation of datagrams (or *packets*). If LAPB or PLP detects an error, it reports the error back to the upper layer protocols.
- **Addressing in X.25** At the network layer, PVCs do not require anything special from PLP in order to be able to communicate. The endpoints are known and statically configured. For SVCs, however, it is necessary to have a way to address the DTE. This is done with X.121 addresses. The X.121 address can be up to 15 digits and contains a National Terminal Number (NTN) and an optional Data Network Identification Code (DNIC) consisting of a country identifier and a PSN number. A null X.121 address (0 digits in length) is treated as though it were bound for the router.
- **X.25 design** X.25 can be designed as any NBMA network using full-mesh for complete fault-tolerance or using partial-mesh for cost savings. However, sub-interface usage is recommended to avoid problems with split horizon and to extend the use of the physical interfaces.
- **X.25 switching** Cisco routers can act as either DCE or DTE and can provide local or remote X.25 switching. This permits calls to be forwarded based on a static map of X.25 DTE.

Summary

Configuring and operating an X.25 environment is quite similar to running a Frame Relay environment, as you have seen. Therefore, many of the design issues of Frame Relay also translate to X.25. It is unlikely that you will ever be asked to design a new X.25 network, because many of the telcos that have traditionally used an X.25 backbone are now finding ways to transport the X.25 traffic over an IP backbone. It is important, however, that you be familiar with X.25, not only for certification tests, but also for an understanding of some of the design issues faced at the service provider level.

Questions

The following review questions have been selected to help you test your knowledge of the subject matter contained in this chapter. You will also find these questions contained in the CD-ROM included with this book. Although these are not the questions you will find in the certification exams, knowing the answers to the review questions in this book will help cement the material in your mind as you prepare for the tests.

1. Which type of protocol is X.25?

- **a.** Connectionless
- **b.** Connection oriented

2. What other WAN protocol is patterned after X.25?

- **a.** ISDN
- **b.** Frame Relay
- **c.** T1/E1

3. X.21bis corresponds to which other physical specification?

- **a.** V.35
- **b.** V.90
- **c.** IEEE 802.3
- **d.** EIA/TIA-232

4. What is the default encapsulation for a serial interface on a Cisco router?
   a. IETF
   b. HDLC
   c. PPP
5. Which command will enable X.25 switching on a Cisco router?
   a. x25 switching
   b. encapsulation x25
   c. x25 routing
   d. route x25
6. X.25 provides flow control at which two layers of the OSI model?
   a. Physical and network
   b. Physical and data link
   c. Data link and network
7. True or False: A sub-interface is point-to-point unless specified as multipoint.
   a. True
   b. False
8. A Cisco router will act as the destination of an X.25 call when which condition exists?
   a. The country code is null.
   b. The IDN is 0 digits in length.
   c. The PSN equals the DTE address of the router.
9. A DTE can be addressed using which type of network address specification?
   a. V.90
   b. V.35
   c. X.121
   d. X.21bis
10. True or False: The call setup mode for PLP is only applicable to SVCs.
   a. True
   b. False

11. Which type of LAPB frame is used as a control frame?
    a. Information
    b. Supervisory
    c. Unnumbered
12. True or False: X.25 addresses are locally significant.
    a. True
    b. False
13. PLP functions at what layer of the OSI model?
    a. Physical
    b. Data Link
    c. Network
14. What aspect of X.25 switching makes it administratively cumbersome?
    a. Maps must be manually configured.
    b. Static routes must be used.
    c. The PSTN provider must enable the process on the switch.
15. What two fields make up the DNIC in an X.121 address? (Select two.)
    a. Country
    b. PLP
    c. PDN
    d. PSN
16. LAPB functions at what layer of the OSI model?
    a. Physical
    b. Data link
    c. Network
17. Which X.25 device provides for buffering?
    a. DTE
    b. DCE
    c. PAD
    d. LAPB

18. What is CCITT now known as?
    a. CIT
    b. ITU
    c. EIA/TIA
    d. ITU-T
19. What is the command to enable a Cisco router to forward incoming calls to another serial interface?
    a. x.25 routing
    b. router x25 *process-id*
    c. x25 routing enable
    d. x25 routing
20. True or False: A multipoint sub-interface is used when you want to run multiple protocols over virtual circuits.
    a. True
    b. False

Answers

1. Which type of protocol is X.25?
   b. Connection-oriented
   Explanation: Remember X.25 is reliable. You cannot guarantee reliability with a connectionless, best-effort delivery protocol.
2. What other WAN protocol is patterned after X.25?
   b. Frame Relay
   Explanation: The development of Frame Relay is closely patterned after X.25 operations.
3. X.21bis corresponds to which other physical specification?
   d. EIA/TIA-232
   Explanation: X.21bis uses much the same physical specifications as RS-232, which is now referred to as *EIA/TIA-232*.

4. What is the default encapsulation for a serial interface on a Cisco router?
   b. HDLC
   Explanation: This is a common configuration error by beginners. Always remember to set the encapsulation to what is needed, even if it is HDLC!

5. Which command will enable X.25 switching on a Cisco router?
   c. x25 routing
   Explanation: It may sound funny, but the command x25 routing does turn on the capability of the router to act as a switch.

6. X.25 provides flow control at which two layers of the OSI model?
   c. Data link and network
   Explanation: Sliding window flow control is provided by both LAPB and PLP at the data link and network layers.

7. True or False: A sub-interface is point-to-point unless specified as multipoint.
   b. False
   Explanation: Cisco sub-interfaces are multipoint unless specified otherwise.

8. A Cisco router will act as the destination of an X.25 call when which condition exists?
   b. The IDN is 0 digits in length.
   Explanation: The IDN can be 0 to 15 digits in length; however, if the field is 0 digits, it is considered a null address and the router will act as the final destination.

9. A DTE can be addressed using which type of network address specification?
   c. X.121
   Explanation: The X.121 specification defines the network addressing that is used for DTEs.

10. True or False: The call setup mode for PLP is only applicable to SVCs.
    a. True
    Explanation: Call setups and teardowns are only necessary with dynamically created virtual circuits, such as SVCs.

11. Which type of LAPB frame is used as a control frame?
    c. Unnumbered
    Explanation: The only purpose for the unnumbered frame is its use as a control frame.

12. True or False: X.25 addresses are locally significant.
    b. False
    Explanation: X.25 addresses enable a source to call a destination by calling its unique identifier. Therefore, X.25 addresses are said to be *globally significant*.

13. PLP functions at what layer of the OSI model?
    c. Network
    Explanation: The Packet-Level Protocol functions at the network (or packet) layer of the OSI model.

14. What aspect of X.25 switching makes it administratively cumbersome?
    a. Maps must be manually configured.
    Explanation: The router will not be able to find the ends of the X.25 calls in a switch setting without a map. As with X.25 and Frame Relay switches, the router must have a manually configured map to locate the destinations.

15. What two fields make up the DNIC in an X.121 address? (Select two.)
    a. Country
    d. PSN
    Explanation: Although the DNIC is optional, when it is present, it consists of a three-digit country identifier and a one-digit PSN.

16. LAPB functions at what layer of the OSI model?
    b. Data link
    Explanation: LAPB is a *link access procedure* and functions at the data-link layer.

17. Which X.25 device provides for buffering?
    c. PAD
    Explanation: The Packet Assembler/Disassembler providers for the handling of the X.25 frames as well as buffering.

18. What is CCITT now known as?
    d. ITU-T

19. What is the command to enable a Cisco router to forward incoming calls to another serial interface?
    d. x25 routing
    Explanation: The forwarding of calls is done when the router is acting as an X.25 switch. The command to enable switching is x25 routing.

20. True or False: A multipoint sub-interface is used when you want to run multiple protocols over virtual circuits.
    b. False
    Explanation: A multipoint sub-interface handles the encapsulation of a single protocol for multiple hosts.

Frequently Asked Questions (FAQs)

1. *What is a hunt group?*

   Hunt groups were introduced with v12.0(3)T of the Cisco IOS in order to provide some load-balancing features for X.25 virtual circuits. You can read more about how to configure hunt groups at Cisco's Web site at **www.cisco.com/warp/public/133/ x25_load_balancing.html**.

2. *What is XOT?*

   RFC 1613 outlines the transmission of X.25 over TCP/IP. This has become known as XOT (X.25 Over TCP). It enables X.25 traffic to be tunneled through an IP backbone in order to provide support for legacy X.25 networks and to link together X.25 networks that have no physical connection. More information is available from the RFC or at Cisco's Web site at **www.cisco.com/warp/customer/ 133/x25_over_tcpip.html**.

Bibliography

Cisco Internetwork Design Course Manual, Version 3.0, April 1997, Cisco Systems, Inc.

Designing Packet Service Internetworks, Cisco Systems, Inc., **www.cisco.com/univercd/cc/td/doc/cisintwk/idg4/nd2009.htm#xtocid1346012**

ITU-T, **www.itu.ch**

Protocols.com, X.25, **www.protocols.com/pbook/x25.htm**

X.25, Cisco Systems, Inc., **www.cisco.com/univercd/cc/td/doc/cisintwk/ito_doc/x25.htm**

CHAPTER 19

Remote Access Design

Overview

As we continue our study of WAN design, we are now going to spend a little time talking about how to establish communication between the remote user and the enterprise network. These users may be telecommuters, who require "on-all-the-time" access to voice, video, and data, or they may be "road warriors"—the sales force and so on. Each particular set of users will have a particular set of requirements. What they will all have in common is the need for fast, reliable service that allows them to get their job done.

In the late 1980s, when many users began to discover the online community through the use of services like CompuServe and "Mom-and-Pop" bulletin board systems (BBSs), it was considered a luxury to have a modem that could transmit and receive at 9600 bits-per-second (bps). These days, it is common for many systems to come with an internal V.90 (56 Kbps) modem. In addition to the slow speeds with which users once had to contend, most online service providers charged by the hour for usage and rarely had local phone numbers—unless you were in a large metropolitan area.

The growing popularity of the Internet drove the need for faster access and lower costs. As rates came down for online services, more users began to sign on. Gradually the business world jumped on the bandwagon and now represents a major percentage of the Internet usage in the United States.

Connection Technology

In this section we will look at the many ways you can physically connect remote users to an enterprise network or a service provider network. Whether a user is dialing into a network over a traditional Public Switched Telephone Network (PSTN) or connecting through a digital line, it is important to select the technology that is going to work best for each particular case. Making the right decision up front will help avoid frustration later on.

Analog Services

The oldest, and still most common, method of connection to a public or private network is through dial-up connection using analog modem technology. Small Office/Home Office (SOHO) users or mobile users connect their PCs to telephone outlets and use the PSTN to send and receive data. This is a very inexpensive connection method and is easily accessible to most users.

As shown in Figure 19-1, mobile users connect through what is called a *local loop* to a Central Office (CO) of a telephone services provider. The data goes through the public phone network (PSTN) and, through a CO at the destination end, the data makes its way to a bank or pool of modems at the destination's central site. If the central site's operations are substantial enough, they could use an access server in addition to modem pools and routers.

Integrated Services Digital Network

In the 1990s, telephone companies introduced Integrated Services Digital Network (ISDN) services in an attempt to create an all-digital network for remote users. Today many home users connect to the Internet and/or their main office by using an ISDN connection.

First we will cover some of the basic terminology related to ISDN. At the user's end of the network is what is called a *terminal adapter* (TA). This is

Figure 19-1
Analog connections

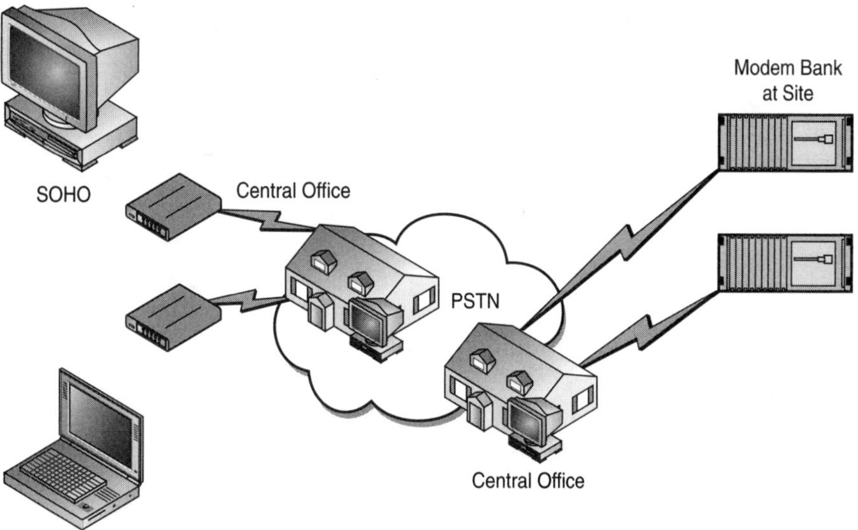

normally an external device that converts the electrical signal between the ISDN network and the non-ISDN equipment (for example, your PC). Equipment that is ISDN-compatible is referred to as *terminal equipment* (TE) *Type 1,* and non-ISDN-compatible equipment is referred to as *TE Type 2.* Type 1 equipment does not require a TA.

There are also a couple of different types of network termination for ISDN lines. In Figure 19-2, we see various equipment types connected together via ISDN. The TE2 device is linked to a TA, which then links to a *network termination* (NT) point. The NT device can either be a Type 1 or Type 2. Type 1 devices connect the four-wire subscriber end to the two-wire line going to the CO (the local loop). A Type 2 device is a "smarter" device, usually a switch, which can direct traffic between different provider services.

Figure 19-2 ISDN equipment

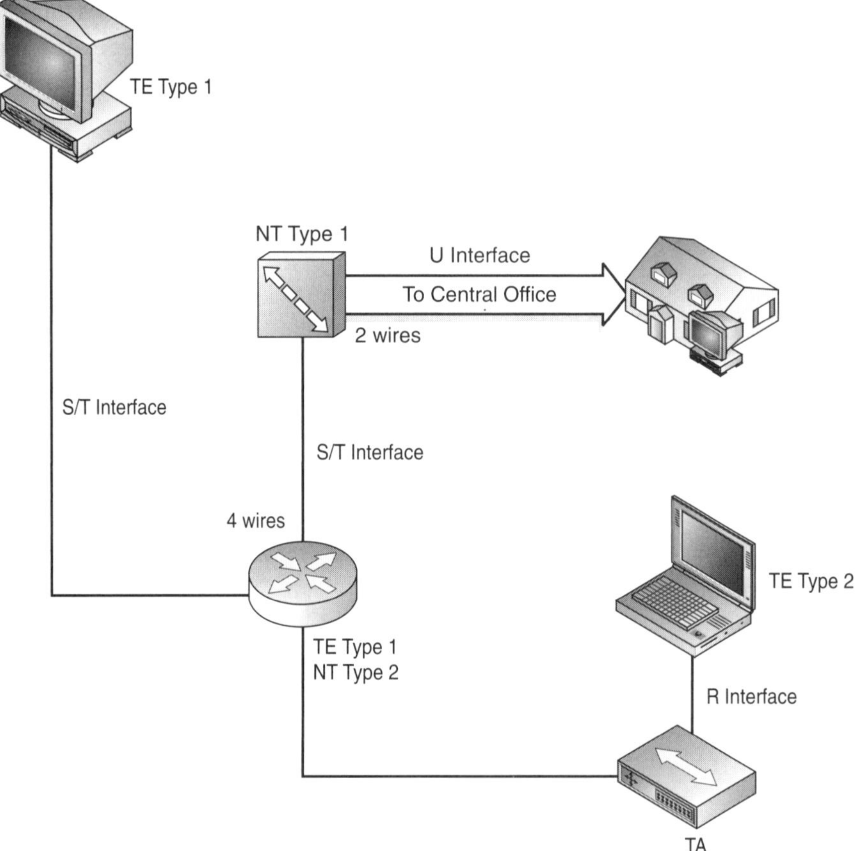

The interface types labeled in Figure 19-2 identify the different types of connections between devices that reside in an ISDN design. An S/T interface links a TE1 device to an NT (of either type). The R interface is used between a non-ISDN compatible device, TE2, and the TA. Finally, the link between the NT and the greater ISDN services network is referred to as the U interface.

There are two main types of ISDN connections:

- Basic Rate Interface (BRI)
- Primary Rate Interface (PRI)

The BRI usually runs on the traditional, twisted-pair copper wiring used to deliver phone service. It is a 144 Kbps line that is divided into two *bearer channels,* called "B" channels, and a *data channel,* called a "D" channel. The B channels are 64 Kbps each and carry voice or data traffic. The D channel is used for signaling, telling the PSTN how to handle the digital traffic. It is operates at 16 Kbps. This three-channel pattern is shown in Figure 19-3.

How does this work in reality? A SOHO user has what amounts to two connections that can be used for voice or data. It is generally implemented with a channel that is "always on" for data and a channel that can be used for voice or multiplexed to the other B channel running data to make a higher bandwidth pipe of 128 Kbps.

A PRI, on the other hand, is designed to handle networks requiring higher amounts of bandwidth, such as corporate offices or central sites where a large number of incoming ISDN calls are terminated. A PRI is made up of 23 B channels to one D channel that is shared among all of the B channels. Figure 19-4 shows how a PRI and BRI might be used in normal application.

One way to look at it is that a PRI is a "T1 worth of BRIs," as one engineer that we met stated it. In other words, where a T1 has 24 64 Kbps channels that can be aggregated into a single T1 or split into single channels or groups of channel, a PRI has 23 64 Kbps channels and a 16 Kbps signaling channel.

Figure 19-3
ISDN BRI

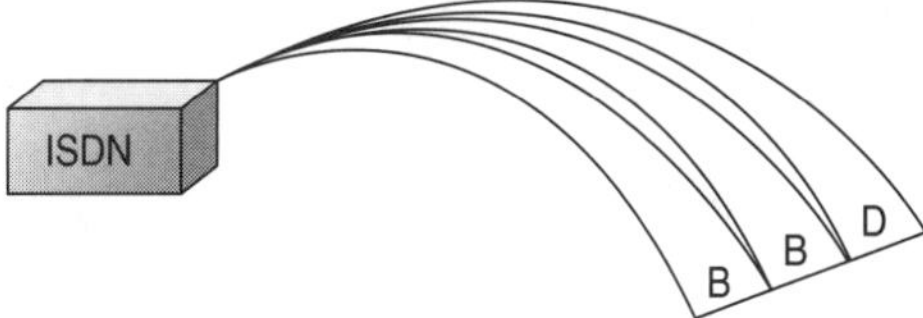

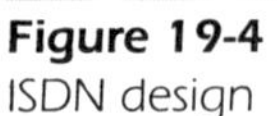

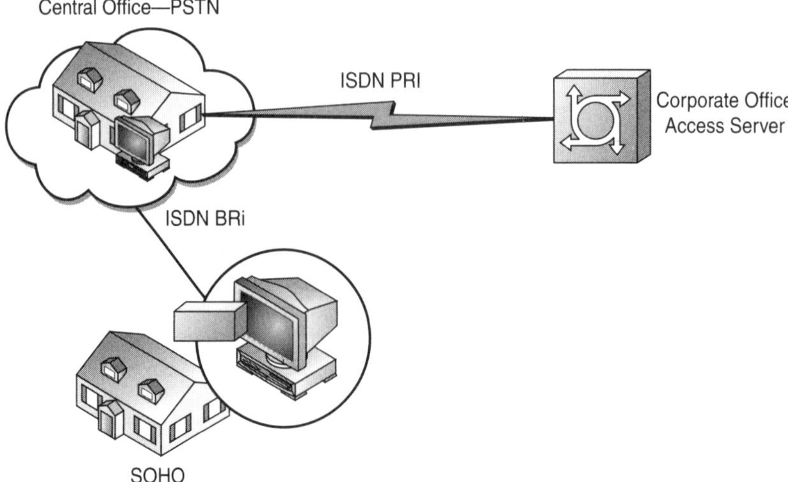

Figure 19-4
ISDN design

In fact the PRI uses either a T1 (in the United States) or an E1 (outside the United States) for its bit-transport layer. If it uses T1, it has the parameters and capacity stated in the paragraph above. If it is using E1, it actually handles 30 B channels and a single, shared-signaling channel.

NOTE: *T1 uses in-band signaling, whereas E1 uses out-of-band signaling.*

So, does ISDN really buy a home user a lot of advantage over a typical dial-up solution? Probably not as much as you might think. It certainly had its advantages in the beginning, when V.34 technology was the order of the day, but with today's modems connecting at 56 Kbps, ISDN has very little bandwidth advantage. The biggest plus for ISDN is that it has very fast call setup, as compared to dial-up services. It is complex to order, install, and configure, however, and despite its having been in use for several years now, it is still fraught with problems.

For the corporate applications, this is not as common a design as it once was, now that Digital Subscriber Line (DSL) is becoming more widely available.

Digital Subscriber Line

Another way to use existing telephone lines to transmit and receive large amounts of data is through DSL. DSL is a true "always-on" technology, eliminating the need for call setup, which is a great benefit over ISDN or analog dial-up.

The different types of DSL are shown in Table 19-1. When dealing with remote users, who download more data than they send, ADSL is the logical choice. Most often, DSL is referred to as *xDSL,* when the type is not known. For our purposes, we will discuss DSL somewhat generically and refer to it as, simply, DSL.

Table 9-2 shows the average transmission rates a DSL user can expect, depending upon the user's distance from the Telco CO. The Telco tests your distance from the closest CO by doing a *loop qualification test.* If you are farther out than 18,000 feet, you will not be able to use DSL. Many customers are still waiting to be eligible for DSL, which can be quite frustrating. If you are close enough to the CO, however, even the worst DSL delivery speed is better than the best speed available through analog or ISDN services.

Table 19-1

Types of DSL

Type of DSL	What It Does
ADSL (Asymmetric)	High bandwidth downstream, lower bandwidth upstream. Great for home users.
SDSL (Symmetric)	Data rate is the same in both directions. Useful for servers, small ISPs, and so on.
IDSL (ISDN/DSL)	Combination of ISDN and DSL technology that provides a 144 Kbps connection.
RADSL (Rate-Adaptive DSL)	Downstream rate varies according to the phone line quality (1.5 Mbps to 7 Mbps).
HDSL (High-Bit-Rate DSL)	Uses two telephone lines. Transmits/receives at about 1.5 Mbps.
VDSL (Very-High-Bit-Rate DSL)	For users within 4,500 feet of CO, downstream rates can be from 15–32 Mbps and 1.5–2 Mbps upstream.
G.lite (Type of ADSL)	Typical type of ADSL for home users. 384 Kbps upstream and 1.5–2 Mbps downstream.
G.dmt (Type of ADSL)	Up to 8 Mbps downstream and 1.5–2 Mbps upstream.

Table 19-2
DSL Rates

Distance from CO (in Feet)	Average Speed
0–9,500	1.568 Mbps
9,501–12,500	1.040 Mbps
12,501–14,900	784 Kbps
14,901–18,000	416 Kbps

With DSL, a user connects to a service provider (usually the same one that sold him the service) with a DSL modem. It doesn't dial up to the provider—you turn it on and it is connected. You can still use your telephone service while online, because the two signals will not interfere with each other. Like ISDN, the ability to use voice and data transmission simultaneously is a big selling point for home users. As you can see in Figure 19-5, the DSL modem then talks to a *DSL Access Multiplexer* (DSLAM) at the CO. The DSLAM differentiates between what is voice and what is data. The data is forwarded on to the Internet backbone—usually through ATM—while the voice traffic is forwarded to a PSTN switch for handling.

Sounds great, right? The catch is that you have to be close to a CO. The closer you are, the faster your speed will be. DSL simply isn't available to everyone. It is a "good news, bad news" technology. The good news is that it's the best technology going, if you can get it. The bad news is, you may not be able to get it at the speeds you want, if at all. If a user does decide to connect to DSL, there may be several "set up" visits, both from the phone company and from the service provider, if different. It can be complex to set up, and this fact alone can make it too frustrating for many users. They want a technology that is easily accessible and comprehensible.

Cable

The final type of connection technology we are going to discuss is the use of the cable system for data connections. Cable companies are now beginning to take advantage of the very large market to which they have access through their television broadcast delivery. It stands to reason that if the large number of television subscribers also uses the cable infrastructure for data communication, the cable companies can expand their services and their profits.

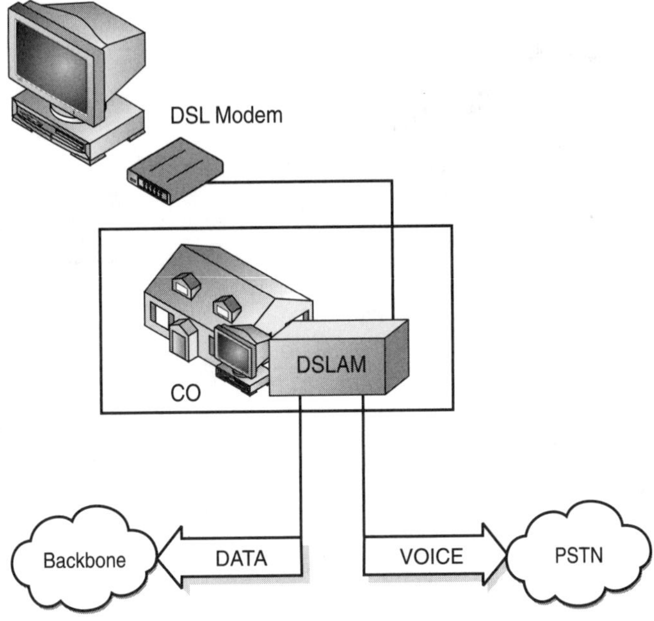

Figure 19-5 DSL connection

NOTE: *Since the data channel is different from the television broadcast channels, you can watch television and surf the Internet at the same time.*

As shown in Figure 19-6, downstream rates can be very fast (up to 5 Mbps, in some instances) over the cable service. By using a cable modem connected to the in-home cable jack and to a mini-hub serving the Ethernet port of a PC, a home user can expect very fast download speeds for general use. Most often, the data stream is asymmetric. The user uploads data through a dial-up modem and downloads it through the cable modem, although some cable companies are beginning to create a bi-directional cable infrastructure. In the beginning, with very few users on the cable data network, the speeds are good, and the service is reliable.

When many users in an area begin to all use cable modems, however, the service begins to slow and become less attractive, as seen in Figure 19-7. The shared backbone speed, of course, will depend greatly upon what each

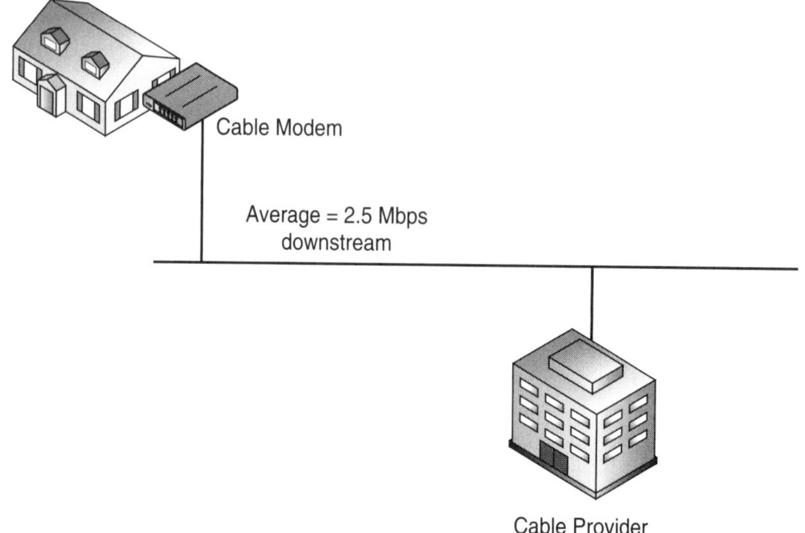

Figure 19-6 Cable modem, scenario one

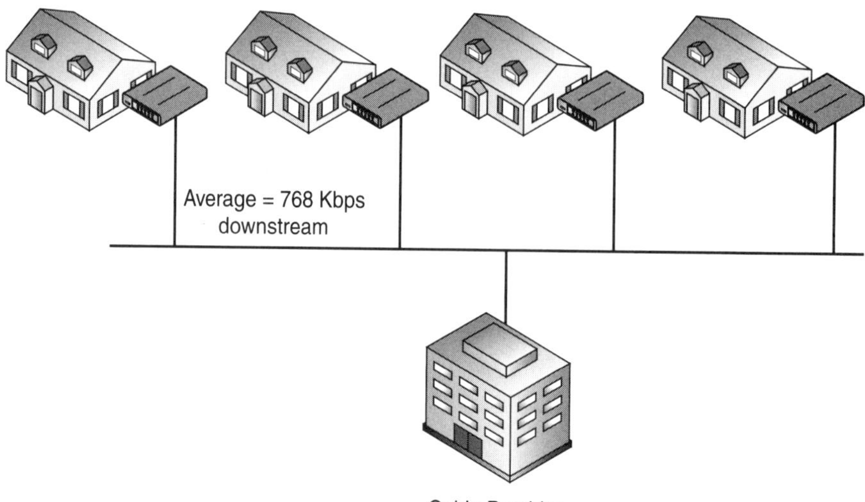

Figure 19-7 Cable modem, scenario two

user is doing on the network. It becomes more like a shared Ethernet (hub) topology and less like a dedicated bandwidth (switch) topology.

Another problem that frequently crops up with the use of cable modems is security. Because "always-on" technology leaves your home system or network vulnerable all the time, it is imperative that you secure your systems with some type of Internet firewall. There are many inexpensive choices on the market that work well with cable modem technology. This is especially important when the home user is accessing the corporate enterprise network (telecommuting). Yet this is one area where corporate security policies seem to be forgotten.

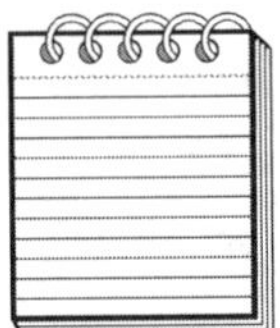

NOTE: *Remember to build security into the remote user design regardless of which method of connection technology is used.*

A Word About Virtual Private Networks

A relatively new technology that is not addressed in the Cisco CID course but that probably will be in the next revision is *virtual private networks* (VPNs). The main focus of the VPN is to create a point-to-point tunnel, sometime with encryption for security, from the remote user to the central site, as shown in Figure 19-8. Microsoft Windows products have had software VPNs included for quite some time. It is, however, somewhat complex for most users to configure and manage. It is also vulnerable to "man-in-the-middle" attacks that eavesdrop on the tunnel and launch attacks from within. A truly secure tunnel will break off communications if a breach should occur.

VPN technology is going to become more prominent as wireless technology advances. Streams of data traffic through radio systems will need to be kept separate. Multiple sites could be using the same private addressing scheme to connect their remote users. The mixing of these traffic streams could result in a breakdown in communication.

Another important area that VPNs will address is the remote access granted to business partners. VPN management will grant access on a per-user or per-network basis, allowing some resources to be accessed while others are hidden. VPNs will not always be managed at the central site, however. More and more, service providers are creating service-level agreements (SLAs) to manage VPNs for their customers. This takes the administrative burden away from the central site and puts it back on the provider. Because providers manage large amounts of traffic and equipment

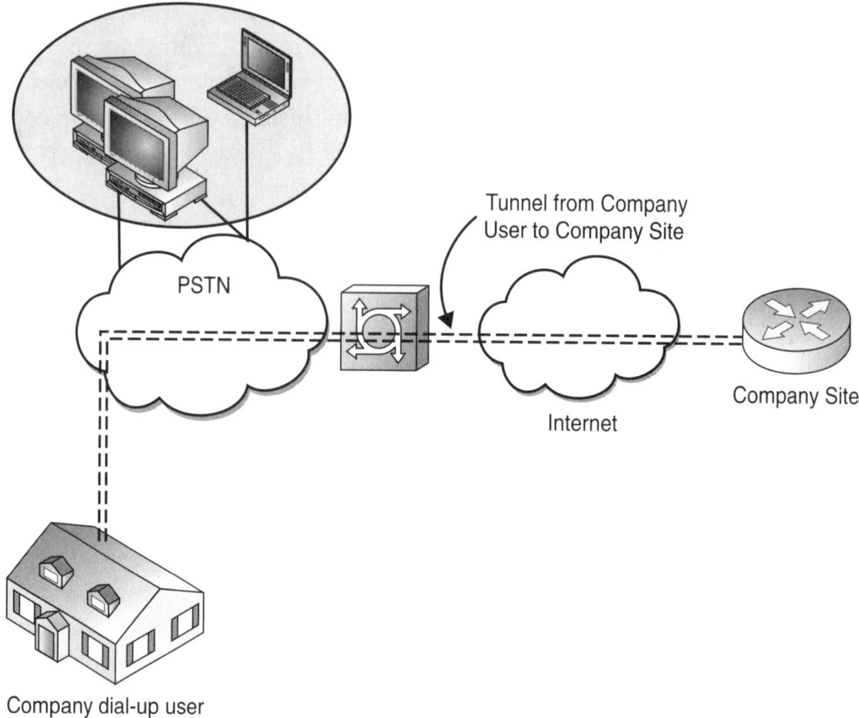

Figure 19-8
VPNs

configuration daily, it is an easier task for them to handle than for a small network engineering staff at a company's central site.

Keep your eye on the VPN headlines. It should prove to be the next big step in remote access.

Remote Access Methods

Now that we have shown you the ways you can connect users to the network, let's talk about how they will access the corporate enterprise network over the telephone or cable lines. There are three methods we will discuss:

- Remote gateway
- Remote control
- Remote node

Remote Gateway

For specific needs, such as e-mail access, the remote gateway method is a good choice. In the example shown in Figure 19-9, a remote user dials in with a laptop computer, from a hotel room or an airplane, for example, and connects to the corporate intranet. This user can open an e-mail program on her laptop and connect to the mail server at the corporate location with very little configuration required.

The drawback in this design is that only one application is accessible. The need for information from other applications or databases is not addressed.

Remote Control

Another method of accessing the corporate LAN from home is to use remote control technology, made popular by the Symantec software PCAnyWhere. Remote control access allows a user to dial directly into a modem connected to a PC in the office, as shown in Figure 19-10. The remote user then controls that PC, which is connected to the corporate network.

As you might imagine, there are several disadvantages to this design. The greatest problem is that of security. The PC at the corporate office must always be powered up with the modem on auto-answer. Anyone can access the modem, with no user authentication whatsoever. Another problem is

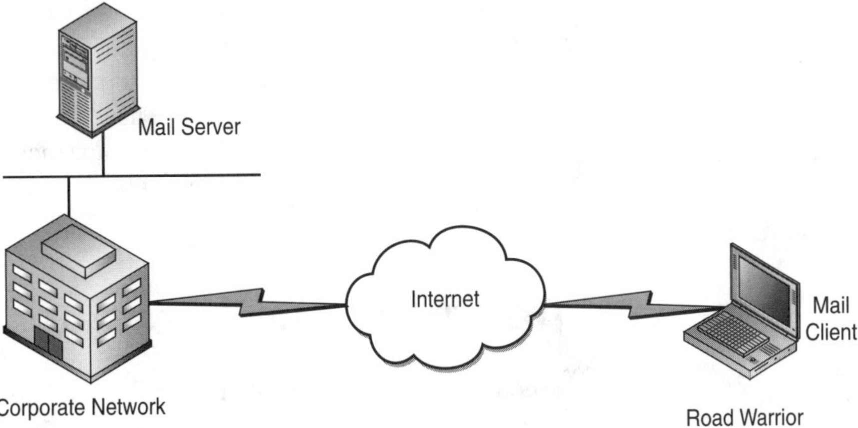

Figure 19-9 Remote gateway

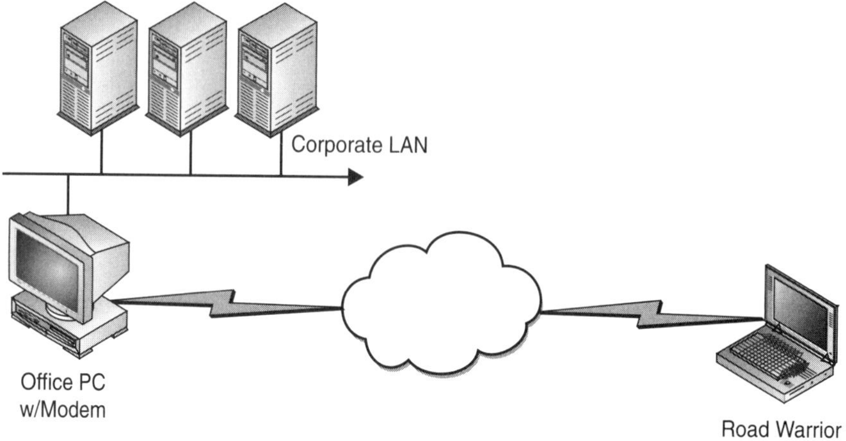

Figure 19-10
Remote control

that each user that needs this method of access must be allocated a home PC and a work PC. In most companies, a user either has a desktop system or a laptop PC with a docking station, not both. For this reason alone, this method of access is not widely used.

Remote Node

The most scalable, secure solution for the remote user is the remote node method, shown in Figure 19-11. The user dials up to the corporate network through an access server. The access server hands off the connection, for authentication, to a RADIUS or TACACS+ server. If the user authenticates successfully, he or she can then proceed to use corporate network resources as though he or she were at his or her desk in the office. The only difference, really, is the connection speed. Rather than having a 100 Mbps dedicated switch port, she may be using a 56 Kbps analog modem, DSL, or ISDN. This is, by far, the most popular design solution for remote users.

Equipment Deployment

The type of network equipment required would depend upon the type of design you need. You may be designing remote access for occasional dial-up

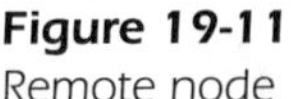

Figure 19-11
Remote node

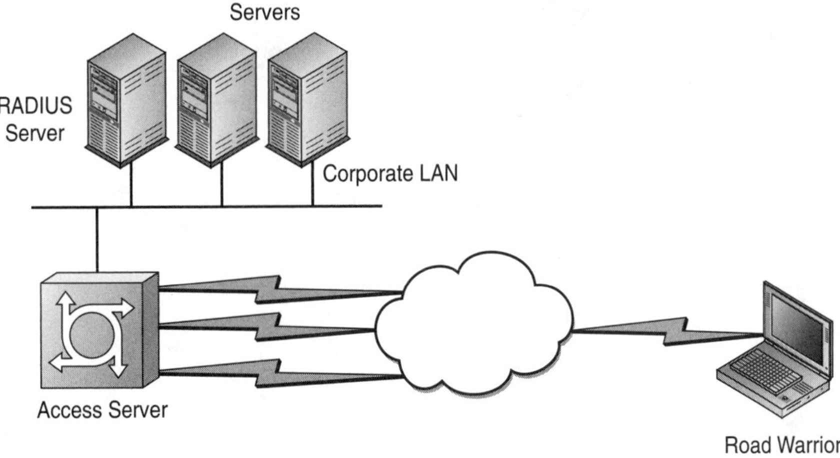

users or for full-time telecommuting employees. The following section will help you decide how to provision the network for the specific problem you are trying to solve.

Mobile Users/Telecommuters

If a user occasionally works from home and needs access to corporate e-mail and other resources, or if a user is traveling and needs to reach the home network from hotel rooms and airports, you do not need to design a complex remote access infrastructure. Figure 19-12 shows how a typical user might access the corporate network. Both the "main office" and the remote user access the PSTN through dial-up, ISDN, or, in the case of the home office, a dedicated line. Depending on the type of access granted, the remote user could get the job done with very little time or equipment investment.

Full-Time Telecommuters

Another type of remote user needs access to the corporate network every day. This type of user is not a "road warrior" and would use a static configuration to dependably reach the resources contained at the central site. Figure 19-13 shows how a typical network configuration might look for a

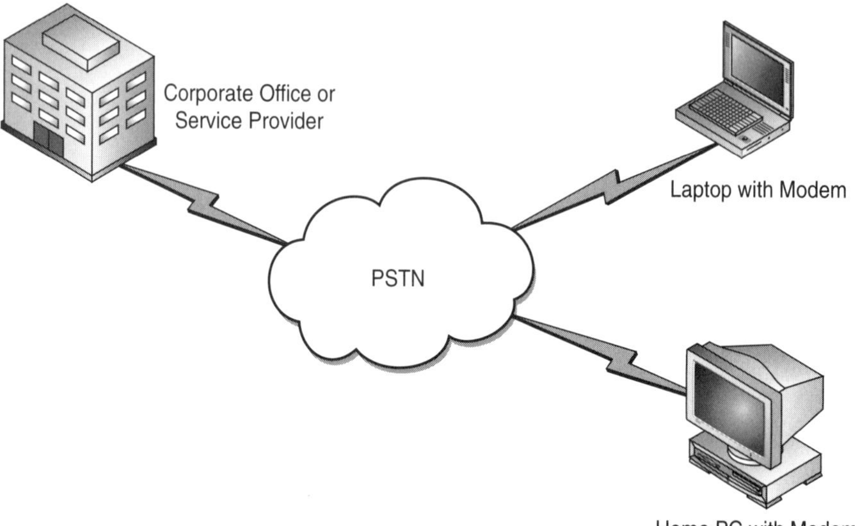

Figure 19-12 Mobile users

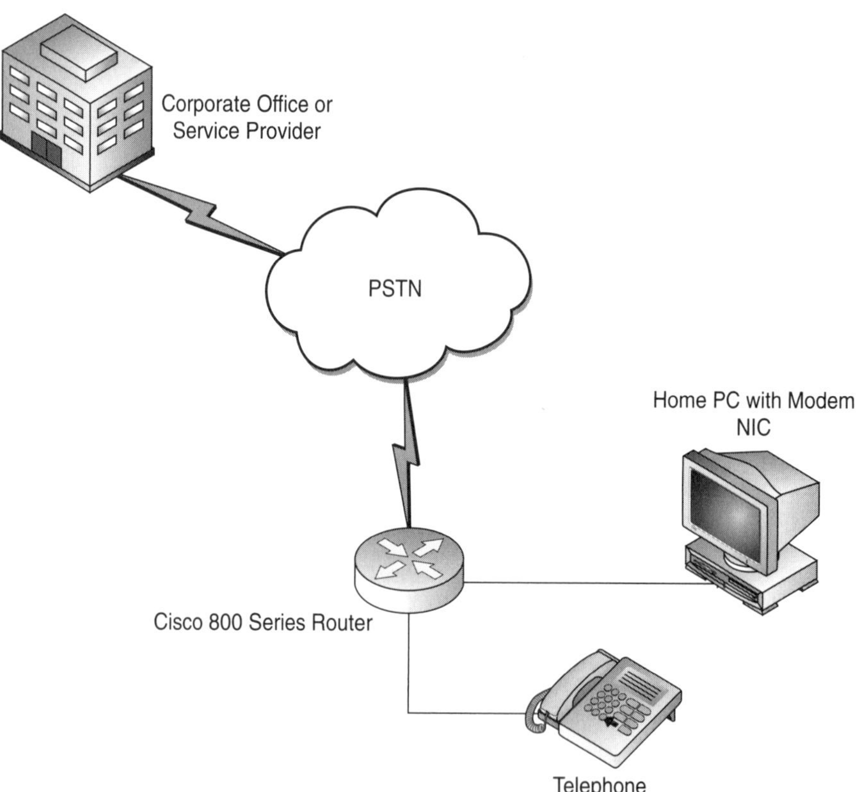

Figure 19-13 Full-time telecommuter

dedicated telecommuting setup. A Cisco 800 series router could be used to allow the telecommuter to use telephone service (in some models) as well as dial-up or ISDN service to the central site, or "home office." This configuration would not apply to an occasional user or traveling employee.

The advantage of a Cisco 800 series router is that it requires the smallest investment while still giving you the ability to use the Cisco IOS software. It can handle ISDN, Frame Relay, dedicated line, X.25, ADSL, IDSL, or asynchronous dial-up.

SOHO with LAN

In the case of a small business office or home office that requires full LAN support, either a Cisco 800 series or a Cisco 1600 series router could be used. The configuration would be similar to that in Figure 19-13, but greater throughput would be supported. Figure 19-14 shows a typical SOHO configuration.

Figure 19-14 SOHO with LAN

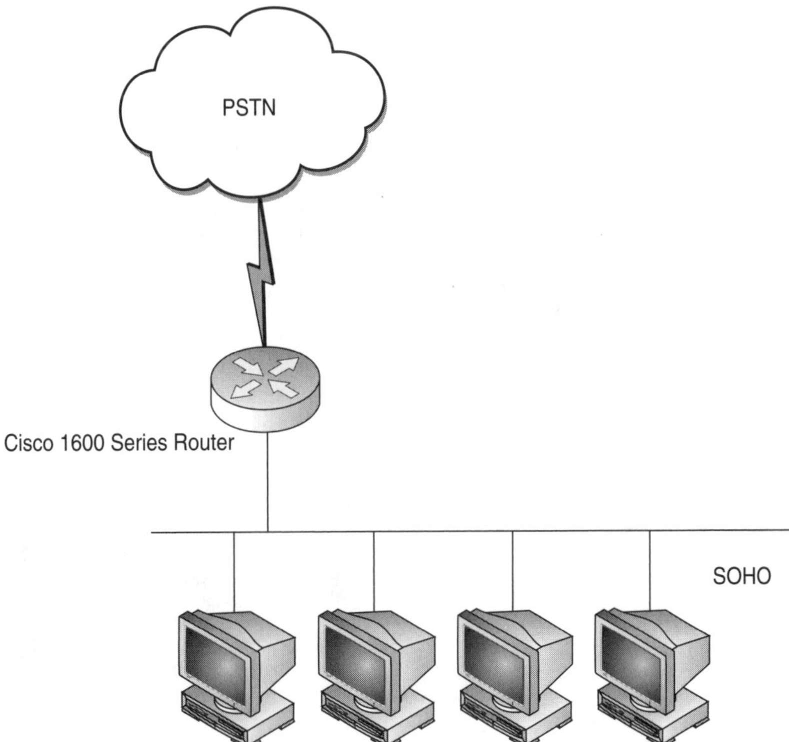

Central Site

At the central site or the location to which remote users will connect, you will need to design for access servers or routers that can handle modem banks. The servers or routers will aggregate all of the incoming traffic and act as a gateway to the central site network and back out again, as shown in Figure 19-15. The access equipment can be a combination of different types as long as it addresses the specific needs of the network (that is, the number of LANs and the type of remote access supported).

One possibility is shown in Figure 19-16, where we see a Cisco 2500 series router supporting a modem bank and also supporting an uplink to a larger router at what may be a headquarters site. The example shown here is a good design for a branch office.

Figure 19-15 Central site equipment

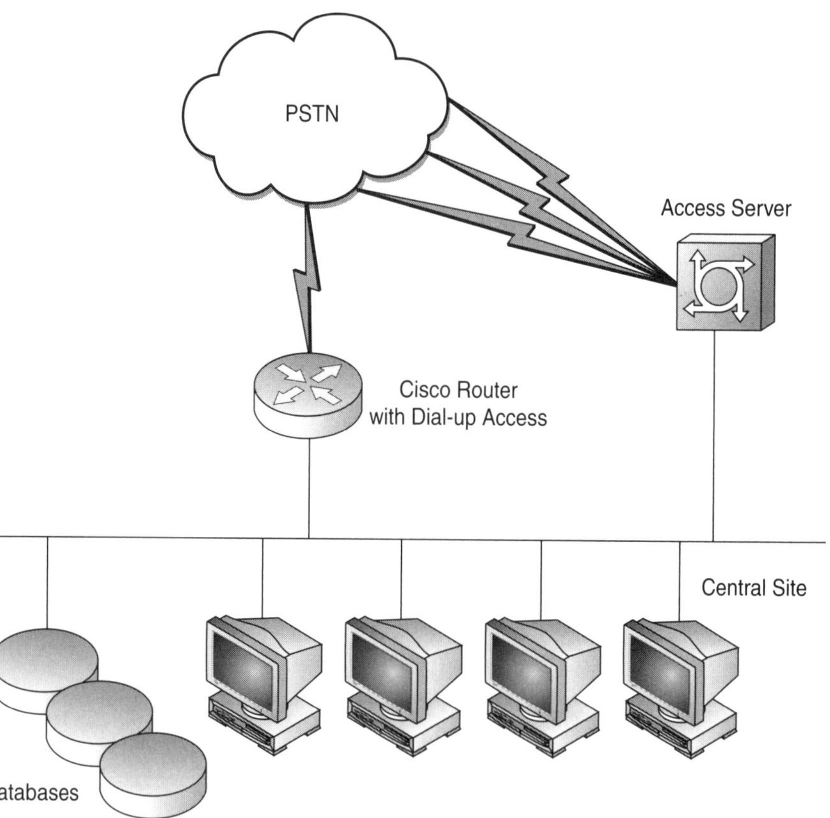

Figure 19-16
Basic design

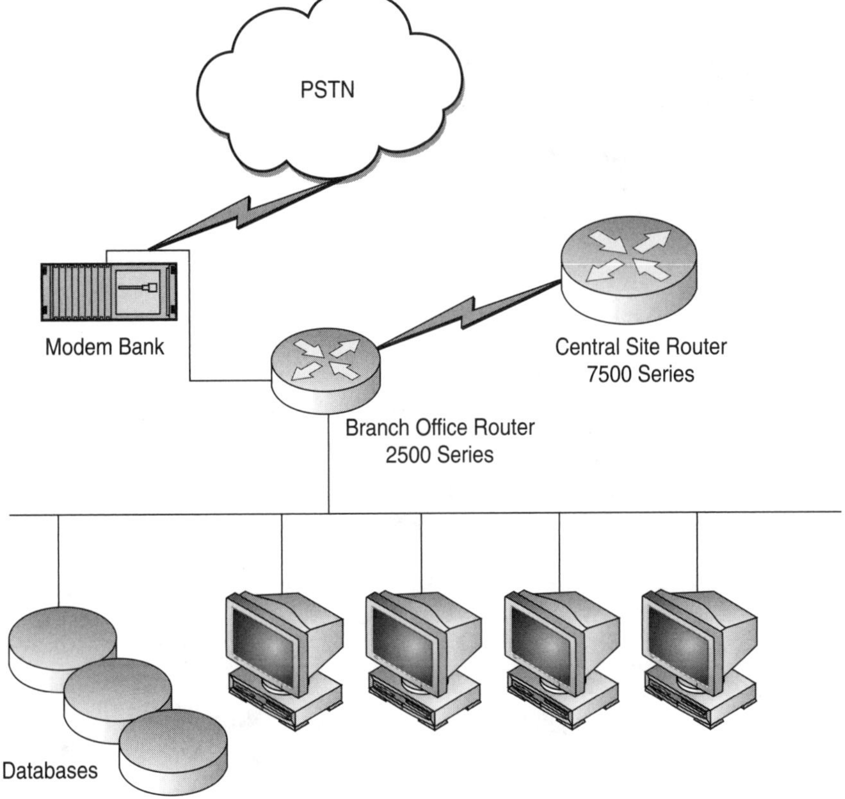

Another design possibility, shown in Figure 19-17, is for the central site handling many dial-up users. This example shows how a Cisco Access Server can be placed in the network. Its integrated modems will negate the need for an external modem bank. Different models support different numbers of modems. The 5800, for example, has 1,400 integrated modems, while the 5300 has only 200 modems. The selection depends upon the design requirements.

Finally, we see how ISDN access can be supported through either an access server or router in a network having remote access through ISDN. Figure 19-18 shows how different requirements can be addressed. Cisco Access Servers can handle ISDN access. Another possibility is to have multiple BRIs coming into a Cisco router. If there are many ISDN lines coming in, the better method might be to use a router with channelized T1/E1

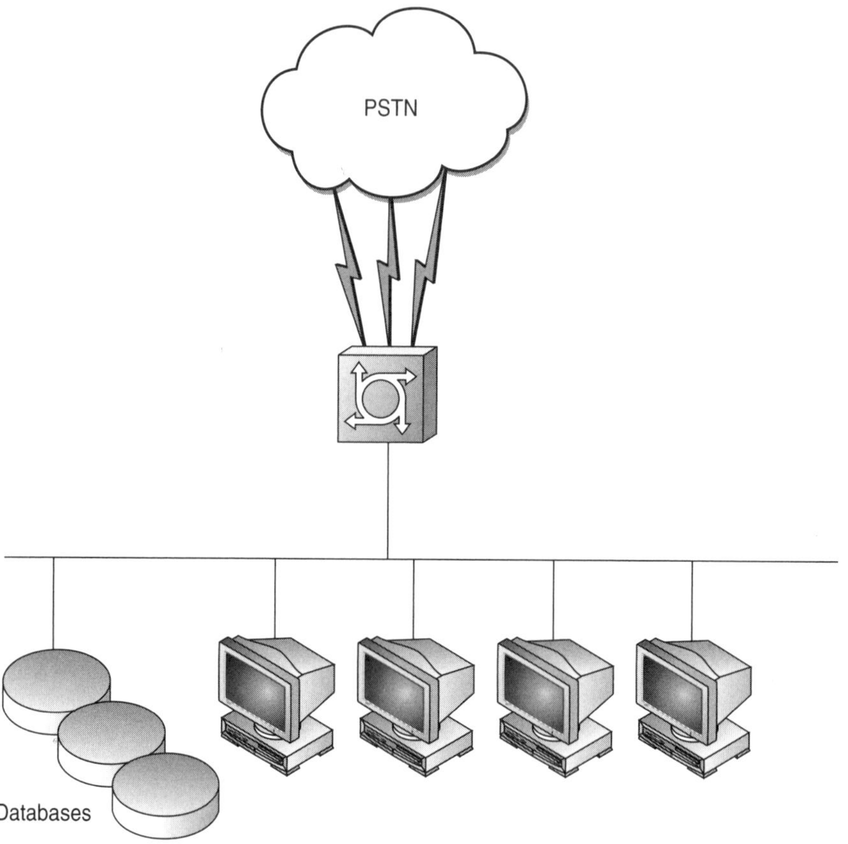

Figure 19-17 Cisco Access Server placement

capability to have a PRI coming in. Any of these works well for central site access. It will depend upon the scaling requirements as well as the site preference.

Data Encapsulation

For remote access, it is likely that you will use Point-to-Point Protocol (PPP) encapsulation at the data link layer. While HDLC is available for ISDN or DSL encapsulation, we will discuss PPP here as the most likely choice

Figure 19-18
ISDN access

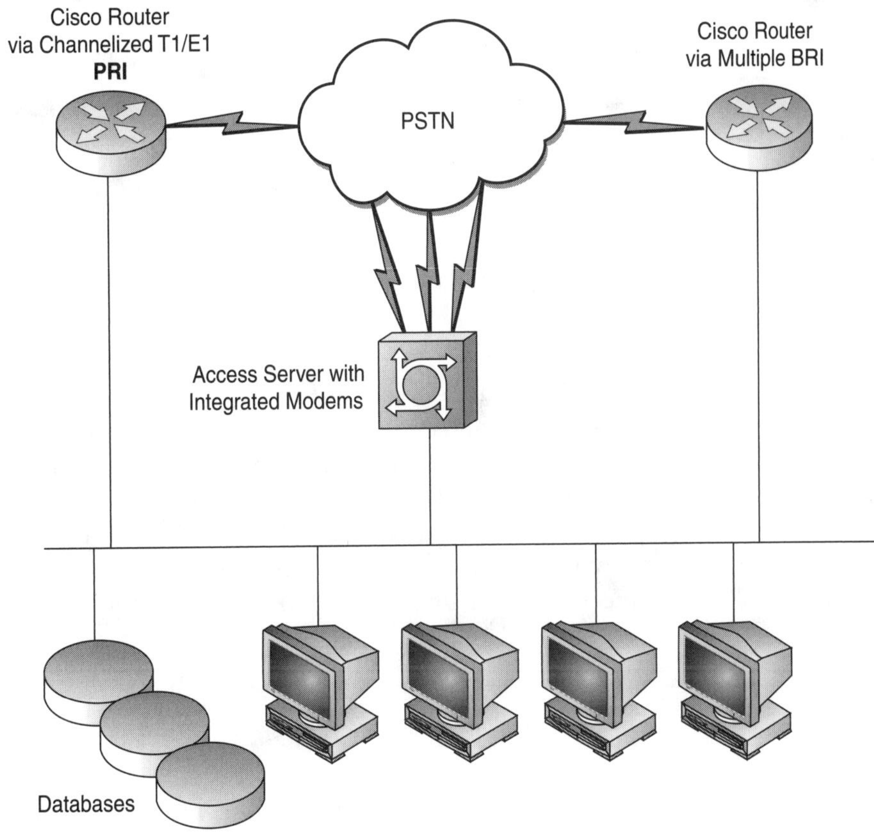

because of its wide use and robustness. It is also, as shown in Figure 19-19, supported for both dial-up and digital line encapsulation.

PPP and Link Control Protocol

RFC 1661 specifies the open standard encapsulation protocol that we know as PPP. When dial-up access first began to be popular, many providers used Serial Line Internet Protocol (SLIP) to encapsulate the traffic. PPP offers several advantages over SLIP, including error checking, authentication, and security.

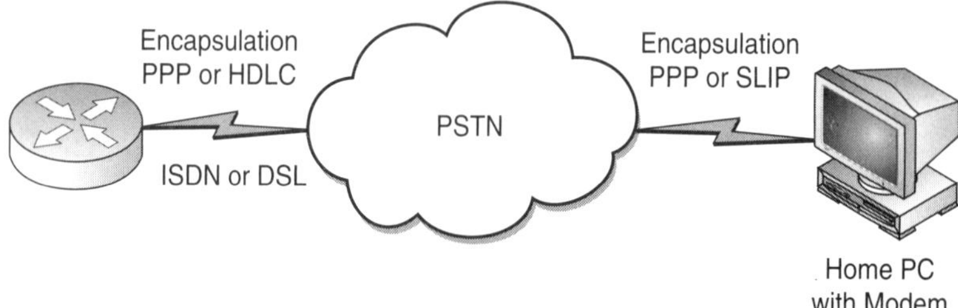

Figure 19-19 Encapsulation

PPP can use either the Password Authentication Protocol (PAP) or the Challenge Handshake Authentication Protocol (CHAP) to provide security at the end points of the connection. Figure 19-20 shows a typical PPP application, where data is encapsulated between two points by the use of PPP.

PPP also uses Link Control Protocol (LCP) to set up the link and agree on parameters, such as framing method. By using different types of control messages, LCP helps to stabilize and regulate the communications between the two end points.

Multilink PPP

RFC 1717 outlined a way of fragmenting and transmitting packets over parallel connections: *Multilink PPP* (MP). The benefit of this is that by using multiple links, latency can be reduced and bandwidth usage can be maximized. As we see in Figure 19-21, data comes into the router or access server from multiple sources. The router or access server can then fragment the packet and send it over the multiple lines being used in a BRI. The resulting packets are 32 bytes each. A 4-byte field is added to the frame header of each frame to control the sequence of the packets as they are encapsulated in PPP and sent to their destination.

Multilink Multichassis PPP

Cisco introduced a concept called *Multilink Multichassis PPP* (MMP) support with Cisco IOS release 11.2. MMP provides for more flexibility in scaling the central site access points. As you can see in Figure 19-22, multiple access servers are grouped into what is called a *stack group*. The access

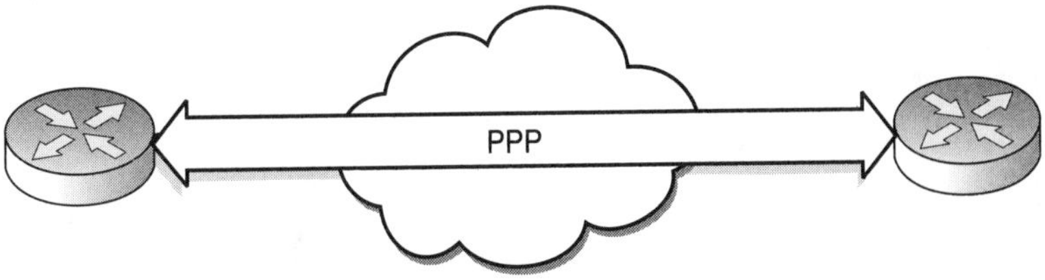

Figure 19-20
PPP design

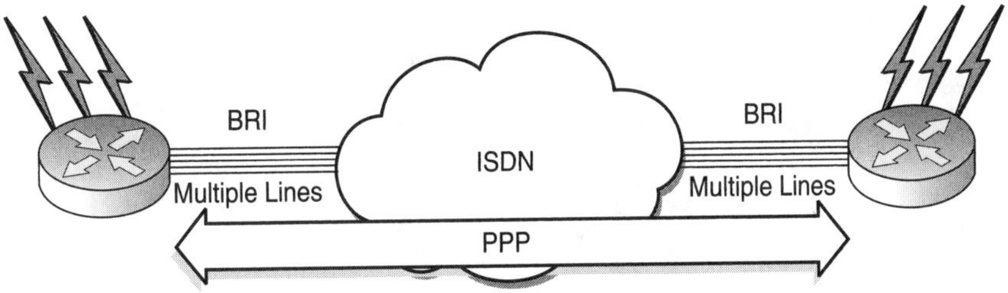

Figure 19-21
Multilink PPP

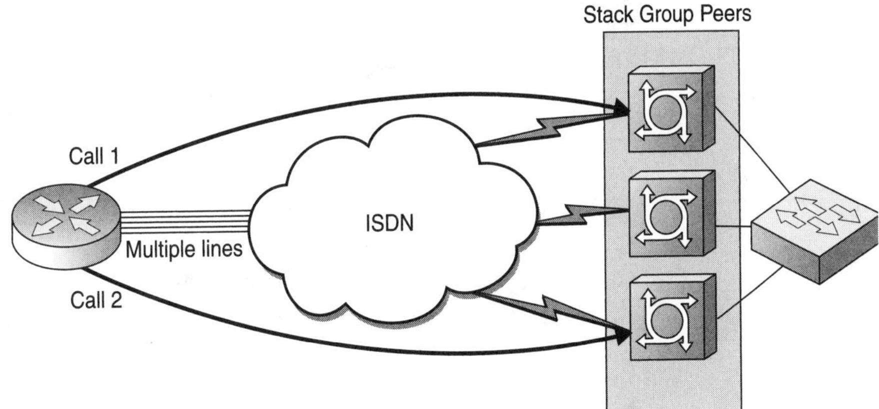

Figure 19-22
Multilink Multichassis PPP

servers are *peers* within the stack group. Multiple calls coming from the same source may terminate at different chassis but reassemble and end up at the same destination. More access servers can be added to the stack group as needed without redesigning the solution.

An important part of large-scale access networks is the MMP Process Server, shown in Figure 19-23. The MMP Process Server can be a dedicated

Figure 19-23 Using an MMP Process Server

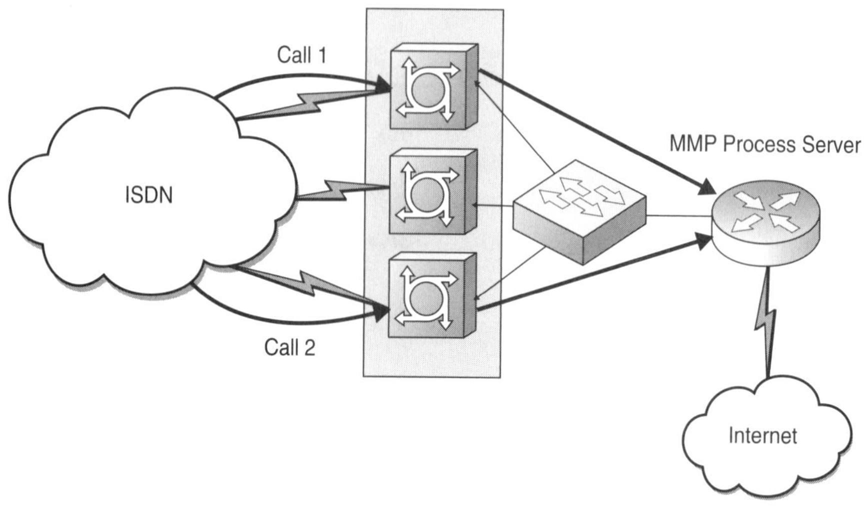

access server but most likely will be a "beefy" router, like the Cisco 7206. The purpose of the process server is to permit the access servers in the stack group to concentrate on answering calls, while the process server performs reassembly of the packets. As we see in the example, the process server can also act as an Internet gateway once packets are ready for forwarding.

A bidding process, using Stack Group Bidding Protocol (SGBP), performs the choice of a process server. A device can be weighted so that it is always chosen as the process server. While configuration of this scenario is outside the scope of this document, you can find more information on the Cisco Web site at **http://www.cisco.com/univercd/cc/td/doc/product/software/ios/12cgcr/dial_c/dcspex.htm#xtocid2505514**.

Security for Remote Access

As we have already pointed out, PPP offers some security for remote access in the form of PAP or CHAP authentication. This enforces a minimal level of security that, unfortunately, is easy to compromise. As with any type of network security, however, you should implement multiple layers of security. The access server or router can enforce the next layer of security with access control lists on a per-user basis. The security can then be further off-loaded to a security server running RADIUS or TACACS+. More information about security methods is outlined in Chapter 23, "Security Design." A typical secure remote access design is shown in Figure 19-24.

Case Study

MetroNet Services is a start-up ISP located in downtown Washington, D.C. The audience they intend to serve is the local community of around 7,000 users who are dissatisfied with any present ISP and don't wish to go with a large online service. There is the possibility that the ISP could grow, if the service they offer is exceptional and unique. For now, they want to plan for less than 10,000 users.

The studies they have done reveal that about one-third of those users could be dialed into the network at any given time. Therefore, they must plan for modem banks or access servers to handle that kind of call volume. They also have about 15 network engineers that work from home (full-time) and will need access into the network either through dial-up or through DSL.

Security is a big concern. MetroNet executives are willing to spend the money up front to make sure hackers launching denial-of-service attacks against the Web servers do not catch them unaware. Currently, they have sold domain name hosting and Web services to 500 companies and need to assure those companies that customer databases will be safe.

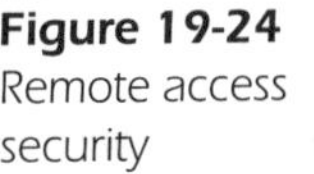

Figure 19-24 Remote access security

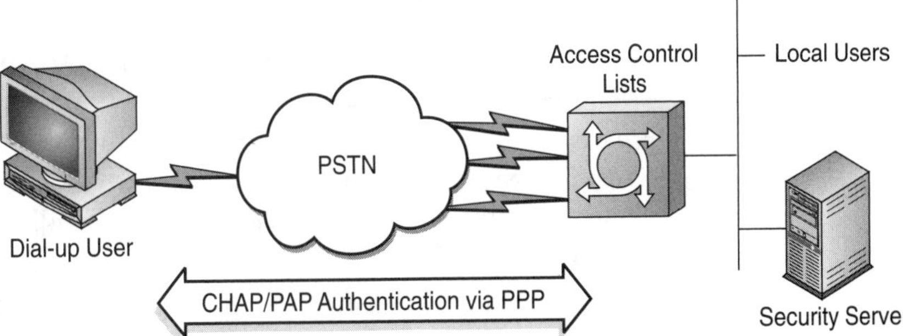

How will your design address these needs? Security, speed, reliability—plus varying types of users—make for an interesting design possibility. See if you can create a viable design with scalability and security. Be creative and have fun with it. Although there is no one right answer to any given design problem, we have suggested one solution in Appendix C, "Suggested Solutions for Case Studies."

Study Hints

Although no one can disclose test items or test content, we can give hints as to what might be valuable to study. For this chapter, there are key facts that need to be reviewed and remembered:

- An **ISDN BRI** is most often used for single household or single user support. It provides two B (bearer) channels at 64 Kbps each. These B channels can be used separately for data and voice or can both be allocated to data—increasing the rate to 128 Kbps. The D channel uses 16 Kbps and handles signaling.
- An **ISDN PRI** is more appropriate for central site connectivity. It provides 23 B channels and one D channel. It is a "T1 worth of B channels." It can be connected into the central site using channelized T1/E1.
- **Security** is an important issue to address in remote access design. Be sure to use whatever authentication methods are available—CHAP/PAP for PPP, RADIUS/TACACS+ for larger designs, and software or hardware firewalls.
- A remote access point must be within **18,000 feet (3.5 miles)** of a CO in order to use DSL service.
- **Road warriors** will most likely be stuck with dial-up service over PSTN for now.
- RFC 1717 outlines the use of **Multilink PPP (MPPP)** for the grouping of access servers into stack groups that can handle the reassembly of calls that have been fragmented and sent over multiple lines. The packets are fragmented and encapsulated into 32-byte frames that include a 4-byte frame header handling the sequencing of the frames.
- **Multilink Multichassis PPP (MMPPP)** can use a single server or router to handle all reassembly of fragmented packets in order to improve overall performance of the stack group.

CCDP Tips

This section contains an abbreviated list of topics covered in this chapter. Think of this section as the equivalent of reading Cliff's Notes™ instead of reading an entire book. You will get the general idea of the chapter but will benefit more from reading the chapter in its entirety.

Connection Technology The connection technology chosen from the four types described in this chapter will be selected according to the problem you are trying to solve.

- **Analog/Dial-up** Traditional modem technology, commonly V.90 (56 Kbps). Useful for mobile users and part-time telecommuters.
- **ISDN** Integrated Services Digital Network. Requires specialized equipment, such as Terminal Adapter (TA), to permit the home user to access the Internet. Available in BRI (2 64-Kbps B channels) or PRI (23 64-Kbps B channels). Always on access without traditional call setup required.
- **DSL** Another method of having "always on" access using traditional telephone lines. Home users can have very high data rates (usually 384 Kbps upstream and 1.5 to 2 Mbps downstream), as well the ability to use the telephone and fax machine all at the same time.
- **Cable** A method of using the cable TV infrastructure to carry data traffic. The current system uses a shared bus topology, so performance suffers in relation to the number of users on the segment.

Remote Access Methods

- **Remote Gateway** A method by which a user may access a single, particular network service at a central site. Works well for e-mail.
- **Remote Control** A method by which a remote PC controls an "always on" desktop PC at a central site. The modem on the desktop system is set to auto-answer calls, which leaves the corporate network vulnerable to attack. This also requires two systems to be allocated to a single user.
- **Remote Node** The best method for secure, remote, dial-up access is by making a remote user appear to be logged into the network at the central site. This requires some software configuration and a login script that authenticates the user.

Equipment Deployment

- **Mobile Users** Normally a mobile user or part-time telecommuter is allocated a laptop computer or desktop system with an internal modem and a dial-up number to allow access to the central site over PSTN. These users could also use ISDN, DSL, or a cable modem, if they work from a fixed location.
- **Full-Time Telecommuters** Today's teleworker population is likely to use DSL or ISDN (sometimes cable modems) to access the corporate network in order to do the job. The investment is a little larger than with a mobile user, but speed and reliability is critical in order to maintain productivity. A Cisco 800 series router can work very well for this design.
- **SOHO with LAN** A Small Office/Home Office that requires LAN support for printers, multiple workstations, and telephones should use a router such as the Cisco 1600 series. It is a "beefier" version of the 800 series. It still uses the Cisco IOS but can handle multiple interface types.
- **Central Site** The type of design used at the central site will vary greatly depending on how remote users will connect. If they connect via direct dial-up, the site may use an access server to handle the calls. If they connect via ISDN, the site may use either a Cisco router with BRI/PRI support or an access server.

Data Encapsulation

- **PPP** is outlined in RFC 1661 and provides data link encapsulation for remote access. It also provides for a modicum of security, with CHAP/PAP authentication.
- **Multilink PPP (MPPP)** is outlined in RFC 1717 and provides for fragmentation of packets that are then encapsulated into 32-byte frames with a 4-byte header included for sequencing. Multiple calls can be handled over multiple lines and can be reassembled at the receiving end within a stack group of access servers.
- **Multilink Multichassis PPP (MMP)** is a method Cisco introduced that can use traditional MMP but can offload the reassembly to a single access server or router (called a process server), thereby improving call-handling performance.
- **Security** is provided in various ways. With PPP encapsulation, CHAP/PAP authentication protocols are supported. As with all security,

you should use a layered approach, however. Deploy access control lists where entry points to the central site network exist. Secure the home systems with software or hardware firewalls (or access control lists on the 800 or 1600 series routers). Use a security server running RADIUS or TACACS+ authentication at the central site to fully secure the network.

Summary

In most modern networks, the intranet does not exist in a vacuum. What used to be a secure, private network of corporate resources now must be accessed by mobile users, teleworkers, and business partners. Understanding how to create a secure, scalable design is, therefore, critical to your success as a network architect. Remember to base the remote access design on the requirements of the network, building in at least 20 percent more for short-term growth. Select products, also, that will scale to the five-year growth projections of the network. Knowing how to create a robust remote access design will round out your portfolio of networking skills.

In our Chapter 20, "What is ATM?," we will discover how to build a scalable network based on some of today's most popular technology.

Questions

The following review questions have been selected to help you test your knowledge of the subject matter contained in this chapter. You will also find these questions contained in the CD-ROM included with this book. While these are not the questions you will find in the certification exams, knowing the answers to the review questions in this book will help cement the material in your mind as you prepare for the tests.

1. ISDN stands for:
   - a. Integrated Signaling Data Network
   - b. Integrated Services Digital Network
   - c. Integrated Services Data Network

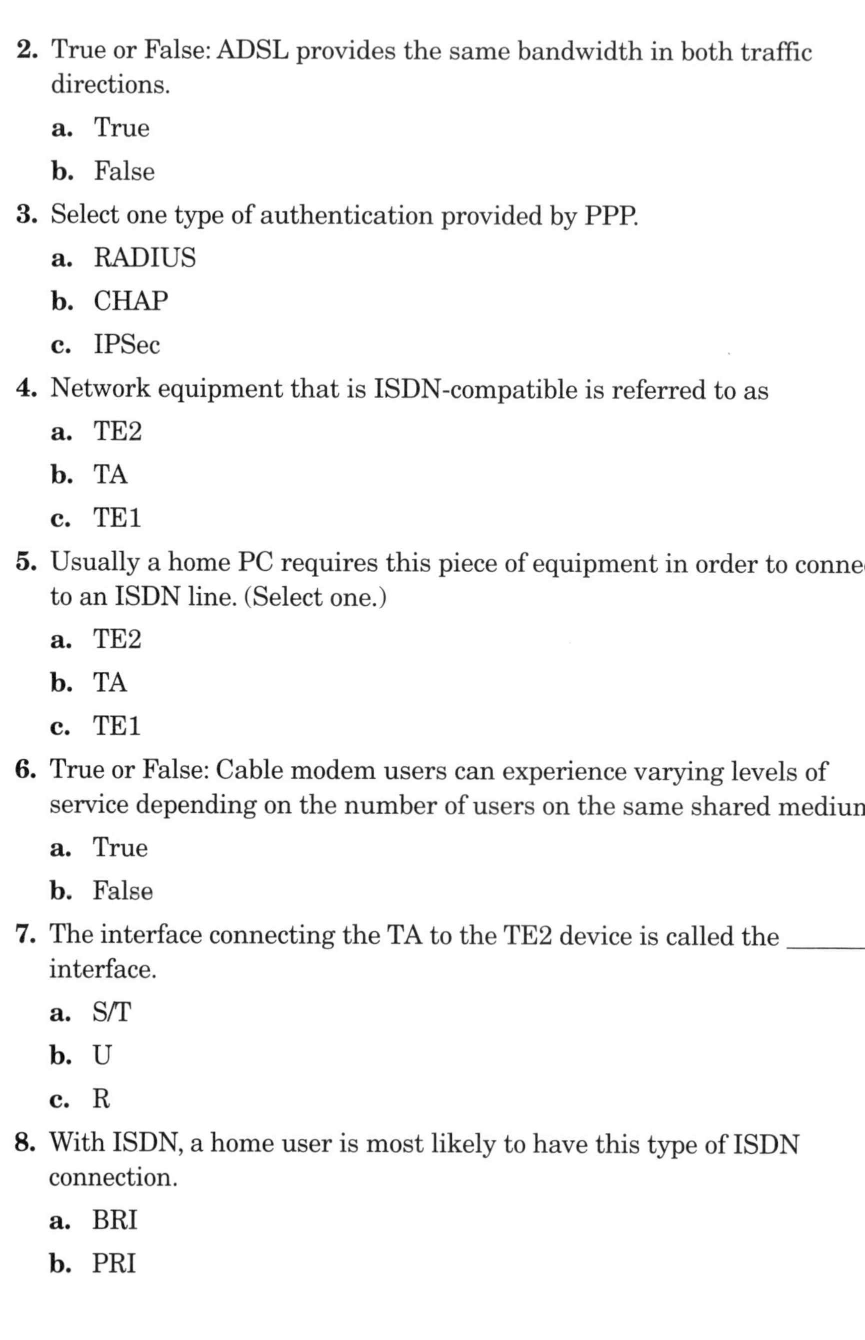

2. True or False: ADSL provides the same bandwidth in both traffic directions.
   a. True
   b. False
3. Select one type of authentication provided by PPP.
   a. RADIUS
   b. CHAP
   c. IPSec
4. Network equipment that is ISDN-compatible is referred to as
   a. TE2
   b. TA
   c. TE1
5. Usually a home PC requires this piece of equipment in order to connect to an ISDN line. (Select one.)
   a. TE2
   b. TA
   c. TE1
6. True or False: Cable modem users can experience varying levels of service depending on the number of users on the same shared medium.
   a. True
   b. False
7. The interface connecting the TA to the TE2 device is called the _______ interface.
   a. S/T
   b. U
   c. R
8. With ISDN, a home user is most likely to have this type of ISDN connection.
   a. BRI
   b. PRI

9. What is the acronym for the bidding process used to elect the MMPPP Process Server?
   a. BGP
   b. SBGP
   c. SGBP
   d. GBP
10. How many B channels are in a single PRI?
   a. 1
   b. 23
   c. 16
   d. 24
11. What is the best router choice for a small branch office?
   a. Cisco 800 Series
   b. Cisco 1600 Series
   c. Cisco 7206
   d. Cisco 700 Series
12. What type of xDSL provides a data rate of 384 Kbps upstream and 1.5 to 2 Mbps downstream?
   a. ADSL
   b. SDSL
   c. IDSL
   d. G.lite
13. What RFC provides the standards for PPP?
   a. 1777
   b. 1661
   c. 1577
   d. 1616
14. In ISDN, what is the D channel used for?
   a. Signaling
   b. Data
   c. Encapsulation

15. True or False: A modem bank is required for an AS5300.
    a. True
    b. False
16. What is the most common way that home users and road warriors connect to the enterprise network?
    a. ISDN
    b. DSL
    c. Cable
    d. Analog dial-up
17. The access servers within an MPPP stack group are called
    a. Servers
    b. Peers
    c. Stack peers
    d. Access groups
18. Traffic can be tunneled through the Internet using
    a. VPNs
    b. ISDN
    c. DSL
19. If a remote user only needed access to e-mail, which type of design might you use?
    a. Remote node
    b. Remote control
    c. Remote gateway
20. True or False: Cable modems are inherently more secure than dial-up access methods.
    a. True
    b. False

Answers

1. ISDN stands for
   b. Integrated Services Digital Network

2. True or False: ADSL provides the same bandwidth in both traffic directions.
   b. False
   Explanation: The key word in the ADSL acronym is "asynchronous." Traffic upstream is allocated less bandwidth than downstream. This works well for most home users.

3. Select one type of authentication provided by PPP.
   b. CHAP
   Explanation: PPP can use CHAP or PAP authentication.

4. Network equipment that is ISDN-compatible is referred to as
   d. TE1
   Explanation: Terminal Equipment Type 1 (TE1) is ISDN-compatible. TE2 is not.

5. Usually a home PC requires this piece of equipment in order to connect to an ISDN line. (Select one.)
   b. TA
   Explanation: Home PCs are likely to be non-ISDN-compatible, which means they will need a Terminal Adapter to connect to their ISDN line.

6. True or False: Cable modem users can experience varying levels of service depending on the number of users on the same shared media.
   a. True
   Explanation: The more users on the media, the slower the data transfer. It also depends greatly on what type of traffic is being sent and received. This is why cable Internet service providers are very strict about allowing users to run any type of server on the network.

7. The interface connecting the TA to the TE2 device is called the ______ interface.
   a. R

8. With ISDN, a home user is most likely to have this type of ISDN connection.
   a. BRI
   Explanation: It is highly unlikely that a home user would ever need the type of bandwidth a PRI carries.

9. What is the acronym for the bidding process used to elect the MMPPP Process Server?
   b. SGBP
   Explanation: The acronym is for Stack Group Bidding Protocol—SGBP.

10. How many B channels are in a single PRI?
    c. 23

11. What is the best router choice for a small branch office?
    b. Cisco 1600 Series
    Explanation: The 1600 series router provides for remote access as well as local LAN support.

12. What type of xDSL provides a data rate of 384 Kbps upstream and 1.5 to 2 Mbps downstream?
    b. G.lite
    Explanation: While ADSL is partially correct, the answer we were looking for is G.lite—a type of ADSL connection that fits the parameters given in the question.

13. What RFC provides the standards for PPP?
    b. 1661

14. In ISDN, what is the D channel used for?
    b. Signaling

15. True or False: A modem bank is required for an AS5300.
    b. False
    Explanation: The modems are integrated into the box.

16. What is the most common way that home users and road warriors connect to the enterprise network?
    f. Analog dial-up
    Explanation: The key here is "road warriors." To date, analog dial-up is virtually the only way road warriors can access their home office.

17. The access servers within an MPPP stack group are called
    b. Peers

18. Traffic can be tunneled through the Internet using
    a. VPNs
    Explanation: VPNs are a method of creating an encrypted tunnel between end points. This permits a tunnel between the remote user and the home office.

19. If a remote user only needed access to e-mail, which type of design might you use?
    d. Remote gateway
    Explanation: Remember, remote gateway permits a single service to be accessed from the dial-up account.

20. True or False: Cable modems are inherently more secure than dial-up access methods.
    b. False
    Explanation: Cable modems are not secure at all. With the "always-on" technology and shared media, cable modem users are a prime target for malicious network activity.

Frequently Asked Questions (FAQs)

1. *How will I know when DSL is available near me?*

   The best way, of course, is to check with your local phone service provider. Usually there is a link on their Web site that will allow you to check for service or request that an e-mail be sent to you when service is available. Another way is to check on **http://www.dslinfo.com**.

2. *Why should I still be using dial-up when all of these other options are available?*

   First of all, everyone has his or her preference. My personal experiences with ISDN have been lousy. For 6 months my access was down more than up. Some folks, however, sing the praises of ISDN. DSL is a great option, but it is not available in a lot of areas yet. Since you have to be within 3.5 miles of a CO, it only serves a slice of the population right now—and I've heard plenty of complaints about the level of service. Cable modems work very well, as long as you install a software firewall for your PC and don't live in a densely populated area. When I first installed a cable modem, I was very pleased. Then everyone else in the neighborhood caught on to the idea and my service started crawling again. In the end, how you access the Internet and your home office is still a matter of both personal preference and company dictates.

Bibliography

Cisco Internetwork Design Course Manual, version 3.0, April 1997, Cisco Systems, Inc

Internetworking Technology Overview: ISDN, Cisco Systems, Inc., **http://www.cisco.com/univercd/cc/td/doc/cisintwk/ito_doc/isdn.htm.**

Point-to-Point Protocol Overview, Cisco Systems, Inc., **http://www.cisco.com/univercd/cc/td/doc/cisintwk/ito_doc/ppp.htm.**

Security Configuration, Cisco Systems, Inc., **http://www.cisco.com/univercd/cc/td/doc/product/software/ios10/12supdoc/dsqcg3/qcsecur.htm.**

CHAPTER 20

What is ATM?

In the last chapter, we showed you how to connect the remote user to the enterprise network through a WAN connection. Now we are going to talk about Asynchronous Transfer Mode (ATM), a cell-based technology that can support multiple service types in both the LAN and WAN, as well as Switched Multimegabit Data Service (SMDS), a packet-switched, datagram-based technology generally seen in telephone company networks. By the end of the chapter, you should have a good idea of how ATM works, how to design for an ATM network, and how to determine whether ATM is right for your design project.

First of all, ATM is a connection-oriented technology that uses fixed-size cells, as shown in Figure 20-1, instead of datagrams. It enables the for-

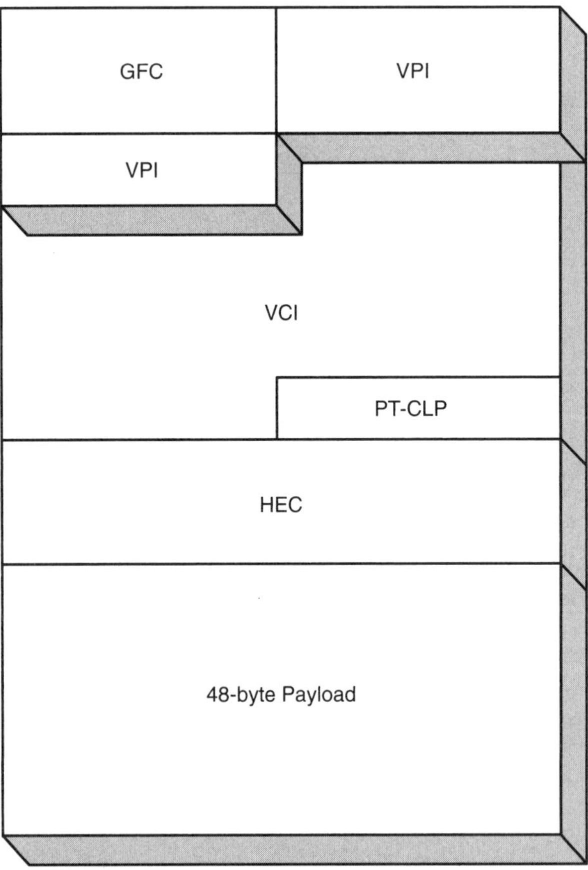

Figure 20-1 The ATM cell format

warding, or *relay*, of these cells through the network. Thus, it is sometimes called *cell relay technology*. ATM itself is a switching standard that describes the asynchronous transfer of information over SONET/SDH. *SONET/SDH* is the standard for the multiplexing and transmission of data over optical networks in isochronous mode. An *isochronous service* is one that is uniform with respect to time and in which the information being transmitted is guaranteed to arrive at regular intervals. In 1991, an organization known as the ATM Forum was founded. The ATM Forum began issuing specifications for ATM standards in 1992.

The ATM cell is 53 bytes in length. It contains a five-byte header and a 48-byte payload. As you can see in Figure 20-1, there are quite a few pieces to this puzzle:

- **Generic Flow Control (GFC)** is used in User-to-Network Interface (UNI) communications to help with short-term overload conditions.
- **Virtual Path Identifier (VPI)** is a one-byte field that uniquely identifies a path through which all traffic to one destination can be bundled. This is a value between 0 and 255. The size depends on whether the interface is UNI or Network-to-Network Interface (NNI).
- **Virtual Channel Identifier (VCI)** is a two-byte field that uniquely identifies a virtual channel circuit. The VPI/VCI is locally significant, as are DLCIs in Frame Relay networks.
- **Payload Type (PT)** can be used for congestion notification, the identification of user data or maintenance data, and is used to indicate the end of a message when using ATM Adaptation Layer (AAL) 5. We will discuss AAL later in this chapter.
- **Cell Loss Priority (CLP)** can be used to set the discard eligibility of a cell—in other words, its relative importance in case congestion occurs.
- **Header Error Control (HEC)** can actually repair single-bit errors in the header as well as some multiple-bit errors. It is an eight-bit cyclical redundancy check (CRC) that is performed on the entire header.
- **Payload** is the remaining 48 bytes of the cell.

Why use ATM? When a design requires a high degree of predictable quality, flexibility, and availability for voice, video, and data, an ATM network can fill the bill. ATM can be used in private enterprise networks, public networks, or hybrid designs that bridge both public and private together.

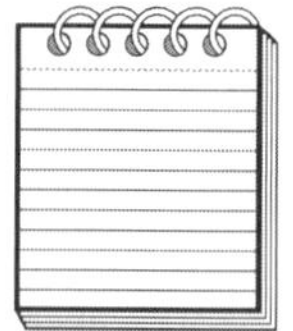

NOTE: *High throughput is no longer the real need or driver for ATM. This used to be true a few years ago when OC12 (622 Mbps) was at least 60 times faster than the current LAN technology. Today, with the availability of OC192 Packet over SONET (POS) and wave division multiplexing (WDM) interfaces on switches and routers, throughput would not be the main driver for using ATM. Currently, the biggest ATM pipes are OC48, and the overhead in the Segmentation and Reassembly (SAR) process is pretty high. However, ATM is still far more mature and comprehensive in terms of Quality of Service (QoS), traffic engineering, and management than IP-based backbones; hence, ATM is especially suitable for voice and video.*

ATM encompasses both hardware and software architecture. Special hardware is required and is usually procured in the form of an ATM switch or an ATM router line card. Software supports circuit emulation for situations in which dedicated bandwidth with guaranteed throughput is imperative. It also provides support for Frame Relay virtual circuits as well as traditional cell relay ATM services. For telephone company networks, SMDS is also supported across the ATM backbone for reliable voice transmission.

A major benefit of using ATM is its capability to support the customization of traffic policies, using methods such as Quality of Service (QoS) to allocate bandwidth to applications that are delay-intolerant. Video streaming, for example, is particularly sensitive to "jitter" caused by latency in the transmission. Voice is sensitive to any problems in transmission because of the extreme importance of frame sequence and reliable speeds.

In today's large networks, it is common to see ATM bridging the gap between the LAN and the WAN. This means that ATM technology is crossing over from the core of the network to the network edge, or the Distribution layer of our three-tier design model.

Benefits of ATM

Today's modern networks can greatly benefit from the migration to ATM in mixed traffic environments. Figure 20-2 shows how bandwidth demand has grown. ATM can handle these increased requirements.

Specifically, the move to ATM is used to

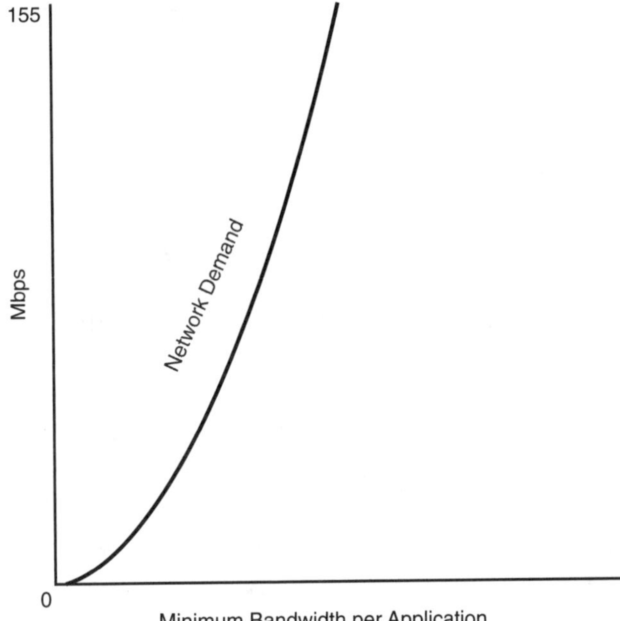

Figure 20-2
Bandwidth demand

- Reduce bandwidth costs
- Improve performance
- Reduce downtime

The price of WAN bandwidth is a big issue when you consider the use of time-division multiplexing (TDM) networks, such as the traditional phone system. In TDM networks, fixed cell sizes are used, but cells are continuously transmitted, even if there is no voice traffic to send. Packet-switched data networks, on the other hand, use variable packet lengths and transmit only when data must be sent. ATM combines the best of both worlds by providing a way to compress voice, silence, and repetitive patterns in addition to allowing for dynamic bandwidth allocation.

Performance in an ATM network is improved by allowing greater flexibility in network usage. Enhanced buffering techniques help guarantee QoS to applications such as voice, which are sensitive to delay and jitter. The use of per-virtual circuit queuing and rate scheduling allows for traffic planning and guarantees. Downtime in an ATM network is also reduced because of ATM's enhanced capability to create redundant paths (in addition to using redundant hardware components) and by its capability to route quickly around trouble spots.

ATM Concepts

ATM can support both permanent virtual circuits (PVCs) and switched virtual circuits (SVCs). It also supports what is called a *soft PVC*, which offers the best of both types of virtual circuits. A VPI/VCI pair uniquely identifies each circuit within the network. Data that will be transmitted across the ATM circuits is prepared by being "chopped" into sections that fit neatly into the payload portion of the cell. In this section, you will learn the difference between the types of virtual circuits and how ATM uses these concepts to provide support for different network requirements.

PVC

A permanent virtual circuit (PVC) is a statically mapped point-to-point link from one network subinterface to another. PVCs can also be point-to-multipoint. As shown in Figure 20-3, the PVC is understood as a logical network on both sides of the connection by the Layer 3 protocols. At the data link layer, the Subnetwork Access Protocol (SNAP) encapsulation is applied. SNAP encapsulation is defined in RFC 1483, which provides for the multiplexing of multiple protocols over a single PVC. Other possible encapsulation types, such as PPP over ATM, are specified in RFC 2225. It is important to note that in a PVC, no negotiation or signaling takes place. Every aspect of the connection is configured manually.

Soft PVC A soft PVC requires some initial manual configuration, but within the provider's ATM cloud, it allows a switch or router to connect to another switch or router that supports signaling. This ensures that the traffic can find another switching path through the provider's network in the event that the primary path fails.

The soft PVC can be configured on a Cisco ATM switch with the following command, along with optional parameters:

```
Switch(config-if)# atm soft-vc source-vpi source-vci dest-address
atm-address dest-vpi dest-vci [enable | disable]
```

Figure 20-3
PVC

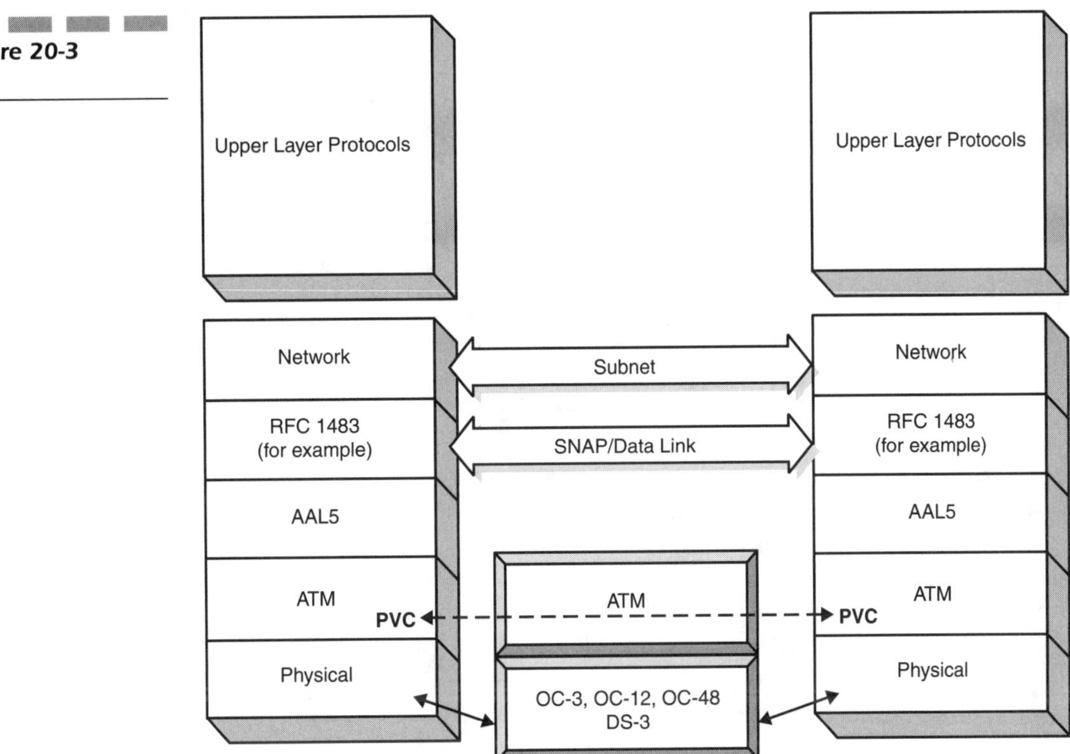

For more information about configuring and using soft PVCs, refer to the Cisco Web site at **http://www.cisco.com/univercd/cc/td/doc/product/atm/c8540/12_0/13_19/sw_cnfig/vir_circ.htm**.

SVC

A switched virtual circuit (SVC) is like a telephone call. It is established when you need it and torn down when you don't. Just as you don't keep a permanent connection up between your home telephone and your best friend's phone line, you don't keep an SVC open all of the time. An SVC requires that some negotiating takes place between two points in a network. The two points have to agree on things like encapsulation and signaling before data transmission can occur.

In Figure 20-4, you can see that an SVC looks a little different at the protocol level than a PVC. From an end-station to an ATM switch, the signaling is User-to-Network Interface (UNI). Between switches, the signaling is called Network-to-Network Interface (NNI). Cells enter an ATM device through a signaling channel and are assembled into frames by the Service Specific Convergence Protocol (SSCOP), following the Q.2931 standard. SVCs can be point-to-point or point-to-multipoint subinterface configurations. Point-to-multipoint is a Non-Broadcast Multi-Access (NBMA) configuration.

VCI/VPI Mapping

At the beginning of this chapter, we talked about virtual path identifiers (VPIs) and virtual channel identifiers (VCIs). What exactly do these identifiers do? As we explained earlier, they are locally significant within the ATM network. Figure 20-5 shows that while our virtual path between Router A and Router B passes through Switch 1 and Switch 2, the path is still identified as VPI 100. The VCI, however, changes as it moves through each hop. This is not necessarily the case in every network. The VCI could potentially be the same all the way through the network. There could not be another path using the same VPI, however.

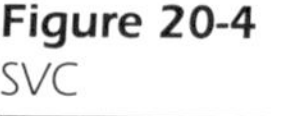

Figure 20-4
SVC

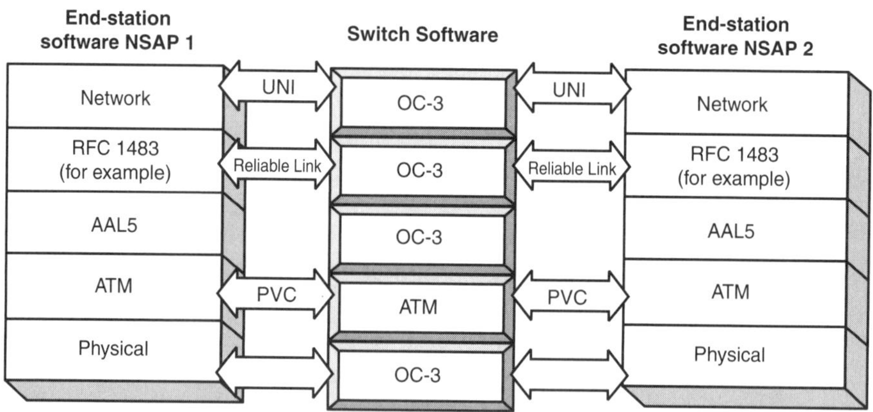

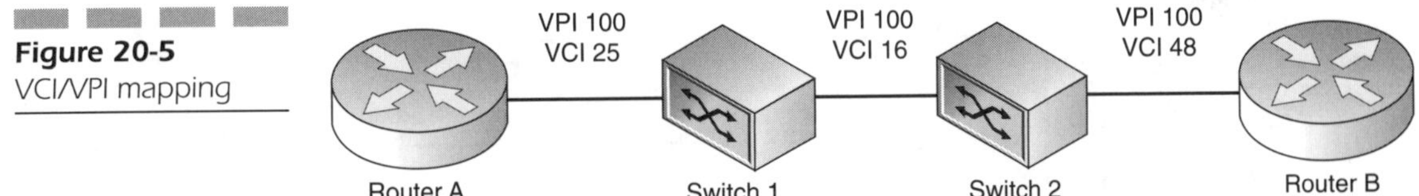

Figure 20-5
VCI/VPI mapping

Segmentation and Reassembly

Segmentation and reassembly (SAR) is a topic that deserves a brief explanation. You will undoubtedly hear this term when dealing with ATM internetworking. SAR is the process by which the sending station *segments* the data into a usable chunk—usually 48-bytes, depending on the ATM adaptation layer used. It then appends the five-byte header and any other special fields required by the adaptation layer. At the receiving end, the SAR process happens again; only this time the data is removed from the cell and is reassembled into its original form.

Because little buffering is done by ATM switches, the amount of latency added to transmit time is important. Oversubscription of a circuit can result in dropped cells and the need for upper layer protocols to request the transmission again. As you will see in the next section, the amount of latency added to the transmission process depends on the type of adaptation layer used as well as its corresponding SAR process.

ATM Adaptation Layers

ATM has a layered reference model of its own, similar to the OSI reference model. In Figure 20-6, we see that in addition to the layers, the model also has reference *planes* that penetrate all layers.

The control plane handles signaling requests, while the user plane handles the transfer of data. Layer management is specific to the ATM layers, detecting and reporting errors and protocol problems. Plane management handles the coordination of functions within the entire structure.

From a protocol layer perspective, the physical layer of both the ATM and OSI models are roughly the same. They handle the proper packaging and

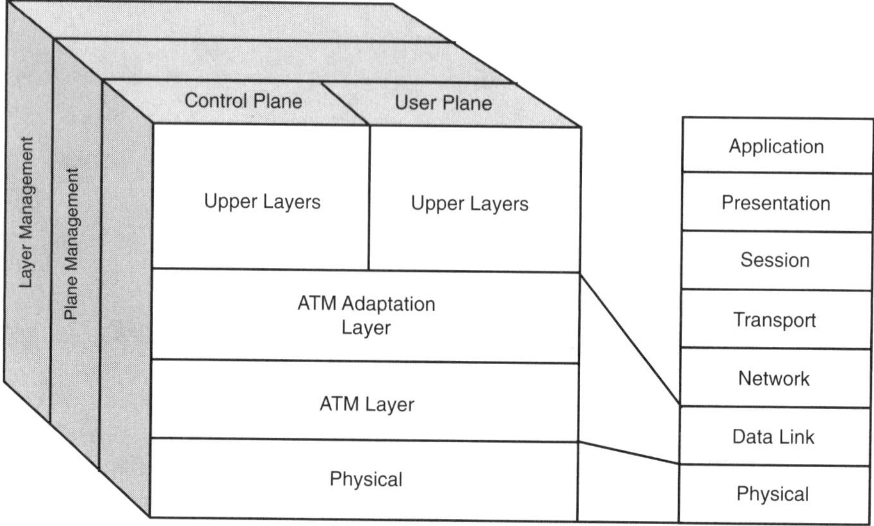

Figure 20-6
ATM reference model

movement of the data onto the physical medium. The ATM layer and the ATM adaptation layer loosely correspond to the data link layer of the OSI model. The ATM layer handles connections and the movement of cells through the network. The ATM adaptation layer (AAL) separates the ATM processes from the upper layer protocols and, as you will see in this section, is unique to the type of information being transferred.

TIP: *An easy way to think of the AAL is that it adapts current or legacy technology to be able to use ATM cells.*

AAL1 and Voice

Voice traffic must be sent at a constant rate. When voice traffic is sent over an ATM network, the traffic is usually digitized using pulse code modulation (PCM). The private branch exchange (PBX) continuously samples the voice at a rate of about 8,000 times per second. The samples are stored in single octet packages, which are then sent continuously over the wire.

The adaptation layer used for voice traffic is AAL1. AAL1 requires that a *sequence number* and a *sequence number protection* field be generated for each cell, in addition to the sampled data. The receiving end needs to know the proper sequence to determine that it has received the data in the proper order. The SAR layer takes out a 47-byte payload of voice traffic and adds a one-byte header, containing the sequencing and clock recovery information. The clock recovery information ensures that the timestamp appears on each cell of the voice call to help reduce jitter. The five-byte ATM header is added and the 53-byte cell is sent over the network at a *constant bit* rate.

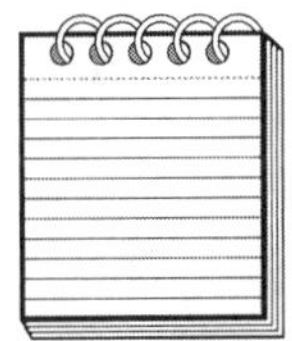

NOTE: *AAL1 requires a physical medium that supports clocking, such as SONET.*

AAL2

With many newer voice services, such as Sprint PCS™, that support voice compression, the AAL2 adaptation is used. AAL2 was originally designed for packetized video, which required variable bit rate (VBR) transmission. VBR is used when traffic is bursty in nature.

By using AAL2, providers are able to use *silence suppression* techniques to squeeze out the unused bandwidth between cells. An upper-layer algorithm is then applied to perform further compression, and bandwidth consumption is reduced by about two-thirds of the original rate. The compression and silence suppression allows voice samples to be much smaller than with AAL1. Additionally, no SAR is used with AAL2, so multiple traffic streams can fit into one cell. A field called an *offset field* delineates the different traffic streams within the cells.

Because of its flexibility, AAL2 is also now being used to support multimedia messaging, voice and telephony to the desktop, and fax to the desktop.

AAL3/4

ATM is a connection-oriented technology. For network service providers and the connectionless protocol SMDS, use AAL3/4. To function with SMDS, a message identifier (MID) and sequence number are added to the cell. This four-byte addition reduces the payload size in AAL3/4 to 44 bytes.

The benefit of using AAL3/4 for connectionless traffic is that many cells from a variety of sources can arrive simultaneously on a channel. Because of the MID and sequence number, the receiver knows how to reassemble the transmission. Consequently, the additional work impacts the latency of this type of transmission. More time is spent doing SAR, because of the additional fields and the CRC that is done to help provide some error checking. The overhead on each 53-byte cell is a minimum of nine bytes, so overhead eats into the efficiency of ATM when using AAL3/4.

AAL5 and Data

For traditional data traffic, like IP and LAN emulation, AAL5 is commonly used. Because no MID or sequence number is needed, the SAR time is negligible. AAL5 computes a 32-bit CRC, so that the receiving station can tell whether errors have occurred during the delivery. AAL5 does not append any additional fields, so the payload is the full 48 bytes. The overhead incurred on an AAL5 cell is five bytes, or about 9.5 percent of the cell size.

ATM Routing

Routing in an ATM network is usually achieved in the same manner as other types of networks: statically or dynamically. Although some implementations may still use the static type of ATM routing, it is unlikely that you will design for this type of network. Generally, when a business looks to ATM as a solution, it does so because of QoS support and the like.

Static ATM routing is provided by the Interim Interswitch Signaling Protocol (IISP), which is supported by Cisco. When you encounter IISP in a network, however, the question would be, "Are there legacy switches in the network that do not have Private Network-Node Interface support?" If so, it would be wise to suggest that these switches be replaced with more modern ATM equipment.

PNNI

The Private Network-Node Interface (PNNI, pronounced *penny*) is a dynamic routing protocol that is an extension of the User-Network Interface

(UNI) protocol for use over Network-Network Interface (NNI) implementations. The ATM Forum developed PNNI to answer the problems of extensive manual configurations that plagued earlier ATM implementations.

The PNNI protocol specifies how signaling requests and data connections are handled in the ATM network. The goal in PNNI's design is to create a protocol that can dynamically create the switch tables necessary for routing signaling setup messages. This dynamic behavior allows for faster overall convergence in the ATM network.

PNNI uses prefix routing and a hierarchical address model and offers support for modern ATM network needs, such as Multi-Protocol Label Switching (MPLS) and QoS. PNNI can also provide support for private or public ATM addressing.

NOTE: *PNNI is said to be dynamic, because it learns the topology of the network, reachability, and operational status through topology state advertisements and the hello protocol. It then shares what it knows about the topology state with other PNNI-enabled devices.*

Although PNNI can function in a flat network topology, it is highly recommended that you design for a hierarchical topology to offer greater scalability. As you will remember from previous chapters, it is almost always suggested that you follow a hierarchical design model, especially when using any type of routing. The hierarchical design reduces the amount of processing that must be done in the upper layers and allows for very fast routing as you approach the core of the network design.

A hierarchical PNNI network has several components, described here and shown in Figure 20-7:

- **Lowest-level nodes** The switches or switching systems at the lowest level of the hierarchy.
- **Peer group** Refers to any group of logical nodes that reside at the same level of the hierarchy.
- **Peer group leader (PGL)** A node within a peer group that is elected to be the group leader. The PGL elects a single node at the next-highest level to act as its "parent node" to represent the entire peer group. The PGL will summarize all peer group information and pass it to the *logical group node* that it has elected.

Figure 20-7 Hierarchical PNNI network

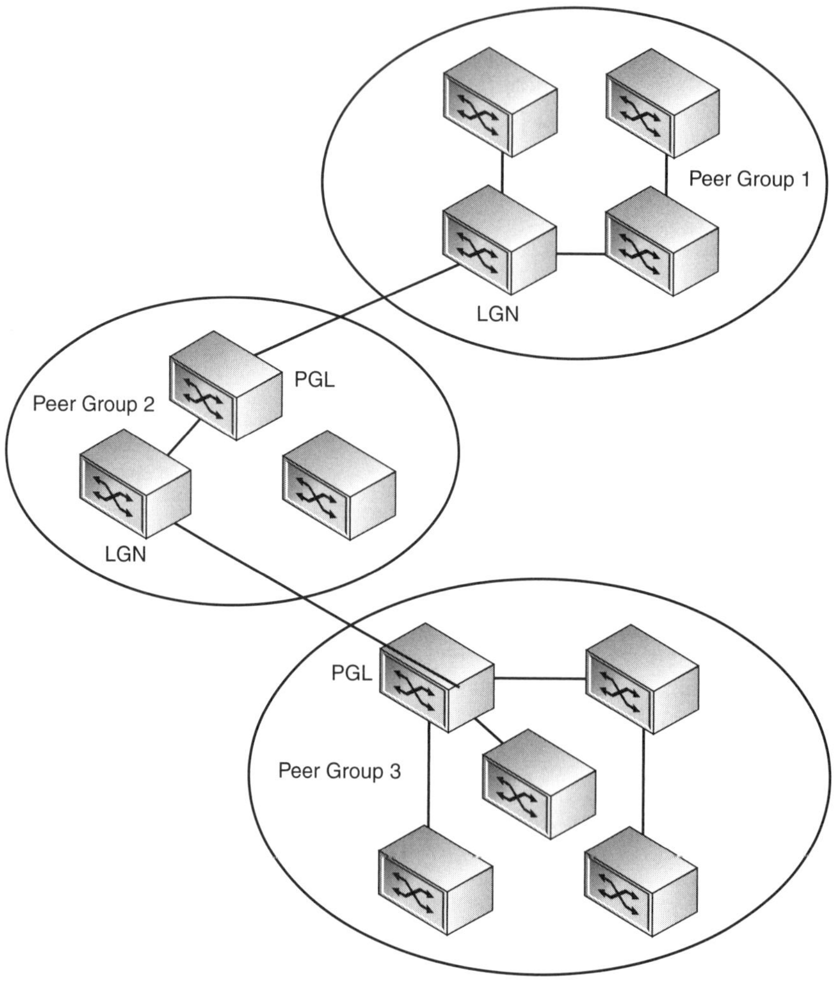

- **Logical group node (LGN)** Elected by the PGL of the next-lowest level. The LGN advertises on behalf of the peer group represented by the PGL.

PNNI supports communication between switches (both public and private), network-to-network interchanges, and what is known as *logical NNI*, which is a private network-to-private network link through a public ATM network. Addressing for public networks is in the E.164 format specification, while private networks use Network Services Access Point addressing. Address formats are shown in Figure 20-8.

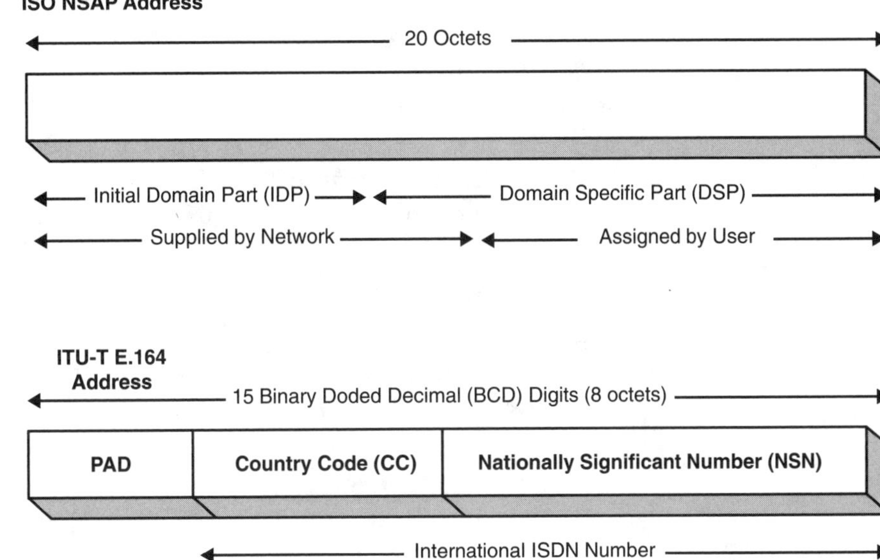

Figure 20-8
ATM address formats

An important final note about PNNI is that although it is a dynamic protocol for use with ATM routing, the most likely design is the use of virtual circuits (VCs) in a network. Once the VCs are set up and operational, the addressing and function of PNNI will be unimportant.

LANE

LANE stands for Local Area Network Emulation, a solution that was developed by the members of the ATM Forum to address the resolution of legacy addresses in the Emulated LAN (ELAN). LANE allows the resolution of a MAC address to an ATM address. It uses the ELAN concept, which means that it uses a logically defined LAN made up of devices that are not necessarily physically connected. The purpose is to emulate a connectionless network like Ethernet or Token Ring so that end nodes can interoperate with the connection-oriented ATM network.

Three servers in LANE are important to the operation of the ELAN:

- **LAN Emulation Server (LES)** Provides for the registration of node addresses and the MAC-to-ATM address resolution (ARP).

- **Broadcast Unknown Server (BUS)** Handles broadcast and multicast functions within the ELAN. Because ATM is a connection-oriented technology, it cannot handle a "go-everywhere" VC. The BUS serves as a point-to-multipoint server that creates VCs to every node in the ELAN.
- **LAN Emulation Configuration Server (LECS)** An optional server that provides central configuration and administration of the ELAN.

Another term used in LANE is the LAN Emulation Client (LEC). An LEC can be defined as any node within the ELAN that is using LANE software. Each type of LANE device is shown in Figure 20-9. As you can see, even a router can be defined as an LEC.

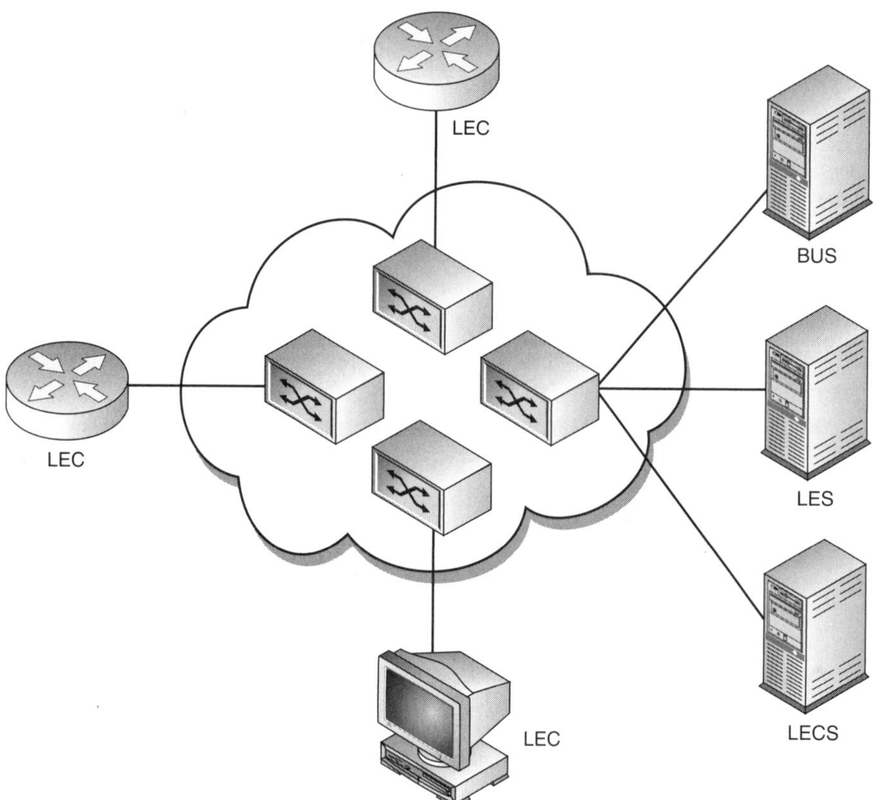

Figure 20-9 Basic LANE design

Each LEC in the LANE must register with the LES for its ELAN. The LEC is normally directed to the ATM address of its LES by the LECS. The LEC contacts the LES and registers its own ATM and MAC address with the LES, which then places the information in its ARP table. The LEC then connects to its BUS and is added to a point-to-multipoint configuration that the BUS will use when sending out broadcasts.

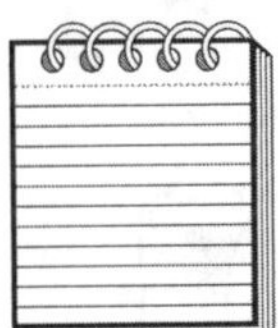

NOTE: *If a LECS is in use, it can serve all ELANs in an ATM cloud.*

LANE has its drawbacks. For instance, it can be used only with a single logical subnet, unless a router is involved. Figure 20-10 shows that if traffic from ELAN 192.168.0.0/16 needs to get to either network 10.10.10.0/24 or network 172.16.10.0/24, it must go through a router. When a router is involved, some of the benefits of ATM are lost. The router must do SAR on each cell received and processed, and it must perform route lookups and filter packets. When an ATM network is using advanced features like QoS, the latency can become a real problem, even with very fast routers.

Although LANE was once thought to be a terrific answer for networks that had legacy equipment but wanted ATM technology, it is not nearly as popular now as faster flavors of Ethernet, such as Gigabit Ethernet. ATM, when compared to Ethernet for the LAN, can be considerably more expensive to implement and maintain.

ATM Design

ATM network design may apply to a WAN or a LAN. It is versatile enough to serve in almost any capacity in a networked environment. Typical ATM network designs include the following:

- Point-to-point links
- Point-to-multipoint links
- High-speed support for workgroups and backbone
- VLAN (Virtual LAN)

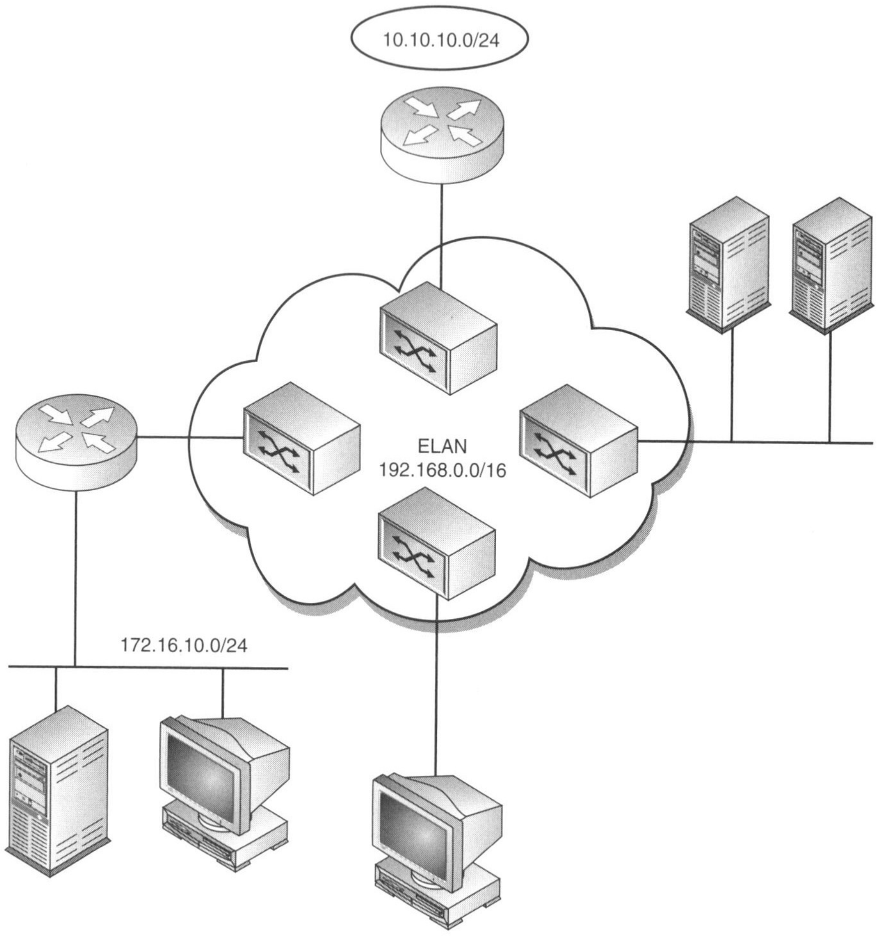

Figure 20-10 Design limitations of LANE

- Backbone router clusters
- Entire LAN/WAN

You can implement virtual circuits in the ATM network design in two ways: Non-Broadcast Multi-Access (NBMA) and hub-and-spoke. The NBMA design, as shown in Figure 20-11, requires a point-to-point virtual connection between each network point. This approach is highly recommended but somewhat expensive compared to the hub-and-spoke approach, also shown in Figure 20-11. The disadvantage of the hub-and-spoke approach is the additional work that the ingress router—that is, the router

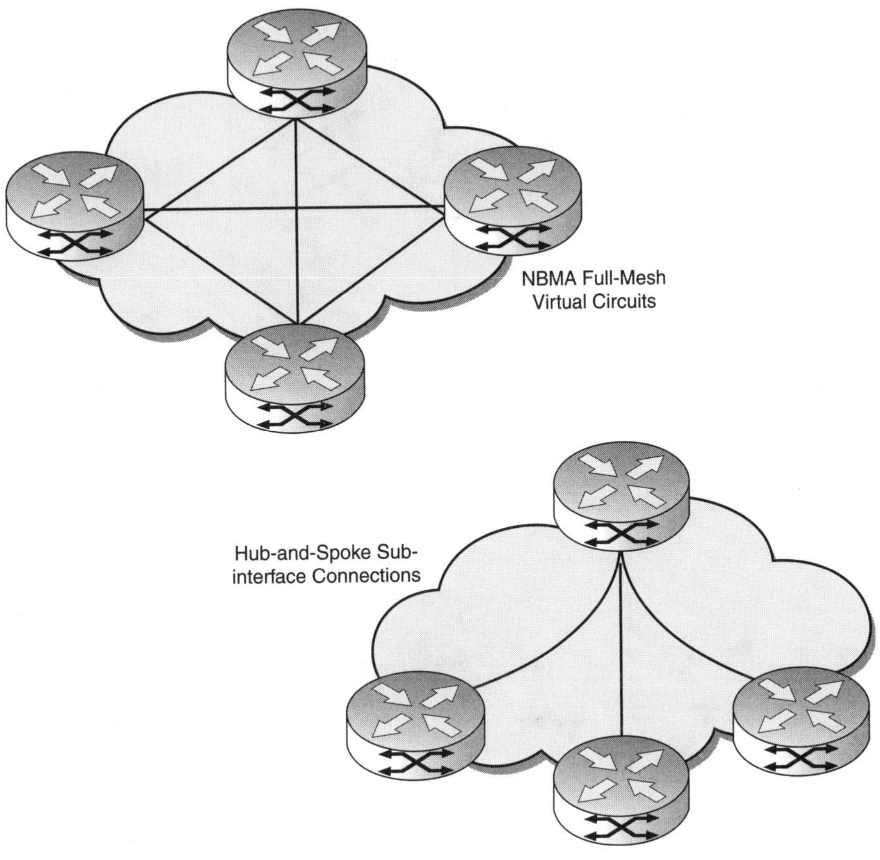

Figure 20-11 Basic ATM design models

receiving traffic—must do for multiple subinterfaces, versus the one-to-one NBMA model.

Figure 20-12 shows the most popular implementation of ATM in the LAN. Here it is used in the campus backbone to provide core as well workgroup support. In this example, different speeds of Ethernet may be used to connect the nodes in each campus to the ATM switch. The switch acts as an uplink for the campus workgroups. Logically, each building in this design is its own broadcast domain, because a router is used at each location. The backbone can then be linked to a router to provide connectivity to the distribution layer of the design model.

In the WAN, ATM can be used by service providers to deliver high bandwidth for extended periods of time with great reliability and service quality.

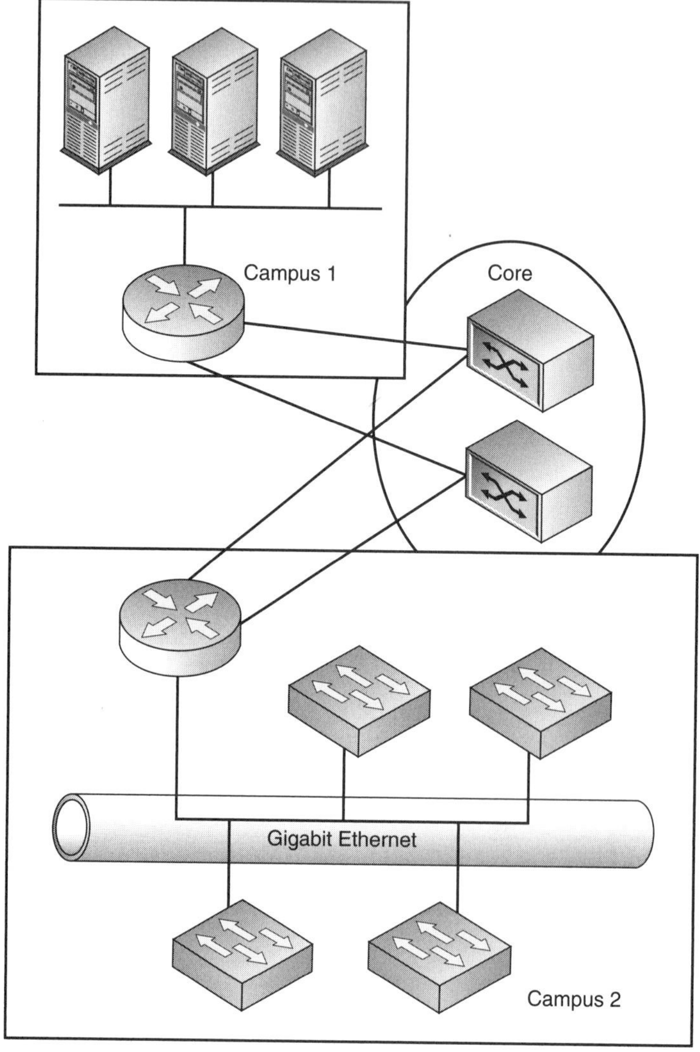

Figure 20-12 Campus backbone—ATM

Many providers are also offering support for all of a business's transmission needs (data, voice, and video) through a single connection. It is like "one-stop shopping" for the customer's in-road to the Internet and telephony clouds. Figure 20-13 shows an ATM WAN with connectivity between a provider edge (PE) router and a customer premises edge (CPE) router. Tunneling or Virtual Private Networks (VPNs) can be run through the provider ATM cloud with guaranteed service levels and throughput while avoiding congestion and delay.

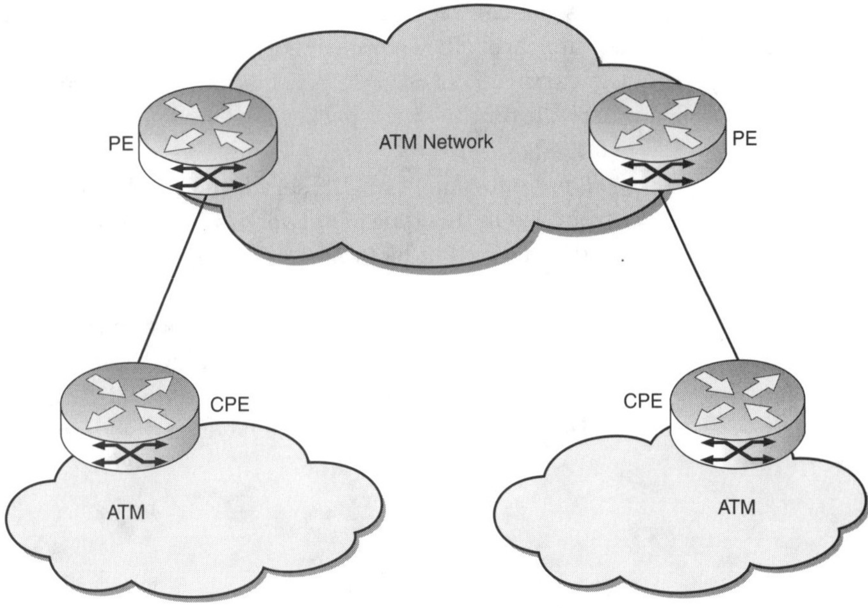

Figure 20-13
ATM WAN design

StrataCom

Cisco StrataCom switches are the product of Cisco's acquisition of StrataCom, Inc. in 1996. Cisco purchased the ATM switch manufacturer to bring a portfolio of ATM offerings to its customers quickly, with little development lead-time. StrataCom switches are easily deployed and managed in the Cisco-based ATM network and are supported by Cisco support services. In the next chapter, we will discuss StrataCom switch models and implementations in depth.

SMDS Networks

The Switched Multimegabit Data Service (SMDS) is based on the IEEE 802.6 metropolitan area network (MAN) standard in conjunction with broadband remote access (BBRAS) ISDN specifications. SMDS provides a way to extend the LAN through a citywide (within 10 kilometers) connection. The SMDS network requires special switching equipment that can be expensive.

As you can see in Figure 20-14, a high-end router with a high-speed serial interface (HSSI) connects to an SMDS DSU (SDSU), usually provided by the carrier. This SDSU performs the cell-to-frame conversion required to carry the data over the packet-switched network beyond the customer's network edge.

The limitation of SMDS service is usually the T3 speed. The adaptation layer used in this type of network is AAL3/4. The connection appears, to the customer's router, like any LAN connection, which is one benefit of SMDS service.

SMDS is a cell-based, connectionless service that takes packetized data, such as Layer 3 protocol data units (PDU), and converts it into 53-byte cells that will be reassembled as packets on the other end of the connection. The SMDS cells consist of a 44-byte payload, five-byte header, and four-bytes of

Figure 20-14 SMDS network service

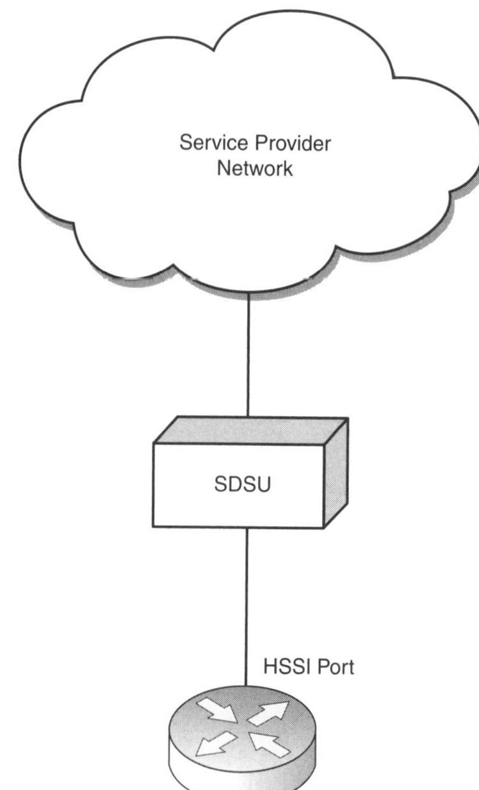

overhead. No call setup or teardown processes are involved in the connection. The SDSU does all of the work.

In Cisco's SMDS implementation, all protocols are supported—IP, IPX, AppleTalk, DECnet, Banyan VINES, XNS, CLNS, and transparent bridging. The address mapping is specific to the protocol being used. Some protocols, such as AppleTalk, may require a static entry, but others, like TCP/IP, can benefit from SMDS multicast and ARP capabilities to obtain addressing. SMDS addressing is usually the responsibility of the carrier or service provider. An example of an SMDS configuration can be found on the Cisco Web site at **http://www.cisco.com/warp/public/132/5.html**.

Case Study

MetraTech, Ltd. is a company that has recently recognized an increase in bandwidth demands both inside its network and to its partner organizations. Because the company provides video teleconferencing to the desktop for staff meetings and over the WAN to its partner organizations, it needs to eliminate some of the problems with network delay and jitter. The network engineering staff would like to have technology in place that will allow them to allocate bandwidth with QoS and IP differentiated services (DiffServ).

MetraTech, Ltd. has its main campus in Houston, with branch offices in San Antonio and El Paso, as you can see in Figure 20-15. Partner organizations include a video equipment manufacturer in San Jose, CA, and a consulting firm in Seattle. The company needs to be able to conduct business securely both with data and with video teleconferencing. Currently, it is paying very high monthly costs to maintain leased T3 lines between Houston, San Antonio, and El Paso, in addition to the fractional T1 between satellite offices that completes the full-mesh design.

The way the company sees it, it needs to increase bandwidth and reliability as well as provide for service-level specifications for certain traffic types. The engineering staff favors the current use of a full-mesh environment, because downtime cannot be tolerated. They would also like to improve the bandwidth and reliability of the links to the partner organizations.

We encourage you to sketch out a design plan, taking the known problems into account along with possible future requirements. Be sure to note the type of adaptation layer used.

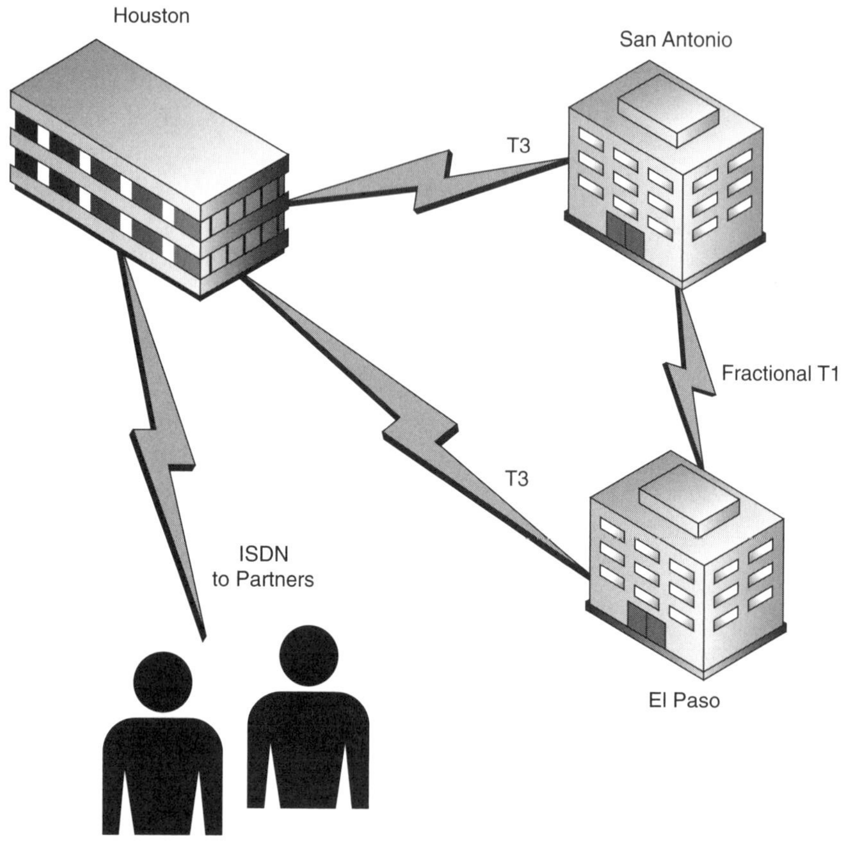

Figure 20-15 The MetraTech, Ltd. network

Although there is no one right answer to any given design problem, we have suggested one solution in Appendix C, "Suggested Solutions for Case Studies."

Study Hints

Although no one can disclose test items or test content, we can give hints as to what might be valuable to study. For this chapter, the following key facts need to be reviewed and remembered.

- **Know your protocol**.
  - ATM is both a hardware and software protocol.

- SMDS is a connectionless software protocol that extends a LAN over the MAN.

- **Understand LANE.**
  - Although some schools of thought say that LANE is quickly receding from real-life designs (and thus from tests), as long as it is a viable Cisco product, you can expect it to be on certification exams.
  - LANE is a way to use ATM technology for legacy addressing (such as Ethernet) in an emulated LAN (ELAN) environment.
  - Study the types of servers described in this chapter and remember the specific functions of each type.

- **Know your ATM service types.**
  - ATM service is specified in bit rates: the constant bit rate (CBR) for traffic types that require dedicated bandwidth at a given level, the variable bit rate (VBR) for bursty traffic, and the available bit rate (ABR) for traffic flows that need to use as much bandwidth as is available at any given time.

- **Understand address types and routing protocols.**
  - Public networks use E.164-specified addresses. These addresses are like telephone numbers with country code identifiers.
  - Private networks use Network Service Access Point (NSAP) addresses that are 20 bytes in length and can be managed dynamically through ARP-like services.
  - Static routing is obtained by using the Interim Interswitch Signaling Protocol (IISP). Dynamic routing is performed using the Private Network Node Interface (PNNI).

CCDP Tips

This section contains an abbreviated list of topics covered in Chapter 20. Think of this section as the equivalent of reading Cliff's Notes™ instead of reading an entire book. You will get the general idea of the chapter but will benefit more from reading the chapter in its entirety.

ATM Technology

ATM is a connection-oriented, fixed-cell technology that provides a reliable delivery of voice, video, and data over the LAN or the WAN. ATM cells are 53 bytes in length, including a five-byte header and up to 48 bytes of payload, depending on the adaptation layer used.

Benefits of ATM

- Handles mixed media types—voice, video, and data
- Reduces cost of bandwidth
- Improves network performance
- Reduces network downtime
- Offers the capability to provide Quality of Service (QoS) to subscribers

Virtual Circuits (VCs) Created in software (versus dedicated lines, which are hardware-based). Each VC has a virtual path identifier (VPI) and a virtual channel identifier (VCI) pair that tell the network how to switch the packets, much like a Frame Relay map. Three types of VCs can be used in ATM:

- **Permanent Virtual Circuit (PVC)** A manually configured point-to-point or point-to-multipoint link that provides a guaranteed, "always on" connection.
- **Switched Virtual Circuit (SVC)** A circuit that is set up when needed and is torn down when the call is completed. The service is available on a first-come, first-serve basis for available bandwidth. Think of it as the telephone service. If all circuits are busy, you cannot place a call, but usually calls can be placed with no problems whatsoever.
- **Soft PVC (SPVC)** A circuit that requires some initial manual configuration, but which provides the benefits of an SVC. The circuit is flexible enough to take alternate routes through the service provider cloud when primary routes are congested or down.

ATM Adaptation Layers ATM adaptation layers are like a thin veneer between the ATM protocol functions and the upper layers. It helps adapt current or legacy technology to be able to take advantage of an ATM network.

- AAL1 is used primarily for voice traffic. It uses a constant bit rate (CBR) service type and depends on the physical medium (SONET) for its clocking. AAL1 uses sequence numbers and sequence number checking to ensure that voice traffic is processed in the order in which it was sent.
- Some wireless service provides greater reliability by using silence suppression and data compression techniques available in AAL2. No SAR is performed in AAL2, so multiple streams can fit into a single cell. The streams are identified by the use of an offset field (OSF). AAL2 is now being used in some networks for multimedia messaging and desktop video.
- AAL3/4 is used to provide reliable network service to connectionless protocols like SMDS. Because of its extensive error checking, AAL3/4 has a good deal of overhead (nine bytes) and spends more time in segmentation and reassembly (SAR) of traffic than other adaptation types.
- AAL5 is used mostly for data traffic. It has low overhead (5 bytes) and permits the full 48-byte payload portion of the cell to be used for data. It provides error checking for connectionless protocols like IP with the use of a 32-bit cyclical redundancy check (CRC).

ATM Routing

- Static routing can be performed by using the Interim Interswitch Signaling Protocol (IISP). This is normally used only when legacy equipment in the network cannot use PNNI routing.
- The Private Network Node Interface (PNNI) is a dynamic routing protocol based on the shortest path algorithm (the same algorithm used in OSPF). PNNI works best with a hierarchical address model and can support the E.164 public network addressing or the NSAP private addressing formats. PNNI uses peer groups and special nodes to handle the exchange of information between the hierarchical layers of the network.
- LAN Emulation (LANE) was developed to provide for ATM support of Ethernet addressing and equipment. By using the emulated LAN concept and special server types, LANE can provide the ARP, broadcast, and configuration technology normally offered only in an Ethernet LAN environment but with the speed and reliability of an ATM network.

ATM Design Models

- Non-Broadcast Multi-Access (NBMA) full-mesh is one way that ATM can be implemented. By using dedicated point-to-point VCs between all nodes in the network, greater reliability is offered by the use of redundancy and multiple paths.
- Hub-and-spoke partial-mesh is another way to set up the ATM network. In this design model, multiple VCs come into a single router through subinterfaces. This simplifies the network and reduces cost but can also create a single point of failure along with extra demand on the ingress router.
- In the LAN, ATM switches can be used in the core to provide reliable, high-speed service between subnets and campuses.
- In the WAN, ATM switches can link a customer premises edge to the provider edge where tunneling or VPNs can provide secure virtual paths between end points.
- StrataCom switches, which will be discussed in more depth in the next chapter, can be used in the LAN or WAN to create an end-to-end Cisco ATM solution.

Switched Multimegabit Data Service (SMDS) Networks SMDS networks are used primarily to extend the LAN into the metropolitan area network (MAN) within a 10-kilometer radius. With special equipment requirements and a limitation of T3 speeds, SMDS is not among the technologies you will frequently encounter. It is sometimes used in school networks. SMDS is a connectionless protocol.

Summary

As we look back at the information presented in this chapter about ATM and SMDS, several points should be emphasized:

- Both ATM and SMDS used fixed-size 53-byte cells for the transport of mixed traffic types over LANs or WANs.
- LANE was once becoming popular as businesses sought to improve LAN bandwidth with ATM to 155 Mbps, but as faster, less expensive technologies such as Gigabit Ethernet became more widely available, LANE use began to drop off.

- Although these technologies require special equipment, which can sometimes be expensive, the use of ATM in the core or over the WAN and the use of SMDS in the MAN can increase the reliability and bandwidth availability required by today's networks.

It should be noted as well that ATM NICs for desktop and laptop computers are difficult to find and prohibitively expensive. The models that are available today cost about four times as much as an Ethernet NIC. It is better to design ATM into the core of the network for MPLS and QoS, and into the WAN for higher bandwidth to destination networks.

In Chapter 21, "Overview of the WAN Design," we will see how StrataCom switches can be used to extend ATM into the WAN using a total Cisco solution.

Questions

The following review questions have been selected to help you test your knowledge of the subject matter contained in this chapter. You will also find these questions contained in the CD-ROM included with this book. Although these are not the questions you will find on the certification exams, knowing the answers to the review questions in this book will help cement the material in your mind as you prepare for the tests.

1. AAL stands for
   - **a.** ATM Adoption Layer
   - **b.** ATM Adaptation Layer
   - **c.** ATM Adaptation Latency
2. SMDS is a way for the LAN to be extended into the
   - **a.** WAN
   - **b.** ELAN
   - **c.** MAN
3. True or False: AAL2 uses a silence suppression technique to squeeze out unused payload space in cell traffic.
   - **a.** True
   - **b.** False

4. Which type of server is used in LANE to provide for the broadcast of routing information, for example?
   a. LEC
   b. LECS
   c. LES
   d. BUS
5. At which layer of the ATM protocol reference model is clocking performed for AAL1?
   a. Data Link
   b. Physical
   c. ATM
   d. Upper layers
6. Static routing in an ATM environment can be provided using which protocol?
   a. UNI
   b. PNNI
   c. IISP
7. What is the algorithm on which PNNI is based?
   a. Shortest path first
   b. First-come, first-serve
   c. First-in, first-out
   d. Longest prefix match
8. What is the speed limitation of an SMDS environment?
   a. T1
   b. T3
   c. DS1
   d. 155 Mbps
9. What is the cell loss priority (CLP) portion of a cell header used for?
   a. Discard eligibility
   b. QoS
   c. Error checking

10. Which statement describes the *primary* benefit of using a soft PVC?
    - a. No manual configuration required
    - b. Guaranteed throughput
    - c. Ease of use
    - d. Its capability to route around problem areas
11. Which function of ATM is responsible for disassembly of a cell?
    - a. PNNI
    - b. SAR
    - c. CRC
12. Of the following ATM adaptation layers, which has the greatest amount of overhead?
    - a. AAL1
    - b. AAL3/4
    - c. AAL5
13. True or False: ATM is a connectionless protocol.
    - a. True
    - c. False
14. To which node does the peer group leader (PGL) pass information about its own hierarchical layer of PNNI routing?
    - a. LGN
    - b. LLN
    - c. NNI
15. What is the cell size used in SMDS?
    - a. 44
    - b. 53
    - c. 48
16. Which identifier is used to track multiple data streams in AAL2 communications?
    - a. OSF
    - b. SPF
    - c. VPI/VCI pair

17. When is it appropriate to use the variable bit rate (VBR) as a service type for ATM traffic?
    a. When traffic is static in nature
    b. When traffic is bursty in nature
    c. When guaranteed bandwidth is not required
18. True or False: PNNI does not support E.164 address types.
    a. True
    b. False
19. How does the receiving station in an AAL5 transmission know if errors have been encountered?
    a. HEC
    b. CRC
    c. SAR
20. ATM technology is also sometimes called
    a. Frame relay
    b. Cell relay
    c. Rapid relay

Answers

1. AAL stands for
   b. ATM Adaptation Layer
   Explanation: The ATM Adaptation Layer provides for adaptation of other technologies so that they can use the ATM protocol.
2. SMDS is a way for the LAN to be extended into the
   c. MAN
   Explanation: SMDS extends the LAN to the MAN within a 10-kilometer radius (usually within the city).
3. True or False: AAL2 uses a silence suppression technique to squeeze out unused payload space in cell traffic.
   a. True
   Explanation: AAL2 is used by some wireless providers to increase the efficient use of the cells while reducing data loss and jitter.

4. Which type of server is used in LANE to provide for the broadcast of routing information, for example?
   d. BUS
   Explanation: The broadcast and unknown server knows about all of the nodes in its ELAN through a point-to-multipoint configuration. When a cell is destined for all nodes or for a node that is unknown, the BUS floods the cell to all known ELAN nodes.

5. At which layer of the ATM protocol reference model is clocking performed for AAL1?
   b. Physical
   Explanation: AAL1 depends on the SONET physical medium to provide the clocking.

6. Static routing in an ATM environment can be provided using which protocol?
   c. IISP
   Explanation: The Interim Interswitch Signaling Protocol (IISP) is used on many older ATM devices and requires static configuration.

7. What is the algorithm on which PNNI is based?
   a. Shortest path first
   Explanation: Like OSPF, PNNI chooses the best route by running the SPF algorithm. It also maintains a topology of its neighbors in a table.

8. What is the speed limitation of an SMDS environment?
   b. T3
   Explanation: An SMDS network is connected to the customer premises by use of a HSSI port, which can accommodate a bandwidth up to 45 Mbps (DS3/T3).

9. What is the cell loss priority (CLP) portion of a cell header used for?
   a. Discard eligibility
   Explanation: The CLP portion of the header assigns a priority to the information being transmitted, so that the switch can make a valid decision on the importance of that traffic, should it need to drop cells due to congestion or other problems.

10. Which statement describes the *primary* benefit of using a soft PVC?
    d. Its capability to route around problem areas
    Explanation: The primary benefit of using a soft PVC is to leverage its capability to find a route through the provider cloud without being tied to a path that could represent a single point of failure.

11. Which function of ATM is responsible for the disassembly of a cell?
    b. SAR
    Explanation: SAR stands for segmentation (disassembly) and reassembly of cells.

12. Of the following ATM adaptation layers, which has the greatest amount of overhead?
    b. AAL3/4
    Explanation: With nine bytes of overhead, AAL3/4 is the most costly ATM adaptation layer.

13. True or False: ATM is a connectionless protocol.
    b. False
    Explanation: ATM is connection-oriented and reliable.

14. To which node does the peer group leader (PGL) pass information about its own hierarchical layer of PNNI routing?
    a. LGN
    Explanation: The logical group node (LGN) acts as the "go-to guy" within the lower echelon peer group and listens to its group leader at the next higher level.

15. What is the cell size used in SMDS?
    b. 53
    Explanation: SMDS uses the same 53-byte cell size as ATM.

16. Which identifier is used to track multiple data streams in AAL2 communications?
    a. OSF
    Explanation: The offset field (OSF) is used to identify the different streams in AAL2 communications.

17. When is it appropriate to use the variable bit rate (VBR) as a service type for ATM traffic?
    b. When traffic is bursty in nature
    Explanation: The use of VBR in network situations where sporadic, bursty traffic is the rule allows for the maximum efficiency of bandwidth utilization. Why build a fat, permanent pipe for traffic that may only occasionally burst to that level?

18. True or False: PNNI does not support E.164 address types.
    b. False
    Explanation: PNNI supports both E.164 and NSAP address formats in ATM.

19. How does the receiving station in an AAL5 transmission know if errors have been encountered?
    b. CRC
    Explanation: A 32-bit CRC is calculated before the cell is forwarded. The receiving station uses the CRC to check the data received.

20. ATM technology is also sometimes called
    b. Cell relay
    Explanation: Because it forwards or relays cells (rather than packets or frames), ATM is sometimes called a cell relay technology.

Frequently Asked Questions (FAQs)

1. *What is IP-to-ATM CoS?*

   CoS stands for class of service, a term that can be used interchangeably with IP differentiated services (DiffServ). DiffServ is a way for service providers to use the IP type of service (ToS) bit to differentiate the type of packet, and thus the level of service to give that type of packet, as it travels through the provider edge. In this chapter, we have introduced you to ATM, which supports QoS. The transition from IP CoS, or DiffServ, to ATM CoS as the traffic enters the ATM cloud is referred to as IP-to-ATM CoS, and vice versa. In this process, the QoS parameters of one technology are mapped into corresponding parameters in the other technology. Cisco has several white papers on their implementation, located at **http://www.cisco.com/pcgi-bin/Support/PSP/psp_view.pl?p=Internetworking:ATM:IP_ATM.**

2. *What is OAM?*

   OAM is a term used for the Operation, Administration, and Maintenance (OAM) enhancement for use in monitoring ATM connections. OAM is used to monitor the number of dropped cells on a PVC. When a configurable number is reached, the PVC will be brought down. This prevents routers with routing table entries that point to a PVC that is no longer passing traffic from continuing to forward cells, which are then dropped. More information on OAM management is available on the Cisco Web site at **http://www.cisco.com/warp/public/121/oam.html**.

Bibliography

Cisco Internetwork Design Course Manual, version 3.0, April 1997, Cisco Systems, Inc. RFC 1483, RFC 2225

StrataCom Strategic Wide Area ATM Networks, Cisco Systems, **http://www.cisco.com/univercd/cc/td/doc/product/wanbu/bpx8600/8_2_0/82over/sysmch01.htm**

The ATM Forum, **http://www.atmforum.com**

Designing ATM Networks, Cisco Systems, Inc., **http://www.cisco.com/univercd/cc/td/doc/cisintwk/idg4/nd2008.htm**

Switched Multimegabit Data Service (SMDS), Cisco Systems, Inc., **http://www.cisco.com/univercd/cc/td/doc/cisintwk/ito_doc/smds.htm**

SMDS Addressing, Cisco Systems, Inc., **http://www.cisco.com/warp/public/132/4.html**

ATM Theory and Applications, McDysan and Spohn, McGraw-Hill, 1999

CHAPTER 21

Overview of WAN Design

Overview

In the summer of 1996, Cisco Systems acquired StrataCom, Inc., in order to add to its portfolio of networking equipment. StrataCom was a manufacturer of ATM and Frame Relay switches. With the acquisition, Cisco was able to add WAN switching to its offerings. In the agreement, the two companies also outlined a plan to put the Cisco IOS on the switches. As with all of its equipment, Cisco maintains a common software infrastructure throughout.

In this chapter we are going to lay out the different switches that are currently offered and show you how they can fit into your overall WAN design. At the end of the chapter, you will have a chance to practice what you have learned with a set of review questions and a short case study.

Today's WAN is becoming large and complex in nature. The network architect must be familiar with ATM, Frame Relay, ISDN, xDSL, dial-up access, and more. The traffic no longer consists of purely data, but contains delay-sensitive video and voice traffic as well. As we can see in Figure 21-1, the types of input into the WAN seem to keep growing. Whereas we once

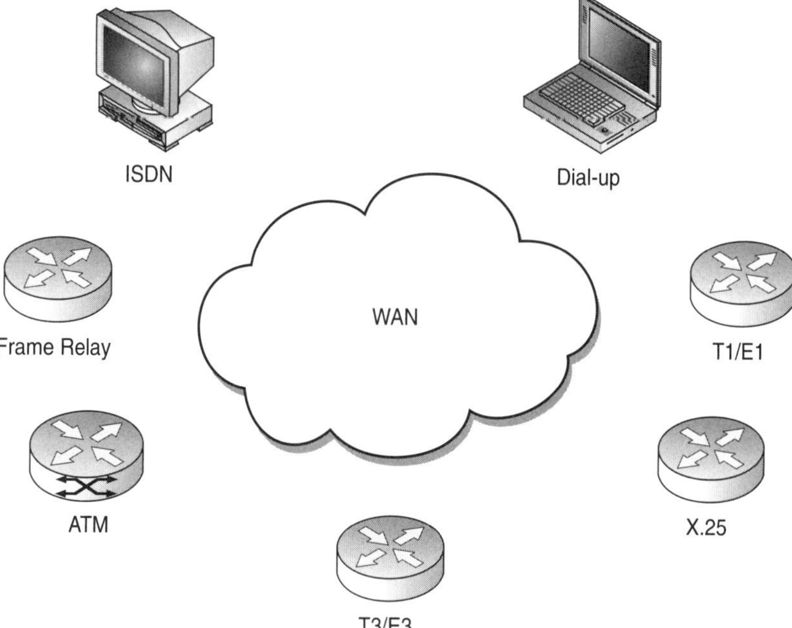

Figure 21-1 WAN design growth

may have imagined that by now we would have a common infrastructure to suit every need, what we have is a myriad of technologies that require our expertise to design and manage.

StrataCom

The StrataCom switches that we will introduce to you in this section support a variety of WAN protocols. In the private WAN sector, they can support multiband ATM applications. In the public sector, they support native ATM and Frame Relay. The switches we are about to discuss are

- BPX Switch
- IGX Switch
- MGX Switch and Concentrator

Each type has a different application for which it was designed.

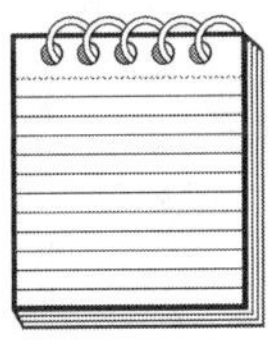

NOTE: *In the CID course material, the IPX switch was still an available product. The IGX 8400 wide-area switch has since replaced it. See the Cisco end-of-life notice for more information:* **http://www.cisco.com/univercd/cc/td/doc/pcat/ipx.htm**.

BPX Switches

The *BPX IP+ATM* switches are robust, 15-slot broadband ATM switches, to be used in larger, busier networks. Three slots are for common equipment cards, and the remaining twelve slots are for interface cards. Each switch operates at 9.6 Gbps and can aggregate existing narrowband networks across the backplane. The BPX switch has available interfaces ranging from T3/E3 to OC-12/STM-4.

In Figure 21-2, we see two BPX switches connecting the LAN and an MGX 8220 concentrator over an ATM backbone. One switch is connecting to both a public carrier and an NNI cloud. The other switch is acting as an aggregation point for the LAN to the ATM backbone.

The BPX switch comes in three models—the BPX 8620, the BPX 8650, and the BPX 8680 Universal Service Node (USN). The major difference

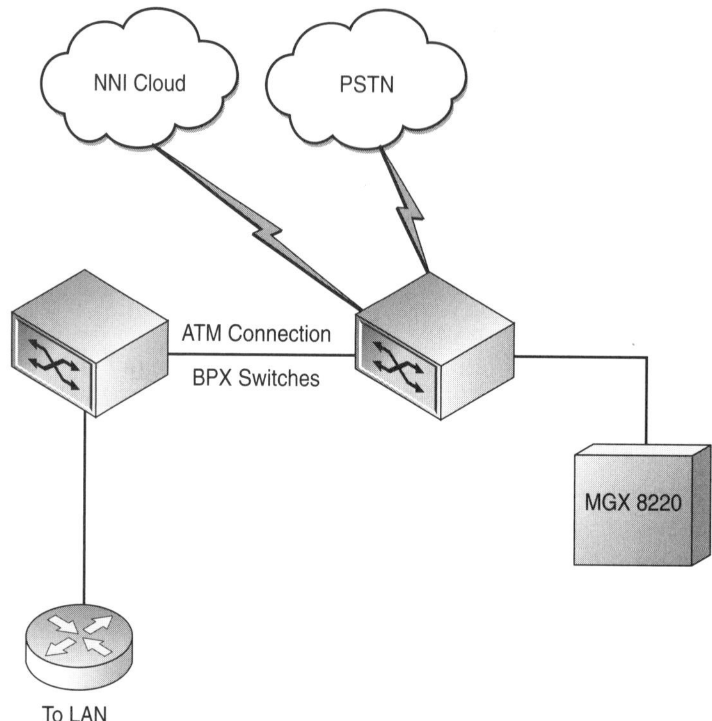

Figure 21-2
BPX/AXI switches

between the 8620 and the 8650 is that the BPX 8650 has added a *Label Switch Controller* (LSC) that provides Layer 3 services, and enables the use of newer technologies, such as Multi-Protocol Label Switching (MPLS) and Layer 3 Virtual Private Networks (VPN). The 8680 USN can provide for all service types—broadband, narrowband, and MPLS.

IGX Switches

The IGX switch is a multiservice ATM switch—meaning that it can handle voice, video, and data traffic—with a 1.2 Gbps backplane. It comes in models that include 8, 16, or 32 slots, depending upon the requirements of the network design. It supports trunk speeds ranging from 256 Kbps to OC-3/STM-1, so it is clearly designed for smaller, lower throughput WANs.

The IGX is perfect in scenarios like the one shown in Figure 21-3, where it is connecting several large points of a campus together. It can also form

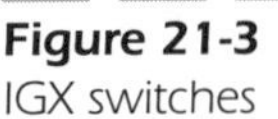
Figure 21-3
IGX switches

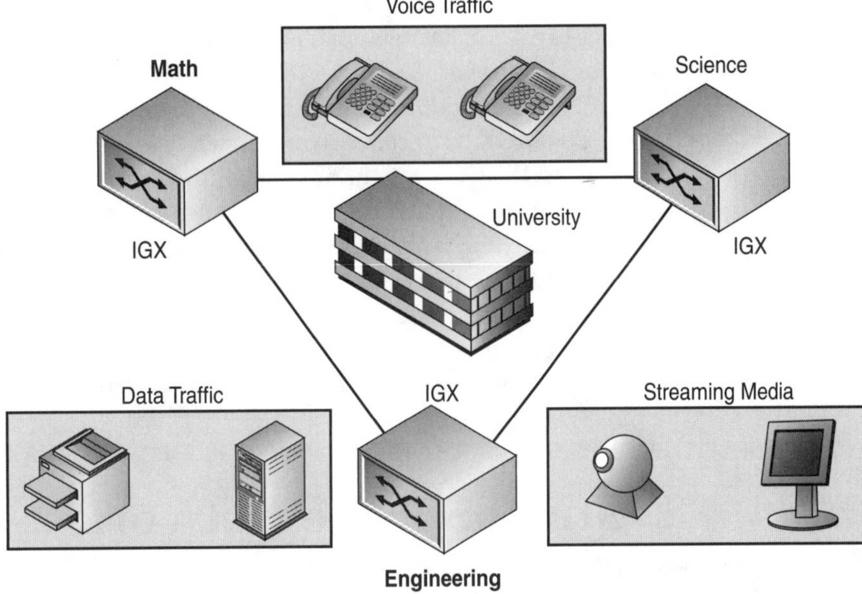

the basis for leased-line traffic or an ATM WAN or MAN, connecting several campuses and carrying mixed service types, as the core switch in the design. In standalone mode, the IGX can also serve as a user access entry point. The IGX can also be configured as a feeder switch to another IGX or to a BPX switch.

MGX

There are two MGX models available to use for narrowband applications at the network edge:

- MGX 8850 Edge Switch
- MGX 8220 Edge Concentrator

The MGX 8850 switch can use many of the same interface cards as the MGX 8220 concentrator. It differs in that it is capable of switching services between service modules or between a service module and the backbone trunk. Designed to enhance Cisco's WAN switching product line, the MGX is capable of both local and remote switching. Port speeds range from DS0 to OC-48c. Trunks are E3, DS-3, OC-3/STM-1, and OC-12/STM-4. All interface cards are hot swappable and support full redundancy. The MGX switch provides support for voice over IP or ATM, VPNs, circuit emulation, wireless or DSL aggregation, and traditional Frame Relay and ATM services.

The MGX 8220 concentrator is what was formerly called the AXIS shelf. The MGX 8220 can handle core functions or network services such as Frame Relay, T1, E1 and Frame-based User-to-Network Interface (FUNI). The 8220 concentrator is an interface shelf (also called a *feeder shelf*) for the BPX 8600 switch, or it can act as an access point to the ATM network, when in standalone mode.

Figure 21-4 shows how the two devices might be used in a WAN. For illustration purposes, different link speeds are shown.

StrataSphere Network Management

StrataSphere is a suite of network management applications, built around the HP OpenView platform, that reside on a single Network Management Station (NMS) in the WAN. StrataSphere consists of these applications:

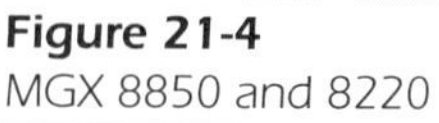

Figure 21-4 MGX 8850 and 8220

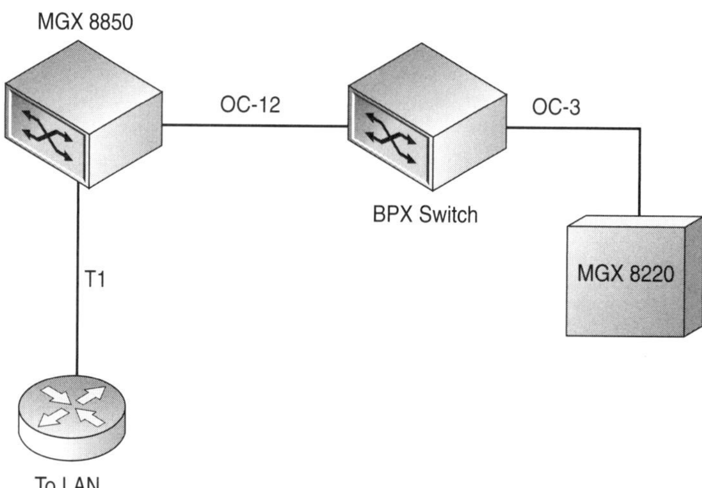

- StrataView+
- StrataSphere BILLder
- StrataSphere Modeler
- StrataSphere Adaptor
- SNMP Service Agent

The various components of *StrataView+* allow for graphical viewing and management of network devices. For instance, the administrator can add, modify, or delete ports and lines on an 8220 concentrator. *StrataSphere BILLder* allows the administrator to input customized billing policies, which it then compares captured traffic flow against for simplification of customer invoicing.

StrataSphere Modeler is a tool built into the StrataSphere suite that does simple, preliminary design work—less complex than what can be done with the modeling tools we will discuss later in this chapter. *StrataSphere Adaptor* provides a third-party interface for the sharing and conversion of data with other, commercial-off-the-shelf (COTS) products. Finally, the *SNMP Service Agent* can be loaded on remote equipment to enable it to send data back to the StrataSphere suite for statistical collection.

Network Services

In a complex WAN design, the StrataCom line of switches and concentrators can support many services. Because of the vast amount of traffic that can potentially cross a busy WAN, it is important that the services are handled rapidly and efficiently. This section will introduce you to some of the ways that the StrataCom products handle these tasks.

Trunk links are full-duplex communication lines between either an interface shelf to a routing node or between two routing nodes. Like trunk links on LAN switches, the WAN trunks handle the passing of all traffic, much like a bridge. The links are meant to be fast, with very low latency. The type of traffic that passes through these WAN trunk links is ATM traffic. The ATM cells can be in standard 53-byte format or can be in the proprietary Fast Packet 24-byte cells, used with IGX switches only.

The StrataCom Intelligent Network Server (INS) handles call setup for the StrataCom network. INS is actually a set of three different software products that come loaded on a Unix-based platform that is rack mountable.

The applications are

- **Dial-up Frame Relay** Uses soft Permanent Virtual Circuit (PVC) configurations that are activated as needed when a call is initiated.
- **Dynamic Network Switching** Provides voice Switched Virtual Circuit (SVC) services across a StrataCom network for PBXes.
- **INS ATM SVCs** Provide SVCs across the StrataCom ATM network. No resources are used unless a call is in session.

Many applications are bursty in nature, unpredictable. As you have already seen in Chapter 17, "Frame Relay Design," with traffic needs that fluctuate, Frame Relay is usually the best choice. Fortunately, StrataCom switches provide for Frame Relay services across the cell relay network. One problem that could occur is that Frame Relay networks work best in a fully-meshed design. In a StrataCom network, however, PVCs are used to carry the data frames. This allows the network to perceive a permanent connection without incurring the overhead or cost associated with it—unless there is data to be transmitted.

One way that Frame Relay traffic is sent over the network is through the User-to-Network-Interface (UNI). This is a method by which frames are sent over a network from a source to a destination. Another method is over the Network-to-Network-Interface (NNI), which allows separate WANs to communicate with each other. No end-stations or users are involved in the communications.

The StrataCom implementation of Frame Relay even plans for the forwarding of frames that do not conform to Frame Relay standards. By recognizing any frame that contains data as a valid frame, the local Frame Relay port will forward these non-standard frames over a single PVC to a remote Frame Relay port. The forwarding process assumes that a valid Frame Relay connection will be found. If not, the frames are discarded at the receiving end.

To avoid congestion in the Frame Relay cell relay network, StrataCom provides software such as Credit Manager. Credit Manager allows for a "save for a rainy day" policy that allows a port to accumulate "credits" that can be used when data transmission is needed. Credits are issued at a steady rate as dictated by the Committed Information Rate (CIR) for the Frame Relay circuit. The fact that credits can accumulate permits those initial large bursts of traffic to go through smoothly but allows the Credit Manager to effectively throttle the traffic back if the high traffic continues.

Another way that StrataCom networks handle congestion is by support of the Explicit Congestion Notification (ECN) bits in the frames. If a port notices that its input buffer is reaching a preset threshold, it sets the Forward ECN (FECN) bit. The destination device is then notified that congestion is occurring. It sets the Backwards ECN (BECN) bit to tell the user device that congestion is occurring. Now the sending device can throttle back the transmission as needed.

StrataCom networks can also handle point-to-point data connections over circuit-mode data ports. Connections between the cell relay network and standard data communication interfaces operate at speeds up to 1.344 Mbps through a variety of interface types. There are several types of compression and multiplexing techniques available to customize the network to suit the needs of the business. For more information, consult Cisco's Web site at **http://www.cisco.com/univercd/cc/td/doc/product/wanbu/84/switch/sysm/syssrvov.htm#2447**.

StrataCom devices support voice and fax connections over the ATM network. These calls can be set up and handled by the INS. Voice calls are received in compressed format for processing by the switch over a T1 line. They can be sent over SVCs by INS Voice Network switching, as shown in Figure 21-5, or simply recompressed and forwarded by the switch to the destination PBX.

Even though the voice traffic is important, it is usually considered less important than the data traversing the network. Therefore, StrataCom switches provide a couple of methods for control of the bandwidth in the network:

- **Courtesy downing** Frees up bandwidth when a call is no longer active.

Figure 21-5
INS Voice Network switching

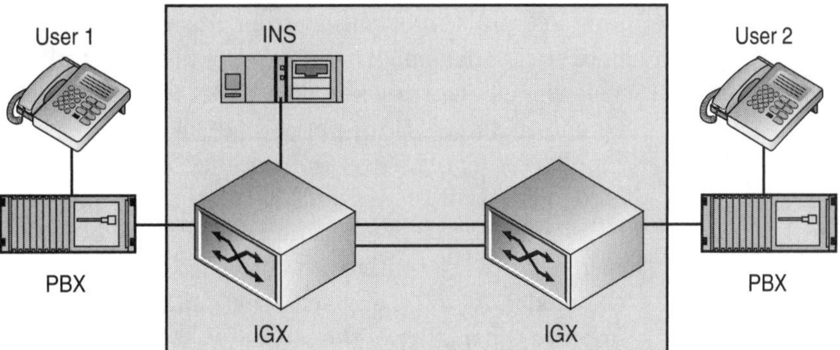

- **Bandwidth reservation** Configures inactive connections to become active at a configurable point in time. This allows for use of the bandwidth for moving large files, for instance, across bandwidth normally used for voice traffic.

Network Design

The aim of this section is to introduce you to the tools Cisco provides to help with the design and modeling of the WAN, as well as to show you a few of the more common network design models you may use.

Tools

Cisco has software tools to help with design of the WAN using StrataCom systems. The software is built around the *Network Modeling Tool* (NMT), which helps you design around the various WAN switches discussed in this chapter, as well as some network edge equipment.

NOTE: *The NMT and related applications must be loaded on a Sun SPARC station.*

As shown in Figure 21-6, NMT can receive data from several sources.

The *Configuration Extraction Tool* (CET), along with two conversion plug-ins, pulls information from StrataView+, part of the StrataSphere network management suite, and puts it right into the topology database. This is a one-way process. The *Third-Party Interface* (TPI) permits data to be output to any third-party analysis tool and read back into the NMT. Finally, the *Spreadsheet Interface* (SSI) allows for information to be gathered and output to Microsoft Excel or any supported database software.

In addition to modeling the topology of a network, NMT will give you the correct software configuration needed to configure the network shown in the model. As with any tool, the quality of the data you put into it will improve the quality of the output. When data entry is complete, the output

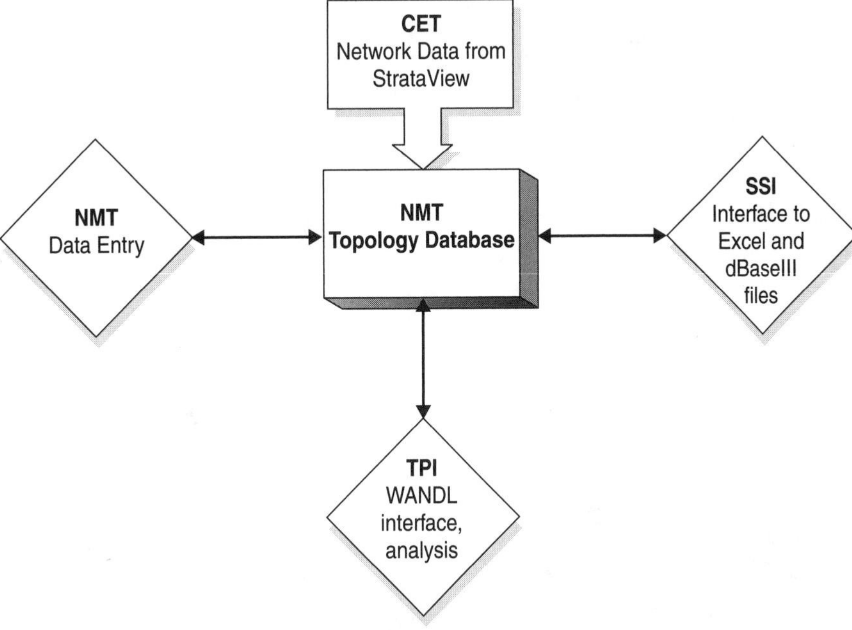

Figure 21-6 Modeling tools

will be in the form of graphical display, reports, and updated tables. NMT meshes nicely with the idea of a well-managed network. As the network grows and changes, you can keep the information updated on the NMT. Likewise, you can respond to changing requirements by modeling any proposed network modifications on the NMT first, to see how it might impact your overall design.

Now we will look at the three most common WAN design models.

Flat Networks A *flat network* can be simply defined as one in which all network nodes have knowledge of each other and can freely communicate with one another. The nodes are connected together using *trunks.* Figure 21-7 shows how a flat network design might look.

Tiered Networks In a tiered network, a node can be either a *routing node* or an *interface shelf*, as shown in Figure 21-8. The interface shelf, sometimes called a *feeder node*, acts as an interface between user devices and a single routing node. Interface shelves are single-trunk devices and cannot serve to link routing nodes or routing and switching nodes together.

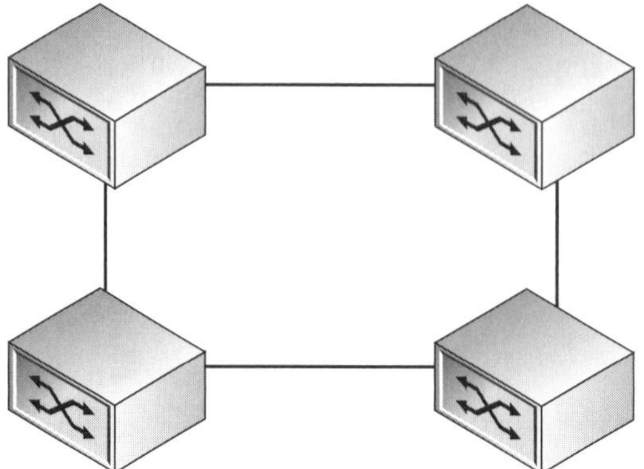

Figure 21-7 Flat network topology

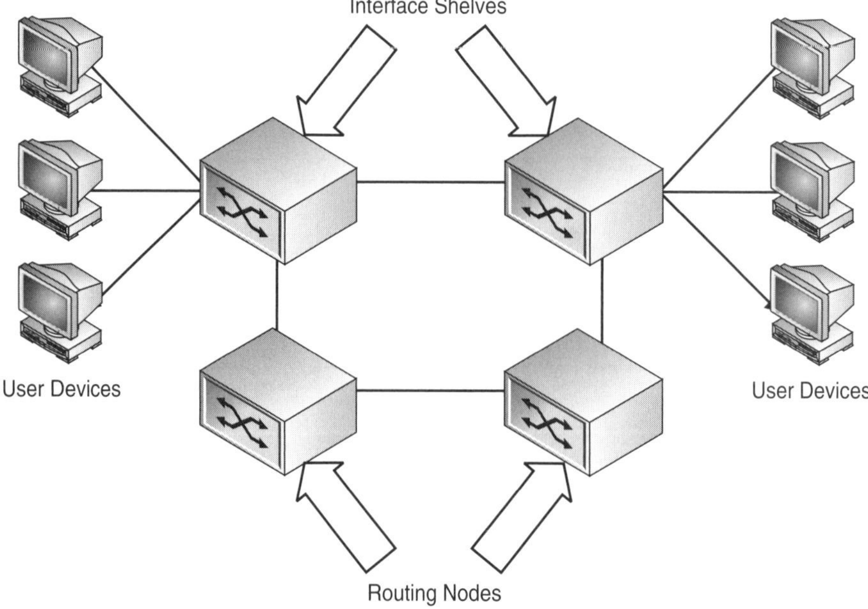

Figure 21-8 Tiered-network topology

Structured Networks Larger, more complex networks require a different approach. The use of a *structured* topology allows for greater scalability as the network grows and changes. In Figure 21-9, you can see that we have separated the WAN into several domains. Our choice was to break out the domains geographically because of the network size. You could also

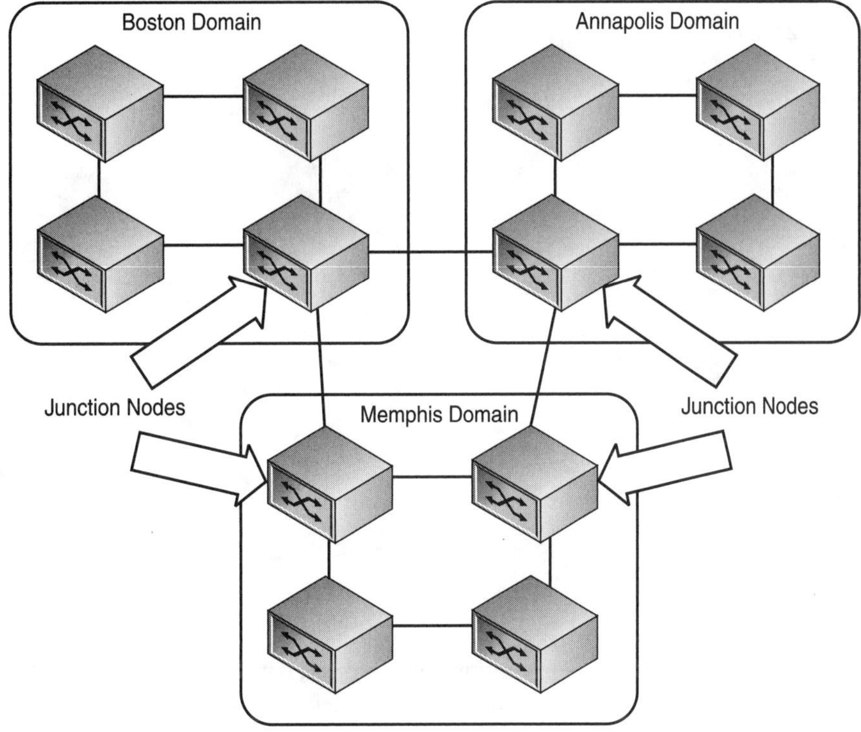

Figure 21-9 Structured network topology

choose to break out the domains along boundaries of interest, such as by department in a large university infrastructure.

Within a domain, the topology can be either tiered or flat, depending upon the needs of the network area. Each domain contains at least one *junction node*, which connects the domains together. This type of WAN design can scale up to about 384 nodes, according to Cisco.

Case Study

FasTransport Systems has asked for a preliminary design of an ATM backbone network. They have three large sites, shown in Figure 21-10, located in Cincinnati, Princeton, and Portland. Each of these sites has been growing at a rapid pace around an ATM infrastructure. The company wants to link all three sites together with OC-12, if possible. The sites currently have

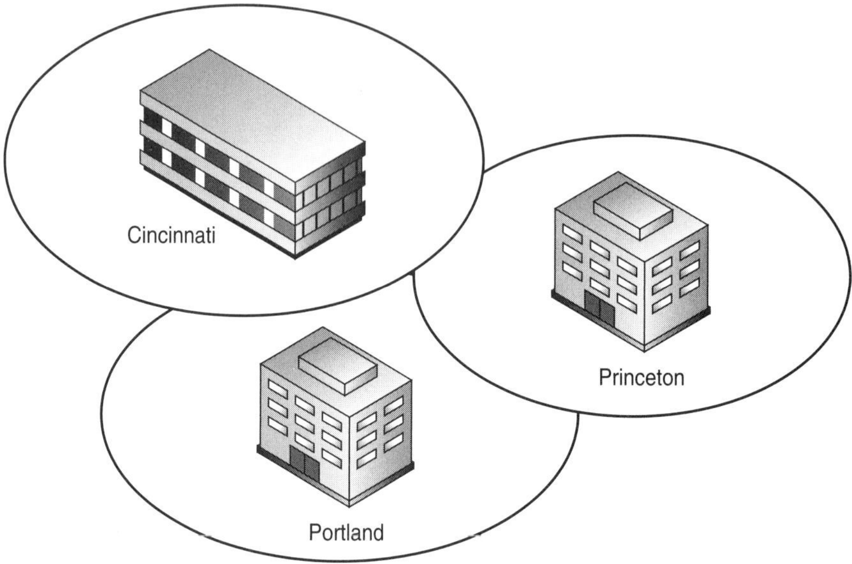

Figure 21-10
FasTransport Systems

another vendor's equipment, which has reached end-of-service. They will be replacing the user interfaces with Cisco equipment.

Given the information you have about FasTransport Systems, what type of topology might you select for them? How would you link the sites together and with what models of WAN switches? Sketch out your ideas on paper and compare them to our solution in Appendix C, "Suggested Solutions to Case Studies.".

CCDP Tips

This section contains an abbreviated list of topics covered in this chapter. Think of this section as the equivalent of reading Cliff's Notes™ instead of reading an entire book. You will get the general idea of the chapter but will benefit more from reading the chapter in its entirety.

Types of Switches

- **BPX** switches are large, 15-slot broadband ATM switches designed for large networks.

- **IGX** ATM switches are designed for smaller networks with lower bandwidth requirements. They come in models with 8, 16, or 32 slots.
- The **MGX** switch and concentrator are designed for the provider edge. The concentrator replaces the AXIS interface shelf.

Network Management

StrataSphere network management consists of a suite of tools, built around the HP OpenView platform, that permit for the configuration, policy, and SNMP management of the StrataCom product line.

Network Services

- **Frame Relay services** are provided by forwarding valid frames across a single PVC to a Frame Relay destination. This is better known as Frame Relay cell relay, as the frames are being forwarded across a cell relay (ATM) network.
- **Congestion avoidance** is performed either by Credit Manager, which allows circuits to accumulate circuit usage "credits" in order to "pay" for large bursts of traffic, or by the use of Forward Explicit Congestion Notification (FECN) or Backward ECN bits in the frame. When a FECN bit is set, the receiving station sets a BECN bit to notify the sending device to slow the transmission because of congestion.
- **Voice and fax transmissions** are accommodated by the StrataCom switches using standard compression techniques or by allowing INS Voice Network switching service to handle the call setup and teardown.

Network Design Network design can be modeled using the Network Modeling Tool (NMT). NMT can extract data from StrataView+ or manual entry and output it in graphical or text format for use in configuring one of the following network types:

- **Flat networks** consist of nodes that have knowledge of and connectivity to one another. All nodes are equal.
- **Tiered networks** consist of routing nodes and interface shelves. The routing nodes connect to each other or to interface shelves via trunk lines. Interface shelves connect to the user devices and to a single routing node, via a trunk line.

- **Structured networks** are built around domains. Domains can contain a variety of switching equipment, including routing nodes. A routing node that is used to connect domains together is known as a junction node.

Summary

As you can now see, StrataCom switches and concentrators can be an important part of any WAN design. They are flexible and robust and can handle the many types of traffic that can pass through the WAN. In Chapter 22, "BGP Design." we will look at BGP design and how the WAN routing protocol of choice can be used to create an efficient and scalable wide area network.

Questions

The following review questions have been selected to help you test your knowledge of the subject matter contained in this chapter. You will also find these questions contained in the CD-ROM included with this book. While these are not the questions you will find in the certification exams, knowing the answers to the review questions in this book will help cement the material in your mind as you prepare for the tests.

1. What switch model replaced the IPX WAN switch?
   a. IGX 8400
   b. BPX 8620
   c. MGX 8850
2. True or False: An interface shelf can support multiple trunk links.
   a. True
   b. False

3. What switch model supports the edge of the carrier network?
   a. MGX 8850
   b. MGX 8220
   c. BPX 8650
4. What software tool is used to bank unused bandwidth in order to accommodate large, initial bursts of traffic?
   a. INS
   b. Credit Manager
   c. NMT
   d. StrataSphere BILLder
5. True or False: In a flat network, all network nodes have knowledge of all other network nodes.
   a. True
   b. False
6. What type of Frame Relay connection facilitates traffic between two WANs?
   a. UNI
   b. NNI
   c. PVC
   d. SVC
7. What WAN switch is designed for smaller networks with lower throughput requirements?
   a. IPX
   b. IGX
   c. BPX
   d. MGX
8. What StrataCom model was formerly the AXIS shelf?
   a. IPX
   b. MGX 8220
   c. IGX 8400

9. In a structured network, what type of node connects domains together?
   a. Routing node
   b. Junction node
   c. Domain node
   d. T-node
10. What part of the Network Management Tool extracts data from StrataView+?
    a. VNS
    b. SSI
    c. TPI
    d. CET
11. In the INS Voice Network switching functionality, what service is provided in order to store unused bandwidth for other types of traffic, such as data?
    a. Courtesy downing
    b. Bandwidth reservation
    c. Credit Manager
    d. StrataSphere BILLder
12. What is the name of the proprietary cell length used by some StrataCom products?
    a. Fast Packet
    b. Frame Cell Relay
    c. D4
    d. LMI
13. True or False: In a tiered network, a network node can only be *either* an interface shelf or a routing node, but not both.
    a. True
    b. False

14. What type of interface, port, or circuit is used by StrataCom for the forwarding of Frame Relay traffic?
    - **a.** T1
    - **b.** SVC
    - **c.** Serial
    - **d.** PVC
15. True or False: Data from the NMT can be output to a spreadsheet for manipulation.
    - **a.** True
    - **b.** False

Answers

1. What switch model replaced the IPX WAN switch?
   a. IGX 8400
2. True or False: An interface shelf can support multiple trunk links.
   b. False
3. What switch model supports the edge of the carrier network?
   a. MGX 8850
4. What software tool is used to bank unused bandwidth in order to accommodate large, initial bursts of traffic?
   b. Credit Manager
5. True or False: In a flat network, all network nodes have knowledge of all other network nodes.
   a. True
6. What type of Frame Relay connection facilitates traffic between two WANs?
   b. NNI
7. What WAN switch is designed for smaller networks with lower throughput requirements?
   b. IGX

8. What StrataCom model was formerly the AXIS shelf?
   b. MGX 8220

9. In a structure network, what type of node connects domains together?
   b. Junction node

10. What part of the Network Management Tool extracts data from StrataView+?
    d. CET

11. In the INS Voice Network switching functionality, what service is provided in order to store unused bandwidth for other types of traffic, such as data?
    b. Bandwidth reservation

12. What is the name of the proprietary cell length used by some StrataCom products?
    a. Fast Packet

13. True or False: In a tiered network, a network node can only be *either* an interface shelf or a routing node, but not both.
    a. True

14. What type of interface, port, or circuit is used by StrataCom for the forwarding of Frame Relay traffic?
    d. PVC

15. True or False: Data from the NMT can be output to a spreadsheet for manipulation.
    a. True

Frequently Asked Questions (FAQs)

1. *Where can I get more information about configuring StrataCom devices?*

   The best place to go is Cisco's Web site. Here is a URL that contains loads of information on these products—everything from field notices to information on loading configurations from a TFTP server: **http://www.cisco.com/warp/customer/74/wansw_index.shtml**.

   Note that it requires a CCO login.

Bibliography

Cisco Internetwork Design Course Manual, version 3.0, April 1997, Cisco Systems, Inc.

Cisco WAN Quick Start, McCarty, Cisco Press, 2000

Network Services Overview, Cisco Systems, **http://www.cisco.com/univercd/cc/td/doc/product/wanbu/84/switch/sysm/syssrvov.htm#2447**

StrataCom Strategic Wide Area ATM Networks, Cisco Systems, **http://www.cisco.com/univercd/cc/td/doc/product/wanbu/bpx8600/8_2_0/82over/sysmch01.htm**

Overview of the WAN Design Tools, Cisco Systems, **http://www.cisco.com/univercd/cc/td/doc/product/wanbu/nmt/91tools/nmtintro.htm**

CHAPTER 22

BGP Design

Overview

By far one of the most complex and interesting routing protocols is the Border Gateway Protocol (BGP). BGP, as outlined in RFC 1771, was originally introduced in the early 1990s to replace the older Exterior Gateway Protocol (EGP) and to address the requirement for loop-free communication between autonomous systems (ASs). As you may recall from earlier chapters, an autonomous system is a group of network nodes and end-user devices that are located within a common administrative framework. This inter-AS communication is handled by what we now know as External BGP or EBGP. BGP can also be used within an AS as Internal BGP (IBGP). IBGP and EBGP are subsets of the current specification for BGP—version 4 (BGPv4).

BGP is a *path vector protocol*, which means that the initial data flow through the backbone makes up the routing table. Two routers that have established communication are known as *peers* and send each other incremental updates when or if a change occurs in their networks. If no data is passing between the peers, TCP keepalives are sent to keep the session open.

This chapter will focus on how BGP works. To do the protocol justice, however, would mean filling an entire book with the nuances of the operations and design possibilities. It is impossible, and impractical, to do so within this book. As of this writing, BGP network design is not included in the CID course, so we will not include study hints. By the end of the chapter, you should have a good basic understanding of what BGP is, what it does, and where you may encounter it in network design.

Protocol Characteristics

The BGP protocol is most often encountered in large enterprise, carrier, or service-provider networks that exchange global routing information with other autonomous systems. In this section, we will discuss the various components of the protocol, examine how it is intended to work, and explain how it makes its routing decisions.

BGP Communication

BGP uses a reliable transport protocol (TCP Port 179) to deliver information, which means that it requires a TCP connection to be established before it allows the exchange of routing information. Once the connection is established, the two routers—called *peers*—immediately exchange the full BGP routing table. Thereafter, only incremental updates about changes are exchanged, which conserves bandwidth and resources, as we have seen with interior gateway protocols in earlier chapters. In Figure 22-1, we see that Router A and Router B are exchanging the routing tables relevant to their own AS.

While the peers maintain this connection, they must also maintain the routing table of each peer to which they are connected. This connection is called an *external link* if the communication is between two different AS's, and it is called an *internal link* if the communication is within the same AS. The information gleaned from the routing tables enables the routers to choose the best path to a given destination, although all paths are "remembered."

BGP Message Types

BGP peers communicate by transferring messages to one another. These messages can consist of the header only, at 19 octets (with no data), or with any amount of data up to 4,096 bytes total message size. The format of the BGP header is shown in Figure 22-2.

Figure 22-1
A BGP session

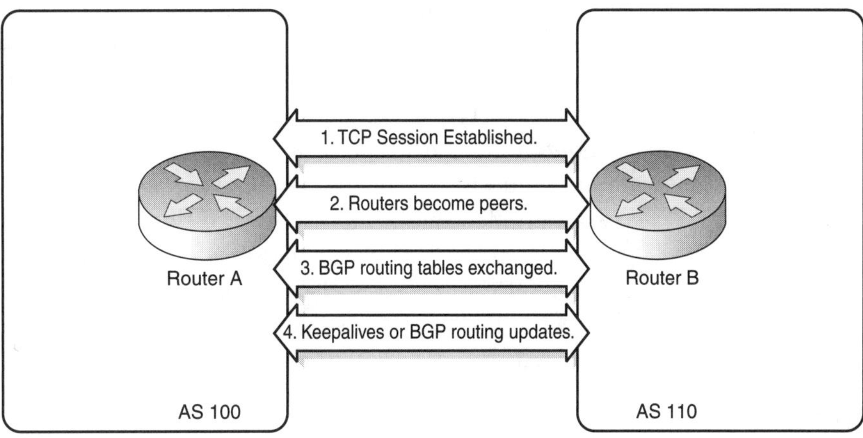
1. TCP Session Established.
2. Routers become peers.
3. BGP routing tables exchanged.
4. Keepalives or BGP routing updates.
Router A
Router B
AS 100
AS 110

Figure 22-2
The BGP header

BGP Header Format

MARKER (16 bytes)	LENGTH (2 bytes)	TYPE (1 byte)	DATA (variable length)

Regardless of the type of message, every message has a fixed-size header containing the following fields:

- 16-octet *marker* that can be used by the receiving peer to make some determination about the message.
- 2-octet *length* field that must be at least 19 octets and no more than 4,096 bytes. It tells the peer how long the total message will be. The message will not be processed until it has been received in its entirety.
- 1-octet *type* field that describes the type of message being sent.

Four types of BGP messages can be exchanged:

- OPEN
- UPDATE
- NOTIFICATION
- KEEPALIVE

The OPEN message type contains several fields, in addition to the mandatory BGP headers, that help establish the peer relationship. These include a 1-octet *version* field, which is always set to 4 (the current BGP version); a 2-octet *My Autonomous System* integer identifying the AS of the sender; and a 2-octet *holdtime* integer proposing a holdtime to be used as a maximum number of seconds between keepalives or updates between the two peers. This holdtime value can be between 0 and 3 seconds and must be agreed upon by both peers to establish the connection successfully.

The OPEN message also contains a 4-octet *BGP Identifier* that is normally the IP address assigned to the BGP speaker. Finally, the OPEN message contains an *Optional Parameters Length* field that is 1-octet in length and identifies the length of the optional parameters, if any, that are included in the message. The optional parameters fields are used for BGP peer authentication.

The UPDATE message is used to help build the "big picture" of the inter-AS topology. It allows for the transfer of routing information between peers to build a loop-free routing environment. As with other message types, the UPDATE message will contain at least the BGP header as well as two mandatory fields: *unfeasible routes length* and *total path attribute length*. If the value of each of those 2-octet bytes is 0, the total UPDATE message length will be 23 bytes total.

The UPDATE message can also carry a lot of other information, however, whose length will be defined by these two mandatory attributes. The UPDATE message can withdraw one or more routes from service (in the *withdrawn routes* field), and it can carry a route to be advertised, if necessary, along with specific attributes of the route or path (in the *path attributes* field). Both fields are variable and optional.

The NOTIFICATION message type is sent when an error condition is detected, at which time the connection between peers is promptly closed. The message will contain the requisite BGP header as well as a 1-octet *error type* code describing the error condition, a 1-octet *error subcode* that is used if a specific subcode identifier is available, and a variable length *data* field that diagnoses the reason for the error condition. Table 22-1 shows possible BGP error codes and their related subcodes.

The KEEPALIVE message contains only the BGP header, and thus is only 19 octets in length. BGP does not use any transport protocol-based keepalive message (i.e., TCP based keepalives). It sends its own KEEPALIVE message type to keep communications open between BGP peers. The interval at which keepalives will be sent is generally one-third the holdtime interval but not less than one keepalive per second. If the holdtime interval is set to 0, no keepalive messages will be sent.

BGP Attributes

UPDATE messages in BGP can contain several path attributes. These path attributes can be characterized as *well-known mandatory, well-known discretionary, optional transitive,* and *optional nontransitive*. Each of these attribute types has significance within the UPDATE message to tell the receiving route the kind of information contained in the packet. Classification of attributes is shown in Table 22-2.

Table 22-1

BGP Error Codes and Subcodes

Error Code	Error Subcode
Message Header Error	1. Connection Not Synchronized
	2. Bad Message Length
	3. Bad Message Type
OPEN Message Error	1. Unsupported Version Number
	2. Bad Peer AS
	3. Bad BGP Identifier
	4. Unsupported Optional Parameter
	5. Authentication Failure
	6. Unacceptable Holdtime
UPDATE Message Error	1. Malformed Attribute List
	2. Unrecognized Well-Known Attribute
	3. Missing Well-Known Attribute
	4. Attribute Flags Error
	5. Attribute Length Error
	6. Invalid Origin Attribute
	7. AS Routing Loop
	8. Invalid NEXT_HOP Attribute
	9. Optional Attribute Error
	10. Invalid Network Field
	11. Malformed AS_PATH
Holdtime Timer Expired	None
Finite State Machine Error	None
Cease—errors other than those already listed	None

Table 22-2
BGP Attribute Types

Attribute	Class	Type Code
ORIGIN	Well-known mandatory	1
AS_path	Well-known mandatory	2
NEXT_HOP	Well-known mandatory	3
MULTI_EXIT_DISC	Optional nontransitive	4
LOCAL_PREF	Well-known discretionary	5
ATOMIC_AGGREGATE	Well-known discretionary	6
COMMUNITY	Optional transitive (Cisco-defined)	7
ORIGINATOR_ID	Optional nontransitive (Cisco-defined)	8
Cluster List	Optional nontransitive (Cisco-defined)	9

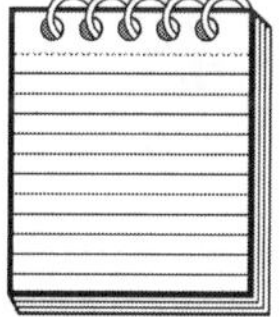

NOTE: *An example of a well-known mandatory attribute is ORIGIN. All BGP routers must support this attribute, and it must be contained in the UPDATE message. A well-known discretionary attribute is LOCAL_PREF. While all BGP implementations must support the use of this attribute, it does not have to be contained in every update message. An optional transitive attribute is COMMUNITY. It is not required to be in a BGP implementation, but any BGP router receiving this attribute within a message should pass it along to the subsequent routers. An optional nontransitive attribute is ORIGINATOR_ID. An optional attribute does not have to be supported by all BGP implementations, and a receiving BGP router does not pass on the information.*

The AS_PATH attribute is a well-known attribute, meaning that all manufacturers selling products that support BGP must support the AS_PATH attribute. It is also a mandatory attribute, meaning that it is contained in every UPDATE message.

The AS_PATH attribute contains information about where the information came from and where it has been on its route to the current destination. To simplify, the example update message in Figure 22-3 may contain an AS_PATH that says "110, 100," as the information came from Router A in AS 100, and has traveled through Router B in AS 110 en route to Router C in AS 200.

Trying to decipher the AS_PATH information can be confusing. The easiest way to read what it means is to remember that it is a mirror image of the autonomous systems that are traversed along a path. In other words, it is like a roadmap back from the destination to the source. If a path goes from AS 100 to AS 110 to AS 200 to AS 220, the BGP speaker at AS 220 will see the path as "200, 110, 100"—which does not include itself in the path.

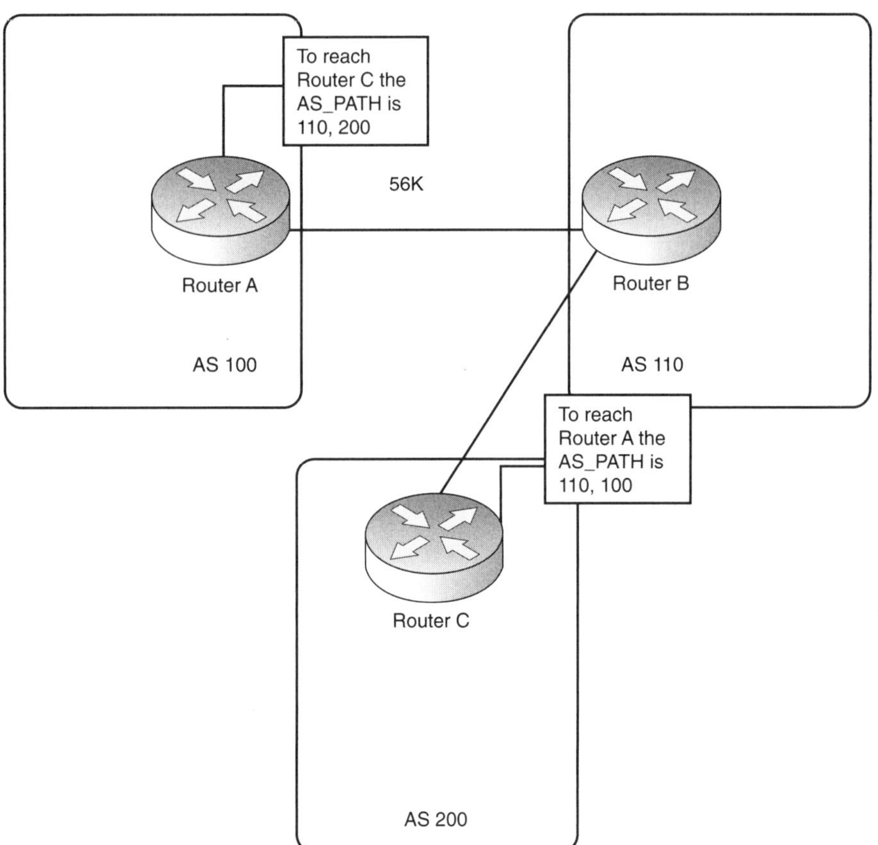
To reach
Router C the
AS_PATH is
110, 200
56K
Router A
Router B
AS 100
AS 110
To reach
Router A the
AS_PATH is
110, 100
Router C
AS 200

Figure 22-3 Example message containing an AS_PATH

The purpose of the AS_PATH attribute is to provide loop-free routing. If AS 100 receives an update message with an AS_PATH that contains its own AS number (100) anywhere in the AS_PATH attribute, it will not listen to the routes enclosed and will discard the update. By doing this, it avoids taking on new routes for which it already has a path.

AS Path Prepend BGP is like OSPF, in that it wants to take the shortest path to a destination. Take a look at Figure 22-4. The direct, and therefore shortest, path from Router A to Router B is a 56 Kbps line. The line from Router A to Router B via a T1 to a T3 circuit goes through Router C. The AS Path in the most direct path is the shortest—"100." The indirect, but faster, AS Path is "100, 110." In many instances, you would want traffic

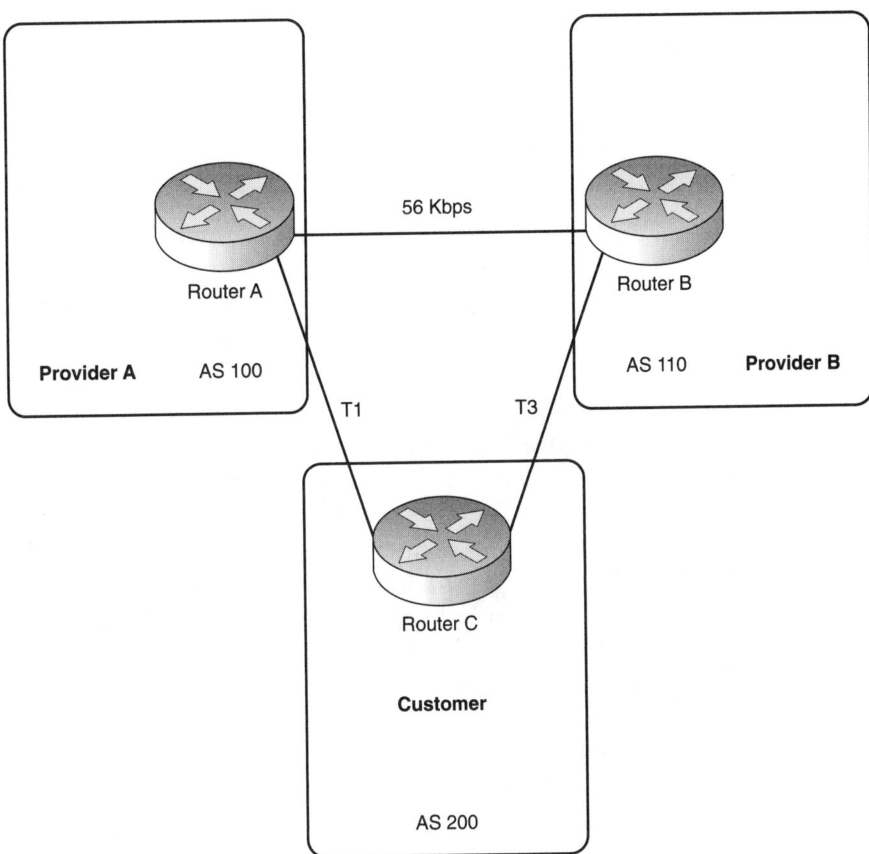

Figure 22-4
An AS Path prepend

to take a faster path versus a shorter path. In such a case, you must then force BGP to not use the shortest path.

You can manipulate the path that traffic will take by using a method known as *AS path prepending*. To do this, a router (or other BGP speaker) will pad the AS Path with multiple instances of dummy numbers (usually its own AS number) to tip the scales of the number of AS hops, so to speak. Using the example in Figure 22-4, Router A would advertise an AS Path of "100, 100, 100" to Router B. The faster route, through Router C, will not be prepended with the dummy AS numbers and would appear as "100, 110," a shorter path. Router A can be selective in its prepending of dummy numbers, depending on to whom it is advertising.

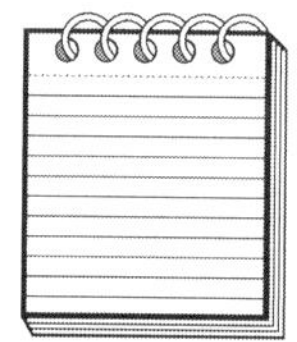

NOTE: *Inserting dummy numbers other than a router's own AS could lead to routing loops and is not a recommended practice!*

IBGP vs. EBGP

You may have heard the terms *IBGP* and *EBGP* and thought it was a rather simple distinction between intra-AS routing and inter-AS routing. This is an oversimplified way of looking at the definitions, but it does serve as an adequate description for most purposes. Let's look at them in depth.

How does one decide to use BGP internally to an AS? Don't most IGPs, especially OSPF and ISIS, serve to create scalable networks for large environments? The answer to this greatly depends on your definition of a large network and on the particular hardware and software in use. The rule of thumb is that when an IGP is handling more than 2,000 routes, it is time to think about segmenting the AS to create *regional routing* within the AS. This can be best handled with a protocol like IBGP.

As shown in Figure 22-5, several IBGP speakers are located within AS 100. The IBGP speakers will exchange information with each other, and IBGP speakers who also have external (EBGP) neighbors will exchange information with them as well. Each IBGP speaker can have its own mini-AS, or region, working within the larger AS.

A few generally accepted guidelines should be followed in respect to configuring IBGP. All the internal peers must be fully meshed within the AS. The configuration of the router must treat each IBGP peer as though it

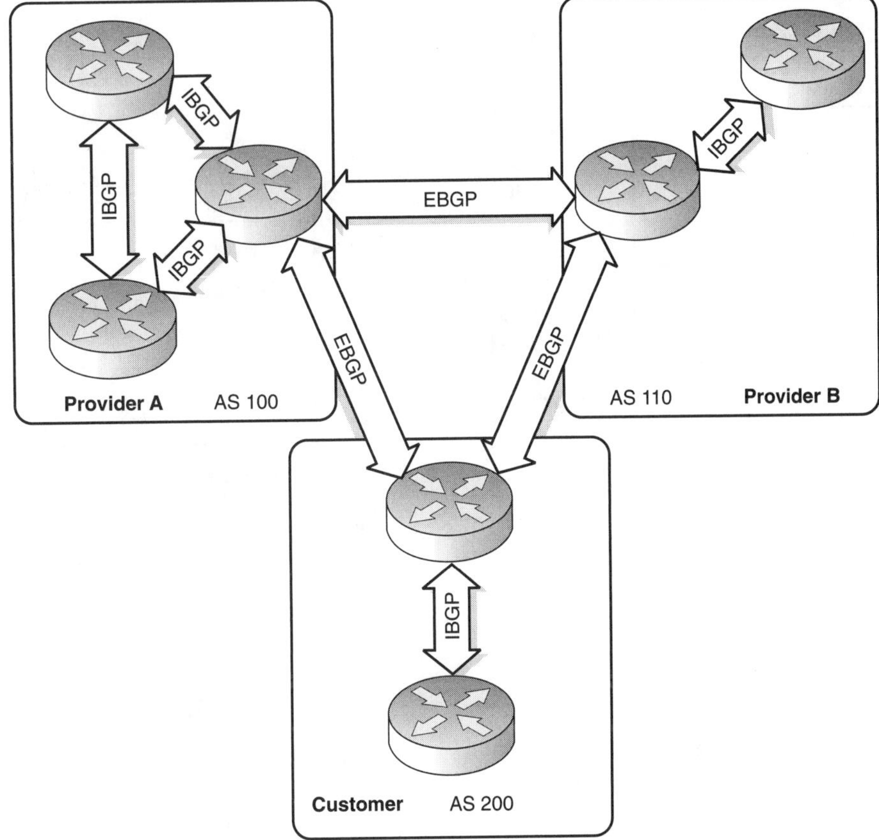

Figure 22-5 Several IBGP speakers are located within AS 100.

belonged to a remote AS, even though it is within its own AS. The identity of the IBGP speaker is usually the loopback address of the router to provide added resilience. (The use of the loopback address, as you may recall, was also recommended for OSPF.) The loopback interface is not subject to failure, as are other types of logical interfaces, and therefore is more stable and reliable.

External BGP is what we could refer to as *traditional BGP*, meaning that it functions in a manner consistent with the spirit of a true EGP—providing communications between more than one AS. In Figure 22-6, we see that AS 100 is talking to AS 110 and AS 200 via EBGP, while still carrying on intra-AS communication via IBGP to other BGP-speaking routers within its AS.

Figure 22-6
AS 100 talking to AS 110 via EBGP

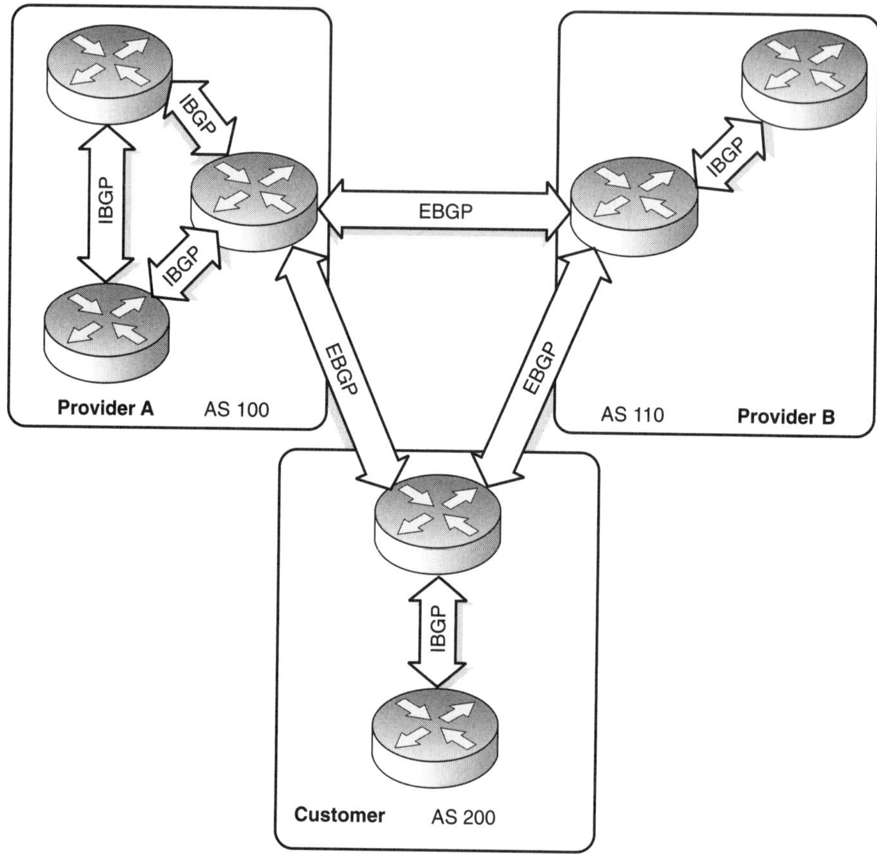

One final note is that a large part of what distinguishes IBGP from EBGP is how the route selection is processed. In other words, BGP will handle UPDATE messages differently depending on whether they came from an IBGP peer or an EBGP peer. We explore the route selection process in the next section.

Route Selection

Each BGP speaker sends and receives route advertisements or route withdrawals between itself and its peers. From the pool of routes received, it applies its own routing policies or inbound filters to choose the best route.

BGP places the best routes in its own IP routing table and filters them again as they are outbound before advertising them to other peers.

The input policy filtering takes place based on parameters such as AS Path, IP prefix, and so on. There are many complex ways to filter BGP routes that are beyond the scope of this chapter.

Once the routes have been filtered, they are entered into the BGP table. BGP then decides on the best path to a destination; if there are multiple paths, the attributes are compared and a selection of the best route is made and entered into the IP routing table.

TIP: *The Cisco Press book Internet Routing Architectures Second Edition, by Bassam Halabi, is still the best source of BGP information on the market today. By reading this book, you will greatly supplement the BGP knowledge you gain from this chapter.*

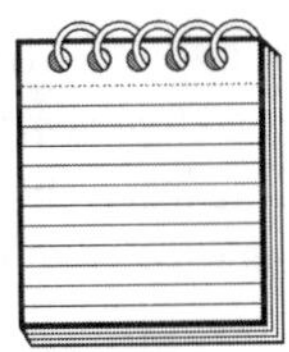

NOTE: *If no filtering is in use, all routes are seen in the routing table with one annotated as the "best" route.*

By default, BGP selects only one "best" route for the routing table, but it is possible to load balance across multiple paths. BGP uses a complex, step-by-step decision process in selecting routes. These steps are listed here:

1. If a route is received for a path in which the next hop is unreachable, BGP will ignore the route. BGP will also ignore a route that is not synchronized or is marked as "received-only" in the output of **show ip bgp <longer-prefixes>**. A route may also be rejected if the AS_PATH contains the AS number of the local AS, and if you have enabled **bgp enforce-first-as** but the UPDATE message does not list the neighbor's AS number as the first AS in the AS_SEQUENCE.
2. Next the router will compare the weights for each route. BGP will prefer the path with the highest weight. Weight is a Cisco-specific parameter.
3. If the weights are equal, BGP will look at the local preference and use the path with the largest local preference value.

4. If the local preferences are the same, BGP will prefer the route that was originated within the local BGP process. This can be from a **network** or **aggregate** statement or via redistribution from an IGP. Paths supplied from **network** or **redistribute** statements will be preferred over those from **aggregate-address** statements.
5. If none of the resulting routes originated locally, BGP will prefer the path with the shortest AS_PATH length. Exceptions to this rule are as follows:
   - It does not apply if **bgp bestpath as-path ignore** is configured.
   - An AS_SET counts as one, regardless of the number of AS's listed in the set.
   - An AS_CONFED_SEQUENCE is not included as part of the AS_PATH length.
6. If all the AS_PATH lengths are equal, BGP will look at the origin types of the paths, of which there are three types, listed here in lowest to highest order: IBGP, EBGP, and Incomplete. BGP will prefer the lowest origin type.
7. If the origin codes are the same, BGP will prefer the path with the lowest MULTI_EXIT_DISC (MED) value. The *multi-exit discriminator* is the cost of using a particular router to get to a destination, when multiple paths exist between two ASs. This value can sometimes be the only "tie-breaker" when all other factors are equal in choosing the best path. For further reading about how the MED value is used in BGP route selection, visit the Cisco Web site at **http://www.cisco.com/warp/public/459/25.shtml**.
8. When a "tie" still exists, BGP will choose the external path that was announced by an external BGP speaker with the lowest router ID over the internal path. The exception: if a route was learned as part of a confederation, it is treated as internal.
9. Paths with the lowest IGP metric to the BGP next-hop attribute are preferred.
10. BGP can load balance over a maximum of six paths. This is configurable with the **maximum-paths *n*** command, where *n* represents an integer from 1 (the default value) to 6. When maximum paths greater than 1 are enabled, BGP will insert up to *n* most recently received paths into the routing table.
11. If all factors remain tied, BGP will choose the external path that was announced by an internal BGP speaker with the lowest router ID. This

can be the loopback interface address or it can be manually set with the command **bgp router-id**. If the path contains route reflectors, the originator ID is substituted for the router ID.

12. In reference to route reflectors, if the originator ID or router ID is the same for multiple paths received, the path with the lowest cluster ID length is preferred.
13. Paths coming from the lowest neighbor address are then preferred by BGP.

BGP Operations

In this section, we cover some of the operational aspects of BGP, including aggregation, filtering, and design structures. While this section is not intended to teach you everything there is to know about BGP operations, it will help you understand some of the concepts that are important if you are to design successful BGP networks.

Single-homed vs. Multi-homed AS

The distinction between a *single-homed* and a *multi-homed AS* is that the single-homed AS has a single connection to one service provider (ISP), whereas the multi-homed AS connects to more than one provider or has multiple connections to a single provider. Things tend to get a little more complicated once you multi-home your AS, however.

There exists what is known as a *multi-homed non-transit AS*, which you can see in Figure 22-7. It has more than one connection to the Internet through ISPs, but it does not advertise routes that it learned from another AS—only its own routes. This is the typical setup for most businesses that require redundant links to the Internet. In this example, AS 200 is advertising its own networks to each ISP independently. The ISPs, in turn, advertise their networks to AS 200. But AS 200 does not advertise the networks learned from one ISP to the other! This prevents routes from Provider A from being shared with Provider B via AS 200, which could cause routing inconsistencies. The AS is not usually required to run BGP, but sometimes the ISP may require that a simple implementation be set up at the edge of the AS, if the customer's network is large enough.

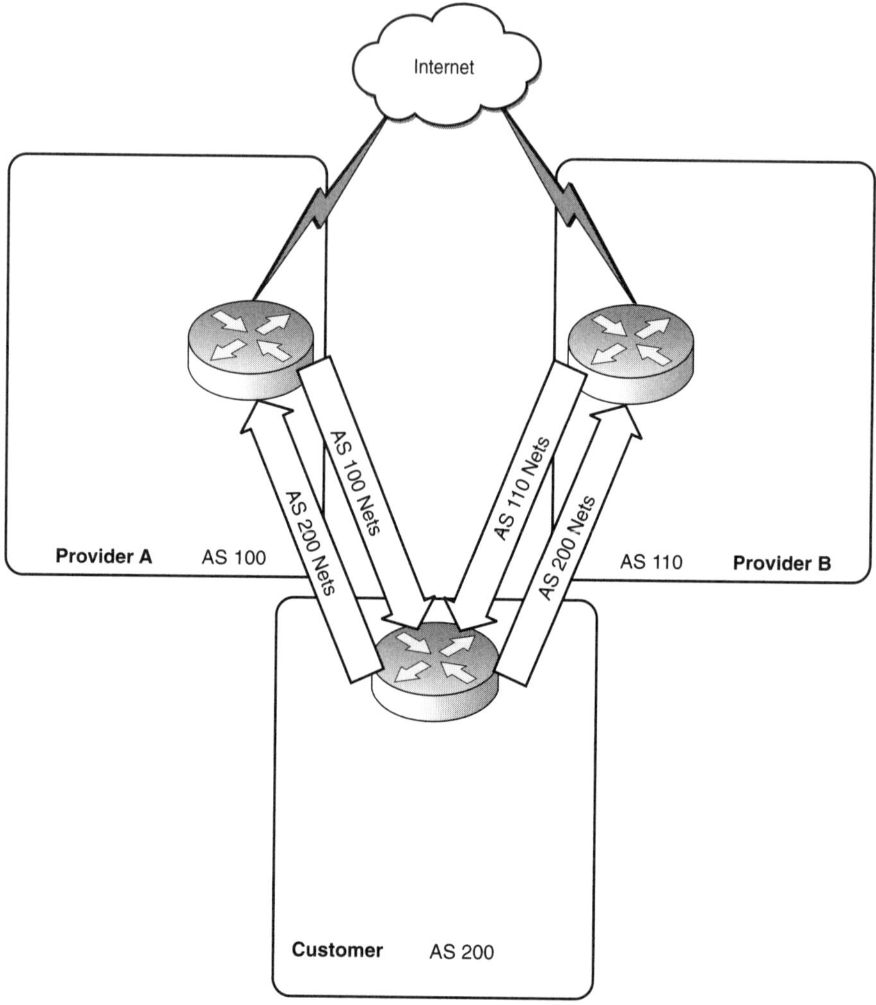

Figure 22-7 Multi-homed non-transit AS has more than one connection to the Internet through ISPs.

A multi-homed transit AS, on the other hand, can pass routes from one AS to another, as shown in Figure 22-8. The AS itself will have more than one connection to the Internet, by definition, and may have a router serving as either a *transit router*, meaning that it pipes BGP traffic through its own AS between other ASs, or a *border router*, meaning that it is running EBGP between its own and at least one other AS. In this example, you can see that AS 200 is now advertising its own networks as well as those learned from

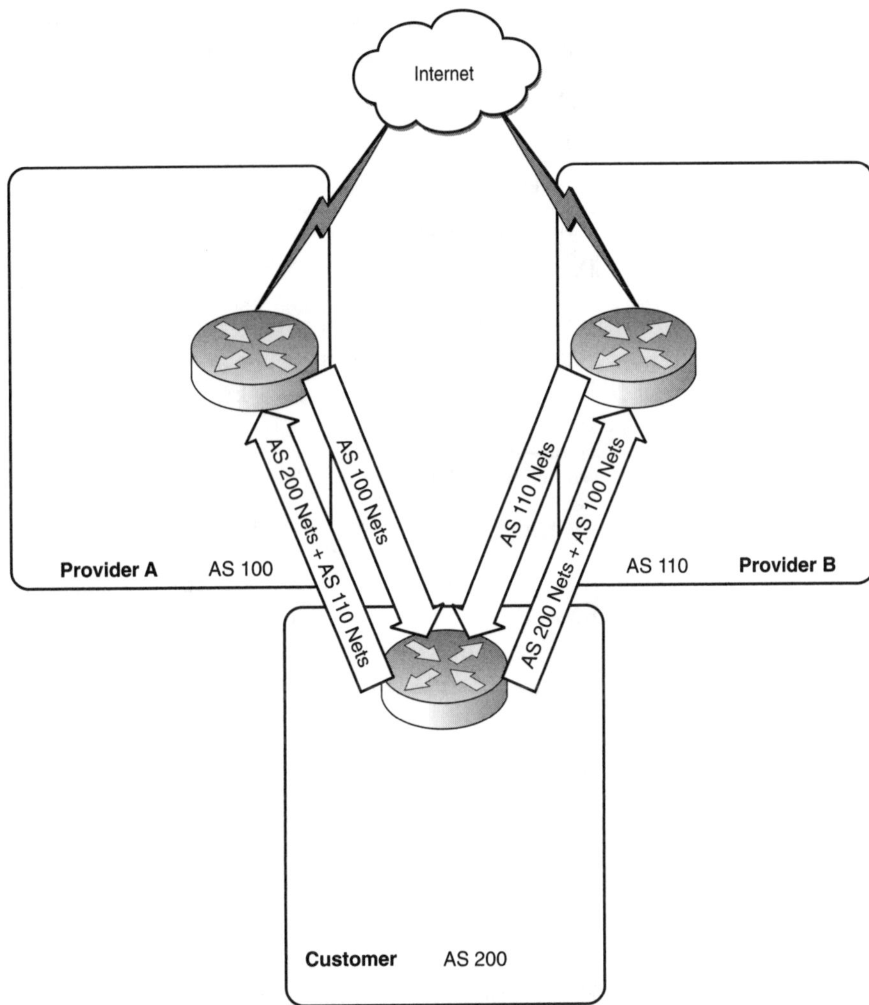

Figure 22-8 Multi-homed transit AS passes routes from one AS to another.

the individual ISPs. While running EBGP externally, it is also running IBGP with intra-AS routers.

Route Filtering

Route filtering in BGP works a lot like any other type of filter in the Cisco IOS, except that it applies only to routing advertisements. With route filters, one can also modify the attributes of a route, such as the ORIGIN. The filters used with BGP can be said to apply the policy of the BGP peer by using the following:

- Route maps
- Route filters based on Network Layer Reachability Information (NLRI)
- Route filters based on AS_PATH
- Prefix lists

A *route map* is a named entity that works like an access list. The following example includes a route map called CENSOR that is used to match the IP address listed in access list 10:

```
route-map CENSOR permit 10
match ip address 110
!
access-list 110 permit 192.168.10.0 0.0.0.255
```

The commands used for route maps are *match* and *set*. Use the *match* command to compare the conditions to a particular access list *permit* or *deny* statement. Use the *set* command to apply an attribute to a route. Here is an example of how a route map using a set command might look:

```
Router BGP 200
Neighbor 3.3.3.3 route-map CENSOR out
Neighbor 3.3.3.3 remote-as 110
!
route-map CENSOR permit 10
match as-path 170
set metric 115
!
ip as-path access-list 170 permit ^110$
```

Route maps are applied to a peer in either an *in* or *out* direction, as shown in the example. In this script, an access list (number 170) is created that will permit paths originating from autonomous system 110. The route map *CENSOR* then sets the metric to 115 on all routes from that AS.

Although it is outside the scope of this chapter to fully explain *regular expressions*, a couple of characters are used in the examples shown. A sample of the meaning of some commonly used characters is included in Table 22-3.

Table 22-3

Regular Expression Characters

Character	Symbol	Meaning
Period	.	Match any single character including white space
Carat	^	Match the beginning of the input string
Dollar sign	$	Match the end of the input string
Asterisk	*	Match 0 or more sequences of the pattern

***NOTE:** For further reading, refer to Mastering Regular Expressions: Powerful Techniques for Perl and Other Tools (O'Reilly Nutshell).*

Route filtering can also prevent the acceptance or re-advertisement of a particular set of routing information. This might happen when you have more than one AS in an EBGP configuration with IBGP running inside at least one AS. The NLRI of a route may be passed to a remote AS, which can then begin to advertise reachability to that network. In actuality, you may not want it to advertise that route, as it would then become a transit AS. In Figure 22-9, Routers A, B, and C are within AS 10. On either side, AS 20 and AS 30 are EBGP peers with AS 10. Routers A, B, and C are talking to each other via IBGP.

If Router A receives an advertisement of 192.168.20.0/24 from AS 30, it will share that NLRI with the other IBGP peers within AS 10. If we do not want Router A to advertise that routing information to AS 20, we can use the following route filter:

```
router bgp 100
no synchronization
neighbor 192.168.10.6 remote-as 10
neighbor 192.168.10.9 remote-as 20
neighbor 192.168.10.9 route-map POGO out
no auto-summary
```

Figure 22-9 Filtering on NLRI

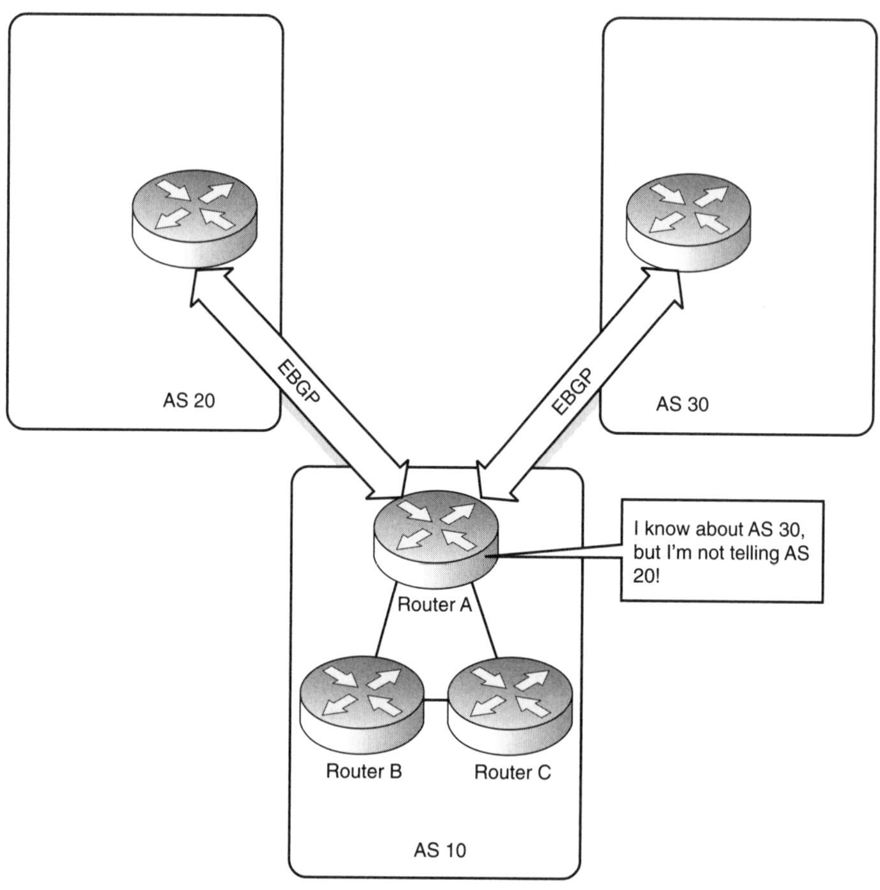


```
!
route-map POGO permit 10
match ip address 5
!
access-list 5 deny 192.168.20.0 0.0.0.255
access-list 5 permit 0.0.0.0 255.255.255.255
```

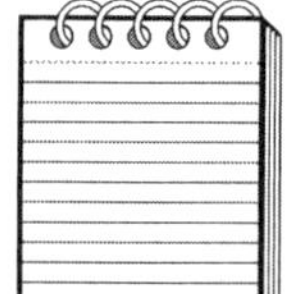

NOTE: *You can also use a distribute list or a filter list instead of a route map, but all examples in this text use route maps.*

The **no synchronization** command in the preceding example is being used to prevent routes learned via IGP from overriding routes learned in a fully meshed IBGP environment. It also prevents the AS from becoming a transit AS.

When you wish to filter all routes from one or more ASs, it is possible to do this using an AS Path access list. By using this type of list, you can greatly reduce the number of lines required to filter the routes. AS Path lists can use regular expressions to make partial matches against route statements.

For example, if we wanted to filter route advertisements coming out of IBGP in AS 10 from going to AS 20, in Figure 22-9, we could use the following configuration:

```
router bgp 100
no synchronization
neighbor 192.168.10.6 remote-as 10
neighbor 192.168.10.9 remote-as 20
neighbor 192.168.10.9 route-map POLY out
no auto-summary
!
route-map POLY
match ip address 12
!
ip as-path access-list 12 permit ^$
```

We have effectively told the router to apply the policy outlined in the route map POLY to all outgoing advertisements to neighbor 192.168.10.9. The policy sends an empty AS Path to the neighbor and thus filters out any outbound advertisements.

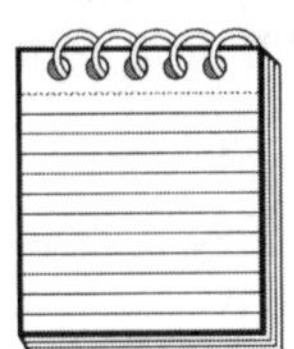

NOTE: *The command* **no auto-summary** *prevents BGP from summarizing networks on major network boundaries.*

Using a *prefix list* to filter BGP routes is similar to using an access list. The statements in the prefix list correspond to route prefixes, which are then permitted or denied as routes are matched against the statements in the list.

An empty prefix list will explicitly permit all routes to pass. If a route matches none of the statements in a list, it will be implicitly denied. If multiple statements in the list match a route entry, the first statement in sequence will permit or deny the route. As with access lists, the order of the statements in the prefix list matters. Be sure that you are specific in the list so that a route will not pass a statement early in the sequence if a deny statement for that prefix comes later in the list.

For specific information on how to create and configure prefix lists on Cisco routers, refer to the following Cisco Web page: **http://www.cisco.com/univercd/cc/td/doc/product/software/iso120/12cgcr/np1_c/1cprt1/1 cbgp.htm#40309**.

Filtering in BGP, as with any protocol, can be as simple or complex as the needs of your network. For more information, see the "Configuring IP Protocols" page on the Cisco Web site: **http://www.cisco.com/univercd/cc/td/doc/product/software/ios11/cbook/ciproute.htm**.

Route Aggregation

Route aggregation is the ability to shorten or summarize routing table entries when advertising them. You can use route aggregation in many ways within BGP. BGP version 4 brought with it the ability to use Classless Inter-Domain Routing (CIDR), which is discussed in earlier chapters. CIDR permits smaller routing advertisements by allowing groups of contiguous addresses to be shrunk into advertisements containing fewer lines. This can conserve both router processing power and bandwidth.

One way to aggregate routes is to advertise the aggregate address only. In other words, as seen in Figure 22-10, if the router in AS 200 has all of 192.168.0.0/16 behind it, it needs to advertise only 192.168.0.0/16 to its neighboring routers, as shown in the following statement. This single statement can stand for 65,000+ possible hosts within AS 200 and reduce the number of routing table entries:

```
aggregate-address 192.168.0.0 255.255.0.0 summary-only
```

Another way to advertise the routes is to advertise the aggregate address (192.168.0.0/16) as well as more specific routes. This would allow the single-homed AS 110 in Figure 22-11 to communicate more information to its provider, allowing better routing decisions to be made by the provider. The provider can in turn still advertise only the aggregate address to the rest of the Internet, thereby limiting the number of routes sent out.

A more complex method of route aggregation is to advertise the aggregate address plus a sub-set of the more specific routes. You can do this by creating a route map to be applied to routing advertisements. If we decide,

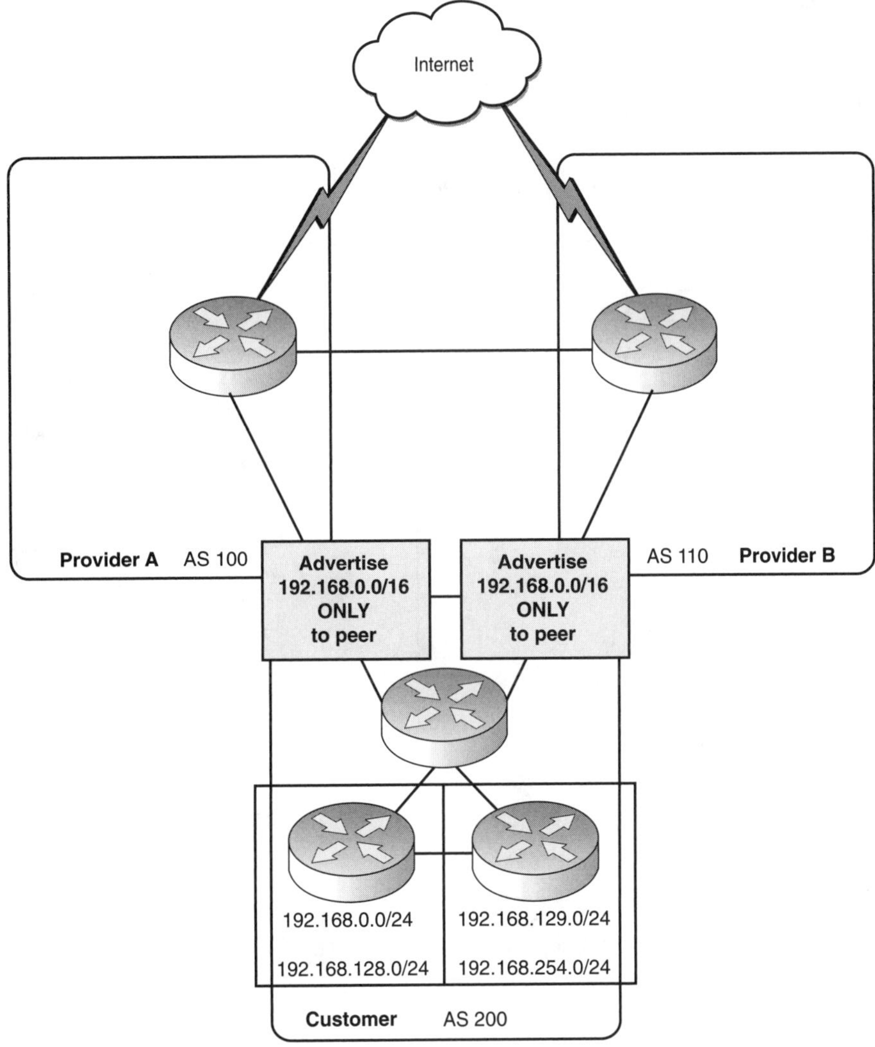

Figure 22-10 Advertising the aggregate address only

for example, to advertise the aggregate address of 192.168.0.0/16 but remove 192.168.10.0 and 192.168.50.0 from the advertisement, it would look like this:

```
router bgp 110
network 192.168.0.0
aggregate-address 192.168.0.0 255.255.0.0 suppress-map SAMPLE
!
```

Figure 11 Advertising the aggregate plus specific routes

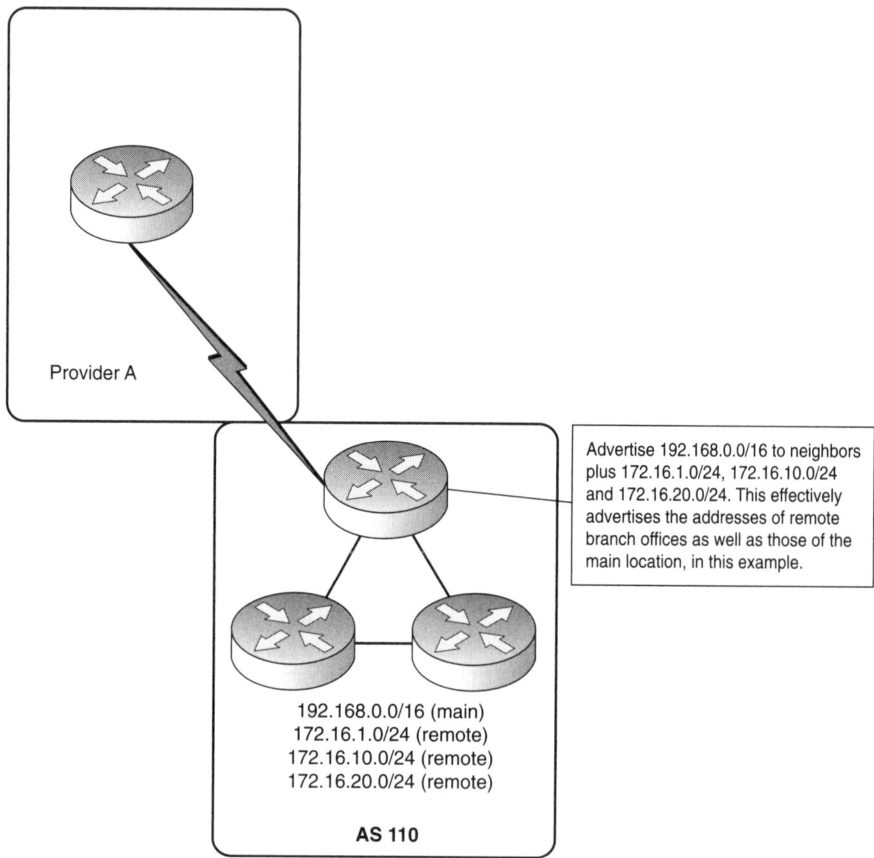
Provider A
Advertise 192.168.0.0/16 to neighbors plus 172.16.1.0/24, 172.16.10.0/24 and 172.16.20.0/24. This effectively advertises the addresses of remote branch offices as well as those of the main location, in this example.
192.168.0.0/16 (main)
172.16.1.0/24 (remote)
172.16.10.0/24 (remote)
172.16.20.0/24 (remote)
AS 110

```
route-map SAMPLE permit 10
match ip address 1
!
access-list 1 deny 192.168.10.0 0.0.0.255
access-list 1 deny 192.168.50.0 0.0.0.255
access-list 1 permit 0.0.0.0 255.255.255.255
```

NOTE: *A route map has an implicit "deny all" at the end, as access lists do.*

Conversely, you could create permit statements identifying a sub-set of routes to be advertised, rather than to be suppressed, along with the aggregate address.

It is also possible to modify the attributes of the advertised routes with attribute maps, available in the Cisco IOS. You could, for example, set the ORIGIN of a route to IGP if you wanted the route to appear to be coming from inside an AS rather than from a BGP process.

For more information on attribute maps and other aggregation topics, refer to the Cisco Web site: **http://www.cisco.com/univercd/cc/td/doc/cisintwk/ics/icsbgp4.htm#xtocid2765137**.

IGP Interactions

In some instances, situations may arise with BGP running at the edges of an AS and interacting with IGP routing decisions and metrics. This could potentially cause routing loops and inconsistencies. For example, in Figure 22-12, Router A is within AS 100 and is using OSPF to communicate with other routers in the AS. It knows nothing about BGP. The edge routers, Router B and Router C, however, are using OSPF to communicate with Router A and are using BGP to communicate with two separate ISPs.

In this situation, some interesting possibilities arise. We could load balance (outbound only) between the two ISPs, provided that there are some peering agreements between them, or we could have one primary route to the Internet with a standby or backup route at the second ISP. If we want the backup route, how do we keep the IGP from load balancing between the two? How do we make one path preferred over the other?

We can manipulate the routing metric that is injected into the IGP by advertising the route to Router B's provider as having a much higher cost. We could also run IBGP among all three intra-AS routers and apply BGP policies to control the routing of the traffic. This latter method would actually be the safest one, because routes could be better controlled through direct BGP interaction rather than by redistribution.

If you do this, it is important that you consider the type of metrics used by an IGP running inside an AS when BGP is running on the edge of the network. It will be imperative that you address routing metric differences as well as the routes you wish to advertise outside the IGP and to BGP speakers on the outside.

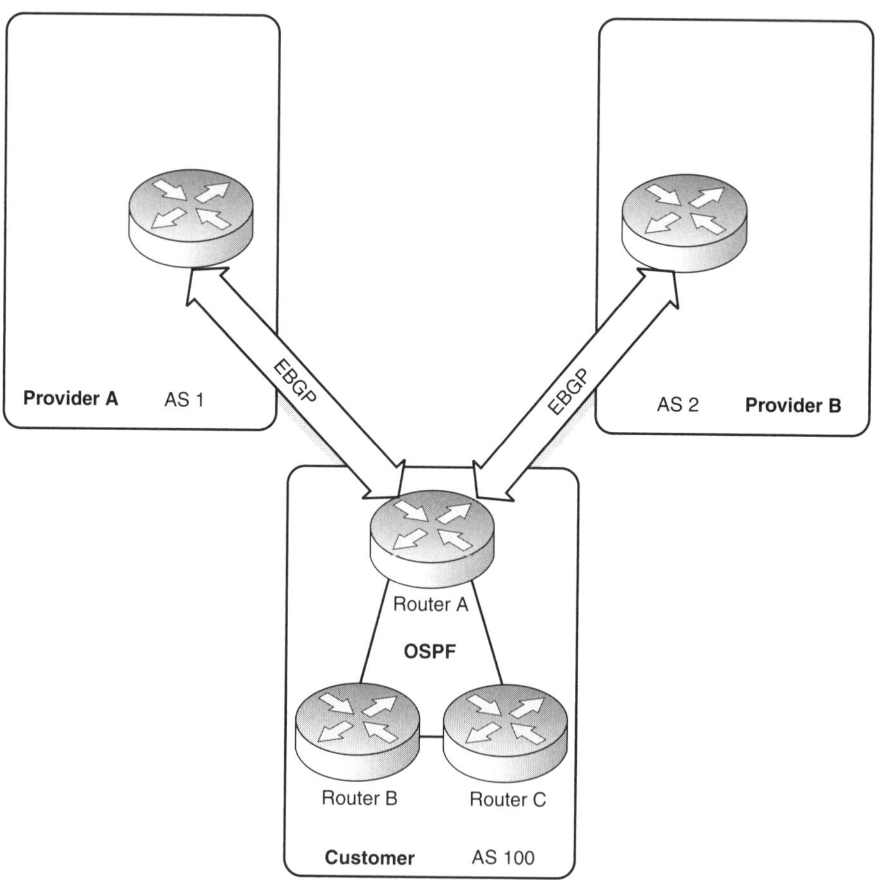

Figure 22-12 BGP-to-IGP communications

BGP Extensions

Creating a BGP network design should be seen as part of an ongoing process, not a one-time event. As you know, BGP4 evolved out of other inter-AS routing protocols and technologies that, at one time, sufficed for the task at hand. It is likely that another version of BGP or another routing protocol will someday be developed to meet the ever-increasing demands of the Internet. Until then, you can use some extensions that are part of BGP4 to create scalable networks that fit the requirements of the design you intend to create.

Improving Scalability

The purpose of adding the BGP extensions was mainly to address the scalability issues inherent to full-mesh networks. As mentioned earlier in this chapter, you must fully mesh a traditionally designed IBGP network, as shown in Figure 22-13, to ensure routing accuracy. In this case, six IBGP sessions are running concurrently in the network, which is a piece of cake for most routers.

The problem is that this doesn't scale well. Four routers? No big deal. Forty routers? Now you are talking about 780 IBGP peering sessions occurring simultaneously, not to mention other work that each router is trying to perform. That is 40 routers multiplied by 40 routers minus 1. Divide by 2 and get the result of the number of interfaces needed for the full-mesh network. With the BGP extensions, *route reflection* and *confederations*, you have more direct control over the scalability of IBGP.

Figure 22-13 An IBGP network without extensions

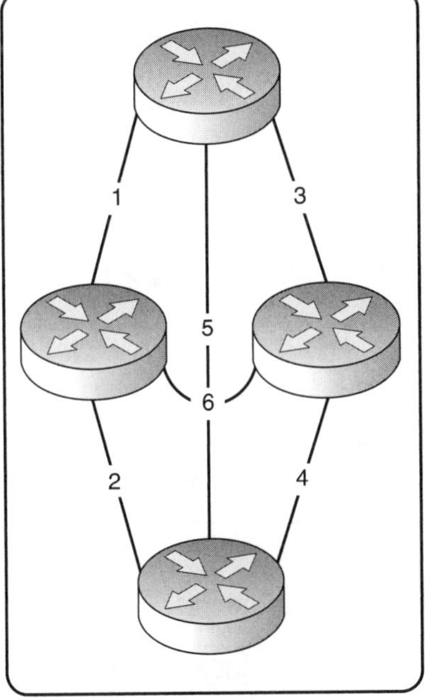

Route Reflection

When the number of BGP peering sessions becomes excessive, it is usually a good idea to begin to look into alternative methods of handling IBGP. Configuring route reflection in an IBGP network allows for the development of a more hierarchical structure, as with routing protocols like OSPF. In route reflection, one router, called a *route reflector*, is permitted to advertise routes to other routers, called *route reflector clients*. This means that the full-mesh concept is no longer applicable. Peering session are reduced, because the route reflector clients can only peer with the route reflector. A route reflector may advertise routes on behalf of many route-reflector clients. In Figure 22-14, we see that Router A is configured as a route reflector. It has six routers that are route-reflector clients. Router A can advertise routes learned from all six clients both internally and externally, if desired. The IBGP sessions have been reduced to 6, versus 21, peering sessions in a full-mesh IBGP environment.

Remember that we said the address of the router should be the loopback interface? This is because the loopback interface is always up and is not

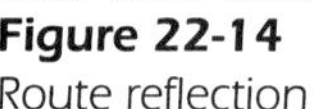

Figure 22-14
Route reflection

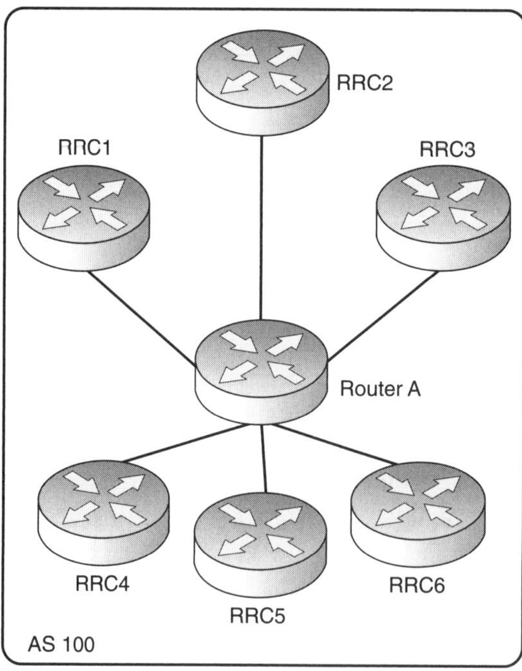

subject to link failures, as are other interface types. As with OSPF, BGP uses the interface with the highest IP address as its router ID. If a loopback interface is present, however, BGP will use the IP address of the loopback interface as its router ID. This reduces the possibility of a lost peering session in the event that one interface fails—provided it is not the actual peering connection. This is an important point to remember as we go into further discussion of route reflection and confederations.

We have changed the configuration of AS 100 somewhat in Figure 22-15. Each router is now labeled with its loopback address. Another important distinction is that Routers A, B, and C are running a traditional IBGP configuration, while Router B is the route reflector for clients RRC4, RRC5, and RRC6.

Router B will not re-advertise routes learned from Router A to Router C, nor will it do so with routes learned from Router C to Router A. These routers are not route-reflector clients and will depend upon the full-mesh (i.e., their peering session with each other) of the traditional IBGP environment to ensure that their routes are known. Router A *will* re-advertise routes learned from both B and C to its route-reflector clients.

Figure 22-15 Route reflector re-advertisement

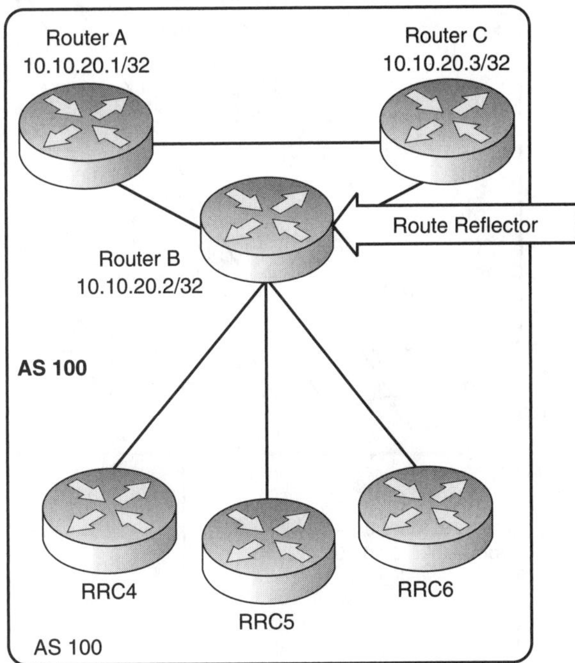

Next-Hop Attribute It is important that certain attributes of the routing information not be changed as routes are re-advertised. One of the most important is the *next-hop attribute*. Because the restrictions of BGP had to be somewhat relaxed to provide for the use of route reflection, the possibility of routing loops increased. One way to prevent routing loops is to ensure that certain important information stays the same.

Take a look at the example in Figure 22-16. Router RR1 is a route reflector for its route-reflector clients RRC1 and RRC2 within the IBGP mesh and for RR2, which is in another region of the AS. The physical connection for RR2 is to RRC2, however RR1 is actually the route reflector for the IBGP mesh, therefore re-advertising the routes to RR2. RR2, in turn,

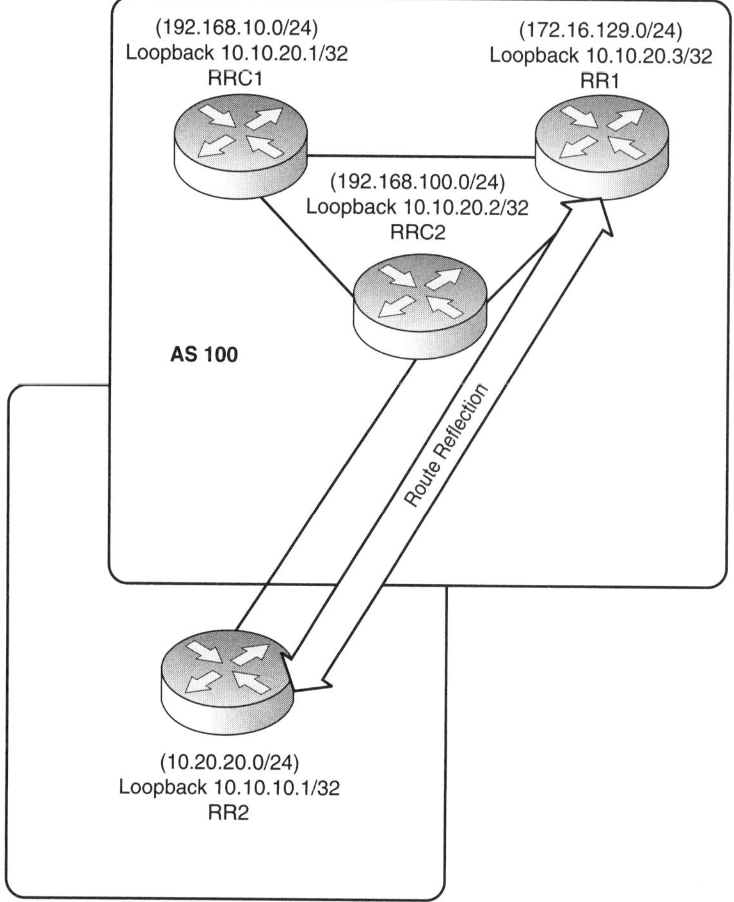

Figure 22-16 Using the Next-Hop attribute in route reflection

reflects routes it learns to the route-reflector clients in the AS. This means that RRC1 and RRC2 are eligible to have their routes re-advertised by both RR1 and RR2. In this figure, the addresses of the loopback interfaces are shown, and the addresses of the advertised networks are shown in parentheses.

Suppose that RR1 sends an advertisement for prefix 172.16.129.0/24 with a next-hop address of its own loopback interface (10.10.20.3/32) to RR2. RR2 will now reflect the routes it has learned to any route-reflector clients. It will advertise the prefix to RRC1 and RRC2 as 172.16.129.0/24 with a next-hop of 10.10.20.3/32. Since RRC1 and RRC2 both know about this route with the IBGP mesh, they will not try to send traffic to that destination through RR2.

If RR2 had changed the next-hop address to its own loopback, a routing loop would result. RR2 would advertise prefix 172.16.129.0/24 with a next-hop of 10.10.10.1/32. Routers RRC1 and RRC2 would begin to send traffic destined for that network to RR2. RR2, having a physical connection to the mesh (and thus to the destination network) through RRC2, would send the traffic back through RRC2! This is why the next-hop attribute is preserved in route reflection.

Originator ID The other attribute preserved by route reflectors is the *originator ID*. This is an optional 4-byte BGP attribute that is added by the route reflector to identify the router ID (the loopback address) of the router that originated the advertisement for a prefix. If an advertisement comes back to the originator, the originator will ignore the route. In a good design, this should not happen, but the originator ID further helps to prevent routing loops.

AS Confederations

Another way to deal with a large IBGP environment is to break up the single AS into multiple *sub-autonomous systems* (Sub-ASs). Each sub-AS is then given a private AS number (64512 to 65535). What happens, in effect, is that multiple ASs exist within a *confederation*, which is the original AS. The use of BGP confederations is outlined in RFC 3065. As shown in the example in Figure 22-17, the entire confederation exists around the private sub-AS structure. Within each sub-AS, routers communicate via IBGP. Between each sub-AS, you will run EBGP. Even though you are still within your AS, you must run an external protocol, because each sub-AS acts like a separate AS.

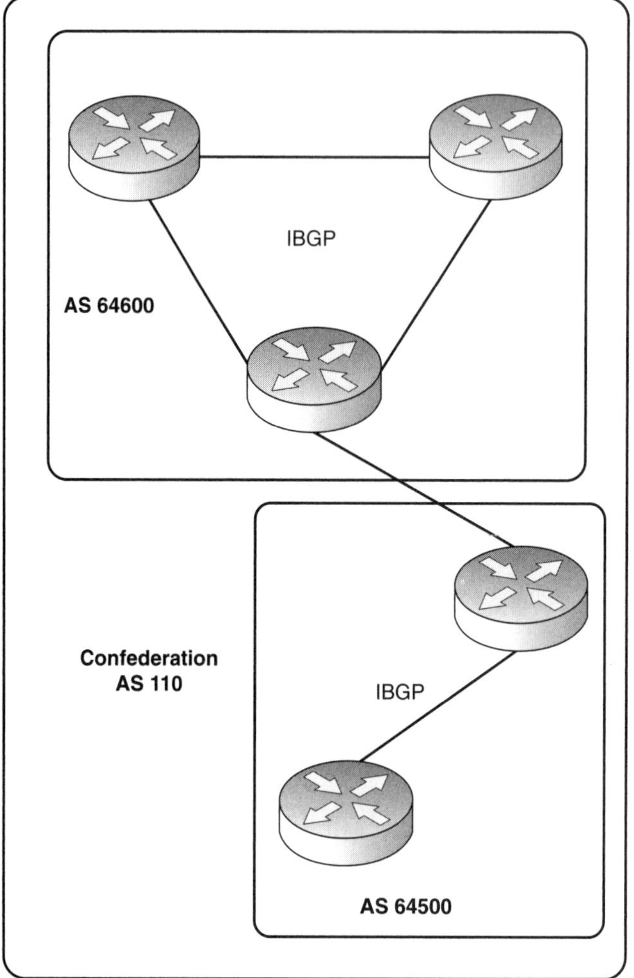

Figure 22-17
Multiple ASs within confederations

As for design issues, the example in Figure 22-17 shows a rather modest confederation design. The problems appear when more than two sub-ASs are present. In this case, it may be necessary to create complex BGP policies that strictly set the AS Path desired for each route. While designing confederations, bear in mind that Cisco recommends centralized structures for confederation design, as shown in Figure 22-18. In the example, sub-AS 64600 is acting as a central sub-AS. Sub-AS 64500 and 64700 will each communicate only with the central sub-AS (64600). This reduces the amount of

Figure 22-18 Centralized confederation design

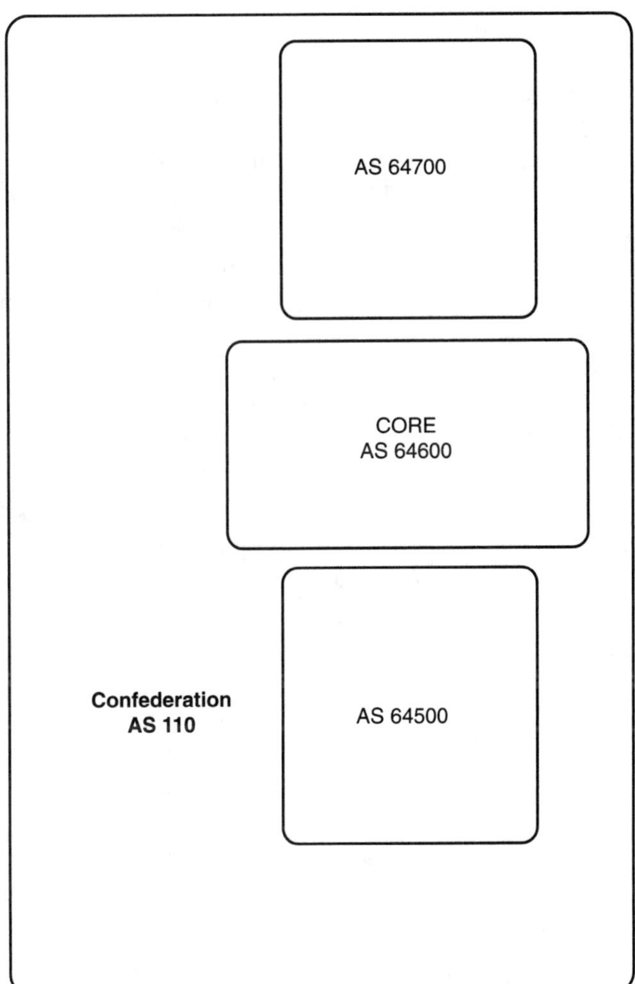

processing each router must do, and it improves the uniformity of path length and routing behavior.

Route Flap Dampening

From experience, every network engineer knows that physical interfaces can become inactive from time to time. Then, as troubleshooting measures are being taken, the gremlins chuckle, and the interface comes back up. This can cause tremendous amounts of CPU time to be consumed by the router's CPU to recalculate peers and routing tables and to reconverge.

When this occurs it is called *route flapping*. In the example shown in Figure 22-19, the physical link from Router A to Router B may have a timing problem on the serial line. The interface protocol may periodically fail. This can cause the route to flap as the interface goes down and comes up again. If the loopback interface is configured, as shown in the example, the router ID will not change and will not cause a recalculation of EBGP. The route between Router B and Router C will remained unaffected.

Note that if a router behind each of the EBGP speakers has a route flap, the other EBGP speakers will not notice the condition if proper aggregation is used. This concept is shown in Figure 22-20.

As mentioned earlier in this chapter, the router ID or BGP process ID is determined as the highest IP address on the router. This address is not necessarily the address of the physical connection to other IBGP peers. If for some reason this interface stops working, all peering sessions with other

Figure 22-19 Possibility of route flaps

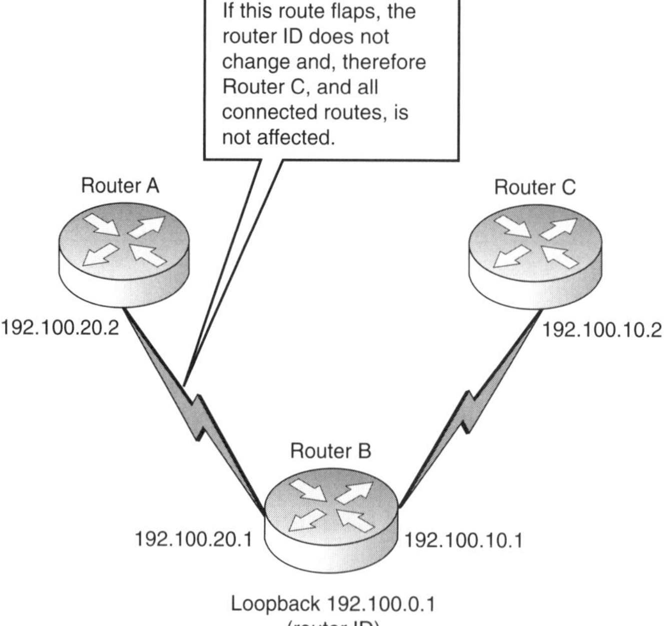

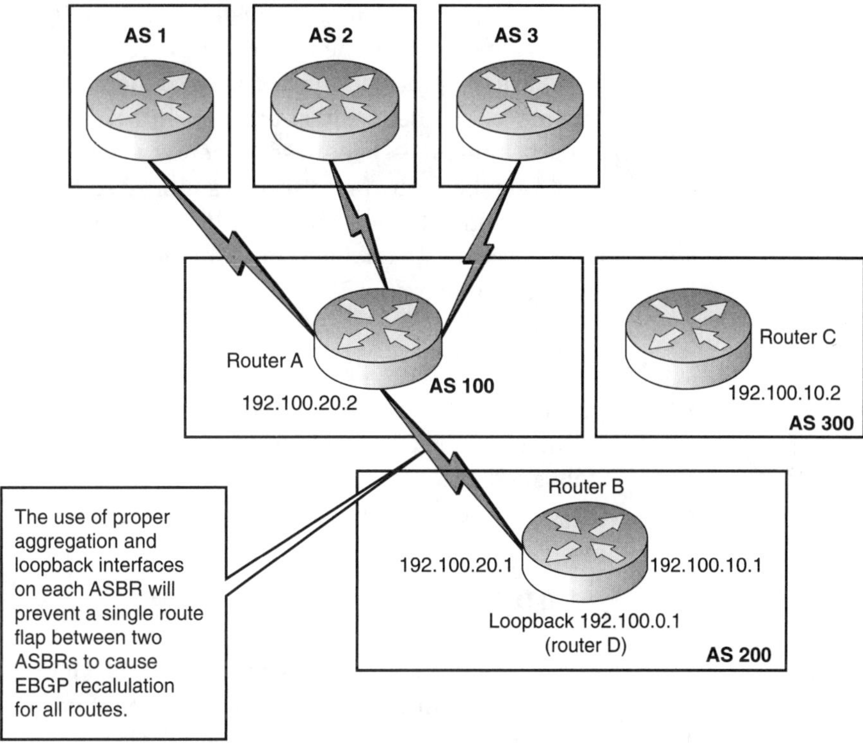

Figure 22-20 Reducing the affect of route flaps

routers will stop. The peers will have to recalculate their routing tables and send updates to their peers. When the interface comes back up, the calculating starts again, and we have a route flap.

One way to prevent this, as stated earlier, is to configure loopback interfaces on all routers in your network. This provides a stable interface that will be advertised as the router ID to all peers. The only time a peer will be lost is if the physical connection between routers goes down, and then the only peers lost will be those relying on that physical connection.

Another way to fix route flapping is to use static routes in the configuration. By statically injecting the routes into BGP, they are assumed to be there regardless of the physical status of the connection. Because configuring static routes does away with the need for and eliminates the usefulness of the protocol being used, however, another method for alleviating route flapping is available—*route flap dampening.*

Route flap dampening, outlined in RFC 2439, is a configurable method that identifies the problem route, reduces its impact on the network, and still allows the protocol to function as configured. Routes are monitored and a history of the behavior is tracked. If a route flaps continuously over a period of time, it is penalized. When the penalties add up to a predetermined threshold, the route will be suppressed for a certain amount of time. An algorithm calculates the penalties and the speed with which the suppression occurs. To enable route flap dampening on a Cisco router, use the following command in BGP configuration mode:

```
bgp dampening
```

By the same token, a route loses its penalties if it stops flapping. Penalties can continue to accrue even if a route is suppressed. So once stability is established, the route can have its penalty increment decayed and its addition to the routing process reinitiated.

Communities

Every publicly addressed destination can be viewed as part of the general Internet community. These destinations, however, can be reached from any autonomous system. When many destinations are known and are reachable from a given AS, it can become quite complex to apply a different routing policy or rule to each individual route.

The *community* attribute for BGP is a way to group a set of routes that have something in common. Think of this as being like the domain structures on the Internet. You know that .gov suffixes represent government entities. Likewise, .edu suffixes represent schools and other education-related entities. Communities can be used like domain structures. You may have a group of routes to which you wish to apply a common routing policy. You can use communities to group these like routes.

NOTE: *The use of BGP communities to group routes into categories is sometimes referred to as route coloring.*

Community lists work in a similar manner to access lists. A series of statements can be configured in the router that will be applied to routes as they are learned or advertised. The community list is a reference line of a route map that will instruct the router on which routes to accept or deny, or which routes to prefer or advertise. To configure a community list, you would use the following command in global configuration mode:

```
ip community-list community-list-number [permit|deny] community-
number
```

NOTE: A community number is formatted as ASN:ID. For example, if the AS number were 110 and the value of the two low-order octets (in hex) were equal to 1 (in decimal), the community number would be **110:1**.

The community attribute in BGP is optional and transitive, using an identifying integer between 1 and 4,294,967,200. While these can be defined locally, there are some globally significant (or well-known) communities:

- **Internet** This community tells the router to advertise this route everywhere. It is part of the general Internet community.
- **No-export** This identifies the route as internal to the AS. It signifies a route that isn't supposed to be advertised to EBGP peers.
- **No-advertise** This tells the router not to advertise the route *anywhere*, internally or externally.

By default, in Cisco routers, the COMMUNITIES attribute is not sent to neighbors. To send this attribute in the routing updates, you must set the following parameter:

```
neighbor {ip-address | peer-group-name} send-community
```

In Figure 22-21, we see that AS 120 is sending a community of **no-export** with its advertised networks of 192.168.0.0/16. This permits both AS 110 and AS 130 to receive the route advertisements, but they will not, in turn, advertise knowledge of these routes to each other directly.

Consider the example in Figure 22-22, however. Internally to AS 120, three routers are IBGP speakers. Each is sending a community of **no-advertise**, which causes the receiver to hear the route but not advertise it to any other router, internal or external. Therefore, each IBGP speaker will send routes only to destinations advertised by a single originator.

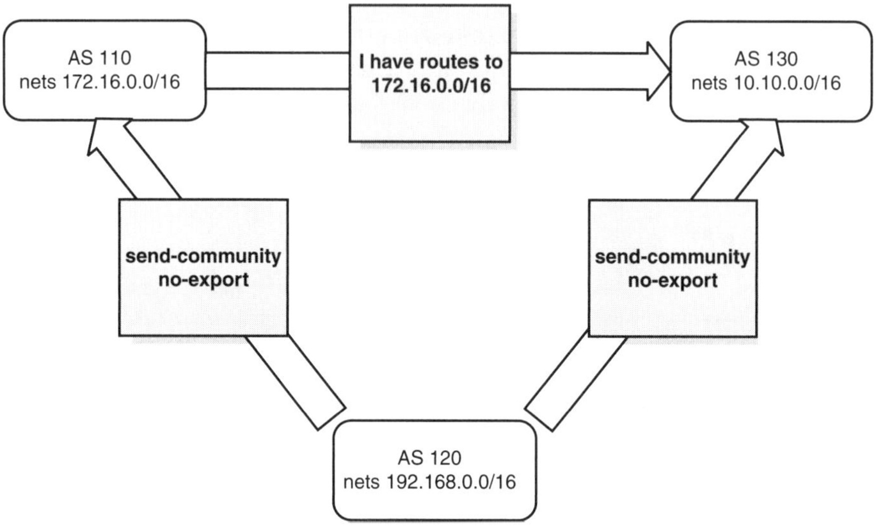

AS 110
nets 172.16.0.0/16
I have routes to
172.16.0.0/16
AS 130
nets 10.10.0.0/16
send-community
no-export
send-community
no-export
AS 120
nets 192.168.0.0/16

Figure 22-21 A no-export community

192.168.15.0/24
192.168.20.0/24
send-community
no-advertise
IBGP
192.168.10.0/24
AS 120

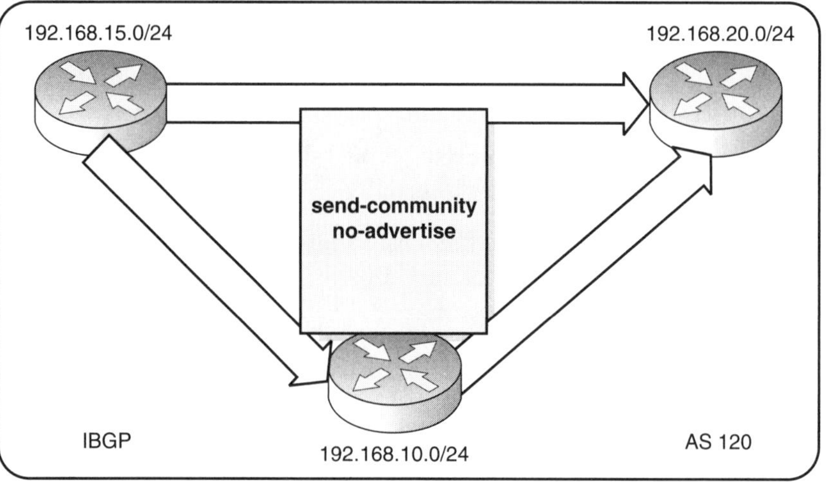

Figure 22-22 A no-advertise community

Configuring BGP communities can be somewhat complex when you first begin, but the use of communities and community lists can be invaluable in creating stable and fault-tolerant WAN designs. Refer to the chapter "Bibliography" section for more reading about the use of this feature.

Authentication

The use of authentication in BGP is designed to secure the TCP connection that occurs between the peering routers. As you can imagine, if a BGP peering session were to be "hijacked" by an intruder, it could wreak havoc against the Internet as a whole by fooling a router into trusting the intruder. The intruder could inject routes or apply policies that could disrupt a cascading hierarchy of Internet routers.

While the authentication specified for the connection is not yet fully mature, it is the best that has been specified to date. TCP authentication in BGP uses the MD5 message digest algorithm. MD5 is a method of taking a given message and running a calculation that outputs the message into a 16-byte digest form. The receiving router runs the algorithm against the message and decrypts it. If the key (password) used to decrypt the digest is the same on both ends, the message will be received and processed. If an intruder tries to send a message, it must guess the shared key.

To configure MD5 authentication for BGP, use the following command in BGP configuration mode:

```
Neighbor neighbor-IP-address password shared-key
```

Case Study

In this case study, you will not be asked to create complex BGP configurations but rather a high-level design to meet the needs of the customer. The situation presented to you is that of Marquette Biomedical, Inc., a large medical research firm that has recently recognized a need to possibly multihome their autonomous system. Problems with the current ISP, while not severe enough to warrant dropping them altogether, have made it clear that fault tolerance is needed for the Internet link. Route flaps at the provider have crippled Marquette's network on more than one occasion.

The network engineering staff would like to understand a little better how this design would appear. They have also begun to struggle with the growth inside the AS to 70 routers. They believe it is becoming unmanageable and that the overall network performance is suffering. Is there a solution with BGP that will allow them some breathing room without buying faster routers? Figure 22-23 shows their network layout today.

Jacksonville is the headquarters for Marquette and serves as the Internet gateway for the rest of the network. The traffic through Jacksonville has

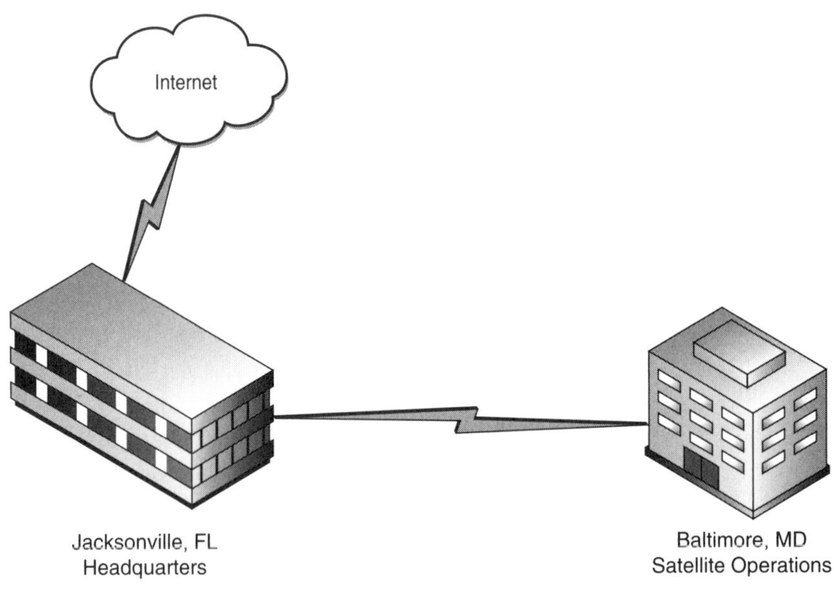

Figure 22-23 Marquette Biomedical

been growing. The staff is wondering if it would be okay to have a link to another ISP from the location in Baltimore, the second busiest location and the site with the highest usage of Internet services. While maintaining the link to their current provider, the staff at Marquette would like to use the proposed new ISP more often than the old one.

Try to create a workable solution for Marquette. Although there is no one right answer to any given design problem, we have suggested one solution in Appendix C, "Suggested Solutions to Case Studies."

CCDP Tips

This section contains an abbreviated list of topics covered in this chapter. Think of this section as the equivalent of reading Cliff's Notes™ instead of reading an entire chapter. You will get the general idea of the chapter but will benefit more from reading the chapter in its entirety.

Protocol Characteristics

- **Internal vs. External BGP** Internal BGP is used inside an autonomous system (intra-AS). In its native state, IBGP requires a full-mesh environment so that all routers can have knowledge of all routes. External BGP is a traditional inter-AS EGP that is used throughout the Internet community.
- **Message Types**
  - **Open** Sets up the BGP session.
  - **Notification** Alerts the BGP peers to an error condition, after which it terminates the connection.
  - **Update** Advertises or withdraws routes.
  - **Keepalive** Consists of the 19-octet BGP header only.
- **Sessions** Established between BGP peers over a TCP connection. Once the session is established, the peers immediately exchange a full BGP routing table, after which they exchange only incremental updates.
- **Authentication** The authentication used between BGP peers is secured by the use of the MD5 hash algorithm, which turns the message into a 16-byte digest form.
- **AS Paths**
  - Identifies the path a packet has taken, in reverse order. Subsequent AS hops prepend their ASN to the beginning of the AS Path.
  - Can use alternate prepending method to add multiple instances of its own ASN to change the preference of the route.
- **Attributes**
  - **Well-known mandatory** Must be supported by all BGP implementations; must be present in all UPDATE messages.
  - **Well-known discretionary** Must be supported by all BGP implementations; not required to be present in UPDATE messages.
  - **Optional transitive** Not required for all BGP implementations; transitive flag is set to tell BGP receiver to forward the attribute along.
  - **Optional nontransitive** Not required for all BGP implementations; quietly ignored by BGP receiver and not passed along.

- **Route Selection** BGP will select one path for a destination. Refer to the "Route Selection" section to see how this process works.

Operations

- **Single-homed vs. Multi-homed** Single-homed BGP networks have a single ISP connecting them to the external community. Multi-homed networks have more than one ISP connection. In the case of multi-homed networks, the AS can act as a transit AS, sharing routes from one provider to another.
- **Aggregation** BGPv4 permits route aggregation via the use of Classless Interdomain Routing (CIDR). Using classless network masks to lump groups of contiguous networks into a single route statement can reduce advertisements. You can advertise aggregate only, aggregate plus specific routes, or sub-sets of the aggregate using route maps.
- **Filtering** Through the use of route maps, filter lists, or distribute lists, you can manipulate the routing advertisements based on match conditions. Filtering can be performed based on AS Path or network layer reachability information (NLRI), as well as standard ACL-type configuration.
- **IGP Interactions** A router will naturally want to prefer a route learned internally, through an IGP, over a route learned externally. When using BGP, you must consider the differences in the routing metrics between the IGP and the EGP and adjust metrics, if necessary, to create the desired behavior. One method of dealing with this is to run IBGP inside the network and run EBGP outside.

Extensions

- **Route Reflection** is a method by which a representative router in the IBGP mesh, called a *route reflector*, acts on behalf of its *route reflector clients* to send and receive routes. This reduces the number of routers participating in the IBGP mesh and improves the overall performance of the intra-AS routing and processing as a result.
- **Confederations** are subsets of a single AS. By using confederations, you can segment the overall AS to limit the number of routers participating in an area of the AS. A subset is referred to as a *sub-AS* and is assigned an ASN from a group of private ASNs (64512 to 65535) to prevent overlap with any other "real" AS that may be using a public

ASN. Inside the sub-AS, IBGP is run, while EBGP must be run between the sub-ASs.

- **Communities** are groups of routes that have something in common. By grouping these routes together (also called *route coloring*), you can simplify the creation and application of routing policy. Rather than create multitudes of route maps, ACLs, and so on, you can create a few standard policies and apply them to different communities, based on requirements.
- **Route Flap Dampening** is the ability to limit the impact of a route that is misbehaving by dropping and coming up again. Route flap dampening penalizes the route that is having the problem, thereby reducing its preference. If the route stabilizes again, the penalties start to diminish until they are gone completely.

Summary

BGP is a complex inter-domain routing protocol designed primarily for use in the Internet. By creating sessions between peering routers, BGP allows for the control of routing advertisements and the path that the traffic will take. When poorly configured, the results can be, at best, less than optimal routing and, at worst, disastrous. The intent of this chapter was to give you an awareness of the possible configurations that can be used in BGP network design. Further reading is absolutely critical to a deeper understanding of the protocol.

Questions

The following review questions have been selected to help you test your knowledge of the subject matter contained in this chapter. You will also find these questions contained in the CD-ROM included with this book. While these are not the questions you will find in the certification exams, knowing the answers to the review questions in this book will help cement the material in your mind as you prepare for the tests.

1. True or False: BGPv4 is primarily an intra-AS routing protocol.
   a. True
   b. False
2. What protocol is used by BGP for peering sessions?
   a. TCP
   b. UDP
   c. ICMP
   d. SNMP
3. Which BGP message type is immediately followed by termination of the peering session?
   a. OPEN
   b. NOTIFICATION
   c. UPDATE
   d. KEEPALIVE
4. The BGP community **no-advertise** tells the next-hop router to advertise routes to
   a. The Internet
   b. The internal AS only
   c. All BGP speakers peering with the next-hop router
   d. None of the above
5. True or False: BGPv4 can handle both internal and external gateway routing.
   a. True
   b. False
6. How many octets are there in a BGP KEEPALIVE message?
   a. 4
   b. 2
   c. 16
   d. 19

7. Select the statement that best describes AS_PATH prepending.
   a. The insertion of dummy numbers into the beginning of an AS_PATH statement to decrease preference for the route
   b. The insertion of the AS number of the AS receiving the packet
   c. The insertion of a dummy number into the originator ID to prevent routing loops
8. Which two of the following attributes, preserved throughout the AS Path, help prevent routing loops? (Select two)
   a. AS_PATH
   b. Next-hop router
   c. Originator ID
   d. Loopback address
9. When performing AS_PATH prepending, what is (are) your best choice(s) for the dummy numbers?
   a. The AS number itself
   b. The AS number of the next-hop router
   c. 64512 to 65535
10. What is the main purpose of the use of authentication with BGP?
    a. To create a tunnel between two peers
    b. To allow for TACACS+ to be used at the distribution layer
    c. To secure the TCP connection between peers
11. Of the three selections given, which origin type would be preferred by BGP for path selection?
    a. Incomplete
    b. IBGP
    c. EBGP
12. What is one purpose of the "no synchronization" command used in BGP?
    a. It can be used to create a transit AS.
    b. It can be used to prevent OSPF routes from overriding IBGP routes.
    c. It can prevent EBGP routes from overriding IBGP routes.
    d. It can be used to segment a transit AS.

13. Of the two selections given, which type of BGP requires a full-mesh design?
    a. IBGP
    b. EBGP
14. The use of BGP communities to group routes into like sets can also be known as
    a. Route reflection
    b. Route coloring
    c. Route flap dampening
    d. Confederations
15. Which statement best describes the key mechanism used in BGP authentication?
    a. It is a one-time password authentication scheme.
    b. It reduces a message to a 16-byte digest.
    c. It uses an SKEY algorithm.
16. Route flap dampening uses the following method for reducing the impact of route flaps on a network.
    a. It penalizes the route that is flapping.
    b. It replaces the problem destination with a destination of loopback0.
    c. It increases the holdtime on the route.
17. When an AS is divided into multiple sub-AS's, it is said to be using
    a. Route flap dampening
    b. Route coloring
    c. Route reduction
    d. Routing confederations
18. True or False: The MED value in BGP is used to set preferences when multiple exit points exist at any point in an AS.
    a. True
    b. False

19. What method can be used in IBGP to negate the need for a full mesh?
   - **a.** AS_PATH prepending
   - **b.** Route reflection
   - **c.** Route flap dampening
   - **d.** Authentication
20. In route reflection, how will routers that are not fully meshed receive adequate routing information for the AS?
   - **a.** They will receive the updates from their route reflector.
   - **b.** They will receive the updates from the router with the highest router ID.
   - **c.** They will receive updates from other route reflector clients.
   - **d.** They will receive no updates.

Answers

1. True or False: BGPv4 is primarily an intra-AS routing protocol.
   b. False
   Explanation: Although it can be both, BGPv4 is primarily an *inter-AS* (meaning between autonomous systems) routing protocol.

2, What protocol is used by BGP for peering sessions?
   a. TCP
   Explanation: Since a handshake must take place between peers, TCP is used for the connection.

3, Which BGP message type is immediately followed by termination of the peering session?
   b. NOTIFICATION
   Explanation: If BGPv4 sends a notification message, it immediately terminates the connection, because an error has occurred in the peering session.

4. The BGP community **no-advertise** tells the next-hop router to advertise routes to
   d. None of the above
   Explanation: The well-known community of **no-advertise** indicates that the route should not be re-advertised to any internal or external routers.
5. True or False: BGPv4 can handle both internal and external gateway routing.
   a. True
   Explanation: IBGP is an Internal Gateway Protocol (IGP), while EBGP is an External Gateway Protocol (EGP).
6. How many octets are there in a BGP KEEPALIVE message?
   d. 19
   Explanation: The KEEPALIVE message consists of the BGP header only, which is 19 octets in length.
7. Select the statement that best describes AS_PATH prepending.
   a. The insertion of dummy numbers into the beginning of an AS_PATH statement to decrease preference for the route.
   Explanation: When AS_PATH prepending is configured, a router inserts its own AS number into the beginning of the AS_PATH a number of times to decrease preference for the route.
8. Which two of the following attributes, preserved throughout the AS Path, help prevent routing loops?
   b. Next-hop router
   c. Originator ID
   Explanation: Both the *next-hop router* and the *originator ID* attributes identify attributes to the network that will prevent routing loops by identifying the origin of the routing information.
9. When performing AS_PATH prepending, what is(are) your best choice(s) for the dummy numbers?
   a. The AS number itself
   Explanation: Using any number other than the router's own AS number can lead to routing inconsistencies and routing loops.
10. What is the main purpose of the use of authentication with BGP?
    c. To secure the TCP connection between peers.
    Explanation: Because a hijacked peering session could have widespread impact on the Internet, the session is secured with the MD5 hash algorithm.

11. Of the three selections given, which origin type would be preferred by BGP for path selection?
b. IBGP
Explanation: Of the three choices given, IBGP has the lowest origin weight. Therefore it would be preferred over the other selections.

12. What is one purpose of the "no synchronization" command used in BGP?
b. It can be used to prevent OSPF routes from overriding IBGP routes.
Explanation: A router will normally prefer a route learned via an IGP rather than via a fully-meshed IBGP environment. The "no synchronization" command will prevent the OSPF-learned route from overriding the IBGP-learned route.

13. Of the two selections given, which type of BGP requires a full-mesh design?
a. IBGP
Explanation: It would be impossible to have a fully meshed EBGP environment, as every router on the Internet that is an EBGP speaker would have to talk to every other EBGP speaker. Therefore, the answer is IBGP.

14. The use of BGP communities to group routes into like sets can also be known as
b. Route coloring
Explanation: Because the routes are being identified as part of a BGP community, it is like highlighting or coloring the route.

15. Which statement best describes the key mechanism used in BGP authentication?
b. It reduces a message to a 16-byte digest.
Explanation: The MD5 hash algorithm creates a 16-byte digest of the message.

16. Route flap dampening uses the following method for reducing the impact of route flaps on a network.
a. It penalizes the route that is flapping.
Explanation: By imposing a penalty on the problem route, the router decreases its preference.

17. When an AS is divided into multiple sub-AS's, it is said to be using
 d. Routing confederations
 Explanation: A confederation is nothing more than a subset of an autonomous system.

18. True or False: The MED value in BGP is used to set preferences when multiple exit points exist at any point in an AS.
 b. False
 Explanation: The MED value is applicable only when multiple exit points exist between two points in a network.

19. What method can be used in IBGP to negate the need for a full mesh?
 b. Route reflection
 Explanation: Route reflection permits clients in the IBGP network to receive and send updates through a route reflector. With this configuration, full mesh is not necessary.

20. In route reflection, how will routers that are not fully meshed receive adequate routing information for the AS?
 a. They will receive the updates from their route reflector.
 Explanation: As with the explanation for question 19, we see that the route reflector will handle full knowledge of the IBGP network and will handle updates within that routing environment.

Frequently Asked Questions (FAQs)

1. *What is a peer group?*

 A peer group is a set of BGP peers that have identical outbound route advertisement policies. The use of peer groups can greatly simplify the configuration of route maps, distribute lists, and the like. For more information on peer groups, see Cisco's Web site: **http://www.cisco.com/warp/public/459/29.html**

2. *If I use private AS numbers in confederations, how do I prevent these from being leaked to the Internet?*

 There is a command in the Cisco IOS to strip off the private AS number before sending the route advertisements. The command is used in BGP configuration mode:

```
Neighbor neighbor-ip-address remove-private-AS
```

When used, this command will remove the private AS number and cause the peer to believe the routes are coming from the AS of the router that removed the AS number. In a sense, the final hop replaces the originating AS number with its own ASN. For more information, refer to the Cisco Web site: **http://www.cisco.com/warp/public/459/36.html**

Bibliography

Internet Routing Architectures—Bassam Halabi, Cisco Press, 1997

Routing in the Internet, Second Edition—Christian Huitema, Prentice Hall, 2000

BGP4: Inter-Domain Routing in the Internet—John W. Stewart III, Addison-Wesley, Pearson Education, 1999

Using the Border Gateway Protocol for Interdomain Routing—Cisco Systems, Inc., **http://www.cisco.com/univercd/cc/td/doc/cisintwk/ics/icsbgp4.htm#xtocid2765125**

Configuring BGP—Cisco Systems, Inc., **http://www.cisco.com/univercd/cc/td/doc/product/software/ios120/12cgcr/np1_c/1cprt1/1cbgp.htm**

RFC 2439, **http://community.roxen.com/developers/idocs/rfc/rfc2439.html**

RFC 1771, **http://www.cis.ohio-state.edu/cgi-bin/rfc/rfc1771.html**

RFC 3065, **http://www.cis.ohio-state.edu/Services/rfc/rfc-text/rfc3065.txt**

CHAPTER 23

Security Design

Overview

Often the most neglected part of any network design, new or old, is security. The reasons for this vary from the lack of trained personnel on staff to ordinary fear of the unknown to a feeling of resignation. Network security is not a one-time decision or task. It is an ongoing task to detect and block malicious activity that can damage the network. New computer viruses and "hacks" are discovered and shared daily around the Internet community, making it easy for users of all experience levels to easily reproduce these often devastating programs.

In this chapter we will explain some of the ways you can implement security in the network design through the use of access control lists, network access tracking, Virtual Private Networks (VPNs), IP Security (IPSec), Network Address Translation (NAT), and firewalls. While this chapter will not make you a network security expert, it will help you to understand some of the ways that Cisco products can help secure the network.

Access Control Lists

Access Control Lists (ACLs) are known in most Cisco texts as access lists. An *access list* is a set of rules with a unique identifying number that is implemented in the Cisco Internetwork Operating System (IOS) configuration. These rules define how the router will handle a packet when it is presented to the router for processing. The rule contains a "permit" or "deny" statement. Either the traffic is permitted to route through or it is denied and dropped. A network engineer who is trained in security should manually enter access lists. Many mistakes are made with access lists that, in turn, can compromise the security of the network.

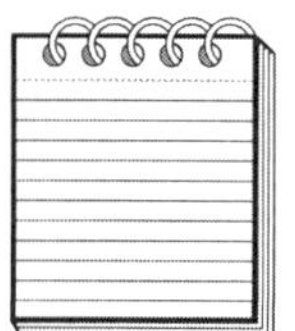

NOTE: *Access lists, Access Control Lists, and filters all mean the same thing.*

When designing for network security, it is important to know a few key points:

- The network access points
- The network assets that need to be publicly accessible
- The network assets that must be strictly guarded
- The services that will be permitted through the perimeter or firewall

In Figure 23-1, the arrows indicate the entry points to the network. At each of these points, outside users can traverse a router in order to access network resources. These entry points are not necessarily all from outside users. It is important to also protect data from users inside the network, unless they have a specific need for the information. A high percentage of malicious network activity originates inside the network, rather than from outside. Access lists can help to secure all of those entry points.

There are two kinds of access lists we will discuss in this section:

- Standard
- Extended

Bear in mind that an access list can be configured on the router but is not active until it is applied to an interface or a terminal line.

Figure 23-1 Points of network vulnerability

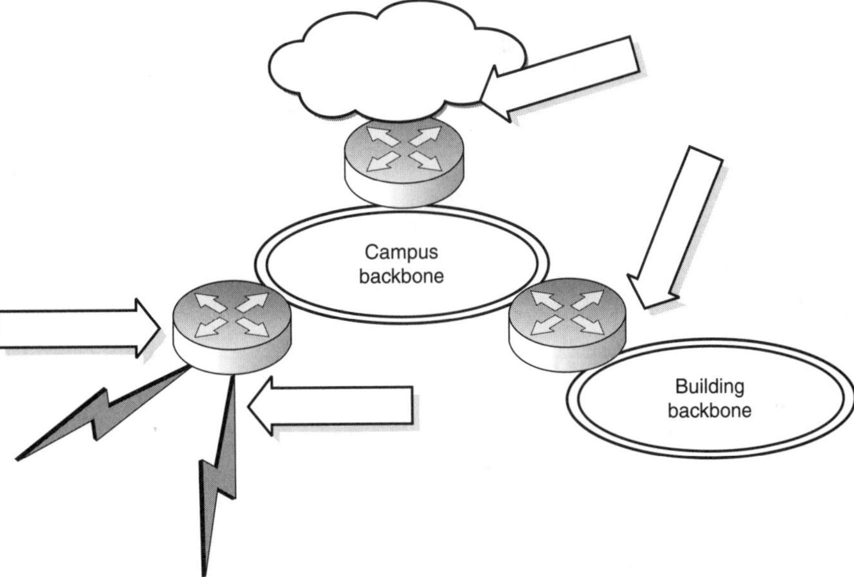

Standard Access Lists

Standard access lists are basic access lists that contain permit or deny statements against which network layer packets will be compared. The packets are compared to the statements in a top-down manner; therefore, the order of the statements is critical in order to obtain the desired results.

Standard access lists are numbered with a range that is specific to a protocol. Refer to Table 23-1 for the numbers that are assigned to each protocol.

The syntax of a line in an access list looks like this:

```
access-list number {permit|deny} address wildcard-mask
```

The *number* is, of course, the number that is manually assigned to the access list. Then either permit or deny is chosen, followed by the unique address or address range with a wildcard mask. For instance, if we were to create access list 1 to permit host 172.16.10.5 to access our network, it would appear like this:

```
access-list 1 permit 172.16.10.5
```

You will notice that in this example, no wildcard mask is used. That is because it is implied, when no wildcard mask is entered, that we wish for the statement to be specific, or 0.0.0.0. In other words, we want only host 172.16.10.5 to be permitted. We could also permit all hosts from 172.16.10.0 to enter the network like this:

```
access-list 1 permit 172.16.10.0 0.0.0.255
```

Table 23-1

Standard Access List Numbers

Protocol	Range of Access List Numbers
IP	1–99
DECnet and Extended DECnet	300–399
XNS	400–499
AppleTalk	600–699
IPX	800–899
IPX SAP	1000–1099

The wildcard mask, as you will notice, is opposite what we have seen with subnet masks. Each 0 in the mask means to be specific. If you look at the values in the following table, you will notice that there are a limited number of values that are allowable. The wildcard specifies how many bits (from the right) will be allocated to the host portion, or number of host addresses covered by the access-list statement.

Number of Hosts	Decimal	Binary
1	.0	00000000
3	.3	00000011
7	.7	00000111
15	.15	00001111
32	.32	00011111
64	.64	00111111
128	.128	01111111
255	.255	11111111

As we said before, access lists work in a "top-down" fashion, meaning that each packet will hit the access list on an interface one line at a time, starting from the top, until a match condition is found. A match condition means that the packet meets the parameters specified in a line of the access list. If a rule is found early in the list that permits all traffic, the remainder of the list is insignificant. It is very important to use great caution when configuring the lists.

NOTE: *Every access list ends with an "implicit deny," which means that if it isn't expressly permitted in the list, then the packet will be dropped.*

Another item to note is that while access lists can be created and removed, they cannot be edited. To "edit" an access list, you must essentially re-write the list. Cisco recommends using a TFTP server to copy access lists to a text-editor program, make the changes, and copy the changed list back to the router. Note that when you do this, your first line in the edited list must be the one that removes the list. Your lines that follow, then, re-create the access list. So, the first line in an edited list should always be

```
no access-list x
```

Learning how to do access lists correctly takes a lot of practice and experience. It can also be helpful to have a tool such as CiscoWorks Routed WAN Management Solution, which allows not only network management but the management of access lists as well. For more information on CiscoWorks, go to **http://www.cisco.com/warp/public/cc/pd/wr2k/**.

Static Extended List

The standard access list is fine for many applications, but when you need the granularity of being able to permit or deny traffic based upon port number, you will need to use *static extended access lists,* usually known as *extended access lists.* The numbers assigned to extended access lists are found in Table 23-2.

Extended access lists are used when packets need to be filtered at the transport layer by specifying either TCP or UDP port number. How would you, for instance, allow IP traffic from any source that is bound for the server, seen in Figure 23-2, at address 172.16.10.0/24 *if* you want to allow FTP only?

Here is how the line of the access list might look:

```
access-list 101 permit tcp any host 172.16.10.4 eq ftp
```

Table 23-2
Extended Access List Numbers

Protocol	Range of Access List Numbers
IP Extended	100–199 and 2000–2699
Extended XNS	500–599
Extended IPX	900–999
Extended VINES	101–200
Protocol type-code access lists	201–300

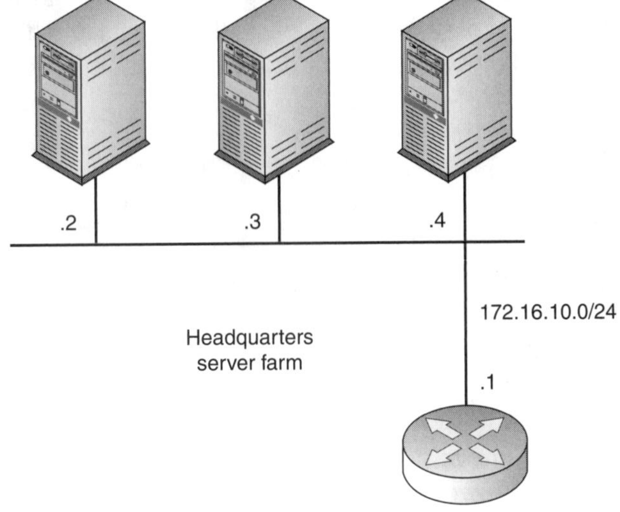

Figure 23-2 Static extended access list

You could also specify the FTP port numbers in place of using the common name of well-known TCP port 21 (FTP). Some well-known ports are listed in the following table, although many more exist. Technically, a well-known port is any port number less than 1,023. Ports above 1,023 are generally not statically assigned. Notice that we are permitting the type of traffic (TCP) from the source (any) to the destination (host 172.16.10.4) with a port number (equal to FTP). This gives you an idea of just how specific you could get with an extended access list. As we said with standard access lists, however, it is important to use caution and to make use of tools that help manage and test access lists before placing them in service on the router.

Port Type/Number	Common Name
TCP/21	FTP
TCP/23	Telnet
TCP/25	SMTP
UDP/69	TFTP
UDP/161	SNMP

The following table shows the suggested format for gathering the data necessary to play your access lists. By using something like this form, your chances of creating successful, secure access lists are increased.

From	To	Permit/Deny?	UDP/TCP?	Port Number
172.16.10.10 0.0.0.0	Any	permit	tcp	23
10.0.0.0 0. 255.255.255	172.16.10.0 0.0.0.255	deny	udp	162

TIP: *Be sure to include all decision-makers in your discussions of the services to permit or deny between network points!*

Authentication, Authorization, and Accounting (AAA)

After securing the network resources and services by placing ACLs on router interfaces, the next step is to apply the same types of security to the users. The passwords for local (or console) logon, line (or remote terminal), and enabled mode are configured, of course, in the router start-up and running configurations. All other types of user authentication or access control must be configured through the AAA model. This model is used to define access control by user or by service.

The AAA model of access control is the Cisco implementation of three security methodologies:

- Authentication
- Authorization
- Accounting

The process of positively identifying a user prior to allowing network access is called *authentication.* In other words, are you who you say you are?

The authentication method for single or multiple interfaces is defined in a named list. The default list is in control if no other lists are defined, and it is called, simply, "default."

The way the router learns what types and parameters of network resource access to grant a user is done through defining an *authorization* method. This can be on the router or access server itself or it can be housed on a TACACS+ or RADIUS server, for example. In Figure 23-3, a remote user wishes to access data on a server located on the corporate network. Through a dial-up connection, the user initiates a request for the server. Assuming that the request passes the ACLs on the router, as well as the user authentication step, it now needs authorization to reach the resources requested.

The request first goes to the RADIUS server, in this example. The network administrator may have configured the network to process in a certain order, with the ingress router acting as the Network Access Server (NAS), the RADIUS server processing incoming packets first, followed by the TACACS+ server if the RADIUS server fails to respond. The NAS will

Figure 23-3
Authorization servers

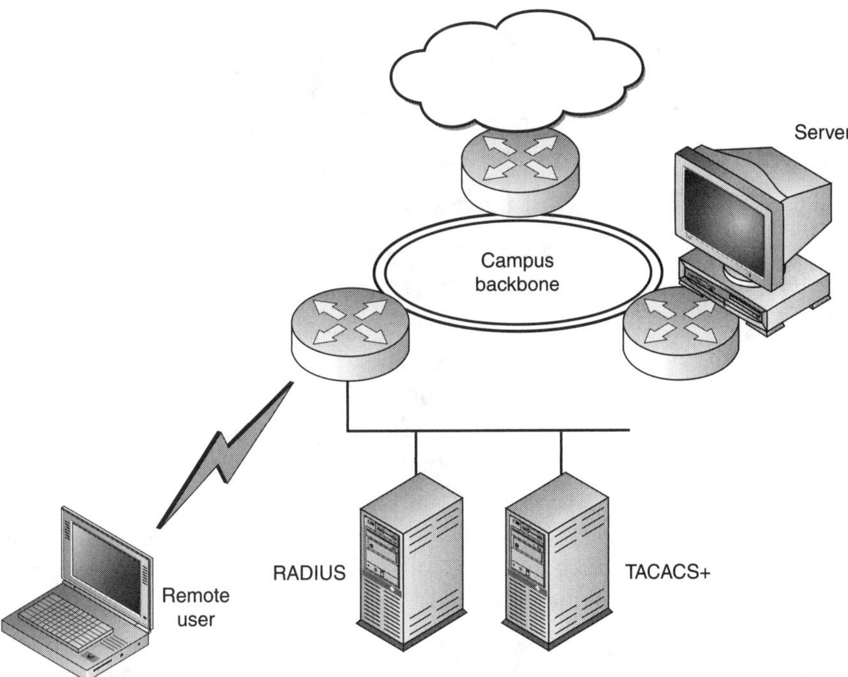

pass the traffic to the RADIUS server. The RADIUS server checks its database against the request made. The RADIUS server can then PASS or FAIL the request. If it returns a decision, its decision is final. The request is either allowed or disallowed. If it does not return a decision, an ERROR condition is noted and the request goes to the TACACS+ server. If no server responds, the traffic is disallowed by default.

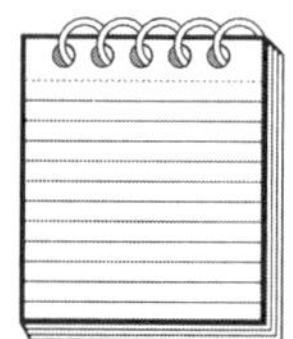

NOTE: *The AAA model is not compatible with TACACS and Extended TACACS. It is only compatible with TACACS+.*

Accounting is the method of logging network traffic and resource access and assembling the data so that it may be used for billing, user access tracking, auditing, or tracking how services are being used. When the AAA model is turned on in the router, all accounting must then be configured on the router itself. Accounting is then applied equally to every router interface. Accounting records for every transaction are sent to either the RADIUS server or the TACACS + server, depending on the type of security server that has been selected. With accounting enabled, the network engineering staff has records that enable them to

- Gather information that assists in managing the network
- Assemble client billing data
- Audit network or user activity

Although the use of AAA is not absolutely necessary for the router serving as the NAS, as you can see, it does allow the network engineering staff to enforce policies, authenticate user identity, and gather valuable data about the usage of the network resources. Because a lot of the heavy processing is being off-loaded to the RADIUS or TACACS+ server, the router's overall performance should not be affected by enabling these services.

AAA policies can also be managed by the use of Cisco's Access Registrar, which is a RADIUS-compliant policy server that is specifically designed to handle the processing of AAA. See more information at **http://www.cisco.com/warp/public/779/servpro/operate/csm/nemnsw/car/prodlit/index.shtml.**

The total control of AAA services can be centrally managed with Cisco Secure Access Control Server (ACS), which is a scalable solution that addresses the need to control user logins, encryption keys, and TACACS+ authentication. It also provides a central repository for the accounting data collected on the network devices. For more information on Cisco Secure ACS, please go to **http://www.cisco.com/warp/public/cc/pd/sqsw/sq/prodlit/sacsd_ds.htm.**

Virtual Private Networks (VPN)

You have secured the network perimeter with ACLs and have forced network users to identify themselves and abide by rules, which are policed by the AAA model. The next step is to examine users who will need to access network resources through non-standard entry points. For these users, whether they are gaining entry via dial-up or from remote branch offices, the solution is a Virtual Private Network (VPN).

There are three basic types of VPNs:

- Access VPN
- Intranet VPN
- Extranet VPN

The *access* (or Internet) *VPN* is targeted toward users who will come in through dial-up access to their own Internet service provider (ISP). An access VPN is a secure tunnel used to create a link from a remote user with an established Internet connection to the internal corporate network, as seen in Figure 23-4. The two main benefits to using an access VPN instead of using traditional remote user dial-up services are that the burden and expense of support for the dial-up services fall to the ISPs, and the company saves money as well by not having to maintain 800 numbers for dial-up.

The remote user, while dialing into his ISP normally, can open an encrypted session with the enterprise router or firewall in order to securely link to the enterprise network resources he needs. This technology is very useful for "road warriors" and corporate users who work from home. They are able to access inside resources as if they were at a desk inside the network.

An *intranet VPN* is very similar to an access VPN. The way it differs is that the VPN is created between internal corporate users and private areas of the enterprise network. For instance, in Figure 23-5 we see that Bob, a corporate user at a branch office, has a need to administer secure servers at the headquarters office. An intranet VPN can be created that will allow for

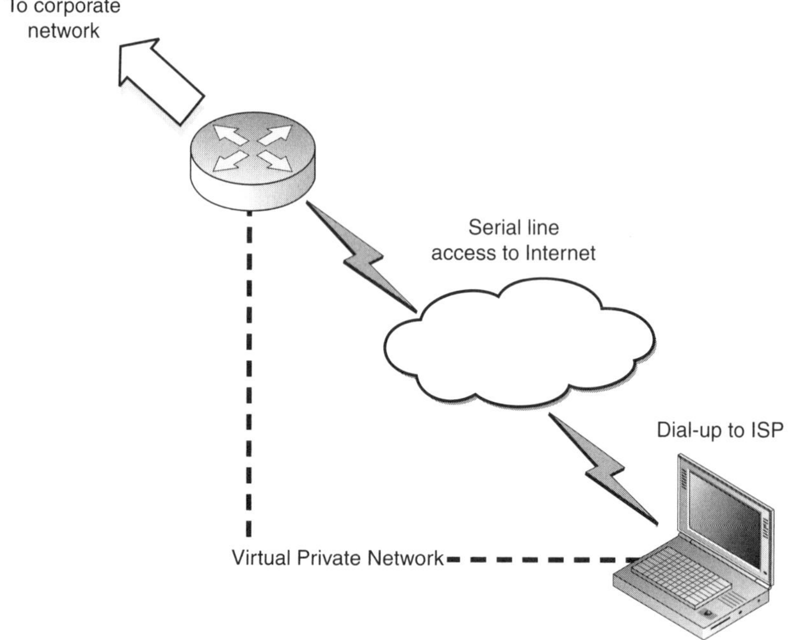

Figure 23-4 Virtual private network

a virtual point-to-point connection between the user and the servers with encryption protection.

An *extranet VPN*, again, is quite similar to the access VPN except that it is designed to support remote users outside the corporate employee structure, such as business partners and employees of joint ventures.

Cisco equipment that supports VPN technology includes the Cisco PIX firewalls, the 2600 Modular Access Router series, the 3600 series, the 7200 series, and the VPN 3000 concentrators. For more information on these devices and Cisco's implementation of VPN security, please go to **http://www.cisco.com/warp/public/cc/so/neso/vpn/vpne/.**

IP Security (IPSec)

Encryption technology provided in most VPNs is done through the use of IPSec. This section will not detail each encryption algorithm, as it is outside the scope of this book, but some suggested reading is included at the end of this chapter.

Figure 23-5
Intranet VPN

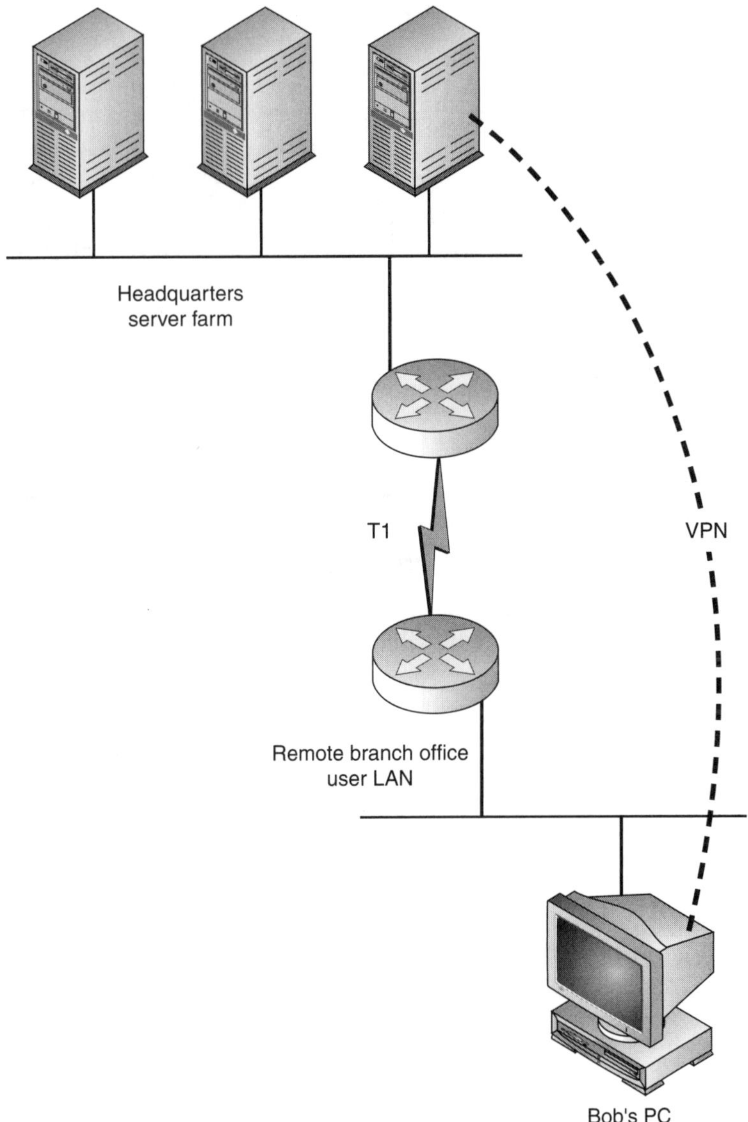

IP Security (IPSec) is not one product but rather an open standards framework, developed by the Internet Engineering Task Force (IETF) for securing private communication over IP networks. It was developed, in part, in response to the rising threat of intercepted communications as more companies and individuals began to access the Internet. It also addresses the need to synchronize the complex task of total network security. Rather than use many different products and technologies, which may leave holes in the network security mesh, the network engineering staff can now employ IPSec to address the entire spectrum of vulnerabilities. The details of IPSec can be found in RFCs 2401-2411 and 2451.

For many years it has been common for organizations such as the Department of Defense (DoD) to use encryption devices to provide link-layer encryption. The encryption devices are still in use today at many military installations and are kept under tight security. That is an impossible task over the Internet, because network administrators have no control over intermediate systems between points.

Take the example shown in Figure 23-6. Bob is trying to send an email to Mary. Between the time Bob sends the e-mail and the time Mary receives it, there may be no problems. But an intruder *could* "hijack" the communication, alter it and send it on—without either Bob or Mary knowing that it had been altered. This is a very real and very easy threat to secure communications. Therefore, it has become necessary to create a way to encrypt traffic between points so that the data contained within would remain safe from potential threats.

Figure 23-6 Message traffic interception

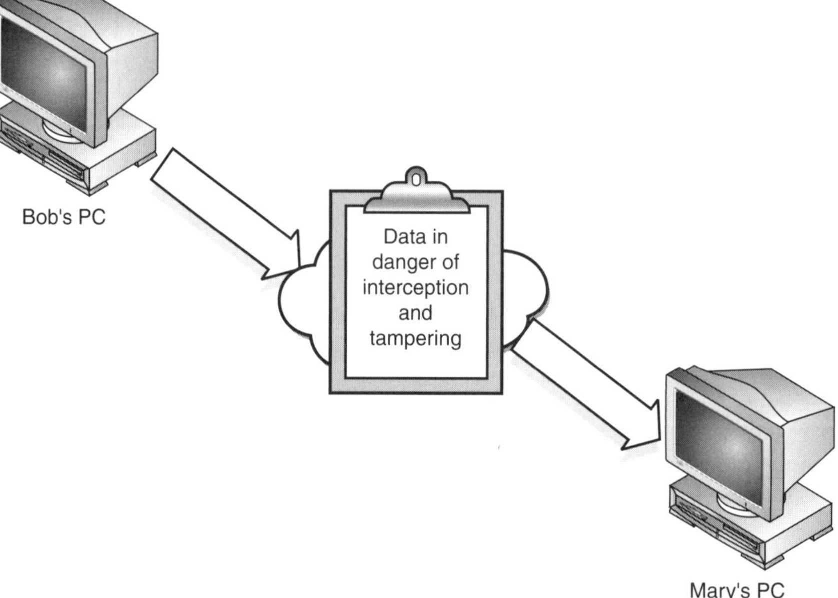

IPSec provides network-layer encryption based on the following security technologies:

- Diffie-Hellman methodology for public key exchange and private digital "signatures" that assure the identity of the sender and receiver
- Bulk encryption, such as Data Encryption Standard (DES), for encrypting data
- Hash algorithms, such as Message Digest 5 (MD5) or Secure Hash Algorithm (SHA), for packet authentication
- Digital certificates from a certificate authority, such as Verisign, that act as virtual ID cards

These technologies were then bundled into a package that represented a new standard for secure IP communication. This bundle now includes

- IP Security Protocol
- Internet Key Exchange (IKE)

IP Security Protocol provides for a new set of headers in the IP datagram. One header is placed before the IP header and another before the Layer 4 Protocol. The Authentication Header (AH) provides for the authenticity of the data contained within the payload. The confidentiality of the data is provided by the Encapsulating Security Payload (ESP). IPSec can operate in *transport mode* or *tunnel mode.*

Transport mode, shown in Figure 23-7, does not encrypt the IP header information. Since this data is sent "in the clear," it is available to intruders so that they can learn something about your network. Once they have an IP address, they have enough information to start digging deeper. Although they have the source and destination addresses, however, the transport portion of the packet is encrypted, so they will not be able to distinguish the type of traffic being sent.

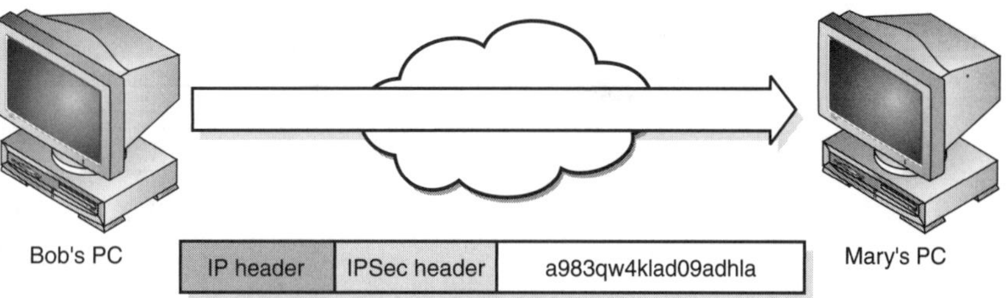

Figure 23-7
IPSec transport mode

Tunnel mode, on the other hand, is a much better choice for remote users. Not only is the payload of the packet encrypted, the IP header is encrypted as well. The sending router performs the encryption, and the receiving router decrypts the packet. This does increase latency on the traffic, but it reduces the amount of customization that must be done to an end-station to protect communication. The example in Figure 23-8 shows that a new IP header is placed on the packet, just before the IPSec header, and the entire IP packet, including original header, is encrypted.

While IPSec can be configured without IKE, IKE adds features and flexibility to IPSec when used. IKE is a hybrid protocol that incorporates Oakley and Skeme key exchanges within the Internet Security Association and Key Management Protocol (ISAKMP) framework. Oakley and Skeme are both key exchange protocols that define how keyring information is shared, but Skeme permits rapid key refreshing.

When IKE is used, there is manual pre-configuration of certain parameters required (such as a lifetime for the IPSec Security Associations (SAs) and all security for the cryptographic maps at both peers). Additionally, it allows for dynamic key peer authentication and automatic key exchange.

The SA is a negotiated policy applied to a peer. The two peers agree to use a specific key exchange on both ends that will be applied to incoming packets associated with the peer relationship. Although one peer may have many SAs in its database, two peers may only use one SA between them.

Cisco has many tools, such as the Cisco Secure VPN Client, that make it easier to use IPSec technology as well as VPNs in general. There is also a lot of good information, including sample configurations and troubleshooting tips at **http://www.cisco.com/warp/public/cc/so/neso/sqso/eqso/dplip_in.htm.**

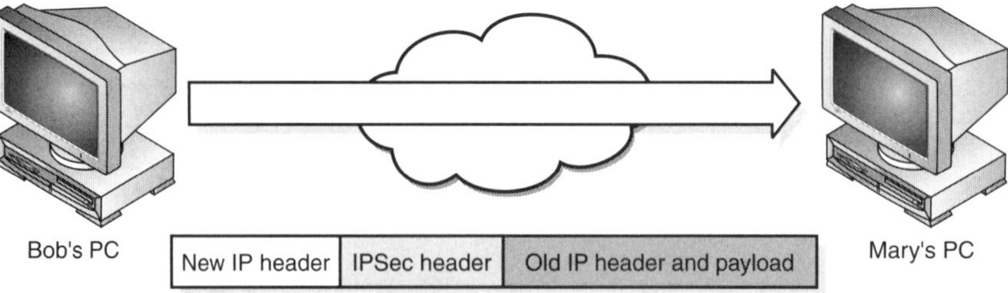

Figure 23-8
IPSec tunnel mode

Network Address Translation (NAT)

Network Address Translation is useful for both networks that use RFC 1918 addresses in private networks and networks that want to hide their "real" addresses from the outside user community. What NAT does is to allow the inside (real) address to masquerade as a false address. NAT can either be configured on the Cisco router or on a firewall. Address mapping can be done in two ways:

- One-to-one (static)
- One-to-many (dynamic)

A one-to-one mapping allows a pool of false addresses to be used against a pool of real addresses. In other words, for every address inside the network that could possibly need to go outside the enterprise network, there exists a false address that is mapped either statically or dynamically to it as packets leave the inside network. The firewall in Figure 23-9 is configured to have a pool of 254 usable addresses to map to traffic leaving from the inside LAN, or the 10.0.0.0 networks. You would, of course, need a more realistic number of addresses in the NAT pool if you were supporting large numbers of users on the inside LANs. Each conversation from an inside workstation to an outside destination will have a source address from the 131.101.111.0/24 NAT pool, rather than the true source address. The firewall then keeps a table of mappings so that it knows how to route return packets.

The other option is to have a one-to-many mapping. This configuration is used primarily when a network has a limited number of valid IP addresses. For instance, if a network engineering staff purchases a small subnet from an ISP that permits them to configure the outside router or firewall only, then a one-to-many mapping would allow for unlimited private addresses to access the Internet by using a single valid IP address. As Figure 23-10 shows, one valid IP exists on the outside interface of the firewall. Every conversation coming from the inside LANs will appear to be from that source IP address. The firewall then tracks the conversations by using an internal conversation "map."

Most networks, however, require a mixture of the two types of NAT mapping in order to support servers in the Demilitarized Zone (DMZ), a topic we will explore in the next section. For now, take a look at the design shown in

Figure 23-9
One-to-one mapping

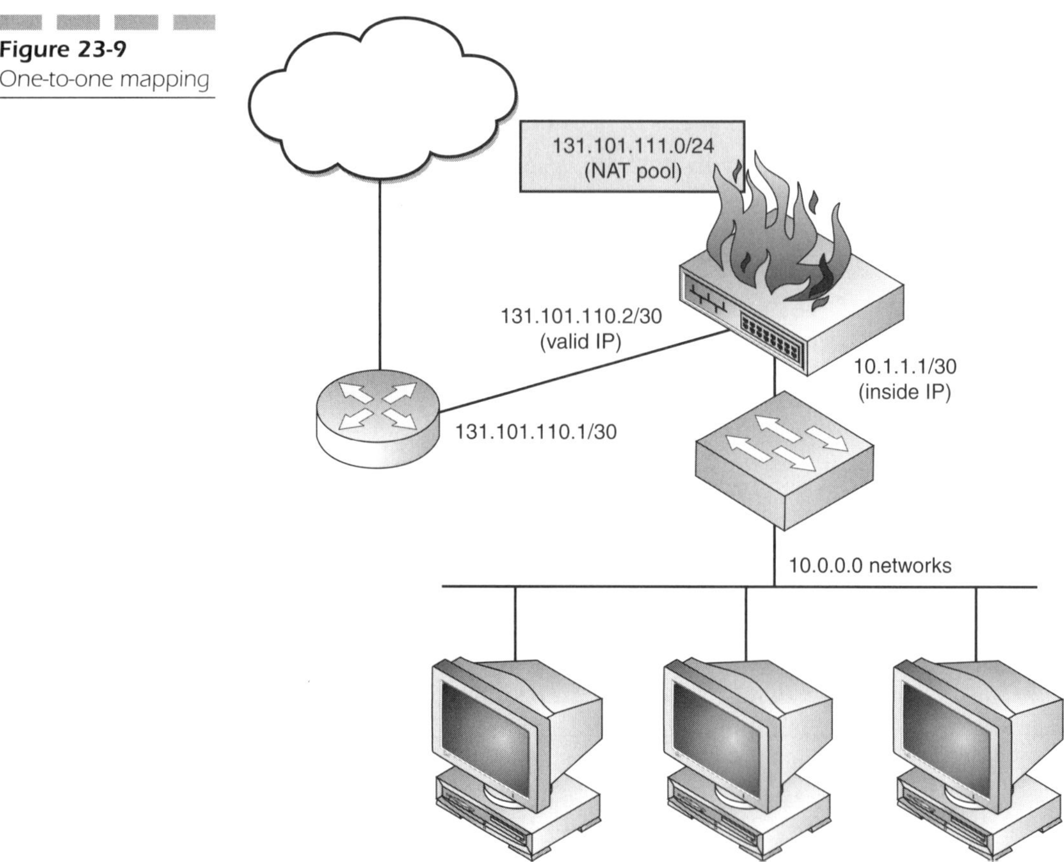

Figure 23-11. For the inside LANs, we can use one-to-many mapping, with all inside sources appearing as the valid IP address of the firewall's external interface. The DMZ, however, requires static one-to-one mapping if the servers must be accessible from external sources by a valid IP address. Normally, the servers will only know the private IP address with which they are configured, but they can be configured as *dual-homed* servers with a private IP on an interface to the internal LANs and a public interface that is publicly routable on the external side. The firewall maintains a table of the valid-to-private IP mappings. All external traffic will see the static valid IP as the source address.

A great source of information for helping you decide how to choose between the available NAT configurations on a Cisco PIX firewall is available at **http://www.cisco.com/warp/public/707/28.html.**

Figure 23-10 One-to-many mapping

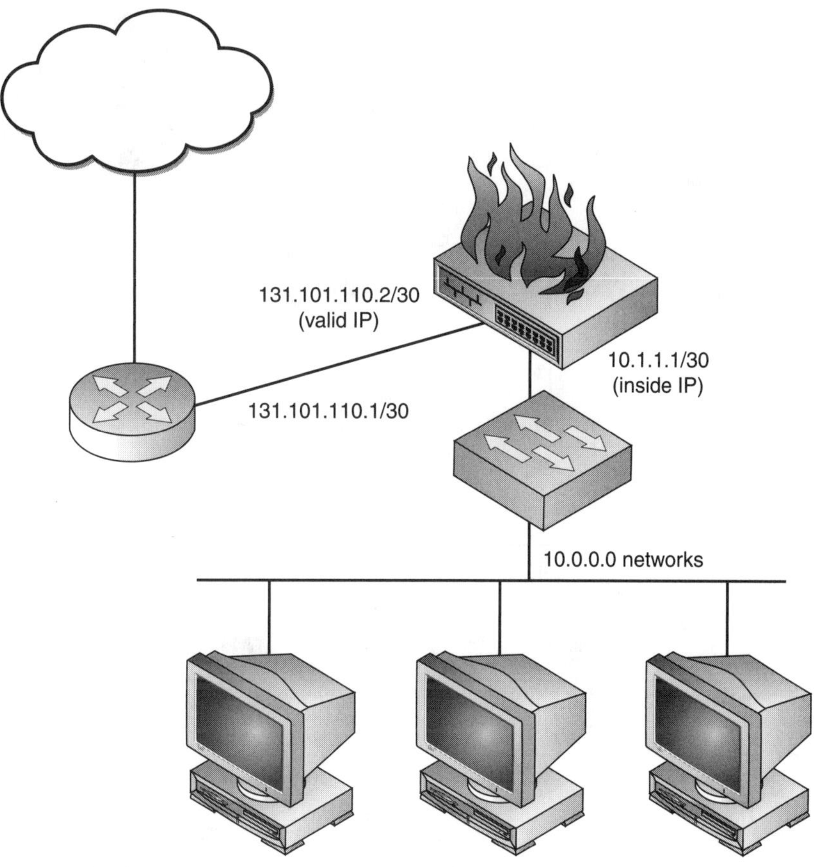

Because you can also configure NAT in the Cisco IOS on the router, another link that is helpful in understanding how to do that is found at **http://www.cisco.com/univercd/cc/td/doc/product/software/ios120/1 2 cgcr/np1_c/1cprt2/1 cipadr.htm.**

Cisco Secure PIX Firewall

The firewall is a critical part of any good network security design, because it is the enforcer of the security policy, which we discussed in earlier chapters. There are as many ways to configure the security in the network as

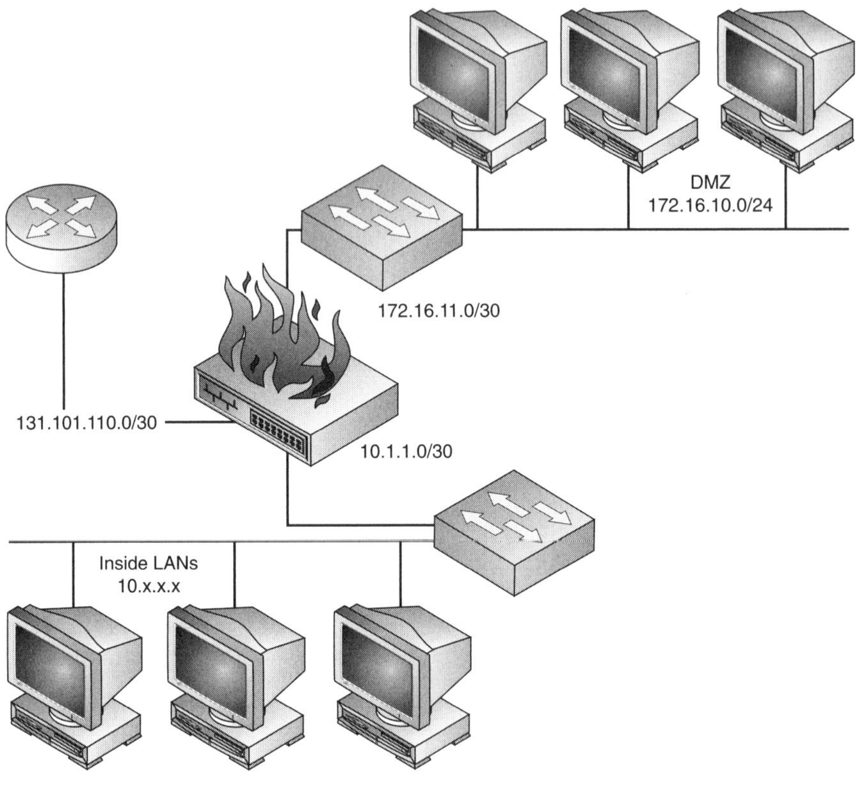

Figure 23-11 Mixed mapping

there are firewalls, but we will cover the most common design concepts here.

There are several different types of firewalls on the market:

- Packet filters
- Application gateways
- Stateful inspection

The *packet filter* is a firewall that is much like an ACL in that there are lists of rules against which incoming packets are compared. If a match condition is found, the packet is permitted or denied, depending upon the action specified in the rule. If no match condition is found, the packets usually are dropped. Specific behavior, of course, depends upon the actual product.

An *application gateway*, or *proxy,* is another type of firewall that compares packets against a set of rules. Usually, this type of firewall is a software package that is loaded onto a Unix or Windows platform. Some application gateways are "bundled" in such a way as to have a proprietary, secure kernel that loads as part of the installation process. The application gateway, which works at the upper layers of the OSI model, starts a proxy-like software daemon for each application that is allowed through the firewall. As this process is carried out, the firewall maintains the session information in its cache. Because of the need to maintain information for each session going through the firewall, this type of firewall lacks the scalability necessary for most networks today. An application gateway tends to be a very secure type of firewall, but performance is highly dependent on the hardware platform of choice, the operating system, and on the amount of throughput it is expected to handle.

Stateful inspection firewalls are those that maintain a state table to keep track of the source/destination pairs, the active conversations, and the security rules. The Cisco PIX firewall, which is also covered in Appendix B, is a "black box" type of stateful inspection firewall, or a network security device. This means that it is a security appliance versus a security software package. There are other stateful inspection firewalls on the market, but many of them depend on a Unix or Windows NT operating system and PC platform to run.

The PIX firewall has a *hardened* operating system, meaning that it has a Unix-like operating system that has had all unnecessary daemons and tools removed. With a software package running on top of a traditional operating system, an administrator would have to manually shut down each service or tool that did not need to be running. Additionally, the administrator would have to ensure that startup scripts did not permit these services to start up again on reboot. This leaves a lot of room for human error.

There are three important network types that you should know in relation to network security and firewall design:

- Trusted (inside)
- Untrusted (outside)
- Demilitarized Zone (DMZ)

The trusted network is considered to be clean and safe and usually refers to the inside LANs or private user community for which the firewall is offering protection. Although many network violations originate inside the network, the term "trusted" is commonly used in relation to the inside, protected network.

The untrusted network is the public or "dirty" network and usually refers to Internet traffic. This side is referred to as untrusted not because more attacks come from the outside but because administratively the network engineering staff has no control over that traffic. Security is usually more stringent on the untrusted traffic.

The DMZ refers to a network that, while under the administrative control of the network engineering staff, must be less stringent in its security policy. The DMZ usually contains Web servers, public FTP servers, and other resources that may need to be accessed by the public or untrusted user community.

The Cisco PIX firewall can be configured for failover with a primary and standby unit, as shown in Figure 23-12. Shortly after power-up, the primary firewall downloads its configuration to the standby firewall. Through a serial cable between the two units and the connected interfaces of each unit, the standby system monitors the health of the primary unit. In the event of a failure, the standby firewall takes over as primary.

The PIX firewall uses the Adaptive Security Algorithm (ASA) to compare each incoming packet against both the security policy and the connection state table. The security policy is the virtual representation of the company security policy. The connection state table is a dynamic table, stored in memory, that keeps a record of all connections that are traversing the firewall. If an incoming connection from the outside, or "untrusted," side of the firewall claims to be a TCP reply to an inside host, the PIX firewall can determine if this is a valid connection or if it is from an intruder. If the connection attempt is in violation of the security policy or does not match the state table, the packets are dropped and a notification is sent to syslog, if configured.

More information about the PIX firewall can be found at **http://www.cisco.com/go/pix.**

Case Study

Bulldog Industries is concerned that their network is not secure enough to allow them to build the e-commerce business that they know is needed. There have been a rash of denial-of-service (DoS) attacks on one of their competitor sites recently, which has caused the other company a great deal of negative publicity. In response to the CEO's concerns, the network engineering staff has hired you to evaluate the security needs of the company and to make recommendations for a security design.

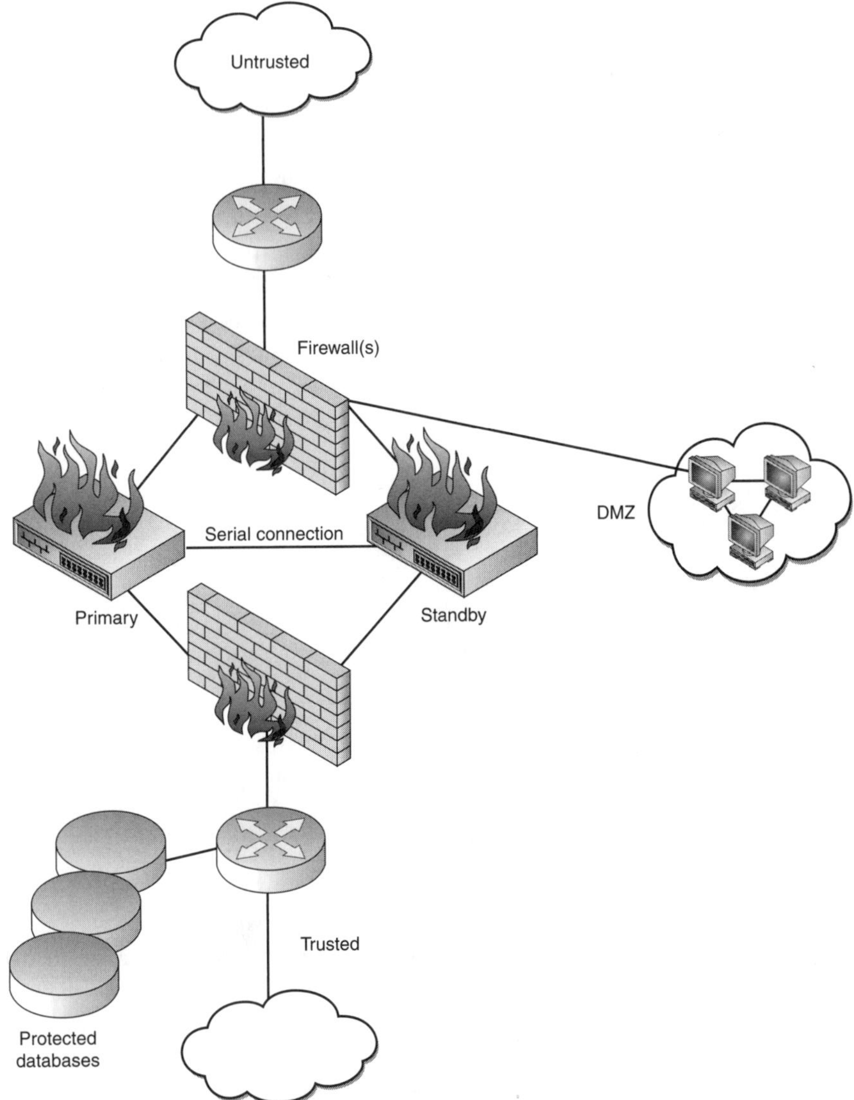

Figure 23-12 Common security design

The company has one office building that houses all of their departments. A main-floor computer room is home to the server farm, which contains both the private databases and the Web and FTP servers. The computer room has a badge scanner that restricts access to the room. Some of the sales people telecommute or are dialing in from their hotels to access the customer databases and product information. Currently, they are all dialing in through a rack of modems and an 800 number. The CFO is finding that this is becoming cost-prohibitive but is aware that the sales force must get to this information.

A single Internet router is currently performing all NAT services for the network and has extensive access lists in place to help protect the network. However, the router interfaces are all in use, and the network engineering staff is concerned that performance isn't what it should be. They do not have a backup in case of a failure.

Your task is to recommend a simple network security design based upon what you know about the network and the Cisco tools that would apply to the issues stated. Although there is no one right answer in any design scenario, a suggested solution can be found in Appendix C.

Study Hints

In this chapter, a lot of material has been covered. Here are areas that you should review before attempting any Cisco network design certification tests.

- *Know your firewall types.* Cisco markets both the PIX firewall series as well as the Cisco Secure Integrated Software (CSIS), formerly the Cisco IOS Firewall. But it is important to know the different types of firewalls—application gateway, stateful inspection, and so on—and their applications.
- *Practice configuring access lists.* Even though it is recommended that you use TFTP or a network management application to edit and load access lists, it may be helpful to find a practice router and some time to test out your access list skills. Not all vendor tests tend to be multiple choice, as are the questions in this book. New testing technology allows for free text in many test questions. Be sure you know how to do these lists.
- *Read up on encryption algorithms and key schemes.* It is outside the scope of this book to cover all of the details of network encryption, but to understand security fully, you should be familiar with how these schemes work on at least a general level.

CCDP Tips

This section contains an abbreviated list of topics covered in this chapter. Think of this section as the equivalent of reading Cliff's Notes™ instead of reading an entire book. You will get the general idea of the chapter but will benefit more from reading the chapter in its entirety.

Access Control Lists (ACL) Before creating the access lists, become familiar with these aspects of the network:

- The network access points
- The network assets that need to be publicly accessible
- The network assets that must be strictly guarded
- The services that will be permitted through the perimeter or firewall

Standard Access Lists

- Work at the network layer
- Perform simple filtering based upon source and destination

Static Extended Access Lists

- Work at the transport layer for greater granularity
- Perform filtering on source/destination, port type, and port number
- Can use the common name of the well-known port

Authentication, Authorization, and Accounting (AAA)

- Authentication asks for positive user identification.
- Authorization consults a database for resources to which the user is allowed.
- Accounting keeps track of and reports all user activity on the network.

Virtual Private Networks (VPNs) A VPN is a software "tunnel" from a remote user to a network resource. The VPN types are

- Access VPN, which generally refers to a VPN for a remote user entering the corporate network from his personal ISP.
- Intranet VPN, which refers to VPNs for internal users to securely access internal corporate resources without "clear text" communication.
- Extranet VPN, which refers to VPNs created for business partners or other users external to the company.

IP Security (IPSec) IPSec is a security framework in which encryption types, key exchange algorithms, and a new header type are specified.

- IP Security Protocol provides a new set of headers for encrypted packets: the Authentication Header (AH) and the Encapsulating Security Payload (ESP), which comes before the Layer 4 Protocol.
- IPSec Transport Mode works by encapsulating the entire packet *except* for the packet header.
- IPSec Tunnel Mode encapsulates the entire packet, even the original header.
- Internet Key Exchange (IKE) is an added protocol that can be used with IPSec. While it is not mandatory, it can simplify the use of IPSec by allowing for many parameters to be pre-configured.

Network Address Translation (NAT) NAT not only allows for the issue of IP address depletion to be solved by the use of private addresses (RFC 1918), it also permits privacy of the real IP addresses in an enterprise network. There are two types of NAT:

- One-to-one, which means there is one phony address for each real address in the network. The firewall or NAT device keeps track of the mapping, one-to-one, in a database or table.
- One-to-many, which means that all addresses masquerade as one address—usually the external address of the firewall or NAT device itself.

Cisco Secure PIX Firewall The Cisco Secure PIX Firewall is a black box, stateful inspection-type firewall that is a simple-to-deploy network appliance.

- The operating system is a Unix-like, pre-hardened kernel.
- The firewall usually is deployed with a minimum of a trusted and untrusted interface. Semi-private networks known as DMZs can also be added on optional, additional interfaces.
- The Adaptive Security Algorithm (ASA) is the proprietary method of packet inspection and traffic control used by the PIX firewall.

Summary

Network security is one of the most important and, unfortunately, most misunderstood of all network design elements. However, with this chapter, you have been given a high-level overview of the tools Cisco has available to assist you with the task of securing the network.

With access lists you can screen traffic as it comes into or leaves router interfaces, thereby securing the network entry points. Users are forced to identify themselves and access only the services for which they are authorized through the use of the AAA model. We also looked at how IPSec technology works to provide encryption for tunneling and VPNs. We saw how NAT can be used to hide "real" network addresses from the world, and how the Cisco PIX firewall can be deployed to act as a physical representation of the network security policy.

Next we will look at an overview of SNA network design as we finish out the last chapter in our main text.

Questions

1. The interface on a firewall that connects to the Internet is known as what type of interface?
   a. Untrusted
   b. Trusted
   c. DMZ
   d. Internet
2. Which term describes a negotiated agreement between two peers using IKE?
   a. Diffie-Hellman
   b. ISAKMP
   c. SA
   d. AH

3. The IPSec mode that encrypts the entire packet is known as ________ mode.
   a. Transport
   b. Tunnel
   c. ISAKMP
   d. IKE
4. This term refers to a tunnel technology that encrypts a data communication session as though two end points were directly connected.
   a. Tunnel
   b. DMZ
   c. SA
   d. VPN
5. What does the Cisco PIX Firewall use to compare incoming packets against the security policy and the state table?
   a. Adaptive security algorithm
   b. Routing table algorithm
   c. Stateful algorithm
   d. Adaptive synchronized algorithm
6. If all packets leaving the enterprise network from the firewall have the same source IP address, what type of NAT mapping is in use?
   a. One-to-one
   b. One-to-many
   c. Many-to-many
   d. Hide mode
7. The primary difference between standard and static extended access lists is
   a. Standard access lists work at the transport layer; static extended access lists work at the network layer.
   b. Standard access lists use wildcard masks; static extended access lists use network masks.
   c. Standard access lists use two-digit numbers; static extended access lists use three-digit numbers.
   d. Standard access lists work at the network layer; static extended access lists work at the transport layer as well.

8. A network that connects to a firewall and hosts servers that are publicly accessible is
   a. Trusted
   b. Untrusted
   c. DMZ
   d. Internet
9. Select the letter next to the line that is *not* valid for an access list.
   a. access-list 101 permit ip any 172.16.10.10 eq telnet
   b. access-list 101 deny udp host 172.16.10.4 any eq 161
   c. access-list 101 permit udp 10.0.0.0 0.255.255.255 any eq syslog
   d. access-list 101 deny tcp any any eq telnet
10. Two PIX firewalls configured in a "hot standby" array are connected by a(n)
    a. Ethernet switch
    b. UTP cable
    c. Serial cable
    d. Standard phone cord

Answers

1. The interface on a firewall that connects to the Internet is known as what type of interface?

   a. Untrusted

2. Which term describes a negotiated agreement between two peers using IKE?

   c. SA

3. The IPSec mode that encrypts the entire packet is known as ________ mode.

   b. Tunnel

4. This term refers to a tunnel technology that encrypts a data communication session as though two end points were directly connected.

   d. VPN

5. What does the Cisco PIX Firewall use to compare incoming packets against the security policy and the state table?

   a. Adaptive security algorithm

6. If all packets leaving the enterprise network from the firewall have the same source IP address, what type of NAT mapping is in use?

   b. One-to-many

7. The primary difference between standard and static extended access lists is

   d. Standard access lists work at the network layer; static extended access lists work at the transport layer as well.

8. A network that connects to a firewall and hosts servers that are publicly accessible is

   c. DMZ

9. Select the letter next to the line that is *not* valid for an access list.

   a. access-list 101 permit ip any 172.16.10.10 eq telnet

10. Two PIX firewalls configured in a "hot standby" array are connected by a

    c. Serial cable

Frequently Asked Questions (FAQs)

1. *Why do I need an access list if I have a firewall?*

   Although having a firewall to protect the network is a good measure of security, access lists can add to a layered security effect, preventing some traffic from ever reaching the firewall. Because firewall performance is dependent to some extent upon the speed of the platform and operating system, offloading some of the traffic that would normally go through the firewall can also improve overall performance.

2. *Can I have more than one DMZ?*

   There can be as many DMZs as there are "extra" ports on the firewall. There must be one trusted port and one untrusted port, by definition, or all you really have is a roadblock. The additional ports, if any, can be configured by customizing the permits and denies in the security policy.

3. *Is there really anything I can do to stop intruders?*

   Let's face it. If someone really wants to crack your network, they will keep trying until they find the single vulnerability you may have overlooked—or they may find a new way to exploit a common network resource. The goal is to make security a layered function, so that an intruder has many layers to traverse before getting the goods, so to speak. Having a firewall with all the bells, whistles, and patches is a good start, but it is not enough for most corporate networks.

Bibliography

http://www.cisco.com/univercd/cc/td/doc/product/software/ssr83/rpc_r/48383.htm

Cisco PIX Firewall Configuration Guide: Introduction, **http://www.cisco.com/univercd/cc/td/doc/product/iaabu/pix/pix_v53/config/intro.htm#34035**

Installing the Cisco PIX Firewall Syslog Server, **http://www.cisco.com/univercd/cc/td/doc/product/iaabu/pix/pix_v52/install/pfss.htm**

Increasing Security on IP Networks, **http://www.cisco.com/univercd/cc/td/doc/cisintwk/ics/cs003.htm#xtocid2185618**

Recommended Reading

Cisco Access Lists Field Guide, McGraw-Hill Technical Series, Kent Hundley/Gilbert Held

Cisco Secure Integrated Software (CSIS) Cookbook, **http://www.cisco.com/warp/public/793/ios_fw/intro_cbac.html**

Cisco Secure Internet Security Solutions, Cisco Press, Andrew G. Mason, Mark J. Newcomb

The Cuckoo's Egg, Doubleday, Clifford Stoll

Increasing Security in IP Networks—Cisco, **http://cio.cisco.com/univercd/cc/td/doc/cisintwk/ics/cs003.htm**

Managing Cisco Network Security, Cisco Press, Michael Wenstrom

Mastering Network Security, Sybex, Chris Brenton

Practical Unix and Internet Security, O'Reilly Press, Simson Garfinkel, Gene Spafford

Rootshell **http://www.rootshell.com**

CHAPTER 24

SNA Design Overview

Overview

In the early 1970s, IBM introduced an internetworking protocol called Systems Network Architecture (SNA) in order to allow its mainframe systems to talk to the "dumb" terminals at the user end. Although this type of technology, based on bridging, has seen its popularity come and go, it is still in use at many locations that are using mainframe-computing designs. These locations include manufacturers, financial institutions, government agencies, and retail.

Like any other technology we have discussed in this book, if it is supported by Cisco and is in use in the real world, then you would be well advised to have a solid understanding of how the technology is implemented. The goal of this chapter is to provide information on the background, components, and design implementation of SNA networks.

Bridging Concepts

This section will briefly introduce you to some of the bridging concepts that allow SNA to work. Although the intent of this section is not to thoroughly cover each topic in great detail, you should have a basic understanding of the concepts when we are through.

Source-Route Bridging

LANs using Token Ring and IEEE 802.5 use a bridging technique called Source-Route Bridging (SRB). The best path to a destination is selected by examining all possible paths and then using predetermined criteria to select one. After the selection is made, all traffic from that source to that destination uses the same path. With Cisco routers, SRB can be used to group multiple Token Ring LANs into a single, logical segment. If Token Ring and non-Token Ring environments are grouped together, the bridging is referred to as Remote Source-Route Bridging (RSRB).

SRB allows for multiple protocols to be routed on Token Ring LANs by letting the router act as both a Layer 3 router and a Layer 2 source route bridge.

Routing Information Field (RIF)

The routing information field (RIF) is inserted into the 802.5 header by the source station. It is entered immediately after the source address field. The destination station will reverse the information in the RIF when sending data back to the source. It is from this behavior that SRB gets its name. The 802.5 frame format is shown in Figure 24-1.

SRB uses explorer frames that are sent by the source station and venture all through the network to learn various paths to a given destination. Two types of explorer frames exist: all-routes explorer (ARE) and spanning-tree explorer (STE). ARE frames are copied by source-route bridges, which then add their own routing information to the frame. If frames are received on ports that are in the spanning-tree state, the source-route bridge will add its own routing information to the STE frame. ARE frames are flooded out all paths to a destination, while only one STE frame is sent to each ring by spanning-tree. Once the best path is determined, it is entered into the RIF of the frame.

Spanning-Tree Protocol (STP)

Token Ring LANs use the spanning-tree protocol (STP) to help ensure a loop-free topology by keeping a single path between two nodes active. If more than one active path exists, a loop condition can occur. The spanning-tree algorithm calculates this "best path."

In a switched environment using spanning tree, all switches learn about each other through the exchange of bridge protocol data units (BPDU). From the exchange of BPDUs, a *root switch* is elected. The root switch is the one with the lowest numerical priority or the lowest media access control (MAC) address. Each bridged or switched segment then elects a designated

Figure 24-1
802.5 frame format

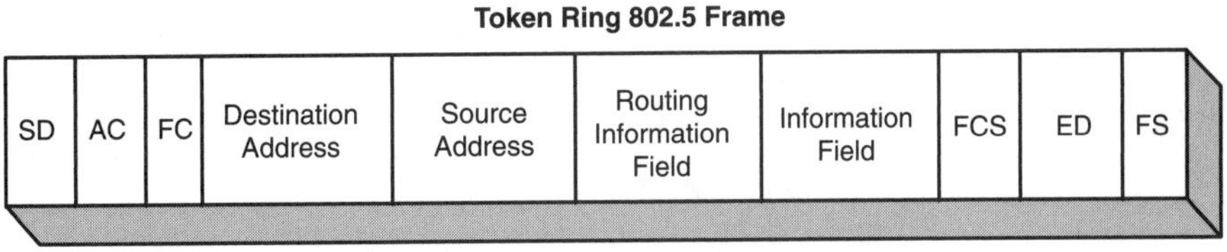

Token Ring 802.5 Frame

SD	AC	FC	Destination Address	Source Address	Routing Information Field	Information Field	FCS	ED	FS

switch that will communicate with the root bridge, which is the logical center of the switched network. The root switch calculates the best path to all other switches in the network and puts all other paths into a blocked state. Although it is outside the scope of this section to go into greater detail about the components and functions of STP, you can read more about it at the following Cisco Web page at **http://www.cisco.com/univercd/cc/td/doc/product/lan/cat5000/rel_5_2/config/spantree.htm**.

Figure 24-2 shows the BPDU used in the IBM implementation of spanning-tree.

In the IBM implementation of the spanning-tree protocol, here is how the process works:

- If a frame is received on a local ring, the bridge learns the MAC address.
- If a frame is received from the other side of a source-route bridge, the bridge learns the route descriptor.
- Frames that are non-source-route are discarded.
- Source-route frames are forwarded based on the route descriptor.
- All-routes explorer and STP explorer frames are issued and forwarded.

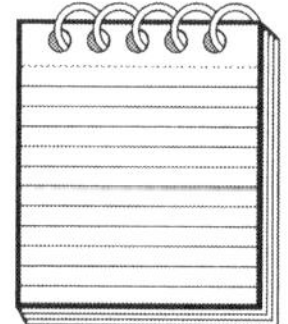

NOTE: *In IBM's implementation, STP is used only to ensure a loop-free topology for explorer frames.*

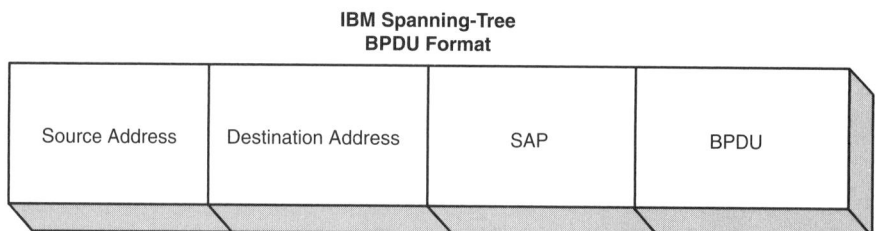

Figure 24-2 IBM BPDU

Systems Network Architecture (SNA)

When SNA was introduced, many things changed in the way communication between the hosts and mainframes was conducted. Hardware communications, for instance, moved away from the mainframe and were offloaded to a front-end processor (FEP) on a model 37xx platform. The FEP took on most of the processing load and let the mainframe do its job as keeper of the databases. The FEPs were loaded up with powerful software called the network control protocol (NCP) to handle tasks like polling. Also, new software called the virtual telecommunications access method (VTAM) was loaded on the mainframe. Figure 24-3 shows the basic host-centric design of the SNA network.

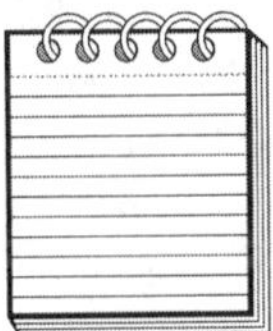

NOTE: *An FEP can also be called a communication controller. A cluster controller is sometimes referred to as an establishment controller.*

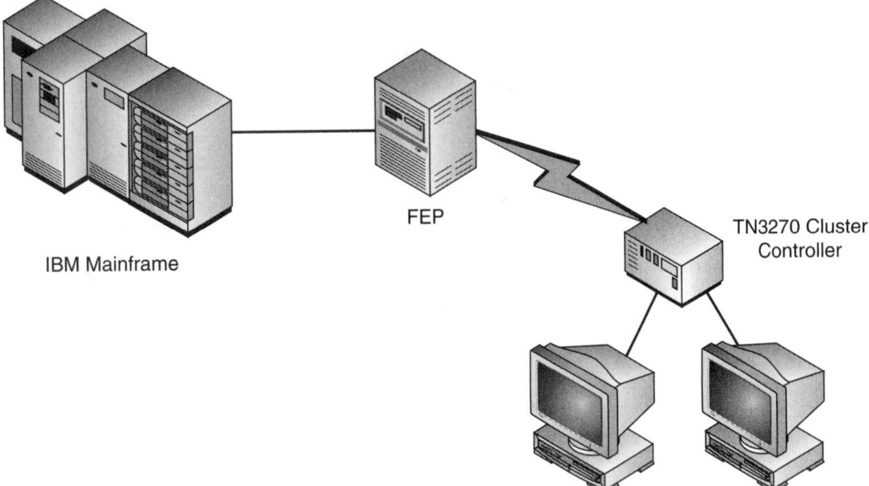

Figure 24-3
SNA basic model

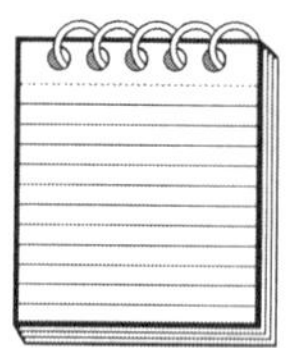

NOTE: The FEP can also be a Cisco 7500 Channel Interface Processor (CIP) router.

Network Addressable Units

Communication within SNA happens between components called network addressable units (NAUs), of which several types exist:

- Logical unit (LU)
- Physical unit (PU)
- System services control point (SSCP)

As shown in Figure 24-4, each type of NAU has a certain purpose within the SNA network. The logical unit can be a primary LU (PLU) associated with a mainframe application or a secondary LU (SLU) associated with the end users.

The *physical unit* is a node type 2, 4, or 5, which will be discussed in the next section, and this physical unit communicates with the SSCP. The PU

Figure 24-4
NAUs

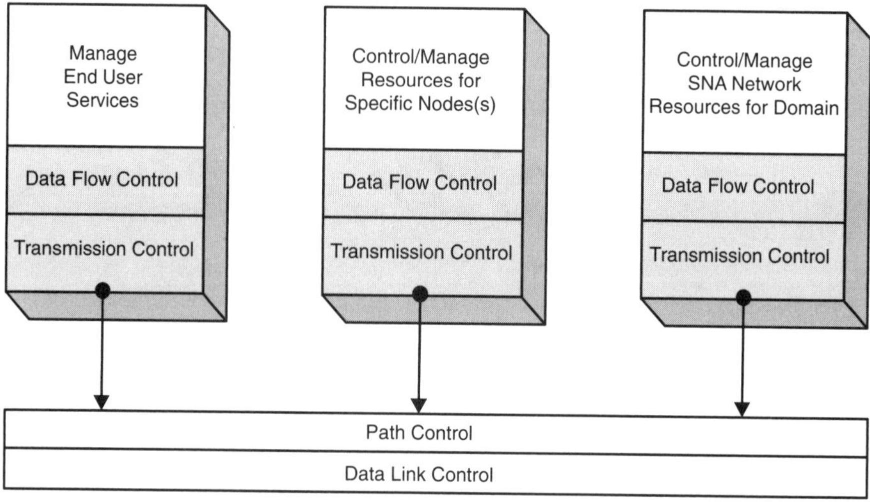

is responsible for tasks such as controlling the physical resources—CPU time, disk space, and so on.

Finally, the SSCP, which is part of VTAM on the mainframe, controls the sessions between the end users and the mainframe.

SNA Hierarchy

Like many aspects of internetworking, SNA is hierarchical in nature. In this section, we will talk about certain nodes that are classified as part of the hierarchy, *subarea nodes* and *peripheral nodes*. The subarea nodes, which can route, are grouped into types 4 and 5. Peripheral nodes are of type 1 or 2 and have no routing capabilities.

NOTE: *Type 1 nodes were "dumb terminals" and are now obsolete. Type 2 nodes reside in intelligent terminals or establishment controllers (a 3270 emulator on a PC, for example).*

Subarea Nodes A subarea node provides routing services to the peripheral nodes attached to it within a certain *domain*. The subarea node can either be a host (mainframe) or a communication controller (FEP), but all traffic from the peripheral nodes must pass through the subarea node.

SNA classifies a host computer or mainframe as node type 5 at the top of the SNA hierarchy. Each mainframe runs VTAM software. An FEP is node type 4 and runs NCP software. Regardless of the node type, each subarea node is assigned a specific subarea number that is unique within the network.

Peripheral Nodes A peripheral node is part of a domain and communicates through its assigned subarea node. Figure 24-5 shows a typical SNA domain with end-user 3270 terminals communicating with the mainframe through its cluster controller and the FEP. Notice the node types and how they relate to one another in the design. In this figure, the mainframe is a type 5 node running VTAM. It communicates with the end users through a node type 4, the FEP, which is acting as the subarea node to the cluster controller. Therefore, the cluster controller is a peripheral node to the FEP. The end-user 3270 terminals are considered to be SLUs. The SLU communicates with the PLU (the mainframe) through a PLU-to-SLU session,

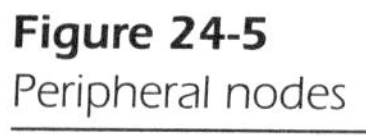

Figure 24-5 Peripheral nodes

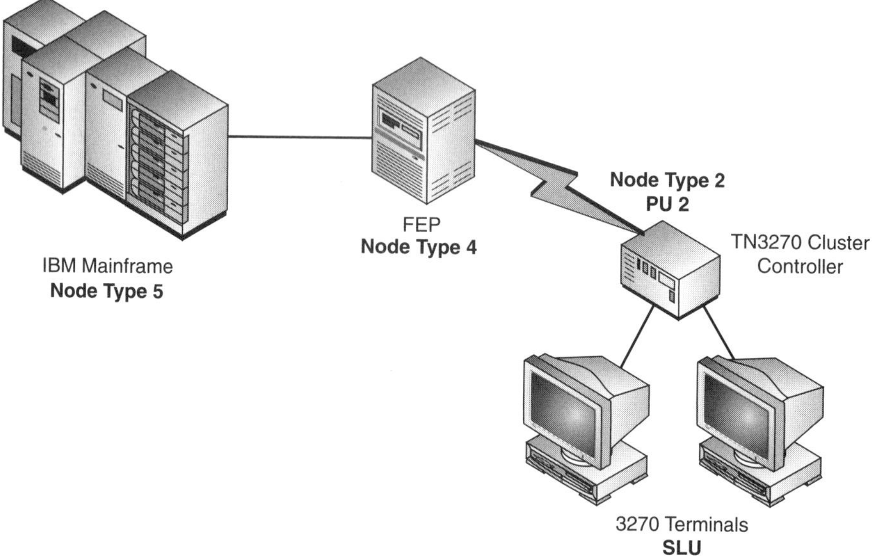

which is initiated through an initial login message to the SSCP (part of VTAM on the mainframe).

SNA Subareas A subarea in SNA consists of the subarea node and all peripheral nodes attached to it. This is sometimes referred to as a domain as well. Figure 24-6 shows a configuration of four subareas within an SNA network. Each subarea is defined in NCP with its own unique number within the internetwork. A subarea usually has an FEP associated with it, but in Figure 24-6, subarea 1 is using the mainframe as its subarea node. A subarea can also have a single FEP with no other node, as in subarea 2. When this is the case, the FEP is referred to as an Internetwork Node (INN) and is essentially a router with a static routing table.

SNA End-User Session Startup So, how does a user initiate a session with the mainframe? This happens through a LU-LU session. The *LU-LU session* is the end result of many other types of sessions taking place first. Consider the simple network shown in Figure 24-7.

In Figure 24-7, the mainframe is the type 5 node and contains the SSCP and VTAM, which is the PU. The mainframe must first establish a session between the SSCP and the PU. The FEP shown in the figure is acting as the

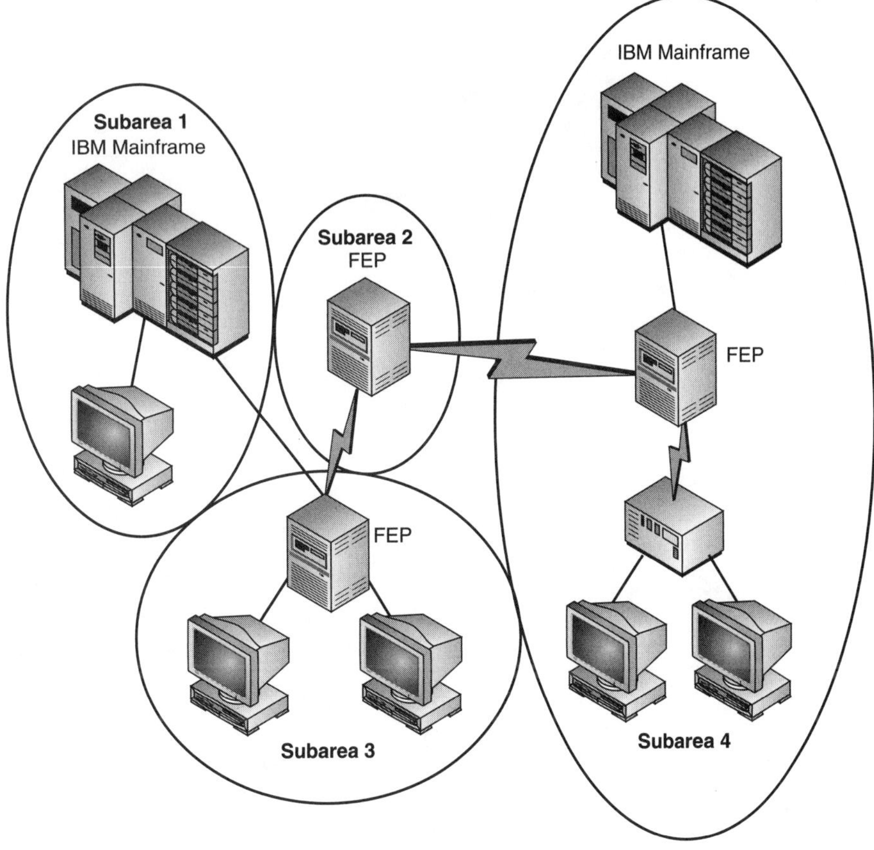

Figure 24-6
SNA subareas

PLU for our subarea. The end-user terminal is the SLU. Now that the SSCP-PU session is established, the SSCP initiates an SSCP-LU session with the PLU that wants to communicate. Remember that the FEP acts on behalf of the SLU in this instance and is handling the hardware communications. Finally, the PLU activates the LU-LU session with the SLU. Now the host system (mainframe) is communicating with the end-user system (SLU). This process is illustrated in Figure 24-8.

The exception to this session setup is when communication is required between two LUs in different subareas. When this occurs, the two host computers must first establish an SSCP-SSCP session before the remainder of the LU-LU session setup can occur.

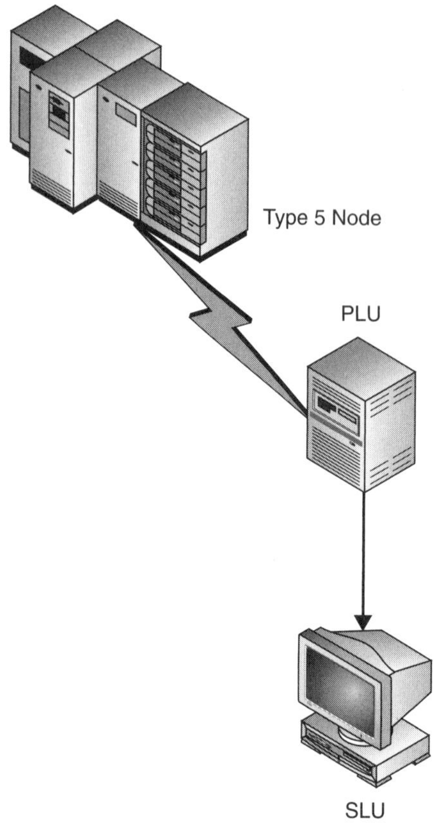

Figure 24-7 End-user communication

Token Ring SNA Gateways

SNA networks are generally implemented over Token Ring. In fact, the IBM mainframe world is still very much based on Token Ring environments. The end users, however, use PCs, just like the users of other network types around the world. These PCs run terminal emulation packages that talk to the IBM host computers.

As you saw in the last section, however, the PC can't just access the mainframe directly. A whole set of processes must happen in order for the session to be established. Additionally, the PC must access the SNA resources through a *gateway* node on the Token Ring. Figure 24-9 shows a

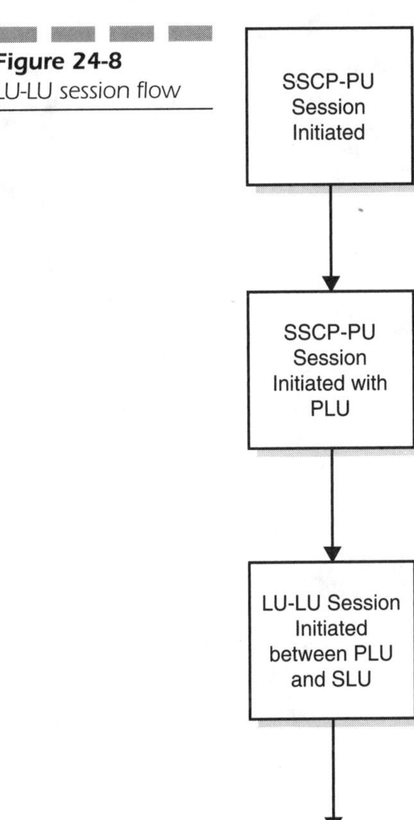

Figure 24-8
LU-LU session flow

typical Token Ring environment with a gateway node and a PC acting as a terminal. The host computer must have each Token Ring device defined as a *switched major node* in its system generation (sysgen) macros.

Three kinds of Token Ring gateways are supported:

- **PU Gateway** This appears as a node type 2.
- **LU Gateway** The Token Ring device appears as an LU and the gateway node appears as a node type 2.
- **Cisco Router** This acts as a downstream PU concentrator (DSPU).

We will now take a closer look at each type of gateway.

Figure 24-9
Token Ring gateway

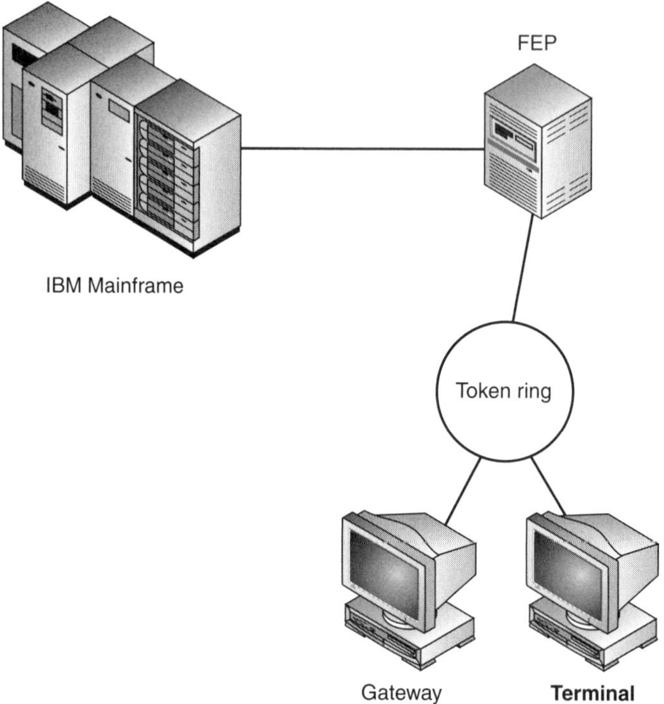

Pass Through

A *pass through* gateway is transparent to the Token Ring-attached PCs and to the host system (mainframe). Because each Token Ring device must be defined in the VTAM processes on the host as a switched major node, the systems that are communicating do not need to know about the pass through gateway. Figure 24-10 shows the PU gateway type, also called a pass through, as it might be configured. Once the session is established, you can see that the PU in the PC communicates directly with the SSCP on the host system.

As you can imagine, this type of gateway requires a lot of overhead and administration on the part of the network engineering staff. Every device must be manually entered into the host system as it is added to the Token Ring network.

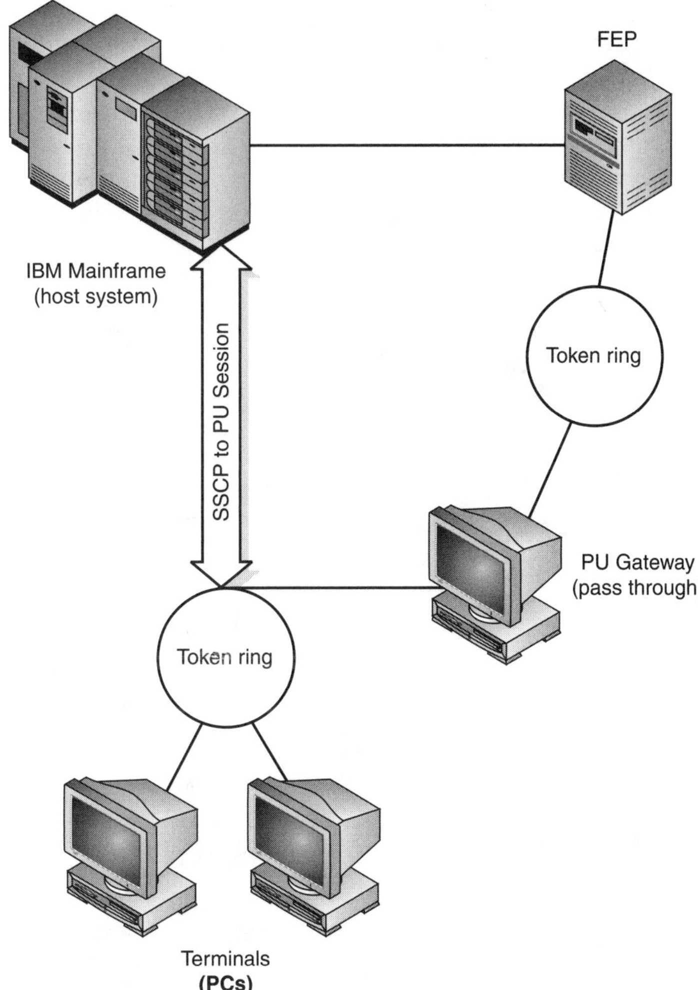

Figure 24-10 Pass through gateway

LU Gateways

With the LU gateway type, the problem of the additional overhead and administration is solved, because the host system never has to have direct communication with the terminal. Instead, the PU in the LU gateway node communicates in an SSCP-to-PU session with the host system. Although some manual configuration is still required, it is far less than if you were to use a PU gateway.

The placement of the LU gateway can either be at the host end of the network, as shown in Figure 24-11, or at the client end.

As you can see, the host system communicates with the LU gateway, and the LU gateway establishes a session to the end user's PC. Depending on how geographically dispersed the network is and how many subareas exist, locating the LU gateway closer to the client can vastly reduce the traffic across the wide area network (WAN). The only polling that will take place

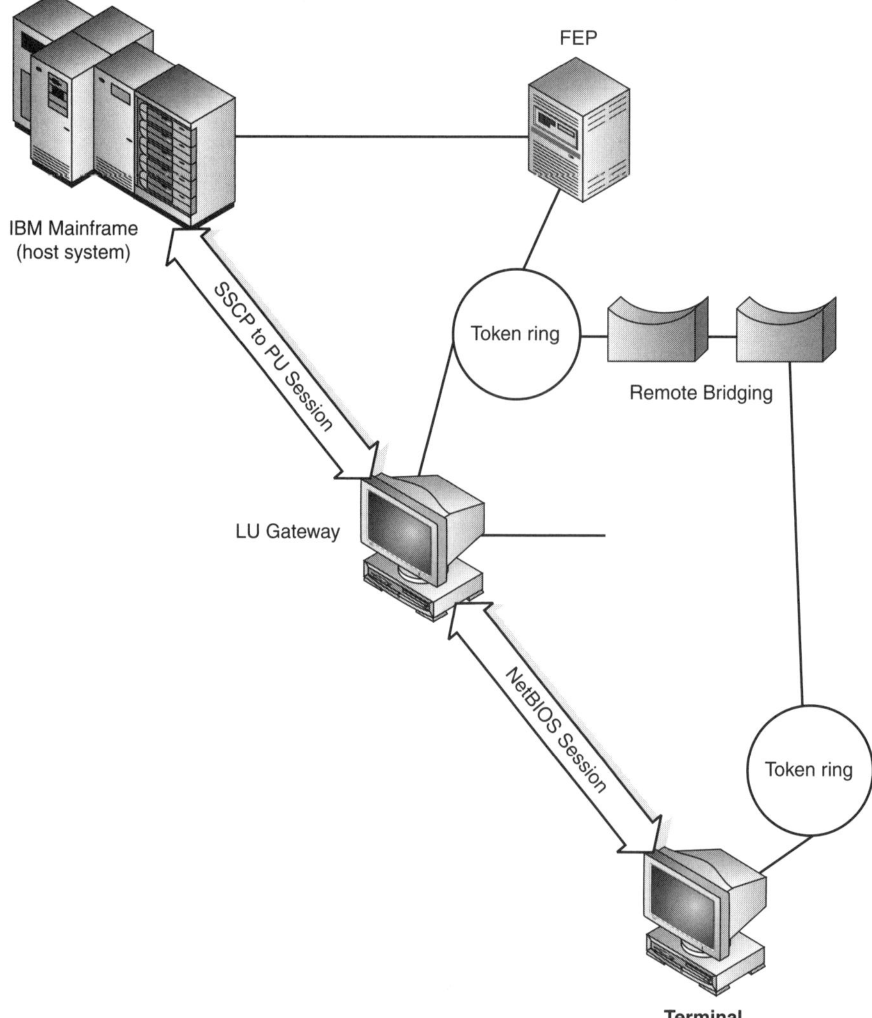

Figure 24-11
LU gateway

is between the LU gateway and the terminals. However, if many subareas require many LU gateways, it may be more logical (and less costly) to collocate the LU gateway with the host system.

In Figure 24-11, we have shown a NetBIOS session between the end user's PC and the LU gateway. In fact, several types of NetBIOS implementations are supported, depending on the type of gateway software used:

- NetBIOS over IPX or native IPX/SPX for Novell SAA gateways
- NetBIOS over LLC2 for Attachmate gateways
- NetBIOS over TCP/IP for Mitec gateways

Downstream PU (DSPU)

A final option is to configure a Cisco router as a DSPU concentrator. This implementation reduces the amount of manual configuration that is required even further. The host system must still know about each LU with which it must communicate, but it only needs to know about a single PU. In Figure 24-12, the router acting as the DSPU concentrator knows about all of the same LUs as the host, but it also knows about two PUs that the host system does not need to have configured as part of its sysgen.

Aside from the reduced administration that this option brings to the table, it also offers some other benefits:

- Support of Token Ring and remote source-route bridging (RSRB) connections to upstream SNA hosts
- Support for IBM NetView network management software
- Support for the dynamic registration of downstream SNA devices
- The reduction of WAN overhead by keeping traffic local

SNA Internetworking

Part of solving a problem is to define the problem you are trying to solve. In this section, we will look at how to determine the requirements for an SNA internetwork, both from a business and a technical perspective. Then we will describe how you can migrate the network from today's design to a design that will prove scalable and robust in order to support tomorrow's applications.

Figure 24-12
DSPU concentrator

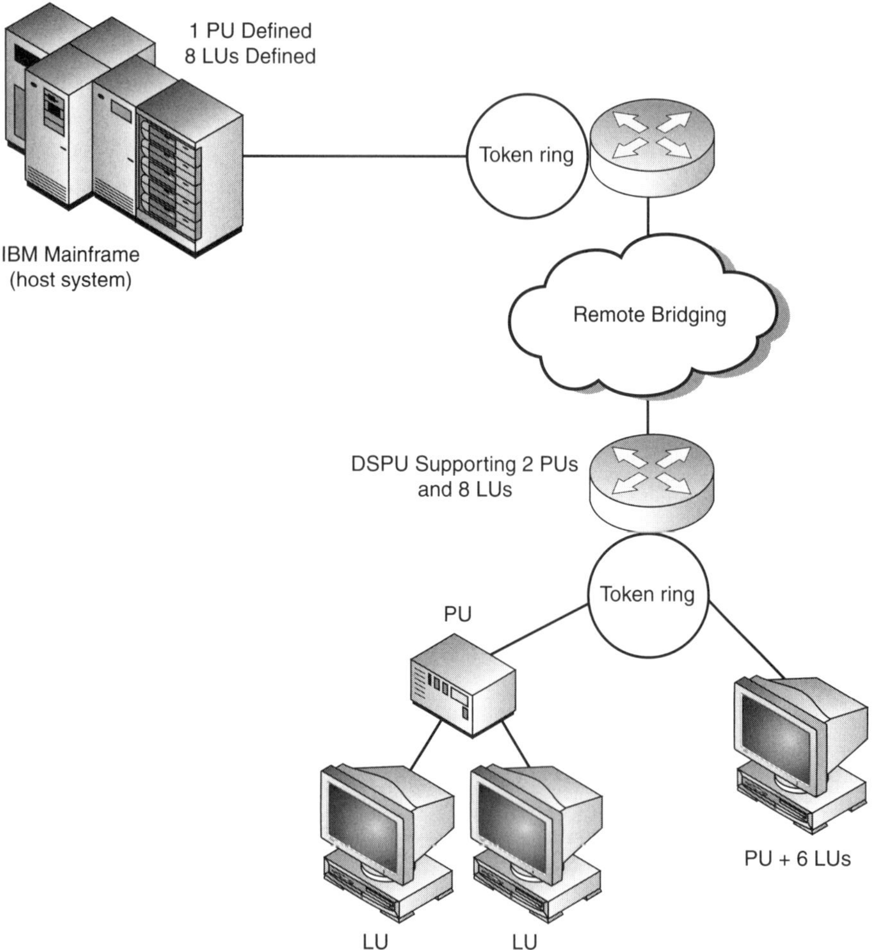

Requirements

When mainframe design was first introduced to the business world, it was as a very large client/server model. The mainframe held all of the information, and the client terminals communicated directly with the mainframe in order to use the information. Between the limited bandwidth available in the early years of networking and the limited technology, the process of client/server communication was slow and cumbersome.

To use yesterday's design to try to support today's requirements is an exercise in frustration indeed. Today a need exists to keep the end-user system "intelligent" by using a PC with its own memory, storage space, and processor. The mainframe has been relegated to the role of a high-speed, high-storage capacity file server. Although the end user must still access the mainframe over the network, new design models are available that can make the entire network run smoothly.

For instance, an upgraded switching infrastructure can help deliver high-speed throughput from end-to-end in the network. Moving gateways closer to the host can reduce the cost of building the network, if the infrastructure can support the bandwidth needed between host and client. Upgrading the technology can also improve overall business productivity by providing support for emerging technologies like multimedia messaging and more efficient databases.

Before we move into a discussion of how to design, or redesign, the SNA internetwork, let's first take a look at how the network might look today. In Figure 24-13, you can see that many FEPs and dedicated lines use Synchronous Data Link Control (SDLC) to communicate. Some support exists for Token Ring, but this network design is fraught with overhead and high-cost components. In the next section, we will show you how to update this design.

Migration Design

Frame Relay (RFC 1490) made its debut in the SNA world at the beginning of the 1990s. The RFC outlined support for SNA networks over Frame Relay, enabling designers to remove remote FEPs and replace them with Cisco routers, which have a lower cost of ownership. The improved design is shown in Figure 24-14.

The SNA network benefited from Cisco routers in two ways:

- RFC 1490 is an optional encapsulation method for RSRB over Frame Relay.
- The router can directly connect to RFC 1490-compliant FEPs.

By using routers, the design shown in Figure 24-14 has fewer SDLC-dedicated lines and fewer costly FEPs. The direct communication between the routers and the FEPs improves the performance, and the cost savings over having many FEPs is substantial. More changes were to come.

The next step was a migration to multiprotocol networks. This meant a replacement of the remaining remote FEPs with Cisco routers. Data Link

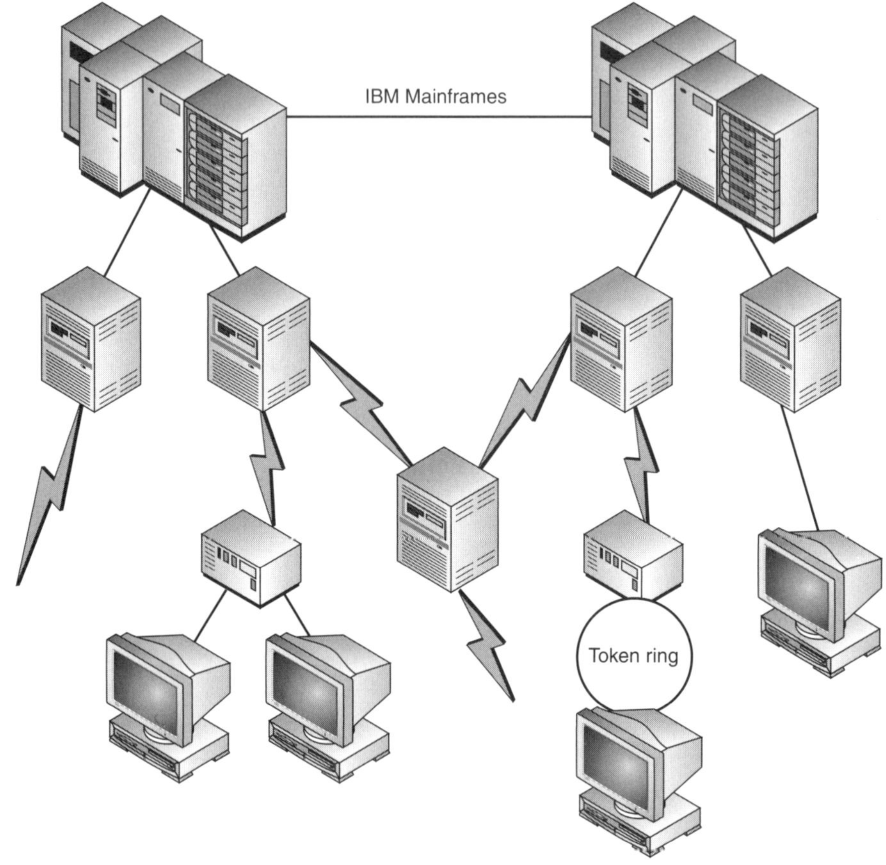

Figure 24-13 Outdated SNA design

Switching Plus (DLSw+) was deployed and bisynchronous links were tunneled. This final design improvement, shown in Figure 24-15, meant that SNA could share the same network as TCP/IP and IPX traffic—a huge step forward from the days of segregated mainframe networks.

SNA Token Ring Internetworking

As the migration from "old-world" mainframe technology took the SNA network into the "new world" of multiprotocol support, several enabling technologies came into play:

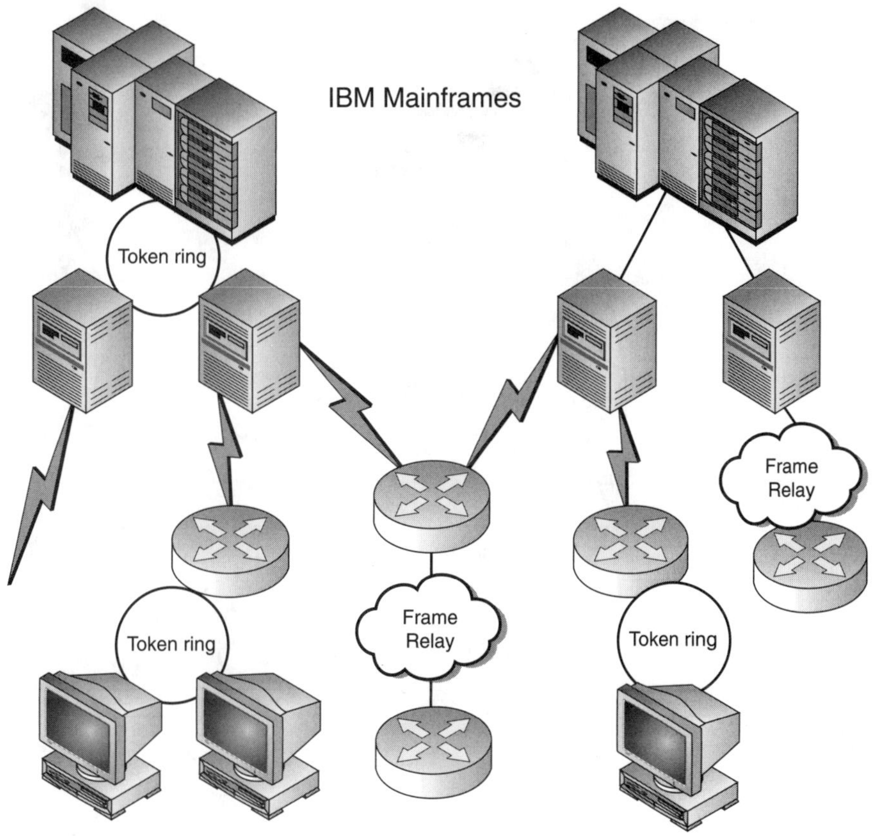

Figure 24-14 SNA migration: phase one

- SNA tunneling with RSRB and SDLC
- DLSw+ and Advanced Peer-to-Peer Networking (APPN)
- APPN for multihost SNA routing
- Router channel attachment with the CIP card

In this section, we will introduce you to each of these integrators.

Data Link Switching (DLSw) and Data Link Switching Plus (DLSw+)

The most common form of SNA tunneling is Data Link Switching (DLSw), which provides a way to integrate SNA and NetBIOS over TCP/IP while

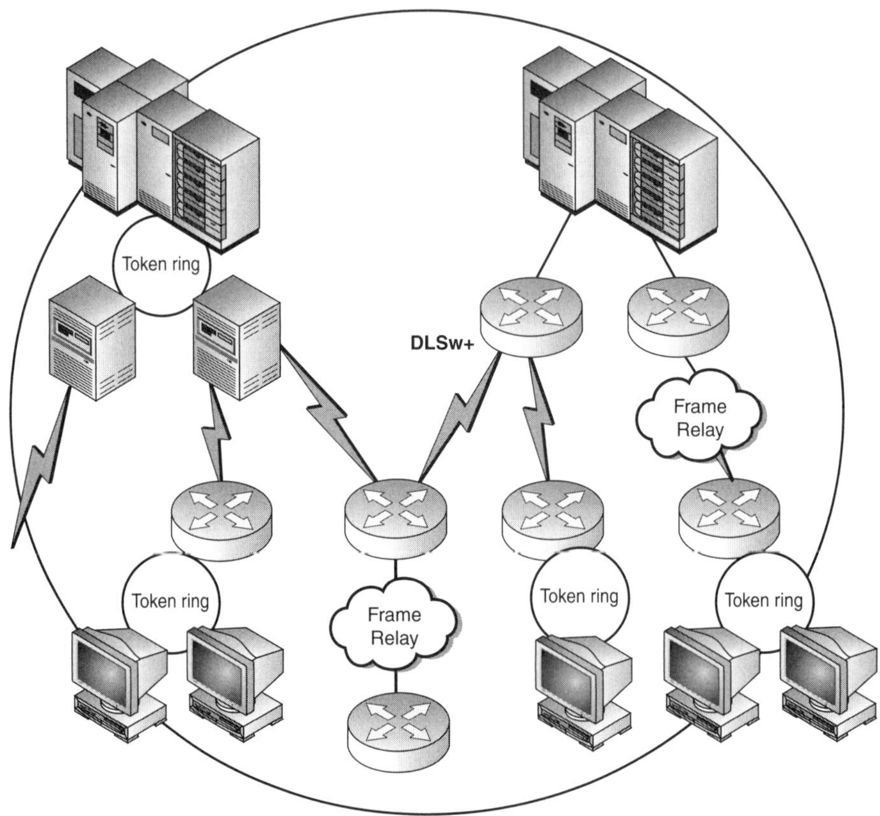

Figure 24-15 SNA migration: phase two

reducing overhead and session timeouts. The DLSw Working Group of the APPN Implementers' Workshop (AIW) first outlined the DLSw standards in 1994. The result was described in RFC 1434, which was later replaced by RFC 1795, then RFC 2166. Cisco routers are fully compliant with the entire DLSw standard and provide support for extensions. Thus, Cisco's implementation is usually referred to as DLSw+.

DLSw+ is based on a peer-group approach that optimizes the Token Ring explorer processing and supports direct communication between network nodes. Cisco also supports explorer firewalls, which permit only a single explorer for a given destination MAC address to be sent over the WAN at one time. Any explorers that are destined for the same MAC address are "remembered" by the router and receive a simultaneous local response when the original explorer receives an answer. This process helps to eliminate explorer "storms" that can result during peak hours.

DLSw+ also supports local LLC2 terminations, which eliminate the need to send LLC2 keepalives and acknowledgements over the WAN. This also helps prevent LLC2 timeouts. Communications between DLSw+ peer routers occur over a construct known as a *circuit*, which is comprised of two data link control connections and a TCP session. This allows DSLw+ to provide reliable delivery and flow control in the network.

The use of remote source-route bridging supports RIF pass through. Using this scenario, the router cloud appears as one ring in the RIF. Notice the RIF in our examples in Figure 24-16. From the client workstation on Ring 10, the last hop in the RIF is to Ring 30. The DLSw+ router cloud could contain multiple router hops, but all are seen as one, allowing for longer paths. Normally, only seven SRB hops are permitted in the RIF. By using DLSw+, up to six additional SRB hops are permitted on either end of the connection. This provides for much more scalable RSRB networks.

SNA Tunneling with RSRB

A less frequently used method of tunneling SNA is by tunneling with RSRB. You may still encounter this, but it is an older technology. In a stable environment, this technology works well. The tunnel is shown in Figure 24-17 in a steady state. The LLC2 Information (I) frames and ACKs

Figure 24-16 RIF termination

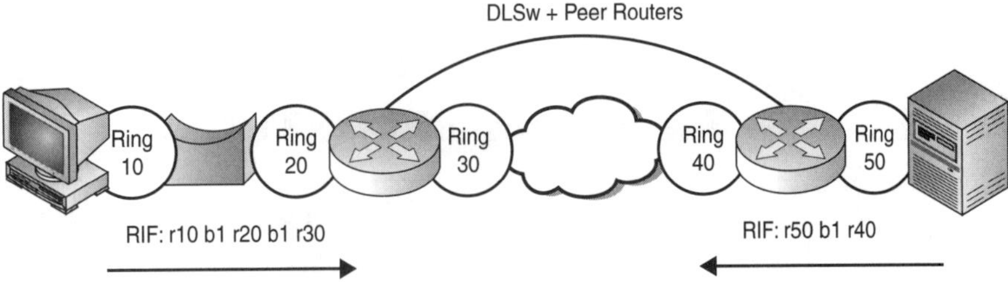

Figure 24-17 RSRB tunnel/ steady state

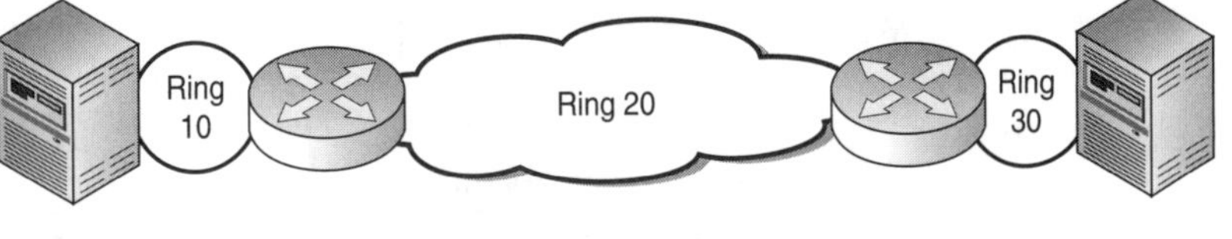

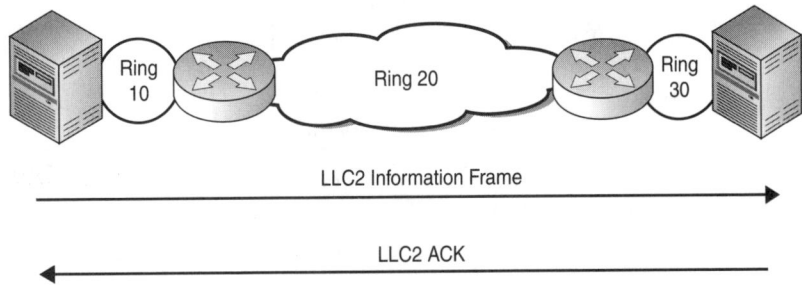

must flow without interruption from end to end, and the routers and tunnel must be transparent to the timing.

Slow WAN links or congestion can trigger the LLC2 T1 timer, which controls the length of time the router will wait for an acknowledgement after an "I" frame is transmitted. When this happens, the retransmission of the frames can cause even more congestion. The SNA session will fail if the T1 retries timer expires as well.

Several choices are available for encapsulation methods for SRB networks:

- Direct encapsulation of LLC2 frames in a data link frame (such as SDLC).
- Frame Relay encapsulation of LLC2 per RFC1490 specifications.
- IP encapsulation using *Fast-Sequenced Transport* (FST). This works well for non-fragmented, in-sequence transmissions and encapsulates the LLC2 frame into an IP datagram.
- TCP transport of LLC2 frames in a TCP segment. This is a better method when fragmentation or out-of-sequence transmissions might occur or when local ACKs are required. This is actually the less "chatty" of the methods.

Use TCP transport with local ACK only when absolutely necessary. It can be useful when communication across a Token Ring network is not possible any other way, but because the router has to maintain a full LLC2 session for each transmission, router performance can be adversely affected very quickly.

Serial Tunneling (STUN)

Serial Tunneling (STUN) is an older SNA encapsulation method used for the WAN. It is unlikely that you will use STUN in any modern designs, but it is still a supported technology. STUN can be used

- To connect router serial ports directly
- To attach to local controllers
- To use TCP encapsulation between routers across an IP network
- To gain the best performance over a serial line

STUN also supports local ACK, which tends to work better with this technology than with RSRB because of the larger timers on SDLC. Using local ACK can give end users the sense of a faster response time over the

WAN and can help in situations where congestion is a possibility. STUN, however, has a higher overhead than HDLC or direct serial connections.

SDLC-to-LAN Conversion

One way to save money in what can be a costly LAN/WAN environment is to use *SDLC-to-LAN conversion* (SDLLC). By adding a *Token Ring interface coupler* (TIC) to the FEP, the high throughput of a 16-Mpbs Token Ring can be leveraged for use by remote SDLC devices. Legacy hardware and protocol conversion is addressed in Cisco's implementation of SDLLC. LLC2 nodes and SDLC devices communicate through Cisco IOS transparently. Figure 24-18 shows a typical SDLLC configuration using a Cisco router that has SDLLC enabled on the interface using SDLC encapsulation.

Figure 24-18
SDLLC configuration

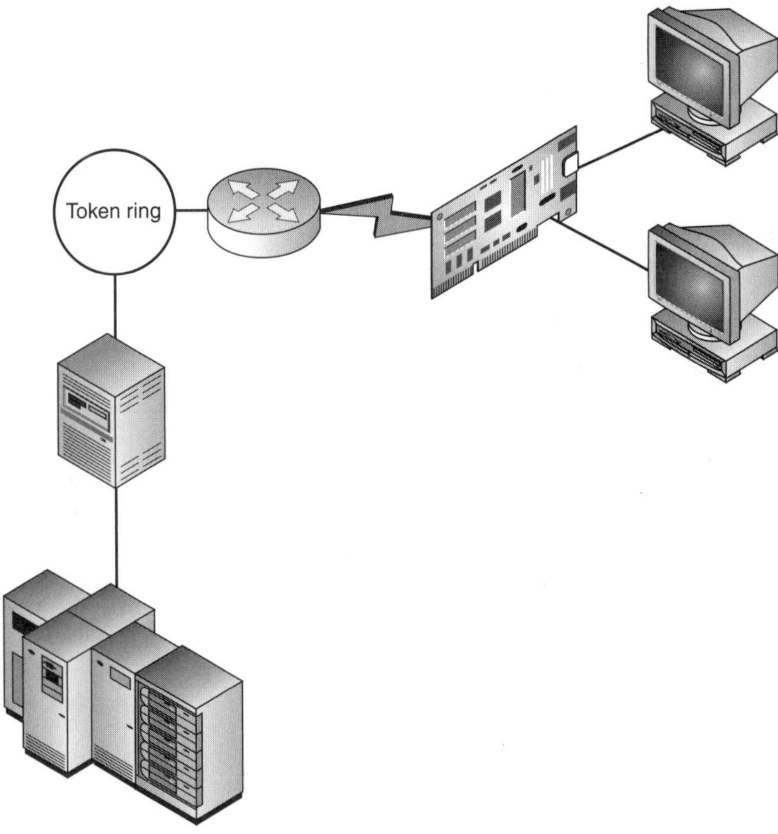

Load Balancing

Load balancing in an SNA network is performed by peer routers caching equal-cost paths to a given destination. The router then uses a round-robin fashion to load balance sessions across the WAN. When load balancing is not enabled, the preferred path to the destination is always used. In Figure 24-19, Router A sends sessions from MAC 1 or MAC 2 destined for MAC 3 over either Token Ring 20 or Token Ring 30. Router C, in turn, can load balance between Token Ring 50 and Token Ring 60 to reach MAC 3.

Advanced Peer-to-Peer Networking (APPN)

IBM introduced a major leap forward into second-generation SNA internetworking with *advanced peer-to-peer networking* (APPN). APPN helped bring SNA into the modern age of networking by providing the following:

- A routing protocol that allowed SNA traffic to flow concurrently with other protocols
- Peer-to-peer networking without a mainframe involvement
- A reduction in requirements for predefined resources and paths

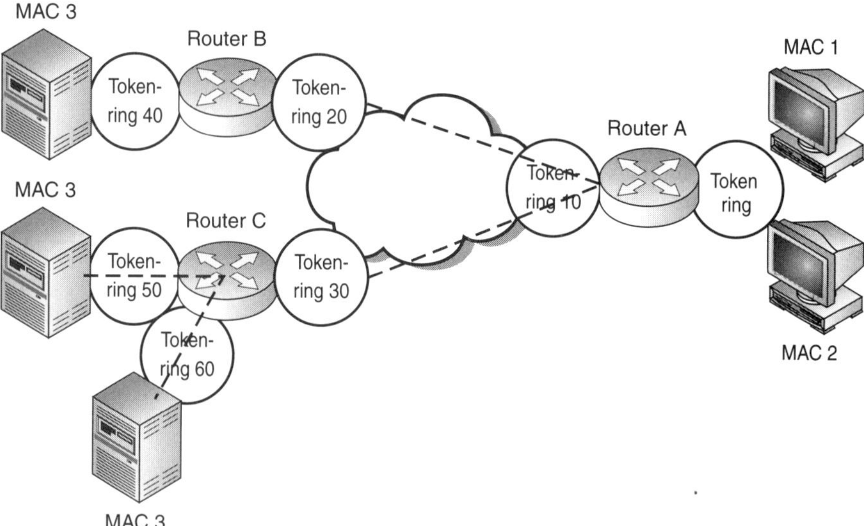

Figure 24-19 SNA load balancing

- The capability to do *Class-of-Service* (CoS) traffic prioritization
- An environment that still supports legacy devices but also supports APPN traffic

APPN uses a *control point* (CP) to activate and deactivate resources either within a node or between nodes. CP also exchanges topology information between nodes. APPN nodes come in four different kinds. It is important to have some understanding of these node types before further discussion of APPN ensues.

- **Network Node (NN)** A router in an APPN network.
- **End Node (EN)** An application host that accesses the resources of the network node.
- **Low Entry Node (LEN)** One of the original peer nodes defined by IBM (AS/400 or S/36). LENs require relay applications or direct connections, because they do not provide for intermediate routing.
- **Composite Network Node (CNN)** Created to describe the APPN functionality in VTAM and NCP. CNN works with NCP to represent a single NN.

In APPN routing, decisions are based upon the route of least weight. All APPN nodes are responsible for communicating changes in the local topology. These updates propagate throughout the network until all nodes have received the information. A node will always pass information it has learned *unless* that information is something it already knows. In that case, it stops forwarding the updates.

A further discussion of how APPN routing works can be found on Cisco's Web site at the following link: **http://www.cisco.com/univercd/cc/td/doc/cisintwk/idg4/nd2006.htm#17531.**

Channel Interface Processor

Cisco 7200 or 7500 series routers can be outfitted with a *Channel Interface Processor* (CIP) that enables the router to establish a channel connection directly with the mainframe. This does away with the need for an intervening FEP and reduces some of the expense. Figure 24-20 shows what a CIP configuration might look like. As you can see, IP datagram support is provided, as is support for SNA and LLC2 traffic types.

A CIP occupies a single slot in the router and can support two mainframes. A router with a CIP connected to a mainframe is referred to as

Figure 24-20
CIP design

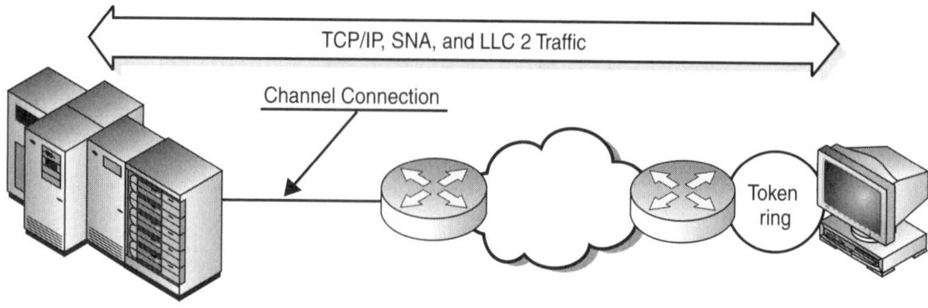

a *channel-attached router*. A channel-attached router can support TCP/IP offload, which moves the transport layer and below from the mainframe to the router for processing. This can greatly enhance performance in the network. Channel connections between the router and the mainframe can be either traditional bus-and-tag (using parallel signal lines within the wire) or Enterprise System Connect (ESCON), which uses a packet-switching architecture. More information about CIP and ESCON can be found on Cisco's Web site at **http://www.cisco.com/warp/public/537/1.html**.

SNA Topologies

Now that you have been given an overview of the components and inner workings of the SNA network, how do you put it all together? In this section, we will show you a few possible designs can be used to solve some common SNA network scenarios.

Redundancy with Dual FEPs

Fault-tolerance and redundancy are key factors in any good network design. SNA networks are no exception. In the design shown in Figure 24-21, dual FEPs and dual rings are in use. The same MAC addresses are configured locally on both FEPs so that redundant paths can be created in Token Ring. Another benefit of this design is that load balancing can be performed on a session-by-session basis. In this design, the traffic destined

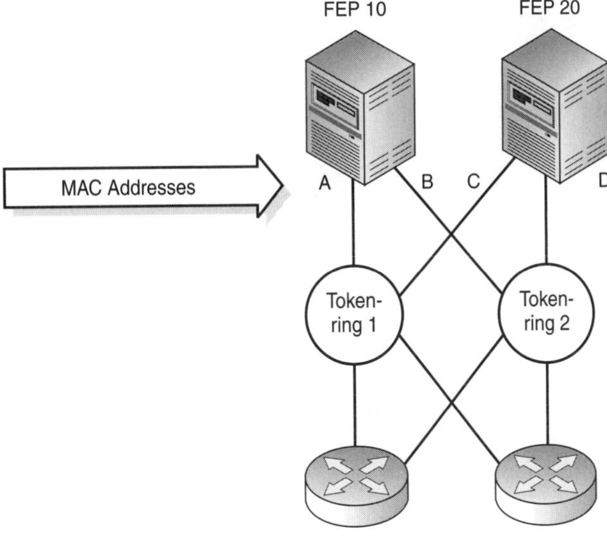

Figure 24-21
Dual FEP design

for either MAC A or MAC B will be rather evenly divided. The drawback is that in the event of a Token Ring failure, the session will still be lost.

Dual Backbone Ring Design

The dual backbone Token Ring design addresses the possibility of a lost session by creating redundancy in the rings. End-user systems are on Token Rings that are local to their work area or wiring closet. The local rings then attach to both building rings in the risers. We have kept the redundant FEPs in Figure 24-22 and added redundancy in the rings. Servers can be connected to the building rings, which are accessible by the end-user client systems.

The explorer frames are controlled at the bridges between the clients and servers. By lowering the normal seven-hop limit and setting the maximum hops to one, for example, the clients can communicate with servers on the building rings, but not with a server that is two hops away. This keeps the propagation of explorer frames to a minimum.

Dual Collapsed Backbone An alternative to the design shown in Figure 24-22 is the dual collapsed backbone model, which provides greater

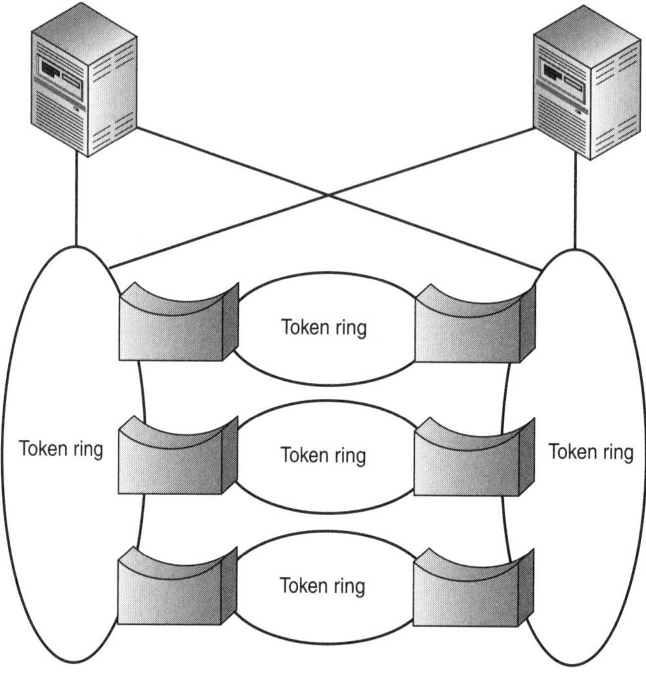

Figure 24-22 Dual backbone Token Ring design

control of the explorer frames while still keeping redundancy. Figure 24-23 shows this design, in which the router has an internal virtual ring and five virtual bridges in its backplane.

Virtual Ring Design

The WAN backbone can be a single *virtual ring* over which the local rings can bridge. This can be set up in a partial-mesh or full-mesh design. The first design model, shown in Figure 24-24, uses a flat design and can be limited. Therefore, you should use the first model only with smaller internetworks.

For larger internetworks, a hierarchical structure is more practical, as shown in Figure 24-25. It is a modular, scalable network design that still controls explorer frames while providing room for the design to grow without a complete redesign.

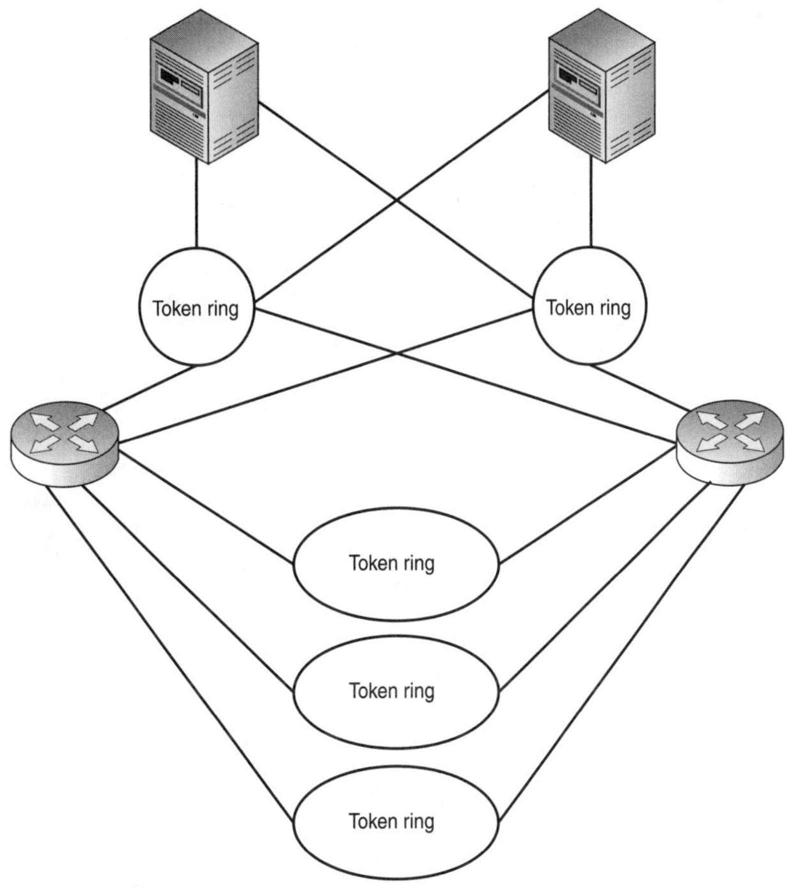

Figure 24-23 Dual collapsed backbone design

Queuing for SNA

The Cisco IOS can be configured for queuing SNA traffic in two ways:

- Priority queuing
- Custom queuing

Priority queuing is performed by setting up four interface output queues —high, medium, normal, and low. These queues use process switching, which is the slowest form of switching in the Cisco routers, because the queues work on CPU queues. The way priority queuing works is that traffic

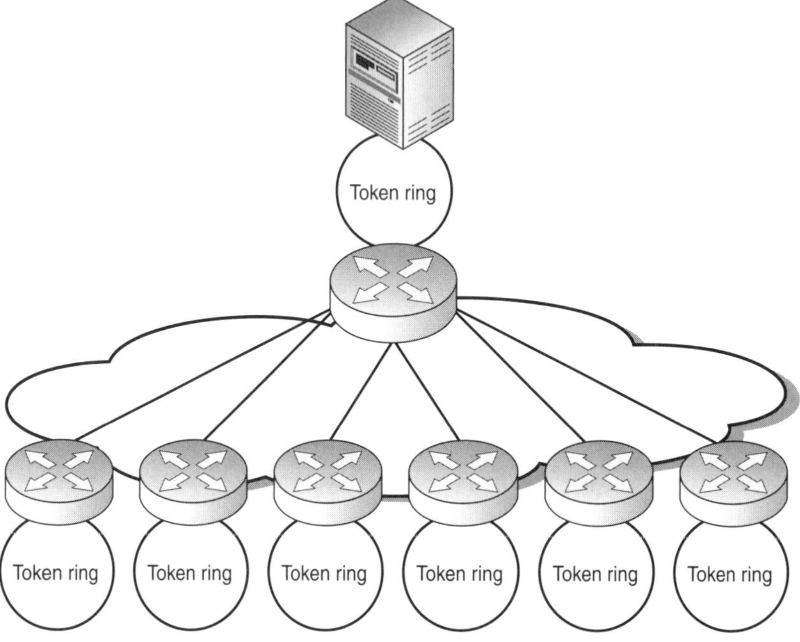

Figure 24-24 Single virtual ring design

in the high-priority queue must always be emptied before the traffic in the medium-priority queue is handled, and so on. This is a drastic scheme and is very CPU-intensive. Use this only if your SNA traffic is of the utmost importance, and if other types of traffic are of very low importance.

Custom queuing, which is also CPU-intensive, uses 16 interface output queues. Custom queuing is somewhat fairer than priority queuing, because rather than having to empty a queue completely before moving on to the next queue, custom queuing is configurable to the number of frames and the byte count. In other words, if your RSRB queue is set to transmit 5,000 frames, it will do so before moving to the next queue. This keeps other types of traffic moving more smoothly than with priority queuing.

Problem Areas

In many network redesigns, the move from RSRB to DLSw+ is a target concern, mainly because development for the enhancement of RSRB

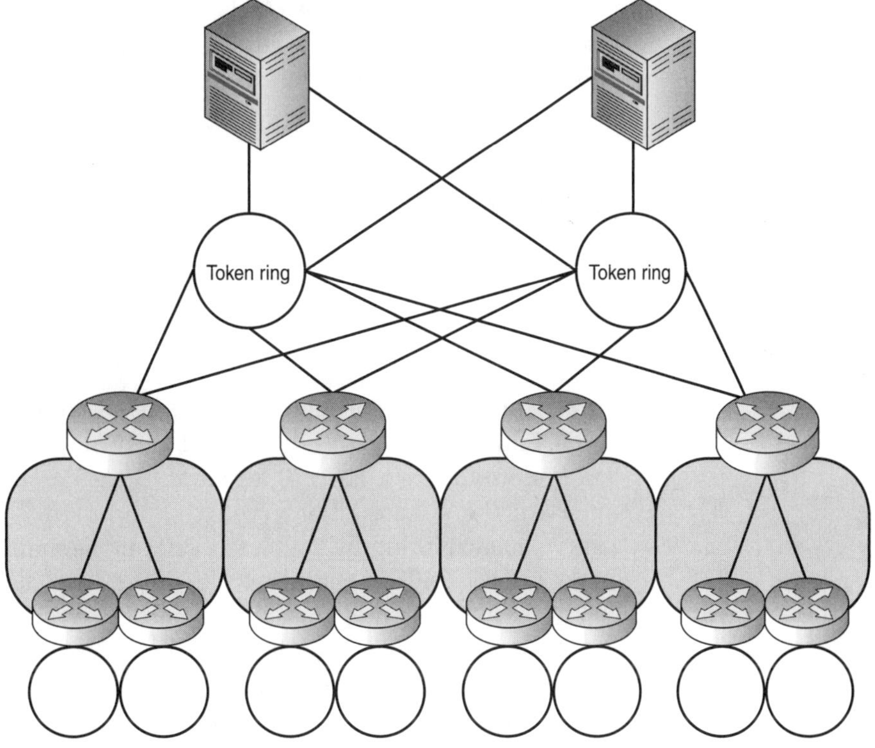

Figure 24-25 Hierarchical virtual ring design

stopped around 1995. Several other benefits can be recognized with a migration to DLSw+, including

- Support for local ACK over Ethernet
- RIF termination
- Multivendor interoperability support

In some cases, however, the migration may not be possible. Here are the reasons you may not be able to migrate from RSRB to DLSw+:

- Routers are using Cisco IOS earlier than 12.0. In this case, you could upgrade the routers, if it is possible to do so. Releases before 12.0 did not include support for RIF pass through, which is required for FEP-to-FEP communication over parallel SRB paths.
- Fast Sequenced Transport (FST) between SDLC and LANs is not currently supported by DLSw+ but will be in future releases of the Cisco IOS.

- Automatic Spanning Tree (AST) is not currently supported. AST is required by some source-route bridges to determine whether or not to forward single-route explorers.

For more information on migration issues and paths, see the Cisco Web site at **http://www.cisco.com/warp/public/cc/pd/ibsw/ibdlsw/prodlit/dlsw8_rg.htm**.

Case Study

Great Wall Bank in Portland, Maine is using an older SNA internetwork design. Bank employees needing access to the mainframe, where all account data is stored, have a TN3270 terminal on the desk as well as a PC, which can access the Windows NT servers that are used for newer office applications. As shown in Figure 24-26, the FEP at the main office is connected to another branch of the bank through a 33.6-Kbps dedicated line. Another 33.6-Kbps dedicated line is used to connect the branch backbone Token Ring to the main branch backbone. The two floors of the main branch are on local rings, which connect to the redundant backbone rings using SRB.

The bank would like to do away with the 3270 terminals at both branches and improve overall performance. Using what you have learned in this chapter, create a redesign for the bank that uses a newer topology and faster services. Find a way to remove the dual-terminal system with which employees currently must deal. Although there is no one right answer to any given design problem, we have suggested one solution in Appendix C.

Study Hints

Although no one can disclose test items or test content, we can give hints as to what might be valuable to study. For this chapter, certain key facts need to be reviewed and remembered:

- Token Ring is defined in IEEE 802.5.
- Support for SNA over Frame Relay is defined within RFC 1490.
- In an 802.5 header, the routing information field (RIF) is inserted after the source address.

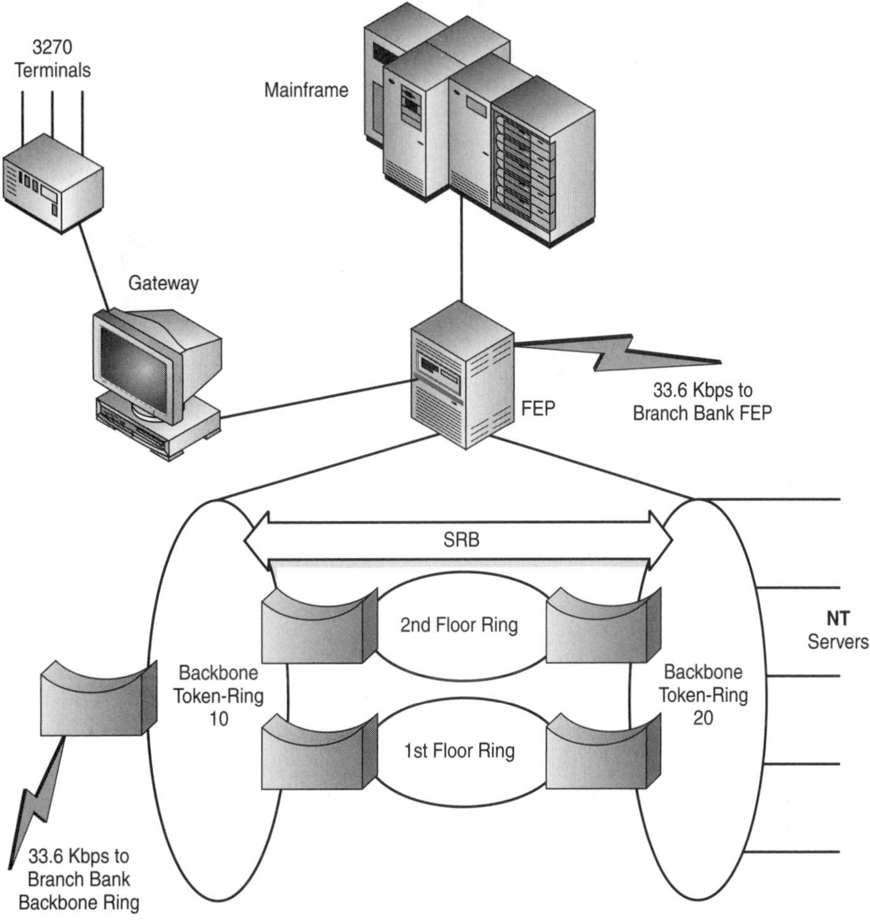

Figure 24-26
Current bank design.

- In an environment using the spanning-tree protocol, switches or bridges learn about each other through the exchange of bridge protocol data units (BPDUs). The spanning-tree protocol is only used in the SNA environment to provide a loop-free topology for explorer frames.
- Communication in an SNA environment takes place between network addressable units (NAU), such as the physical unit (PU), the logical unit (LU), or the system services control point (SSCP).
- In SNA, the mainframe (also called a host) runs some software called the virtual telecommunications access method (VTAM). The mainframe is a node type 5 and is considered to be at the top of the SNA hierarchy.

- In SNA, the FEP handles the hardware communication and runs the network control protocol (NCP) software. An FEP can be the only device in the SNA logical group known as a subarea. When this occurs, the FEP can be referred to as an Internetwork Node (INN). In its INN role, the FEP acts as a router with a static routing table. An FEP is a node type 4.
- In SNA, the end-user workstations are normally intelligent terminals, such as desktop PCs, and run a terminal emulation software that enables them to engage in sessions with the mainframe. Intelligent terminals are node type 2 and never communicate directly with the mainframe but through a gateway node.
- The SNA hierarchy contains subareas, which are logical domains containing subarea nodes and peripheral nodes. An FEP is an example of a subarea node, while an end-user PC is an example of a peripheral node.

CCDP Tips

This section contains an abbreviated list of topics covered in Chapter 24. Think of this section as the equivalent of reading Cliff's Notes™ instead of reading an entire book. You will get the general idea of the chapter but will benefit more from reading the chapter in its entirety.

Bridging Concepts

- Source-route bridging (SRB) can be used on Cisco routers to group multiple Token Ring LANs into a single, logical segment. The best path is chosen by examining all possible paths and selecting the best one, based on predetermined criteria.
- The Routing information field (RIF) is a field entered into the header just after the source address. The source station enters it in order to identify the path to the destination. The destination station reverses the information when sending traffic back to the source.
- The Spanning-tree protocol (STP) is used in SNA to provide a loop-free topology for explorer frames. A root bridge learns about all possible paths to all other bridges and then keeps only one path in active mode. Bridges within a network using STP communicate with each other using bridge protocol data units (BPDU).

Systems Network Architecture (SNA) SNA is a network architecture introduced by IBM that eliminated the need for the mainframes to communicate directly with the end-user terminals. Processing was offloaded to front-end processors (FEPs) and to cluster controllers, such as a TN3270 controller.

- Network addressable units (NAUs) are nodes within the SNA network between which communication occurs.
  - Logical units (LUs) can be either associated with a mainframe (primary LU) or with an end-user station (secondary LU). The LU communicates with other nodes and with SSCP.
  - Physical units (PUs) control the physical characteristics of the node, such as disk utilization and so on.
  - System services control points (SSCPs) reside in the virtual telecommunications access method (VTAM) and control sessions between end users and the mainframe.
- Hierarchy
  - Subarea nodes provide routing services to the peripheral nodes attached to the subarea nodes within a domain. This can be a router, FEP, or mainframe.
  - Peripheral nodes communicate with a subarea node and do not provide routing services. Peripheral nodes can be 3270 terminals, for example.
  - Subareas are uniquely numbered domains within the SNA network. A subarea usually contains an FEP or a mainframe system. When an FEP is the only device in a subarea, it is referred to as an Internetwork Node (INN), and is essentially a router with a static routing table.

Token Ring Gateways Token Ring gateways act as the go-between device from the end user to the mainframe. Three types of Token Ring gateways exist:

- **Pass through gateways** Passive devices that are transparent to both the end user and the mainframe. Pass through gateways incur a lot of overhead on the network and a lot of administration on the part of the network engineering staff.
- **LU gateway** Requires less administration. It sets up a NetBIOS session directly with the LU on the end-user system. It then acts on

behalf of the end-user system to communicate with the SSCP on the mainframe.

- **Downstream physical unit** (DSPU) A Cisco router acting on behalf of a group of LUs and PUs behind it. Less information has to be entered into the mainframe, as it only needs to know about the router as a PU and any LUs attached to the router. The router processing power is usually greater than alternative gateways also.

Token Ring Internetworking

- DLSw+ has the following characteristics:
  - It is based on a peer-group approach that optimizes the Token Ring explorer processing and supports direct communication between network nodes.
  - It provides a way to integrate SNA and NetBIOS over TCP/IP.
  - It supports explorer firewalls, which permit only a single explorer for a given destination MAC address to be sent over the WAN at one time.
  - It also supports local LLC2 terminations, which eliminate the need to send LLC2 keepalives and acknowledgements over the WAN.
- **Tunneling with RSRB** Works best in a stable WAN environment and can be performed over Frame Relay as well as serial lines. The LLC2 Information (I) frames and ACKs must flow without interruption from end to end, and the routers and tunnel must be transparent to the timing.
- **STUN** An older encapsulation method that can use local ACK and provides the following benefits:
  - It enables you to connect router serial ports directly.
  - It enables you to attach to local controllers.
  - It enables you to use TCP encapsulation between routers across an IP network.
  - It improves serial-line performance.
- **SDLLC** SDLC-to-LAN conversion, which allows different media and protocol types, including legacy equipment, to leverage the faster 16-Mbps Token Ring environment. SDLLC does this through the addition of a Token Ring interface coupler (TIC) to the FEP.

- **Load balancing** When enabled, can do round-robin, per-session load balancing across equal cost paths.
- **APPN routing** Decisions are based upon the route of least weight. All APPN nodes (NN, EN, LEN, and CNN) are responsible for communicating changes in the local topology. These updates propagate throughout the network until all nodes have received the information. A node will always pass information it has learned *unless* that information is something it already knows. In that case, it stops forwarding the updates.
- Cisco 7200 or 7500 series routers can be outfitted with a Channel Interface Processor (CIP) that enables the router to establish a channel connection directly with the mainframe. This does away with the need for an intervening FEP.

Queuing Both types of queuing that are available for SNA traffic are CPU-intensive and process-switched:

- **Priority queuing** Uses high, medium, normal, and low queues. Starting with the high queue, each queue must be completely emptied before the traffic in the next queue can be sent. Only one traffic type is allowed per queue, so if SNA traffic is in the high queue, all other traffic will receive poor performance.
- **Custom queuing** Uses 16 interface output queues. Queues are set up with the numbers of frames associated with a given traffic type. Rather than filling up a queue and emptying that queue with a single traffic type, traffic priority can be allocated based on percentages or the relative value of the traffic.

Summary

SNA is still in use at many locations that are using mainframe-computing designs, such as banks and manufacturers. SNA is still supported by Cisco and is in use in the real world. This chapter has provided you with a solid overview of the components and technology behind SNA, along with some understanding of the logic behind the designs in use today. We also gave you some design models to use for networks that require greater scalability and fault-tolerance. Although SNA is not as popular now, in the day of inexpensive client/server models, as it once was, it is still a robust and viable networking alternative.

Questions

The following review questions have been selected to help you test your knowledge of the subject matter contained in this chapter. You will also find these questions contained in the CD-ROM included with this book. Although these are not the questions you will find in the certification exams, knowing the answers to the review questions in this book will help cement the material in your mind as you prepare for the tests.

1. Select the proper definition of SNA.
   - **a.** Systems Network Architecture
   - **b.** Systems Non-Ethernet Architecture
   - **c.** Software Network Architecture
2. An end-user PC is an example of what SNA node type?
   - **a.** 5
   - **b.** 4
   - **c.** 2
3. Select the card type that, when placed in a Cisco 7200 or 7500 series router, enables the router to establish a channel directly with an IBM mainframe.
   - **a.** RSP
   - **b.** CIP
   - **c.** VIP
4. Which bridging type allows both Token Ring and non-Token Ring LANs to be grouped together into a bridge group?
   - **a.** SRB
   - **b.** DLSw+
   - **c.** RSRB
   - **d.** TB
5. The RIF is inserted after which field in the SRB header?
   - **a.** Source address
   - **b.** Destination address
   - **c.** Frame check sequence

6. Name the type of frame used by a bridge or switch to communicate its information to other bridges or switches.
   a. Explorer
   b. Bridge protocol data unit
   c. Information
7. Select the type of queuing that uses four interface output queues: high, medium, normal, and low.
   a. Priority
   b. Custom
   c. Weighted fair
8. An IBM mainframe is which type of SNA node?
   a. 5
   b. 4
   c. 2
9. A physical unit (PU) is an example of this type of SNA component.
   a. Type 4
   b. Internetwork node
   c. Network addressable unit
10. When an FEP is the only device within a subarea, what is the FEP also referred to as?
    a. PLU
    b. Internetwork node
    c. Network addressable unit
11. Select the RFC that defines support for SNA over Frame Relay.
    a. RFC 1771
    b. RFC 1490
    c. RFC 1483
12. A Cisco router that is directly attached to an IBM mainframe can also be referred to as this.
    a. Channel-interfaced router
    b. Channel-to-channel router
    c. Channel-attached router

13. When a Cisco router is acting as the downstream physical unit (DSPU), which nodes will not be seen or administered on the mainframe?
    a. Any PU beyond the DSPU
    b. Any LU beyond the DSPU
    c. All nodes beyond the DSPU
14. On what route information are APPN routing decisions made?
    a. Number of hops
    b. Shortest path
    c. Least weight
15. SNA nodes are grouped into logical domains known as what?
    a. Subareas
    b. LUs
    c. Peer groups
16. Select the statement that best describes the function of SDLLC.
    a. SDLLC allows multiple Token Ring LANs to be attached to a single router interface.
    b. SDLLC allows a 16-Mbps Token Ring to be leveraged for support of slower remote SDLC devices.
    c. SDLLC does not require any FEPs in the network design.
17. Which type of Token Ring gateway is completely transparent to the network?
    a. PU gateway
    b. LU gateway
    c. DSPU
18. Which desktop protocol is used for communication between a PLU and an SLU in a Token Ring LU gateway design?
    a. TCP/IP
    b. IPX
    c. NetBIOS
19. What is the most common form of SNA tunneling in use today?
    a. STUN
    b. DLSw+
    c. SDLLC

20. The use of local ACK gives an end user the sense of which network characteristic?

a. Fast performance

b. Slow response

c. Transparent routing

Answers

1. Select the proper definition of SNA.
   a. Systems Network Architecture
2. An end-user PC is an example of which SNA node type?
   c. 2
   Explanation: SNA node type 2 usually refers to an intelligent terminal or a desktop computer that uses an emulation software package in order to access the mainframe.
3. Select the card type that, when placed in a Cisco 7200 or 7500 series router, enables the router to establish a channel directly with an IBM mainframe.
   b. CIP
   Explanation: A channel interface processor (CIP) enables a direct channel connection between the Cisco router and the IBM mainframe.
4. Which bridging type allows both Token Ring and non-Token Ring LANs to be grouped together into a bridge group?
   c. RSRB
   Explanation: Remote source-route bridging allows for Token Ring and other LANs types such as Ethernet to be grouped together into a single bridge-group. This differs from SRB, which only permits Token Ring LANs to exist in the bridge-group.
5. The RIF is inserted after which field in the SRB header?
   a. Source address
   Explanation: Source-route bridging gets its name from the fact that the source (the sending station) dictates the path that will be taken. The destination station reverses the RIF in order to send data back to the source.

6. Name the type of frame used by a bridge or switch to communicate its information to other bridges or switches.
   b. Bridge protocol data unit
   Explanation: A bridge protocol data unit (BPDU) contains the information about the sending switch.

7. Select the type of queuing that uses four interface output queues: high, medium, normal, and low.
   a. Priority
   Explanation: Priority queuing uses four interface output queues. Each queue handles a given protocol type. Starting with the high queue, each queue must be completely emptied before the data in the next queue is addressed. This usually works very well for the protocol using the high queue, but other protocols or traffic types suffer.

8. An IBM mainframe is which type of SNA node?
   a. 5
   Explanation: An IBM mainframe is always classified as node type 5 for SNA.

9. A physical unit (PU) is an example of this type of SNA component.
   c. Network addressable unit
   Explanation: Physical units (PUs), logical units (LUs), and system services control points (SSCPs) are all examples of network addressable units (NAUs).

10. When an FEP is the only device within a subarea, what is the FEP also referred to as?
    b. Internetwork Node (INN)
    Explanation: An FEP that exists in a subarea with no peripheral devices is known as an INN. It is essentially a router with a static routing table.

11. Select the RFC that defines support for SNA over Frame Relay.
    b. RFC 1490

12. A Cisco router that is directly attached to an IBM mainframe can also be referred to as this.
    c. Channel-attached router
    Explanation: The name says it all—channel-attached router. It is literally attached directly to the mainframe and establishes a direct channel with the host.

13. When a Cisco router is acting as the downstream physical unit (DSPU), which nodes will not be seen or administered on the mainframe?
    a. Any PU beyond the DSPU
    Explanation: Think of it this way—the downstream PU (DSPU), which is the router, is acting on behalf of the other PUs behind it. Therefore, the other PUs do not need to be directly known by the mainframe.

14. On which route aspect are APPN routing decisions made?
    c. Least weight
    Explanation: APPN only chooses the best path to a destination by looking at the path of least weight.

15. SNA nodes are grouped into logical domains known as what?
    a. Subareas
    Explanation: The logical domains used to group nodes within an SNA network are known as subareas.

16. Select the statement that best describes the function of SDLLC.
    b. SDLLC allows 16-Mbps Token Ring to be leveraged for support of slower remote SDLC devices.

17. Which type of Token Ring gateway is completely transparent to the network?
    a. PU gateway
    Explanation: A Token Ring PU gateway is also known as a pass through gateway. It is transparent to the nodes it sits between.

18. Which desktop protocol is used for communication between a PLU and an SLU in a Token Ring LU gateway design?
    c. NetBIOS
    Explanation: The LU gateway is a primary LU (PLU) acting on behalf of the secondary LUs (SLUs) behind it. It establishes a standard SSCP-to-PU session with the mainframe and establishes a NetBIOS session with the SLU.

19. What is the most common form of SNA tunneling in use today?
    b. DLSw+
    Explanation: According to Cisco, the most common form of SNA tunneling is DLSw+.

20. The use of local ACK gives an end user the sense of which network characteristic?
    a. Fast performance
    Explanation: By performing the local ACK for the LLC2 session, the router gives the end user the sense of fast network performance. With busy or congested networks, however, the router can quickly become overwhelmed by taking on the task of maintaining all of the LLC2 sessions, and performance could degrade as a result.

Bibliography

Cisco Internetwork Design, Cisco Press, 2000, Birkner.

Cisco Internetwork Design Course Manual, version 3.0, April 1997, Cisco Systems, Inc.

Configuring Remote Source-Route Bridging, Cisco Systems, Inc., **http://www.cisco.com/univercd/cc/td/doc/product/software/ios121/121cgcr/ibm_c/bcprt2/bcdrsrb.htm**

Configuring Spanning Tree, Cisco Systems, Inc., **http://www.cisco.com/univercd/cc/td/doc/product/lan/cat5000/rel_5_2/config/spantree.htm**

Designing SRB Internetworks, Cisco Systems, Inc., **http://www.cisco.com/univercd/cc/td/doc/cisintwk/idg4/nd2004.htm**

DSPU Product Announcement, Cisco Systems, Inc., **http://www.cisco.com/warp/public/cc/pd/ibsw/ibdlsw/prodlit/dspu_pa.htm**

IBM Mainframe Channel Attachment, Cisco Systems, Inc., **http://www.cisco.com/warp/public/537/1.html**

Positioning SNA Switching Services and Data Link Switching Plus, Cisco Systems, Inc., **http://www.cisco.com/warp/public/cc/pd/ibsw/ibdlsw/tech/dlsw_wp.htm**

SNA over Frame Relay: Technology Overview, Cisco Systems, Inc., **http://www.cisco.com/univercd/cc/td/doc/cisintwk/dsgngde/snafr/fr_ch1.htm**

APPENDIX A

Multiservice Design

Overview

The purpose of this appendix is to introduce you to some of the terms related to multiservice network design—particularly networks carrying voice traffic. Because the scope of this appendix is simply to introduce the topic, further reading is suggested from the many references included in the bibliography at the end of this appendix.

Public Switched Telephone Network Fundamentals

The *Public Switched Telephone Network* (PSTN) is the primary means of the transmission of voice and data today. It evolved from the original human-operated analog circuit-switching systems and is now almost completely digital, except for "the last mile" to the end-user. The last mile is normally made up of twisted-pair cable carrying an analog signal back to the telephone company (telco) to be sampled at a rate of about 8,000 8-bit samples per second. The samples are then digitized and sent through a DS0, 64-Kbps channel. These channels can then be bundled for greater bandwidth. Twenty-four DS0 channels make up a single T1 line (1.544 Mbps).

PSTN provides a means for users to connect phones, fax machines, and modems to telephone switching equipment (either "wireline" central offices [COs] or "wireless" mobile switching centers [MSCs]). The information can be transmitted over voice trunk lines or over fault-tolerant data networks. An example of PSTN architecture is shown in Figure A-1.

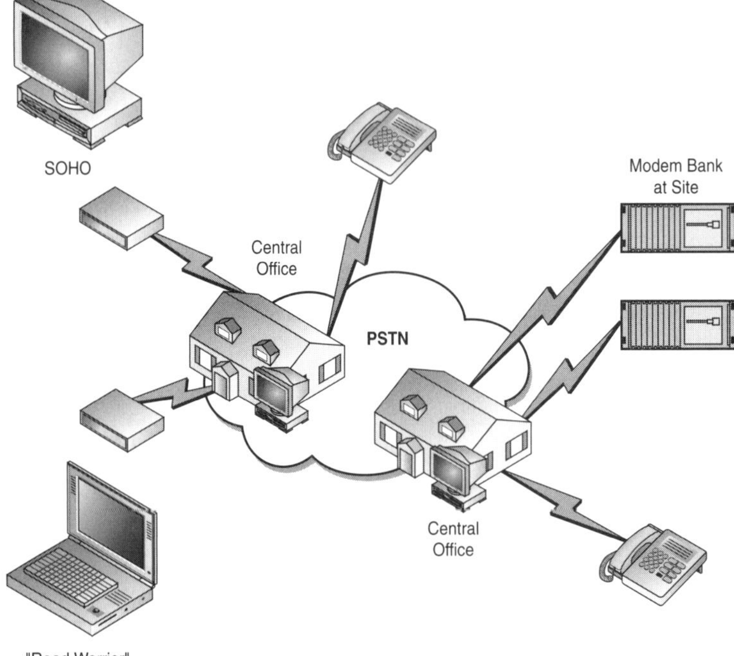

Figure A-1 PSTN architecture

The oldest, and still most common, method of data connection to a public or private network is through dial-up connection using analog modem technology. A user in a Small Office/Home Office (SOHO), or a mobile user, connects the PC to a telephone outlet and uses the PSTN to send and receive data. This is a very inexpensive connection method and is easily accessible to most users.

As shown in Figure A-1, the mobile user connects through what is called a *local loop* to a CO of a telephone services provider. The data goes through the public phone network (PSTN) and, through a CO at the destination end, the data makes its way to a bank or pool of modems at the destination's central site. If the central site's operations are substantial enough, they could use an access server in addition to modem pools and routers.

Communications usually occur between two similar end-user devices, such as two telephones or two PCs. The end-user device initiating the call will use the destination address of the other end-user device. This could be an IP address, a telephone number, or a fax number. The CO handles this request for a call through a circuit-switched synchronous path. All call setup and clearing (tear down) is the responsibility of the CO.

There are two kinds of connections within the CO: trunk lines and the signaling network. The trunk lines actually carry the data (or voice) between source and destination.

The signaling network is used to negotiate the call through to the destination PSTN switch. The signaling used is signaling system seven (SS7). There are IETF drafts currently under discussion to use SS7 to merge PSTN and Internet internetworking into a technology called PINT, which is the moniker for *PSTN and Internet Internetworking*. This new proposed technology could someday change the way calls are made both for voice and for data.

Cisco Architecture for Voice, Video, and Integrated Data Fundamentals

Like many internetworking solutions today, Cisco *Architecture for Voice, Video, and Integrated Data* (AVVID) is a framework upon which the solution can be built. Rather than a fixed product consisting of a set of components, AVVID addresses the structural component of building a scalable solution for companies wanting to merge voice, video, and data networks together.

AVVID consists of software, tools and industry "best practices" to act as a foundation, or "jumping-off point," for enterprise customers to begin this merging of technologies. Because today's network depends on open standards such as TCP/IP, Ethernet, and so on, Cisco found it was important to bring the same open standards design to the AVVID framework.

This open architecture approach can be categorized into several concrete benefits:

- **Speed** The AVVID framework allows for new tools and technology to be rapidly integrated into the existing structure—without a complete redesign!
- **Reliability** All parts of the framework are consistent in architecture and design, making it easy to create and maintain a stable networked environment.
- **Interoperability** Because of the open standards approach, it is less likely that there will be interoperability problems between tools and software based on the AVVID framework.

- **Ease-of-Deployment** It becomes much easier to select and deploy tools and software when they fall under an umbrella framework. It takes the guesswork out of product procurement.

The key components of AVVID are shown in Figure A-2. The basis for the infrastructure is in *network platforms*, which can include routers, switches, hubs, and so on. These are the building blocks for the rest of the solution. These devices do not have to be Cisco devices, but they must adhere to the AVVID open standards.

The *intelligent network services* run on the network platforms, or clients. The software can include tools to do network management, policy-based routing, accounting, network security, and more. Both *service control* and *communication services* are important parts of the AVVID framework. These layers provide tools for partners and customers to allow for access

Figure A-2
AVVID Structure

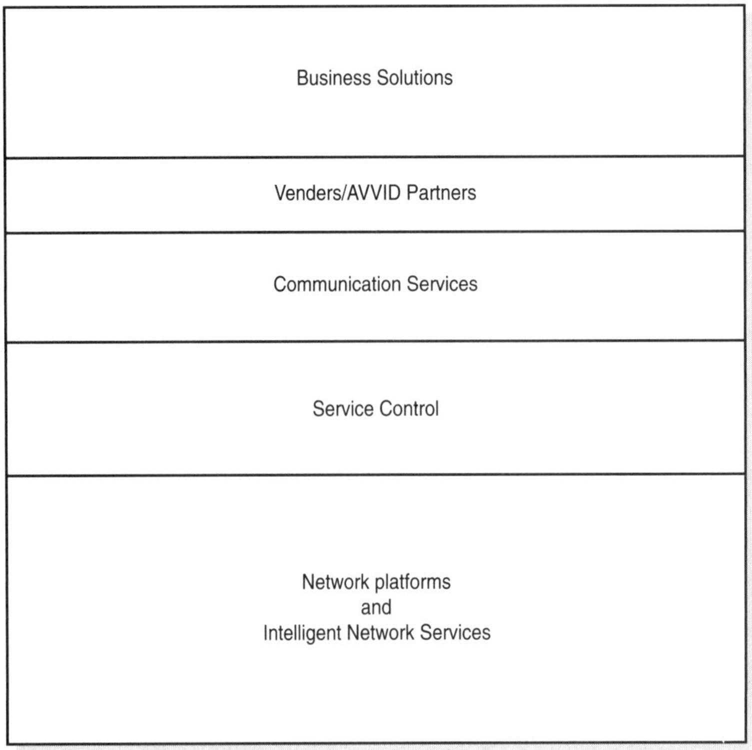

Business Solutions
Venders/AVVID Partners
Communication Services
Service Control
Network platforms and Intelligent Network Services

management, perimeter security, traffic management, and so on. Whereas in the past these features may have been vendor-specific, AVVID allows multiple vendors to interoperate by adhering to a set of open standards.

The *vendors'* section of the framework, of course, refers to the network integrators and partners who are familiar with and trained on the AVVID model. These integrators can help customers quickly design and deploy the AVVID infrastructure. Finally, the *business solutions* section at the top of the AVVID model refers to the applications that are marketed by Cisco and other companies, such as HP and Oracle, that are all part of the AVVID open standard solutions.

Voice over IP

When voice traffic is sent over IP, which is a connectionless, best-effort delivery method, special consideration must be taken of the path, delay, and overhead incurred. IP works well for data traffic, because it ensures that traffic takes the path of least resistance —that is, the path with the lowest amount of congestion.

The IP header is used to make sure that the packet reaches the right destination and helps with the reassembly on the receiving end. The header itself, however, adds a great deal of overhead to any transmission—20 bytes versus 2 bytes for Frame Relay and 5 bytes for ATM. Add Quality of Service (QoS) to the mix, and you now need to make all traffic take the same path so that you can make certain assurances about the delivery of the packets.

Prioritization of IP traffic for QoS was originally handled by the use of Resource Reservation Protocol (RSVP). The IETF is now proposing the use of Differentiated Services (DiffServ) that allows for the use of the Type of Service (ToS) bit in the IP header. The ToS bit is used to classify traffic between the customer premises edge (CPE) and the provider edge (PE) or between PEs.

Voice over IP (VoIP) takes up a great deal more bandwidth than over ATM or Frame Relay networks because of the size of the IP header. Fragmentation of data packets is allowed, but the large header size causes the use of VoIP to take up to 50 percent more bandwidth than over ATM or Frame Relay. Future implementations of header compression may help alleviate this problem.

Other methods of dealing with voice traffic over an IP network include *jitter buffering*, which mitigates the problem of varying delays between packets, echo cancellation, and silence suppression. *Echo cancellation* helps eliminate the reflection of the signal back to the caller, which can result from a four-wire to two-wire hybrid connection between the PBX and the data lines. *Silence suppression* means that packets are not sent during pauses in the conversation, saving up to 60 percent of the bandwidth that would be consumed if the full-duplex signal were consumed by empty transmissions.

Voice over Frame Relay

Frame Relay is a packet-switched WAN architecture that is available in a variety of bandwidths—typically 56 Kbps, 64 Kbps, and 1.544 Mbps. It is a more inexpensive method of creating a redundant, efficient network versus using point-to-point links through leased lines, for instance. Leased lines represent a circuit-switching method that works very well for steady-stream applications like voice and video. For data traffic, which tends to be bursty in nature, Frame Relay provides a high-performance alternative. For networks already using Frame Relay for the WAN, it is a logical "next step" to progress to carrying their voice traffic over Frame Relay as well. Figure A-3 shows Voice over Frame Relay (VoFR) architecture.

NOTE: *The Voice Frame Relay Access Device (VFRAD) can be a router alone or a router along with an H.323 device external to the router.*

Voice Frame Relay Access Devices (VFRADs) work by connecting the router and PBX to the Frame Relay network. The VFRAD can be part of an integrated router. VFRADs also allow for tagging of traffic types in order to prioritize delay-sensitive traffic, such as voice. Because voice transmission is usually compressed and short in nature, the prioritization of the voice traffic does not generally have a negative impact on the data traffic sharing the network.

The use of a VFRAD also gives carriers the ability to market QoS to their customers. The highest rate would be paid for real-time voice traffic,

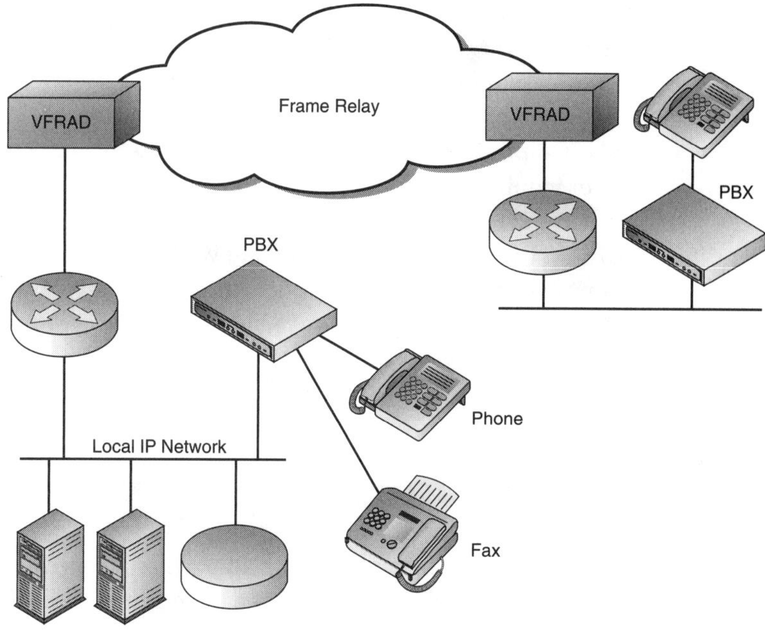

Figure A-3 VoFR architecture

whereas the lowest rate would be charged for traffic using available frame rate (AFR) or unspecified frame rate (UFR), such as e-mail traffic.

Most VFRADs also allow for fragmentation of data packets so that voice traffic can sail through without delay. This, of course, adds to the overhead and number of data frames being sent. Some VFRADs also allow for jitter buffering and voice compression, which help to keep the voice sounding natural as it passes from the source to the destination by eliminating delay and silence in the call.

Voice over ATM

ATM provides what is probably the best alternative to PSTN voice transmission. ATM has fragmentation naturally built in, with its tidy, 53-byte cells carrying predictable chunks of information. The header is small (5 bytes) and can be used for assuring QoS.

You might think, after having read Chapter 20, "What is ATM?" on ATM design, that you would naturally use AAL1 as your ATM adaptation layer for voice. However, there are some issues with using AAL1 for Voice over ATM (VoATM). For one thing, AAL1 uses constant bit rate (CBR), which takes valuable bandwidth away from other applications that could use it. By doing so, partially empty cells are sent in the interest of reducing delay. Why would ATM want to wait for a cell to fill up? With CBR, it just keeps them moving.

Instead of AAL1, the standard of choice is AAL2, which uses variable bit rate (VBR) and a variable payload within cells. What this means is that it allows multiple short payloads to be entered into a single cell, thus wasting less bandwidth. AAL2 also supports silence suppression and voice compression, which AAL1 does not.

Migration Issues

There are several issues to consider when designing for multiservice networks. These include delay, jitter, different types of codecs, and QoS. Each of these is discussed in this section.

Delay

Delay is something we all experience in our every day lives. You are supposed to be at an appointment across town. The drive routinely takes 30 minutes, so you leave about 35 minutes before your appointment. Wouldn't you know it? You are driving along and suddenly end up in a backup due to road construction. The lanes are all congested, and you are delayed in reaching your destination.

It is the same for network traffic. The time it takes for a packet to move from the sender to the destination is called *end-to-end delay*. There are two kinds of delay—fixed network delay and variable network delay. To refer back to our traffic analogy, the *fixed delay* would be the time it normally takes you to go from Point A to Point B. The *variable delay* is, of course, the road construction. It impacts your normal trip time. We know something

Table A-1

Fixed Network Delay

Link Bandwidth	64	128	256	512	1024	1500
56 Kbps	9	18	36	72	144	214
64 Kbps	8	16	32	64	128	187
128 Kbps	4	8	16	32	64	93
256 Kbps	2	4	8	16	32	46
512 Kbps	1	2	4	8	16	23
768 Kbps	0.640	1.28	2.56	5.12	10.24	15

Packet Size (in bytes, shown in bold) **results shown in milliseconds*

Delay (shown in lightface)

about the fixed network delay for packets of various sizes traversing links of various bandwidths. Those facts are shown in Table A-1.

The Cisco IOS is designed to help move packets to the output queues as quickly as possible, thereby minimizing delay. After the packet arrives in the queue, there are methods you can use, such as QoS, to prioritize the traffic in order to expedite its delivery.

Jitter

The term *jitter*, also called *variable delay,* refers to the delta between the end-to-end delay of two different packets in the same data, voice, or video stream. It can also be characterized as the difference between when the packet is expected and when it actually arrives. If you were expected at your appointment at 3:30 P.M. and actually arrived at 3:45 P.M., 15 minutes would be the jitter experienced, to say nothing of your nerves!

To design a network that has reduced jitter, use the Cisco 7200 VXR router with PA-MCX port adapters. It handles jitter by setting up a playout buffer, which uses Real-Time Transfer Protocol (RTP) encapsulation.

Quality of Service

Providing the best service possible to customers is the goal of any good multiservice provider. Many of today's customers want a *service level agreement* (SLA) that ensures a certain level of guarantee on the delivery of voice, video, or data traffic. In order to have any hope of providing these types of guarantees, the service provider must use a technique such as QoS in order to manage traffic flows. There are several components of QoS that are important to understand:

- **Classification of Traffic** This means that a packet is inspected (usually at the ingress port) to determine the traffic type.
- **Traffic Policing** This is a technique used to limit or deny certain traffic types or amounts of traffic to enter the network.
- **Packet Marking** Once traffic has been classified and policed, it is marked (usually at the edge router) to indicate that it does not need to be classified again. Packet marking can include setting the discard eligible (DE) bit on a Frame Relay frame, setting the 802.1p/q ToS field in Ethernet, or a DiffServ Code Point (DSCP) in an IP packet.
- **Queuing** This is an important technique performed by the egress interface in order to reduce jitter and move voice traffic to the "front of the line" in the outbound queue.
- **Traffic Shaping** This is a way to move traffic through the egress interface in a predetermined fashion without dropping packets. It also helps even things out when the two interfaces on either side of a network are of different speeds, which helps to reduce jitter.

Mean Opinion Score

The *mean opinion score* (MOS) is a rating of different types of coding techniques used in transmitting voice over digital media. Each ITU-T specification listed on the following page corresponds to a different coder-decoder (codec) technique. Each codec provides a different quality of speech. The MOS is the benchmark used to rate the speech quality. The ITU-T specifications are listed in Table A-2, with corresponding framing size, bit rate, and MOS. The scores are based on a sampling of listeners rating the quality of speech on a range of 1 to 5, where 1 is bad and 5 is excellent.

Table A-2

Mean Opinion Score

Codec	MOS	Bit Rate	Framing Size
G.711 PCM	4.1	64	0.125
G.726 ADPCM	3.85	32	0.125
G.728 LD-CELP	3.61	16	0.625
G.729 CS-ACELP	3.92	8	10
G.729 × 2 Encodings	3.27	8	10
G.729 × 3 Encodings	2.68	8	10
G.729a CS-ACELP	3.7	8	10
G.723.1 MP-MLQ	3.9	6.3	30
G.723.1 ACELP	3.65	5.3	30

Although it may seem logical that one would design a network with low bit codecs, this is not always the best solution. Low bit rate solutions can cause codec-induced delay. Voice compression also can cause signal distortion when a signal is encoded multiple times.

Bibliography

IP Applications with ATM, Amoss and Minoli, McGraw-Hill, 1998

Migrating to Multiservice Networks—A Planning Primer, Cisco Web site, **http://www.cisco.com/warp/public/cc/pd/rt/2600/tech/st10_wp.htm**

A Proposal for Internet and Public Switched Telephone Networks (PSTN) Internetworking, **http://www.bell-labs.com/mailing-lists/pint/draft-faynberg-telephone-sw-net-00.txt**

Public Switch Telephone Network, **http://www.linuxguruz.org/foldoc/foldoc.php?PSTN**

Toward the PSTN/Internet Inter-Networking Pre-PINT Implementations, **http://www.bell-labs.com/mailing-lists/pint/draft-IETF-pint-pre-implement-00.txt**

Voice Primer, Cisco Web site, **http://www.cisco.com/univercd/cc/td/doc/product/core/7200vx/portadpt/voice_pa/pa_mcx/6799over.htm**

APPENDIX B

Cisco Hardware and Applications

In this appendix you will find brief product information about Cisco hardware and certain software applications that you may want to include in your network design solutions. Where products have reached or will soon reach end-of-life (as of this writing), we have made note of such, along with Cisco's recommended replacement.

Cisco Catalyst Switches

This section of the appendix covers Cisco layer-2 and layer-3 Catalyst switches for the workgroup, wiring closet, and data center. Whatever problem you are trying to solve, as well as the sizing of your network, will determine your choices.

Cisco Catalyst 6500 Series

With the Catalyst 6500, Cisco has implemented better redundancy and resiliency. Positioned to support increased requirements for gigabit scalability, the 6500 switch works as well in the core or distribution layer as it does at the access layer. The switch not only recognizes layer 2 and layer 3 packets but can decode layer 4 as well. This opens up a wide range of possibilities for traffic management, which is provided with Quality of Service (QoS) support.

The 6500 switch is available in either a six-slot 6506 or a nine-slot 6509. Both models offer support for up to 384 10/100 Ethernet ports, 192 100FX ports, 8 OC-12 ATM ports, or up to 130 Gigabit Ethernet ports. The Supervisor engine can hold up to 32,000 MAC addresses in the table, and with a scalable switching bandwidth of up to 256 Gbps and multilayer switching support at 150 Mpps, this switch is robust enough for most backbone applications.

The 6500 can support eight Fast Ether-channel or Gigabit Ether-channel links for logical connections up to 16 Gbps. Additionally, Ether-channel can be aggregated across several modules for even higher available connectivity.

The 6500 supports either IP-only or multiprotocol environments, with the optional *Multilayer Switch Feature Card* (MSFC). With the MSFC, the switch can support wire-rate IP, IPX, IP multicast, AppleTalk, DecNet, or VINES traffic, as well as Web-caching techniques.

All components are hot swappable and field-serviceable, reducing the amount of potential downtime from a failed line card or power supply, for instance. Specifically, the switch can be configured with redundant supervisor engines, redundant load-sharing power supplies and fans, redundant system clocks, redundant uplinks, and redundant switch fabrics. The switches also support Cisco's Hot Standby Routing Protocol (HSRP) for fast failover to a backup unit in the event of a system failure.

Memory availability is as follows:

- Supervisor 1: 64MB dynamic RAM (DRAM)
- MSFC 64: 128MB DRAM
- Optional PCMCIA flash memory in 16 or 24MB size

Cisco Catalyst 5000 Series

The workhorse of the Catalyst switches is, without a doubt, the 5000/5500 series switch. Available in a multitude of configurations, the 5000/5500 series is the premiere data center or wiring closet solution for medium to large enterprise networks. The switch is 19-inch rack-mountable with a 1.2 Gbps backplane that can use any available supervisor engine.

The 5002 model is a small, two-slot chassis that works well in smaller wiring closets and for smaller applications, such as a localized server farm. One of the slots is dedicated for the supervisor engine that contains two built-in Fast Ethernet ports. The other slot can house either an Ethernet, Fast Ethernet, Token Ring, FDDI, or ATM interface processor module. Redundant power supplies are standard on this model. It will also support a *Route Switch Module* (RSM), if required.

The 5500 model is a high-end 13-slot Gigabit Ethernet-ready switch that scales up to 50 Gbps full-duplex switching capacity. Additionally, it can use interface processor modules from the 5000, 8500, or LS1010 switches to provide investment protection in the network. The modules are all hot swappable, including the power supplies and fans.

The 5505 model is a five-slot variation of the 5500. This model can also use interface processor modules from the 5000 switch and can be configured to house redundant supervisor engines and power supplies.

The 5509 model is the nine-slot big brother of the 5505. It is a high-density, low-cost solution to most data center or wiring closet needs. It can be configured for 10/100/1000 Ethernet or dedicated Token Ring. The switch will support up to 38 Gigabit Ethernet ports and can be configured for Gigabit Ether-channel, providing up to 8 Gbps full-duplex switching.

In this series of switches, the supervisor engine acts as a hardware-based, media-independent switching backplane that can handle up to 16,000 MAC addresses in the table. It also contains the uplink ports and the network management processor. Proprietary NetFlow switching offers layer-2 and layer-3 support, while the Route Switch Module (RSM) provides true multi-protocol layer-3 routing.

Three levels of priority on the backplane provide

- Support for ATM and Token Ring (which use priorities)
- Port-based priority settings
- Server and bursty traffic accommodation

Cisco Catalyst 3500 XL Series

The Catalyst 3500 XL switch has a small footprint and is designed to be stackable and highly scalable. It is applicable only to 10/100 or Gigabit Ethernet environments, so it is not for every network. This unique switch works with Cisco's switch clustering technology, which allows for the management of several switches over a single IP address. Cisco Visual Switch Manager (CVSM) is also deployed with the switch to allow easy management via a Web-based GUI, if desired.

Several models of the Catalyst 3500 switch are available, as shown in Table B-1. Each has two priority forwarding queues on each 10/100 port and eight priority forwarding queues on each Gigabit Ethernet port. All ports can be configured for full-duplex. The switch is positioned to be able to support video applications with future software releases.

Table B-1
3500 XL Models

Model	Throughput	Miscellaneous
3548	8.8 mpps	- 5.4 Gbps max forwarding rate
3508G	7.5 mpps	- 10.8 Gbps switch fabric
3524	6.5 mpps	- 4MB shared memory architecture
3512	4.8 mpps	- 8192 MAC address capacity in table
		- 8MB DRAM
		- 4MB flash

You can use the switch in the stacked manner in three ways:

- Create an independent stack bus.
- Use point-to-point stacking.
- Employ switch clustering.

The independent stack bus method uses a true daisy-chain method, with each switch connecting to the one above it, up to eight switches high, and linking to a "master" switch forwarding packets for the entire stack. This does, however, create a single point of failure for the stack. If a switch at the top of the stack fails, everything below that switch fails to pass traffic up the line as well. This method may also be implemented in conjunction with the GigaStack GBIC, that is a lower cost alternative to using a GBIC for each port. Up to nine 3500 XL switches or eight Gigabit-enabled 2900 XL switches may be daisy-chained together for a 1 Gbps maximum forwarding rate—2 Gbps in a point-to-point configuration.

The point-to-point method links a single port from a 3500 XL switch, or Gigabit-enabled 2900 XL, to another 3500 switch. This would be preferred to the independent stack bus if you wanted to ensure traffic would pass from all other switches if one switch failed.

The switch clustering method allows up to 16 switches in a wiring closet to be aggregated to a single IP address. This simplifies traffic flow to and from the wiring closet and permits management of up to 380 ports through the one address.

Cisco Catalyst 2900 XL Series

The 2900 Series XL encompasses a line of five auto-sensing Fast Ethernet switches geared to the smaller wiring closet or server farm. The various models all support Virtual LANs (VLAN) and Inter-Switch Link (ISL) VLAN trunking. Up to 64 VLAN trunks can be supported. The switches can handle from 2048 (2912MF XL and 2924M XL) to 8192 (2912 XL, 2924 XL, 2924C XL) MAC addresses in the table. The maximum forwarding bandwidth is 1.6 Gbps with 14,880 bps on a 10 Mpps port and 148,800 bps on a 100 Mpps port. The switch fabric scales up to 3.2 Gbps with a 3 Mpps forwarding rate. The switch supports Fast Etherchannel for up to 800 Mpps bandwidth between switches.

The best design application for this series of switches is in workgroup and server aggregation. Figure B-1 shows several basic 2900 XL 10/100 switches connecting to the 2924M XL model and then to a Catalyst 6500 in a central wiring closet. The 2924M XL model is a 24-port modular switch that works well when applied in this manner.

The same design could also be applied to a workgroup and server aggregation combined, as seen in Figure B-2.

The available models of the 2900 XL series are listed in the Table B-2.

Figure B-1 Workgroup aggregation

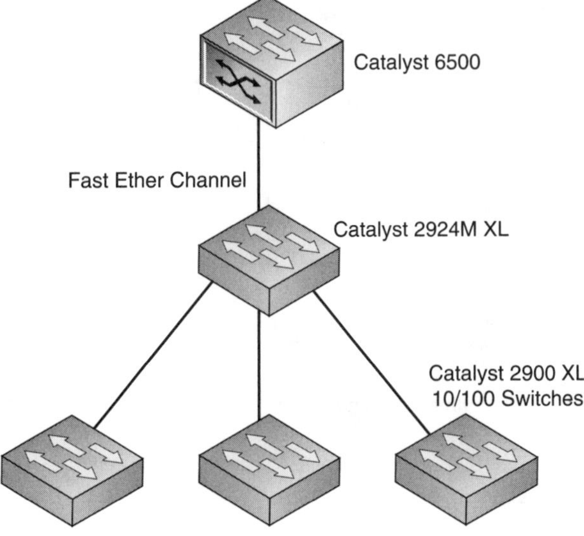

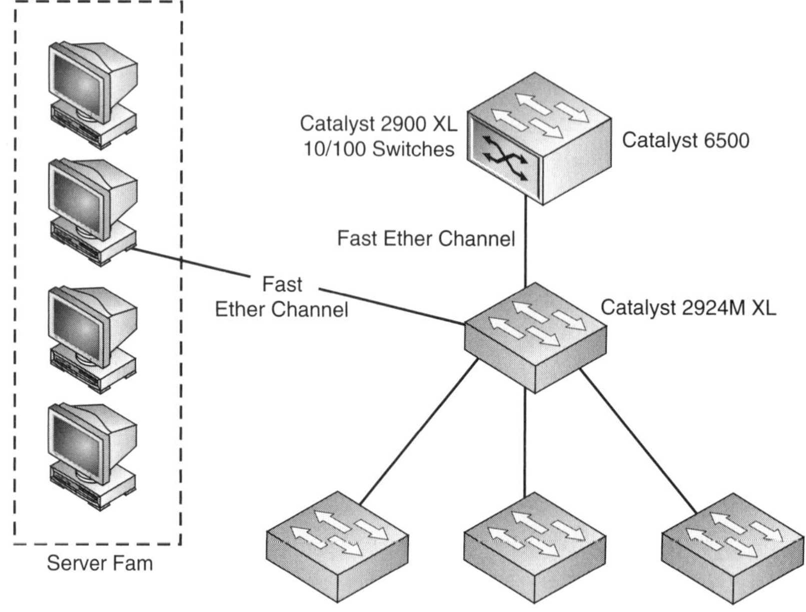

Figure B-2 Server and workgroup aggregation

Table B-2 2900 XL Switch Models

10/100	RJ-45	100 Base-FX	Gigabit Ethernet	ATM
2926F	24	2	n/a	n/a
2926T	24 + 2 100BaseTX	n/a	n/a	n/a
2912 MF XL	n/a	12 + 2 module slots	n/a	Available Modules
2912 XL	12	n/a	n/a	n/a
2924 XL	24	n/a	n/a	n/a
2924C XL	22	2	n/a	n/a
2924M XL	24 + 2 module slots	n/a	n/a	Available Modules
2948G	48	n/a	2	n/a
2948G-L3	48	n/a	2	n/a
2980G	80	n/a	2	n/a

Cisco Routers

In this section, we will cover Cisco's most popular routers that are used in most enterprise network designs. Products that have reached or soon will reach end-of-life (as of the time of writing) have been noted.

Cisco 7500 Series Router

The 7500 series routers are by far the most popular, marketed as voice, data, and video-integration routers. Using *Cisco Extended Bus* (CyBus) technology, these routers are usually the workhorses of an enterprise network. Each router contains at least one *Route Switch Processor* (RSP), which is the "brains" of the unit, with the route processor and all memory functions held within.

Modular cards for network interfaces can be a combination of ATM, channelized/clear channel T3, Ethernet, Fast Ethernet, FDDI, T1/E1, Gigabit Ethernet, IBM Channel Attachment, Token Ring, HSSI, synchronous serial, and OC-3c *Packet Over Sonet* (POS). Shown in Table B-3, the different models in the series are the 7505, 7507, 7513, and 7576. The general rule of thumb is that the last number identifies the number of slots in the chassis. The 7576 is the exception.

The 7576 actually houses *two* routers within the same footprint as the 7513. Router A is a seven-slot configuration, with a single RSP and six interface slots. Router B is a six-slot configuration, with a single RSP and five interface slots. As you can see, the RSPs have no capability for

Table B-3

7500 Router Models

Model	Number of Slots	CyBus	RSP slots	Interface Processor Slots
7505	5	One	1	4
7507	7	Two	2	5
7513	13	Two	2	11
7576	13	Four	Router A=1	Router A=6
			Router B=1	Router B=5

redundancy, which is a drawback if that is important to your overall network design.

Choice of RSP determines the horsepower of the router. The RSP2 will work on all models except the 7576. It has an external clock speed of 50 MHz and an internal clock speed of 100 MHz. All 7500 series routers can use the RSP4, with an external clock speed of 100 MHz and an internal clock speed of 200 MHz. DRAM is available in 32MB to 128MB. The units ship with 128MB of *Non-volatile RAM* (NVRAM) and 16MB of flash memory—upgradeable to 110MB.

Cisco 7200 Series Router

The 7200 series routers are primarily geared toward edge services such as broadband subscriber aggregation services, VPN gateways, and multiservice capabilities. Additionally, the *Versatile Interface Processors* (VIPs) on these devices can use the same port adapters as the 7500 series, bringing flexibility and investment protection to the customer. What differs from the 7500 series, however, are the services targeted.

Like the 7500, the 7200 supports voice, data, and video but also supports high-density LAN and WAN interfaces including channelized T1/E1 ISDN PRIs, channelized T3, ISDN BRI, as well as light-density integrated Ethernet switching. ATM, Frame Relay, and layer-3 functionality come together in this series supporting mixed IP traffic, frame to ATM conversion, and circuit emulation all on the same WAN link. Service providers using *DSL Access Multiplexers* (DSLAMs) and *Cable Modem Termination Systems* (CMTS) are able to provide secure services using the 7200 series router. The various available models are compared in Table B-4.

With the introduction of the 7204VXR and 7206VXR systems, Cisco included a multiservice capability, called *Multiservice Interchange* (MIX). MIX is positioned to support voice applications, which are in development for the open multiservice architecture, which will provide for end-to-end call management in packet and digital voice services. This will allow for the router to connect to both legacy PBX and newer PSTN call equipment, providing the same call control capabilities for all VoIP calls. With multichannel port adapters, digital and packet channels will be combined on a channelized access link without requiring a separate TDM multiplexer. Up to 128 DS0 channels can then be switched from a channelized WAN link to PBX, video codec, or other TDM-oriented devices.

Table B-4

7200 Router Models

Model	Number of Slots	Memory	Processor
7206	6	Comes without SRAM—can add 1 or 4MB	PXF is 263 MHz RISC processor
7204VXR	4	PCMCIA flash 6–40MB	
7206VXR	6		

The 7206VXR can support up to 48 Ethernet or serial (channelized or clear channel) ports, or up to 24 Token Ring ports, 12 HSSI ports, or 6 Fast Ethernet or ATM ports.

This series of routers is being marketed as having a long future. Next-generation engines and services, such as MPLS and QoS at layer 2, are being developed for this platform. Using the same Parallel eXpress Forwarding (PXF) architecture as the 10000 Edge Services Router (ESR), the 7200s are designed to permit upgrading the firmware over the network with a simple software download. This, coupled with future development of services for this line, should extend the life and flexibility of this model.

4700 Router

The 4700 is based on a 133 MHz IDT Orion RISC processor. It has three slots available for Network Processor Modules (NPMs) that can use any variation of Ethernet, ATM, FDDI, HSSI, ISDN PRI, ISDN BRI, serial interfaces, or Token Ring. One caveat is that whereas the platform can support up to two high-speed interfaces, only one ATM OC-3 interface may be supported per router.

The 4700 router ships with 128KB DRAM NVRAM. Flash memory is available in 4MB to 16MB. Main memory is available in 16MB to 32MB, and shared memory is available in 4MB to 16MB.

The 4700 router should not be seen as an answer to robust network needs, but it is an excellent choice for medium throughput needs and when a modular edge device is needed in the network design.

As of this writing, the Cisco 4000 series has reached end-of-life but, is still included in Cisco course materials and possibly tests. Its recommended replacement is the Cisco 3600 series.

Cisco 3600 Series Router

The 3600 series is a modular, high-density access router used to combine dial-up access, LAN-to-LAN integration, and routing in a single box. It is a combination of the best features of the 2600, 1700, and 1600 routers. This platform supports dial-up services, ISDN PRI, ISDN BRI, serial interfaces, ATM networking, and both analog and digital voice (both VoIP and VoFR), so it is excellent for medium-sized offices and smaller ISPs. This series is available in a two-slot, four-slot or six-slot version—the 3620, 3640, and 3660, respectively.

The 3620 model has an 80 MHz IDT R4700 RISC processor and can be configured with from 32MB to 64MB DRAM for shared system and packet memory. Flash memory can be configured from 8MB to 32MB.

The 3640 model is based on a 100 MHz IDT R4700 RISC processor. Shared memory is available in amounts from 22MB to 128MB DRAM. Flash memory is the same as in the 3620 model.

The 3660 is a beefier version, with a 225 MHz processor and 32MB to 256MB DRAM for shared memory. There are two models created specifically for Telcos—the 3662-AC-CO and the 3662-DC-CO. Each of the Telco models ships with 16MB flash memory. The remaining models 3661AC, 3661DC, 3662AC, and 3662DC—contain 8MB flash.

In the 3660 model, Cisco uses the *Advance Integration Modules* (AIMs) on two internal slots. The AIMs take over data compression, normally done by the router's CPU, thereby theoretically improving router performance. Data compression can be important to the overall cost of a link as well, when usage-based tariffs are involved. By reducing packet size, more data can be transmitted over links; reducing packet size lessens the hunger for bandwidth.

TIP: *Order the Cisco 3600 Modem Bundles: you'll get the maximum connection speeds for the most users and the ease of ordering just one line item instead of multiple line items.*

Cisco 2600 Series Router

Whereas the market for the 2600 Modular Access router is the same as the older 2500 series, discussed in the next section, Cisco provides more versatility in this series. The 2600 can use modules for the 1600, 1700, and 3600 series routers, providing investment protection for the enterprise network.

Some of the applications that are supported in this series of routers are multiservice voice/data/fax integration, analog and digital dial services, VPN access, firewall protection, four- to eight-port serial device concentration, mixed WAN services, and LAN-to-LAN service. The 2600 also provides for lower cost of ownership because the functions of CSU/DSUs, ISDN Network Termination devices, modems, firewalls, and encryption and compression devices are all bundled into a single unit.

The 2600 can support up to 36 high-speed asynchronous ports or up to 64 ISDN B channels. In addition, the router can support up to 32 remote dial-up over PPP, SLIP, ARA, or Xremote. Integrated 8 or 16 analog modem modules provide for a single-box *Remote Access Server* (RAS) solution.

All models of the 2600 ship with a minimum of 24MB DRAM, upgradeable to 64MB, and 8MB flash memory, upgradeable to 16MB. Memory is partitioned, with 12MB used for processor memory and 8MB used for packet memory, on a 16MB card, for example. Redundant power supplies are available. The unit has 25,000 bps throughput and can support up to eight dedicated 128KB synchronous connections. Model specifics are shown in Table B-5. Note that all models come with two WAN slots, one network module slot, and one AIM slot.

Table B-5

2600 Router Models

Model	Slots	Processor
2610	1 Ethernet	Motorola MPC860 40 MHz processor
2611	2 Ethernet	
2612	1 Ethernet	
	1 Token Ring	
2613	1 Token Ring	
2620	1 10/100 Auto-sensing	Motorola MPC860 50 MHz processor
2621	2 10/100 Auto-sensing	

Cisco 2500 Series Router

The 2500 models are fixed configuration units that serve nicely in small branch offices or at remote sites. Any given model (except the Mission-Specific model, which has 4MB standard) will come with 8MB of flash memory and at least two of the following types of interfaces: Token Ring, Ethernet, 10BaseT Ethernet hub, ISDN BRI, and synchronous or asynchronous serial port. Additional flash memory may be required to support some IOS versions. See Cisco's Web site for more product information at **http://www.cisco.com/univercd/cc/td/doc/pcat/2500.htm**.

In addition to the flash memory, each router has two types of DRAM: primary and shared. *Primary memory* is used to store the operating configuration, routing tables, caches, and queues. *Shared memory* is used to store incoming and outgoing packets. DRAM is shipped in 4-, 8-, or 16-MB portions.

The routers come in very specific configurations, depending on the application. Refer to Table B-6 for more information.

Table B-6

Cisco 2500 Configurations

Application	Models
Single LAN	2501, 2502, 2503, 2504, 2520, 2521,2522, 2523
Mission-specific/Entry-level	2501CF, 2501LF, 2502LF, 2503I, 2504I, 2520CF, 2520LF, 2521CF, 2521LF, 2522CF, 2523CF, 2523LF
Router/Hub Combo	2505, 2507, 2516
Access Servers	2509, 2512
Dual LAN	2513, 2514, 2515
Modular	2524, 2525

Cisco 400 Series LocalDirector

The Cisco 400 Series LocalDirector is a load-balancing network appliance for TCP and UDP traffic across multiple servers or mainframes. With full redundancy, including hot standby and stateful failover, the product contributes to high-availability, scalable server farms. In the area of e-commerce, products like LocalDirector are a necessity. Downtime and HTML page timeouts can mean lost business and reduced revenue. Figure B-3 shows a typical application of LocalDirector. A primary set of servers is backed up by a second set of identical servers. All servers are connected on the LAN via a switch. LocalDirector handles the incoming and outgoing sessions by maintaining a state table in its database.

LocalDirector comes in two models: 430 and 416. Both models are rackmountable in a standard 19-inch rack and have 2MB of flash memory. The 416 has three, four-port 10/100 Ethernet interface cards and 32MB of DRAM. The 430 comes with four, four-port 10/100 Ethernet interface cards and is scalable to 16 10/100 cards or a maximum of four FDDI ports. Additionally, the 430 ships with 384MB of DRAM, for use in larger server farms.

LocalDirector is configurable through a console port or a GUI and requires only 10 commands, unless customization is required. The product also features transparent support for common TCP/IP services including FTP, HTTP, Telnet, and SMTP without requiring custom configuration.

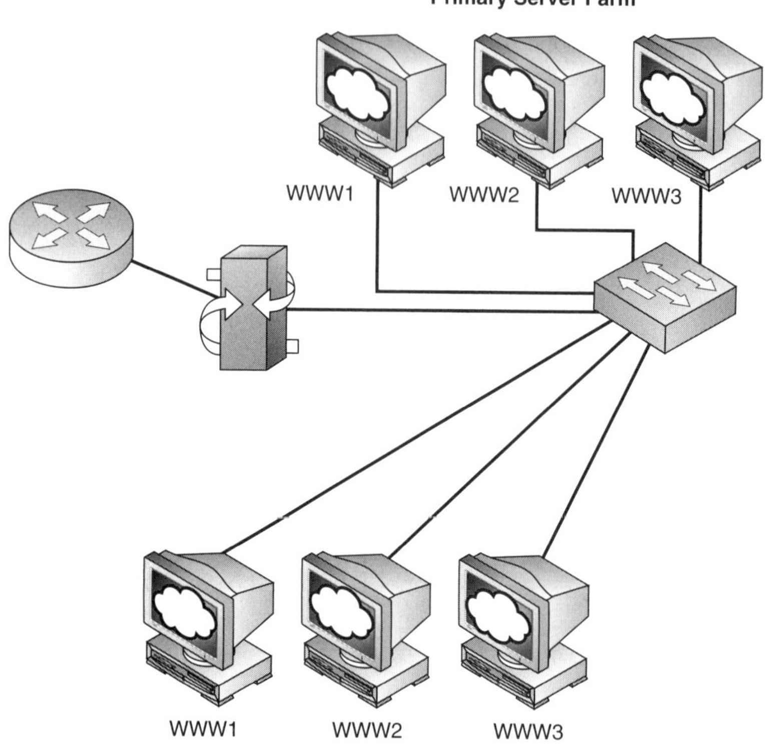

Figure B-3 Distributed environment

LocalDirector is compatible with any operating system, so server farms with Unix and Windows NT Server operating systems present no problem.

For network security, Network Address Translation (NAT) is supported on the platform, enabling internal private addresses to be translated into valid, public addresses for routing to the Internet. Other security features are integrated into the product, such as protection against IP spoof attacks.

LocalDirector uses the Session Distribution Algorithm, which will support up to 1 million simultaneous TCP sessions on the LocalDirector 430 model. It will also support up to 64,000 real or virtual servers, offering flexibility in network configuration.

PIX Firewall

The Cisco PIX Firewall is a rack-mountable "black-box" type of security and VPN device. With a stateful inspection engine and the Adaptive Security Algorithm (ASA), the PIX can handle up to 250,000 simultaneous connections coming in at a rate of more than 6,500 connections per second.

The box is neither a full-time proxy server nor a network security appliance, although it greatly resembles the latter. Using a Cisco, non-Unix operating system, it uses the connection-oriented ASA design to create flows based on source and destination addresses, TCP sequence numbers, port numbers, and additional TCP flags. Security policies are managed through a Java-based GUI for ease of use.

The PIX Firewall is a real-time security platform, meaning that the security policy is applied to all connections, or flows, present in the state table. This means real-time alarms, by e-mail or pager, when an intrusion is detected.

The PIX Firewall can be part of a high-availability architecture when two firewalls are running in parallel, as shown in Figure B-4. The state tables are synchronized and identical, as are the firewall configurations themselves. A heartbeat protocol monitors the availability of the master firewall. If a failure is detected, the slave firewall becomes the master and the sessions continue.

The PIX Firewall must be managed by a PIX Firewall Manager, which must be hosted on a Windows NT/SP4 or better platform. The Firewall Manager can handle the management of up to 10 PIX Firewalls by communicating over a secure conversation protected by the MD5 algorithm.

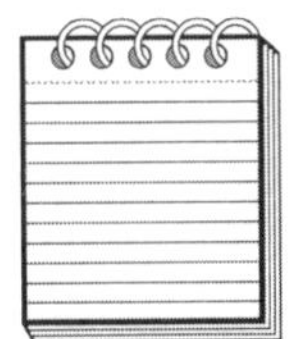

NOTE: *As of this writing Windows 2000 compatibility is in the planning stages for the PIX Firewall.*

Other features of the PIX are

- Cut-through proxy authentication using Cisco Secure Access Control Server Software
- Ability to use TACACS+ or Radius authentication
- Mail Guard to eliminate need for external mail relay server

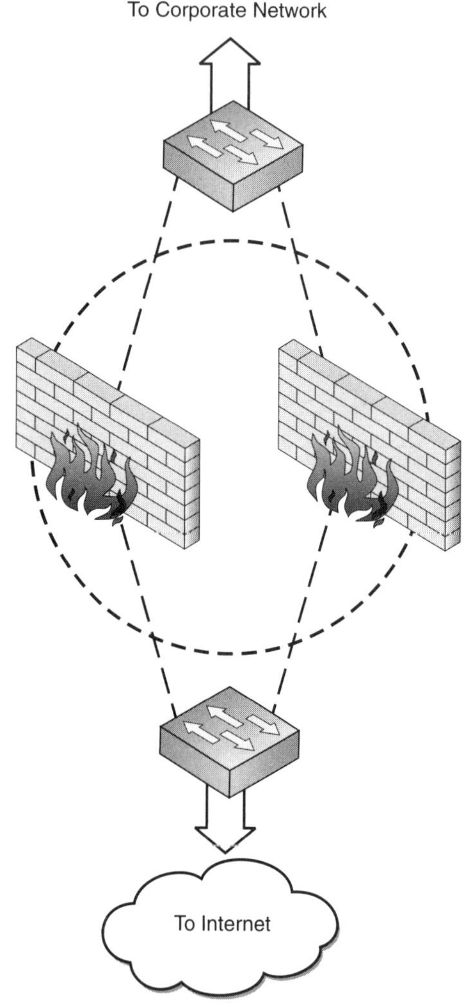

Figure B-4
High-availability firewall configuration

- DNS Guard to protect outbound name and address lookups
- Flood Guard and Fragmentation Guard to protect against denial-of-service (DoS) attacks
- Network Address Translation (NAT) support as specified in RFC 1631
- Port Address Translation (PAT) can allow one IP address to support more than 64,000 hosts
- Java-blocking capability

- Cisco command-line interface
- URL filtering
- Extended authentication, authorization, and accounting (AAA) capabilities
- Net Alias merges overlapping networks with the same address space
- Extended access list support
- Customizable protocol ports (allows for non-standard port usage)
- Customizable syslog messages
- SNMP manageable

Cisco MCS-7830 Media Convergence Server

The Cisco MCS-7830 Media Convergence Server is a high-availability server platform for support of Cisco Architecture for Voice, Video, and Integrated Data (AVVID). Cisco CallManager software comes preinstalled on the server, allowing for easy, out-of-the-box IP telephony implementation. Although the platform is a Pentium III/500-MHz system with 256MB SDRAM and RAID support for dual 9.1GB hot-plug hard drives, the server is intended to run only the CallManager software. The server operating system is Windows NT with Microsoft Internet Information Server (IIS) for remote access to the database.

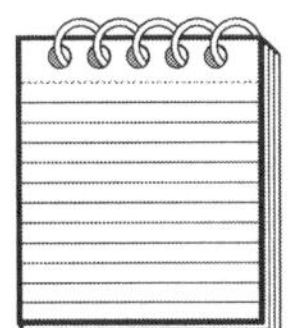

NOTE: *Cisco Media Convergence Server and CallManager software are Windows 2000 compliant.*

With the 7830, Cisco introduced the *Cisco Unified Open Network Exchange* (Cisco uOne), a voice- and unified-messaging application. Essentially, this is a voice messaging application over IP that will support up to 100 mailboxes with four simultaneous sessions (upgradeable to eight sessions).

The CallManager software provides integrated voice applications to support telephone conferencing, manual Web attendant console, click-to-call (from a browsable directory service), and typical voice functions such as forward, transfer, hold, multiple lines, speed-dial, redial, and conferencing. Because IP telephony is handled by software, upgrades are a matter of loading a new software version with no complicated hardware upgrade process.

Currently, redundancy is available by connecting two 7830 servers with one acting as a hot standby server. This is due to be improved in future releases. CallManager may be linked across many servers using H.323 signaling interfaces.

Cisco Network Registrar (CNR)

Cisco provides DNS/DHCP services with its Cisco Network Registrar (CNR) system. The product is available for almost any operating system, including Windows 2000. The primary features of this product are a multithreaded DNS server, DHCP server with BOOTP, dynamic BOOTP, multihoming, and secondary address support on routers. Redundant DHCP using the Safe Failover Protocol eliminates DHCP as a single point of failure without problems with duplicate address assignment.

DHCP, in fact, can be extensively customized based on MAC address, device type, and so forth. Addresses may be assigned from separate address pools, a nice feature for larger networks using a single DHCP server.

CNR processes can be managed via Simple Network Management Protocol (SNMP), and the product allows Open Database Connectivity (ODBC) database exports. The base product will support 1250 nodes, but license upgrades are available in increments of 1250 to 25,000 nodes per license.

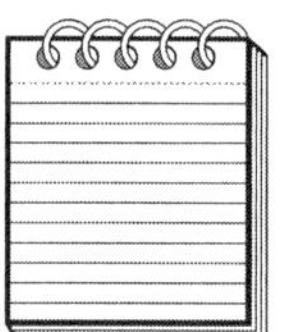

NOTE: *CNR is Windows 2000 compliant.*

Network Verification Tool (NVT)

The *Network Verification Tool* (NVT) toolset is a bundle consisting of an NVT server, Cisco routers running a special software image, and a test tool suite that includes large network emulators, session emulators, traffic analyzers, traffic generators, custom scripts, and custom queries. Generally speaking, the NVT toolset is part of a service package offered to customers by Cisco for the purpose of network auditing and assessment using Cisco Network Test Consulting Engineers (NTCEs).

The toolset can populate the routing tables on the Cisco routers with RIP, BGP, and OSPF, and can generate data traffic to simulate a busy network. Standard traffic generators and analyzers can send and break down multiprotocol traffic streams as well as raw traffic across the network model. The custom queries and scripts serve to automate and control the devices, profiles, and activities while retrieving and displaying tasks such as utilization rates, status information, or routing information.

APPENDIX C

Suggested Solutions to Case Studies

Chapter 3 Case Study

For this case study, our subject was Campus Research Corporation's two locations: Detroit and St. Louis. The current topology is as follows:

- Detroit
  - The building has three major departments spread over five floors.
  - A data center is located on the first floor along with the reception area and Customer Service. The data center houses a server farm that must be reachable from all departments and from the St. Louis campus.
  - On the second and third floors, administration includes Human Resources, Accounts Payable, Accounts Receivable, and Collections.
  - On the fourth and fifth floors, Engineering maintains a staff of 120 engineers along with a testing lab and a separate intranet server.
- St. Louis
  - The building has three departments in a three-story building.
  - On the main floor is a reception area and five training rooms. The training servers are housed in the single wiring closet that services the floor.
  - On the second and third floors, the administration staff for the training center and a small staff of accounting clerks share space with the Research and Development engineers.
  - A server room in the R&D lab is located on the third floor.

Your first assignment was to evaluate the current network infrastructure and make recommendations on

- Wiring
- Location of servers
- Technology in the wiring closet (hubs versus switches, for example)
- The use of routers, where appropriate
- Connectivity recommendations between buildings

Our suggested solution to the design issues in Detroit is shown in Figure C-1.

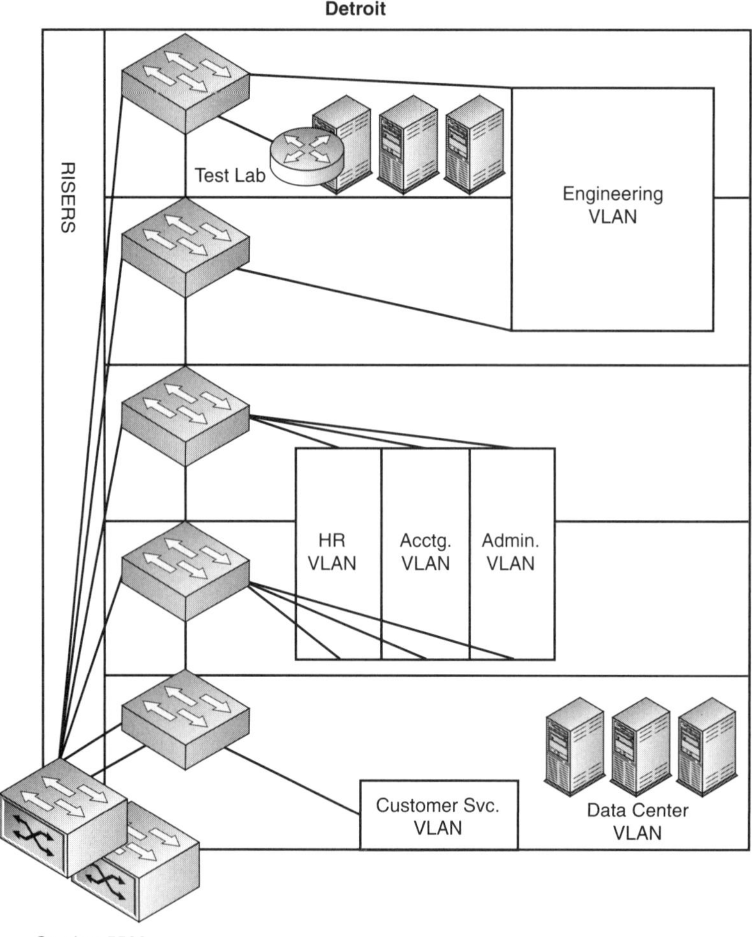

Figure C-1 Detroit redesign

The first recommendation is for wiring. The best solution is to provide fiber-optic cabling in the risers, connecting all switches. Category-5 UTP can then connect the switches to the wall plates and then to the end user devices.

We recommend that a Catalyst 5500 switch be used in the first floor to serve as a connecting point for the remaining floors. This switch contains a *Route Switch Module* (RSM) that is essentially a router. For redundancy, we would recommend a second switch that connects to all other switches in the building as well as to the "sister" switch in the main floor. This would be a costlier solution, but the case study points out that money is not an issue.

Departments are assigned to VLANs by function, which means that they can reside on any floor, adding flexibility to the overall corporate infrastructure. Trading the current hubs for switches in all wiring closets provides this flexibility. The building in St. Louis is shown in Figure C-2 using VLANs and a similar architecture for redundancy and scalability. Note that we are using Catalyst 5505s because of the reduced requirements for this building. A leased line connects the existing router to the headquarters building in Detroit.

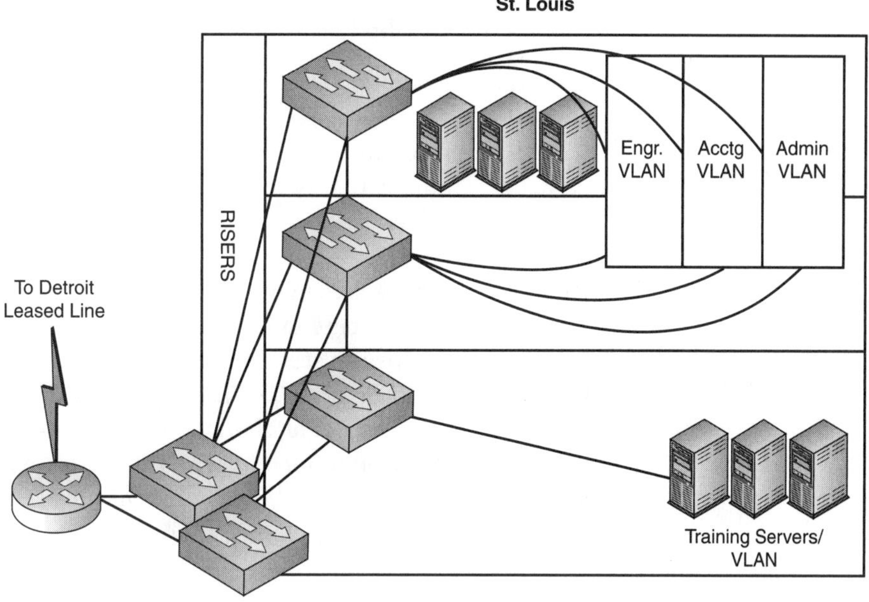

Figure C-2 St. Louis redesign

Redundancy is still provided by dual switches in the main wiring closet, connected to switches on the remaining floors by fiber-optic cabling. We would recommend the addition of wiring closets on each floor, along with the replacement of the hubs by smaller Catalyst switches. Category-5 UTP connects the switches to the end users. Training, and every other department, is segregated into the VLAN architecture for flexibility.

Chapter 4 Case Study

The case study for Chapter 4, "Campus LAN Technology," asks you to consider a set of questions and requirements for Campus Research Corporation.

- Will there be a centralized server farm or a set of servers in each location?
- Define a naming convention for the servers and network devices.
- Define the new connection between buildings. Should they have a backup connectivity method?
- Make recommendations on LAN topology and use of VLANs if appropriate.
- Should the 10 Mbps Ethernet connections to the servers be faster?

The company would like for you to come up with a suggested naming convention for the server farm(s) as well as for their network devices. You were also requested to build on what you recommended to the client in the previous assignment to create a high-level diagram with LAN connection speeds properly labeled. Let's first look at our recommended design for Detroit in Figure C-3.

All links to servers are shown at 100 Mbps. This will mean upgrading the NICs in the servers. Keeping the servers centralized in server farms is not really a concern. This is a standard practice, although some businesses tend to want redundant server farms in multiple locations. This variation is not shown here. The other major change in Detroit is the reuse of the existing Cisco router to provide connectivity to the Catalyst 5500s and to provide a serial port for a T1 link to St. Louis with a backup ISDN link in case the primary link fails. St. Louis is shown in Figure C-4.

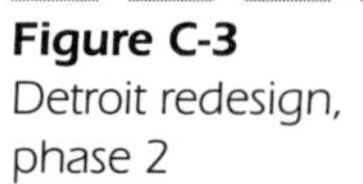

Figure C-3 Detroit redesign, phase 2

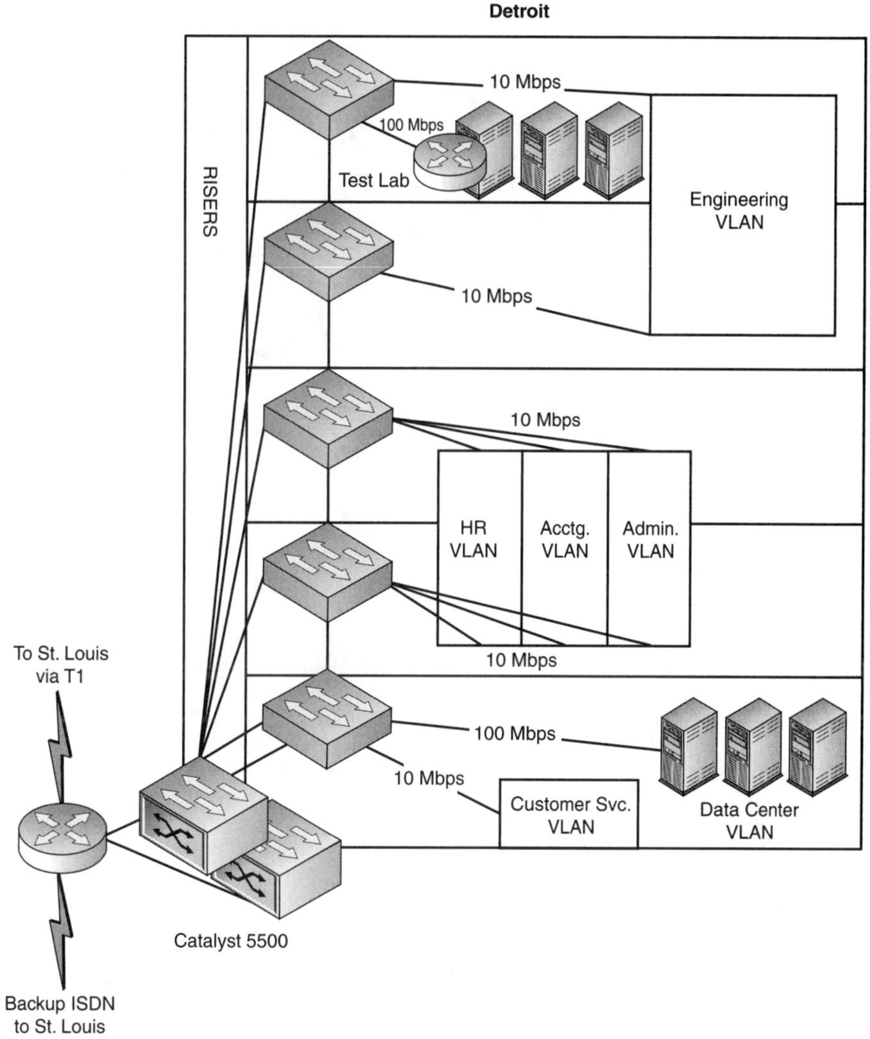

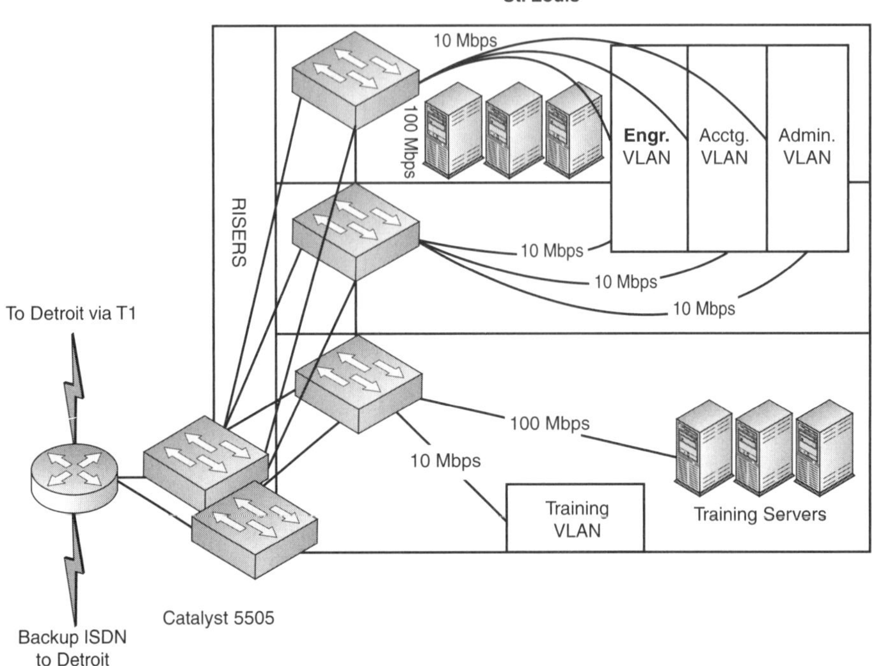

Figure C-4 St. Louis redesign, phase 2

As you can see, we stayed with the same theme in both buildings for simplicity and standardization of the design. The naming convention recommendations are not labeled on the drawings, but here is a suggested sample:

- **Training servers** TRN01 or TRN*function*01, up to the number of servers needed; *function* could be Web, DNS, and so on.
- **Engineering servers** ENG01 or ENG*function*01, up to the number of servers needed.
- **Data center servers** CRC01 or CRC*function*01, up to the number of servers needed. CRC = Campus Research Corporation.
- **Wiring closet switches** CRC_SL_0101, could stand for the first switch on the first floor at St. Louis. CRC_DT_0501, could stand for the first switch on the fifth floor at Detroit.
- **Routers and RSMs** CRC_SL_R01, could simply be router number one in St. Louis.

Chapter 5 Case Study

For this case study, you were to apply both the distributed backbone model and collapsed backbone model to the new design for both locations of Campus Research Corporation. Then answer the following questions:

- Which network design model worked better for your original recommendations?
- What were the drawbacks of each design?
- What were the benefits?

Because you have already seen the collapsed backbone design in the Chapter 3, "Campus LAN Overview," and Chapter 4, "Campus LAN Technology," case studies, we will show you the distributed backbone version of these designs and answer the questions after. First, take a look at Detroit's distributed backbone design in Figure C-5.

Now look at Figure C-6 to see how St. Louis might look.

In both designs, we show an FDDI ring in the risers connecting all wiring closets together "equally." While we can still use Catalyst switches in the closets, we show small Cisco routers connecting the wiring closets to the backbone. This represents added expense and complexity to the design, but it does eliminate a single point of failure that a data center switch in a collapsed design could present.

Whereas either type of backbone design could work, the collapsed backbone is by far the most popular in use today, and, when created with redundancy at the most critical points, it can be both scalable and reliable.

Chapter 7 Case Study

The case study for Chapter 7, "TCP/IP Addressing Design," asks that you make some recommendations to Campus Research Corporation about its TCP/IP addressing scheme. To refresh your memory, here are the assumptions we made at the outset:

- A single router at each building provides routing within the building and connectivity via a T1 link between locations.
- A switch has been deployed on each of the five floors at the Detroit location and on each of the three floors at the St. Louis location. Wiring

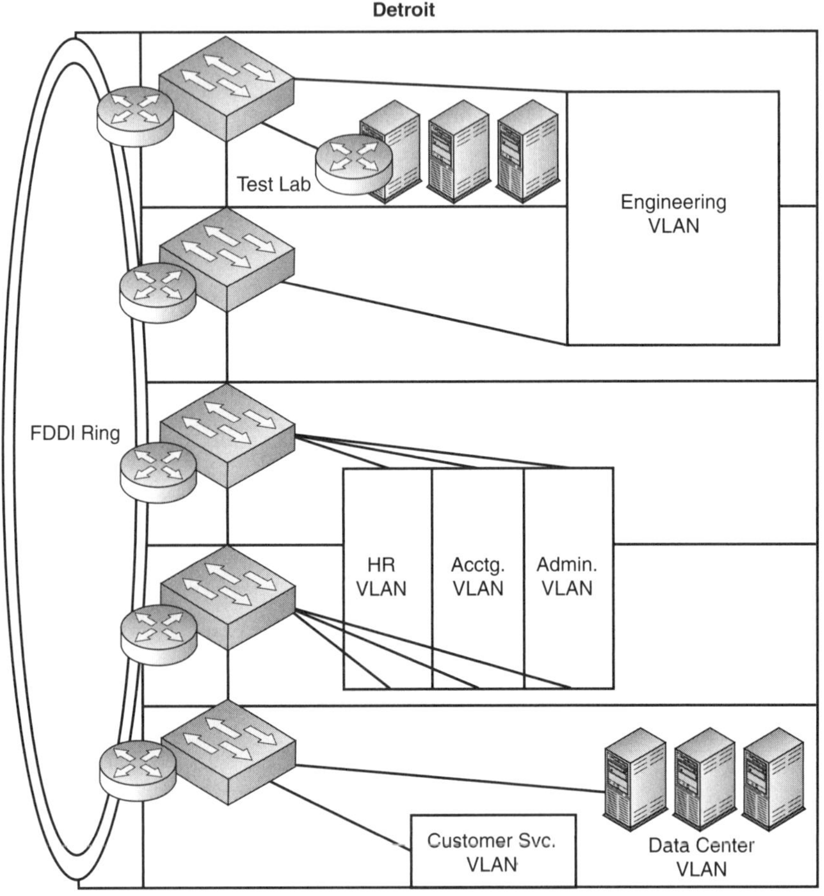

Figure C-5 Detroit distributed backbone

has been upgraded to Category-5 UTP between the closets and LAN drops, with multimode fiber in the risers.

- Server farms have been centralized in the Detroit Data Center and the St. Louis R&D center.
- Accounting clerks in St. Louis need to be able to FTP files at the end of each day to the servers in Detroit.
- Engineering needs to be able to reach the R&D server farm to browse Web pages, download files (via FTP), and update code (via TFTP).
- Data Center personnel need to be able to use Telnet and TFTP to manage network devices in both locations. They also need to be able to manage servers.

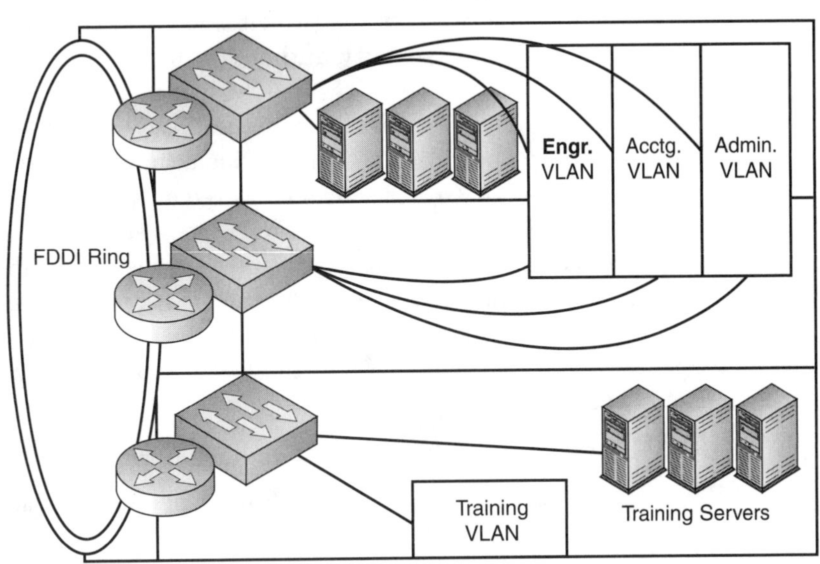

Figure C-6 St. Louis distributed backbone

One of the biggest questions is whether or not to use the six Class C networks that are currently being leased from the ISP or to use private address space. Some other questions you will need to answer with the design will be

- If RFC 1918 addresses are used, what device will handle network address translation?
- Will firewalls be needed at both locations?
- Will a DHCP server be placed at both locations? If placed at only one location, how will traffic between buildings be affected?
- How will authentication be handled in order to verify personnel that are managing network devices and servers?
- What services need to be allowed to pass between buildings?
- What addresses will you select for the networks and departments contained within the locations?

A high-level design for this case study is shown in Figure C-7. A router at each site connects the two sites via a T1 line. A firewall at each site is used to provide security, authentication, and network address translation (NAT).

We would recommend a private addressing scheme within each campus to save money. The ISP will provide a small subnet for the leased line connection. A DHCP server can be placed at each location, keeping traffic off of the T1 line unless it must go to the other building. FTP, Telnet, HTTP, HTTPS, and TFTP traffic will be controlled through the rule sets in each firewall, limiting the traffic to the source and destinations determined by the network engineering staff.

Here is a sample of how the RFC 1918 addresses could be allocated for each location:

- Detroit uses 10.1.0.0/16 with further subnets for various departments.
- St. Louis uses 10.2.0.0/16 with further subnets for various departments.

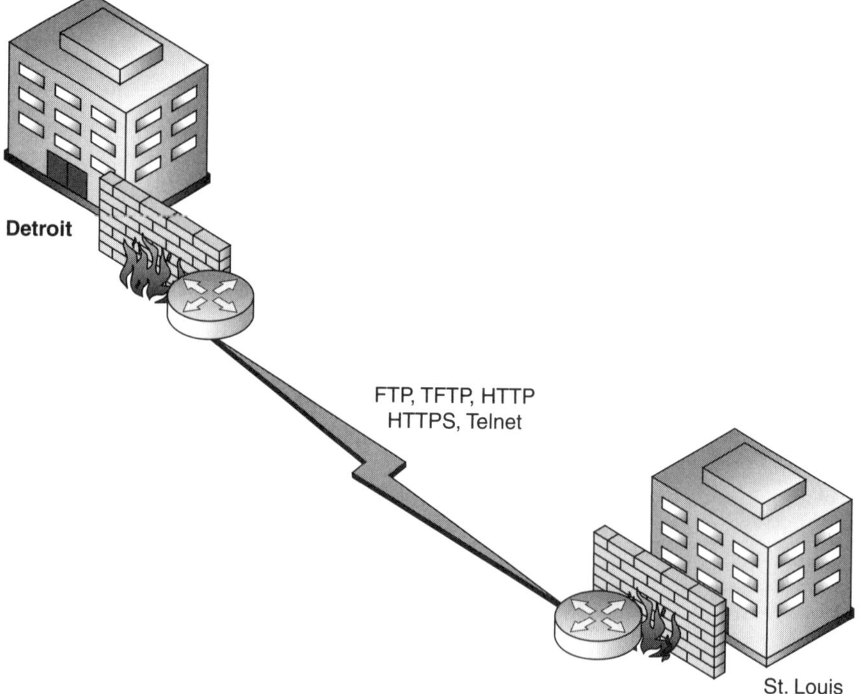

Figure C-7 Campus Research Corporation, phase 3

- NAT occurs at the firewall.
- Servers, which need to be addressed with a public number, are translated in a one-for-one fashion on the firewall. A small public subnet can be used for this purpose. This would require the purchase of a subnet adequate for the number of servers.
- End-user devices, such as PCs, are translated at the firewall in a one-to-many fashion, with the external (valid) address of the firewall substituted for the RFC 1918 address of the actual device.

Chapter 9 Case Study

For our case study on OSPF, we examined Calabash Shipping Company, which is currently using RIP as its routing protocol. It has five locations—headquarters in Detroit, and regional offices in Denver, Boise, Columbus, and Raleigh, as shown in Figure C-8.

Your objectives for this case study were to

- Minimize protocol traffic.
- Use RIP and OSPF together.
- Allow for scalability.
- Summarize where possible.
- Identify your areas in a simple design.

A simple OSPF design is shown in Figure C-9, which lays out the area topology by geographical region. The robust, core routers are in Area 0, the backbone, at the Detroit location. One router acts as the autonomous system boundary router (ASBR) to other autonomous systems. Areas are summarized at the area border routers (ABR) and kept totally stubby. They have a single default route through the ABR to the backbone.

Notice also that our RIP networks at Detroit are injected into our backbone area. These routes are redistributed into OSPF so that they are reachable by all areas.

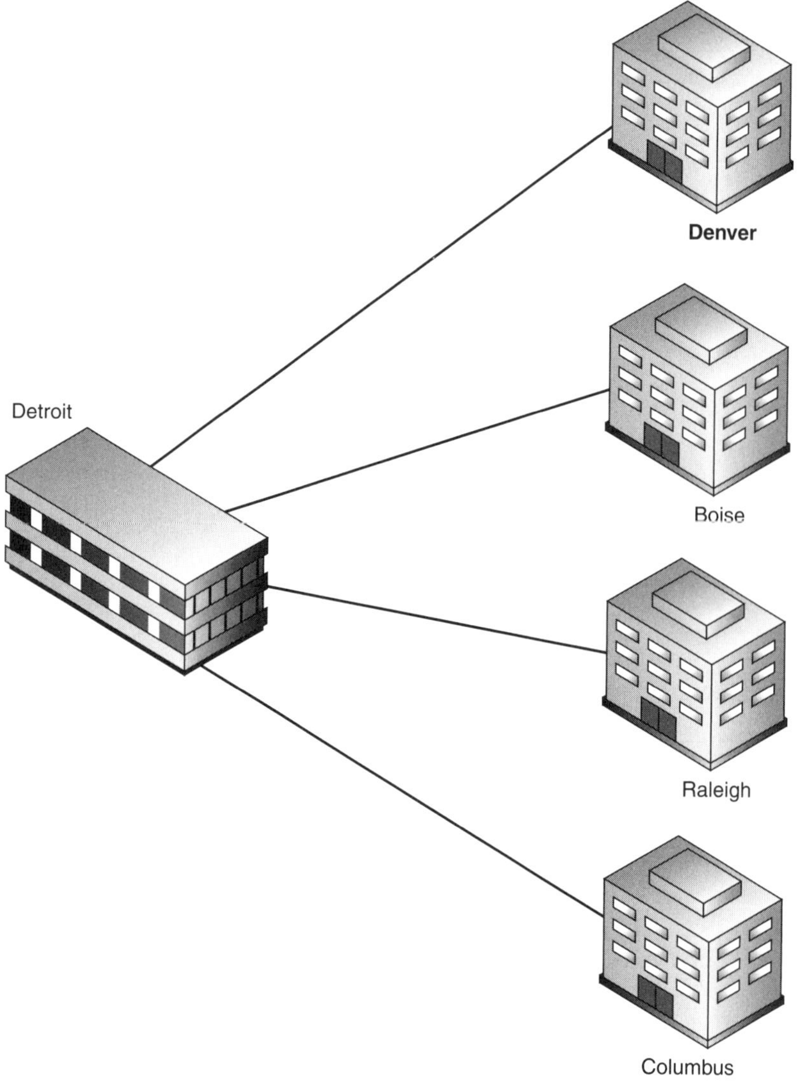

Figure C-8 Calabash Shipping Company

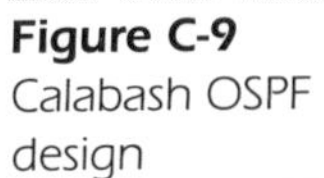

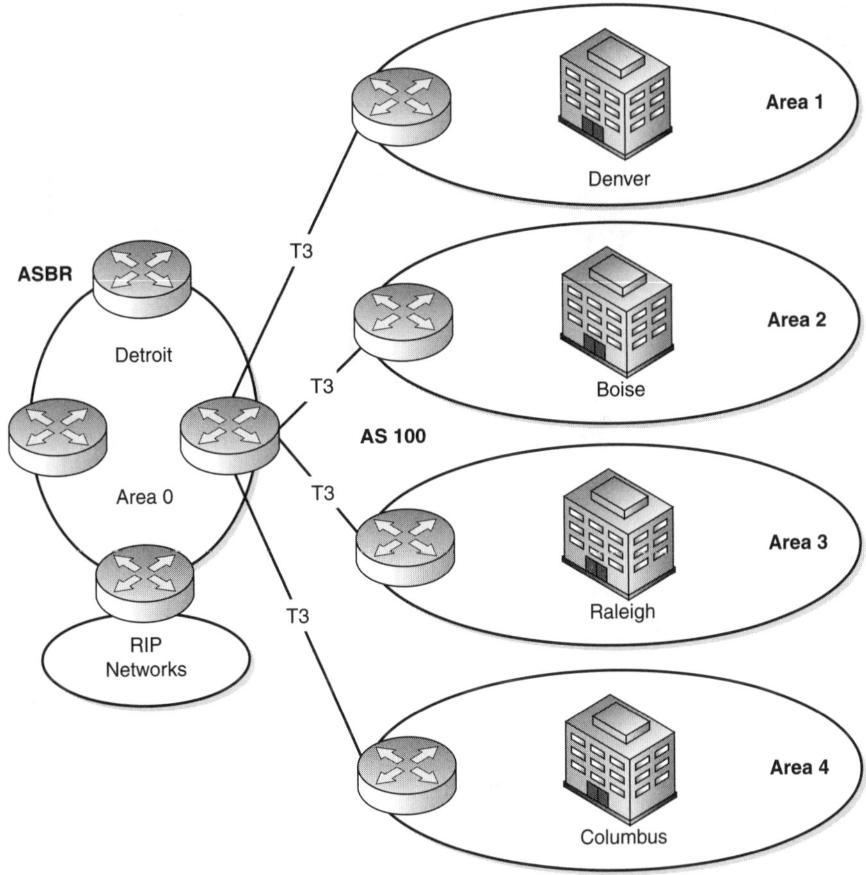

Figure C-9 Calabash OSPF design

Chapter 10 Case Study

Chapter 10, "IGRP-EIGRP Design," concerned IGRP and EIGRP design. Tesla Oil Company has three major locations and requires a redesign of its network due to a recent acquisition. Two of the locations are using the same private address space. Some locations use EIGRP, and some use IGRP. Dallas and Austin are part of AS 200. Houston is in AS 110. The company needs to consolidate and standardize its network infrastructure. The current design is shown in Figure C-10.

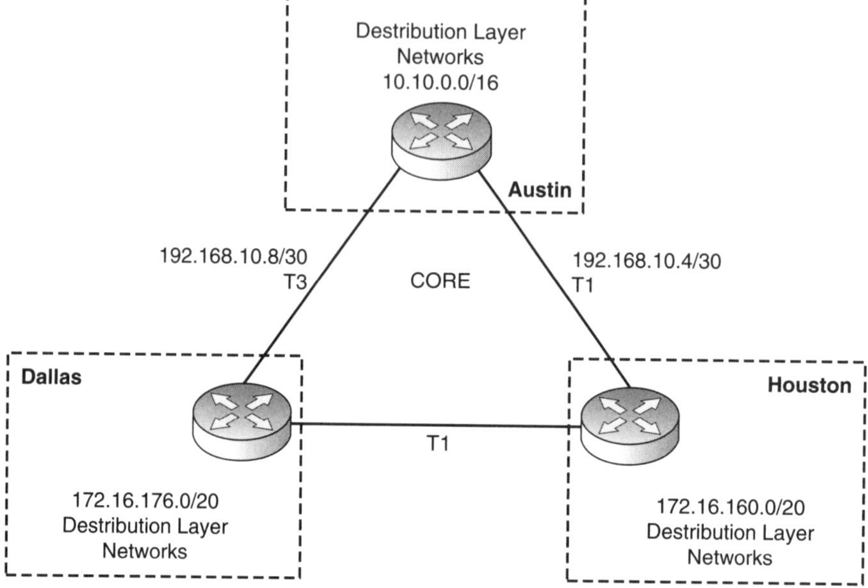

Figure C-10
Tesla Oil Company.

Here are the questions and concerns you were presented with:

- How will redistribution occur between EIGRP autonomous system 200, in Dallas and Austin, and IGRP autonomous system 110, in Houston?
- How will the discontiguous major network that is split between Houston and Dallas be resolved by EIGRP?
- The serial links also contain discontiguous network numbers. How will these be handled by EIGRP? Will they need to be renumbered?
- Will Houston be able to load-balance between the direct T1 to Austin and the T1 to T3 route through Dallas? If so, how will this be accomplished?

The best recommendation for this network is to change it all to a single autonomous system and implement EIGRP on all routers. This simplifies routing and reduces the headache of administration for this network. Although the routers must be reconfigured to reflect the changes, it is a minor amount of work for a maximum benefit.

Turning off auto-summary on all routers and entering the networks individually under the EIGRP process handles the discontiguous networks. Setting the variance factor to 2 can invoke unequal cost load balancing. This will allow Houston to take either the direct route to Austin via its own T1 connection or to take the T1 to T3 route through Dallas. Setting the variance factor to 2 causes the router in Houston to consider all routes that are up to twice the metric of the current best route, which is through the T1 to Austin.

Chapter 12 Case Study

In this case study, Campus Research Corporation has acquired a small manufacturing company in Milwaukee that uses Novell NetWare throughout its LAN with an IPX stack running on the end-stations. Part of the group will move to the company's headquarters in Detroit and will still need to reach the servers in Milwaukee. Already there are problems with slowness and the number of SAPs being advertised.

You were asked to design a network that will allow the users in Milwaukee to continue using Novell for their NOS and that will allow the division that is moving to Detroit to remain on a Novell NetWare platform. You will need to specify a high-level design that meets the needs of the company without discounting the needs of the users.

Figure C-11 shows one way to handle the issues and requirements of this acquisition.

We have installed the TCP/IP stack on the Novell workstations so that the end-user devices can be addressed in the same manner as the existing end-user devices in Detroit. This simplifies the addition of workstations as well as the movement of the department to Detroit. The Novell servers remain in Milwaukee, but the local routers, with the use of watchdog spoofing, answer keepalives for sessions. The routers can also be configured to respond to GNS queries, if desired.

EIGRP routing in the WAN introduces a more scalable environment for the growth of the network.

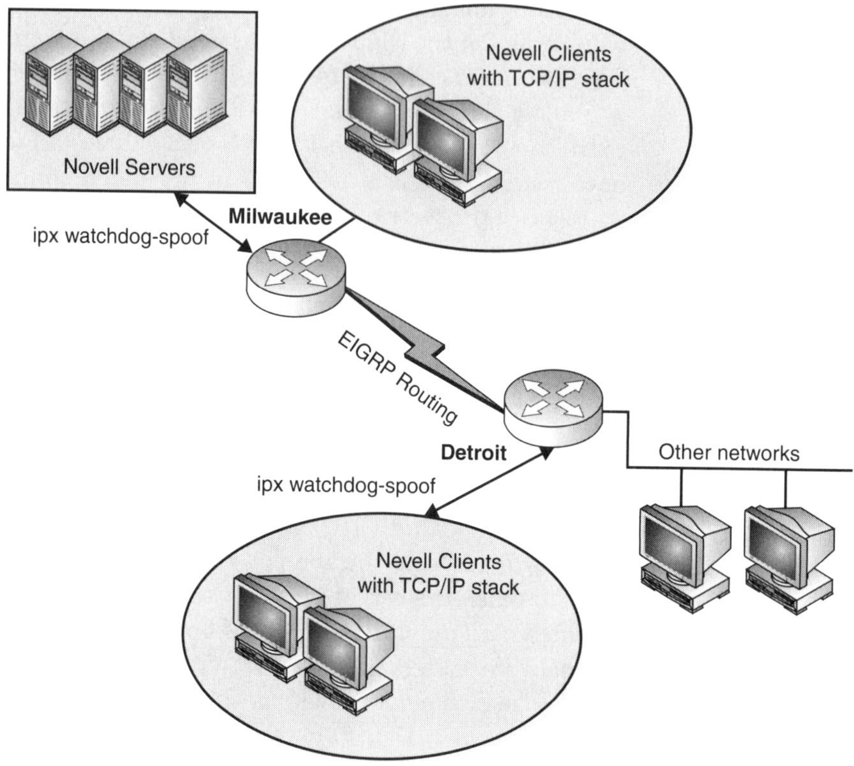

Figure C-11 Campus Research Corporation, post acquisition

Chapter 13 Case Study

The case study for Chapter 13 involved the acquisition of a small design-consulting group by our St. Louis-based Campus Research Corporation. The design group needs to communicate with the manufacturing unit in Milwaukee. They were staunchly defensive of their decision to use Macintosh computers, and are running MAC OS 6.0 over AppleTalk Phase I.

First of all, you must upgrade the operating system on the Macintosh computers to a newer version like MAC OS 7.0, which fixes some of the problems with MAC OS 6.0. Next you would keep their AppleTalk traffic local to one segment of the network using AppleTalk Phase II. As shown in Figure C-12, you could use EIGRP to communicate between St. Louis and Milwaukee over the WAN.

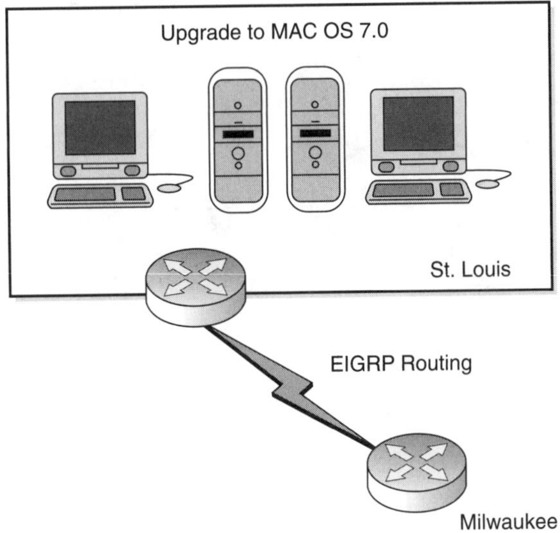

Figure C-12 Campus Research AppleTalk solution

Chapter 14 Case Study

For this case study, you were given a scenario in which several unique departments within Valley Manufacturing were to be integrated into a single Windows networked environment. Only the Human Resources department required continued support for Novell servers. In addition, the Engineering department wished to have the ability to dial-in to the network when necessary. Figure C-13 shows one way to address the company's requirements.

For authentication and domain control, we are recommending a WINS server for address registry and centralized browsing and management. Domain and name lookups are handled by a central DNS in the master domain. Our PDC and BDC are also present in the master domain. The IT department will control the server farms for the master and sub-domains in a special, controlled-access server room.

We have created a centralized bank of modems for the Engineering group users through which they can access the company domain. Using standard CHAP or PAP authentication or offloading the security task to a token-based authentication method (not shown here), the home user may log on to the Windows master domain and be granted access to resources as specified by the domain administrator.

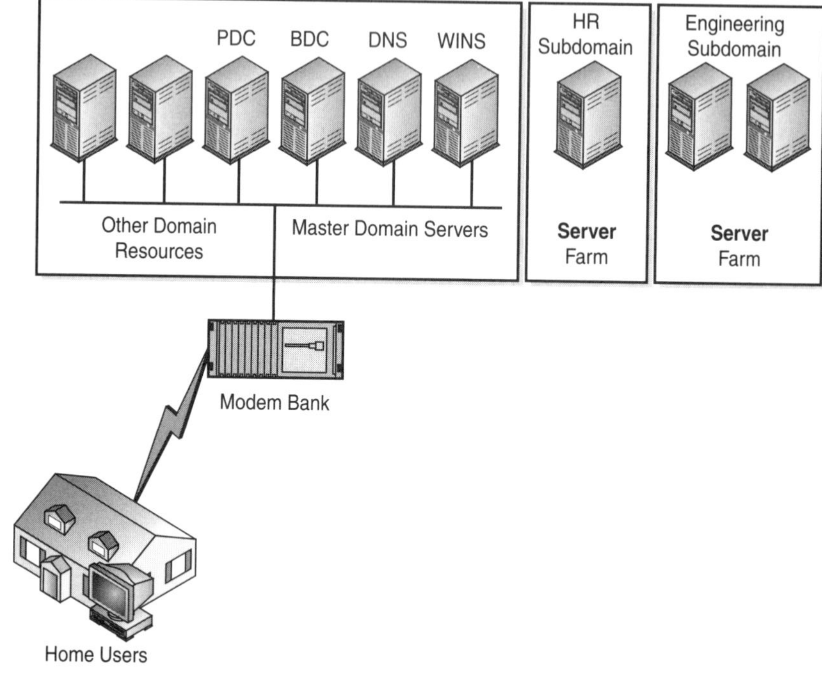

Figure C-13 Valley Manufacturing's Windows infrastructure

The HR department should be upgraded to the latest version of the Novell operating system. HR workstations may then be configured with NetBIOS over TCP, which will allow the use of DHCP and network browsing capability. Because sensitive information may be contained on the HR servers, we show these servers in a separate sub-domain.

The Engineering department may also have sensitive or proprietary information on its servers, so we have shown a separate domain for Engineering servers as well. Based on the information given about Valley Manufacturing, you may even break out the sub-domains further, as shown in Figure C-14. As you can see, all departments, except for IT, are segregated into sub-domains by function. IT, which typically must control the domain, is part of the master domain.

The type of domain structure shown here is the *master domain model*. The master domain trusts nothing from its sub-domains, but the sub-domains trust the master domain implicitly.

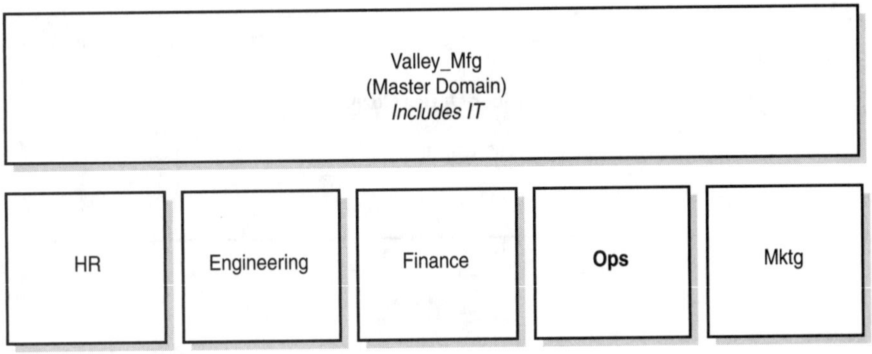

Figure C-14 Valley Manufacturing domain structure

Valley_Mfg (Master Domain) *Includes IT*				
HR	Engineering	Finance	**Ops**	Mktg

Chapter 16 Case Study

In Chapter 16," Dedicated Lines," you were asked to design connectivity for some new Detroit-area acquisitions by Campus Research Corporation. The following information was provided:

- Chip Components has a Cisco 2611 router in its wiring closet and was running over a T1 line to an ISP locally.
- Michigan Fiber-Optics has two Cisco 7513 routers in its main computer center, which will connect to Campus Research.
- Argyle Industries has a different vendor's router in the wiring closet.

The company has given you the following requirements:

- Bandwidth requirements are estimated in Table C-1. These estimates are shown for connectivity between the new offices and the headquarters building.
- The link between headquarters and Michigan Fiber-Optics will be critical to daily business and cannot afford failure. Therefore, cost is not an issue.
- The other two new offices need to have costs kept to a minimum. Refer to Table C-2 for costs associated with the dedicated lines.

Table C-1

Bandwidth Requirements

Location	Bandwidth Needed (in Mbps)
Michigan Fiber-Optics Corp.	30
Argyle Industries, Inc.	8
Chip Components, Ltd.	<1

Table C-2

Cost of Connectivity

Type of Connection	Base Monthly Cost	Monthly Cost per Mile
T-3/DS-3	$1,750	$50
T-1	$1,500	$50
512 Kbps	$1,300	$50
256 Kbps	$1,000	$50
64 Kbps	$350	$50
ISDN (backup line)	$159	N/A

Using this information, you were asked to draw up a simple design of what the WAN needs to look like to support the estimated traffic between buildings. You should show scalability, redundancy, encapsulation type, and line type. We were not provided with a distance, so we are assuming 50 miles between buildings. Figure C-15 shows what the design might look like. An explanation follows.

Part of the cost for hardware will be the purchase of a new router for Argyle Industries so that all routers are the same across buildings. The Cisco 2611 at Chip Components is fine for the design requirements. Assuming 50 miles between points, we see the cost, type, and distance of each leased line shown on our diagram. At Michigan Fiber-Optics, where we have the greatest availability requirement, a second router is available, although the site may or may not want total redundancy, which would mean the lease of a second T1 or T3 line. An ISDN backup line is in place for total routing failures.

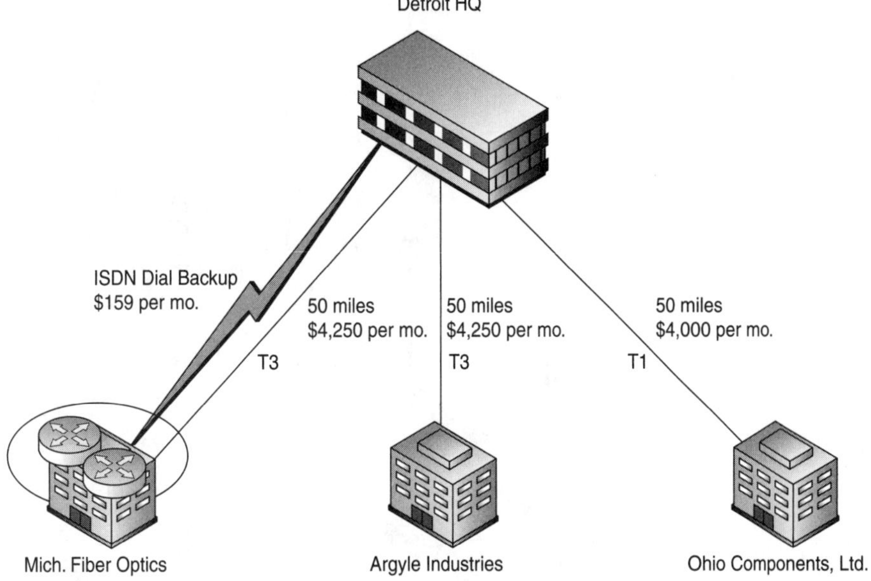

Figure C-15 WAN connectivity for Campus Research

Chapter 17 Case Study

This case study focused on the reduction of the cost of maintaining leased T1 lines between the Campus Research Corporation headquarters and its remote sites. They are using IGRP for their routing protocol, have determined that the traffic tends to burst between 1 and 3 P.M., and are facing more growth in their WAN. Specifically, you were asked to

- Determine whether Frame Relay would work better for the remote site connectivity than dedicated lines.
- Recommend a protocol that might scale better for the company than IGRP.
- Choose a topology model that would work well for this solution and sketch out a design.

As you can see in Figure C-16, Frame Relay works well for this infrastructure. Although we do not have the costs associated with the Frame Relay circuits, we estimate that we can save the company hundreds of dollars per month over the current $1,625 per T1 line. We have created a

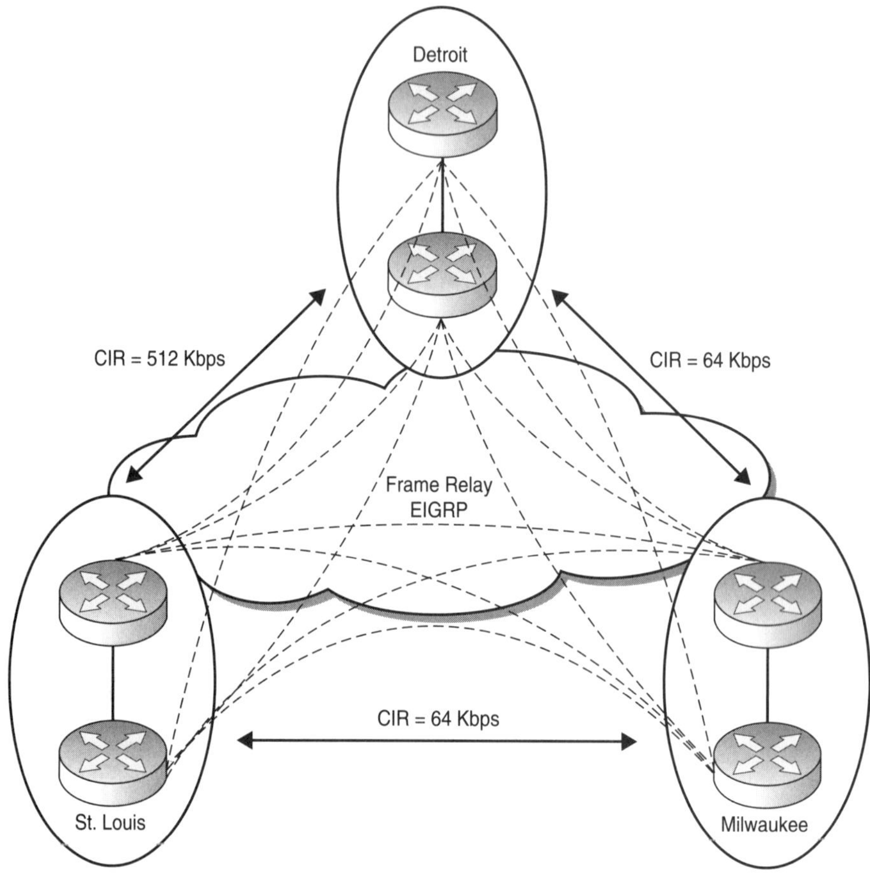

Figure C-16 Campus Research Frame Relay design

full-mesh design using the maximum burst rate as our guideline for the circuits between St. Louis and Detroit and a very low CIR for Milwaukee to Detroit. With this design, we can also get rid of the ISDN backup circuits. Redundancy is already present.

The best routing protocol for this design is likely to be EIGRP. Split-horizon should be disabled so that we may use sub-interfaces to save money on our hardware investment. If discontiguous networks are a problem, EIGRP should also be configured with the **no auto-summary** command.

Chapter 18 Case Study

Our frequent customer, Campus Research, may want X.25 in its WAN to provide fault tolerance and reliability. The company is more interested in extreme fault tolerance between the three Michigan sites. In Figure C-17, we show one possible solution to the design problem.

As you can see, we have created a full-mesh design within the Michigan sites. These can be on sub-interfaces or not, depending upon your preference. By not using sub-interfaces, you provide physical port mesh but incur more total hardware cost. If you use sub-interfaces of a single physical port, the physical port becomes the single point of failure for hardware problems.

Figure C-17 Campus Research X.25 WAN

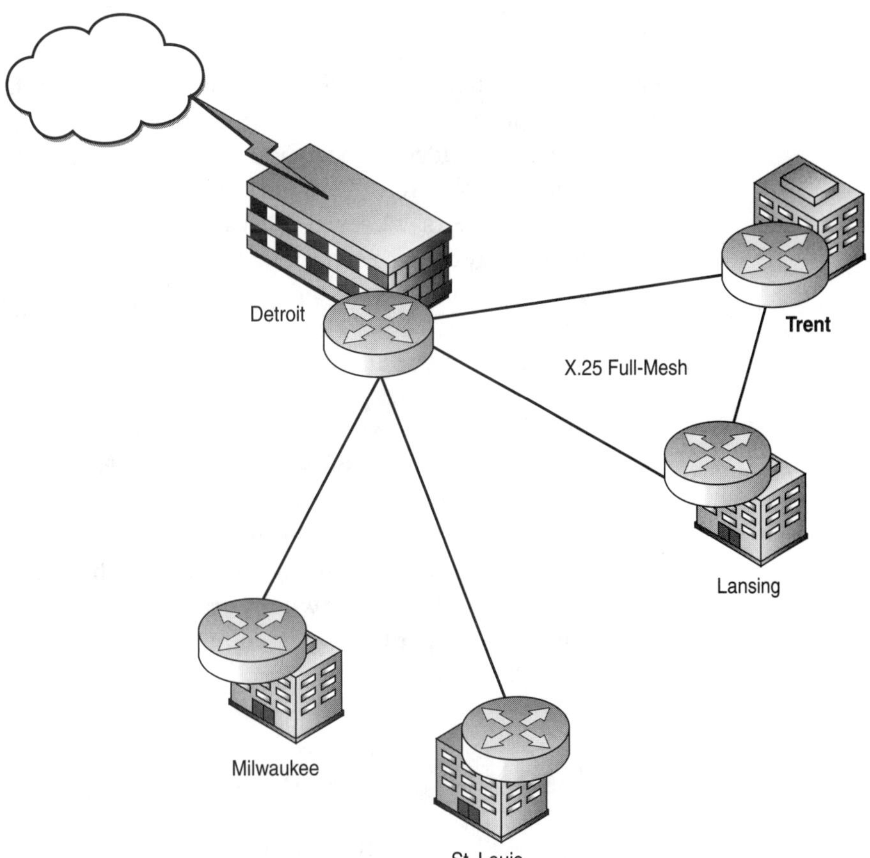

St. Louis and Milwaukee are connected to the headquarters network through a hub-and-spoke connection, partially meshed, as their need for redundancy is not as great. Regardless of the topology type, X.25 is a good choice for this network as long as bandwidth remains under T3 speed and reliability is paramount to their requirements.

Chapter 19 Case Study

For the case study in Chapter 19, we asked you to design a remote access solution for a start-up ISP with a potential of 10,000 users. They need modem banks or access servers for the dial-up users and DSL termination for the telecommuters to be able to access the corporate network. In addition to the access requirements, they are providing Web-hosting services to about 500 sites and need to be sure that security is addressed. Although part of the security solution was outside the scope of this chapter, firewall placement is added here in Figure C-18 to demonstrate what a secure solution might look like.

The engineers who are telecommuting through DSL connections are doing so through a rack of DSLAMs at the Washington, D.C., location. Remote customers are entering through either a rack of ISDN termination points or through 5800 series access servers. With a rack of five 5800s, the scalability is to 7,000 modems. This more than meets the stated requirements of the site.

All remote users are routed through a pair of robust core routers in a redundant array. The routers may use access lists or other means of performing basic security, but we have chosen to allow a firewall to handle this. Authentication can be performed on the firewall or can be offloaded to a security server, which is not something we show in the figure. Once a user is authenticated, the user will be granted access either to the public server, the private LAN, or both, depending upon privileges granted.

Chapter 20 Case Study

For our ATM case study, you were asked to look at a company called MetraTech, Ltd., which provides video teleconferencing to the desktop for staff meetings and over the WAN to their partner organizations. They need

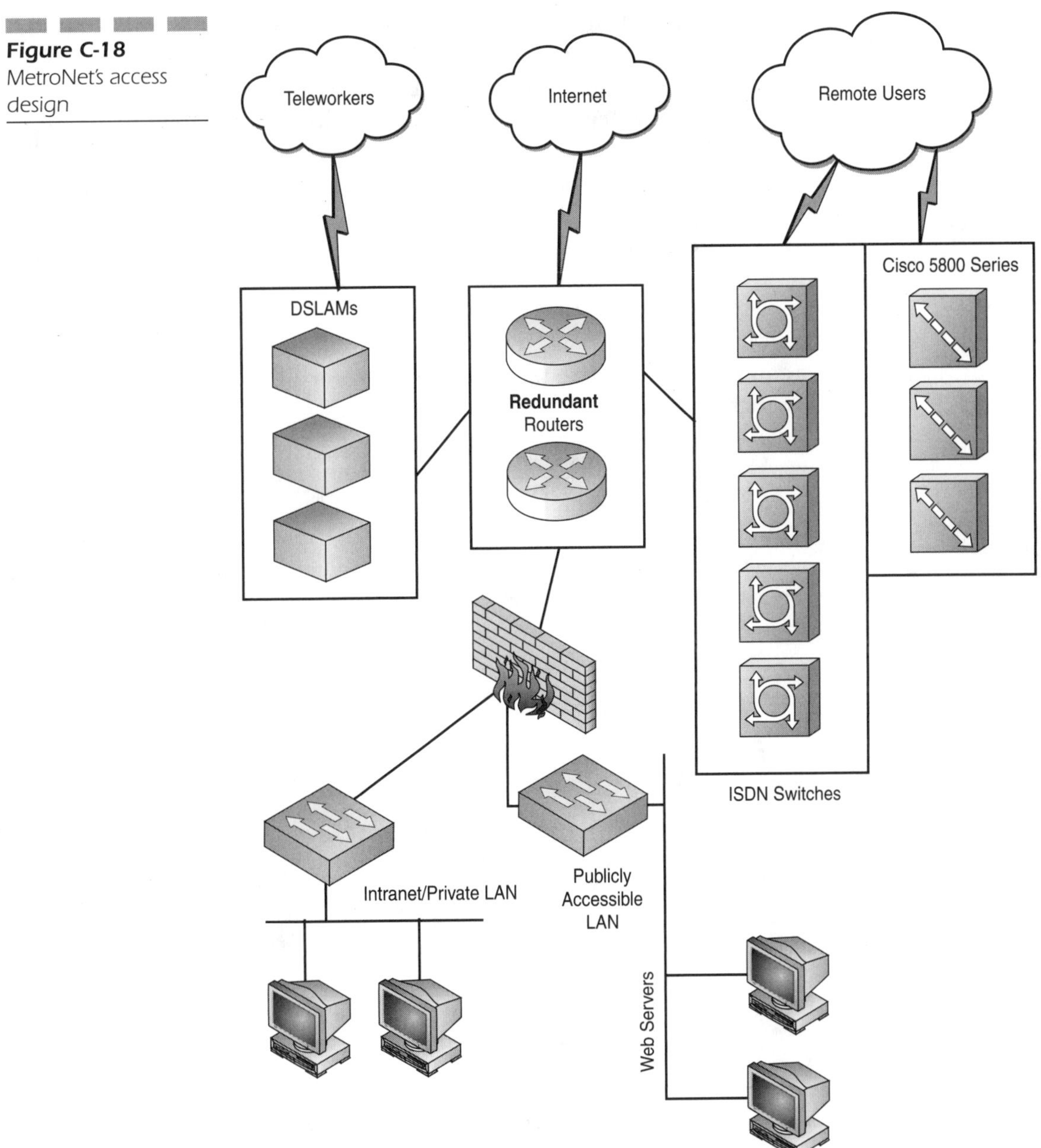

Figure C-18 MetroNet's access design

a design that will eliminate some of the problems with network delay and jitter. The network engineering staff would like to have technology in place that will allow them to allocate bandwidth with QoS and DiffServ.

The company needs to increase bandwidth and reliability, as well as provide for service-level specification for certain traffic types. They like the current use of a full-mesh environment, because downtime cannot be tolerated.

You were asked to sketch out a design plan, noting the type of adaptation layer used. One possible solution is shown in Figure C-19. Each site has its own ATM-enabled router that communicates with all other sites over a fully meshed ATM cloud. PVCs connect all of the sites together. Partner organizations receive data, voice, or video over VPN tunnels that allow for secure transmission.

For voice transmission, you can use AAL1 as the adaptation layer. We would recommend AAL2, however, for the multimedia support to the desktop. Additionally, you could use AAL5 for traditional data and allocate bandwidth based on the traffic type. Data is much more tolerant of delay, so by using QoS to reserve bandwidth for delay-sensitive applications like video, you assure better service for the internetwork and the partners.

Figure C-19 MetraTech ATM WAN

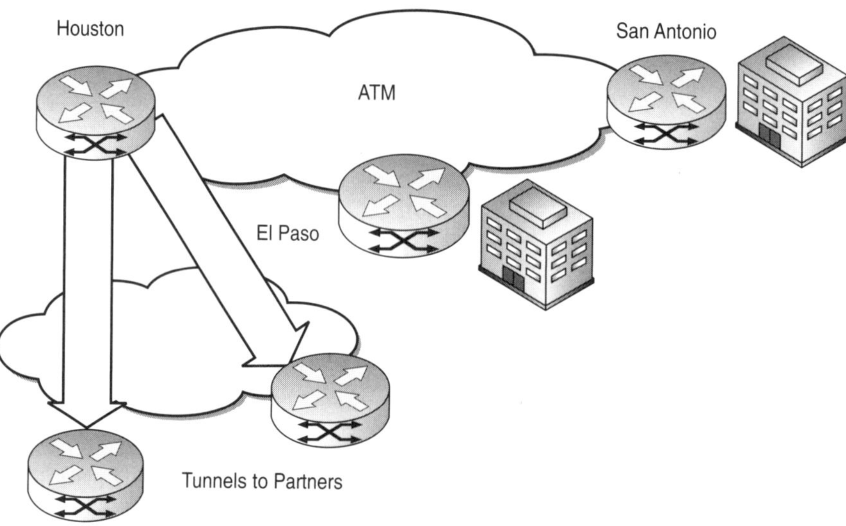

Chapter 21 Case Study

The Chapter 21 case study asked you to propose a topology and switch selection for an ATM backbone. The customer, FasTransport Systems, has three large sites located in Cincinnati, Princeton, and Portland. The company wants to link all three sites with OC-12 over Cisco equipment. The most likely solution to this design problem is outlined in Figure C-20, with comments following.

We have drawn up a design for the ATM backbone between the FasTransport Systems locations in a structured topology. Each site has an MGX-8850 switch connected to the other sites through an OC-12 trunk interface. Inside each domain (geographically chosen), the MGX-8850 can support whatever StrataCom equipment is in use at the site—such as BPX switches or an MGX-8220 concentrator. This design provides exactly what the customer asked for plus scalability and redundancy.

Chapter 22 Case Study

In this case study, you were asked to create a high-level design to meet the needs of Marquette Biomedical, Inc., based in Jacksonville, Florida—a large medical research firm that wants to multi-home their autonomous system, giving preference to the new ISP. The network engineering staff has also begun to struggle with the growth inside the AS to 70 routers. They feel it is becoming unmanageable and would like the second ISP to be homed out of their Baltimore location. A possible solution to this problem is shown in Figure C-21. Specific comments about the design follow.

Note that we are showing you the design for only the two main locations of Marquette. Any other branch office could be added in a similar manner.

As you can see, we have created two fully meshed IBGP confederations in Baltimore and Jacksonville. The total number of routers participating in each confederation is now lower than the original number of routers (70) that were participating in IBGP. Additionally, this gives us the flexibility to filter routes or color routes between each confederation with map lists, distribute lists, or BGP communities.

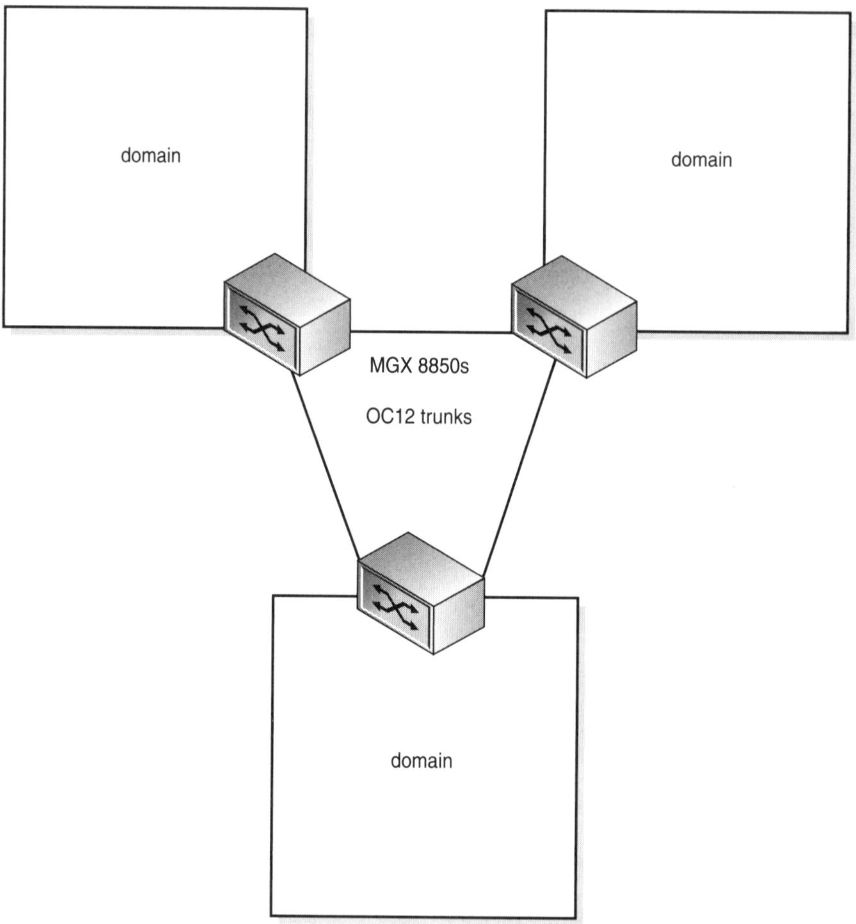

Figure C-20 New FasTransport Systems WAN design

Each location is connected to its own ISP, so the entire AS is now multihomed. Between the two confederations, we are running EBGP. We are also running EBGP to each of the ISPs. We are proposing a higher metric on the route to the ISP out of Jacksonville, since it has more problems. This will cause it to be a less-favorable exit point while still allowing it to back up our new primary ISP. In addition, we are enabling route-flap dampening on both links to the ISPs to help prevent their problems from becoming our problems. You could also use static routes to both ISPs to ensure an "always-on" route.

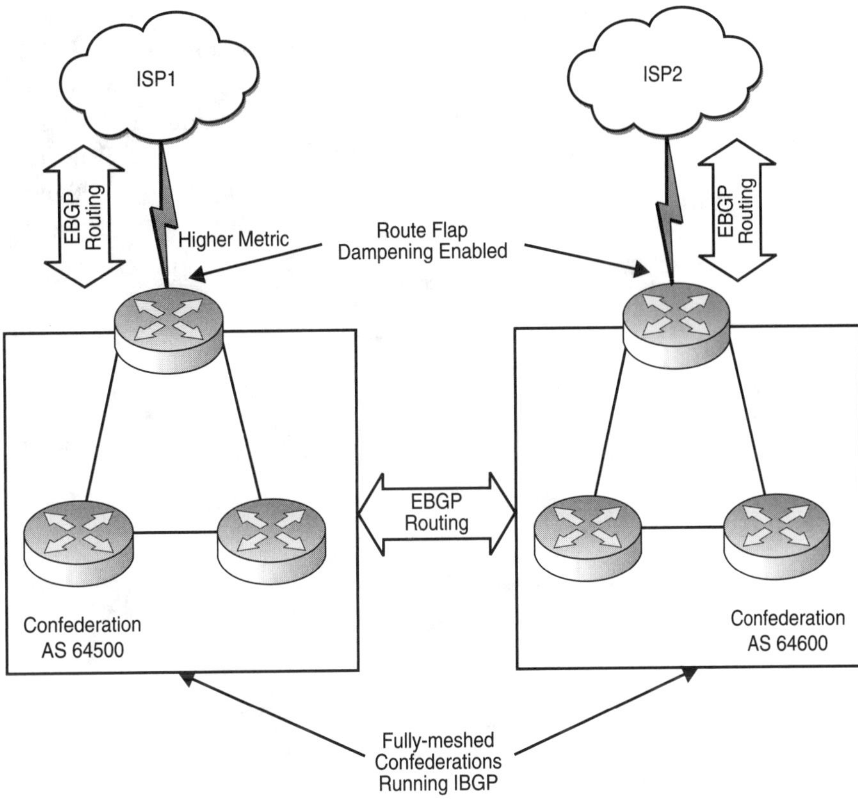

Figure C-21 New Marquette BGP design

To reduce the likelihood of routing problems caused by having a multihomed AS, we would also propose that only routes that originate within the AS be advertised to either service provider. In other words, the routes learned from ISP1 are not advertised to ISP2 and vice versa.

Chapter 23 Case Study

In the security design chapter, the case study is for Bulldog Industries, which is concerned about security for its emerging e-commerce business. This case study involves not only the overall network design but also the security practices company-wide.

The server room is secure, having a badge scanner at the door. The private databases and the servers that need to be publicly accessible, however, must be divided into different networks. This will allow for the easy application of security rules. Telecommuting employees can stop dialing into the 800 numbers if we use VPNs through a PIX firewall. This will save costs for the company. Our proposed security design is shown in Figure C-22.

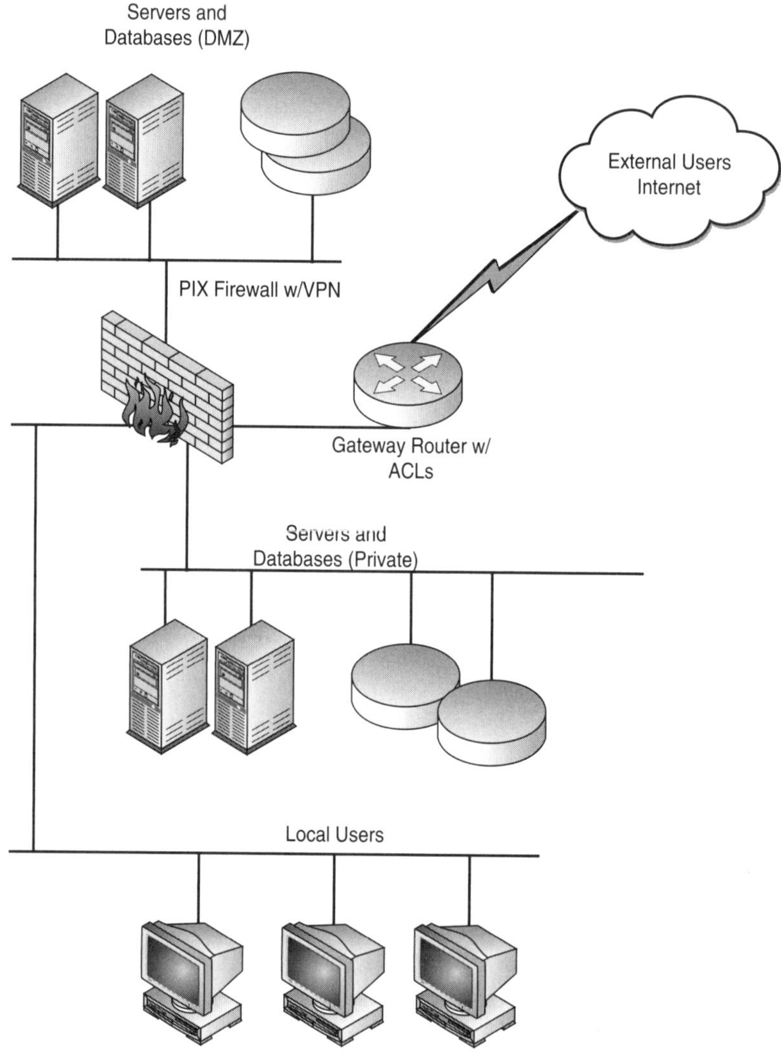

Figure C-22 Bulldog Industries security design

NAT services can be moved from the router to the PIX firewall, leaving only basic access lists in place on the router. The firewall will then do all the work of authentication, security policy enforcement, and VPN administration. The router will be free to do routing once again. The servers and databases that are publicly accessible are segregated into a "demilitarized zone (DMZ)." Private information is kept in a separate network. Access is granted only to those who need to have it.

Local users access the Internet by first going through the firewall. Internet users access company resources through the firewall, as well. For redundancy, you could also use two PIX firewalls in a redundant array (not shown here).

Chapter 24 Case Study

For this chapter, you were asked to look at the current design for Great Wall Bank, which is using SNA for its financial network. Employees are dealing with a TN3270 terminal on their desks along with their PCs. The other branch of the bank is connected to the Token Ring over a 33.6 Kbps dedicated line. The current topology is a redundant backbone ring design. The goal therefore is to get rid of the dual systems on employees' desks, increase the bandwidth for the branch bank, and possibly upgrade the topology.

When we examined the bank's current practices, we revised the design as follows:

- Add software that allows for 3270 terminal emulation on each user's PC. Remove the additional hardware currently on the desks.
- Get rid of the 33.6 Kbps dedicated line used to connect the branch bank (and future branches) to the main branch. Replace the connectivity with a Frame Relay connection with a committed information rate of 64Kbps (or higher, if necessary).
- Replace the FEPs with channel-attached routers.
- Do away with any bridges or cluster controllers. Allow the routers to do the work.
- Keep the redundant backbone ring design and extend the redundancy to the routers.

- Put the Windows NT servers and SNA gateways on the Token Rings. While our design shows redundancy in the servers, this is up to the requirements of the customer, which are not specific in this case.
- Use the DSPU features to allow the router to do PU concentration and reduce traffic to and from the mainframe.

The resulting design is shown in Figure C-23. Bear in mind that this is just one of many possibilities.

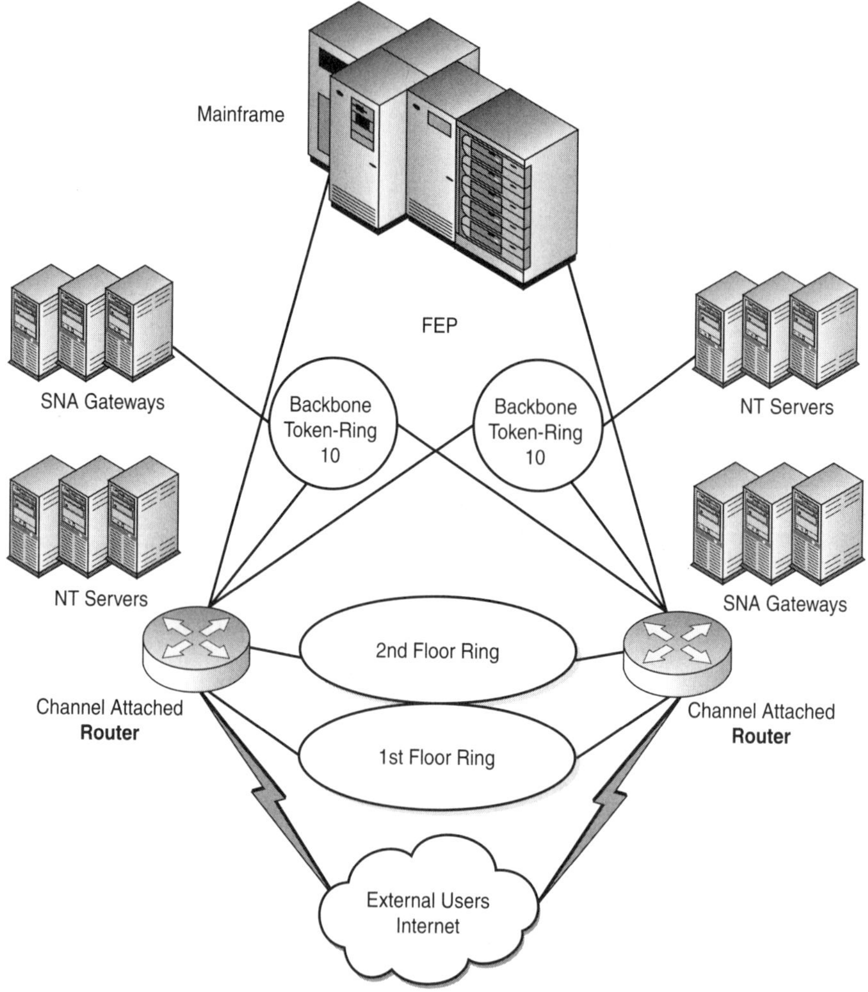

Figure C-23 Great Wall Bank redesign

INDEX

A

D

E

K–L

Q–R

U

V

W

INTERNATIONAL CONTACT INFORMATION

AUSTRALIA
McGraw-Hill Book Company Australia Pty. Ltd.
TEL +61-2-9417-9899
FAX +61-2-9417-5687
http://www.mcgraw-hill.com.au
books-it_sydney@mcgraw-hill.com

CANADA
McGraw-Hill Ryerson Ltd.
TEL +905-430-5000
FAX +905-430-5020
http://www.mcgrawhill.ca

GREECE, MIDDLE EAST, NORTHERN AFRICA
McGraw-Hill Hellas
TEL +30-1-656-0990-3-4
FAX +30-1-654-5525

MEXICO (Also serving Latin America)
McGraw-Hill Interamericana Editores S.A. de C.V.
TEL +525-117-1583
FAX +525-117-1589
http://www.mcgraw-hill.com.mx
fernando_castellanos@mcgraw-hill.com

SINGAPORE (Serving Asia)
McGraw-Hill Book Company
TEL +65-863-1580
FAX +65-862-3354
http://www.mcgraw-hill.com.sg
mghasia@mcgraw-hill.com

SOUTH AFRICA
McGraw-Hill South Africa
TEL +27-11-622-7512
FAX +27-11-622-9045
robyn_swanepoel@mcgraw-hill.com

UNITED KINGDOM & EUROPE (Excluding Southern Europe)
McGraw-Hill Publishing Company
TEL +44-1-628-502500
FAX +44-1-628-770224
http://www.mcgraw-hill.co.uk
computing_neurope@mcgraw-hill.com

ALL OTHER INQUIRIES Contact:
Osborne/McGraw-Hill
TEL +1-510-549-6600
FAX +1-510-883-7600
http://www.osborne.com
omg_international@mcgraw-hill.com

ABOUT THE CD-ROM

FastTrakExpress™

FastTrak Express provides interactive certification exams to help you prepare for certification. With the enclosed CD, you can test your knowledge of the topics covered in this book with over 200 multiple choice questions.

To Install FastTrak Express:

1. Insert the CD-ROM in your CD-ROM drive.
2. From your computer, choose Run. Select the CD-ROM drive and Run the file called "setupfte.exe." This will launch the Installation Wizard.
3. When the Setup is finished, you may immediately begin using FastTrak Express.
4. To begin using FastTrak Express, enter your license key number: 312873677081

FastTrak Express offers two testing options: the Adaptive exam and the Standard exam.

The Adaptive Exam

The Adaptive exam style does not simulate all of the exam environments that are found on certification exams. You cannot choose specific subcategories for the adaptive exam and once a question has been answered you cannot go back to a previous question.

You have a time limit in which to complete the adaptive exam. This time varies from subject to subject, although it is usually 15 to 25 questions in 30 minutes. When the time limit has been reached, your exam automatically ends.

To take the Adaptive Exam:

1. Click the Adaptive Exam button from the Main window. The Adaptive Exam window will appear.
2. Click the circle or square to the left of the correct answer.

NOTE: *There may be more than one correct answer. The text in the bottom left corner of the window instructs you to Choose the Best Answer (if there is only one answer) or Mark All Correct Answers (if there is more than one correct answer.*

3. Click the Next button to continue.
4. To quit the test at any time, click the Finish button. After about 30 minutes, the exam exits to review mode.

After you have completed the Adaptive exam, FastTrak Express displays your score and the passing score required for the test.

- Click Details to display a chapter-by-chapter review of your exam results.
- Click on Report to get a full analysis of your score.

To review the Adaptive exam After you have taken an Adaptive exam, you can review the questions, your answers, and the correct answers. You may only review your questions immediately after an Adaptive exam. To review your questions:

1. Click the Correct Answer button.
2. To see your answer, click the Your Answer button.

The Standard Exam

After you have learned about your subject using the Adaptive sessions, you can take a Standard exam. This mode simulates the environment that might be found on an actual certification exam.

You cannot choose subcategories for a Standard exam. You have a time limit (this time varies from subject to subject, although it is usually 75 minutes) to complete the Standard exam. When this time limit has been reached, your exam automatically ends.

To take the Standard exam:

1. Click the Standard Exam button from the Main window. The Standard Exam window will appear.
2. Click the circle or square to the left of the correct answer.

NOTE: *There may be more than one correct answer. The text in the bottom left corner of the window instructs you to Choose the Best Answer (if there is only one answer) or Mark All Correct Answers (if there is more than one correct answer).*

3. If you are unsure of the answer and wish to mark the question so you can return to it later, check the Mark box in the upper left hand corner.
4. To review which questions you have marked, which you have answered, and which you have not answered, click the Review button.
5. Click the Next button to continue.
6. To quit the test at any time, click the Finish button. After about 75 minutes, the exam exits to review mode.

After you have completed the Standard exam, FastTrak Express displays your score and the passing score required for the test.

- Click Details to display a chapter-by-chapter review of your exam results.
- Click on Report to get a full analysis of your score.

To review a Standard Exam After you have taken a Standard exam, you can review the questions, your answers, and the correct answers.

You may only review your questions immediately after a Standard exam.

To review your questions:

1. Click the Correct Answer button.
2. To see your answer, click the Your Answer button.

Changing Exams FastTrakExpress provides several practice exams to test your knowledge. To change exams:

1. Select the exam for the test you want to run from the Select Exam window.

If you experience technical difficulties please call (888) 992-3131. Outside the U.S. call (281) 972-3131. Or, you may e-mail `brucem@bfq.com`. For more information, visit the BeachFrontQuizzer site at `www.bfq.com`.

LICENSE AGREEMENT

THIS PRODUCT (THE "PRODUCT") CONTAINS PROPRIETARY SOFTWARE, DATA AND INFORMATION (INCLUDING DOCUMENTATION) OWNED BY THE McGRAW-HILL COMPANIES, INC. ("McGRAW-HILL") AND ITS LICENSORS. YOUR RIGHT TO USE THE PRODUCT IS GOVERNED BY THE TERMS AND CONDITIONS OF THIS AGREEMENT.

LICENSE: Throughout this License Agreement, "you" shall mean either the individual or the entity whose agent opens this package. You are granted a non-exclusive and non-transferable license to use the Product subject to the following terms:
(i) If you have licensed a single user version of the Product, the Product may only be used on a single computer (i.e., a single CPU). If you licensed and paid the fee applicable to a local area network or wide area network version of the Product, you are subject to the terms of the following subparagraph (ii).
(ii) If you have licensed a local area network version, you may use the Product on unlimited workstations located in one single building selected by you that is served by such local area network. If you have licensed a wide area network version, you may use the Product on unlimited workstations located in multiple buildings on the same site selected by you that is served by such wide area network; provided, however, that any building will not be considered located in the same site if it is more than five (5) miles away from any building included in such site. In addition, you may only use a local area or wide area network version of the Product on one single server. If you wish to use the Product on more than one server, you must obtain written authorization from McGraw-Hill and pay additional fees.
(iii) You may make one copy of the Product for back-up purposes only and you must maintain an accurate record as to the location of the back-up at all times.

COPYRIGHT; RESTRICTIONS ON USE AND TRANSFER: All rights (including copyright) in and to the Product are owned by McGraw-Hill and its licensors. You are the owner of the enclosed disc on which the Product is recorded. You may not use, copy, decompile, disassemble, reverse engineer, modify, reproduce, create derivative works, transmit, distribute, sublicense, store in a database or retrieval system of any kind, rent or transfer the Product, or any portion thereof, in any form or by any means (including electronically or otherwise) except as expressly provided for in this License Agreement. You must reproduce the copyright notices, trademark notices, legends and logos of McGraw-Hill and its licensors that appear on the Product on the back-up copy of the Product which you are permitted to make hereunder. All rights in the Product not expressly granted herein are reserved by McGraw-Hill and its licensors.

TERM: This License Agreement is effective until terminated. It will terminate if you fail to comply with any term or condition of this License Agreement. Upon termination, you are obligated to return to McGraw-Hill the Product together with all copies thereof and to purge all copies of the Product included in any and all servers and computer facilities.

DISCLAIMER OF WARRANTY: THE PRODUCT AND THE BACK-UP COPY ARE LICENSED "AS IS." McGRAW-HILL, ITS LICENSORS AND THE AUTHORS MAKE NO WARRANTIES, EXPRESS OR IMPLIED, AS TO THE RESULTS TO BE OBTAINED BY ANY PERSON OR ENTITY FROM USE OF THE PRODUCT, ANY INFORMATION OR DATA INCLUDED THEREIN AND/OR ANY TECHNICAL SUPPORT SERVICES PROVIDED HEREUNDER, IF ANY ("TECHNICAL SUPPORT SERVICES"). McGRAW-HILL, ITS LICENSORS AND THE AUTHORS MAKE NO EXPRESS OR IMPLIED WARRANTIES OF MERCHANTABILITY OR FITNESS FOR A PARTICULAR PURPOSE OR USE WITH RESPECT TO THE PRODUCT. McGRAW-HILL, ITS LICENSORS, AND THE AUTHORS MAKE NO GUARANTEE THAT YOU WILL PASS ANY CERTIFICATION EXAM WHATSOEVER BY USING THIS PRODUCT. NEITHER McGRAW-HILL, ANY OF ITS LICENSORS NOR THE AUTHORS WARRANT THAT THE FUNCTIONS CONTAINED IN THE PRODUCT WILL MEET YOUR REQUIREMENTS OR THAT THE OPERATION OF THE PRODUCT WILL BE UNINTERRUPTED OR ERROR FREE. YOU ASSUME THE ENTIRE RISK WITH RESPECT TO THE QUALITY AND PERFORMANCE OF THE PRODUCT.

LIMITED WARRANTY FOR DISC: To the original licensee only, McGraw-Hill warrants that the enclosed disc on which the Product is recorded is free from defects in materials and workmanship under normal use and service for a period of ninety (90) days from the date of purchase. In the event of a defect in the disc covered by the foregoing warranty, McGraw-Hill will replace the disc.

LIMITATION OF LIABILITY: NEITHER McGRAW-HILL, ITS LICENSORS NOR THE AUTHORS SHALL BE LIABLE FOR ANY INDIRECT, SPECIAL OR CONSEQUENTIAL DAMAGES, SUCH AS BUT NOT LIMITED TO, LOSS OF ANTICIPATED PROFITS OR BENEFITS, RESULTING FROM THE USE OR INABILITY TO USE THE PRODUCT EVEN IF ANY OF THEM HAS BEEN ADVISED OF THE POSSIBILITY OF SUCH DAMAGES. THIS LIMITATION OF LIABILITY SHALL APPLY TO ANY CLAIM OR CAUSE WHATSOEVER WHETHER SUCH CLAIM OR CAUSE ARISES IN CONTRACT, TORT, OR OTHERWISE. Some states do not allow the exclusion or limitation of indirect, special or consequential damages, so the above limitation may not apply to you.

U.S. GOVERNMENT RESTRICTED RIGHTS: Any software included in the Product is provided with restricted rights subject to subparagraphs (c), (1) and (2) of the Commercial Computer Software-Restricted Rights clause at 48 C.F.R. 52.227-19. The terms of this Agreement applicable to the use of the data in the Product are those under which the data are generally made available to the general public by McGraw-Hill. Except as provided herein, no reproduction, use, or disclosure rights are granted with respect to the data included in the Product and no right to modify or create derivative works from any such data is hereby granted.

GENERAL: This License Agreement constitutes the entire agreement between the parties relating to the Product. The terms of any Purchase Order shall have no effect on the terms of this License Agreement. Failure of McGraw-Hill to insist at any time on strict compliance with this License Agreement shall not constitute a waiver of any rights under this License Agreement. This License Agreement shall be construed and governed in accordance with the laws of the State of New York. If any provision of this License Agreement is held to be contrary to law, that provision will be enforced to the maximum extent permissible and the remaining provisions will remain in full force and effect.